IN LIGHT AND SHADOW

IN LIGHT AND SHADOW

A PHOTOGRAPHIC HISTORY FROM
INDIGENOUS AMERICA

Brian Adams and Sarah Stacke

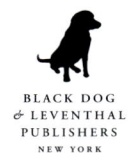

BLACK DOG
& LEVENTHAL
PUBLISHERS
NEW YORK

Black Dog & Leventhal Publishers
Hachette Book Group
1290 Avenue of the Americas, New York, NY 10104
www.blackdogandleventhal.com

 BlackDogandLeventhal   @BDLev

First Edition: October 2025

Published by Black Dog & Leventhal Publishers, an imprint of
Hachette Book Group, Inc. The Black Dog & Leventhal Publishers
name and logo are trademarks of Hachette Book Group, Inc.

The Hachette Speakers Bureau provides a wide range of authors for
speaking events. To find out more, go to hachettespeakersbureau.com
or email HachetteSpeakers@hbgusa.com.

Library of Congress Cataloging-in-Publication Data
Names: Adams, Brian, author. | Stacke, Sarah, author.
Title: *In Light and Shadow: A Photographic History from
Indigenous America* / Brian Adams and Sarah Stacke.
Description: First edition. | New York : Black Dog and Leventhal,
[2025] | Includes bibliographical references and index.
| Summary: *In Light and Shadow: A Photographic History from
Indigenous America* contributes to a comprehensive
understanding that Indigenous people have been making
photographs for their own purposes since at least the 1860s.
This book offers an extensive collection of images that
emphasizes the depth of Indigenous photography originating
in the Americas and Hawai'i from the 19th century forward.
—Adapted from the introduction.
Identifiers: LCCN 2024015779 (print) | LCCN 2024015780 (ebook)
| ISBN 9780762482467 (hardcover)
| ISBN 9780762482474 (ebook)
Subjects: LCSH: Indians of North America—Pictorial works. |
Indians of South America—Pictorial works. | Indians of
Mexico—Pictorial works. | Indian photographers—Biography. |
Photography in historiography. |Photography in ethnology. |
America—History—Pictorial works. | LCGFT: Illustrated
works. | Biographies.
Classification: LCC E77.5.A33 2025 (print) | LCC E77.5 (ebook) |
DDC 970.004/970222—dc23/eng/20240723
LC record available at https://lccn.loc.gov/2024015779
LC ebook record available at https://lccn.loc.gov/2024015780

Printed in China

1010

10 9 8 7 6 5 4 3 2 1

For
Elliott, Ellis, and Ash
Errol, Oscar, Arlo, and Bryan

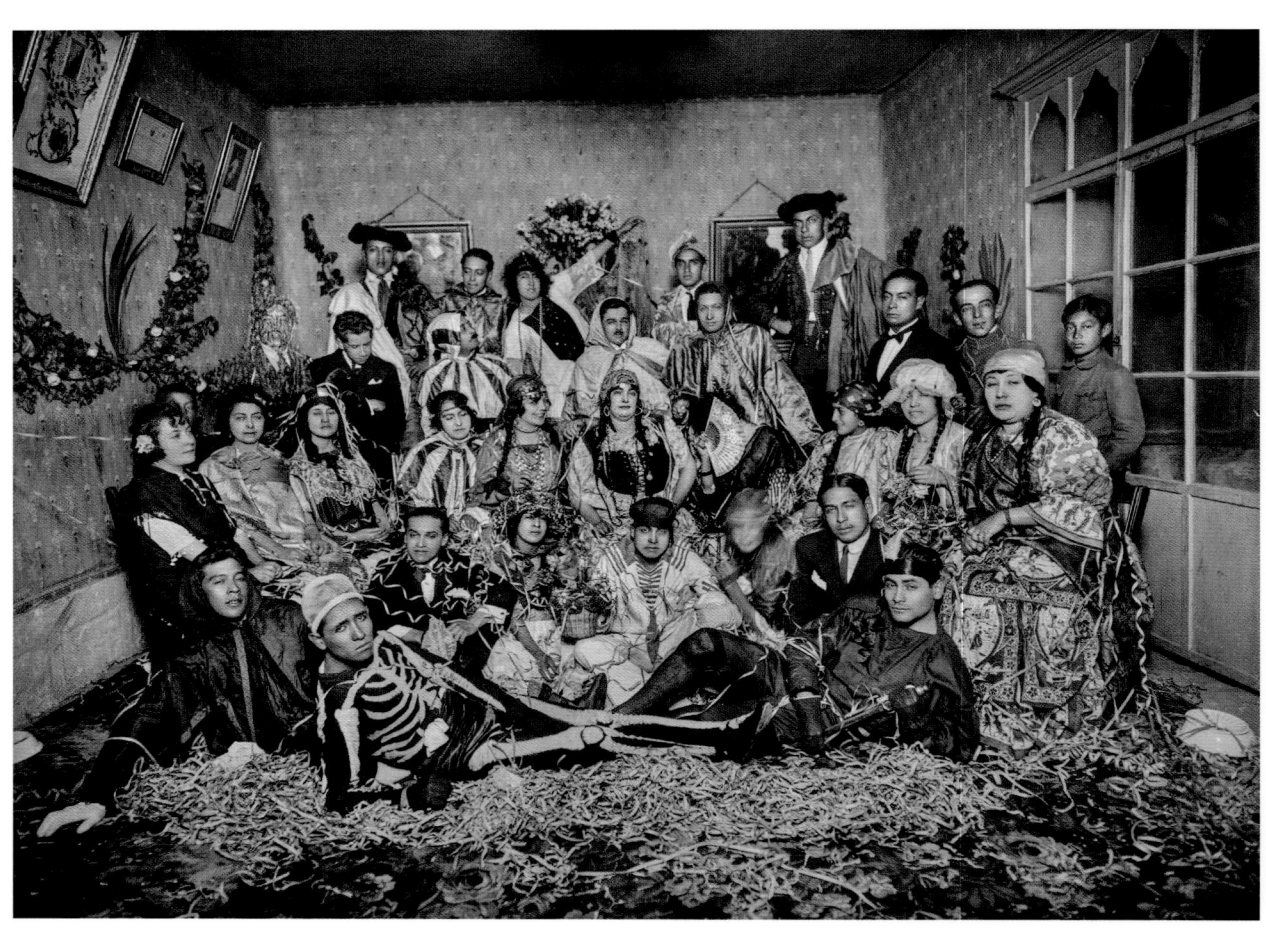

Contents

viii Introduction
1 Photographs

275 *Conclusion*
276 *Acknowledgments*
276 *Authors*
277 *Contributors*
277 *Image Credits*
278 *Notes*
289 *Selected Bibliography*
291 *Index*

Introduction

Brian Adams and Sarah Stacke

In the 1940s, on the Blackfeet Nation in Montana, Ella Mad Plume Yellow Wolf candidly photographed her rich community life and work as a rancher, intentionally creating a visual legacy for the next generations. At the same time in western Canada, James Patrick Brady used his camera as a tool to advocate for the rights of his fellow Métis. The images he made of people connected to the land encapsulate the self-determination he championed. And in Perú's Sacred Valley, Aymara and Quechua members of the Cusco School of Photography welcomed families and compatriots into their studios, generating diverse portraits that challenged simple narratives about their country. During the century preceding these photographers' work, and into the present, Indigenous people have embraced photography, authoring a multitude of experiences.

In Light and Shadow: A Photographic History from Indigenous America offers an extensive collection of images that emphasizes the depth of Indigenous photography originating in the Americas and Hawai'i from the 19th century forward. Along the way, we highlight that learning photography is often a family affair within Native communities, passed from one generation to the next. The artists and images show how the camera is employed as a means of Indigenous power and visual sovereignty.[1]

Photographs made by Indigenous people do not only serve as counterhistories to settler-colonial narratives. They generate a photographic record that enriches Indigenous lives, societies, and collective well-being. Indigenous photographers are expressing their subjectivity—reconstructing and driving the portrayals of themselves as individuals, their identities in a wide sociopolitical landscape, their communities, and their relationships to the environment. These artists and images are reclaiming cultural spaces and histories while developing fresh visual languages that arise from the storytelling and imagery of their forebears.

Though long known within Native circles, the number of Indigenous American photographers receiving recognition in the wider art, documentary, editorial, and commercial realms has increased with each decade since the 1980s. This is thanks to the hard work of Indigenous artists, curators, writers, and scholars. This book is a part of that larger conversation and follows vital publications and exhibitions, including *Silver Drum: Five Native Photographers* (1986), *A Circle of Nations: Voices and Visions of American Indians* (1993), *Our People, Our Land, Our Images: International Indigenous Photographers* (2006),[2] *Yuyayninchis: fotografías inéditas de César Meza y Horacio Ochoa* (2020), *Through a Native Lens: American Indian Photography* (2020), *Speaking with Light: Contemporary Indigenous Photography* (2022), and *In Our Hands: Native Photography, 1890 to Now* (2023).

In 1993, *exposure*, a popular photography journal, released an issue entirely dedicated to Native American photography. In 1995, *Aperture* magazine did the same, and in 2020, they reflected upon Native North America. The library of monographs illuminating the work of Indigenous photographers is expanding. Examples include *Martín Chambi: Photographs, 1920–1950* (1993), *Menadelook: An Inupiat Teacher's Photographs of Alaska Village Life, 1907–1932* (2016), *Dana Claxton* (2021), *Wendy Red Star: Delegation* (2022), as well as the many other titles included in this book's notes and bibliography.

In early 2020, with the 400th anniversary of the *Mayflower*'s arrival to North America looming, we began developing a photography project that looked at the evolution of Indigenous American identity and representation. It was named "The 400 Years Project," and we commissioned original photo essays, licensed existing ones, and created a digital library of Indigenous photographers from the 19th century to the present. Commitment to the craft was the library's criterion, and this resulted in a collection of images by enthusiasts to professionals.

The main goal of this project was to contribute to a comprehensive understanding that Indigenous people across North and South America and Hawai'i have been making photographs

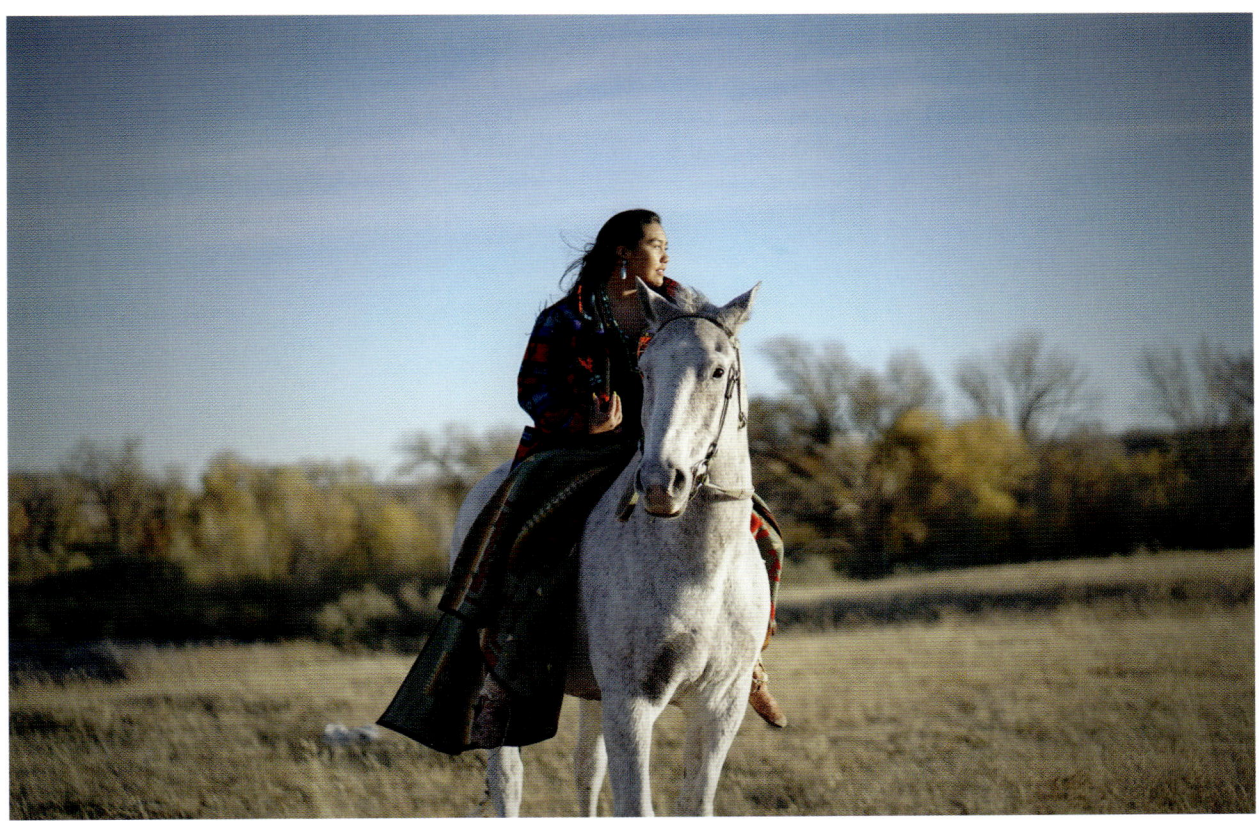

for their own purposes since at least the 1860s. Over time, we believe the archives will reveal Indigenous photographers who were creating imagery in the first two decades following the daguerreotype's 1839 introduction in Paris, after which it spread across oceans and barriers with astonishing speed.

We compiled a list of historical photographers who had, through research prior to ours, been noted. Seeking to add names and Indigenous-led photo publications (such as yearbooks) to the catalog, we consulted Native communities and networks, historical societies, museums, and government and university archives. Much of history is written from encounters with the archives, which are themselves political and cultural constructions. The gradual uncovering and awareness of early Indigenous photographers are confirming the breadth and bedrock of the canon and, at the same time, interrogating the logic and limits of national and dominant institutional archives, where Indigenous photographers are often not credited, if they are included at all.

With a focus on the relationships between the photographs and their makers, *In Light and Shadow* is an expansion of the work we began with the 400 Years Project in 2020.

Selecting the photographers for this book, we considered Indigenous society or nation, geography, and generation. While it is evident that Indigenous people have commissioned photographs of themselves from non-Indigenous practitioners since the 1840s, the earliest photographer mentioned in this book is John Kanipoʻokalani Meek Jr. II, a Native Hawaiian who opened a studio in Honolulu in 1867. Meek auctioned his negatives in 1869 and they have yet to be recovered. The oldest images presented here were made by Jennie Fields Ross Cobb (Cherokee Nation), George Hunt (Tlingit), and B. A. Haldane (Tsimshian) in the 1890s. From this time forward, each decade is represented, as well as numerous technologies (glass plate negatives, celluloid films, digital) and genres. We include family pictures, ethnography, documentary, portraiture, landscape, multimedia, and fine art. Many of the artists work across multiple platforms.

Each entry is accompanied by a text with a biographical sketch and information about the photographer's practice or, in the case of group projects, the scope of the final outcome. For several of the earlier photographers, this is their first publication

Alia Kipp-Heavyrunner rides her horse, Martini, at her family ranch, Blackfeet Nation, Montana, 2020.
PHOTOGRAPH BY WHITNEY SNOW (B. 1991), BLACKFEET NATION.

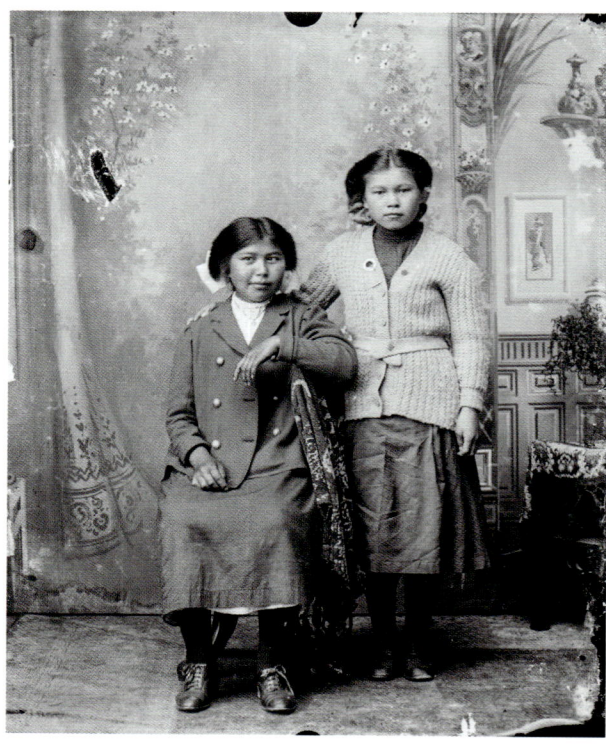

outside hyperlocal media. Details in images are read for the insight they provide into historical context and place. Visual metaphors drawn by photographic compositions are studied. Most of the contemporary texts are informed by interviews the authors conducted with the photographers. As much as possible, the historical texts were shared with and shaped by a descendant, an associated person, or the related archive.

Outside of quotations, capitalization and punctuation do not always heed a conventional style guide. They reflect artist and descendant wishes, feedback from trusted sources, Indigenous style guides, and the authors' best judgment at the time of publication. With the exception of quotes, we do not use extractive or violent language common to photography: *take*, *shoot*, *capture*, *subject*. These terms have been questioned since the nascent days of the medium, yet until relatively recently, the movement to shift away from this language has not gained acknowledgment outside of small circles. In 1847, the *Sandwich Islands News* admitted the "ominous sound" of asking "whether you have 'been taken yet' or 'when are you going to be taken,'" when inquiring if you had visited the local daguerreotypist.[3] Moving away from this oppressive photographic vernacular is one way to acknowledge how Indigenous people across the Americas and the world have been affected by the camera's use as a weapon of colonialism. Photographs have played a role in government surveys, scientific and missionary activities,

expansionism, and tourist spectacles. The camera has invaded sacred and private spaces. In the early 20th century, it was used as an instrument to erroneously proclaim Indigenous people a "vanishing race," and it has abetted the enduring conceptual erasure of Indigenous people from their lands and cultures.[4]

This book is not an exhaustive list of Indigenous American photographers. Many more exceptional contemporary photographers are working across the Americas and Hawai'i than we were able to include in these pages. In addition to the early practitioners acknowledged here and elsewhere, there are unlimited collections from the 19th and 20th centuries lying in wait in institutional, community, and family archives. With the establishment of Indigenous newspapers, a demand for Indigenous photojournalists was created and prodigious archives, still mostly unexamined, were generated.

The artists and images of *In Light and Shadow* demonstrate that the canon of Indigenous American photography has been developing on its own terms since the 19th century. The work here centers Indigenous communities and stories and rewrites history. It is influenced by ancestral memory, transformation, healing, astute observation, imagination, kinship, and continuity. As photographer Nīa MacKnight says with prescience, "We turn to our ancestors' photographs to remind us of where we came from and why we're here today."

Two young women inside B. A. Haldane's photography studio, Metlakatla, Alaska, c. 1910.
PHOTOGRAPH BY B. A. HALDANE. COURTESY OF KETCHIKAN MUSEUMS.
KM 2018.2.30.90

Photographs

JENNIE FIELDS ROSS COBB

Cherokee
Cherokee Nation
Tahlequah, Oklahoma
United States

The life of Jennie Fields Ross Cobb (1881–1959) raises questions about what it means to be a "first." Did her wish to create photographic tapestries of her Cherokee Nation community interlace with some sense that she might later be known as the earliest Native American woman photographer on record?

Cobb began experimenting with photography around 1895, yet the majority of her images were made between 1902 and 1905. Before getting married and turning her attention to teaching at Cherokee Nation public schools, she made images that anchored her deep sense of place, while simultaneously conveying an intention to narrate the complexity and beauty of her surroundings. Through intimate images of people and interior spaces, Cobb's work became vital to a wider illustration of life in the initial years of Cherokee Nation, established in 1839. Her inner fire and a playful sojourning spirit seemed to inspire her documentary and portrait photography beyond any sense that her work would later be considered pioneering.

Cobb studied at the Cherokee Female Seminary in Tahlequah in the mid-1890s, graduating in 1900. Although little information is available about her personal life, some suggest that her father gifted her with her first camera. Through photography, she sought to document her community just as they lived—in everyday rhythms and social spaces. While she artistically orchestrated some encounters, her work largely turned to creating images of unprompted daily existence.

Many of Cobb's photographs focus on women—at school, at play, and in private life. The images she made reflect an intimacy with those she photographed, along with an evident ease of relations that allows the viewer to feel almost a part of the scene. In a picture of two women peering through an open window at the seminary, Cobb's consistent attention to detail shows up in the relationship between the leafy windowsill plants and the dormant vines hanging from the building. Even at a distance, the photo conveys the connection between the photographer and the people she's photographing. Another image places the organic shape of a young woman's hat against a bleak sky; her layered dress and the wintertime trees communicate the cold weather. While the house in the background is unidentified, according to Jon May, photo archivist at the Oklahoma Historical Society, "it was probably a residence near Park Hill in the Cherokee Nation (present Cherokee County, Oklahoma)."[1]

In a 1902 photograph that has become a signature of the collection, three friends walk along the Ozark and Cherokee Central Railway under construction in Tahlequah. And in the leisure of summer, Cobb made a striking image of a group of women swimming in what is likely the Illinois River. Scenes like these could only be made by a member of the community. These photographs reflect Cobb's own spirited character and a break away from the more serious trends of the time.

Cobb's photos speak to a sharp ability to place people in contexts that provide important historical commentaries. An independent woman photographer, she placed women in the city, engaged in flaunting their public selves by promenading through the streets in fine attire. Her photographs often depicted women in transit, rather than the posed formality of imagery typical of this era. This collective work points to a clear interest in telling a story of modern Cherokee womanhood. According to Joan Jensen, "Cobb's Cherokee women defied the stereotypical photographic views of Native women of the time. They were poised, self-assured, fashionable, confident carriers of two cultures."[2]

Through Cobb's life work, both Cherokee identity and the emergence of a dominant U.S. sociocultural landscape can be recognized. According to Karen Shade-Lanier, Cobb's work showed a segment of Native American culture "largely assimilated in dress, custom, language and religion to European-American ways. Yet, their Cherokee heritage was part of a fundamental identity uniting all Cherokee people, traditional and progressive, even as their government was soon to be dismantled to make way for Oklahoma statehood."[3] Cobb's photographs show a fusion of cultures that now reflect the complexities of power and identity inscribed in the struggles of many Native American communities to date. These images can be interpreted today as symbols of resilience and survival. Shade-Lanier surmised, "Just as the Cherokee Nation and its people survived U.S. attempts to dissolve its government and recovered to become the strong sovereign body it is today, Jennie Cobb's work withstands the ages. As a photographic record of life, they defy

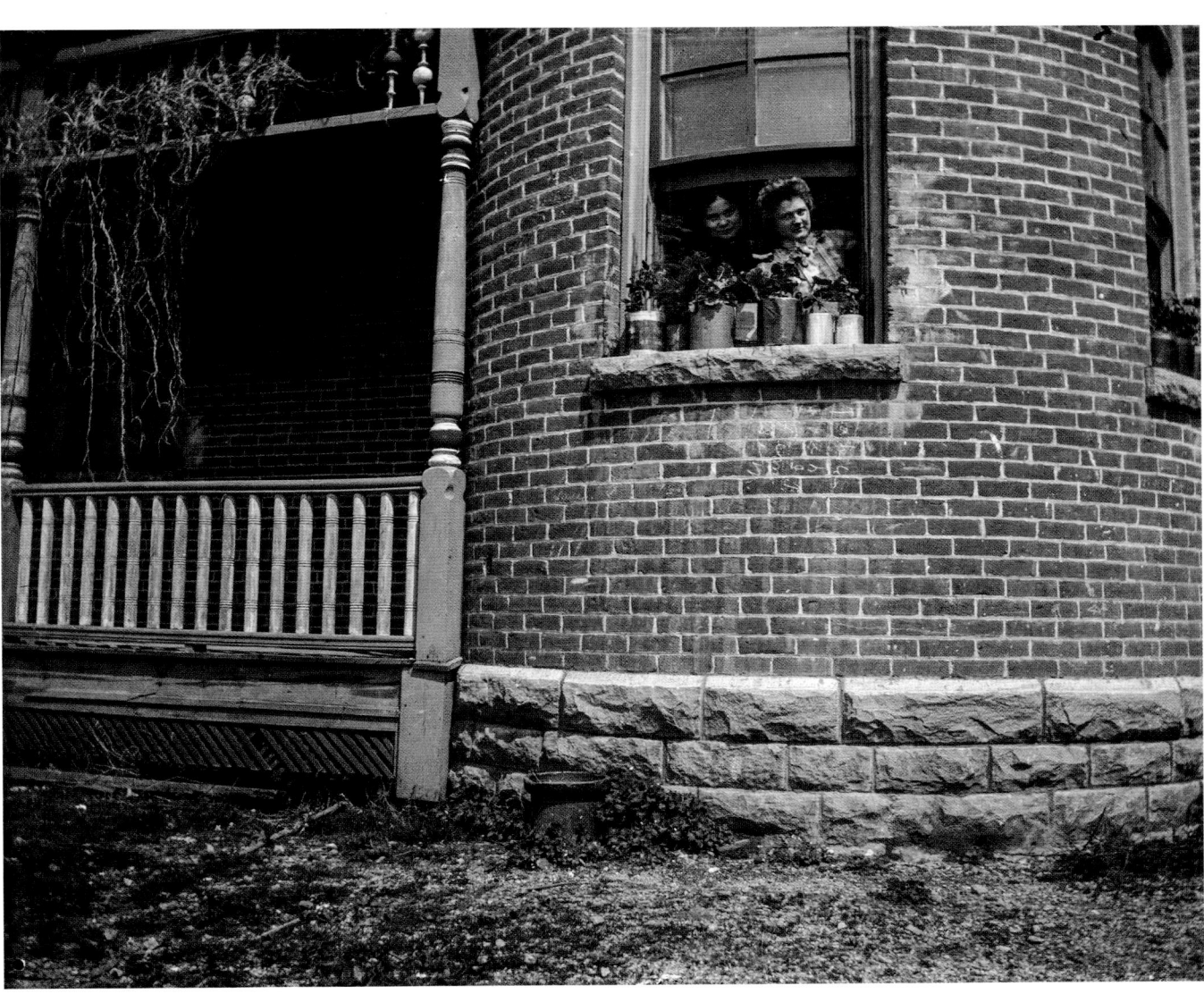

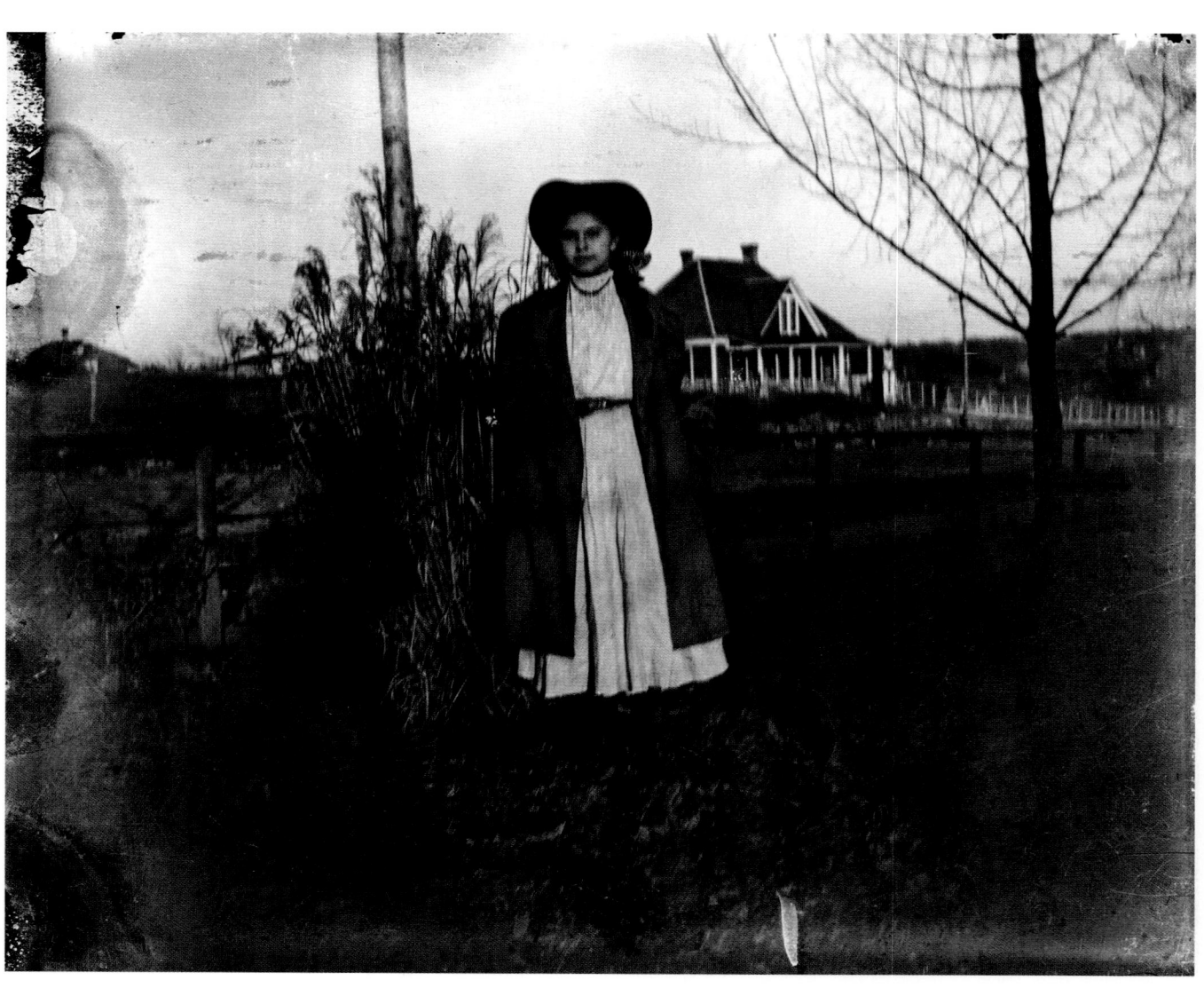

Woman in front of an unidentified house, likely near
Park Hill, Oklahoma, c. 1896–1905.

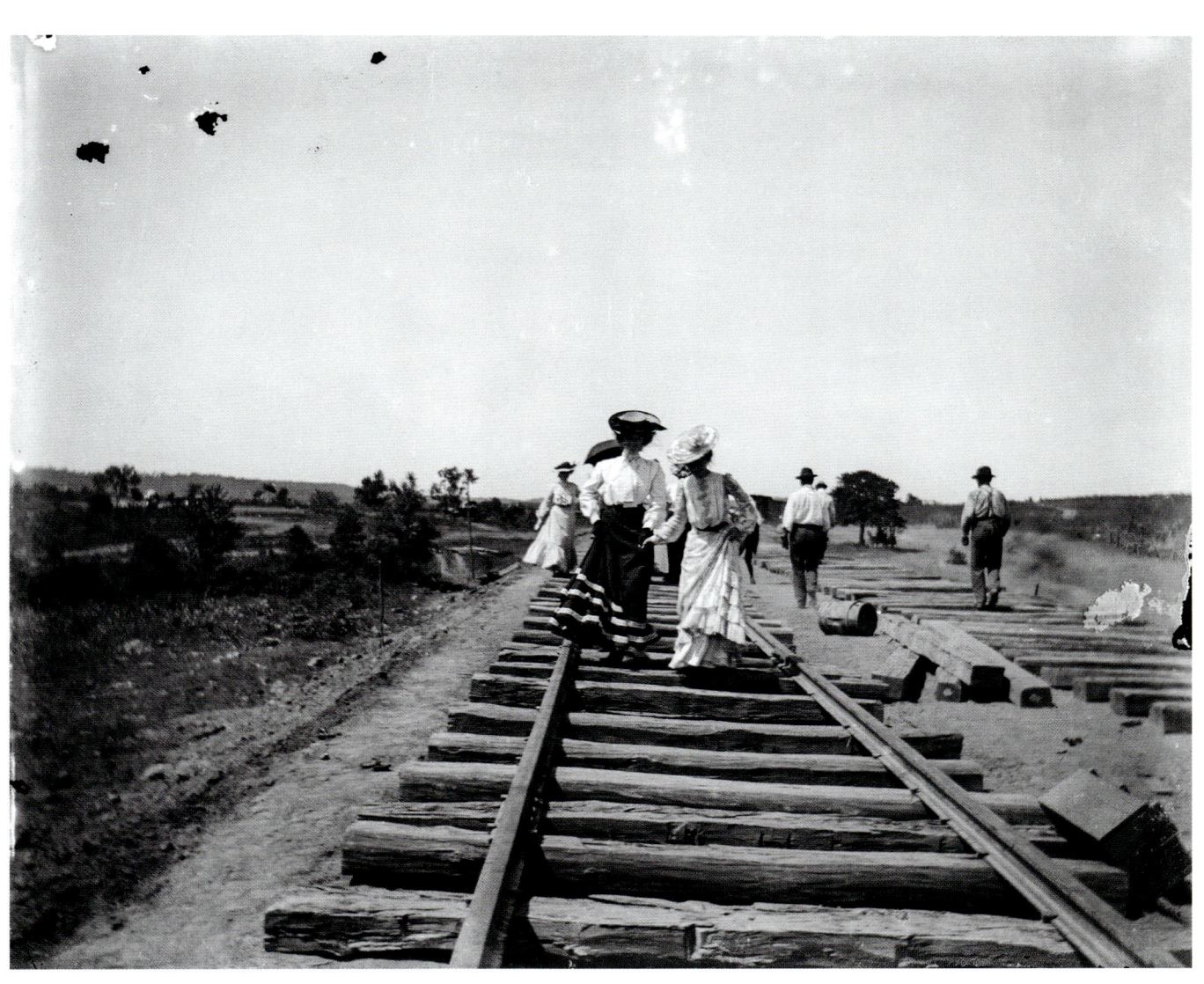

Friends walk along the Ozark and Cherokee
Central Railroad under construction, Tahlequah,
Oklahoma, 1902.

simplified attempts to define the Cherokee experience. As a collection of Cobb's memories, her photos reveal a dimension of humanity connecting Cherokee people today to their shared past."[4]

Across Cobb's photographs, a clear thread of continuity can be seen in her wish to "preserve a piece of her people's heritage."[5] She is often referenced by her documentation of Hunter's Home, considered "the most opulent house in Indian Territory."[6] It was here, as a young woman, that she made a closet into a darkroom to process her glass plate negatives. The home, where Cobb and her family lived from 1894–1907, became a symbolic site for her identity as a photographer. "Quite literally, she maps out the domestic scene with her lens. The fact that her family did not own Hunter's Home is moot—this is *her space*, and she stakes claim to the entire estate through her photography."[7]

Cobb saw her photographic work as part of a contribution to a larger historical record of Cherokee society. A member of the elite herself, she engaged with political life, including work with the Cherokee Temperance Society. From 1949 to 1959, she was the curator of Hunter's Home, her former residence, and a newly established historic site, where she used her own photographic collection to faithfully restore the interior. A study of Cobb's collection today shows how she made use of her own identity—both as a woman and a member of upper-class society—to tell a wider story of Native American life. She became "a leader in the preservation of her family's and tribe's heritage."[8] While she most likely did not see herself as a pioneer, Cobb's life work certainly displays a deep commitment to documenting her own signature outlook on celebrations of life—in women, community, and a wider Cherokee Nation.

—Jennifer Natalie Fish

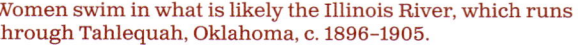

Women swim in what is likely the Illinois River, which runs through Tahlequah, Oklahoma, c. 1896–1905.

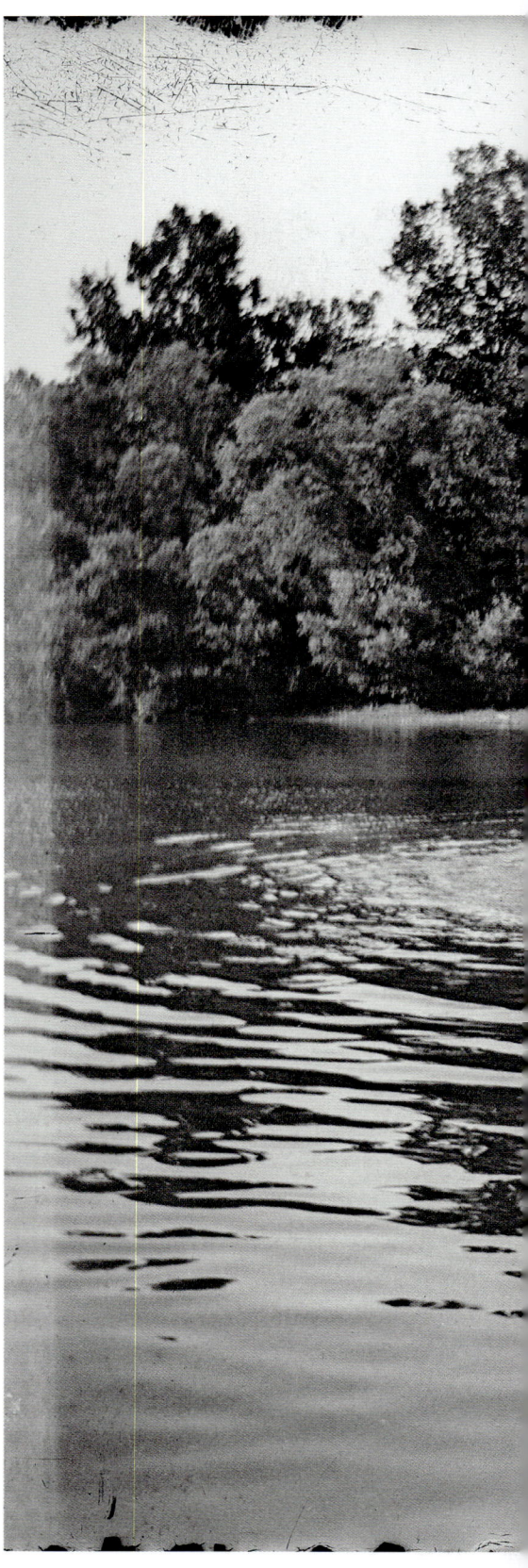

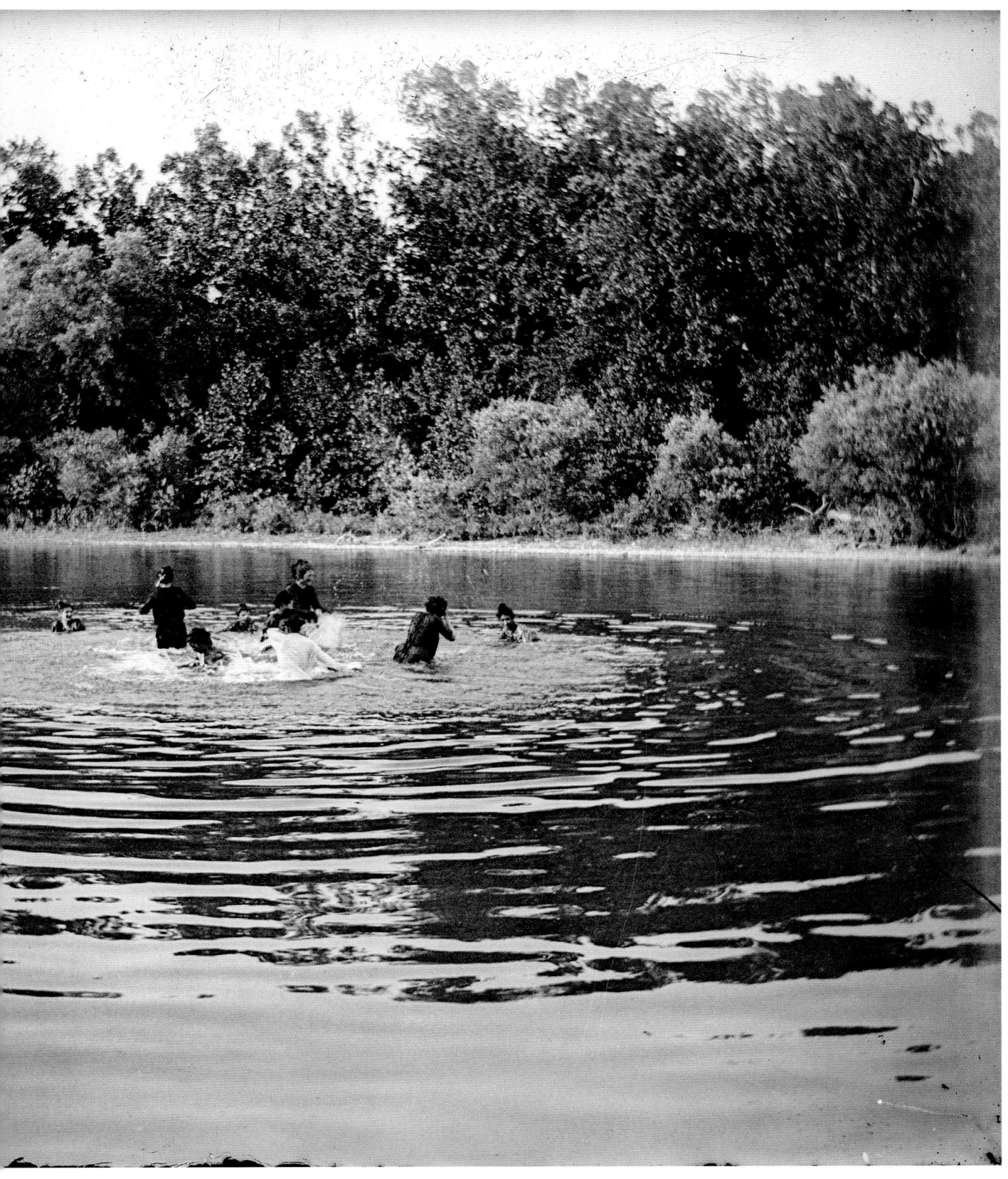

RICHARD ALBERT THROSSEL

Cree
Apsáalooke Nation (Crow Nation)
Montana
United States

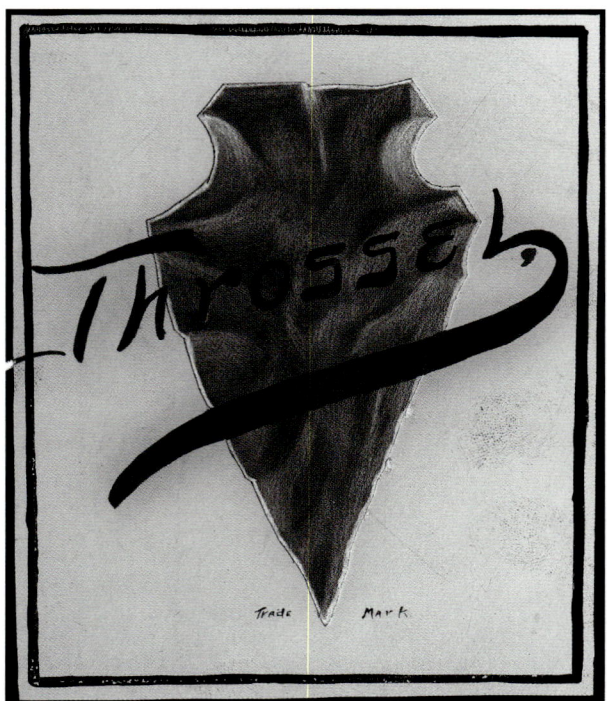

"It somehow felt spiritual to find her," says Apsáalooke (Crow) artist Wendy Red Star about locating a photograph of her great-great-grandmother, Her Dreams Are True (Julia Bad Boy), in the Richard Throssel Papers at the American Heritage Center, University of Wyoming. "Throssel's portraits of women are extraordinary," she adds.[1]

From 1902 to 1911, Richard Throssel (1882–1933), who was, in his own words, of "French canadian cree parentage,"[2] lived on the Apsáalooke reservation in south-central Montana, where he produced a distinct body of work marked by familiarity. He arrived there from Roy, Washington, just 20 years old, needing a drier climate for his rheumatism. Along with his older brother Harry, he found employment as a clerk with the Bureau of Indian Affairs (BIA) Indian Service office. But Throssel's most sincere ambitions lay in the arts.

Throssel's "artist's life," reported the *Billings Gazette*, began with his residence among the Apsáalooke.[3] Under the mentorship of the prolific Joseph Henry Sharp, who was then based on the reservation, he pursued painting and drawing. At the same time, he bought a small camera and learned photography by studying magazines and textbooks. In 1904, Throssel married Florence Pifer, an Indiana-born white woman who reportedly spoke the Apsáalooke language and taught it to her husband. They were debating the economic viability of painting while starting a family, when a persuasive event occurred in 1905: Photographer Edward Sherriff Curtis passed through the reservation. It "was a revelation, indeed," wrote Throssel later. "This was really the starting point in my work."[4]

Curtis is a monumental and controversial figure in the history of photography. Historically, his portfolio has outweighed those of his Native contemporaries, many of whom were working in the same locations Curtis visited. When Throssel met him, he was in the midst of a 30-year project that encompassed 40,000 photographs of more than 80 Tribes. His efforts culminated in *The North American Indian*, published from 1907 to 1930 in 20 volumes. In the decades Curtis spent producing it, he was trusted by some Tribal members, invited by others, kept out, and thrown out. Curtis is rightly slammed for his "lack of ethnographic veracity."[5] He staged and retouched photographs for dramatic effect. He avoided and eliminated signs of modernity. He used a soft focus that obscured details and lent a quality of romance and nostalgia to his images. Collectively these techniques—rooted in the pictorialism movement of the time—espoused the widespread and harmful belief that Native Americans were facing extinction. "While mistaken in his conviction that he was recording the last days of a 'vanishing race,'" writes art critic and curator Lucy Lippard about Curtis, "he was right in believing that his photographs would be invaluable (not infallible) documents of a historical process of representation."[6]

The commercial success Curtis achieved in his lifetime was attractive to Throssel, and the influence of his imagery is particularly apparent in Throssel's close-up studio portraits of men in traditional adornment and regalia. Throssel's training with Sharp is evident across the collection. "When he began to photograph like a painter, using an artist's knowledge of light and composition…and a personal technique evolved from experimentation, he made pictures of real beauty," proclaimed the *Yellowstone News*.[7] Mostly, it's Throssel's Cree heritage and genuine relationships with the Apsáalooke, formed in the time he lived with them, that characterize his images.

With his eye for gesture, hundreds of photographs showing everyday activities—cooking, bathing, playing games, arrow making, hunting, horseback riding—are infused with a relaxed kinship. He lingered on tipi-filled landscapes and paid close attention to ceremonies and public events. He didn't eschew Western wear like cowboy hats and button-down shirts. Women appear unguarded in many portraits and candid moments. Captions Throssel typed point to the respect he held for them. "The woman of the camp takes up her portion of the work, for she is the real worker," reads part of one. An image of a mother holding her newborn inside

Throssel Photocraft Company trademark, c. 1911–33.

Opposite: Making sausage, Apsáalooke Nation, c. 1905–11.

PHOTOGRAPHS BY RICHARD THROSSEL. RICHARD THROSSEL PAPERS (2394). AMERICAN HERITAGE CENTER, UNIVERSITY OF WYOMING. AH02394_1547, AH02394_0274, AH02394_0775, AH02394_0884, AH02394_0648, AH02394_0292, AH02394_0726, AH02394_0893, AH02394_0645

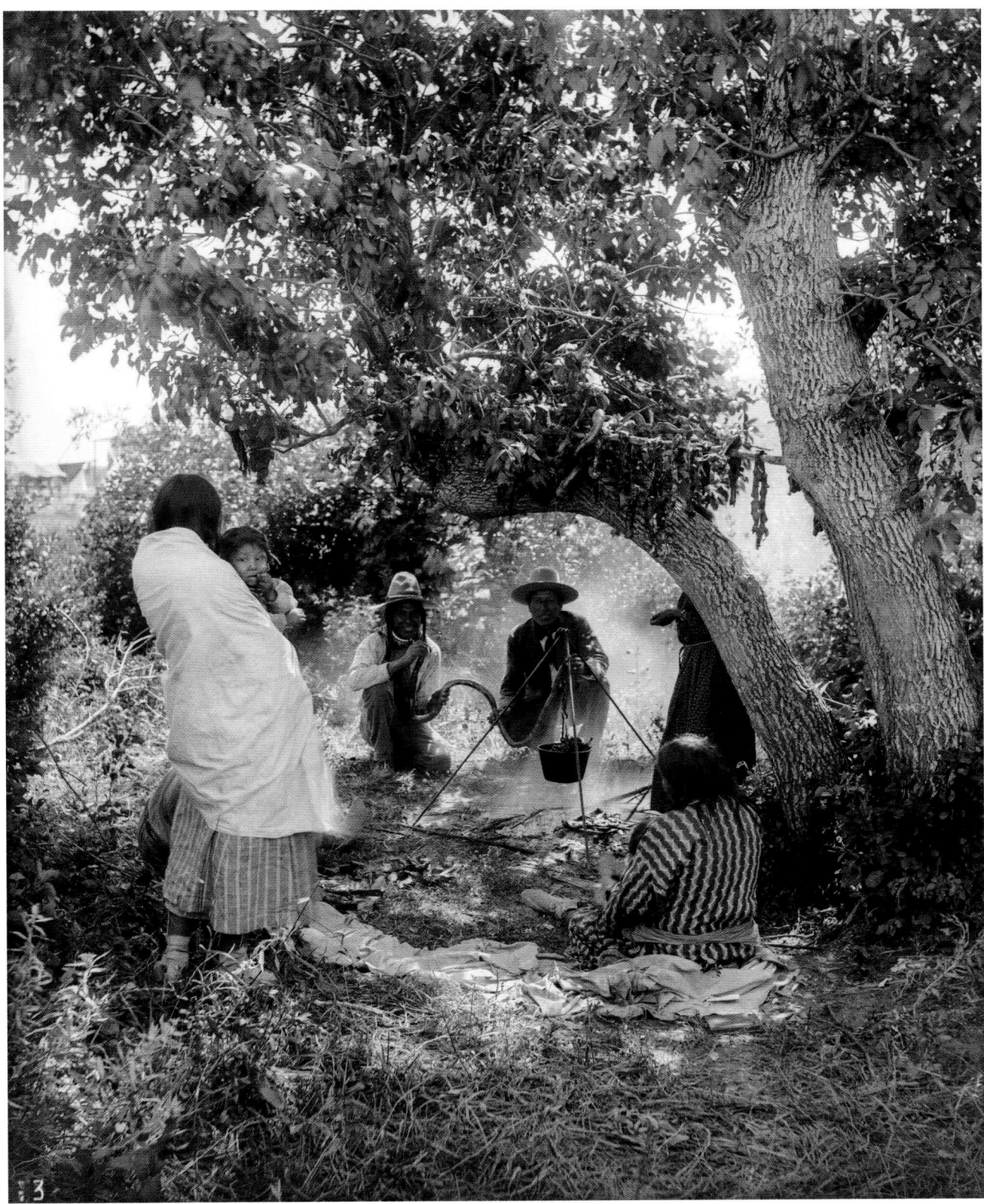

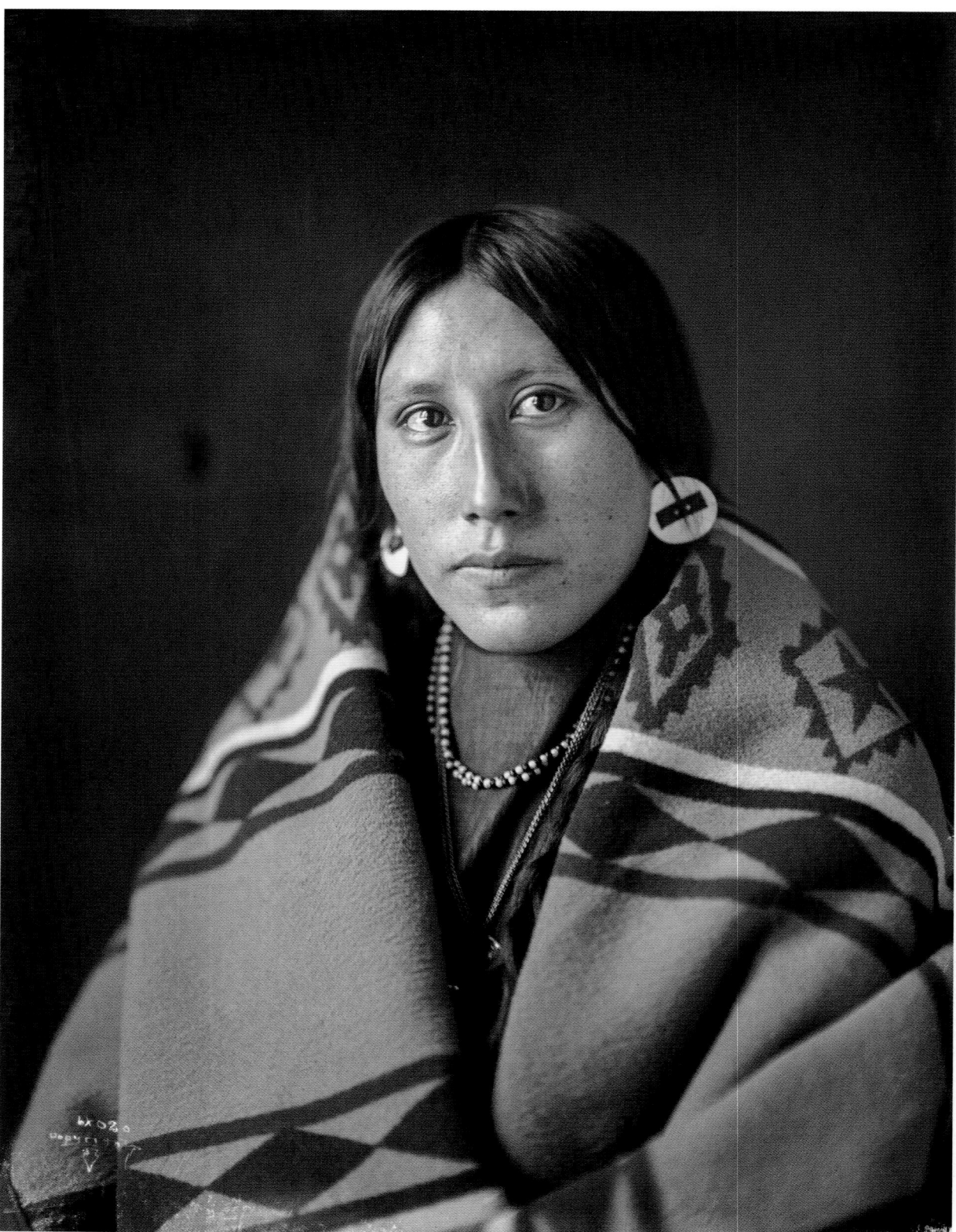

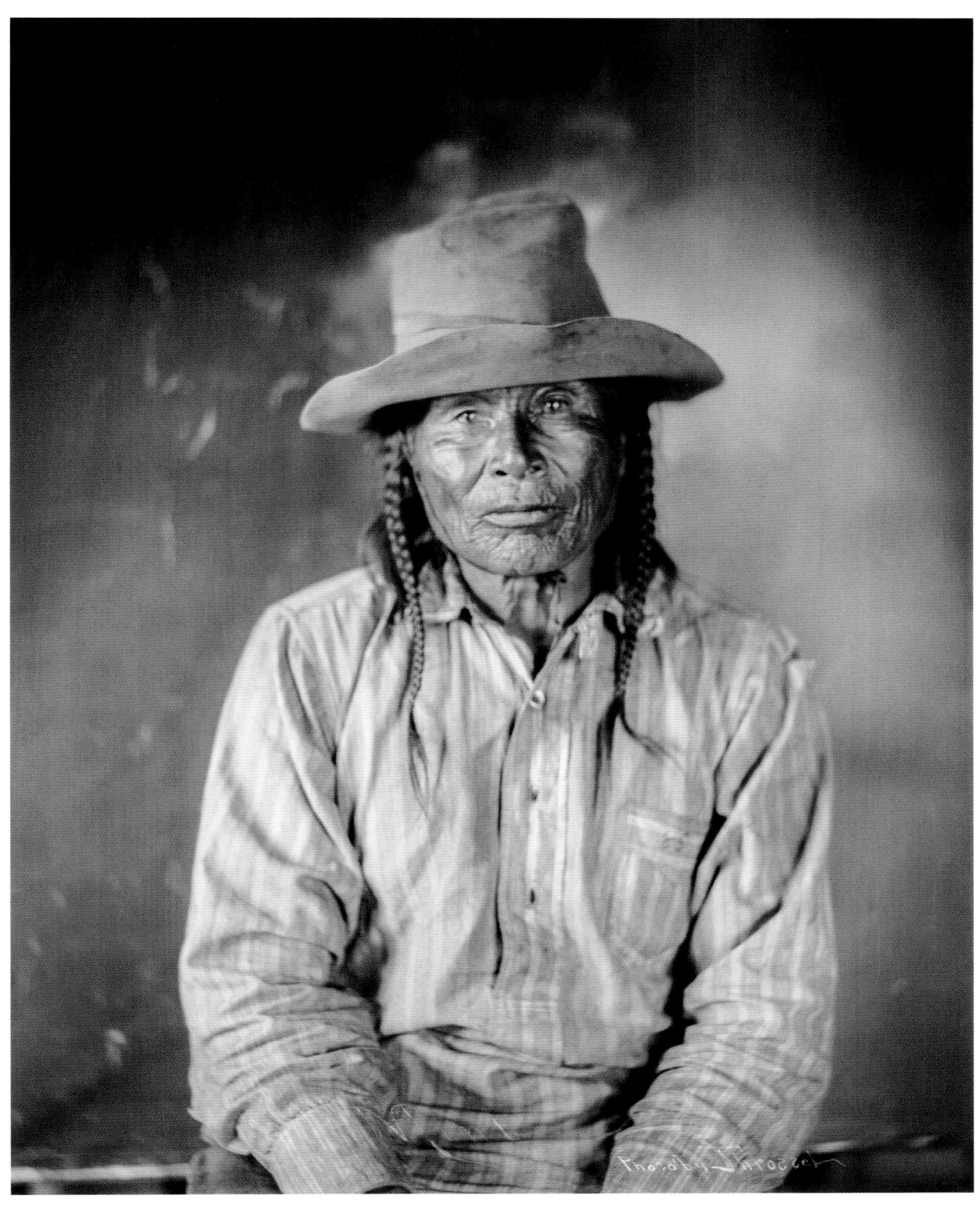

A portrait of Mint, an Apsáalooke man, Apsáalooke Nation, c. 1905–11.

Opposite: An Apsáalooke woman, Apsáalooke Nation, c. 1905–11.

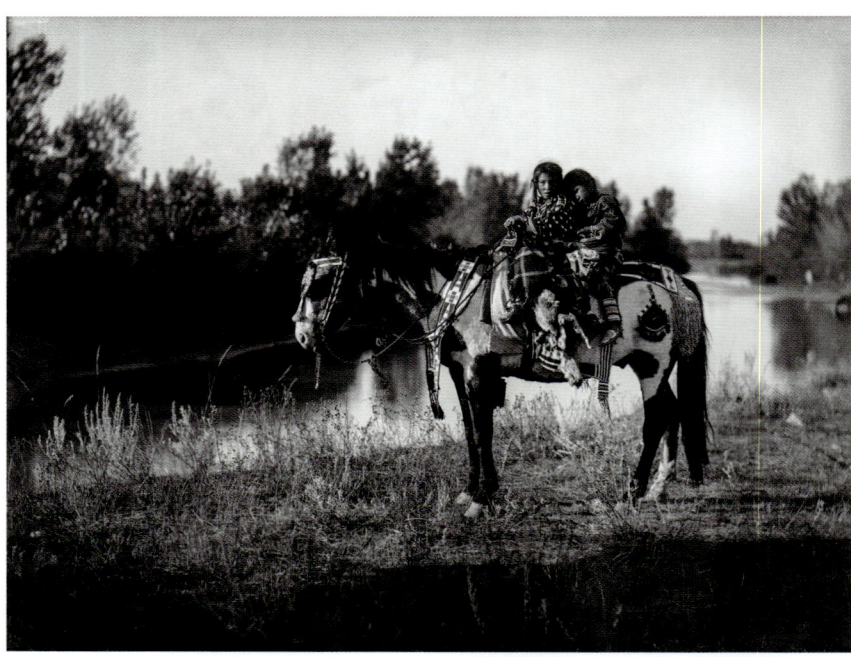

a tipi flooded with light is paired with the words, "The Modern Madon[n]a pictures the home life of one of the younger women. To say she is proud of her baby is needless, for Indian parents rarely punish a child for any offense."[8]

The Apsáalooke adopted Throssel in 1906 and gave him a parcel of land. The decision was propelled by the Dawes Act and the politics of allotment. Inviting him and others into the Tribe helped the Apsáalooke by increasing their property and reducing acreage available for public sale. Throssel's Apsáalooke name was Esh Quon Dupahs ("Kills Inside the Camp"), also spelled Ashua Eshquon Dupaz.

Until 1909, when Throssel was hired by the Indian Service as a field photographer, he pursued his personal photography on "sundays and after hours."[9] In 1910, he was assigned to illustrate an Indian Service lecture meant to battle the spread of tuberculosis and trachoma in Native nations. The photographs Throssel was directed to make (and stage) portrayed traditional activities the government deemed "unsanitary," like sitting on the ground or sharing a pipe in ceremony. Alternative images he made promoted conventional household scenes—for example, dining around a table draped in cloth and set with chinaware. With a goal of acculturation, the illustrated lecture traveled across the country, leaving "cultural destruction in its wake."[10]

In 1911, Throssel resigned from the Indian Service. He, Pifer, and their two daughters moved to Billings, where he opened a commercial photography business called the Throssel Photocraft Company. Leveraging his Indigenous heritage, he marketed his personal collection of images featuring Apsáalooke life. His most well-known product, in which he strived to meet the commercial likings of his early 20th-century Euro-American audience, was a set of 39 idealized photographs called the *Western Classics from the Land of the Indian*. He frequently returned to Apsáalooke Country with hopes to "complete the set of pictures" he started there.[11] He wrote short stories about Apsáalooke battles and lore, and he worked as a photographer and photoengraver for the *Billings Gazette*. After Throssel was issued U.S. citizenship at age 34, he advocated for the Apsáalooke and, in an effort to affect policy, served two terms as a Montana state legislator. In 1933, at age 51, he died from a heart attack, leaving behind a multidimensional portfolio of more than 1,000 images he made with the Apsáalooke.

In a brief autobiographical statement, Throssel alluded to the way his heritage contributed to his career: "Doubtless my Indian blood gives me a keener insight to the lives of the Indians and brings me much more in sympathy with them. At the same time the interpretation of these things comes easy because of the understanding of the white ways and methods."[12]

Despite his efforts, Throssel's pictures did not gain wide recognition in his lifetime. In 1997, Peggy Albright authored *Crow Indian Photographer: The Work of Richard Throssel*. The impressive biography preceded a 2003 exhibition at the Smithsonian National Museum of the American Indian: *Telling a Crow Story: The Photographs of Richard Throssel*.

Two children on a horse, Apsáalooke Nation, c. 1905–11.
Opposite: Bather, Apsáalooke Nation, c. 1905–11.

—Sarah Stacke

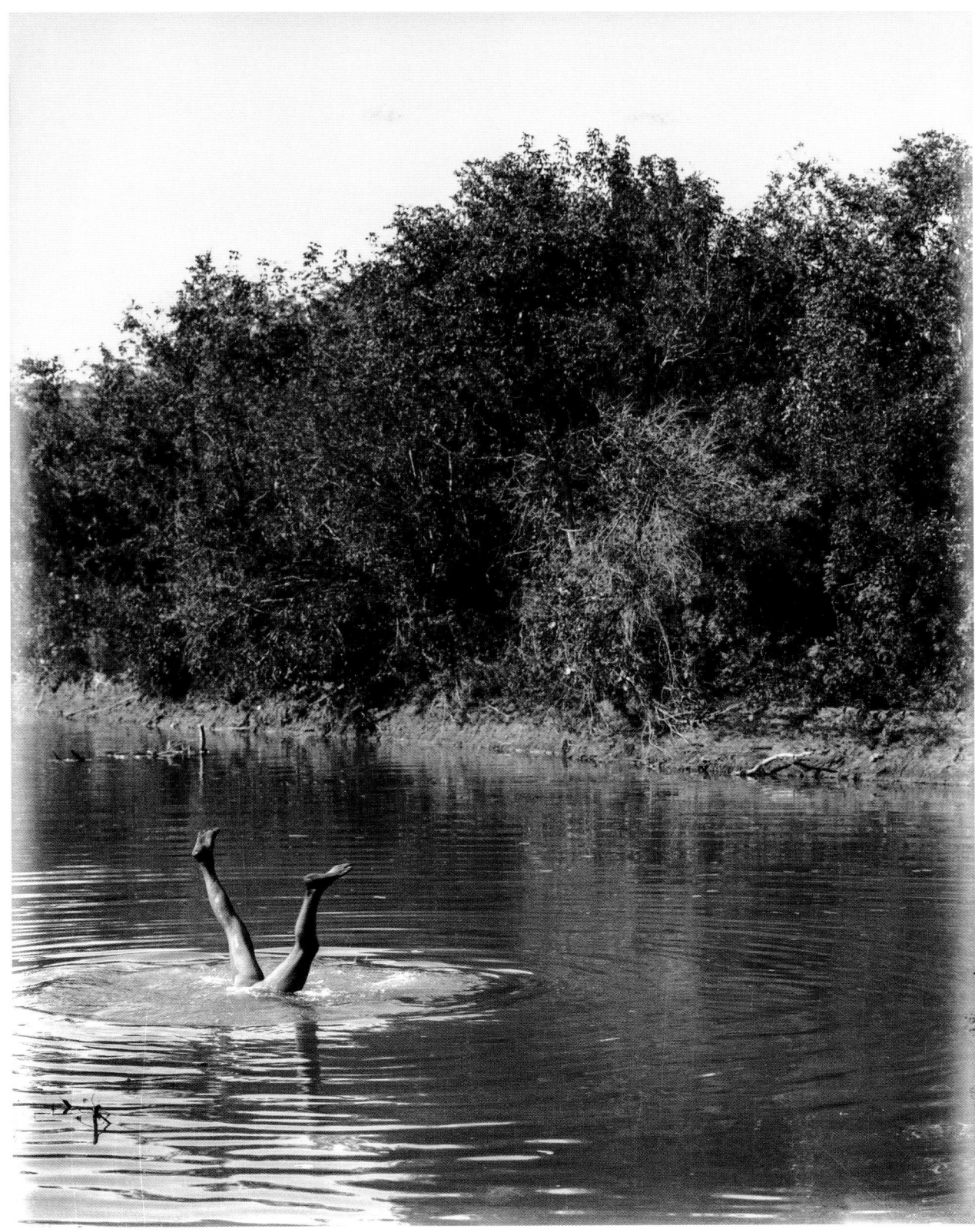

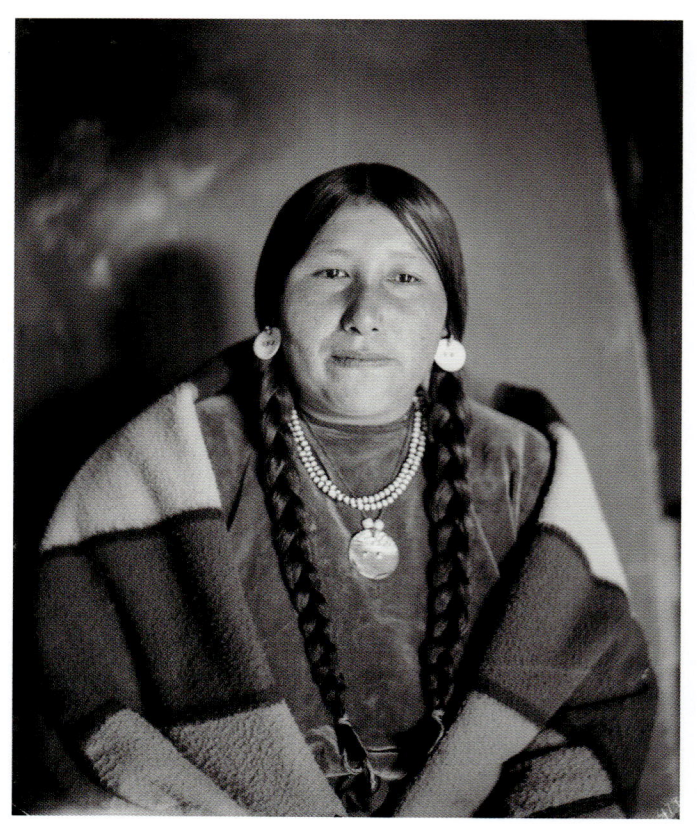

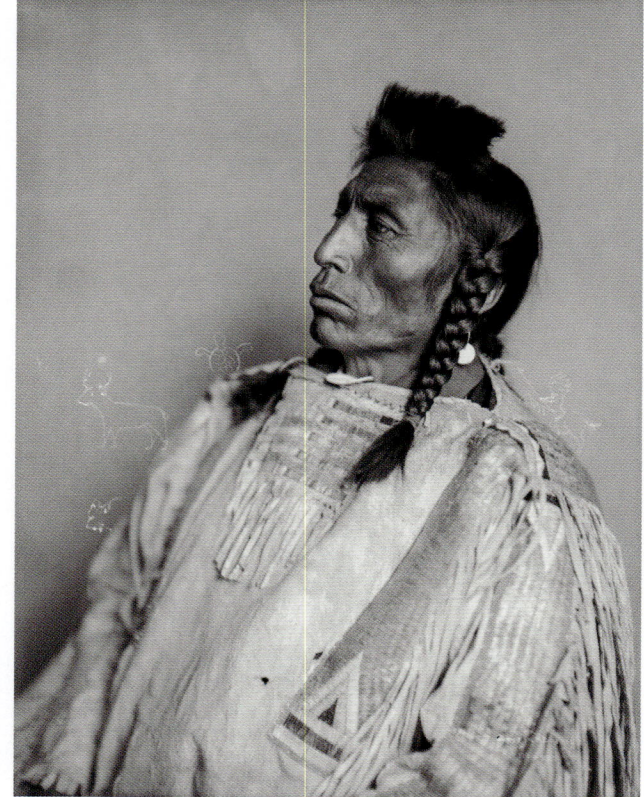

Her Dreams Are True (Julia Bad Boy),
Apsáalooke Nation, c. 1905–11.

Chief Medicine Crow, who is in mourning following the
death of a son, Apsáalooke Nation, 1908.

Opposite: Apsáalooke dancers, Apsáalooke Nation,
c. 1905–11. Caleb Bull Shows with drum; standing (left
to right): Harry Bull Shows, son of Caleb; Frank Hawk;
man once identified; Mortimer Dreamer.

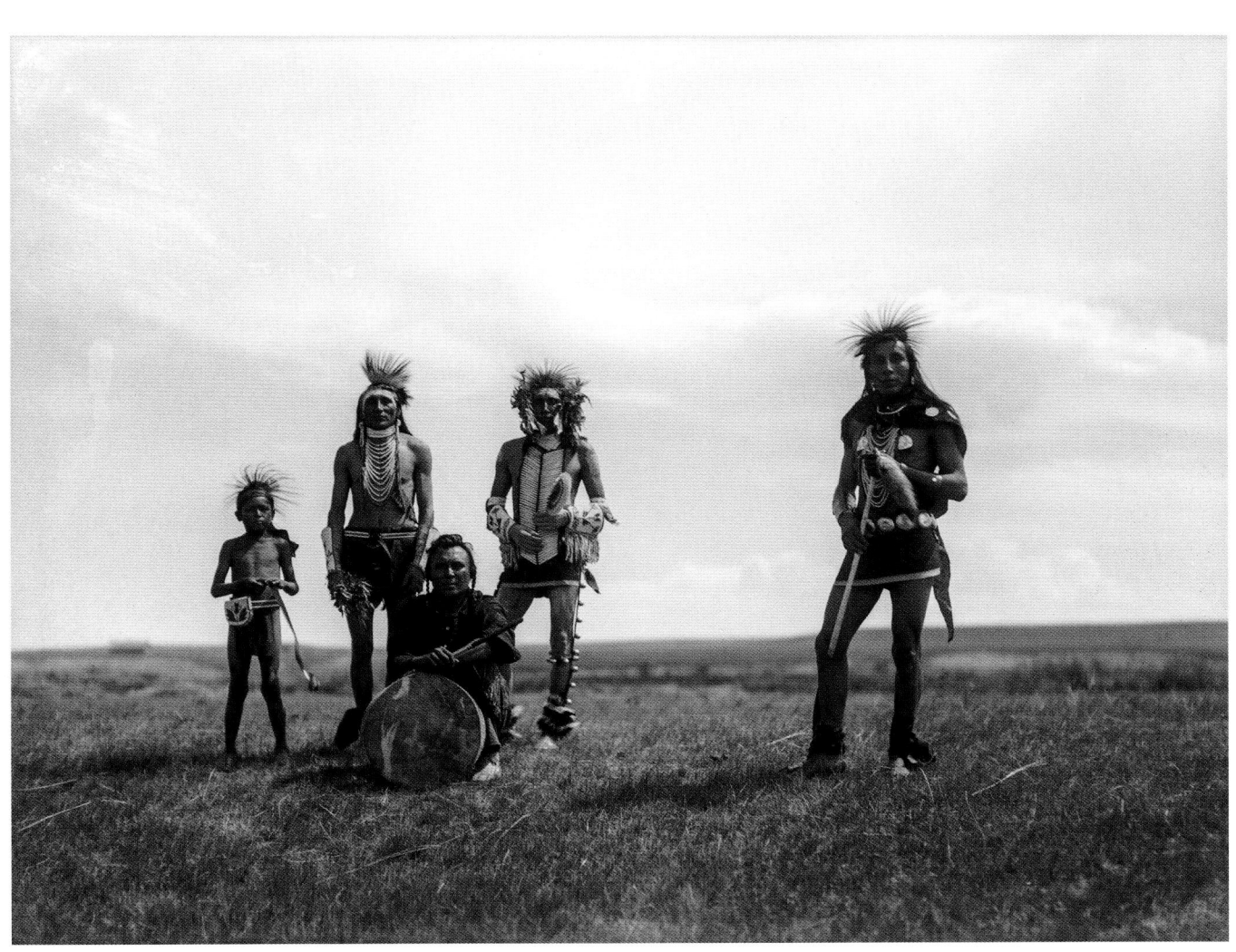

BENJAMIN ALFRED HALDANE
HENRY S. HALDANE

Tsimshian
Tsimshian Nation
Annette Island Indian Reserve, Metlakatla, Alaska
United States

Around 1900, Benjamin Alfred Haldane (1874–1941)—nicknamed B. A.—composed a self-portrait inside his studio in Metlakatla, Territory of Alaska. Seated in the center of the frame, he placed two cameras and a pair of slide lanterns to his left. On his right he arranged a megaphone, a gramophone with multiple earphones, and an open case full of wax cylinders.

The portrait expresses Haldane's love of photography and music, and his steadfast resistance to the colonial rule of William Duncan, the local lay missionary. Haldane, calm and intent, chose to rest his right arm on a model totem pole that displays his Laxgyibuu (Wolf Clan) crest at the bottom. "In this image, B. A. confidently positions himself as physically and metaphorically supported by our cultural values and beliefs," says Mique'l Dangeli, a Tsimshian art historian raised in Metlakatla.[1] Haldane's seemingly small act continued Tsimshian "ways of being and knowing,"[2] despite Duncan's strict governance that tried to outlaw traditional practices, demand Christian living, limit education, and enforce a self-sufficient cash-based economy.

In 1887, when Haldane was 13 years old, his family joined more than 800 Tsimshian people who, accompanied by Duncan, left Metlakatla, British Columbia, in search of government-sanctioned land rights and founded Metlakatla, Territory of Alaska, on Annette Island. The community, highly publicized as a Christian utopia by assimilation-minded media, gained federal recognition four years later and established itself as the Annette Island Indian Reserve, the only reservation in what is now the state of Alaska.

At age 16, Haldane began making portraits using homes, textiles, and the forested land as backdrops. He described himself as self-taught,[3] though he may have traded techniques with his older cousin Henry S. Haldane (c. 1858–1936), a priest turned photographer with a much smaller existing archive than Haldane's. By 1910, Henry was living 15 miles south of Metlakatla in Ketchikan, where he worked at the Salvation Army and as a fisher.[4]

B. A. Haldane opened his studio in Metlakatla in 1899, if not earlier, advertising himself as a "Scenic and Portrait Photo-Grapher." He acquired props, painted backdrops, and decorative flooring, and his sitters used the space to emphasize and record their prosperity—both wealth and abundant loved ones. Haldane's business attracted community members, including the family of Dangeli, who grew up with images he made of her grandmother and great-grandparents. Other Native clients traveled from neighboring communities, perhaps drawn by the opportunity to have their portraits made within the walls of the only Native-owned photography studio known on the Northwest Coast at the time. "B. A.'s photography was a medium through which they could construct the telling of their own histories," says Dangeli.[5]

Regardless of Duncan's efforts and sweeping false narratives, the Tsimshian of Metlakatla did not reject their Tsimshian identities after participating in their conversion to Christianity. Haldane's photographs attest to this. Outside of his studio, he made portraits of Tsimshian and Nisga'a people dressed in ceremonial regalia, attending Potlatches (then illegal in the United States and Canada), and declaring Clan lineage and status with ceremonial belongings. As a child, Dangeli's grandmother Corrine Reeve wore petite gold bracelets engraved with the family's Laxsgiik (Eagle Clan) crest. She

B. A. Haldane self-portrait inside his photography studio, Metlakatla, Alaska, c. 1900.
PHOTOGRAPH BY B. A. HALDANE. COURTESY OF KETCHIKAN MUSEUMS.
KM 89.2.14.21

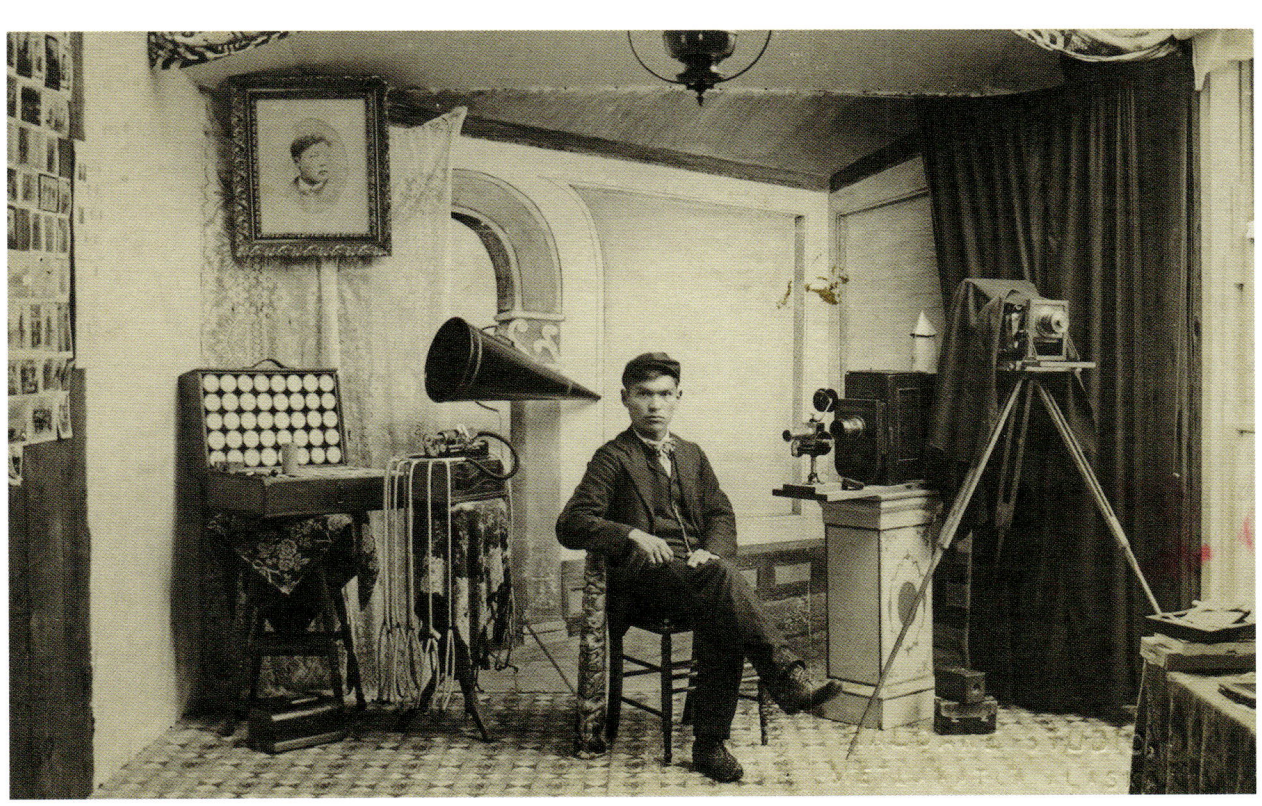

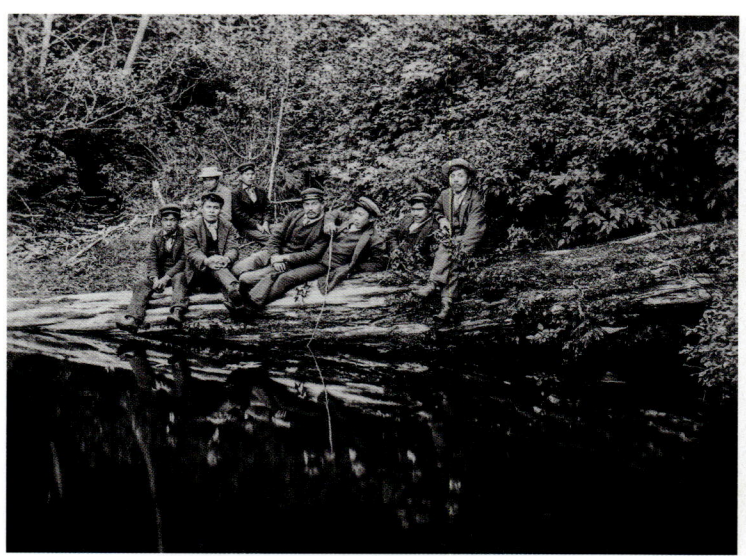

had them on when Haldane photographed her on a boardwalk with her arms wrapped around a hefty bouquet of summertime flowers. "Seeing the bracelets," recalls Dangeli, "was a visual affirmation for me of my great-great-grandparents' efforts to maintain and instill our clan identity into their grandchildren during one of the most intense times of our cultural oppression. Their resilience is the reason for the survival of my family's clan identity today."[6]

In addition to having a four-decade career as a photographer, Haldane was a gifted musician, composer, and band director. He played the piano, pipe organ, cornet, trombone, and violin, and he taught music (and made photographs) in Alaska Native and First Nations communities in southeast Alaska, Washington State, and British Columbia. With eleven children, Haldane was a leader in Metlakatla's civic affairs, especially the movement, against Duncan's wishes, for an improved education system. Haldane's own formal schooling ceased when Duncan expelled him after he finished third grade, claiming "there was nothing more" for him to learn.[7]

In 2003, exactly 163 of Haldane's glass plate negatives, probably a fraction of what he produced in his lifetime, were rescued from the flames of Metlakatla's waste facility by resident Dennis Dunne. It was just one year later that Dangeli learned about Haldane's photography practice, igniting a 20-year-long mission to uncover and share, through his pictures, stories of the Tsimshian of Metlakatla's cultural continuity and opposition to Duncan's colonial code. A large part of her research is locating Haldane's photographs in scattered archives, often reattributing his name in the process, and then reclaiming copies of the images for Metlakatla families. "Enabling B. A.'s photography to re-acquire a living context requires bringing his images and their history home," she says.[8]

—Sarah Stacke

A fishing party at Skeena River, British Columbia, with men from Metlakatla, Alaska, and Port Simpson, British Columbia, 1908.
PHOTOGRAPH BY HENRY S. HALDANE. NATIONAL ARCHIVES, SIR HENRY WELLCOME COLLECTION. NAID 297546

Opposite: A family in regalia, likely in the Nass River valley, British Columbia, c. 1899–1910. This glass plate negative was rescued from the Metlakatla waste facility in 2003.
PHOTOGRAPH BY B. A. HALDANE. COURTESY OF KETCHIKAN MUSEUMS. KM 2018.2.30.54

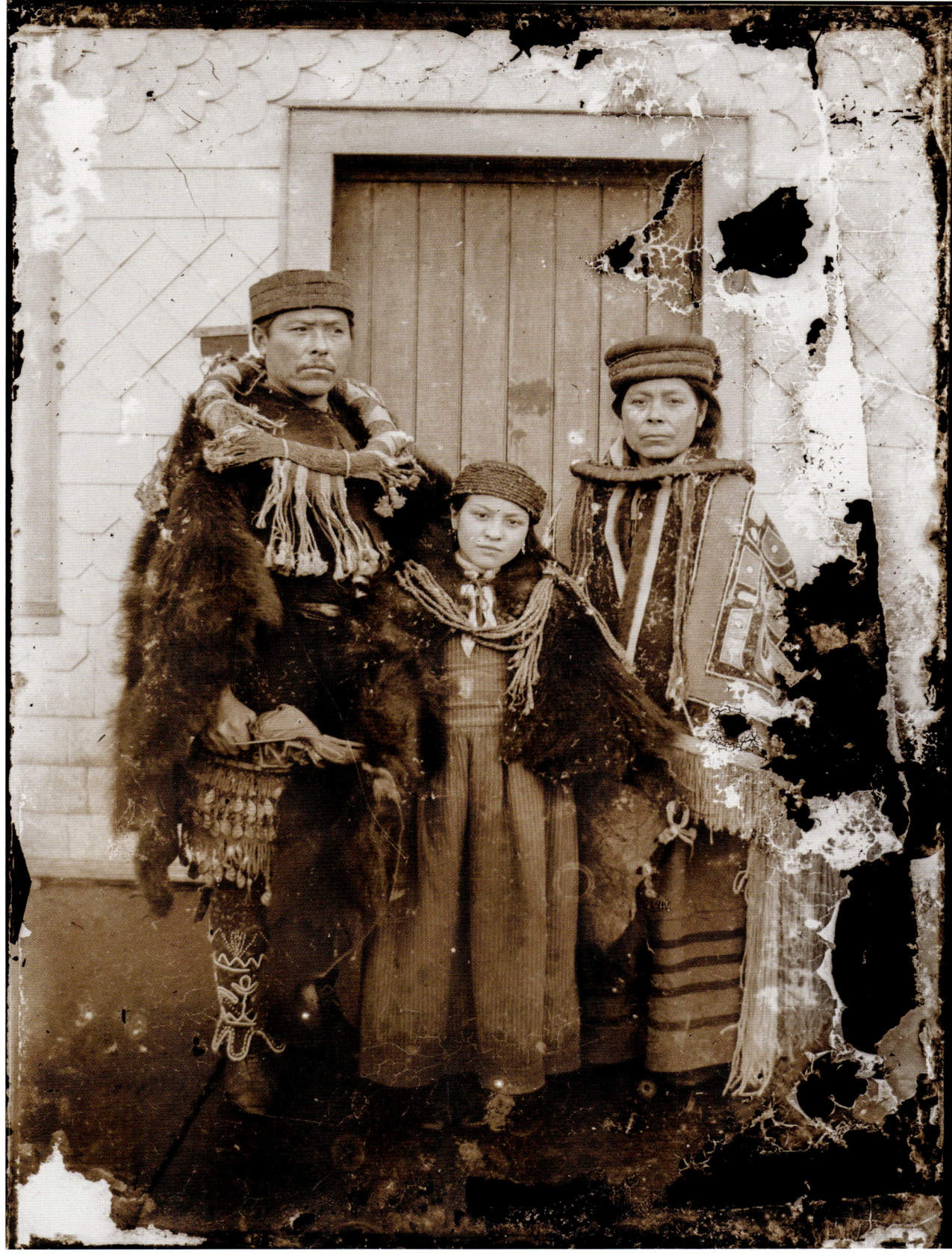

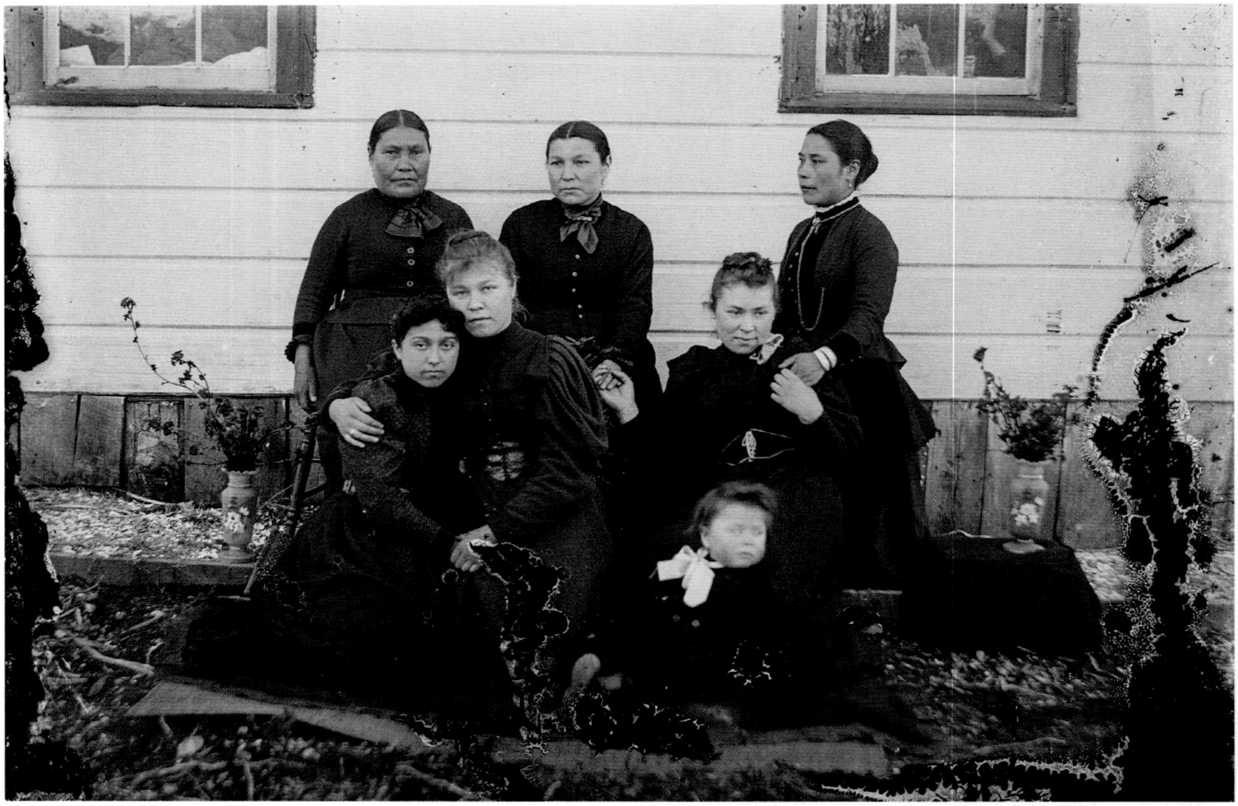

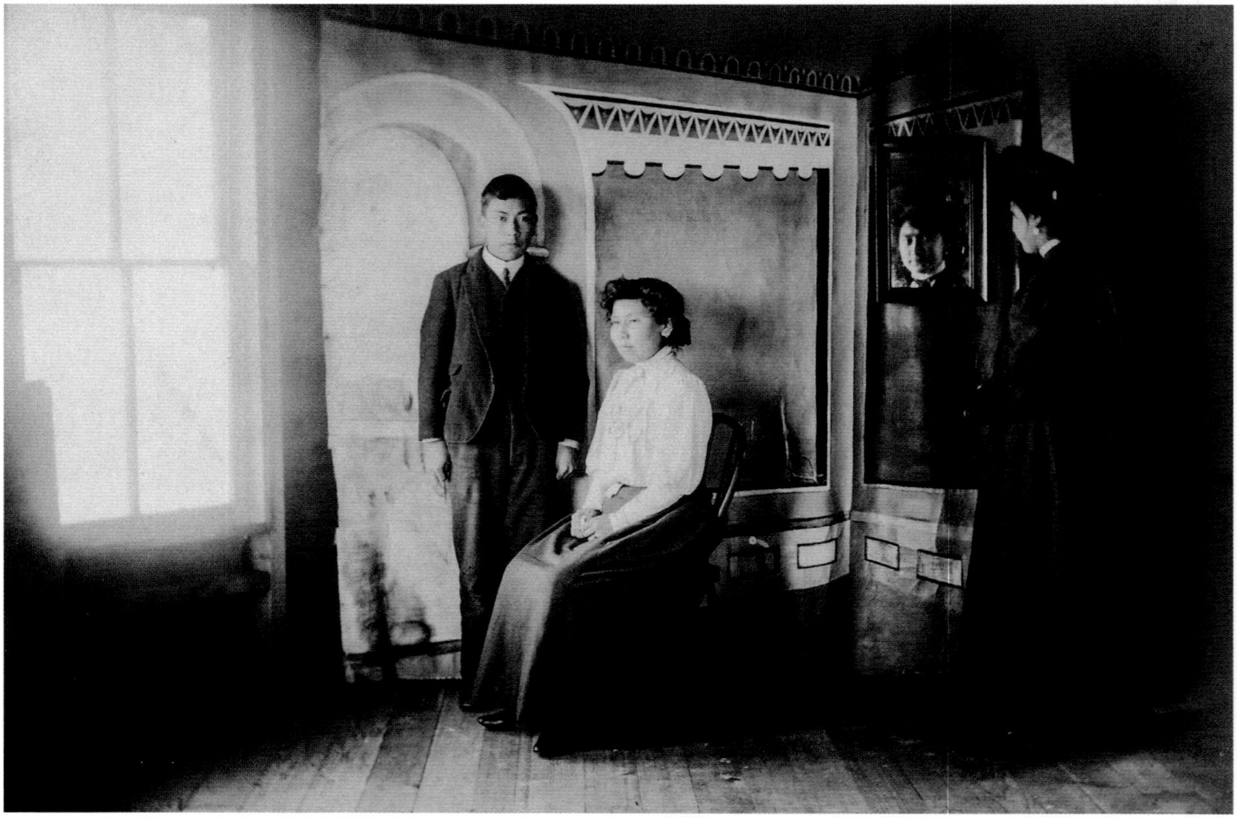

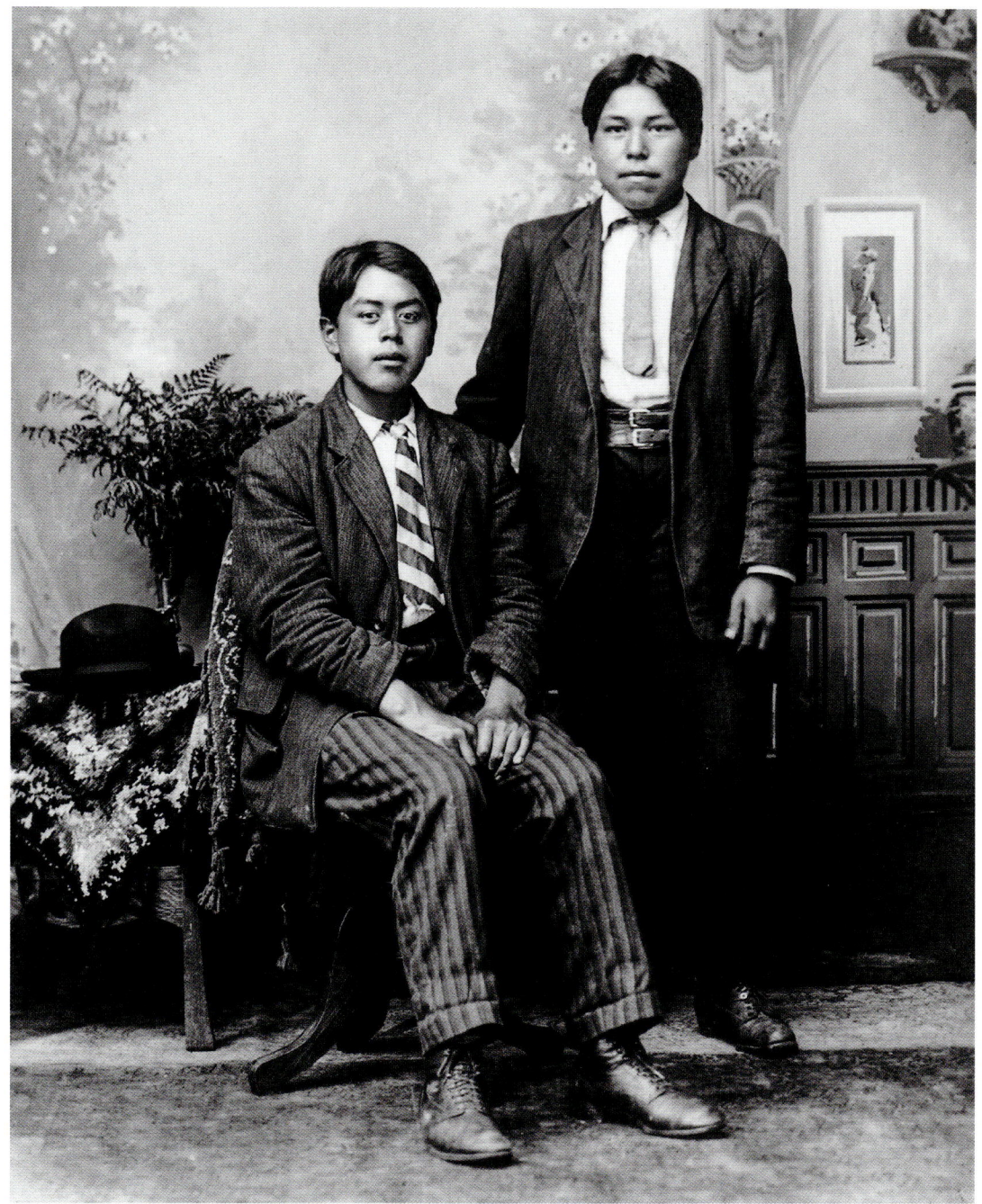

Two young men inside B. A. Haldane's photography
studio, Metlakatla, Alaska, c. 1910.
PHOTOGRAPH BY B. A. HALDANE. NATIONAL ARCHIVES, SIR HENRY WELLCOME
COLLECTION. NAID 297540

Opposite: Six women and a child in front of a home,
Metlakatla, Alaska, c. 1890–99.
PHOTOGRAPH BY B. A. HALDANE. COURTESY OF KETCHIKAN MUSEUMS.
KM 2018.2.30.66

Opposite: Fred Eaton, Mary Eaton (seated), and a friend
inside B. A. Haldane's studio, Metlakatla, Alaska, c. 1900.
PHOTOGRAPH BY B. A. HALDANE. NATIONAL ARCHIVES, SIR HENRY WELLCOME
COLLECTION. NAID 297587

GEORGE HUNT

Tlingit
Kwakwa̲ka'wakw Territory
Vancouver Island, British Columbia
Canada

In the mid-1890s on Vancouver Island, British Columbia, Franz Boas and George Hunt (1854–1933) held a cloth backdrop behind a Kwakwa̲ka'wakw woman sitting on the grass. She's spinning yarn and rocking a cradle hung over a branch, using a thin cord tied around her toe. Boas and Hunt confront the camera, while the woman looks at the spindle in her hands. Rows of fresh wooden fences and a house with pillars are visible behind the staged scene, visualizing the encroachment of settler society.

Boas, widely known as the father of American anthropology, and Hunt, a Tlingit ethnographer, worked together for more than 40 years, recording and collecting the Kwakwa̲ka'wakw culture of the Northwest Coast. Hunt (also named X̲awe, 'Maxwa̲lagalis, K̲'ixitasu, and Noɫq'oɫala)[1] was the son of a Tlingit mother, Anislaga (Mary Ebbets), and a British fur trader, Robert Hunt. Although Hunt was not Kwakwa̲ka'wakw, he was raised among them and Anislaga's Tlingit relatives in Fort Rupert, participated in Kwakwa̲ka'wakw customs and ceremonies, and spoke Kwakawala. He was also fluent in Tlingit and English. Both of Hunt's marriages were to high-ranking Kwakwa̲ka'wakw women —T'ɫaliɫi'lakw (Lucy Homiskanis) in 1872 and Tsukwani (Francine T'ɫat'ɫaɫawidzamga) in 1916.

Boas and Hunt made significant contributions to the ethnographic records of the Kwakwa̲ka'wakw Nation. The first book they coauthored, *The Social Organization and Secret Societies of the Kwakiutl Indians*, a seminal anthropological work, was published in 1897. In the decades they collaborated, Hunt produced "tens of thousands of hand-written manuscript pages"[2] with descriptions of Kwakwa̲ka'wakw lifeways, now archived at the American Philosophical Society (APS), Columbia University (where Boas was a professor), and the American Museum of Natural History (where Boas was a curator).

Hunt was an aggressive collector of ethnographic objects from the Northwest Coast, possibly responsible for 80 percent of Kwakwa̲ka'wakw material culture found in museums today. He incorporated ample photography into his work, imaging Shamans, rites, and other Kwakwa̲ka'wakw practices. Boas frequently requested photographs of particular items,[3] and when he published Hunt's images and texts, he often did so under his own name.

From 1911 to 1914, Hunt was the principal assistant to Edward Sherriff Curtis, who was in Kwakwa̲ka'wakw Territory making photographs for Volume X of *The North American Indian* and filming *In the Land of the Head Hunters*, a silent movie featuring an entirely Kwakwa̲ka'wakw cast. Hunt's wife Tsukwani was intensely involved in both productions. She modeled for photographs, acted in the film, constructed traditional garments, and advised on cultural details.[4]

Hunt's letters and field notes reveal he depended heavily on his mother, sisters, and especially his high-status wives for access to information and insight throughout his relationship with Boas. Their crucial offerings, however, were "accorded neither authority nor authorship" in the publications, observed scholar Margaret M. Bruchac.[5] This history, brought to light by Bruchac and others including Sarah Hunt, Lucy Homiskanis and Hunt's great-great-granddaughter, can be read in the photograph of Boas and Hunt standing over the Kwakwa̲ka'wakw woman with the yarn. With a cloth, their bodies, and their eye contact, the men are creating a frame around her and claiming ownership of the data she is presenting.

The work that Boas and Hunt did together has come to be known as salvage ethnography, a problematic practice focused on the collection of Indigenous cultures believed to be rapidly disappearing, rather than in motion. A photograph Hunt made on the coast around 1900 shows canoes and longhouses made of cedar planks, the traditional dwelling of the Kwakwa̲ka'wakw. Two totem poles are visible on the horizon. The photo is, hauntingly, void of people.

In 2015 and 2016 the APS was invited to attend two Kwakwa̲ka'wakw Potlatches. For these traditional gift-giving and feasting ceremonies, the APS prepared and gave away books compiled from hundreds of pages of unpublished manuscripts written by Hunt in Kwakawala and English. The books contained stories, family histories, maps, and depictions of late 19th- and early 20th-century lifeways. It is "precisely" the Kwakwa̲ka'wakw, said the APS, who are the intended audience and authorities of these manuscripts.[6]

—Sarah Stacke

Kwakwa̲ka'wakw woman spinning yarn and rocking a cradle using a cord tied to her foot, Vancouver Island, British Columbia, c. 1894–95. Franz Boas (left) and George Hunt are holding up the backdrop.
PHOTOGRAPH BY OREGON COLUMBUS HASTINGS. AMERICAN MUSEUM OF NATURAL HISTORY LIBRARY. IMAGE 11604

Scene at the coast with canoe, longhouses, and totem pole, Vancouver, British Columbia, c. 1897–1902.
PHOTOGRAPH BY GEORGE HUNT. AMERICAN MUSEUM OF NATURAL HISTORY LIBRARY. IMAGE 104466

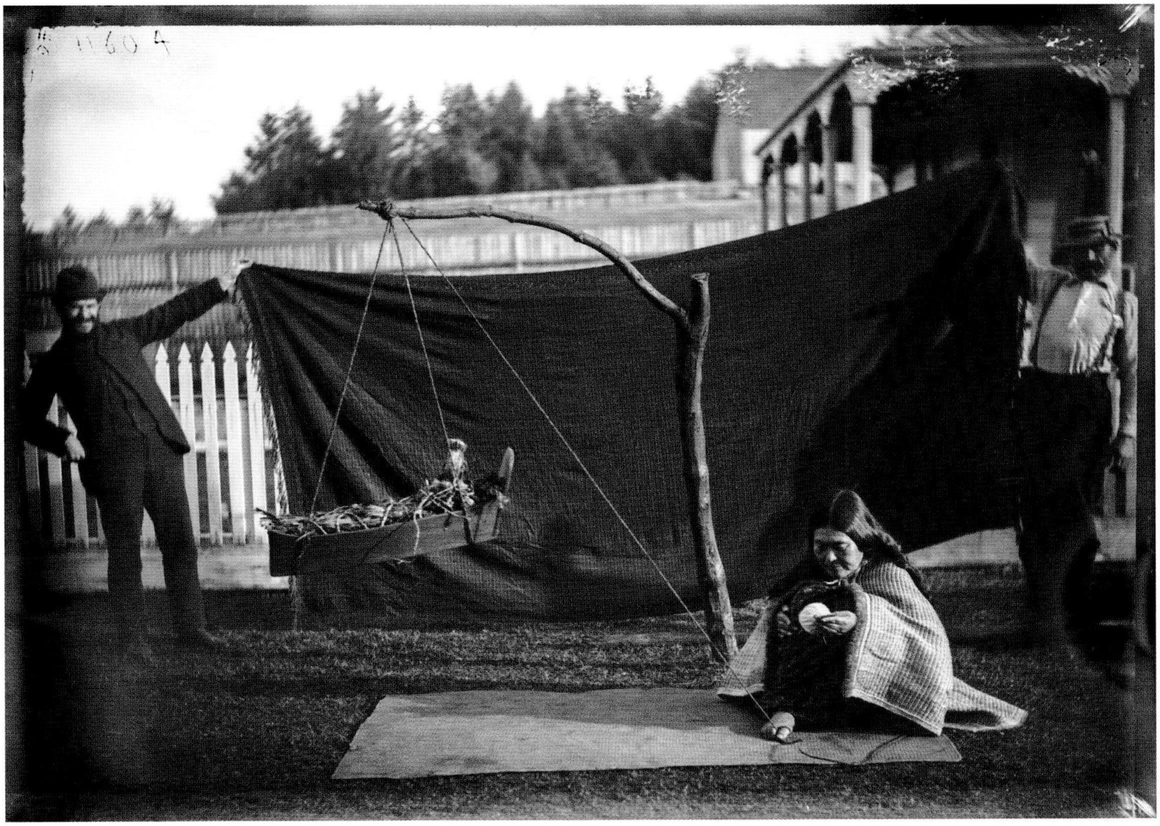

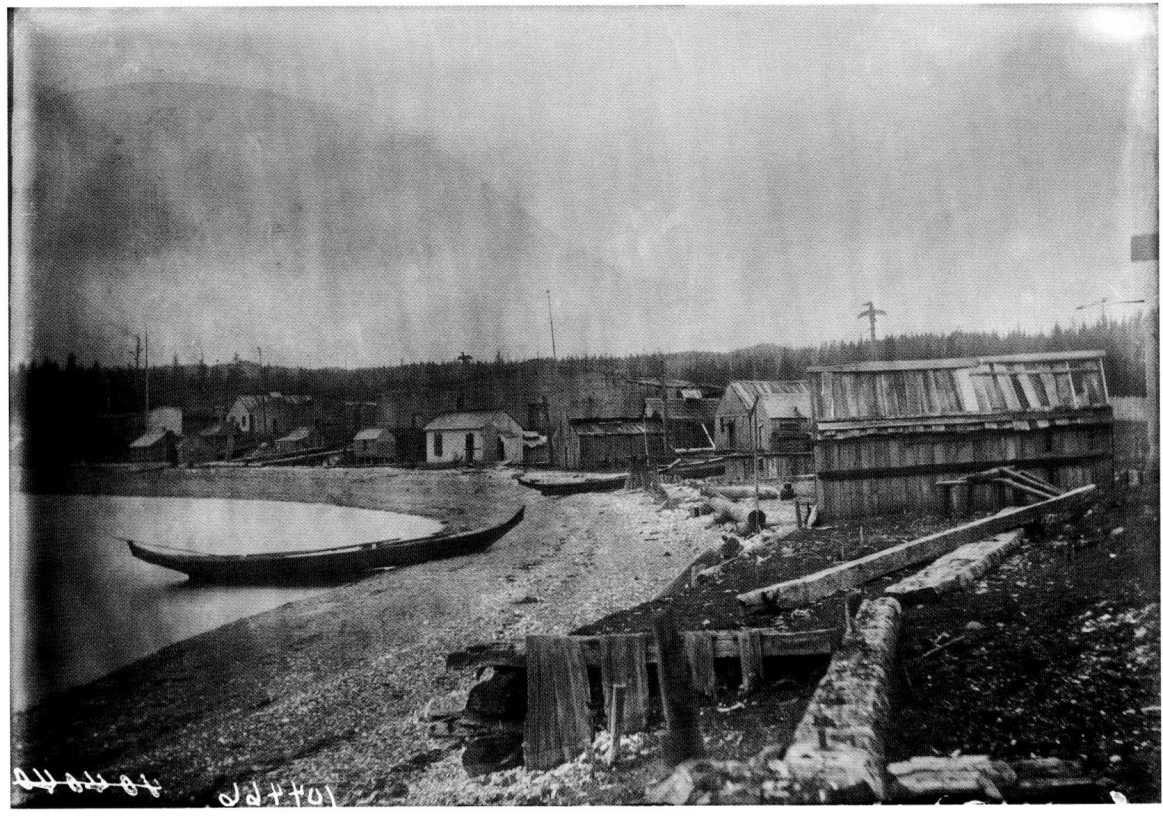

STOOWUKHÁA (ASTUTE ONE) / LOUIS V. SHOTRIDGE

Tlingit
Klukwan, Alaska
United States

Prompted by members of the Tlingit community, in 2006 the Penn Museum began preparing the Louis Shotridge Digital Archive, a project rendering 570 collected objects, 2,600 written documents, 500 black-and-white photographs, and eight sound recordings, accessible online. Some of these Tlingit items have now been repatriated; others are in dispute.

For 20 years, from 1912 to 1932, Louis Shotridge (c. 1882–1937) was a staff member at the Penn Museum in Philadelphia, working as a curator, collector, and exhibit preparer. Over half of his employment was spent doing fieldwork among his own people in southeastern Alaska. His early work at the museum and on expeditions was in collaboration with his first wife, Kaatxwaaxsnéi (Florence Dennis), an ethnographer and accomplished Chilkat weaver, who died from tuberculosis in 1917.

Shotridge was born in Klukwan, Alaska, into a leading Tlingit family. His mother, Kudeit.sáakw, was a member of the Killer Whale Fin House of the Kaagwaantaan Clan. Tlingit society is matrilineal, and Shotridge followed Kudeit.sáakw into her house group and Clan. His father, Yeilgooxú, was the Hereditary Chief of the Whale House, and belonged to the Gaanax.teidi Clan. Shotridge attended high school in the nearby town of Haines, at the Presbyterian Mission School. Later, he enrolled in Penn's Wharton School of Finance and Commerce and attended lectures by anthropologist Franz Boas at Columbia University. For two months, Shotridge and Boas collaborated on the study of Tlingit phonetics.

Shotridge's purchase and collection of sacred material culture for the Penn Museum has led to a controversial legacy within the Tlingit community and among academics and journalists concerned with the history of anthropology. In an argument for a broader understanding of the sociopolitical context in which he worked, Maureen Milburn states, "Louis Shotridge participated actively in both the anthropology museum system and the multiple facets of Tlingit society."[1]

By the late 19th century, radical change and incessant attempts to assimilate Indigenous societies were underway. Congress passed the Religious Crimes Code in 1883, banning Native American ceremonial practices and dancing. Christianity and patriarchy were promoted. Social customs and Native languages were stifled. "European contact created conflict between the Tlingits and the newcomers, but it also created conflict within the Tlingit community, by presenting an array of new choices, options, and strategies for addressing the forces of change," said Tlingit poet and scholar Nora Marks Dauenhauer and her husband, Dr. Richard Dauenhauer.[2]

With descriptive titles, the 500 photographs Shotridge deposited at the Penn Museum are a detailed visual journal of his fieldwork. He photographed local events, like sports competitions, parades, and funeral processions, and daily activities such as fishing and boating. With few exceptions, the portraits he made show Tlingit people in Euro-American-style clothing. When photographing an object, he often placed it against a dark cloth backdrop. Masks, ceremonial hats, and carvings are common, reinforcing his interest in recording with both images and words the art, politics, and history of the region's most prominent Tlingit Clans. He traveled by foot, dog sled, horse, and in a boat he named *Penn*, photographing the mountainous coastal landscapes of southeastern Alaska. Self-portraits reveal a tall man with a penchant for tweed, a camera bag slung over his shoulder.

In 1930, Shotridge was elected Sitka Grand President of the Alaska Native Brotherhood, the oldest known Indigenous persons' civil rights organization in the world. Two years later, amid budget cuts at the museum, his curatorial position was eliminated. He eventually secured employment in Sitka as a government salmon cannery inspector. While on the job in 1937, he was found at the bottom of scaffolding with a broken neck. He died in the hospital 10 days later, survived by his third wife and five children. As befits his contentious life story, theories later developed about the nature of his fall—was it cosmic retribution, murder, or a terrible accident?

—Sarah Stacke

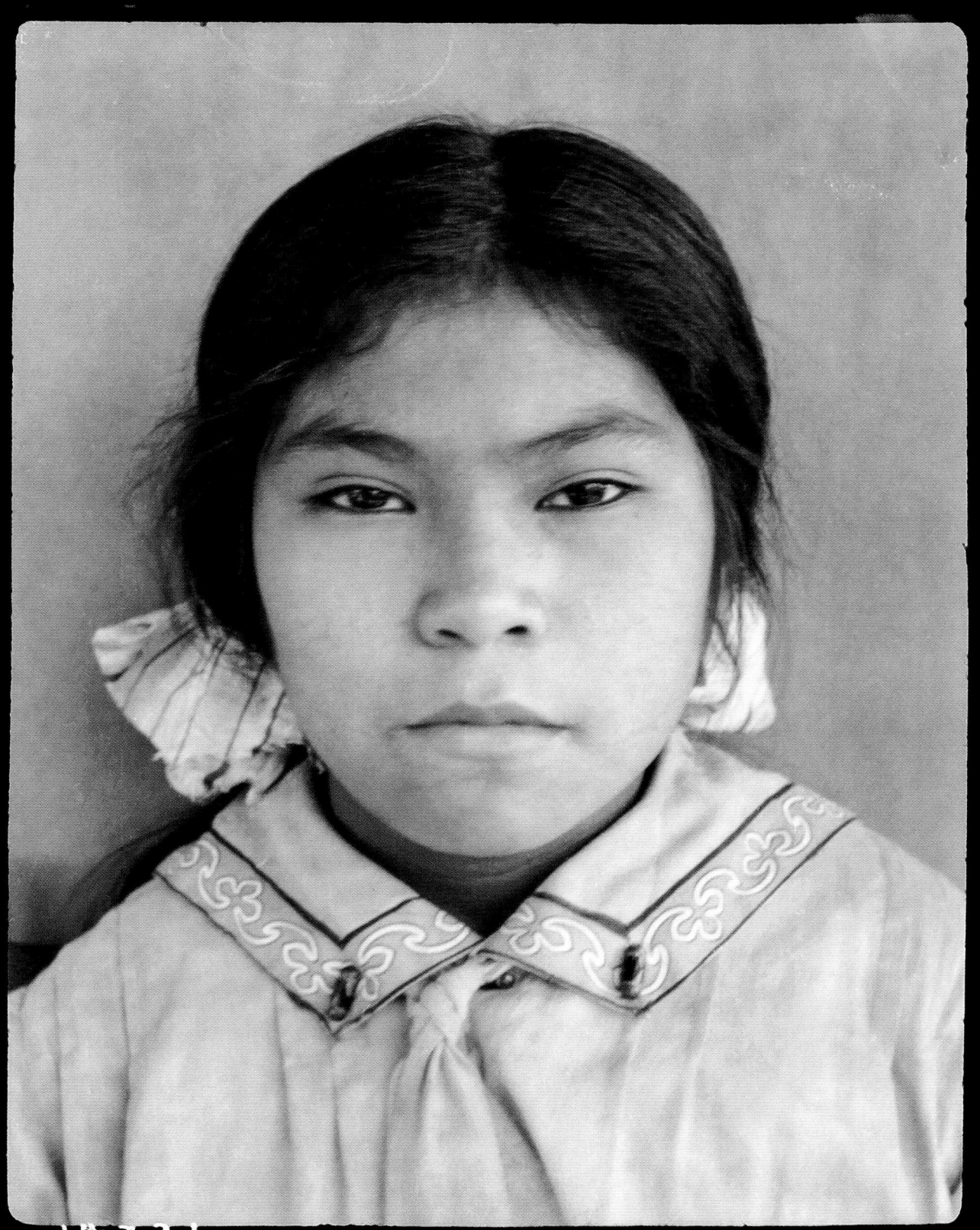

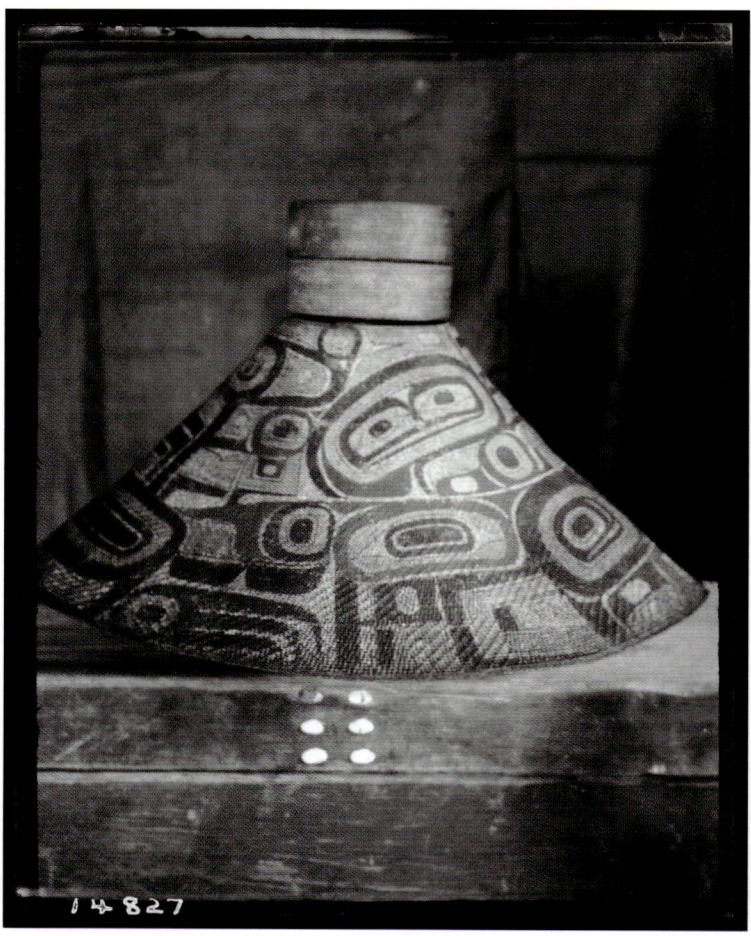

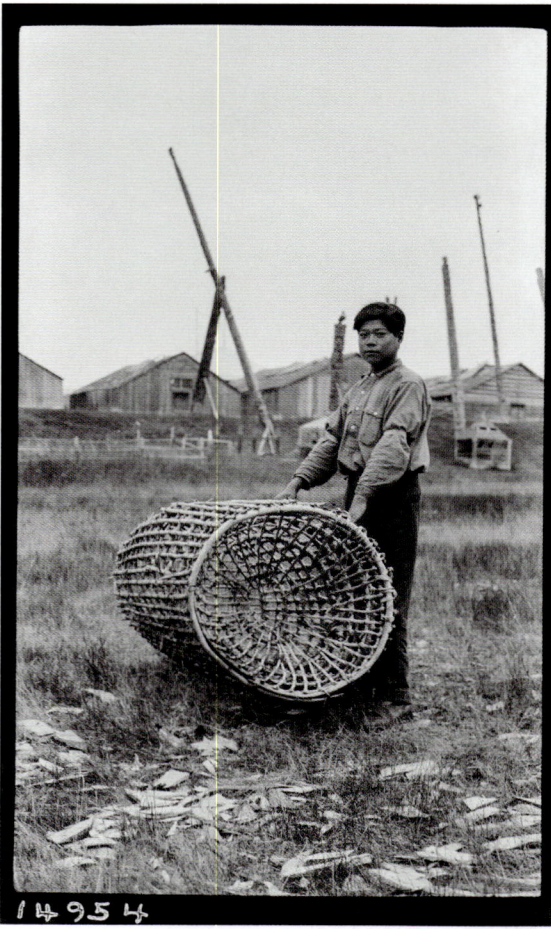

Painted, woven, twined ceremonial hat, Whale House of
Klukwan, Alaska, c. 1920.

Git-keen youth with salmon trap, Git-wen-tqul, British
Columbia, October 1, 1918.

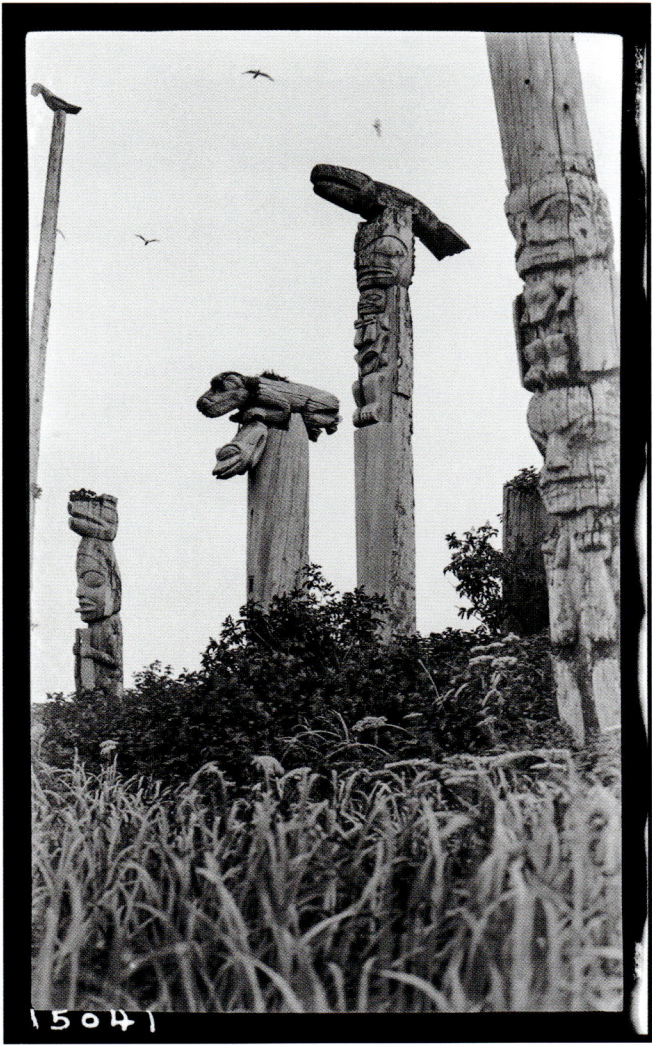

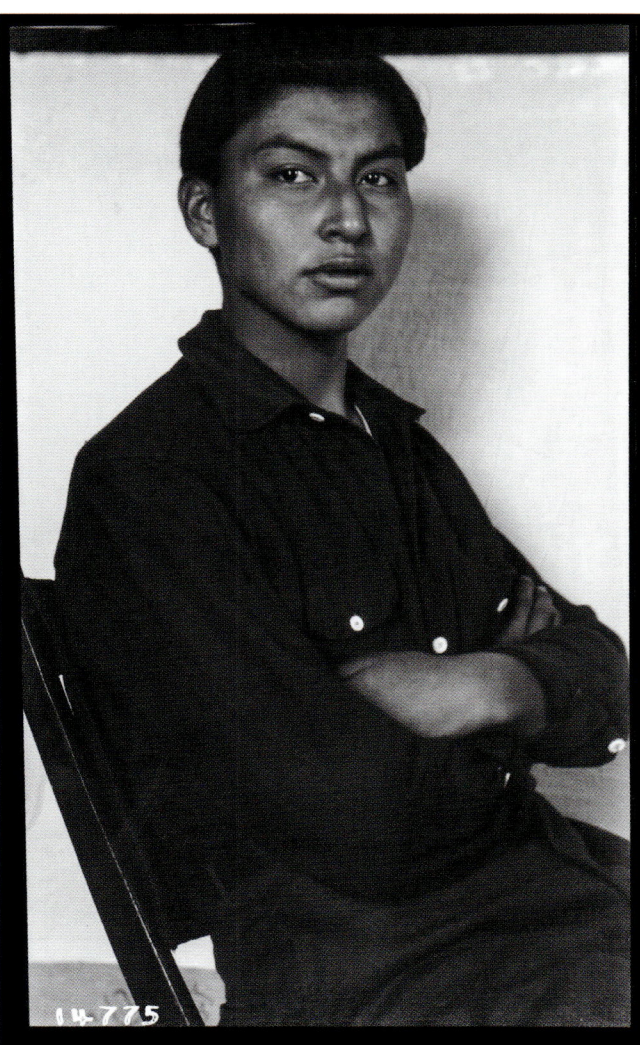

Poles sculpted by the Taant'a K̲wáan (Tongass people),
Southeast Alaska, June 19, 1924.

Tsutsx-xu, a young Chilkoot man, Southeast Alaska,
summer 1915.

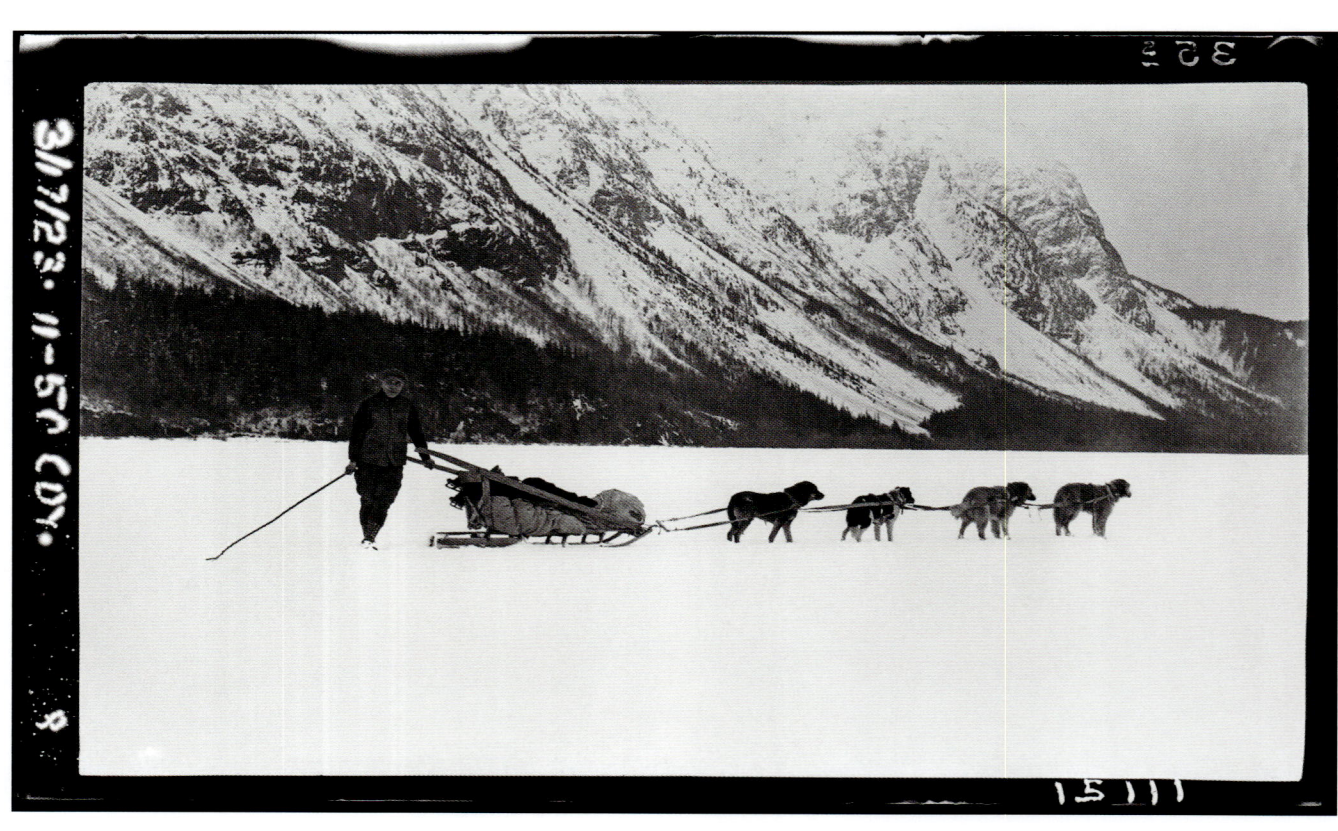

Louis Shotridge mushing on the Chilkat River,
Southeast Alaska or British Columbia, March 1923.

Opposite: A visit to the fishing camps, Southeast Alaska
or British Columbia, August 1918.

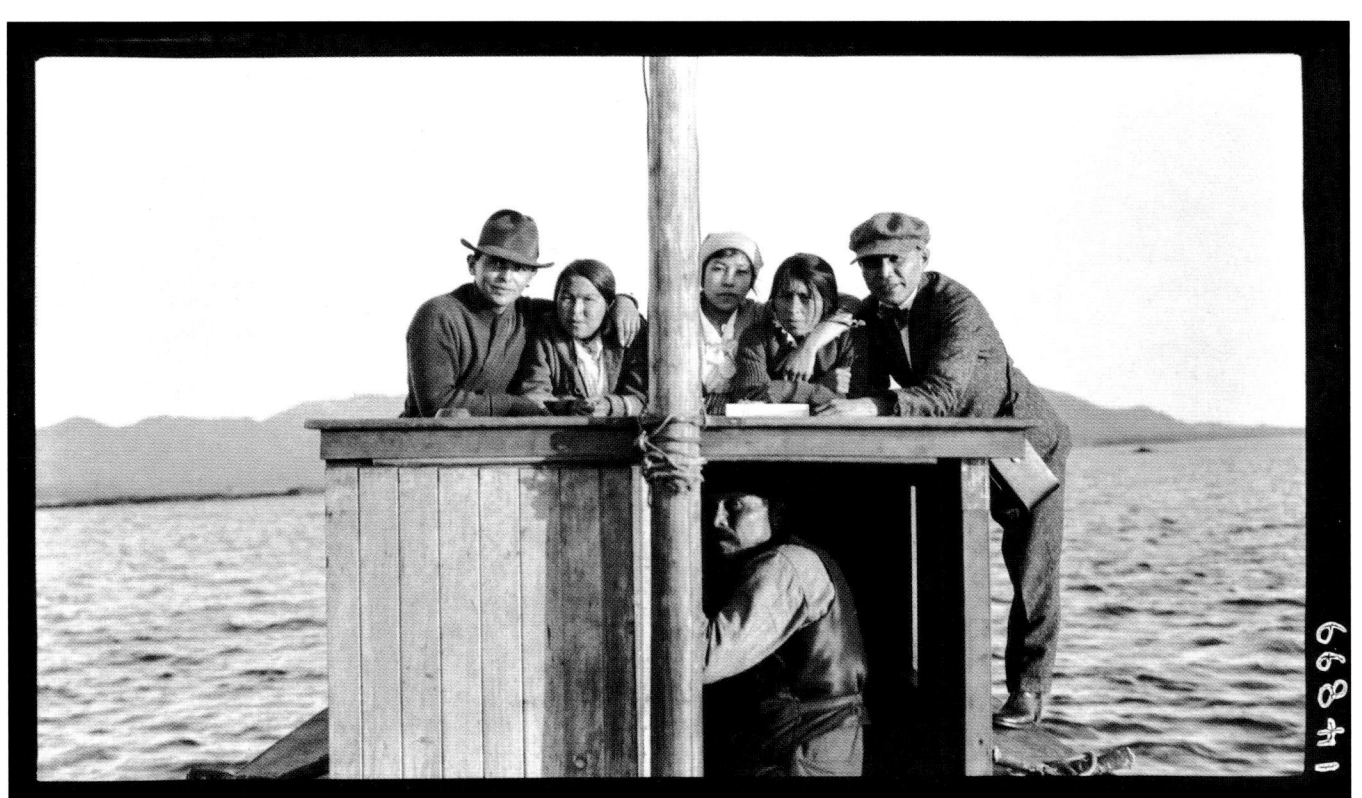

JOHN NAPOLEON BRINTON HEWITT

Tuscarora (Skarù:rę²)
Tuscarora Nation
New York State
United States

The photographs in Lot 155 at the National Anthropological Archives are engaged, warm—neighborly. They were made by John Napoleon Brinton Hewitt (c. 1857–1937), known as J. N. B. Hewitt, an ethnologist and linguist with the Smithsonian's Bureau of American Ethnology (BAE). Unlike nearly all of the photographs made in the field by his contemporaries at the BAE, Lot 155 is the work of a community member.

Hewitt was born on the Tuscarora Nation (Skarù:rę² Nation) in Niagara County, New York, where the north-flowing Niagara River divides the United States and Canada. His father, David Brainard Hewitt, was of Scottish and English descent. Orphaned as a boy, David was adopted by a Tuscarora family and raised accordingly. Hewitt's mother, Harriet (née Printup), was of Tuscarora, French, English, and Oneida (Onyota'á:ka) descent—and an enrolled member of the White Bear Clan of the Tuscarora Nation, as was Hewitt through this lineage.

Although Hewitt's parents spoke Tuscarora fluently, it seems they preferred English at home, where they taught Hewitt and his siblings to read and write. At age 11, he began attending the reservation school. English was used in the classroom, but his peers conversed and played in Tuscarora, laying the foundation for Hewitt's fluency and lifework.

In 1880, while farming, working as a newspaper correspondent, and running a night school for Tuscarora men on the reservation, Hewitt was introduced to Erminnie Adele Platt Smith (née Platt). A historically overlooked anthropologist with the BAE studying Haudenosaunee (Hodinǫhsǫ́:nih) folklore and languages, Smith has been noted as "the first woman field ethnographer."[1] Groundbreaking—again—for her efforts to collaborate with Indigenous consultants, Smith swiftly employed Hewitt as an assistant. Six years later, in 1886, she died at just 50 years old. Hewitt, gripped by the work, requested support from the first director of the BAE—geologist, explorer, and Civil War soldier John Wesley Powell—to complete the Tuscarora-English dictionary he and Smith were writing. With a positive answer from Powell, Hewitt moved to Washington, D.C., and remained an active staff member with the BAE for over half a century.

Largely self-taught, and proud of it, he was referred to as "Dr. J. N. B. Hewitt" in his *New York Times* obituary.[2] The prefix is incorrect, but it rightly reflects his status as the "leading anthropological authority"[3] on the Haudenosaunee at the time of his death.

When the BAE dissolved in the 1960s, Hewitt's manuscripts were transferred to the National Anthropological Archives. Several papers have been published about his respected work as an ethnologist and linguist, but recognition of his photographic practice remains rare.

The 307 photographs that endure in Lot 155 show men, women, youth, and families from the six nations that form the Haudenosaunee Confederacy (Hodinǫhsǫ́:nih Confederacy): the Mohawk (Kanien'kehà:ka), Cayuga (Gayogohó:nǫ²), Seneca (Onöndowa'ga:'), Onondaga (Onoñda'gegá'), Oneida (Onyota'á:ka), and Tuscarora (Skarù:rę²). People of Tutelo descent are also pictured.

Many of the images are family or individual portraits inside or outside the sitters' homes. Hewitt photographed numerous Chiefs—like Cayuga Chief Abram Charles—alone or alongside their wives, children, and grandchildren. Other photographs show babies in cradleboards, Wampum Belts and pipes, traditional longhouses, women selling crafts, a lacrosse club, and a mother and son tilling ceremonial tobacco. Most of the photographs were made between 1897 and 1937 during research trips on or near the Six Nations of the Grand River in Ontario, Canada, and on or near the Tuscarora Nation in New York State. Every year until his death, Hewitt devoted as much time as possible to working within Haudenosaunee communities.[4]

The collection reveals Hewitt as a steadfast photographer who maintained relationships over several decades with advisers, interpreters, and Knowledge Keepers vital to the preservation of Haudenosaunee culture. A cursive note on an undated print of a self-assured and youthful man sitting at a desk in a fresh suit and tie reads, "Joshua Buck (31 years old)…'Bout the best informed rooster there is over here this devil is." When Buck appears again, his face and demeanor are drawn with age. His jacket and vest are fatigued; a tie is absent.[5] Hewitt used this later photograph to illustrate an article he authored in the 1926 edition of *Explorations and Field-Work of the Smithsonian Institution*. The caption reads, "Mr. Joshua Buck, (obit 1923), Onondaga-Tutelo, Iroquoian stock, ritualist and native physician."

Almost all of the original prints in Lot 155 bear handwritten captions penciled by Hewitt or Mae W. Tucker, his administrative assistant,[6] with names, lineages, locations, and a numbering system—a sign Hewitt considered the photographs integral to his work. The original negatives represent a variety of film and camera types, a clue Hewitt tracked the medium's developments and upgraded his gear accordingly.

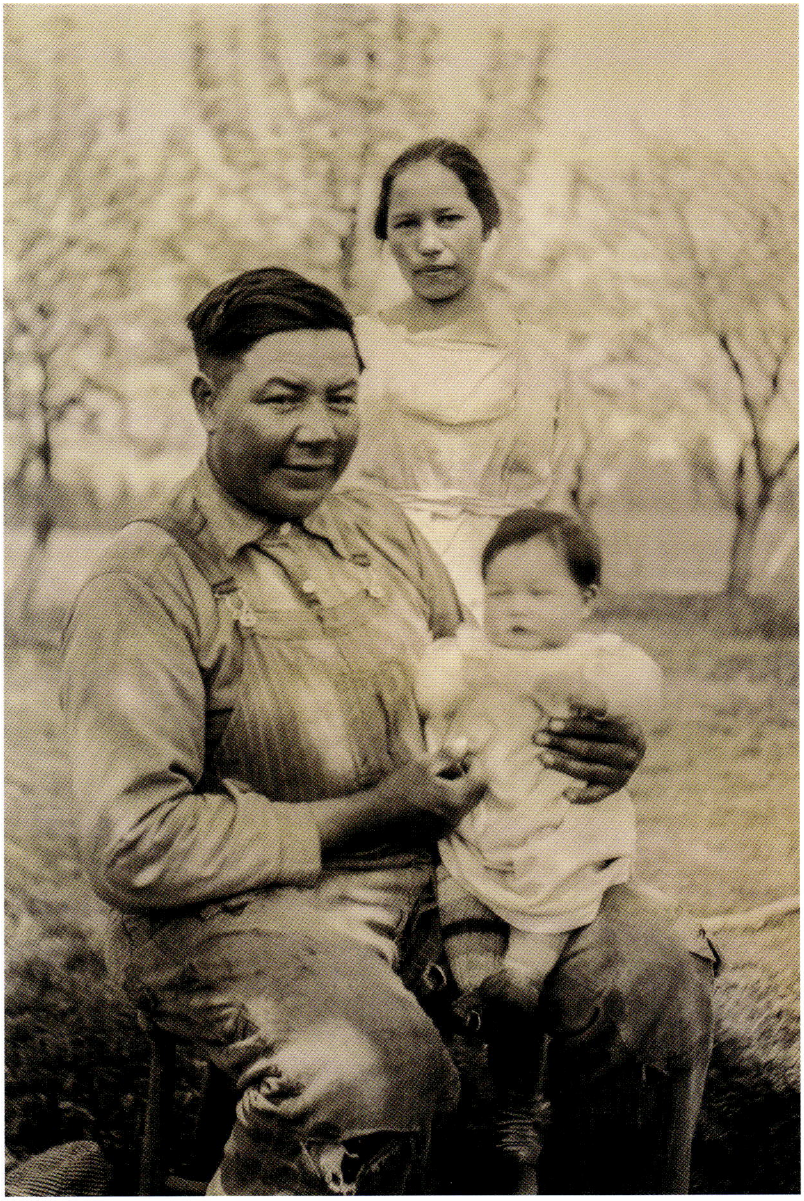

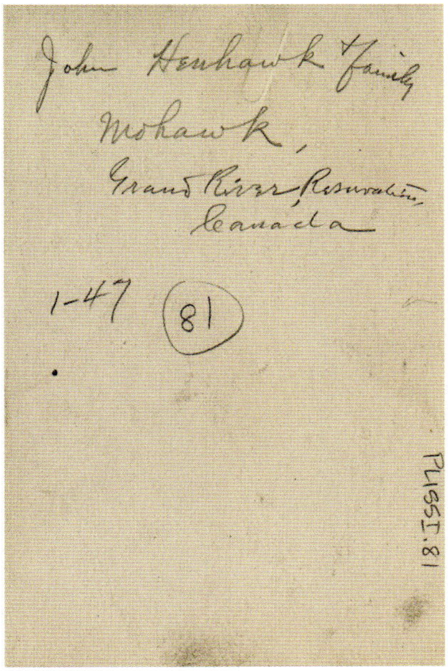

Mohawk man John Henhawk with his family on the Six
Nations of the Grand River, Ontario, c. 1900–37.

Handwritten caption on the back of Item I.81.
PHOTO LOT 155, J. N. B. HEWITT PHOTOGRAPHS OF IROQUOIS INDIANS ON
THE SIX NATIONS RESERVATION, NATIONAL ANTHROPOLOGICAL ARCHIVES,
SMITHSONIAN INSTITUTION. ITEM I.81, ITEM II.12, ITEM II.16, ITEM IV.1,
ITEM I.28

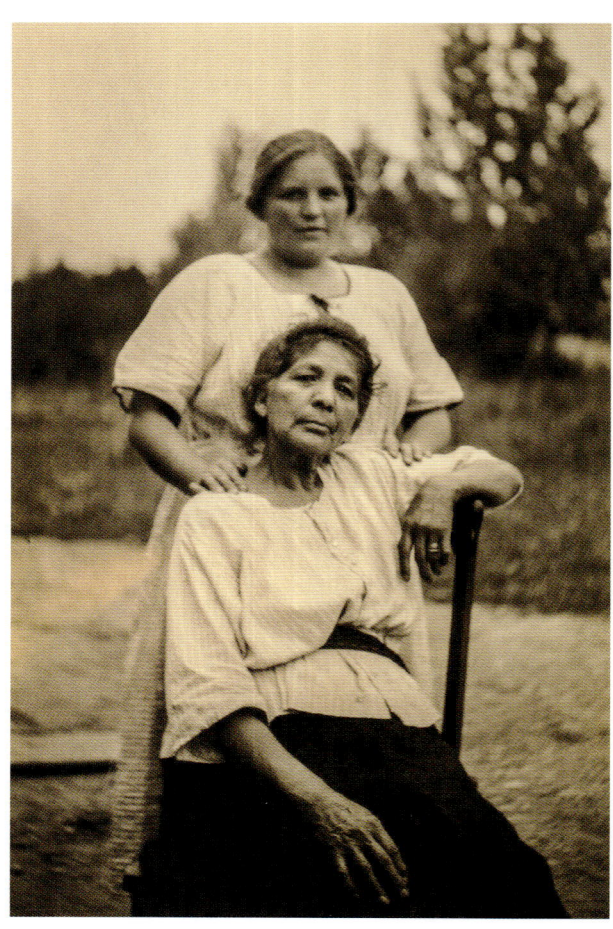 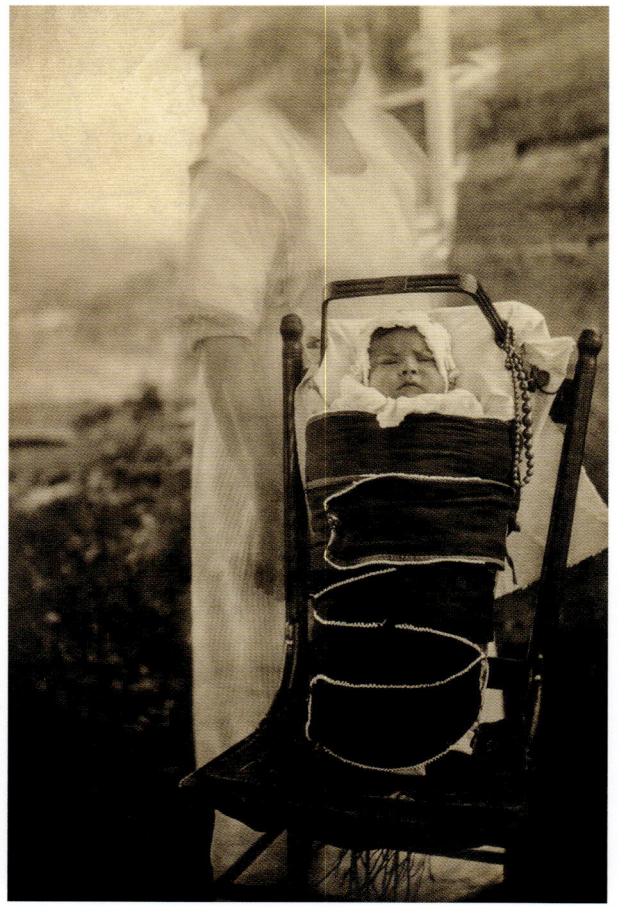

Onondaga Tuscarora woman Phoebe Lyons (née Patterson, 1860–1928) with a young woman, Nedrow, New York, c. 1900–25. Lyons was engaged with Cornell University, giving a cooking and basketmaking demonstration in 1914, and mediating the representation of Haudenosaunee culture at the 1914 Cayuga Indian Festival.

Onondaga woman and baby Van Every in cradleboard, Onondaga, New York, 1925.

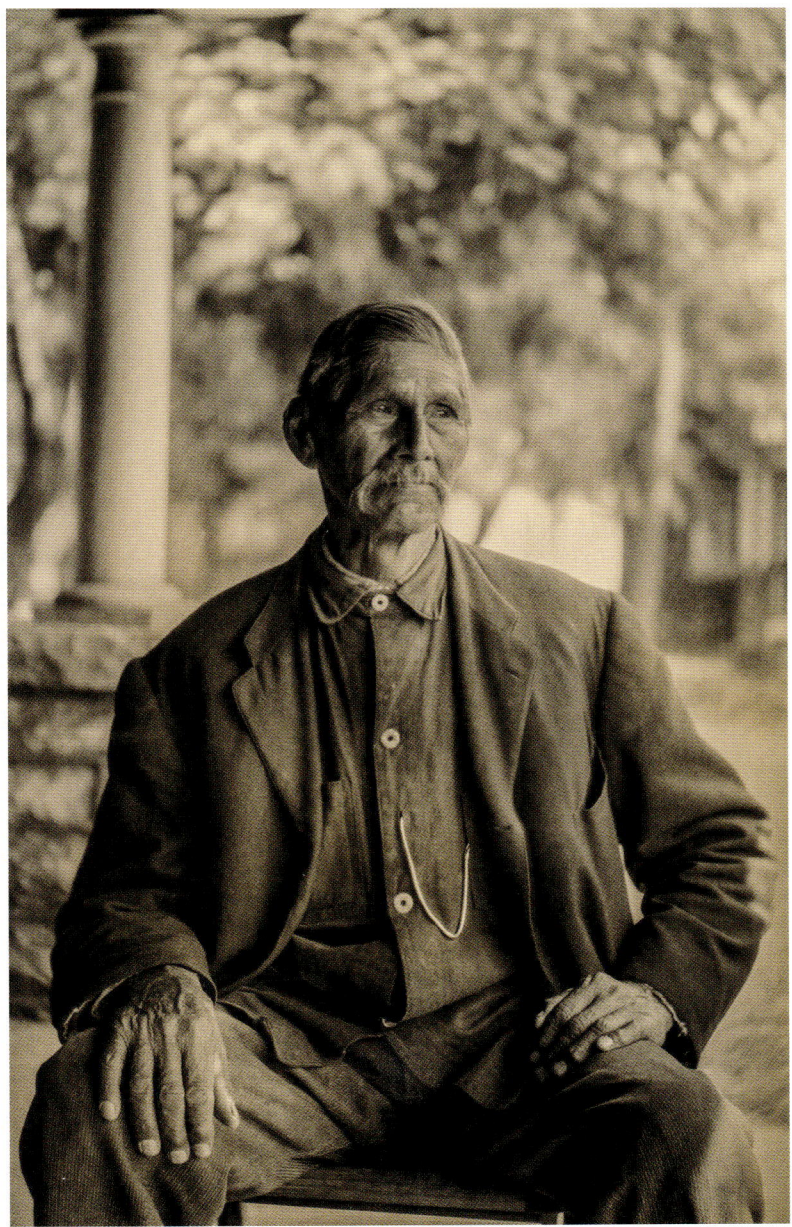

Handwritten caption on the back of Item IV.1.

Cayuga Chief Abram Charles, "Prophet and Statesman"
(d. 1929), Six Nations of the Grand River, Ontario, c. 1900–29.

A self-portrait, made when Hewitt was maybe in his early thirties, shows him seated in an office or classroom. He holds the cable release in his right hand. Somehow, the camera rotated just after Hewitt released the shutter, creating the effect of a faint double exposure. In the photographic apparition, which was exposed first, Hewitt laughs. He then becomes serious—with a hint of levity remaining in his eyes—as he completes the portrait. Whether he moved the camera intentionally or not, perhaps by pulling on the cable release a little too hard, we'll never know. We do know he decided to keep the shutter open, even after the camera moved. The clever image hints at Hewitt's wit, as well as his grasp of advanced photographic techniques.

Hewitt devoted his career to studying and recording the history, language, customs, legends, and myths of the Haudenosaunee and other Indigenous nations. Described as having a "quiet, even disposition" and a "keen sense of humor" by his friend and colleague John R. Swanton, Hewitt also had a reputation for being "painstakingly conscientious."[7] He was notorious among his colleagues for delaying the publication of his work. His tendency to procrastinate probably came from multiple factors, like his "obsession with accuracy," his drive to collect extensive data, and a genuine awareness that he was documenting matters "so central to the society and culture" of his own people. "It is, of course, one thing to write about another people; quite another to write about one's own," reflect Dr. Elisabeth Tooker and Dr. Barbara Graymont in an article about Hewitt's life and work.[8]

Hewitt undoubtedly recognized that the scholarship and photographs he left behind would shape the knowledge held by future generations of his fellow Haudenosaunee about where they come from and who they are.

—Sarah Stacke

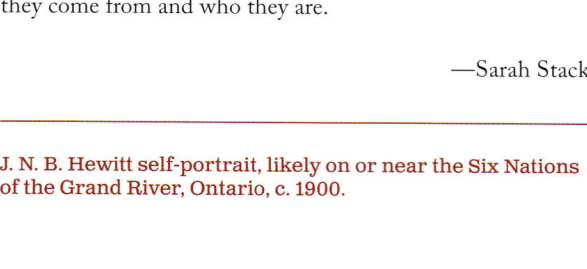

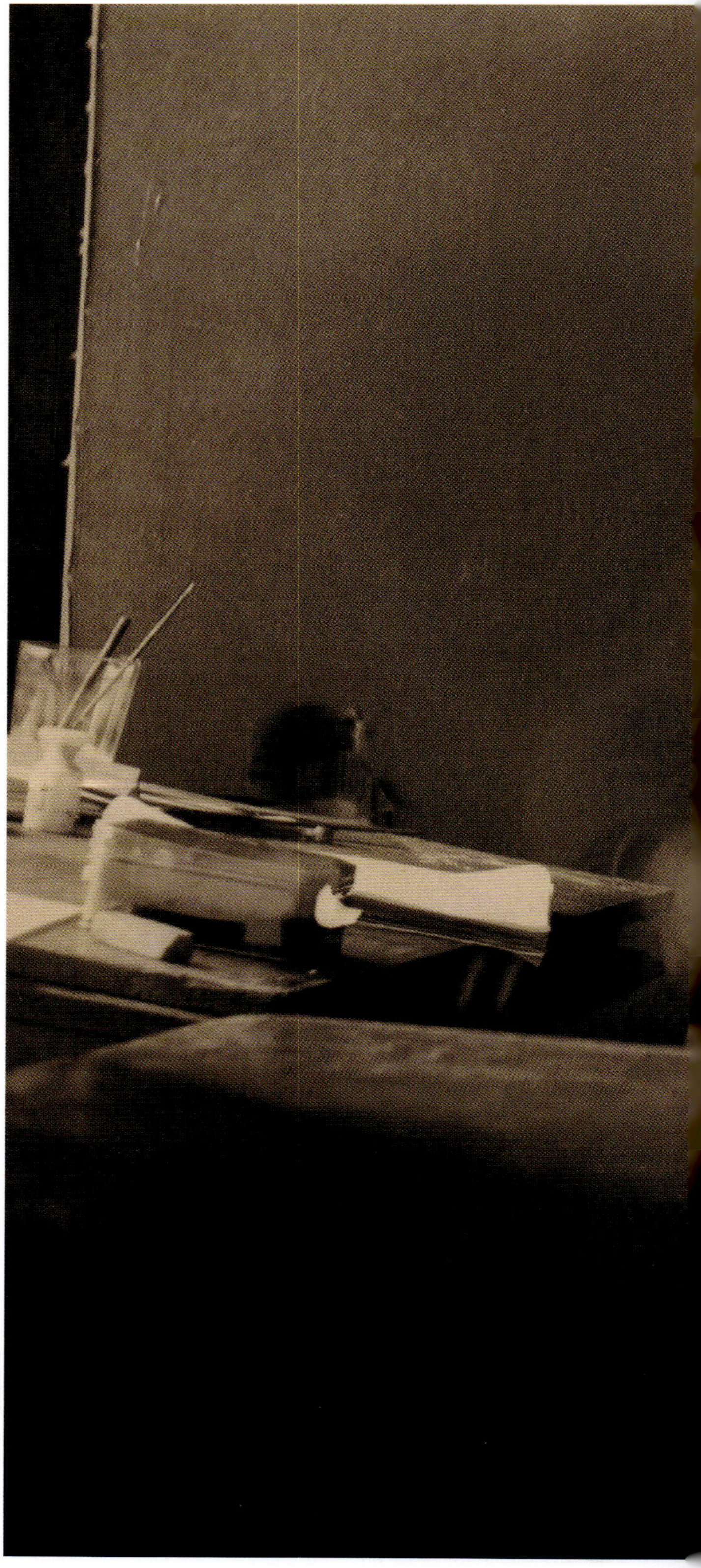

J. N. B. Hewitt self-portrait, likely on or near the Six Nations of the Grand River, Ontario, c. 1900.

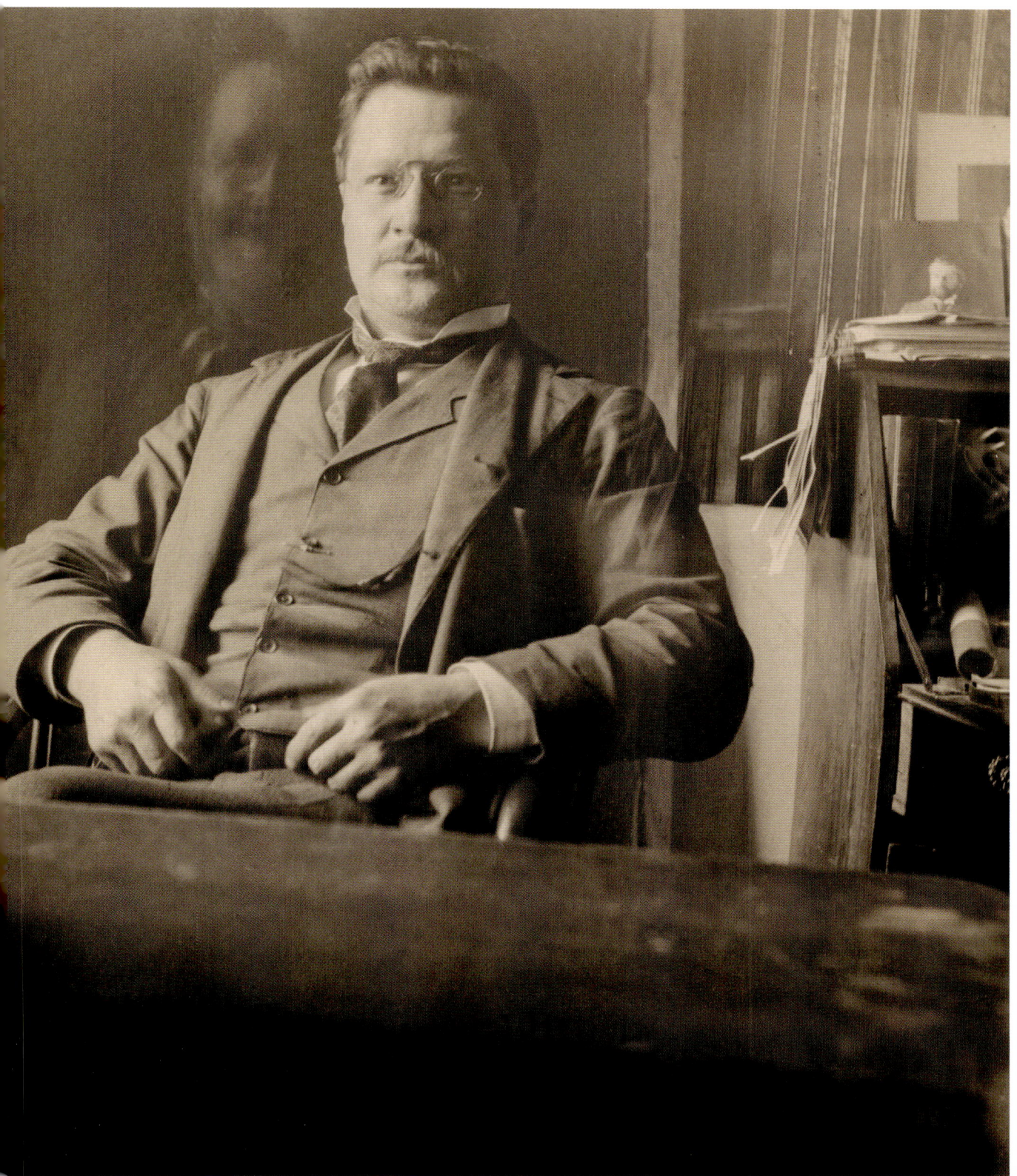

ROBERT GEORGE BEAULIEU

Anishinaabe (Ojibwe), French Canadian
White Earth Nation
Minnesota
United States

The Beaulieu family home in Crow Wing State Park sits alone on a bucolic prairie, where the Crow Wing and Mississippi Rivers meet in central Minnesota. Built by the prosperous and political fur trader Clement H. Beaulieu in 1849, nine years before Minnesota became a state, the Greek Revival house once overlooked the village of Crow Wing, a long-time Anishinaabe (Ojibwe) settlement that became the foremost trading post in the region after European contact. At its peak in the mid-1860s, the village had one of the most diverse populations in Minnesota, with an estimated 600–700 Anishinaabe, white, and mixed-ancestry residents.

In 1867, the White Earth Reservation was established in northwestern Minnesota with a treaty engineered to concentrate the state's Anishinaabe—those who hadn't already been displaced by the 1855 Treaty of Washington—in a single location, freeing millions more acres of premium lands to logging, mining, and agriculture. This, along with the Northern Pacific Railway's decision to cross the Mississippi 10 miles north of Crow Wing, led to the village's end.

Robert G. Beaulieu (1858–1935), the tenth and youngest child born to Clement and his wife Elizabeth (née Farling), was a teenager when the family moved from Crow Wing to White Earth in 1873. Robert was allotted 160 acres on the reservation, where he kept "but one horse."[1] He built himself a house in town, about 12 miles from his parcel, and moved there. By one second-hand account, he was the "black sheep of the family," apparently because the Beaulieus were "very prominent in the White Earth vicinity, and Robert's drinking was frowned upon."[2]

By 1887, Robert was a postmaster for the White Earth Agency. In the first town election, in 1906, he was appointed town clerk. A 1908 photograph of the White Earth Town Band positions him front and center holding his cornet. The musicians are in suits, ties, and hats, and a mustached Robert is described as "Bob," the "leader" of the band.[3]

At age 62, Robert listed his occupation as "Photographer" on the 1920 federal census.[4] Approximately 100 black-and-white prints attributed to him are housed at the Minnesota Historical Society. They're dated c. 1910–25, indicating Robert's interest in making photographs began in his early fifties. The images reflect the sweeping and calculated changes imposed upon the Anishinaabe, the influence of timber interests in northern Minnesota—and the conspicuous presence of his family in White Earth.

One of many photographs in the Robert Beaulieu collection of loggers at work depicts three young log drivers standing on a raft made of sawed pine; a fourth, older driver floats near-by in a small boat. A handful of images picture the annual June Fourteenth Reservation Day Celebration, a festival commemorating the arrival of the first Anishinaabe to White Earth from Crow Wing on June 14, 1868. Several prints document prominent Anishinaabe Chiefs and Elders; many exhibit buildings in White Earth, like the Saint Columba Episcopal Church, the bank, the hospital, and the B. L. Fairbanks Co. Store. A couple show men playing the Moccasin Game, a popular traditional gambling game.

In an image Robert made about 1910, two young men stand next to a printing press inside the headquarters of the *Tomahawk*. Launched in 1903 by Robert's brother Augustus, known as Gus, the *Tomahawk* was White Earth Nation's second weekly newspaper. The first was the *Progress*, which ran from 1886 to 1889. Gus was the publisher and Theodore H. Beaulieu, Robert and Gus's brother-in-law (and second cousin), was the editor. While Gus and Theo used the *Progress* to advocate for Anishinaabe rights and oppose the pervasive anti-Indian rhetoric of the time, they also used it to disguise and advance their own political and economic agendas.

A stark 1908 photo of Theo's future business, real estate, frames his office and a sign boasting "Prairie Brush and Timber Lands. Choice Lake Shore Acres. First Mortgage Loans on Realty." The photograph visually entwines the Beaulieus with the lucrative trade of White Earth lands following the Dawes Act of 1887, the Nelson Act of 1889, and the Clapp Rider of 1904. Collectively, these acts broke up communal ownership of Tribal lands through individual allotments, opened Native property to white settlement, and were part of the U.S. government's efforts to exterminate Tribal sovereignty and culture. While the Dawes Act was nationwide, the Nelson Act and Clapp Rider were specific to Minnesota and were designed to accommodate timber and mining businesses—"with the greatest possible detriment to Indian people."[5]

From Crow Wing to the earliest decades of the White Earth Nation, Clement attained wealth and power through remarkably duplicitous and criminal business practices and politics that positioned family members to exploit the Anishinaabe for personal gain. In 1911 the Tribe tried, unsuccessfully, to withdraw Tribal enrollment from members of the Beaulieu family and others accused of fraudulent and predatory behavior.

Robert lived in White Earth until his death in 1935, at age 77. His obituary was short: "Mr. Robert G. Beaulieu passed away last Thursday at the hospital where he was a patient for several months. He is survived by one daughter, Julia, a sister, Mrs. Theo. Beaulieu, and several nephews. Funeral services were conducted Saturday at the Catholic Church."[6]

—Sarah Stacke

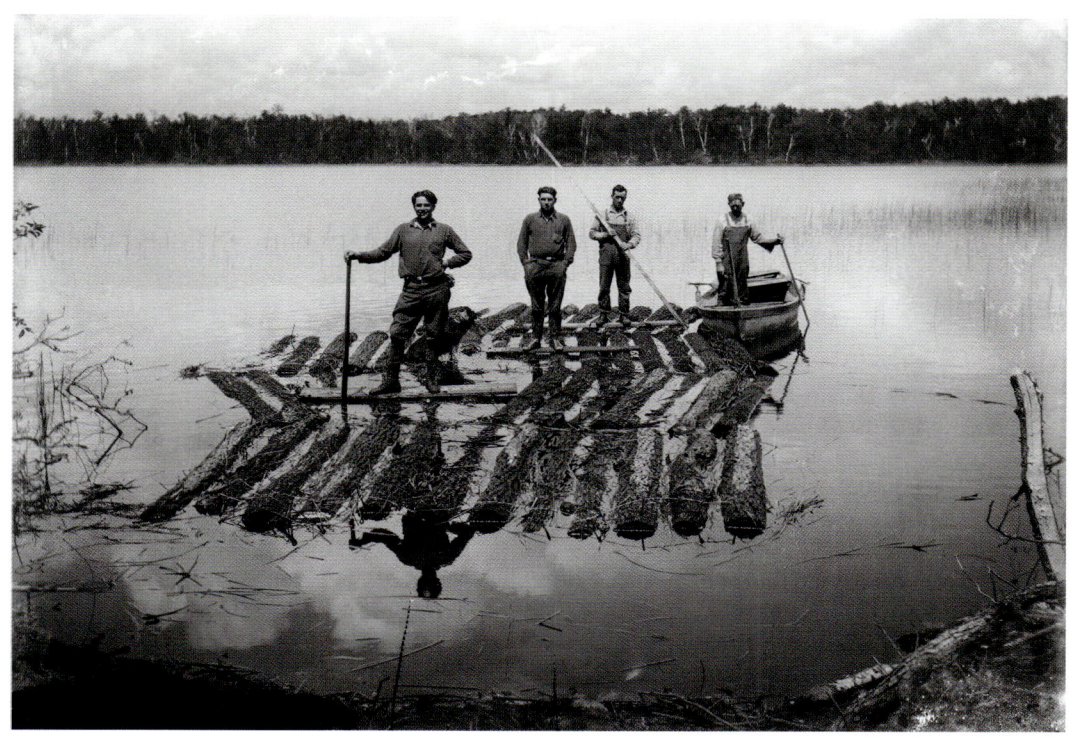

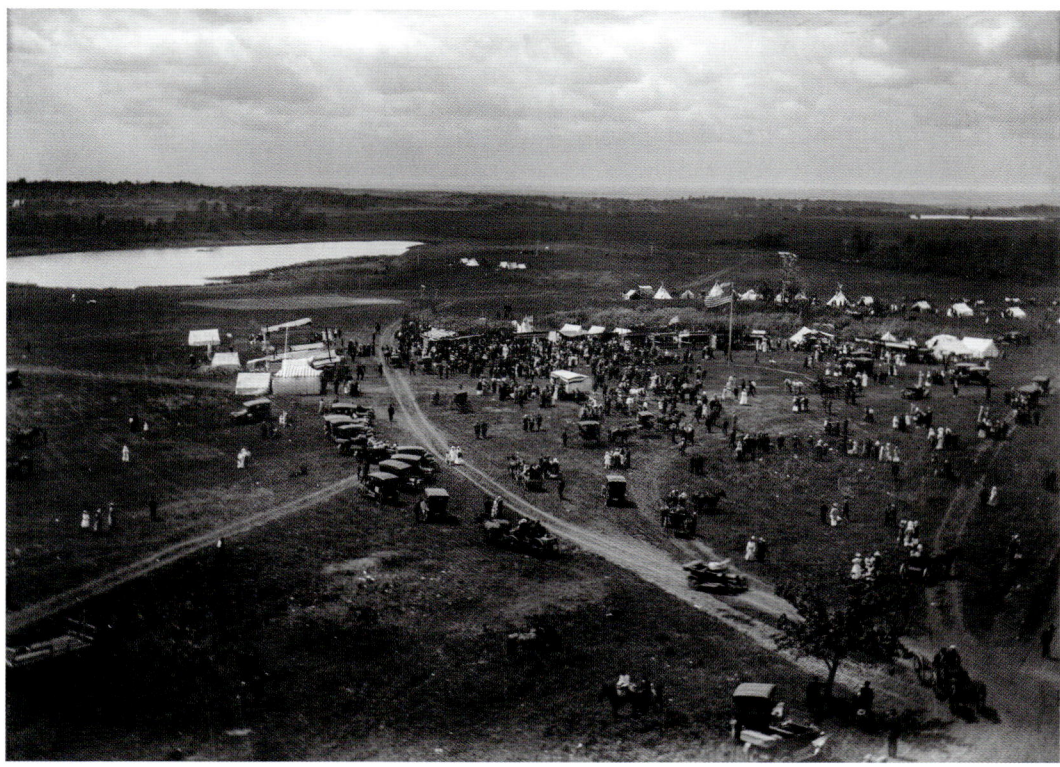

Log drivers on a raft, likely near White Earth, Minnesota, c. 1910–25.

June Fourteenth Reservation Day Celebration, White Earth, Minnesota, c. 1910.

PHOTOGRAPHS BY ROBERT BEAULIEU. SCENES FROM WHITE EARTH INDIAN RESERVATION AND SURROUNDING AREA PHOTOGRAPH COLLECTION, MINNESOTA HISTORICAL SOCIETY. NEGATIVE NUMBER 6410-A, NEGATIVE NUMBER 6425-A

MARTHA MCGLASHAN MONSEN

Unangan, Russian, Scottish, Irish
Aleutian Islands and Bristol Bay, Alaska
United States

Photography played a bountiful role in the McGlashan Monsen family. Hundreds of photographs made and collected by Martha McGlashan Monsen (1890–1981) were donated to the Archives and Special Collections at the University of Alaska Anchorage by her son Melvin Monsen Sr. in 2018, a year before his death.[1] The pictures span nearly a century from the 1880s to the 1970s and reflect a large, close-knit family entwined with the sea and land of the Aleutian Islands and Bristol Bay.

Martha McGlashan was born in 1890 on Akutan Island, a traditional Unangan coastal community within the 1,200-mile chain of volcanic islands that form the Aleutians and divide the fierce Bering Sea from the Pacific Ocean. Her husband, Martin Monsen, was from Stavanger, Norway. After sailing across the world as a mate, he settled in Naknek, a village on the shores of Bristol Bay, roughly 460 nautical miles northeast of Akutan. Though many white men had passed through Naknek, particularly with the advent of commercial fishing, Martin was considered the first white settler to call the Native village home.

With the arrival of the 20th century, a familiar presence in the region was the S.S. *Dora*, a storied 112-foot wooden steamship that carried cargo and passengers to Alaskan coastal towns and settlements unreachable by road. From 1905 to 1912, the mail clerk aboard the *Dora* was John E. Thwaites. Employed by the federal Railway Mail Service, Thwaites was an enthusiastic photographer. At some point during his service aboard the *Dora*, perhaps while the vessel was docked in Akutan Harbor, he was introduced to McGlashan and the two became friends. She acquired one of his old cameras, and photography grew to be a part of her everyday life.

Eighteen years old and still living at home in Akutan, McGlashan birthed a son, Steven William Gardner. Raised by his grandparents, he later became the Chief of Atka, an island southwest of Akutan occupied by the Unangax̂ for thousands of years. As he grew, married, and became a father and a Chief, McGlashan quietly followed her firstborn from a distance.[2] He died in 1943 at age 34.

In 1912, looking for work, McGlashan traveled to Nushagak, a small village west of Naknek, where she met Martin. They married in the local Russian Orthodox church. In a photograph believed to be made by Thwaites, the wedding party is seen filing out of the small hilltop chapel onto a narrow stairway sculpted among willowy grasses. McGlashan moved into her husband's clapboard home in Naknek—reportedly one of only five frame buildings there at the time.

Martin worked as a winter watchman, tugboat captain, and beach foreman at the Naknek Packing Company cannery. He helped establish Naknek's first school in 1922 and led its operations until 1950. McGlashan was a midwife who delivered over 40 children to Naknek parents, an agent for Star Airlines, and the Naknek postmaster for 23 years.

Between 1912 and 1935, McGlashan gave birth to 14 children, 13 of whom were delivered in the McGlashan Monsen home overlooking the Naknek River.[3] All but one reached adulthood. The couple also raised nine children from Martin's first marriage, to Helena Achuksuk, who died at age 26. Apart from Achuksuk's children, it's presumed all her relatives perished in the summer of 1919 when the influenza pandemic struck Naknek.

For more than half a century, McGlashan photographed what was in front of her: a growing family, lively holiday parties, birthdays, weddings, dogs, sailboats, the first motorcycle in Naknek, fishing nets, sleds, reindeer, trapping cabins, and more.

The kitchen table appeared often. Mel Monsen Jr., McGlashan's grandson, described it this way: "It always served as a setting for locals to communicate the news of the day. When I was very young it was the bar during community Christmas parties, it was where cribbage and pinochle was played, it was where the family's commercial fishermen met on the way home after an opening to brag about their catch, (before my time) it was where early Star Airline (now Alaska Airlines) pilots told stories to wide-eyed Monsen children (my grandmother was the local agent for the airline and pilots often spent the night during short daylight winter days) and, almost as importantly, where a young boy could always get a sugar cube on the sly."[4]

A charming photograph from the late 1940s shows McGlashan's three youngest sons—Melvin, Oscar, and Nicky—placing barrels of heating fuel next to the house in the afternoon

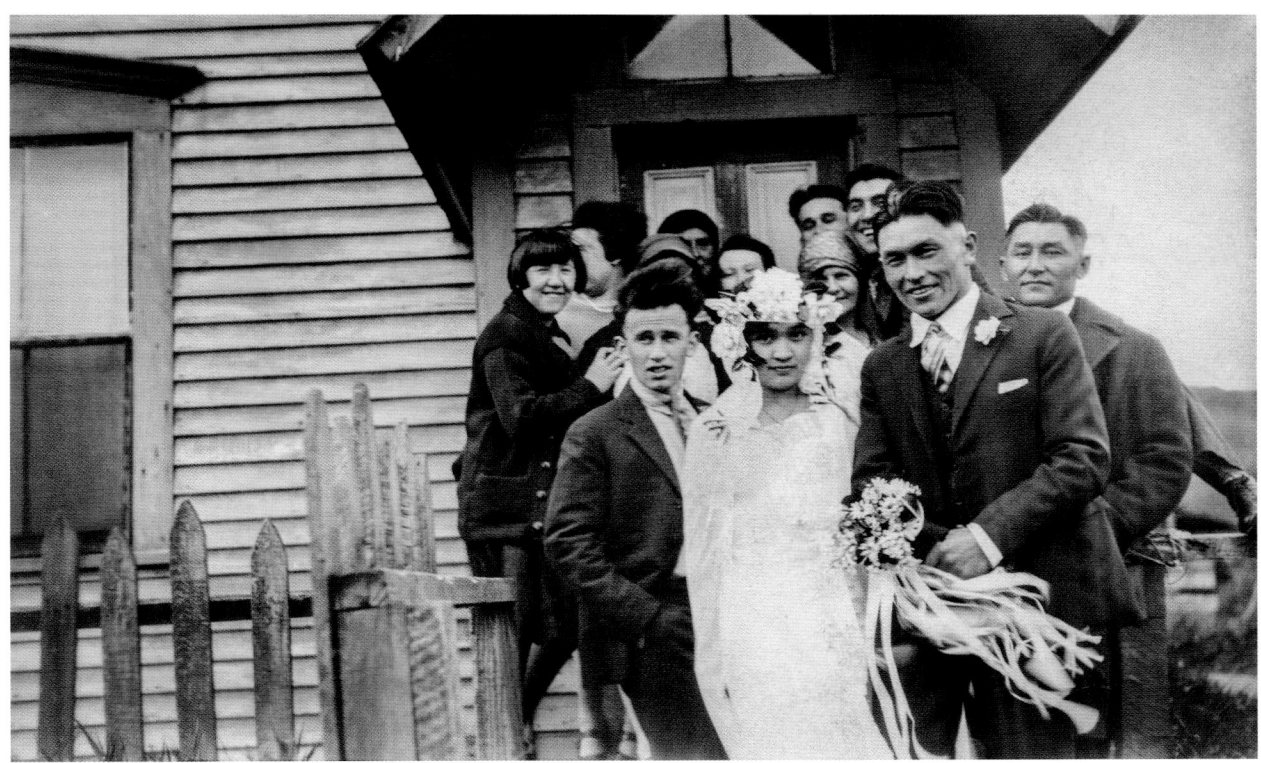

sun. In their twenties, or close to it, they are strong, full of brio, and they shine with their mother's gaze upon them.

The photographs vary in size and format, an indication that McGlashan owned several cameras of various models over the years. It's unknown where she developed the film, but there was a darkroom in the Naknek Packing Company cannery as early as 1918.[5] Some of the pictures carry the remnants of album pages, left when they were pulled from the black or brown paper sheets. Many bear the script of more than one family member, tracing edits and suggesting the photographs were attended to across generations. A handful were delivered to McGlashan with notes from friends and family. "Dear Mom," reads a c. 1945 letter from her oldest daughter, Zenia, on a picture made on Saint Paul, a windswept isle in the middle of the Bering Sea. "This is a picture taken last Xmas eve. I put an x on the church. We are both well. We are leaving soon to winter in Akutan with our little boy. Regards to all."[6]

Nearly 30 of the photographs in the collection picture McGlashan—a young woman, a mother, a grandmother, a pillar of Naknek. In a photograph from 1912, she stands behind Martin, who is seated in a wooden chair outside their Naknek home. Her brown hair is pulled into a low bun; she looks into the distance and leans lightly on Martin's shoulder. They had just married. In one of the latest images, from 1972, McGlashan sits before half-full bookshelves, and her son Nicky stands alongside her. It is 22 years since Martin's death, and it is the dedication ceremony of the Martin Monsen Regional Library in Naknek, a tribute to his role in fostering education in the community. Martha McGlashan Monsen has neat, short gray hair. She looks straight into the camera and rests her hands in her lap.

—Sarah Stacke

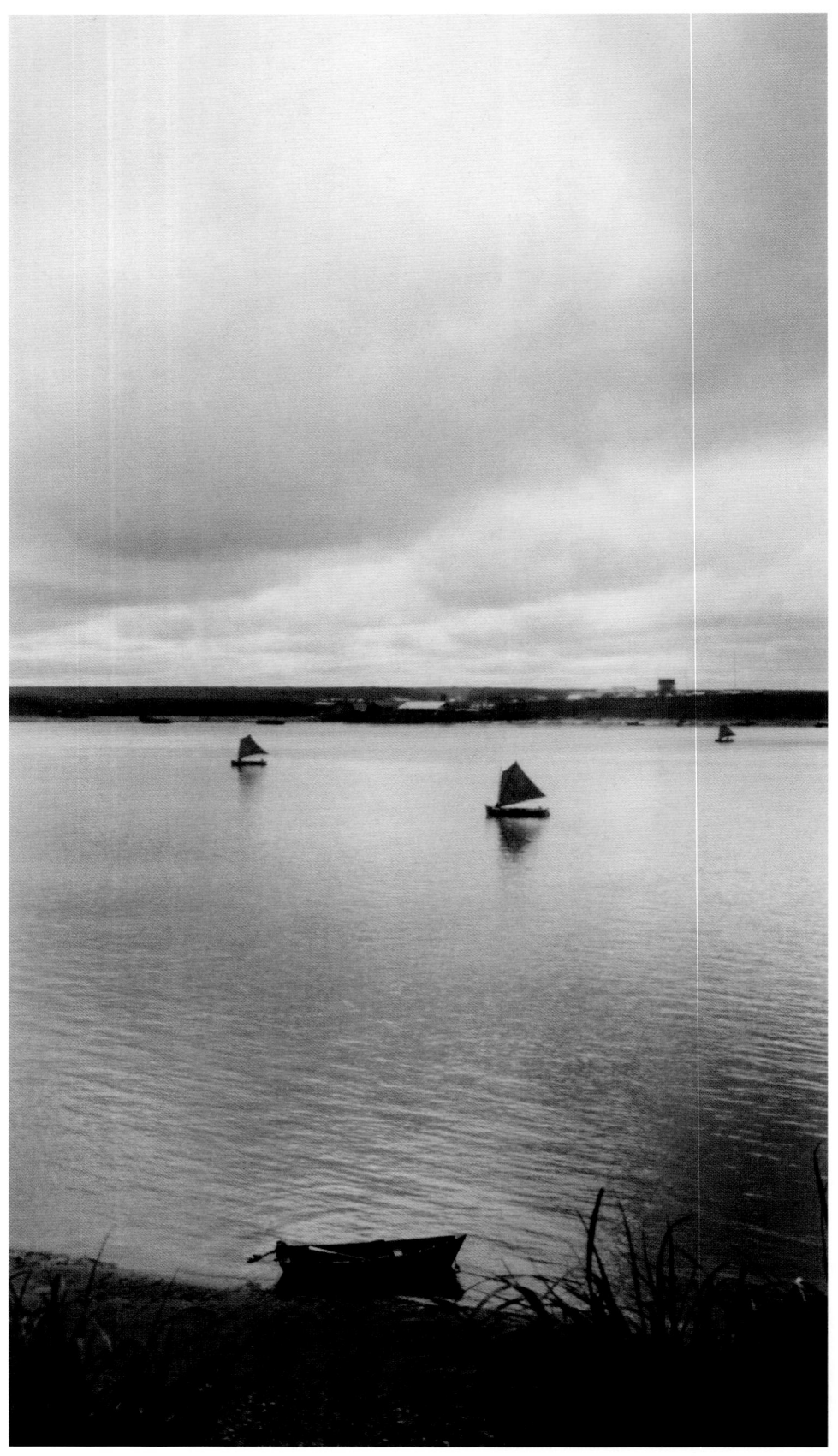

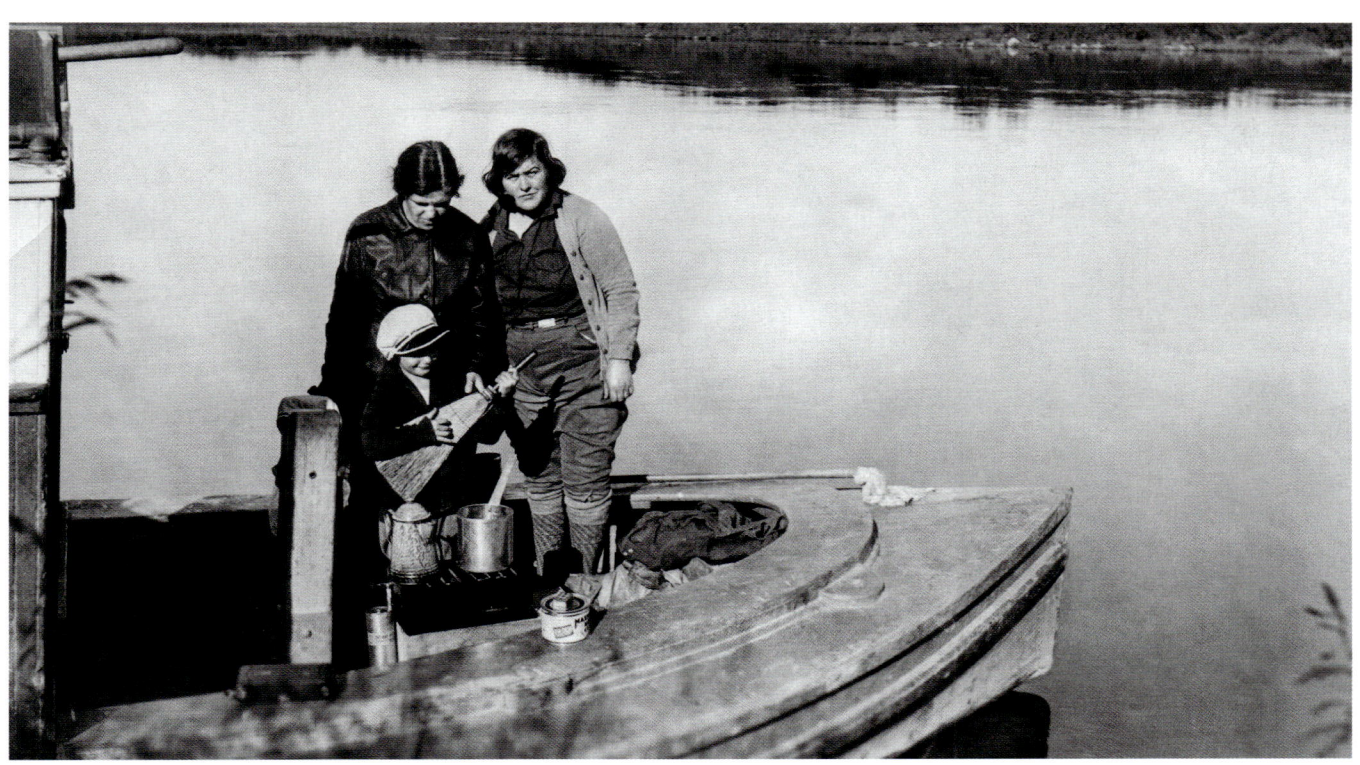

Mrs. Mendenhall (left) with Elsa Lundgren and
her daughter Elizabeth, Naknek, Alaska, c. 1930–38.
Elsa's husband, Oscar Lundgren, was the first winter
watchman at the Red Salmon Cannery, which opened in
1916 and still operates today.

Opposite: A view of the Naknek River looking southeast
from the riverbank below the Monsen house, Naknek,
Alaska, date unknown. Alaska Packers cannery is visible
on the south side of the river.

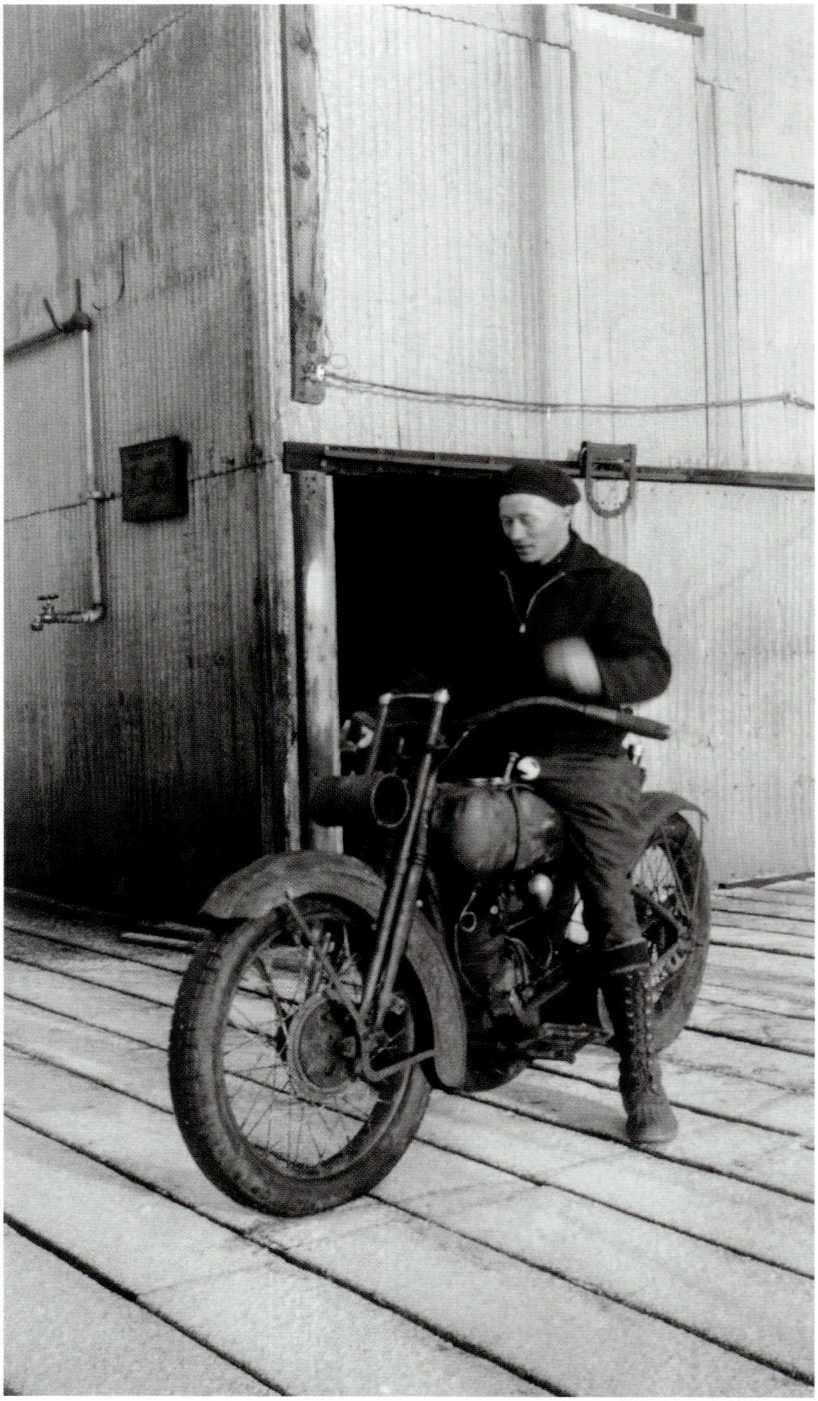

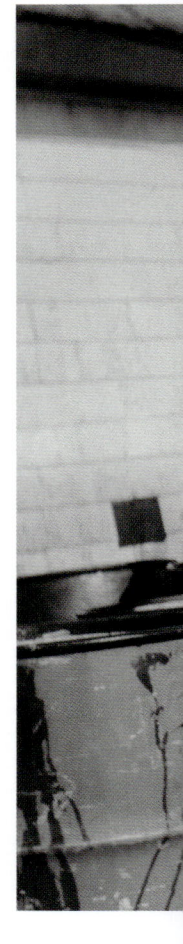

Matt Anderson on the dock of Naknek Packing Co., Naknek, Alaska, c. 1938. The motorcycle is remembered as Naknek's first.

Opposite: Melvin, Oscar, and Nicky Monsen putting barrels of heating fuel for winter beside the Monsen house, Naknek, Alaska, c. 1948–49.

Opposite: Martha McGlashan Monsen's nephew, bush pilot Eddie Hansen, at the Alaska Packers Association Diamond J Koggiung cannery on the Kvichak River, 15 miles north of Naknek, Alaska, c. 1933–35.

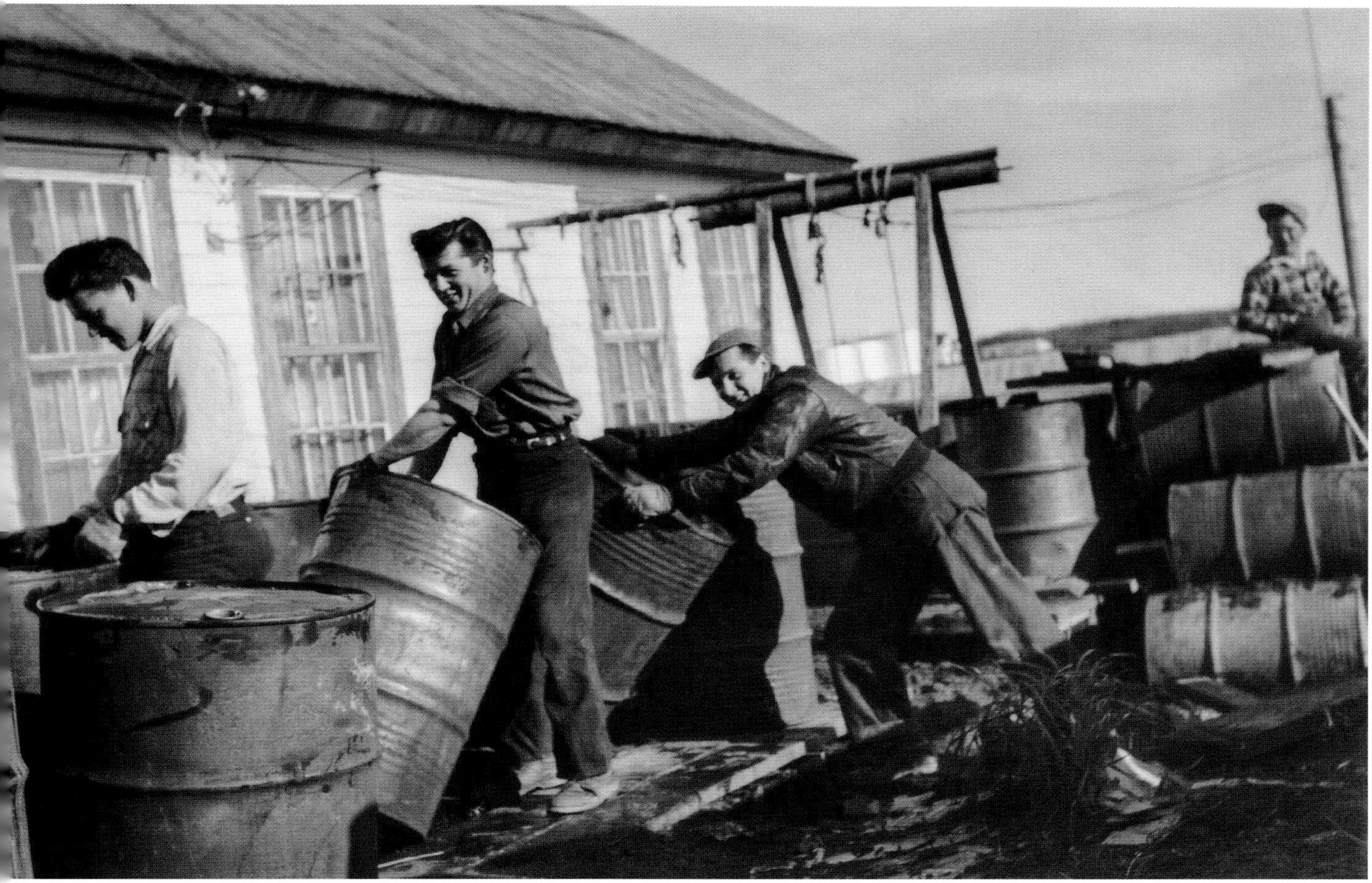

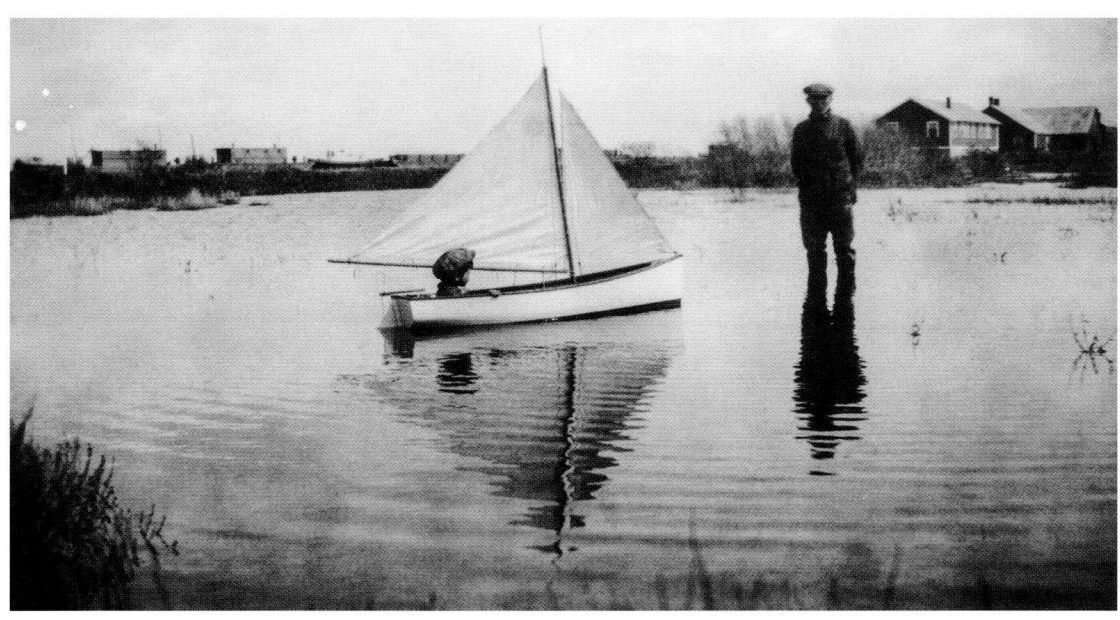

CUSCO SCHOOL OF PHOTOGRAPHY
Perú

The arrival of the first train to Cusco in 1908 was documented by Miguel Chani (1860–1951), whose photograph brought the hulking train engine into relief amid a bloom of smoke and against the backdrop of the Andean foothills. Pitted against the expectant crowd—bent to scrutinize this highly anticipated technological innovation or eager to greet the passengers crowded into train cars—is a lone child keeping a distance in the foreground. The small, poncho-clad figure has one foot firmly on the ground, while the other balances precariously on a discarded rail.

In a 1940 portrait by Fidel Mora (1916–1993), three unidentified women, one holding a babe in arms, pose upon a stairwell. A fourth figure wearing men's clothes has been scratched out—a spectral presence melting into a city wall. The women's silhouettes are arresting—the loft of montera hats, the ample folds of wide pollera skirts, the peek of bare feet beneath. A closer look reveals more details: the motion blur of the baby's leg, a clay pitcher set securely on a step, the glint of matrilineally passed tupus fastening the woven llikllas drawn over their shoulders. A cross section of the city's history of Incan infrastructure, colonial architecture, and mid-century smoothed edges opens behind them.

A wooden cross pierces the mountain landscape in a 1940 Horacio Ochoa (1905–1978) photo. Beneath it, a crowd gathers for a First Communion ceremony. Women and children hold bundles of white flowers. Elsewhere a single stem adorns a lapel. A priest in vestments clutches a prayer book; a band plays quenas and drums as men loft the cross's beams forward to the precipice.

A 1945 studio portrait by César Meza (1912–2003) shows a young family perched on a bench in front of an ornately painted backdrop. Behind the bulk of a double-breasted suit and the parents' forward-facing gazes, an intricately woven textile is just visible where it hangs over the backrest.

Historians count these four artisans of Aymara and Quechua descent among the 20 to 40 members of the eclectic Cusco School of Photography. The images of this informally organized group represent a heterogeneity of perspectives that emerged out of the southern part of Perú during the first half of the 20th century. Far from a consolidated aesthetic movement, the Cusco School encompasses a broad range of photographic impulses, which include documentary chronicles, portraiture of peasants and the emergent bourgeoisie, landscapes, folkloric studies, and art-historical and archeological images that preserve the residues of Incan and colonial pasts. Its practitioners set up formal studios in the region's cities of Arequipa, Puno, and Cusco; they traveled to outlying towns and villages; and they hawked photographs in the Imperial City's Plaza de Armas. Despite biographical and archival lacunae brought on by bank collapse, looting tourists, and the devastating 1950 earthquake that, for many, marks the end of this proliferative photographic golden age, there are upward of 70,000 extant images that show the collaboration of aesthetic, commercial, and activist interests.[1]

While the simultaneous pan–Latin American intellectual movement of indigenismo sought to mobilize Indian populations in nation-building projects largely driven by the mestizo elite, the Cusco School of Photography challenged easy European- and North American–inflected narratives of modernity's arrival to the Sacred Valley.[2]

Among many enduring legacies of this diverse cohort is a structuring of the burgeoning tourist industry that both preceded and outlasted Hiram Bingham's infamous 1911 "discovery" of Machu Picchu circulated in the pages of *National Geographic*. In 1921, for instance, U.S.-born rector of Cusco's National University Albert Giesecke extolled the virtues of postcards and photographic vistas made by the city's artisans. "Chani's collection of 80 distinct views at 50 cents apiece, is especially valuable," he wrote.[3] Certainly, there is an economic importance to such productions, but they also represent the Cusco School's entreaties to view their patria with the informed, contextualized, and expansive perspectives that these photographers were making available.

—Brenna M. Casey

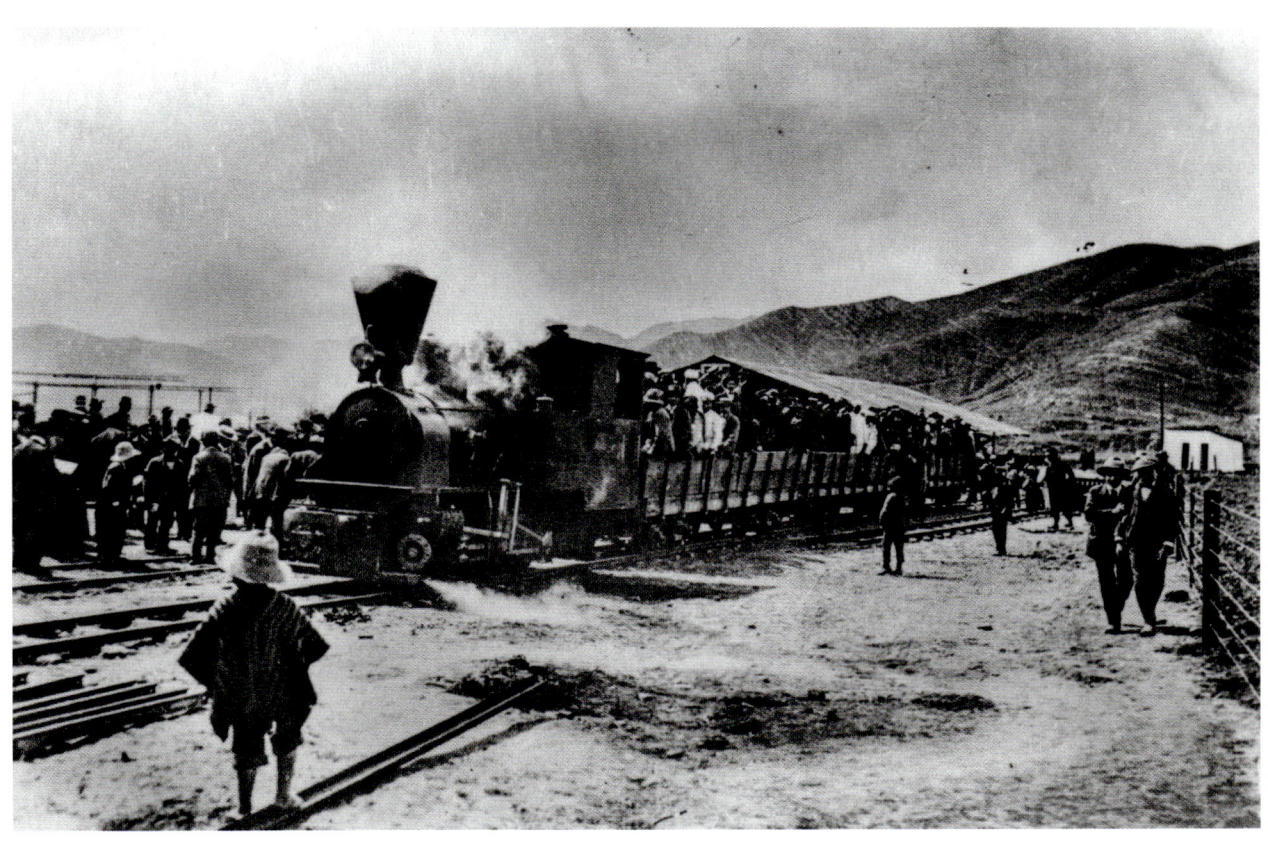

The first train arriving in Cusco, Perú, 1908.

PHOTOGRAPHS BY MIGUEL CHANI. COURTESY OF FOTOTECA ANDINA CBC.
CHAN00124, CHAN00035, CHAN00004, CHAN00127

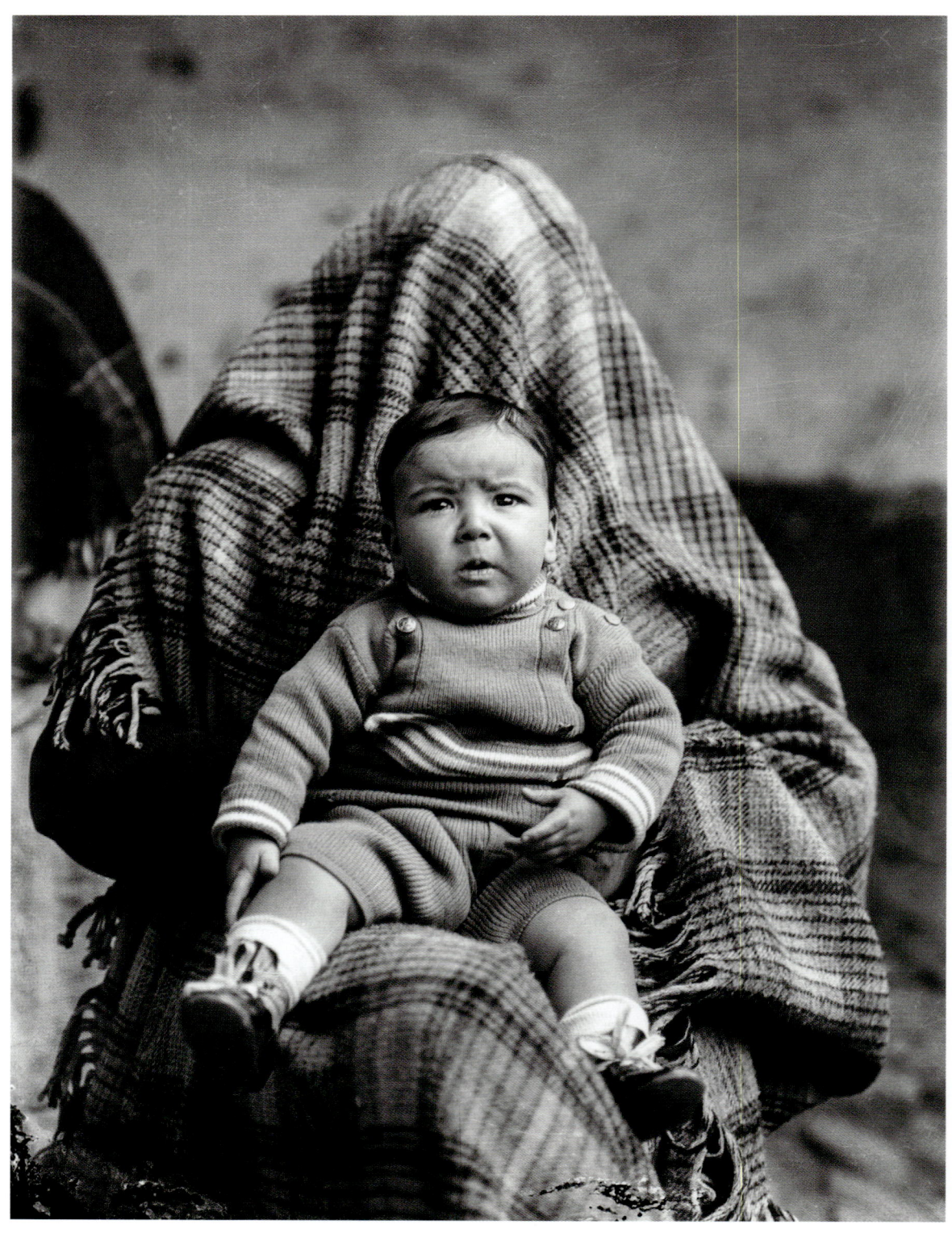

A child held still in the arms of a hidden woman,
likely the mother, Perú, 1920.

Opposite: Three women, Perú, 1920.

Opposite: Campesino in front of an Incan wall,
Huchuy Qosqo, Perú, 1930.

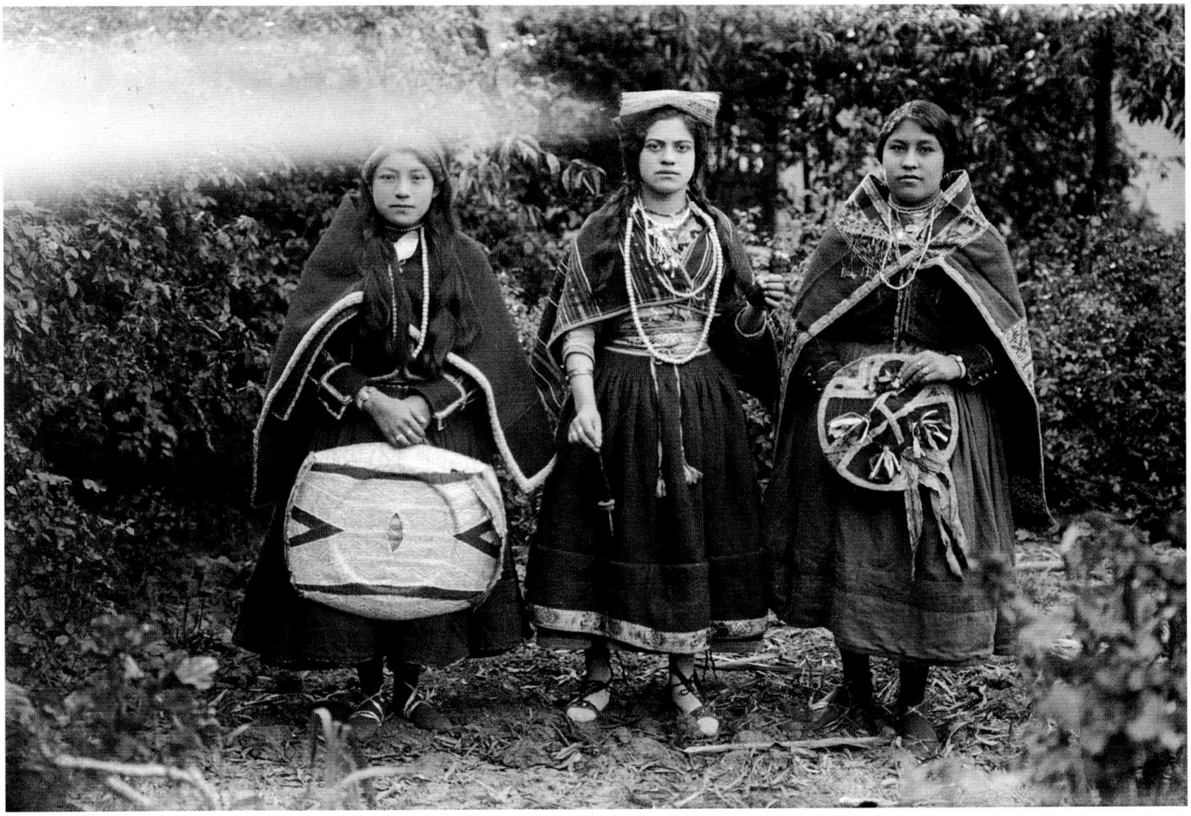

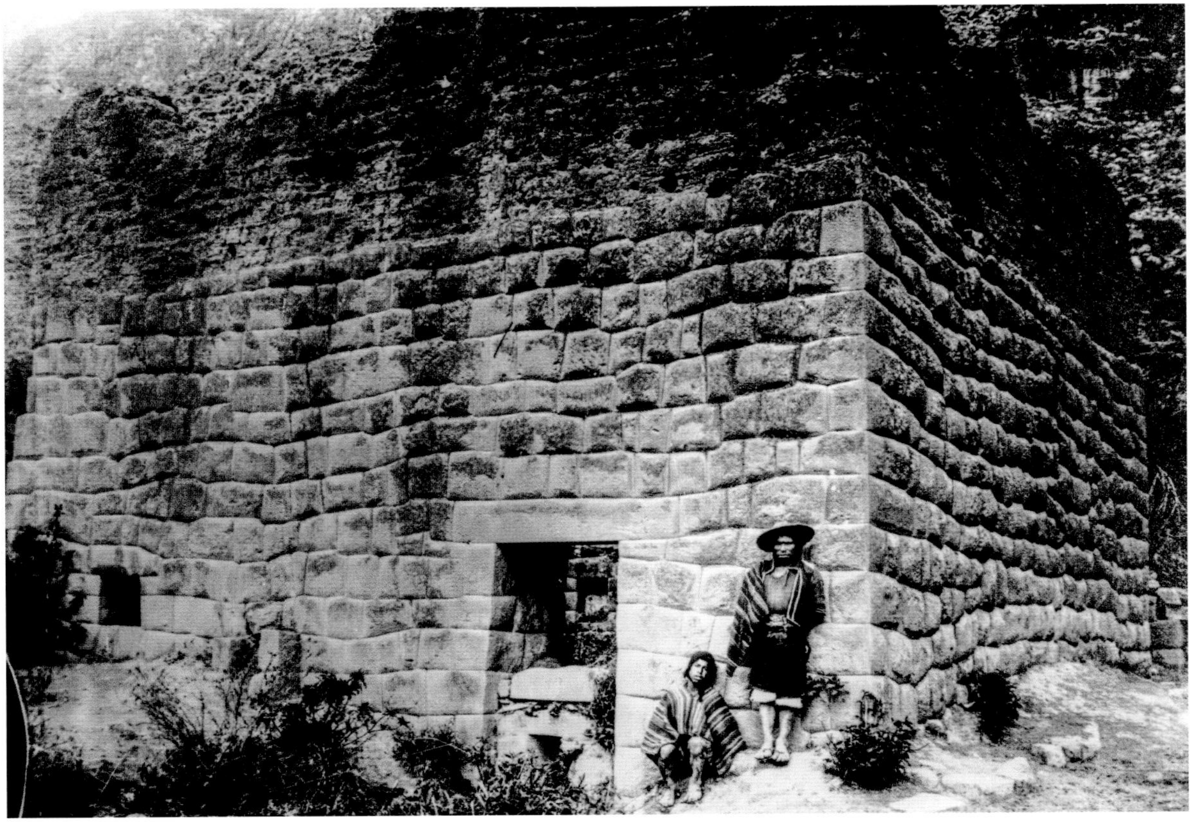

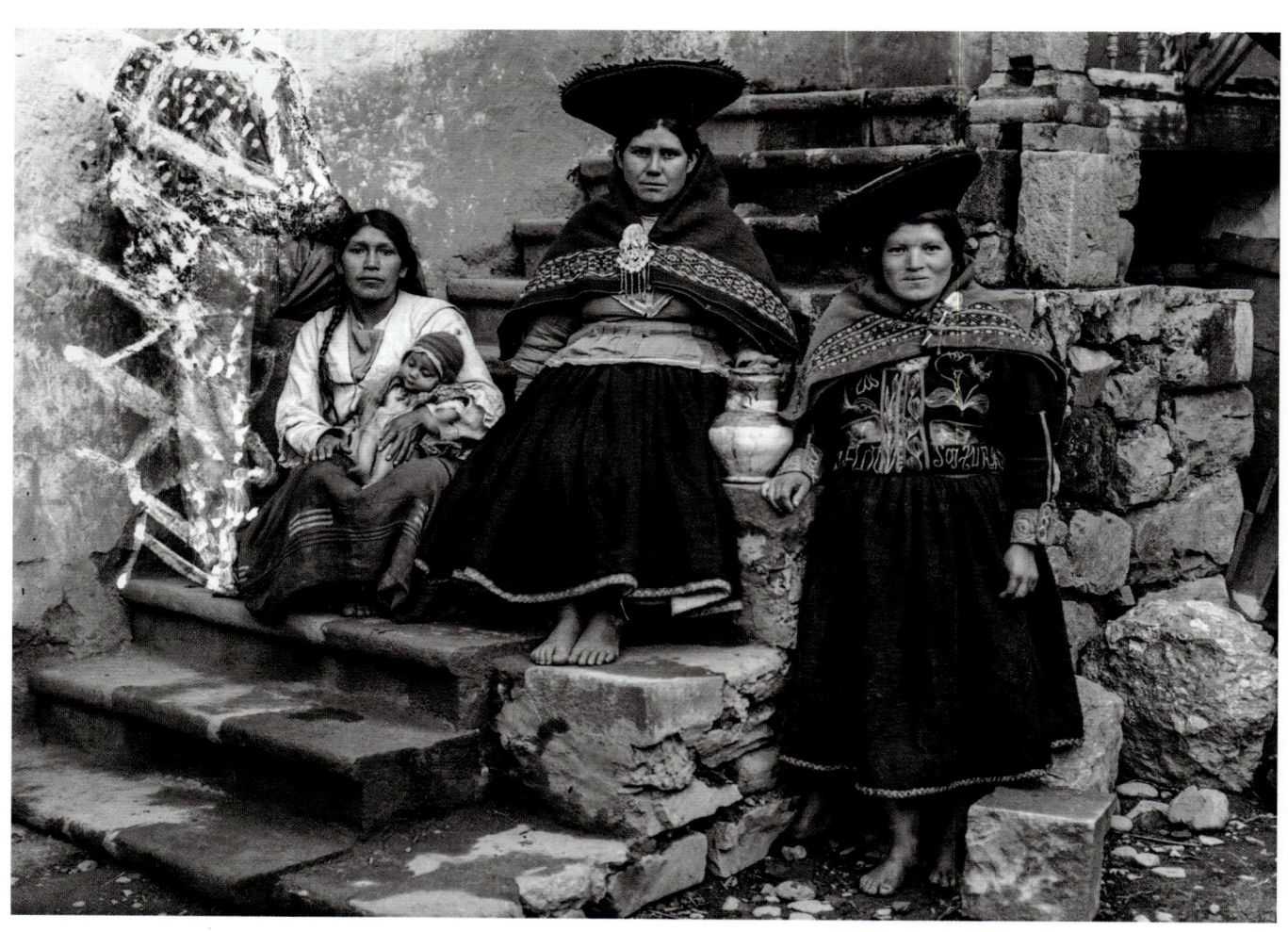

Three women at home, Perú, 1940.

Opposite: Woman on a horse in front of her home, Perú, 1945.

PHOTOGRAPHS BY FIDEL MORA. COURTESY OF FOTOTECA ANDINA CBC.

 MOR00010, MOR00017, MOR00089

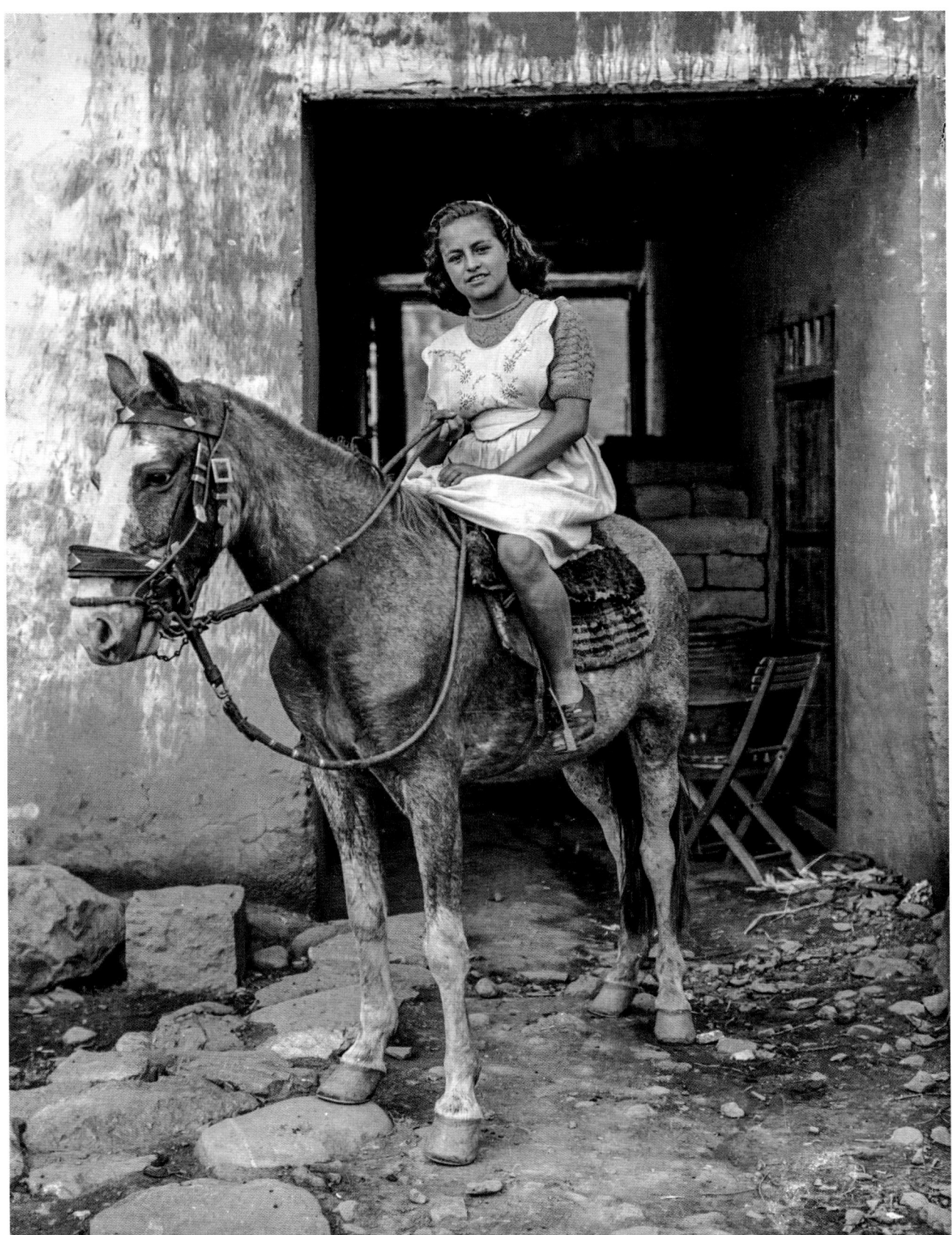

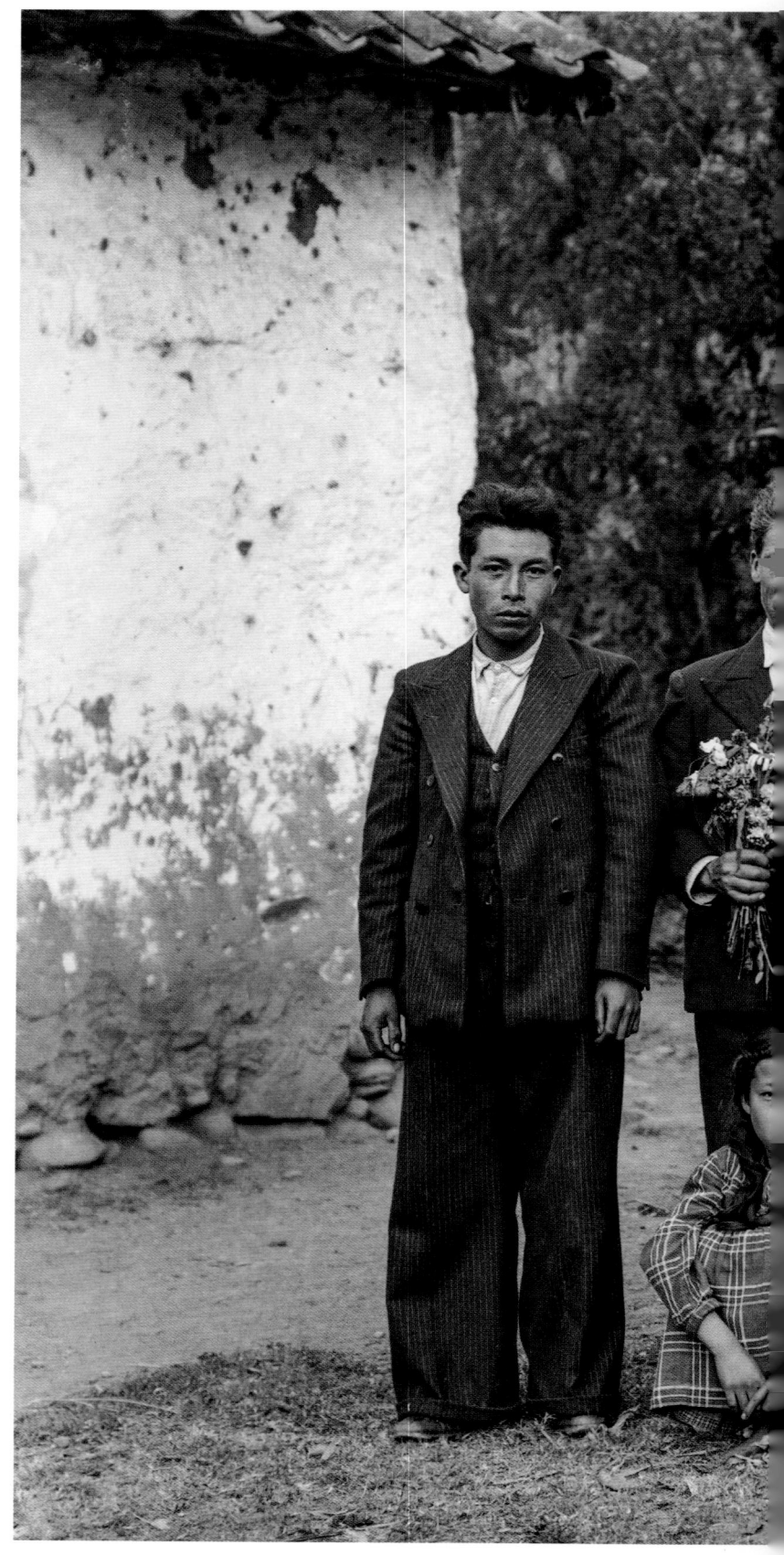

50   Wedding in Calca, Perú, 1945.

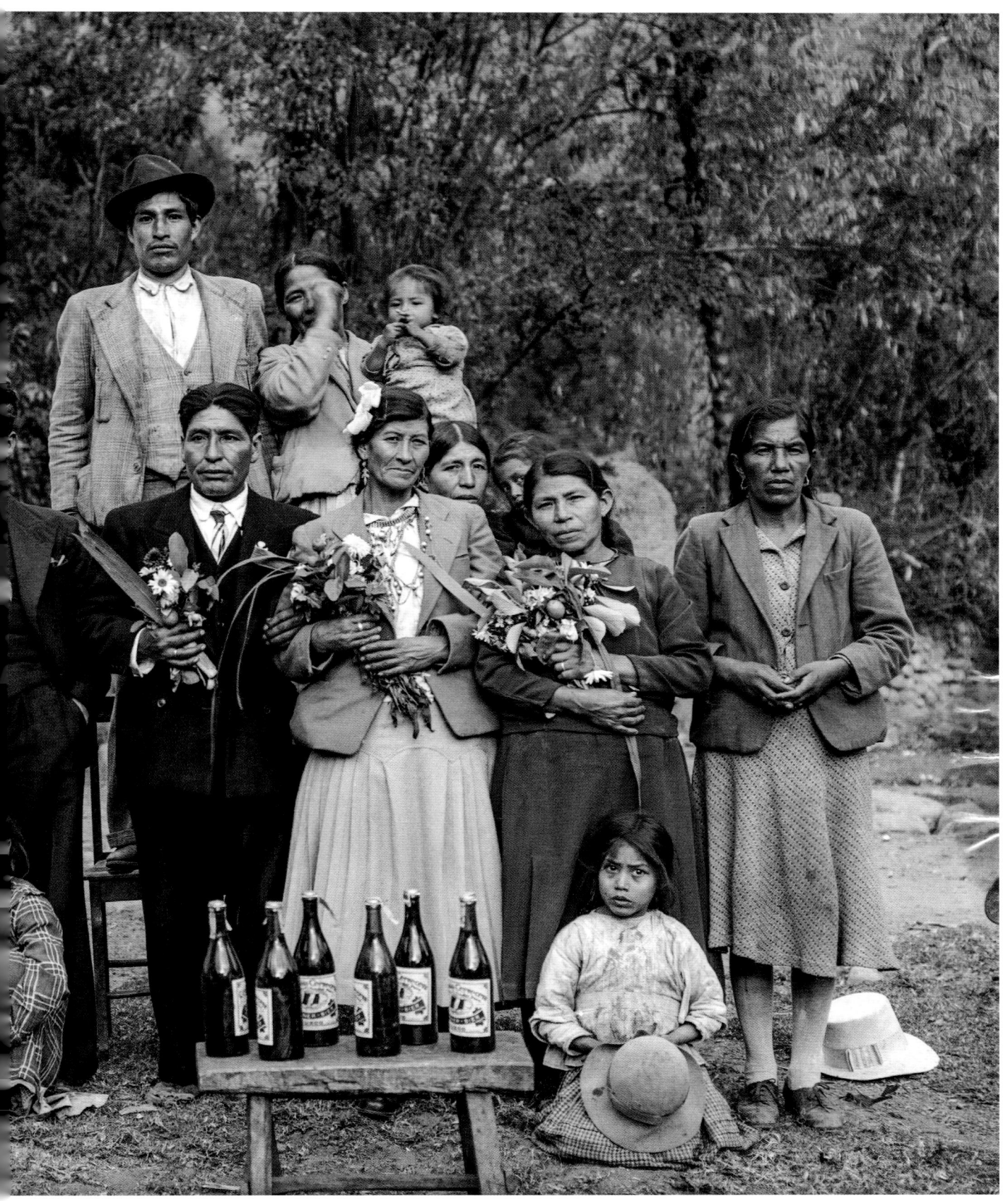

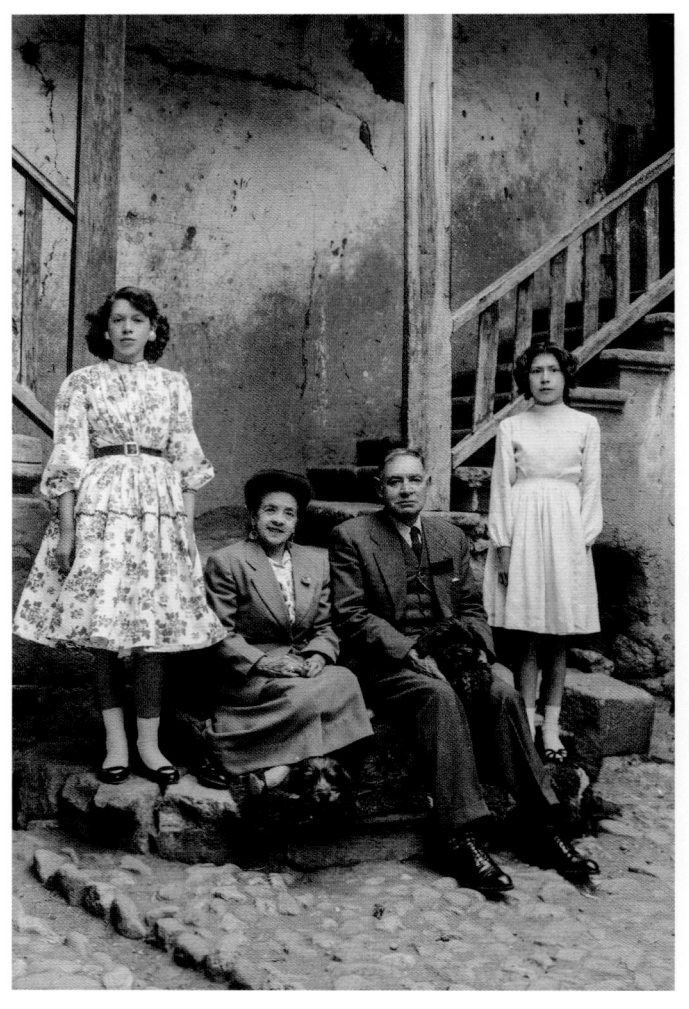
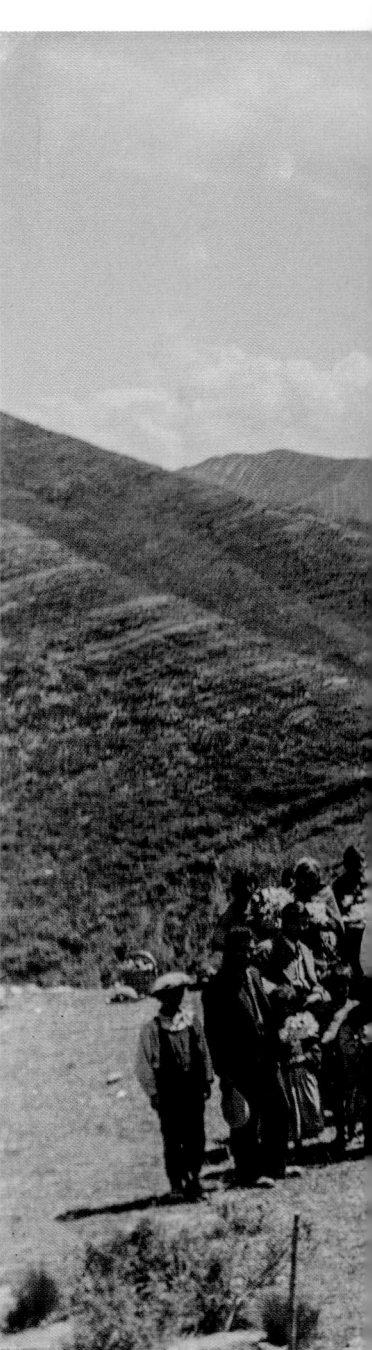
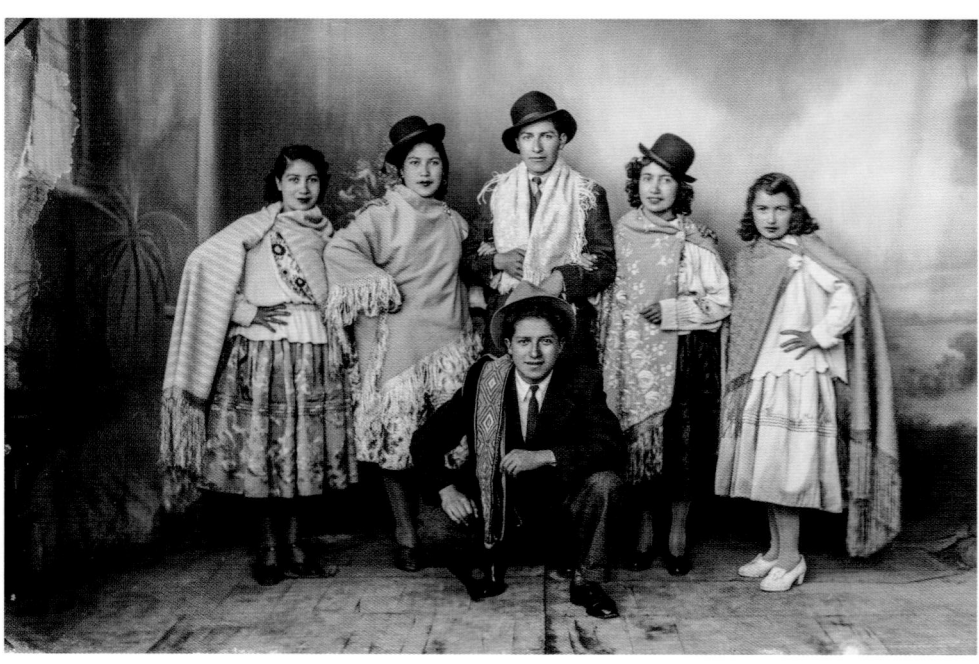

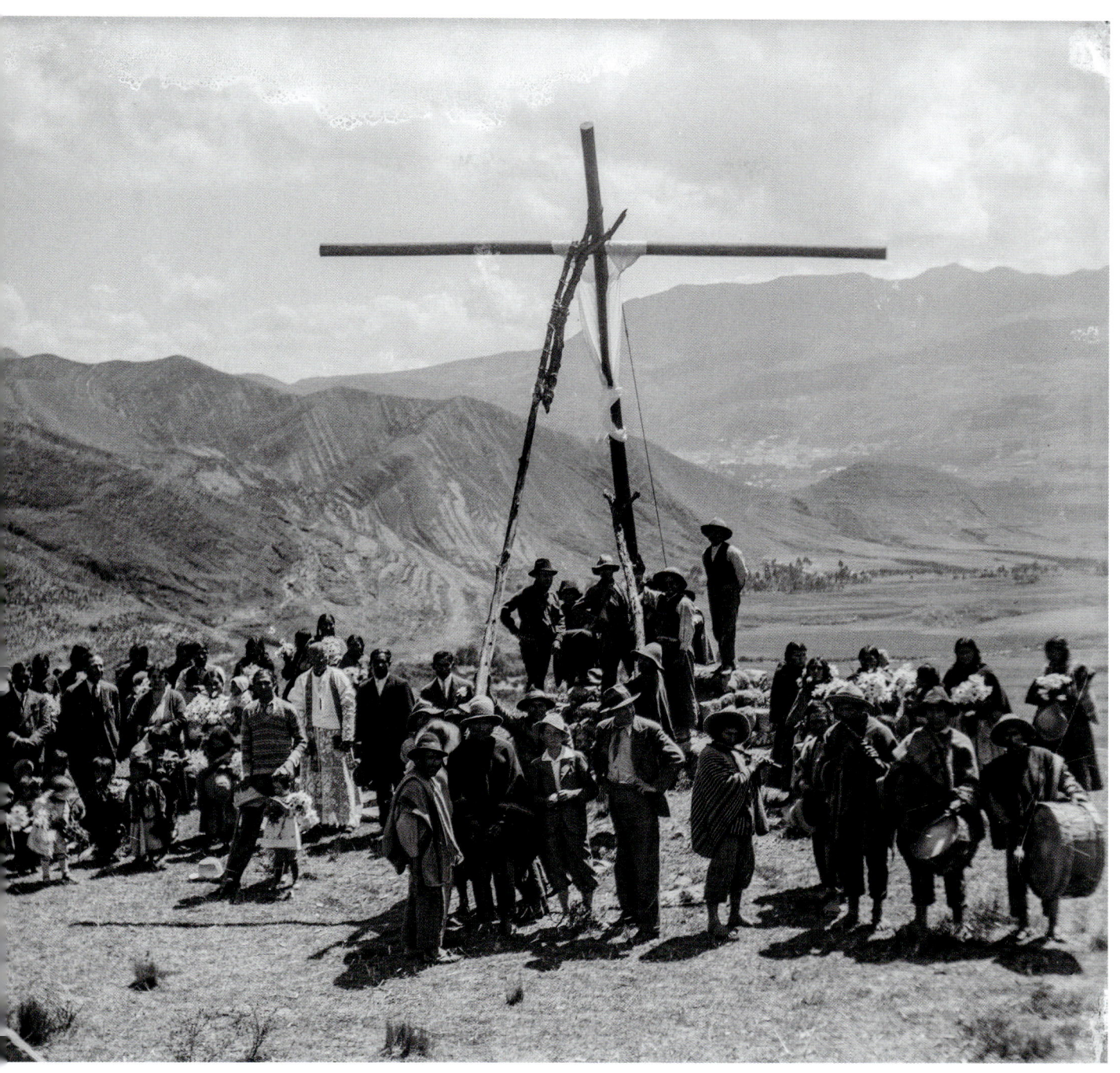

Girls of First Communion, Perú, 1940.

Opposite: Portraits, Perú, c. 1930–60.

PHOTOGRAPHS BY HORACIO OCHOA. COURTESY OF FOTOTECA ANDINA CBC.
OCHOA 6816, OCHOA 8154, OCHOA 8153, OCHOA 6587, OCHOA 410, OCHOA 7111

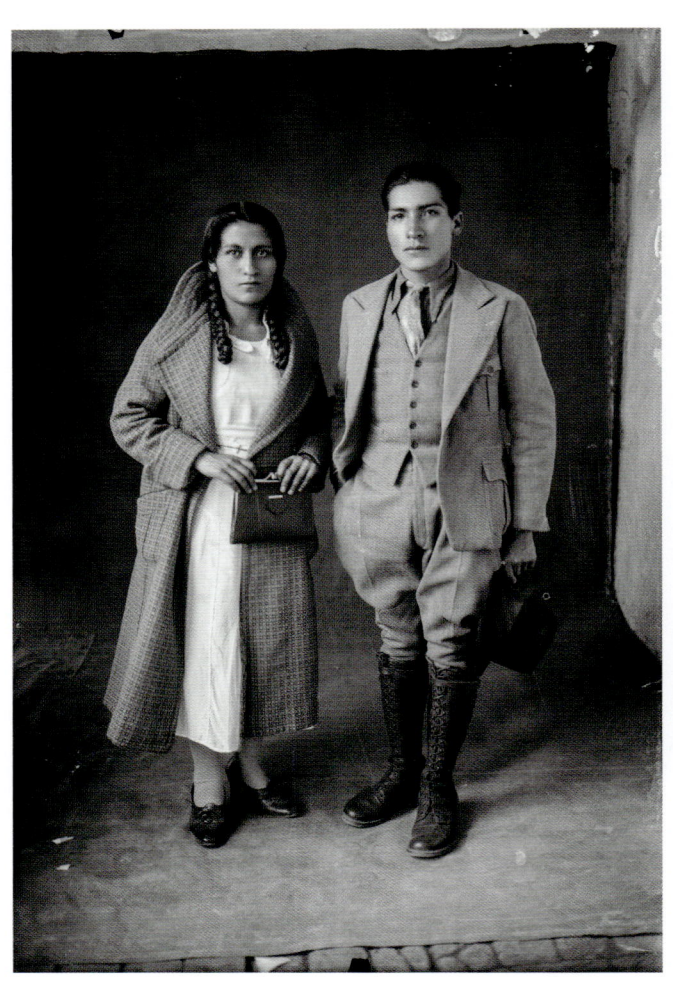

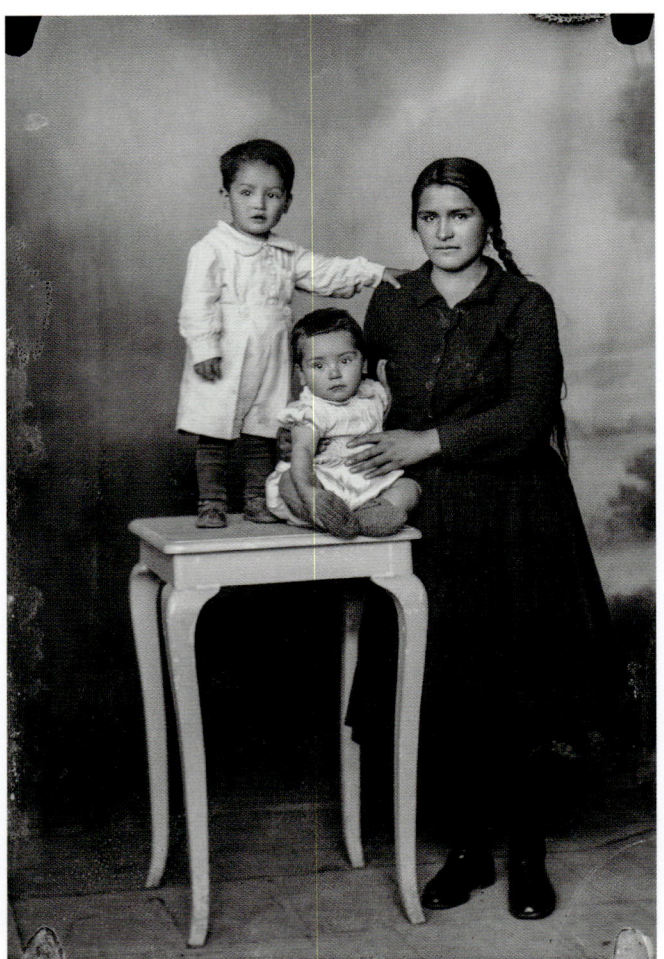

Man in riding costume and partner, Perú, c. 1930–60.

Mother and daughters, Perú, 1950.

54   Opposite: Portrait, Perú, c. 1930–60.

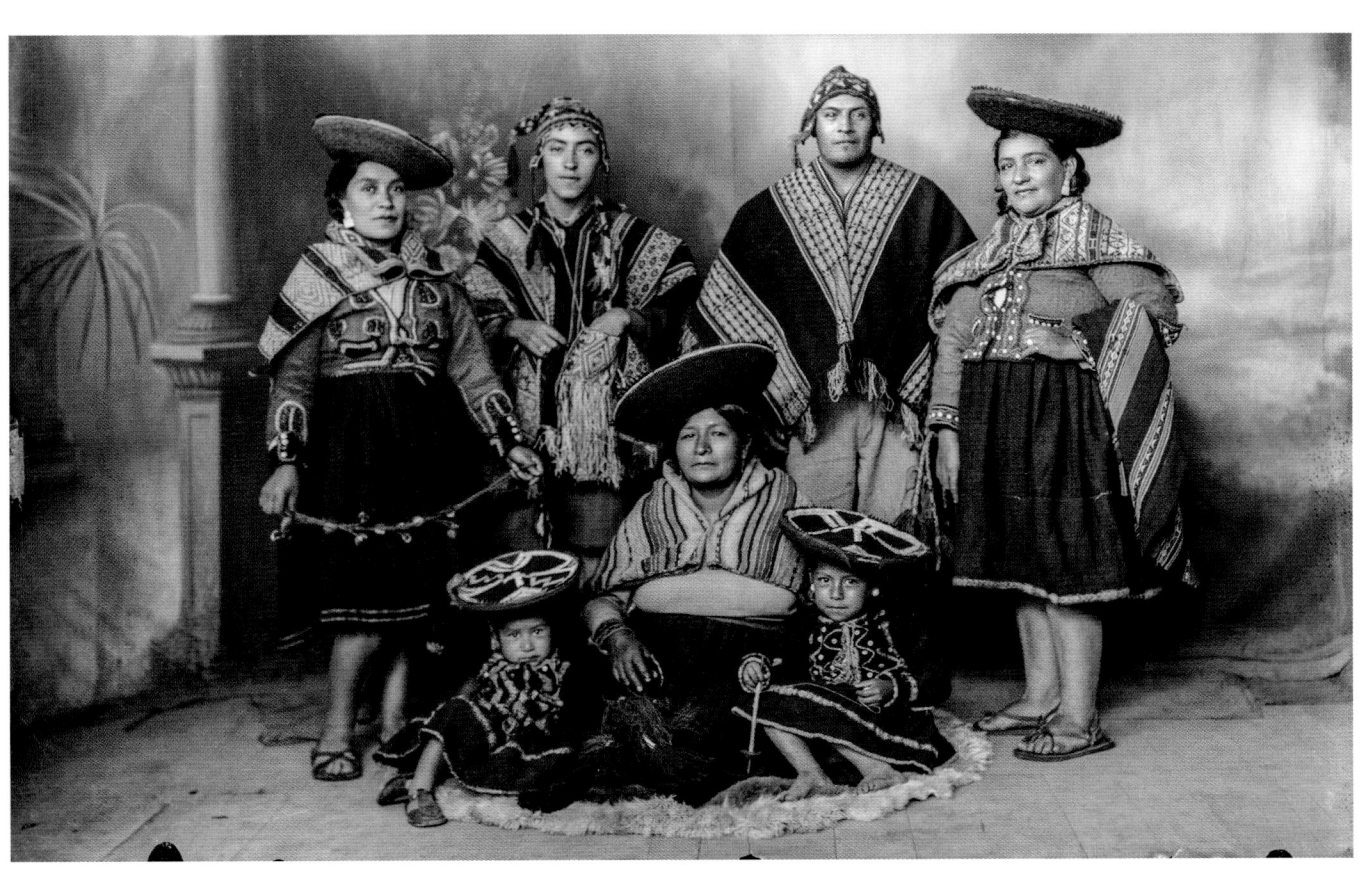

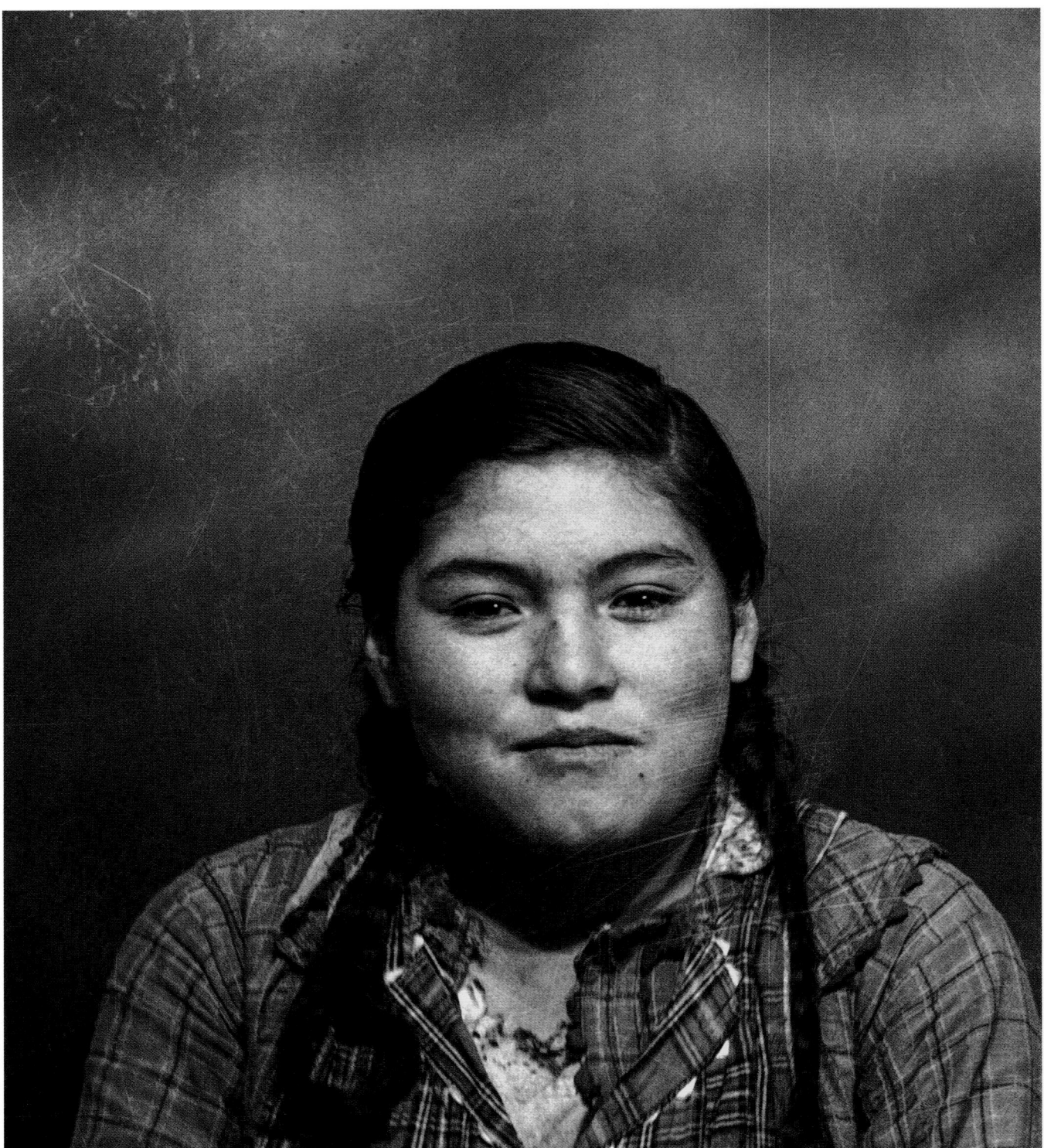

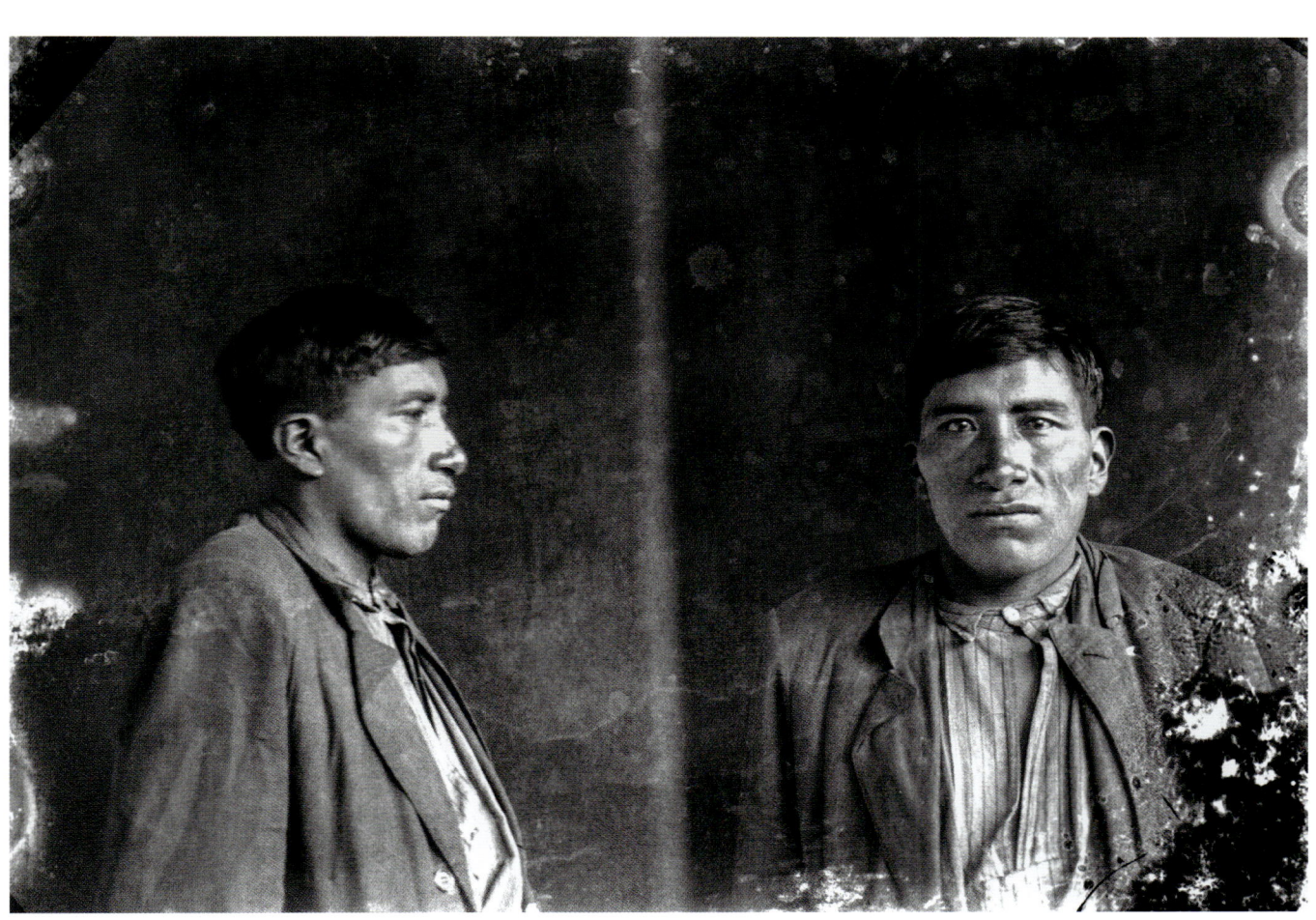

A man pictured in profile and head-on, Perú, 1930.

Opposite: A woman at the atelier, Perú, 1930.

PHOTOGRAPHS BY CÉZAR MEZA. COURTESY OF FOTOTECA ANDINA CBC.
MEZ00109, MEZ00003, MEZ00009, MEZ00186, MEZ00686

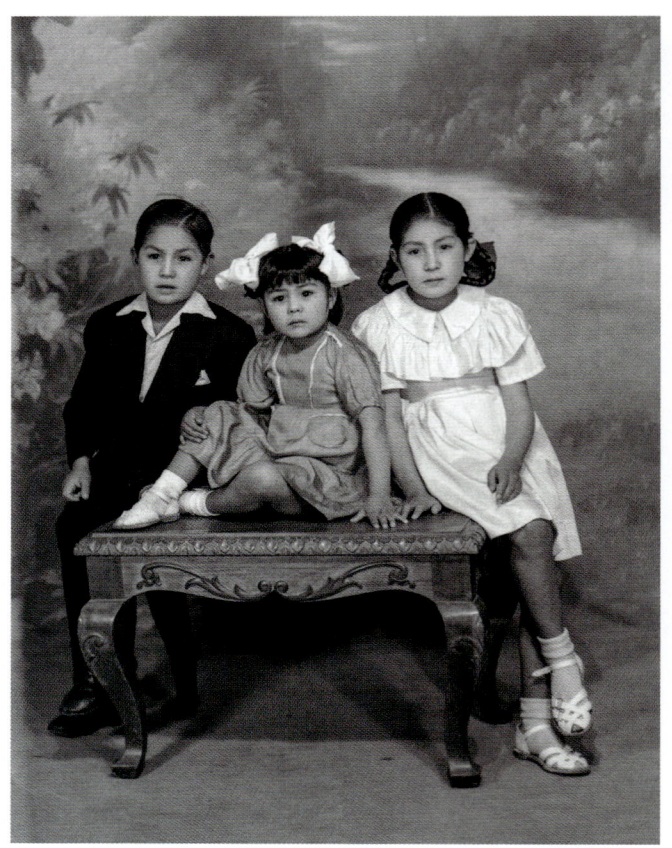

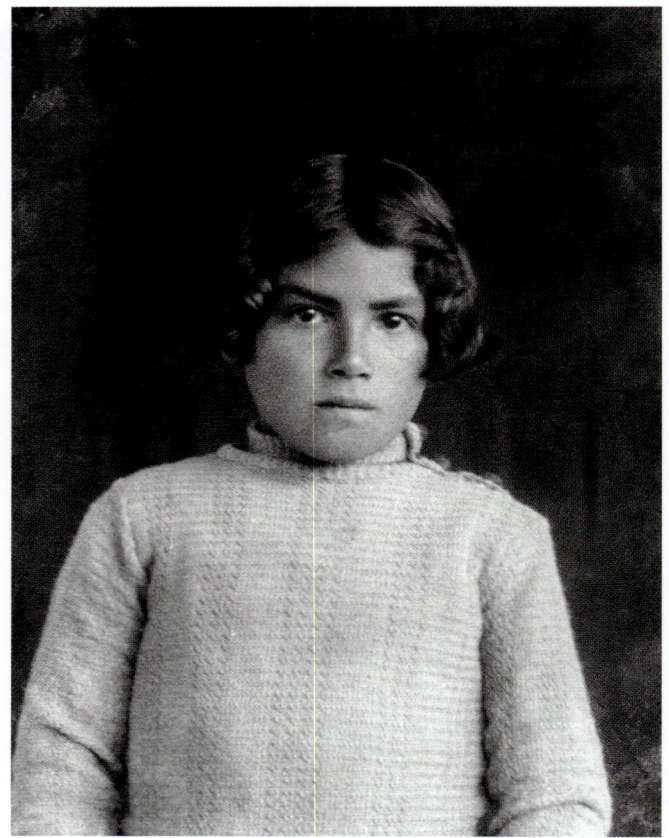

Three children at the atelier, Perú, 1945.

A girl at the atelier, Perú, 1930.

58   Opposite: A family at the atelier, Perú, 1945.

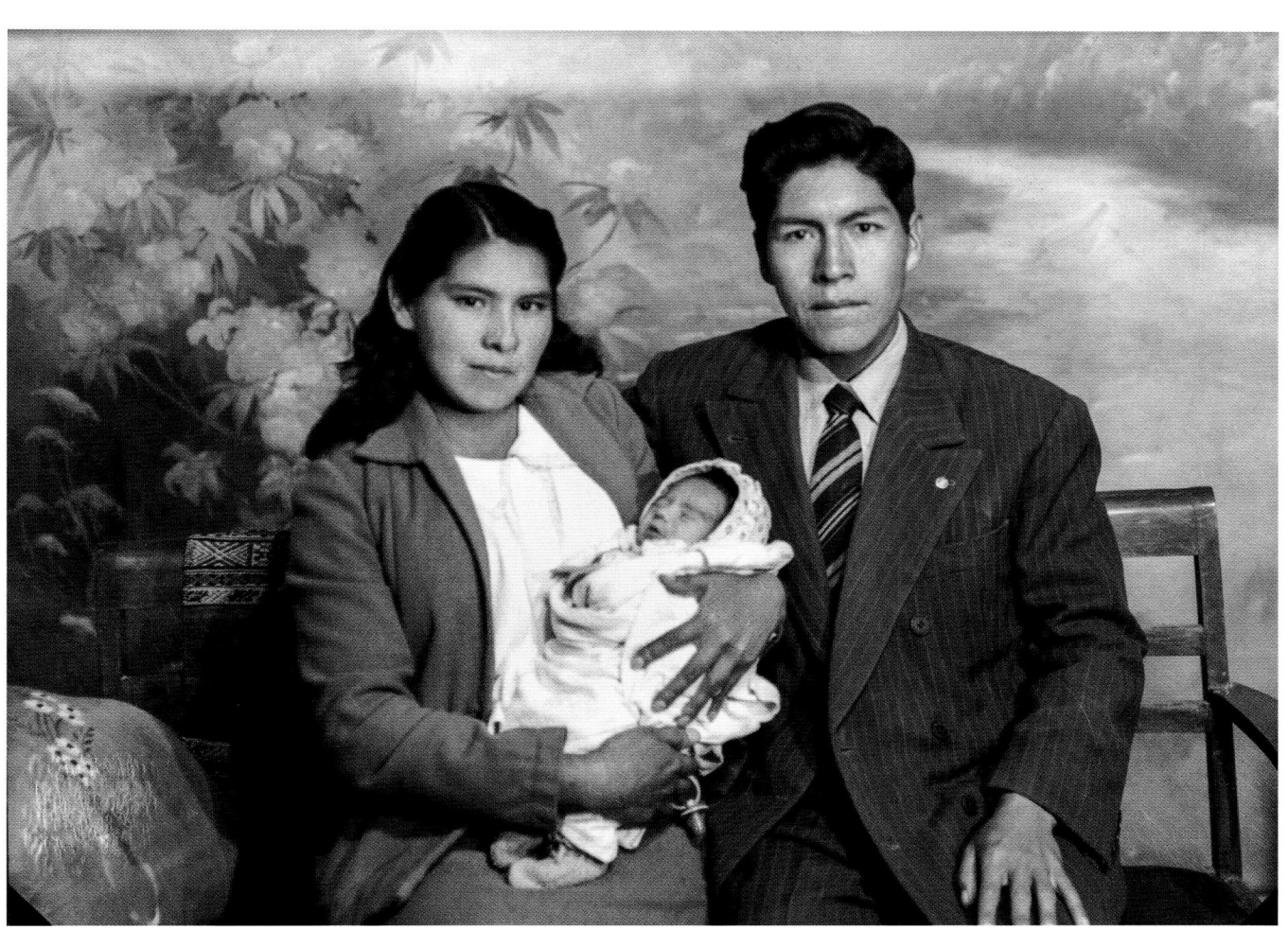

MARTÍN CHAMBI AND FAMILY
Quechua
Cusco
Perú

Perhaps the most noted of the Cusco School of Photography's practitioners is Martín Chambi (1891–1973), whose introduction to photography at the mine where his father was employed has taken on near mythical status. From this chance encounter with the company photographer, Chambi, who is of Quechua descent, went on to enjoy international success during his lifetime. His portraits, folkloric studies, and archeological images circulated throughout Latin America and the United States in exhibits and frequently in the budding periodical press. Chambi's work has been lauded by many distinguished critics, including the Peruvian Nobel laureate Mario Vargas Llosa. He had the capacity, as his son Manuel, an influential filmmaker, once described it, of making a photograph look both "old and new at the same time" (como viejo y nuevo a la vez).[1]

In one such image from 1926, Social celebration of the Cusco Carnival (*Celebración social de carnaval cuzqueño*), a group portrait appears both bourgeois and bohemian (see page vi). Revelers pose against a lush background of patterned wallpaper, ornate carpet, gilt frames, and festoons of flowers and palms that bespeak the wealth and status of the room's occupants. The party-goers mug for the camera, showing off lavish costumes—a skeleton, a sailor, a bullfighter in an elaborate "suit of lights." Women are bedecked in beads and bonnets; they duck behind fans or exchange furtive glances across the crowd.

But, like those of other photographers of the Cusco School, Chambi's images were wide-ranging and encompassed many of Perú's most famous archeological sites, including Machu Picchu. "Since I began to take photography seriously," Chambi told the periodical *El Pueblo* in 1958, "I've had only one goal: to give the whole world an understanding of the natural beauty of my patria and the image of the exceeding splendor of the ruins that speak of our history."[2]

Chambi's distinguished career has given way to three generations of Chambi photographers, creatives, and archival stewards.

His children Julia (1919–2003) and Víctor (1917–1985) began assisting their father in his Cusco-based studio from an early age and were prominent photographers in their own right. A 1964 dual portrait of Martín and Víctor Chambi in the studio pictures father and son mirroring the gaze of the cameras in the foreground. While both Víctor and Julia pursued themes of interest to their father—local festivals and archeological sites—Julia, in particular, distinguished herself as a deft portraitist, illuminating family photos in the style known as "foto-óleo" or black-and-white photos embellished with color by the application of oil paints. In the 1970s, Víctor dedicated himself to the conservation and circulation of his father's work, paving the way to the wide recognition it receives today.

Martín's grandchildren Teo Allain, Peruska, and Oscar would also go on to prominent careers as photographers and directorial positions at the family-founded Asociación Martín Chambi, which promotes and safeguards the work of this venerated artist. Another grandson, Roberto, is president of the association.

The Martín Chambi Digital Catalog (searchable as Catálogo Digital Martín Chambi) is a project undertaken by the association, which makes available some tens of thousands of images created by Chambi and his associates, and serves as an incredible resource for preserving and proliferating this invaluable archive.

Peruska (b. 1958) avows her commitment to the rich Andean histories her family has long chronicled. Of a series of photographs she made of the Dance of Las Pallas, a traditional folk dance derived from Incan culture, she says, "Dance and history mix in these photos" (La danza y la historia se mezclan en estas fotos). The images show young women, representing Incan nobles, dressed in intricately crocheted and beaded costumes. "I think this rituality is part of my essence. I look for that wherever I go, that which is typical of our Andean culture and that carries something of my roots." (Pienso en esta ritualidad que es parte de mi esencia, a donde voy busco eso, que es propio de nuestra cultura andina y que lleva algo de mis raíces.)[3]

—Brenna M. Casey

Portrait of a woman in Sicuani, Canchis, Cusco, Perú, c. 1918–24. Glass plate negative, 10" × 15".
PHOTOGRAPH BY MARTÍN CHAMBI. COURTESY OF ASOCIACIÓN MARTÍN CHAMBI.

Machu Picchu, Perú, 1972. Celluloid negative, 6" × 7".
PHOTOGRAPH BY VÍCTOR ADRIÁN CHAMBI LÓPEZ. COURTESY OF ARCHIVO FOTOGRÁFICO VÍCTOR A. CHAMBI LÓPEZ.

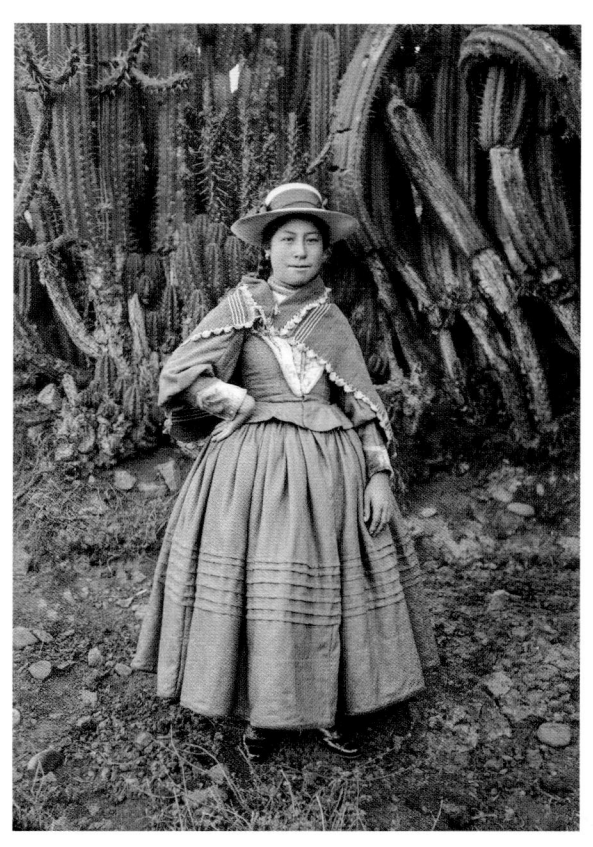

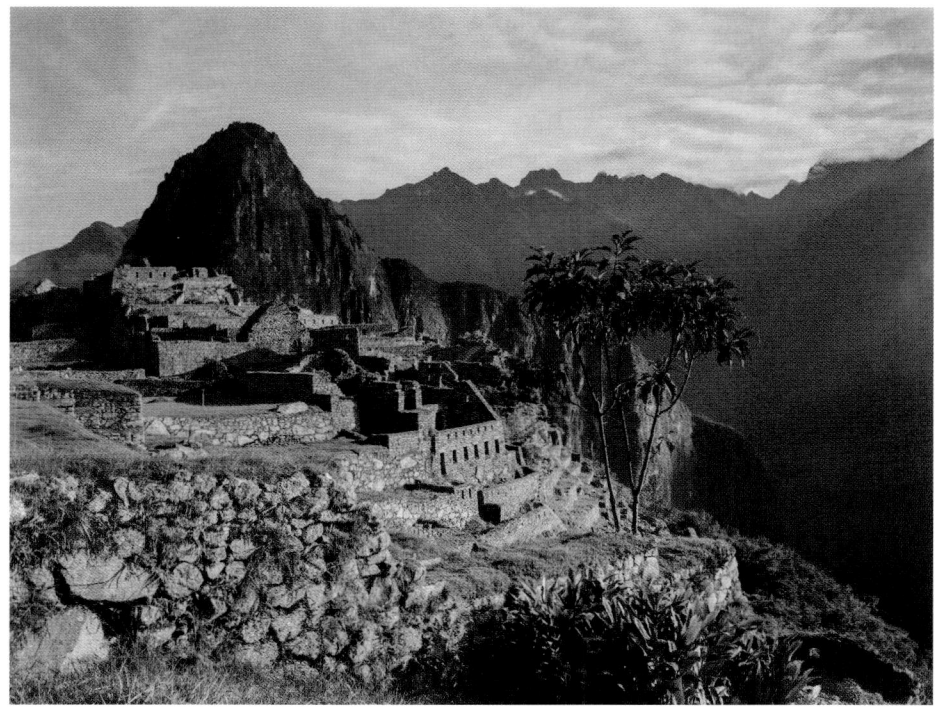

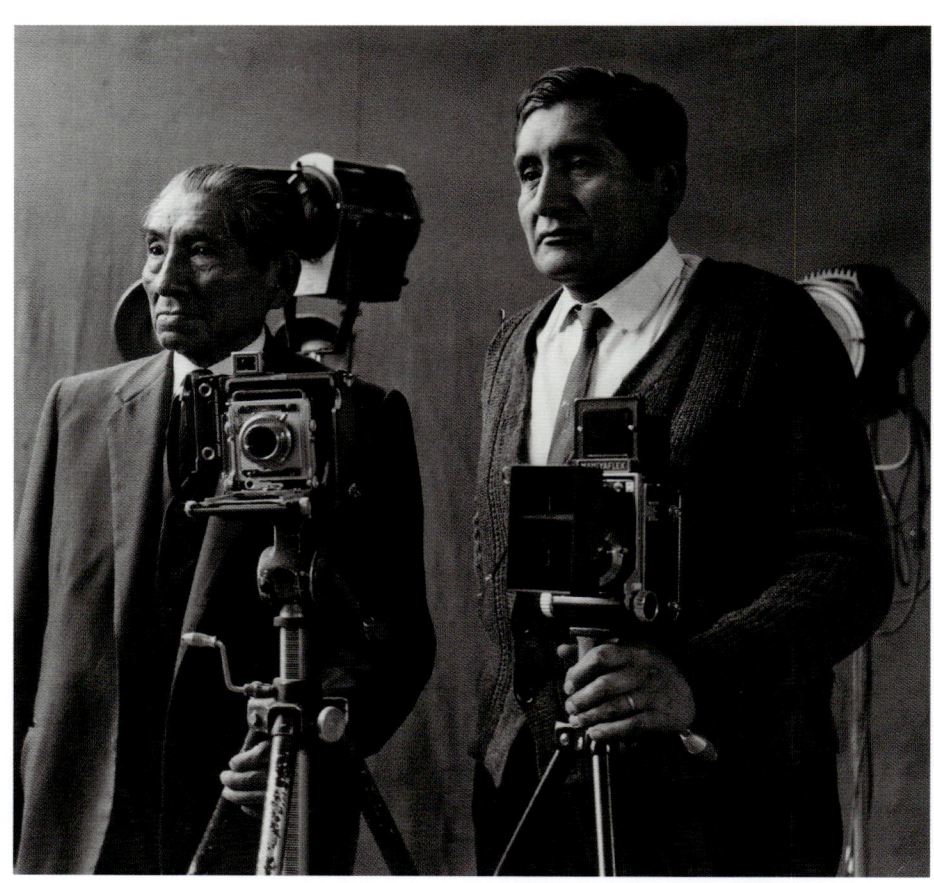

Martín and Víctor Chambi in the studio, Cusco, Perú, 1964.
Celluloid negative, 6" × 6".
PHOTOGRAPH BY VÍCTOR ADRIÁN CHAMBI LÓPEZ. COURTESY OF ARCHIVO
FOTOGRÁFICO VÍCTOR A. CHAMBI LÓPEZ.

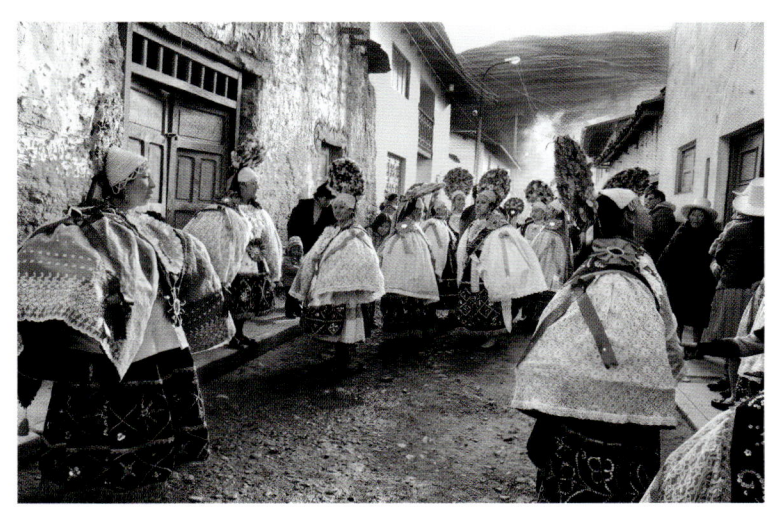

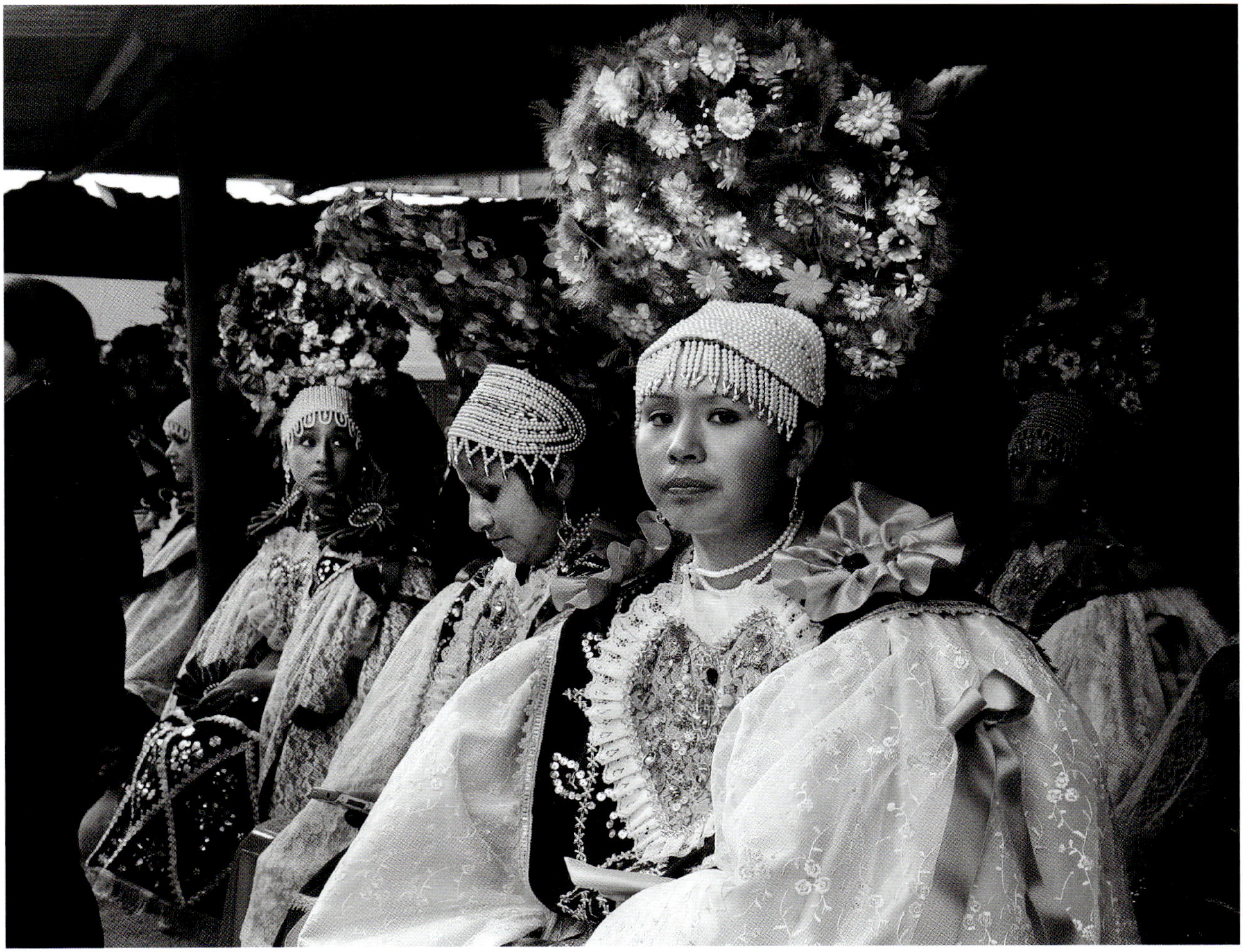

Dance of Las Pallas at dawn, Corongo, Ancash, Perú, 2014.

Dance of Las Pallas, Corongo, Ancash, Perú, 2014.

NETTIE ODLETY
LUCY SAUMTY

Kiowa (Cáuigú)
Mountain View, Oklahoma
United States

On a bright afternoon in Arizona, two teenaged friends living far away from home take turns making photos of each other. They are Nettie Odlety (1897–1978) and Lucy Saumty (1897–1980), students at the Phoenix Indian School. Inside the girls' dormitory they move between the floor and the bed, positioning themselves in wide streams of sunlight. They're having fun, it seems, documenting themselves in this familiar space.

The photographs divulge a self-made sanctuary within the rigid and oppressive boarding school system. In these fleeting, unsupervised moments, the dorm transforms into a space where friendships are forged.[1] Here, students can indulge their youthfulness and create intimate, shared experiences. The closed door and pulled curtains behind Odlety hold hushed conversations or conceal mischief. The beds remind us that the dorm is also a place for rest. Alongside Saumty, the wide-open windows stubbornly gesture to the ever-impinging campus—and world—outside.

Odlety and Saumty are Kiowa (Cáuigú) from Indian Territory, present-day Oklahoma. They were raised in large families in or near Mountain View and, after school, returned to Oklahoma for the rest of their lives.

In 1919, the year she graduated, Odlety married Kiowa linguist Parker Paul McKenzie, her classmate and boyfriend at Phoenix Indian School. They had five children and were married for 59 years before Odlety died at age 80. The camera was a household fixture; the couple made hundreds of pictures of family and "important scenes and milestones."[2] In one insouciant photograph from 1952, Odlety and McKenzie stand in the midday light, shoulder to shoulder.[3] McKenzie, with arms akimbo in a suit shirt, tie, and ironed trousers, chews on a cigar. Odlety, in a floral short-sleeved dress, folds her hands at her waist and peers into the camera. Odlety's great-granddaughter Josie Lampone said her forebear "was an incredibly talented seamstress and quilter," adding, "She was known as a loving yet fierce woman."[4]

Saumty, who had 15 brothers and sisters,[5] passed away at 83 years old. It appears she outlived all but one sibling, Rev. George Saumty. She married Richard Pipestem (Otoe) in 1916, and they later divorced. In the early 1930s, she wed World War I veteran Ludie Napoleon Goins (Chickasaw). Like her friend Odlety, Saumty had five children.[6] Along with her brother George, Parker McKenzie, and several others, she is a contributing storyteller to the 2022 publication *Plains Life in Kiowa: Voices from a Tribe in Transition*. In the book, which contains texts from a medley of sources, a 1970s recording of Saumty speaking in Kiowa about Satanta, a revered Kiowa figure, is transcribed in both English and Kiowa. The genesis of this audio is the Kiowa Culture Program, a group of Elders who regularly recorded themselves at roundtable meetings discussing, in Kiowa, "various aspects of Kiowa culture and history, in order for later generations to listen and learn from them."[7]

In the dorm photographs, Odlety and Saumty are both sitting. Odlety rests on her left hand and Saumty on her left elbow. The pictures are made from a slight distance, allowing the space around them to fill with tangible materials—wood floors, patterned wallpaper, white cotton sheets. The air is awash in enduring realities—the formative years of childhood, the ways boarding school has, and will, change them. They are two young women on the cusp of marriage and children, a life's worth of delicate hopes and sharp uncertainties before them.

—Sarah Stacke

Nettie Odlety inside the girls' dormitory at Phoenix Indian School, Phoenix, Arizona, c. 1915.
PHOTOGRAPH BY LUCY SAUMTY.

Lucy Saumty inside the girls' dormitory at Phoenix Indian School, Phoenix, Arizona, c. 1915.
PHOTOGRAPH BY NETTIE ODLETY.

PARKER MCKENZIE COLLECTION, OKLAHOMA HISTORICAL SOCIETY. COLLECTION NUMBER 19650.68, 19650.92

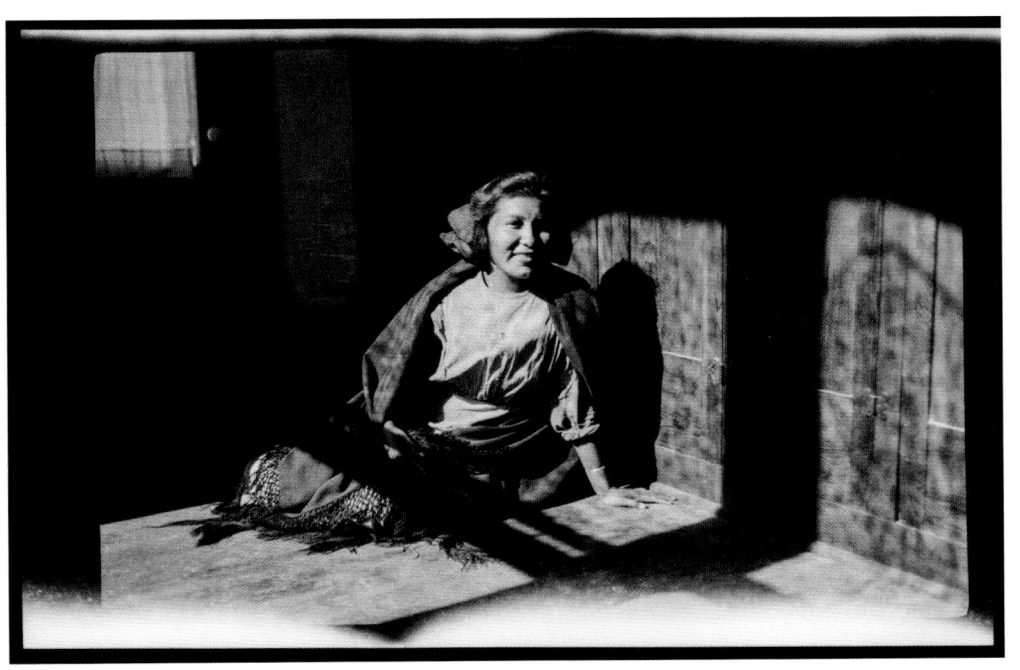

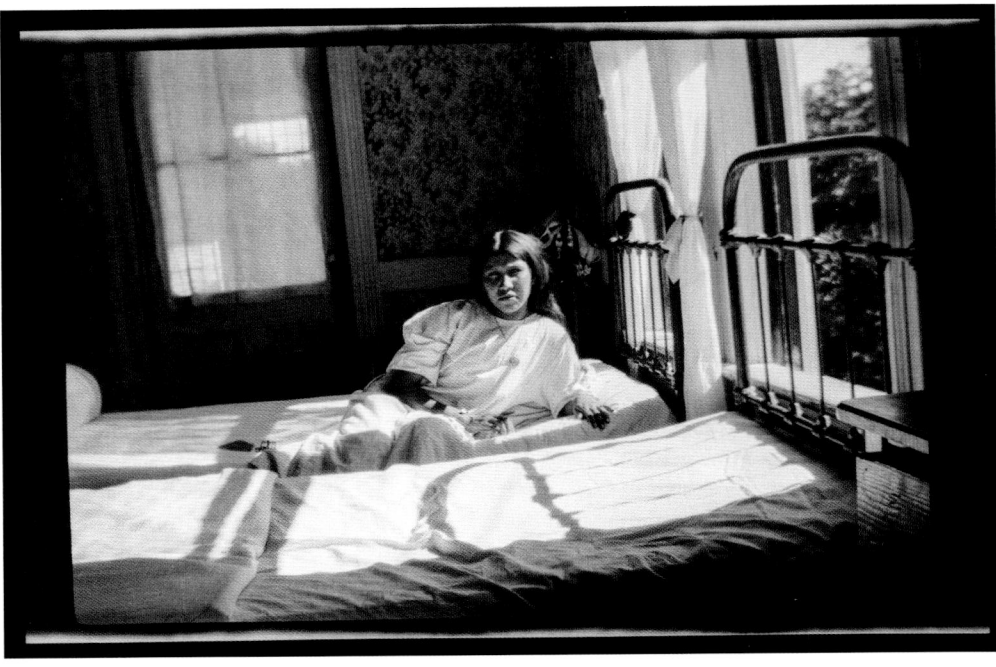

YIŚÀUM (TWICE LOOKED AT) / PARKER PAUL MCKENZIE

Kiowa (Cáuigú)
Mountain View, Oklahoma
United States

In case one of the notes Parker McKenzie (1897–1999) and Nettie Odlety (1897–1978) passed to each other in class at Rainy Mountain Boarding School was intercepted by a sharp-eyed teacher and read aloud, they penned them in elemental phonetic Kiowa (Cáuijògà). An established written form of the language didn't exist, but that would change.

The couple's notes, rather than fading into a sweet memory of young love, sparked McKenzie's interest in the Kiowa language. "The innocent practice was beginning to fascinate me, if not my partner," he wrote many years later. "It led me to experiment with words and simple expressions."[1]

McKenzie became a linguist and developed a Kiowa orthography. He authored books, published papers, and received an honorary doctorate from the University of Colorado. But before all that, he married Odlety, his very first Kiowa correspondent.

Born in his family's tipi and raised in Mountain View, Oklahoma, McKenzie had a Kiowa name: Yiśàum (Twice Looked At). From his grandparents and other Elders, he was taught Old Kiowa—in short, the dialect used before contact with English. In 1904, when McKenzie first attended Rainy Mountain, nine miles southeast of Mountain View, his sole language was Kiowa. Assimilation was the rule; only English was allowed at the school. "We beginners just kept our mouth shut when staff members were around for fear of punishment if caught slipping into the native tongue," recalled McKenzie, who added, "The prohibition slowed down the learning process."[2]

After completing the highest level of education at Rainy Mountain in 1914, McKenzie and Odlety enrolled at the Phoenix Indian School, nearly 1,000 miles away in Arizona. There, McKenzie continued to refine his Kiowa writing system, and both he and Odlety became interested in photography.

Using a Kodak Brownie, McKenzie recorded his surroundings during scheduled breaks. Odlety, it appears, held the camera's attention more than anything, or anyone, else.[3] In an image he made of her relaxing on a patch of grass next to her friend Frances Ross, Odlety beams at McKenzie with a bow in her hair and her left hand raised to her chin. Ross, with a grin, looks resigned to this mirthful exchange of affection between the pair.

In another image, a self-portrait, McKenzie situates himself at a desk outside the school's main building. A typewriter is placed on the desk and the budding scholar rests his hand on it. Asked by the administration what trade he wished to learn at the school, McKenzie, who wanted access to a typewriter, requested and received a clerical assignment. The self-portrait is a prescient affirmation of his lifelong linguistic work and contributions to Kiowa (Cáuigú) cultural heritage. In a place where he was, once again, forbidden to speak Kiowa, McKenzie pictures himself with the very tool he would use to preserve the language. His strong sense of self is palpable in the photograph.

After two years at the boarding school, McKenzie transferred to Phoenix Union High School and later took some college prep courses at Oklahoma A&M (now Oklahoma State University) until the death of his father compelled him to return to Mountain View to work on the family farm and be close to his mother.

In early 1918, McKenzie accepted a job at the Kiowa Agency office of the Bureau of Indian Affairs (BIA) in Anadarko. He remained employed with the agency—first as a steno typist and then as an accounting clerk—until his retirement in 1958. In 1919, he and Odlety married. She had recently graduated from Phoenix Indian School and returned to Oklahoma.

While working at the BIA, McKenzie's bookish pursuits never foundered. The self-taught linguist made time for academic collaborations, independent research, and documentary endeavors to preserve Kiowa language and history. Retired and back in Mountain View, he ardently made audio recordings, authored texts, and traced family genealogies, generously sharing copies of his work with scholars, interested visitors, and Tribal members.

McKenzie spent close to 85 years perfecting a Kiowa writing system. After Sequoyah, who was Cherokee, he was only the second Indigenous person from what is now the United States to complete an orthography of their own language. Though others created systems for writing Kiowa, McKenzie's rises above them for its accuracy, thoroughness, and consistency, and for being developed by a native Kiowa speaker.[4] It also stands out for its accessibility. McKenzie—uniquely and logically—designed his orthography so that it was compatible with the letters and symbols of a standard typewriter.[5] Communicating his wish that the language would not only be preserved but embraced, he asked, "How can Kiowa be kept for posterity's sake if it is not a language in simplified-written form?"[6]

Cameras, along with typewriters, remained a constant in McKenzie's life. Through nearly six decades of marriage, five children, grandchildren, and great-grandchildren, McKenzie and Odlety devotedly photographed their life together.[7] When Dr. Parker Paul McKenzie died at age 101, he was the oldest member of the Kiowa Tribe of Oklahoma.

—Sarah Stacke

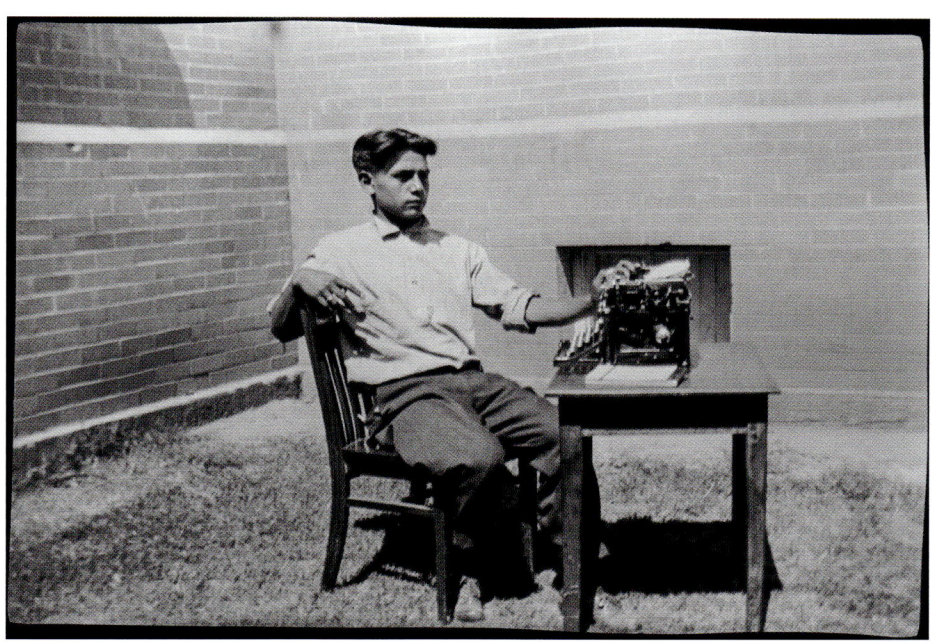

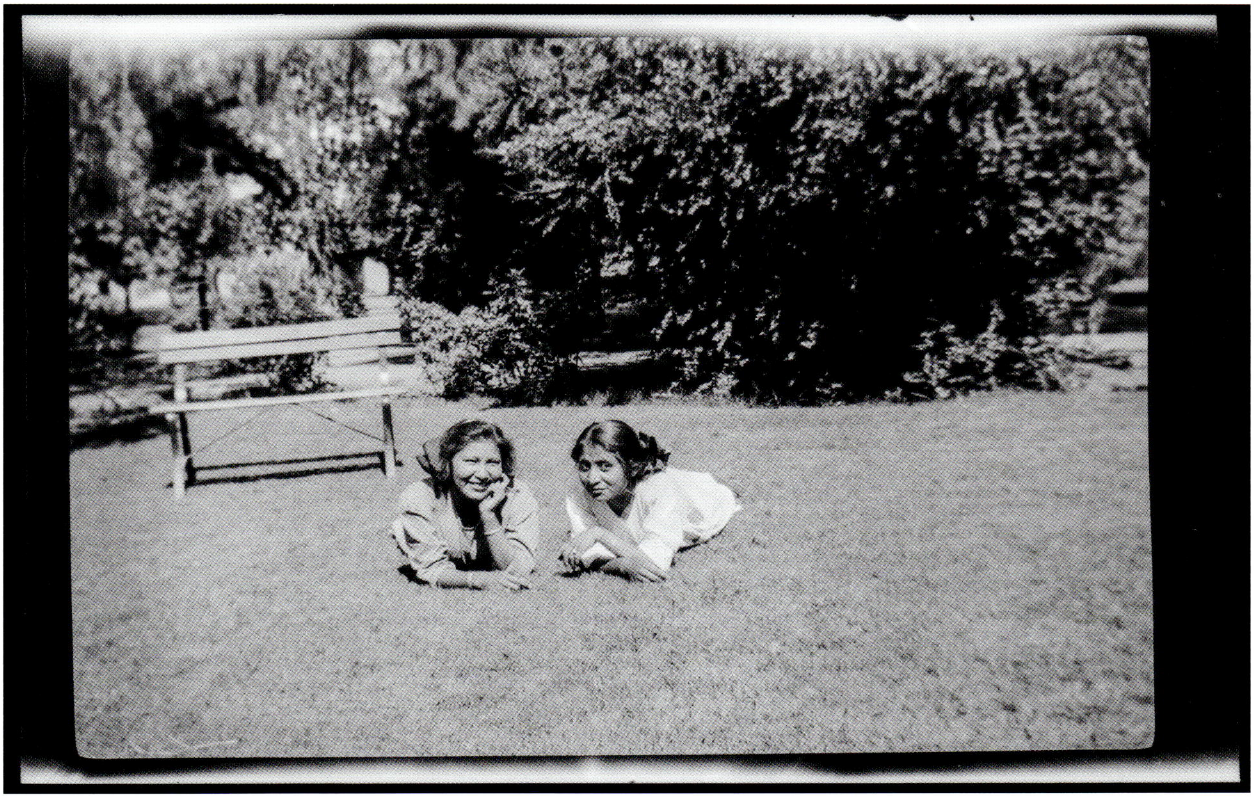

Parker McKenzie self-portrait at Phoenix Indian School main building, Phoenix, Arizona, c. 1916.

Nettie Odlety (left) and Frances Ross, who is Wichita, on the grounds of Phoenix Indian School, Phoenix, Arizona, c. 1915.

SOTERO CONSTANTINO JIMÉNEZ
Zapotec
Juchitán de Zaragoza, Oaxaca
México

In the first half of the 19th century, the Juchiteco photographer Sotero Constantino Jiménez (c. 1890–?) created a photographic collection of studio portraits, documenting and narrating the Native population of the Isthmus of Tehuantepec in Oaxaca, México. Very little is known about his life, work, and practice as an artist in the history of Mexican photography. However, his legacy as a photographer of Zapotec Indigenous origin is a precedent for contemporary and future Indigenous decolonial narratives. His images date back to México's postrevolutionary era between 1917 and 1940, and were created in a region with economic and political power, where the first Zapotec Indigenous president of México, Benito Juárez, came from.

Constantino Jiménez produced his photographs as a craftsman of light and shadows. It is not known whether he had a studio in his home or traveled from town to town to offer his services as a photographer to his neighbors, compatriots, family, and friends. His archive was rescued by the artist Francisco Toledo and is currently housed in the Manuel Álvarez Bravo Photographic Center in Oaxaca.

Through black-and-white images, Constantino Jiménez dedicated his work to portraying his community, its families, but above all, the women of the Isthmus: mothers, grandmothers, and daughters. In his images he rendered the memory of a people that continues to resist culturally against time —poetic images that demonstrate in each scene the agency and decision-making power that his collaborators possess. Elegance and autonomy. A community that raises its voice through its photographs.

From Constantino Jiménez's work, three images that narrate the identity of Istmeña feminine culture can be appreciated. His photographs have a harmonious composition, an aesthetic concordance that proclaims the beauty of Zapotec women who uphold the richness of a territory through their textiles and their brown bodies. Women who wear their traditional attire on their skins, like texts: verbs, words, and prayers. Zapotec clothing is part of the worldview that represents their people. It also represents their town, Juchitán, a word that in the Nahuatl language Ixtaxochitlán means "Place of White Flowers," and their region, Tehuantepec, "Hill of the Wild Beasts." Here in this visual microcosm, these images reveal the souls of flowery and fierce women.

From a feminist perspective, Constantino Jiménez portrays the women of his region, known as Tehuanas, Juchitecas, or Istmeñas.

In the first image, Constantino Jiménez uses the light of his camera to draw a proud woman, joyfully wearing her traditional Istmeño attire embroidered with flowers on crumpled satin fabric. Her hands delicately hold her enagua (skirt), as if she were ready to dance a polka or the traditional sandunga. Is she a married woman? In the Isthmus of Tehuantepec, it is through clothing that the social and marital status of women is announced. There are traditional gala or semi-gala garments that are worn in everyday life and others at weddings, patron saint festivals, or wakes. In the image, we see that the woman's hair is braided with a ribbon headdress that protrudes from her head in a bun shape. Around her neck she wears two typical gold necklaces shaped like medals, one short, known as an ahogador (choker), and the other long. With the arrival of the railroad to the Isthmus of Tehuantepec in the 19th century, American coins became famous among potters, and since then, they have been used to create the jewelry that is part of the garments worn by women. Among the most used coins are ounces, half ounces, five-dollar coins, and two-dollar coins. With a fixed and tender gaze at the camera, the woman observes and constructs a moment. Is this image commissioned? Who is this woman? Her round face, her black eyes, and her bushy eyebrows penetrate the viewer.

Printed in gelatin silver, this image was made in the 1930s or '40s. During the presidency of General Lázaro Cárdenas, with the impetus of nationalism in México, a Mexican 10-peso bill began to circulate featuring an image of a Tehuana woman similar to that in this photograph.

In the second photograph, two women stand looking at the camera. Both are touching their hip with their hand, showing a hint of confidence, empowerment, and pride. The younger woman has placed her left hand on the shoulder of the other woman, who lightly touches her huipil; their haughty gazes pierce the camera. Gestures and poses of a distinct narrative. The woman on the left has her hair braided with ribbons, topped with a bow at the end, which she has placed in front of her body, near her bust. Does it mean that her marital status is single?

Could she be her mother, the one with a headdress made of ribbons in the shape of a bow on top of her head? Does it mean she is married? In Indigenous communities, headdresses fulfill social, cultural, aesthetic, and symbolic functions, hence the importance of using them.

Both are in semiformal Istmeño attire; their huipiles are stitched with geometric figures in the technique called cadenilla. Their skirts have a white flounce, lace, brocade, or braid at the bottom. Between the frills of their skirts, the toes of their bare feet peek out. Although there is nothing to confirm it,

I would like to think they are a mother and daughter. It is a genealogical image. A family image. They wear gold jewelry that, according to the custom of the region, is inherited by daughters from mothers. Cinnamon skin, almond-shaped eyes, a rigid posture, and the sound of a click. A lens that records the essence of a geography. Two women in silence who speak with their eyes and stand in time as political territories.

In the third image, we see a mother carrying her daughter. Could she be her firstborn? Like the other women, she wears typical Zapotec clothing, but her portrait is different. Sitting with the baby in her arms, she looks attentively at the camera. Her braids hang down her back. Her hand subtly touches her skirt, which is embellished with flowers. She wears shoes. Her perplexed face announces an emotional moment. A bond that intertwines through an image—the baby is unaware that the photographer is present as her mother wraps her with her left hand. The baby's soft dress contrasts with the flowers that surround her mother's body.

All the images use a similar background, an allegory of the family environment: a house sheltered by the foliage of trees; fictitious windows and stairs. A metaphor for domestic life.

Although these images were created in a past time, they are timeless. These portraits represent a historical continuity of Zapotec cultural and ethnic idiosyncrasy. The women of the Isthmus of Tehuantepec continue to wear their traditional clothes today, using their headdresses, petticoats, and huipiles embroidered with colorful flowers in chain stitch on velvet, satin, or cotton.

Constantino Jiménez narrates not only the history of Zapotec women but also their ancestral legacy and knowledge. His photographs account for affective bonds and Indigenous femininity, both alternative and communal. In a time when photographs were a social act, and only a small group of the Mexican population could afford to have portraits made, Constantino Jiménez envisioned the importance of representing his community, and above all, of documenting the important role that Zapotec women play in the community structure. What Sotero left in the history of Indigenous photography in México are symbols and emblems of the Isthmus peoples. He petrified moments, gazes, and essences.

—Cinthya Santos Briones

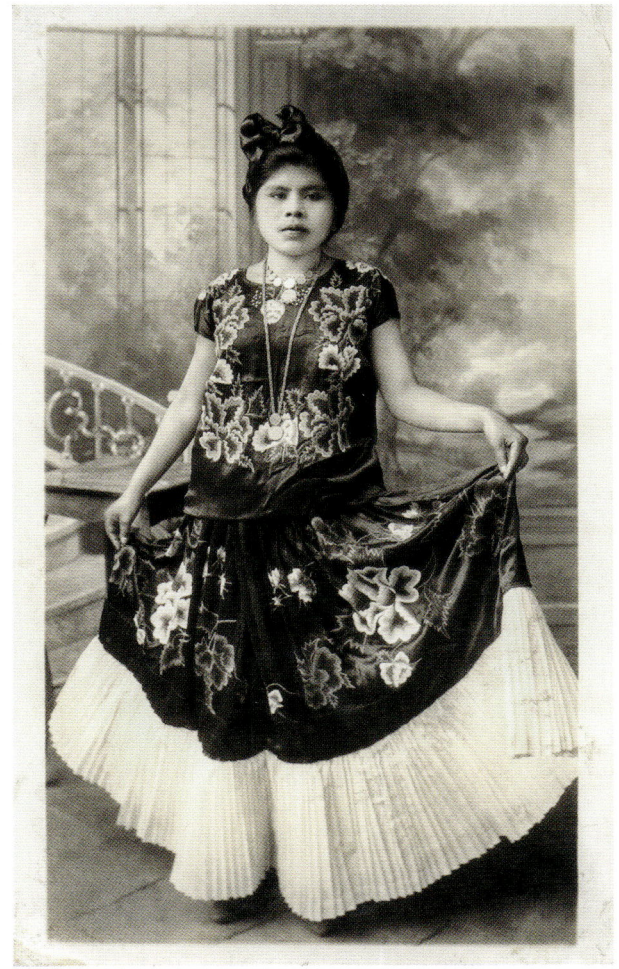

Portraits, Isthmus of Tehuantepec, Oaxaca, México, c. 1920–50.
PHOTOGRAPHS BY SOTERO CONSTANTINO JIMÉNEZ. TOLEDO COLLECTION, MANUEL ÁLVAREZ BRAVO PHOTOGRAPHIC CENTER. REGISTRATION NO. 707, NO. 705, NO. 734

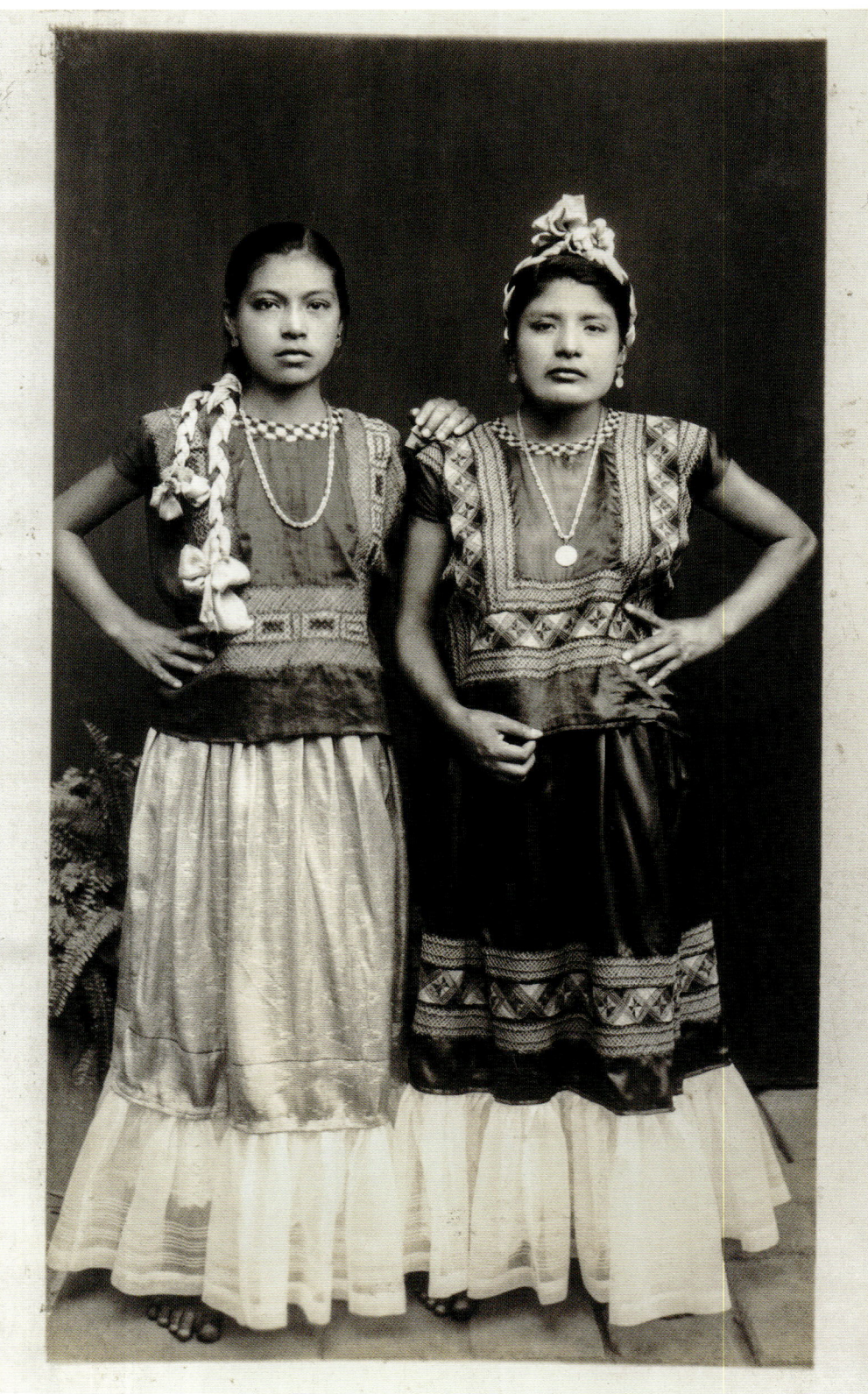

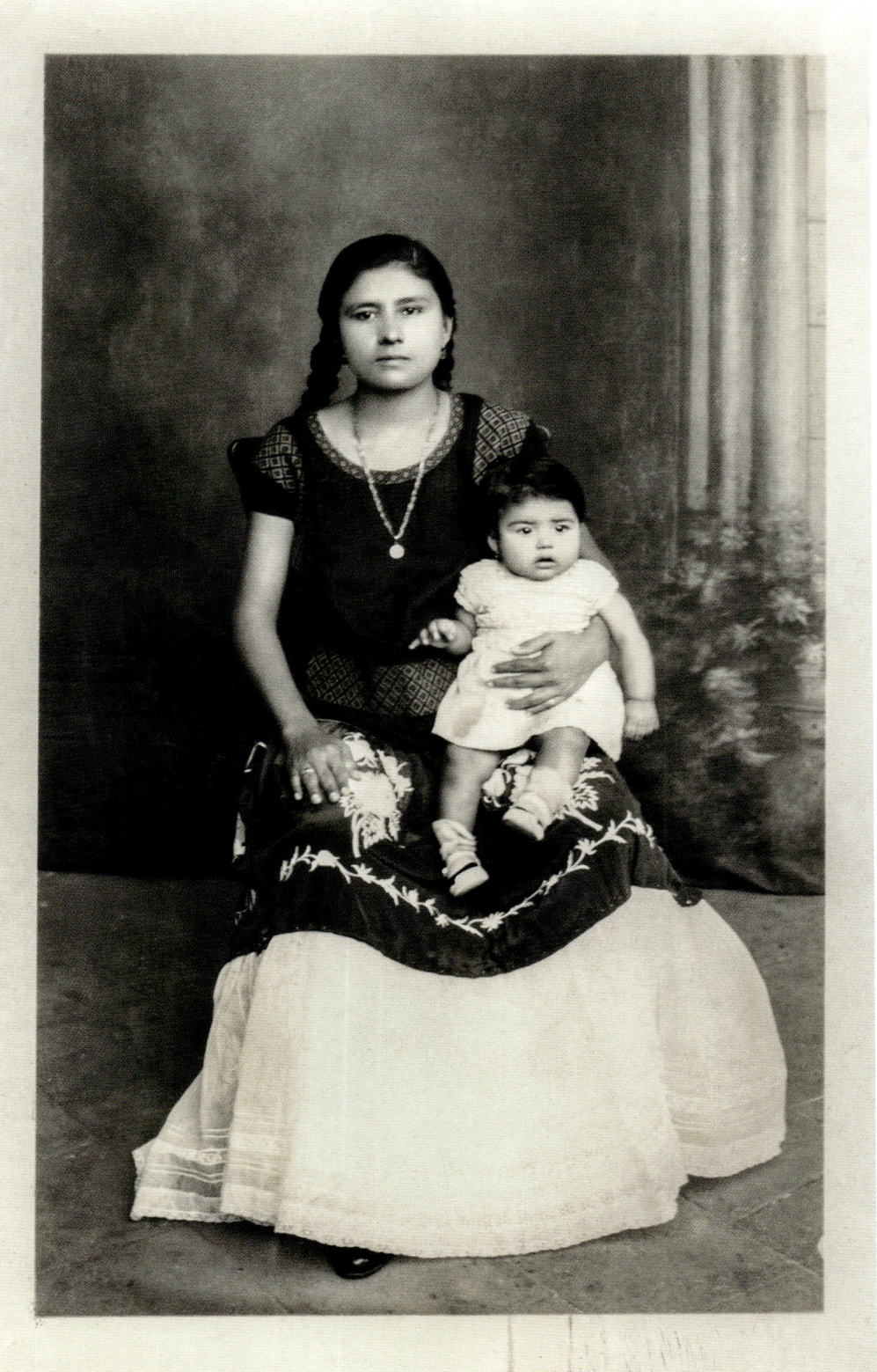

KAASH KLAÕ / GEORGE JOHNSTON
FREDDIE JOHNSTON

Inland Tlingit
Teslin, Yukon
Canada

"These pictures tell the story of the Inland Tlingit people," said Tlingit filmmaker Carol Geddes about the archive George Johnston (c. 1884–1972) left behind. "Where they were and where they are going, and of a man of my village who chose a camera to tell stories; stories needed by those yet to be born."[1]

When George was a young man, he bought a Kodak camera from an Eaton's mail-order catalog. It was delivered to his home in Teslin, a hunting, trapping, and fishing village in the Yukon, and George embraced the medium, creating a familial portrait of his community over four decades. "He always had a camera with him, no matter where he went," recalled his nephew Sam Johnston.

George's photographs, developed in a darkroom he built inside his cabin, illustrate the "golden times" of the Teslin Tlingit before the missionaries moved in and the Alaska Highway was built. Nearly everyone in the village was engaged with trapping, and profits were generous. Many images show the bountiful results of George's community's—and his own—talent for living off the land. Lynx, coyote, fox, mink, and wolverine furs hang from cabins, beaver pelts stretch across hoop frames, and hunters stand alongside moose and bear. Teslin Lake, which reaches into British Columbia, appears frequently. The Johnston family had a fishing camp, "Johnston Town," on its southern shore.

Other pictures document Teslin's treasured youth, gatherings on Dominion Day (later renamed Canada Day), and friends and family in the village and surrounding terrain. At a church picnic, George photographed the local girls baseball team. A player posing with the bat and a dangling cigarette looks especially dashing. In another frame, George stands among them, his kind spirit matching the young women's smiles.

In 1928, George bought a car—a black Model AB Chevrolet. The first car in Teslin, it was delivered by boat, and he was famous for it. Friends helped cut the maiden road in the village, and George offered taxi rides for two dollars per person. He painted the car white in winter (less intimidating to game) and used it to hunt on the frozen lake.

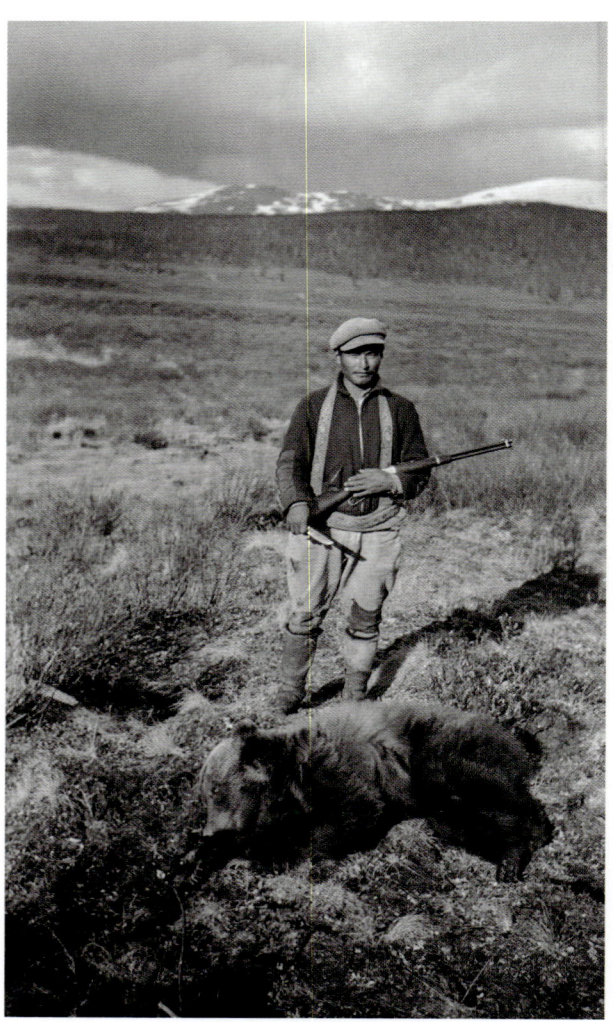

George Sidney and a bear, Yukon or British Columbia, c. 1930–42.

Opposite: Girls baseball team at a church picnic at the mouth of the Nisutlin River, Yukon, c. 1941.

Opposite: Dolly Johnston, George's daughter, with lynx, coyote, and wolverine furs, Teslin, Yukon, c. 1938.

PHOTOGRAPHS BY GEORGE JOHNSTON. YUKON ARCHIVES, GEORGE JOHNSTON FONDS. 82/428 #43, 82/428 #33, 82/428 #39, 82/428 #86, 82/428 #69, 82/428 #46, 82/428 #49

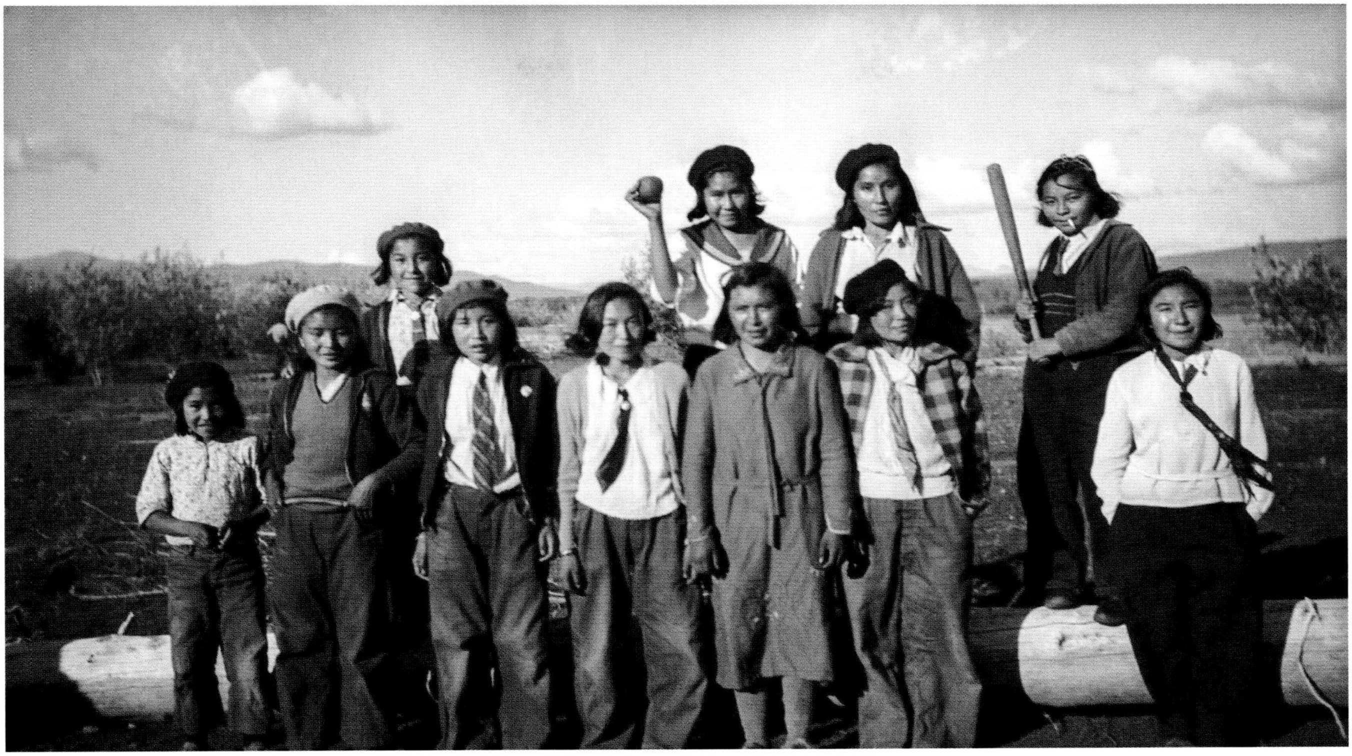

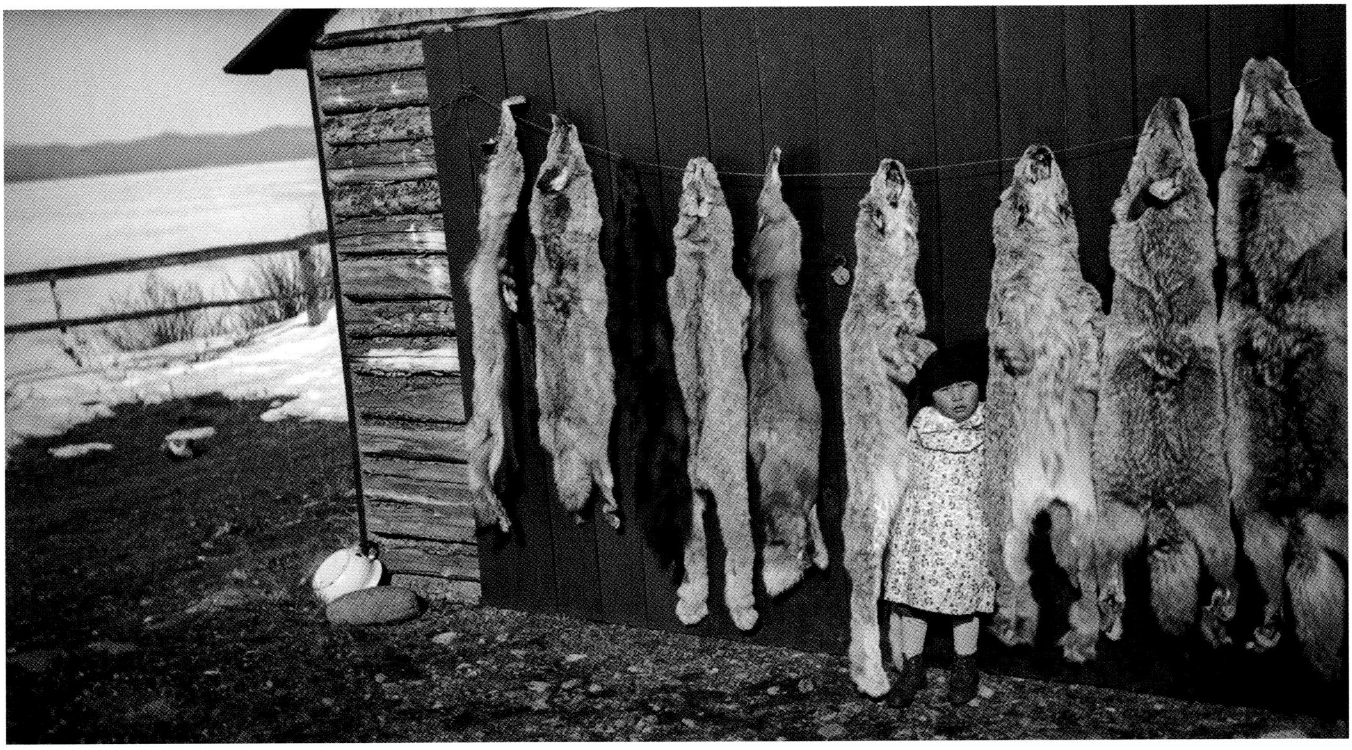

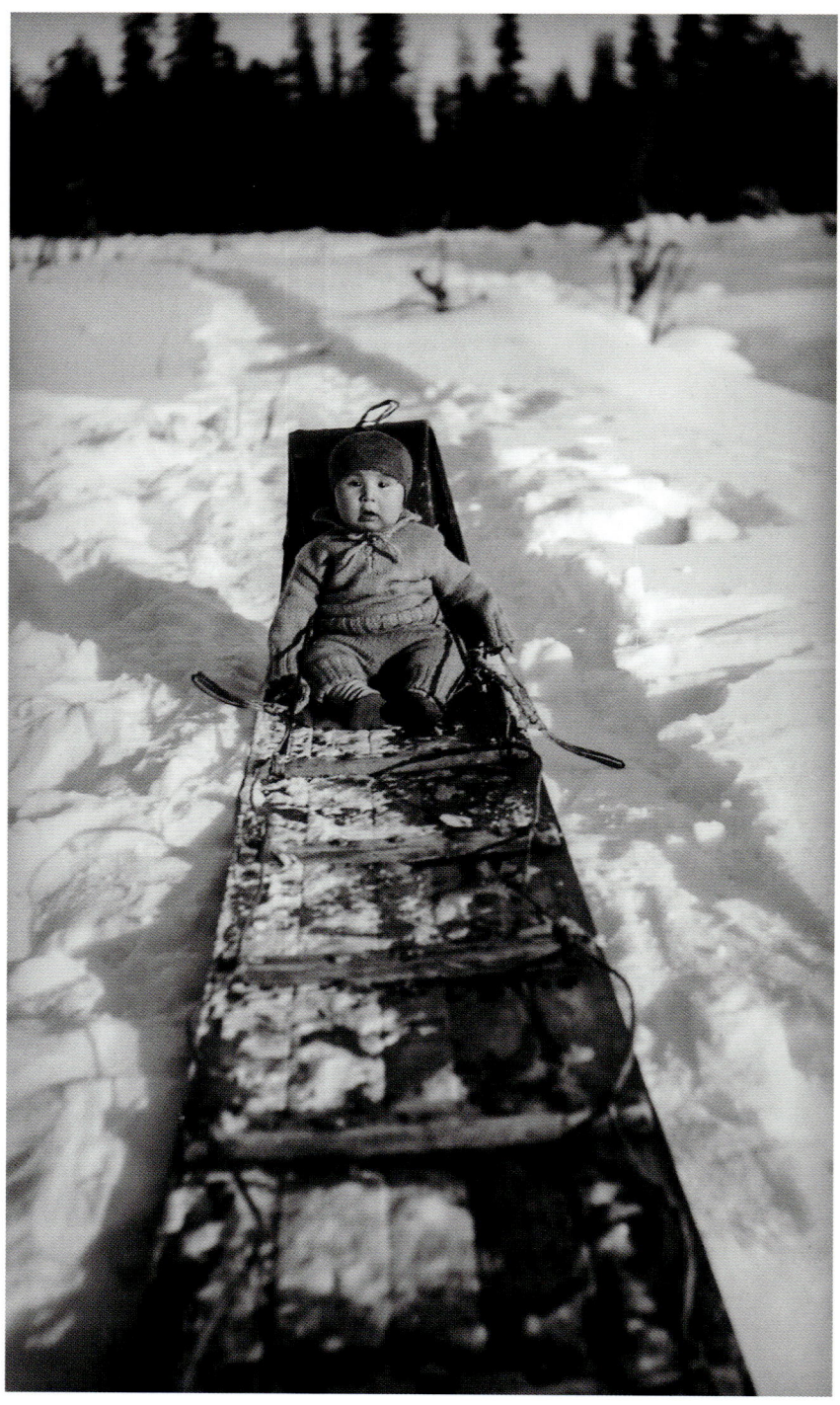

Matthew Thom on a Teslin-built birch toboggan, Yukon or British Columbia, c. 1940.

Opposite: Five children playing funeral, likely Teslin, Yukon, c. 1943.

Opposite: David Johnston and Maude the horse traveling to Johnston Town, British Columbia, on Teslin Lake, c. 1950. George Johnston felled the two moose, who thought Maude was a moose and charged, with just two shots.

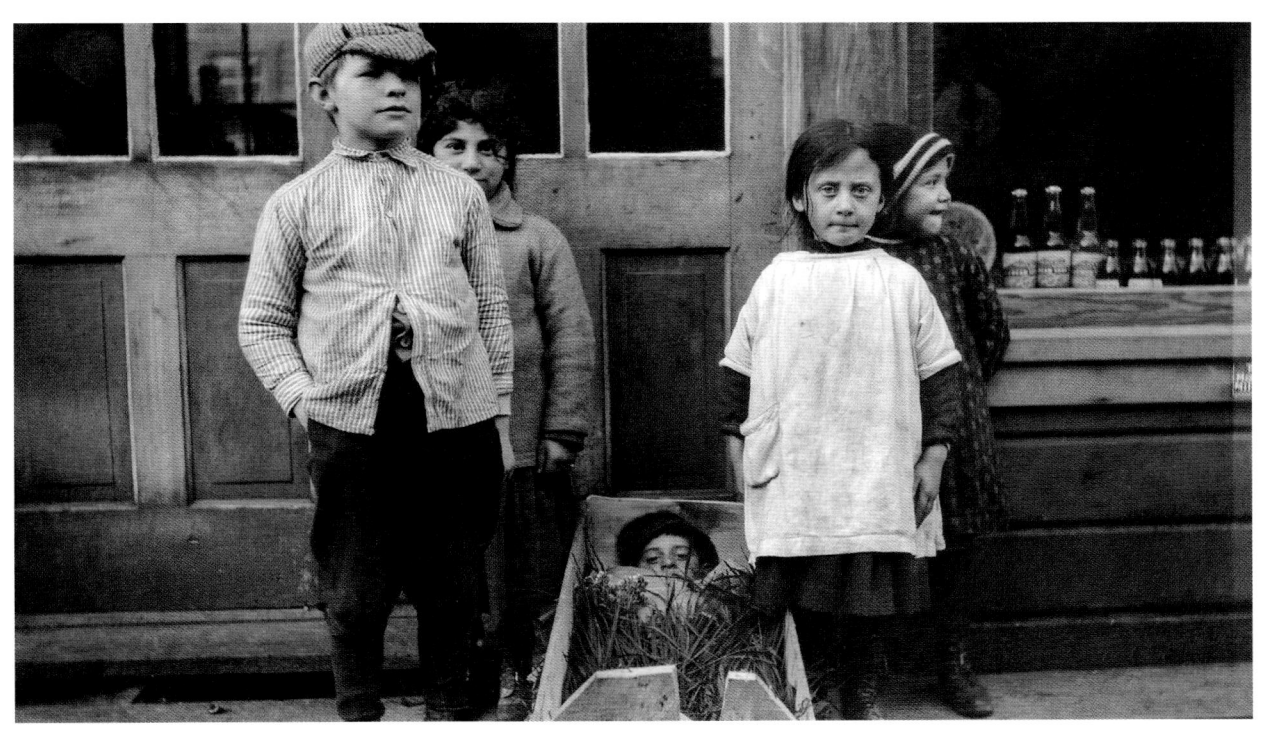

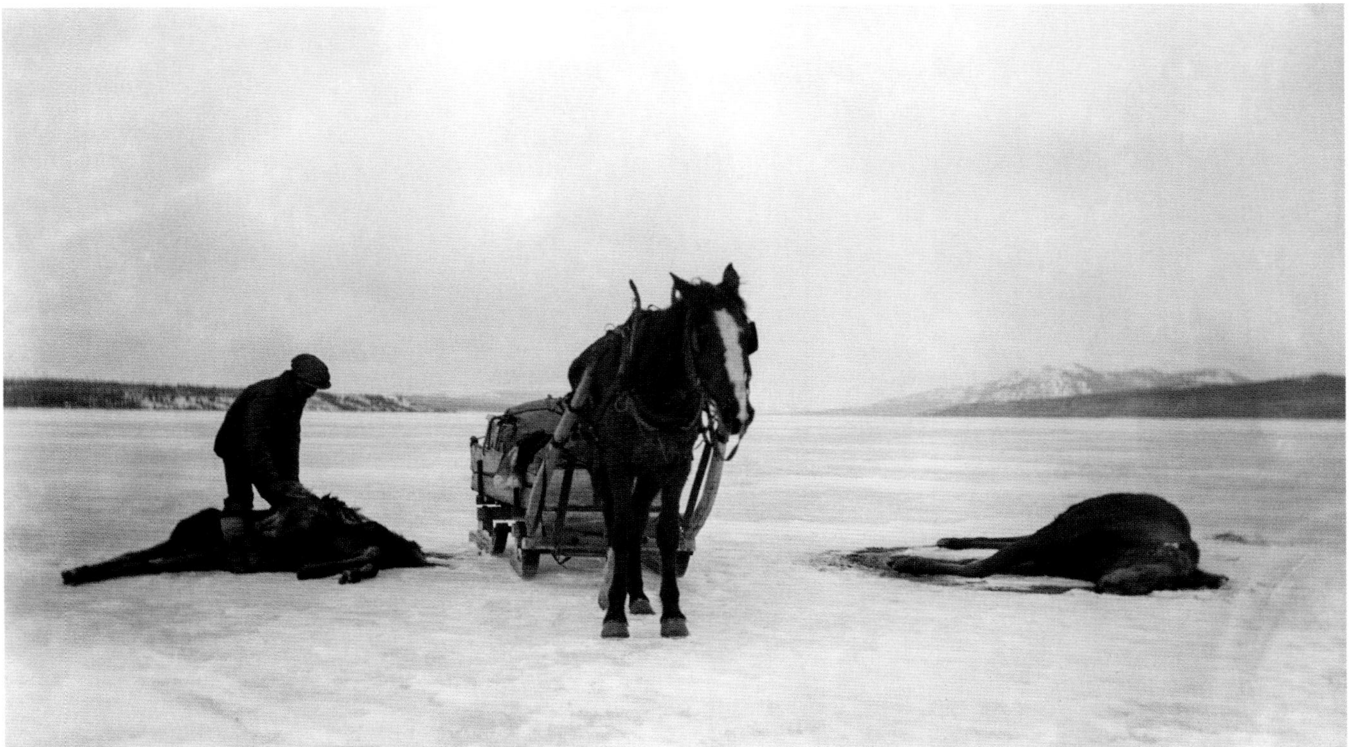

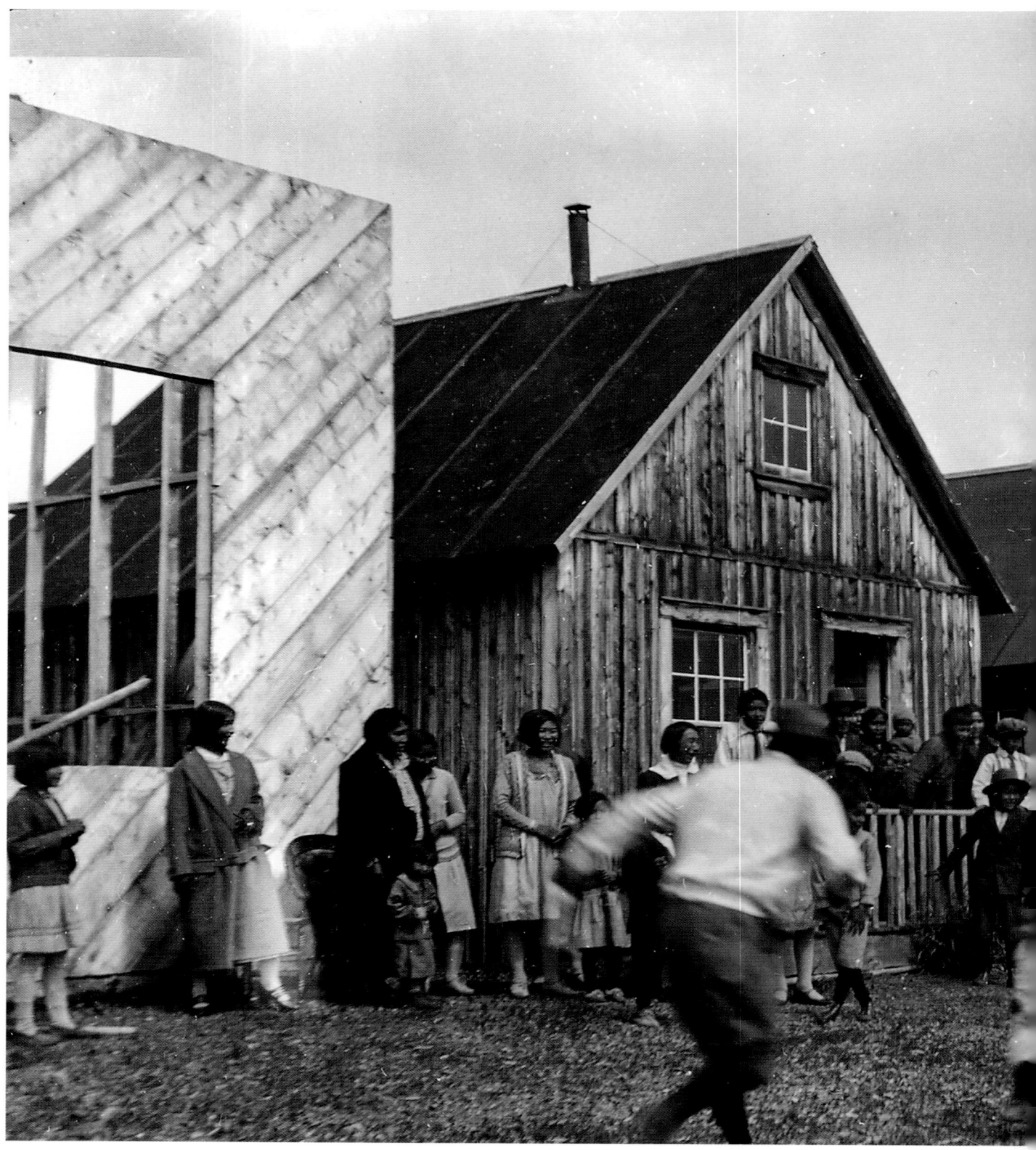

Dominion Day (July 1), Teslin, Yukon, c. 1940.

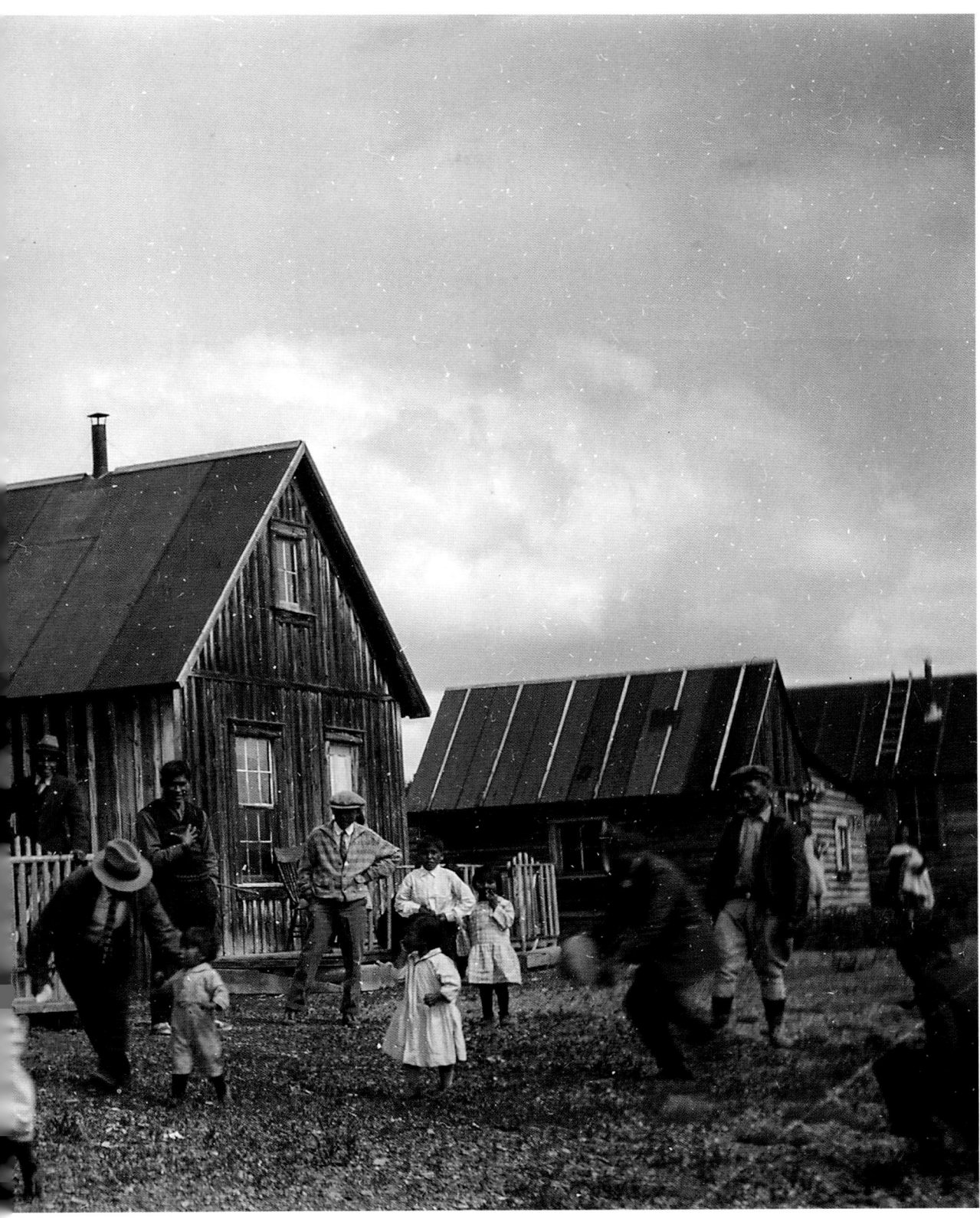

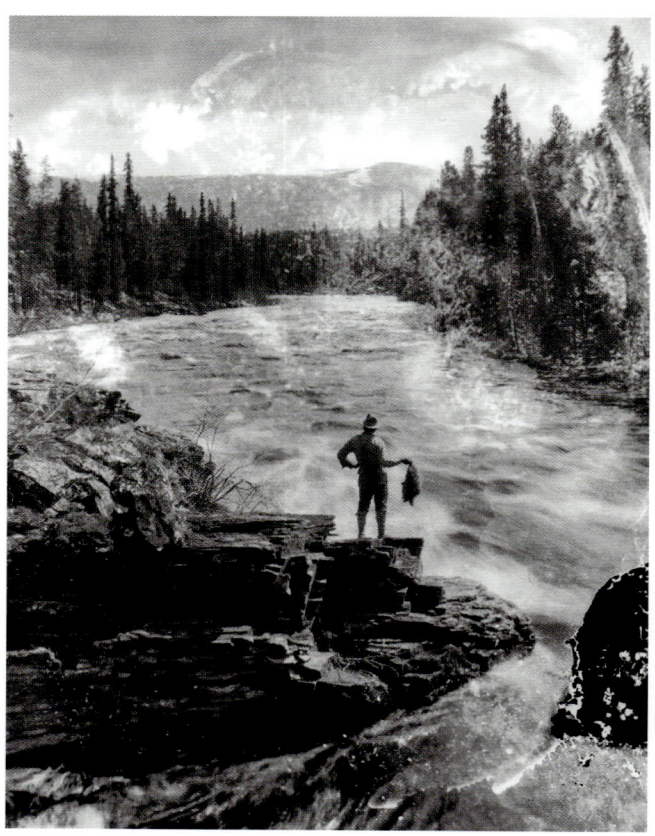 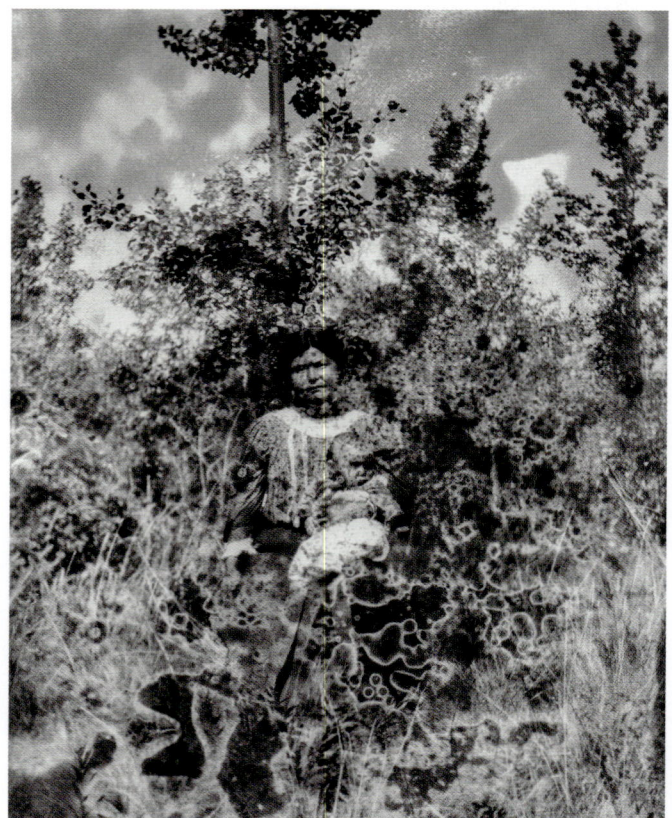

Man standing by a river, Yukon or British Columbia, c. 1920–30.

Mrs. Jenny Johnston holding a baby, Teslin, Yukon, c. 1920–30.

Opposite: Freddie Johnston wearing his camera case, standing with his family in front of their cabin in Johnston Town, British Columbia, c. 1920–30. It is possible George Johnston made this photograph with Freddie's camera.

PHOTOGRAPHS BY FREDDIE JOHNSTON. YUKON ARCHIVES, FREDDIE JOHNSTON FONDS. 79/119 #135, 79/119 #37, 79/119 #32, 79/119 #106, 79/119 #2, 79/119 #126

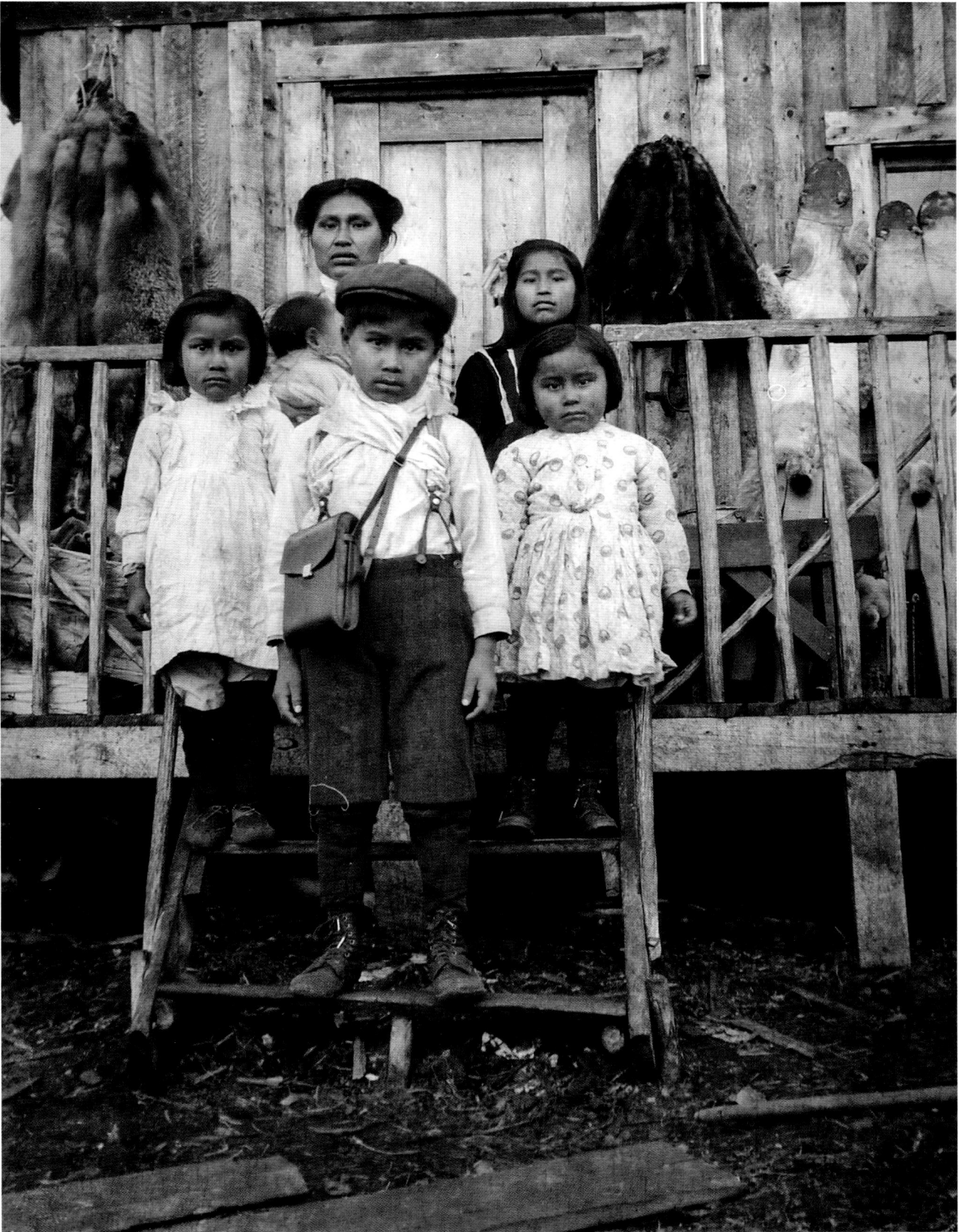

George's nephew Freddie Johnston (c. 1900–?) was a fellow photographer. One hundred forty-eight of his negatives were found in his Johnston Town cabin and passed on to the Yukon Archives in 1979. Multiple pictures feature seasonal scenes from Johnston Town. There are images of gardens, piles of potatoes and turnips, sled dogs, and camping trips. Similar to his uncle's archive, the Johnstons' large extended family and subsistence activities predominate. Spirituality is visualized in an atmospheric picture of a memorial Potlatch. Gifts of new clothing for family of the deceased hang from fences that will soon be relocated to the cemetery, where they will surround the gravesites. A young Freddie appears alongside his parents, Shorty and Annie, and siblings in a handful of photographs. One frame shows him, about 10, standing precociously in front of his cabin in Johnston Town. His camera case, made for a Kodak folding camera, hangs at his side.

In 1938, missionaries settled in Teslin. "There began a struggle for Tlingit souls that was to shake the very roots of kinship and family," said Geddes. Not long after, World War II commenced, giving rise to the Alaska Highway. The Teslin Tlingit learned of the construction when thousands of U.S. soldiers suddenly appeared in 1942, armed with bulldozers, trucks, and diseases new to Teslin Tlingit bodies. By autumn, reported Geddes, 128 out of 135 people in the village were sick with measles. A grim photograph George made of children "playing funeral" attests to how devastatingly common illness and death became. The three-mile road George built for his prized car became a part of the new highway. Motorists arrived and alcohol consumption increased. In this period of great change, "despair took over a once vital community."

George stopped making photographs. He continued trapping and opened a popular general store. In the 1970s, the Teslin Tlingit embarked on a long, successful campaign for self-government. The idea for a museum emerged and George, who collected Tlingit art and artifacts, donated them to the burgeoning institution. The George Johnston Museum opened in 1975, three years after George died in the winter of 1972.

"Although he did not live to see his people regain their self-government, his photos provided to the young a much needed beacon of light for their path ahead," voiced Geddes. "Your legacy, Kaash Klaō, was to help us dream the future as much as to remember the past."

—Sarah Stacke

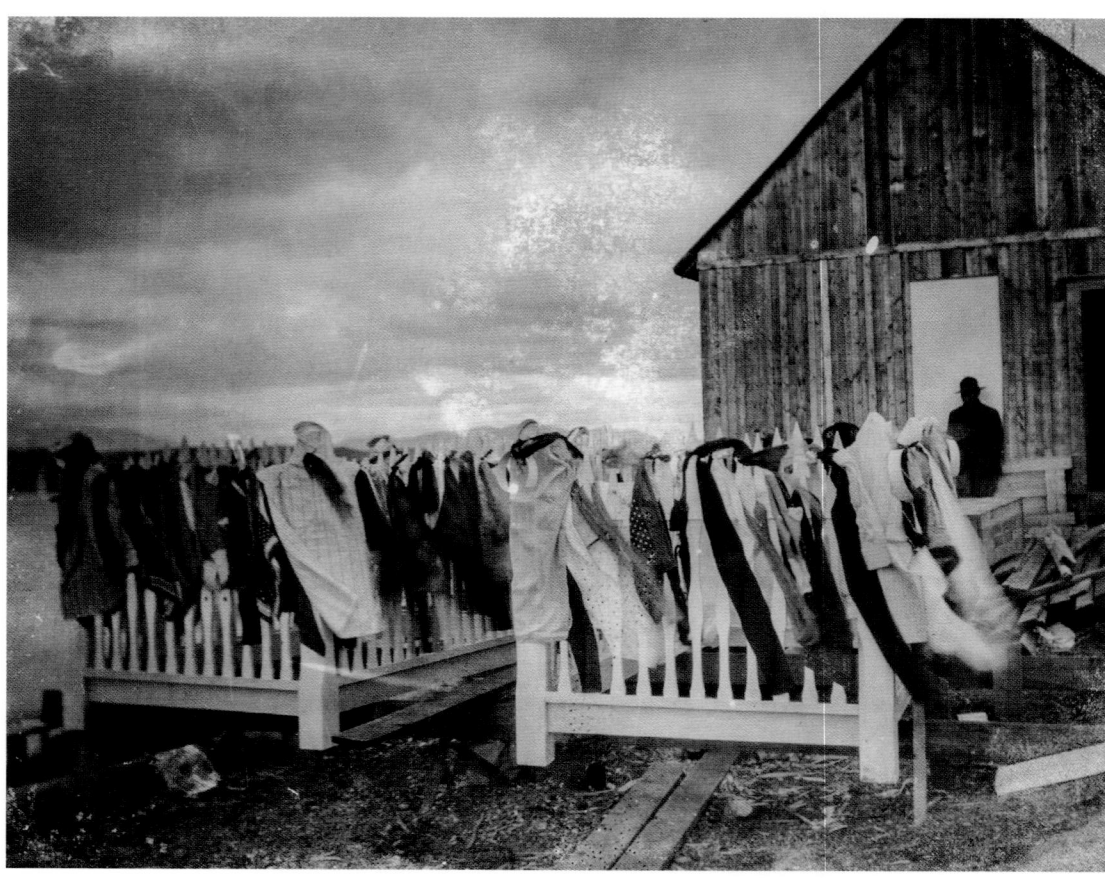

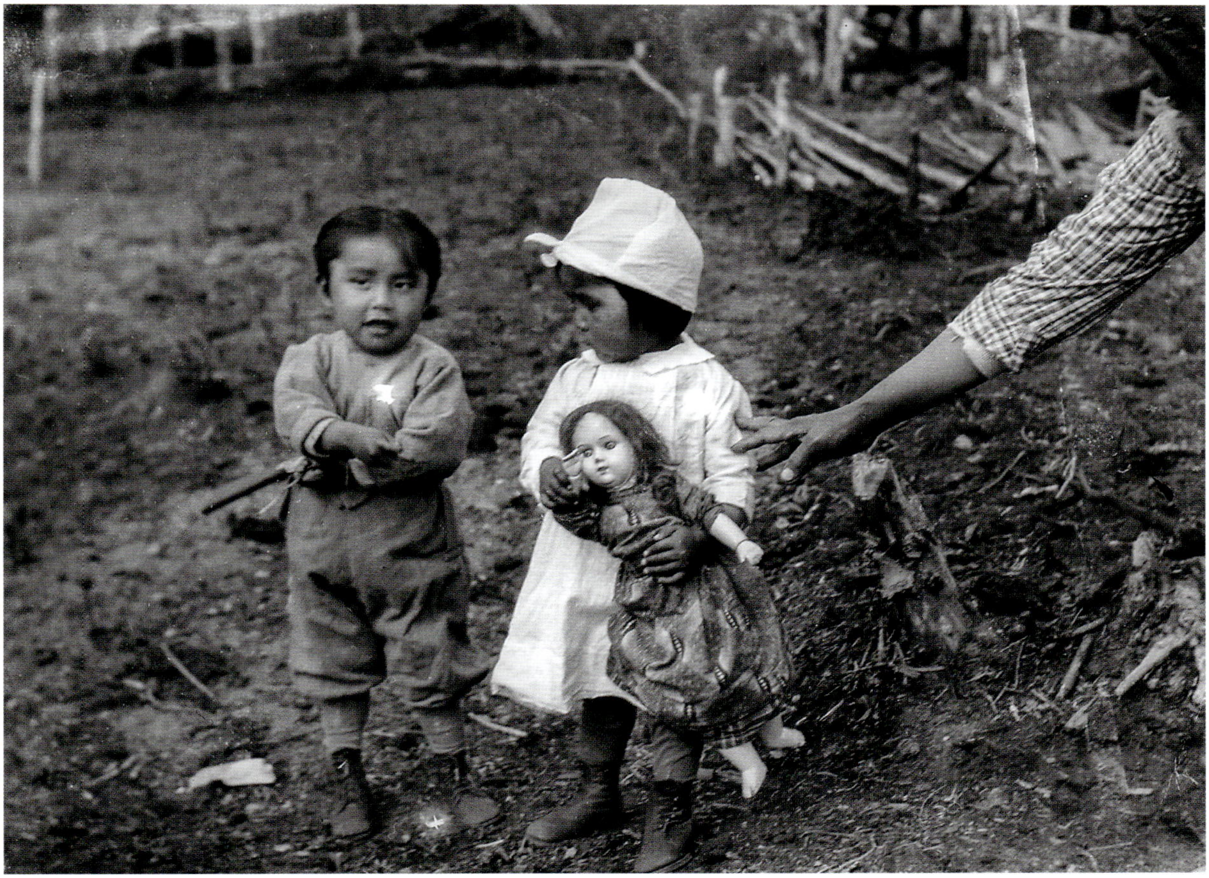

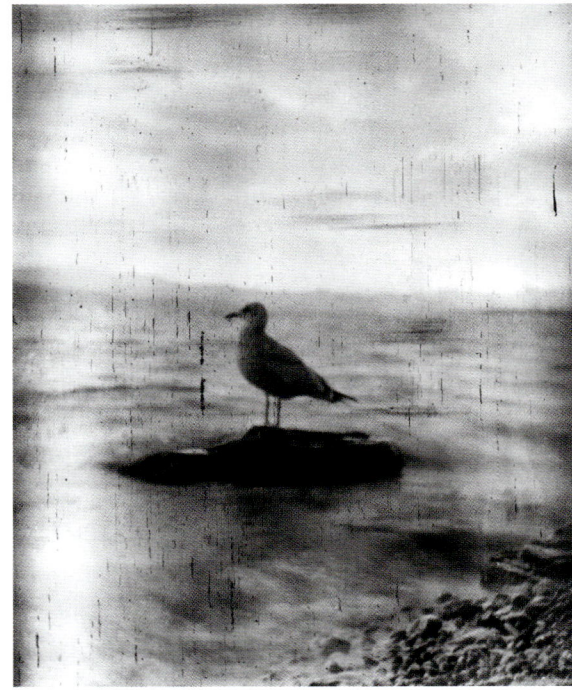

First Jimmy Johnston, Ida Bob, and Nina Johnston,
Johnston Town, British Columbia, c. 1920–30.

Bird standing on a rock, Yukon or British Columbia,
c. 1920–30.

Opposite: Old dance hall and Crow Potlatch next to Charlie
Bob's house, Teslin, Yukon, c. 1920–30.

PETER PITSEOLAK
AGGEOK PITSEOLAK
Inuk
Kinngait, Baffin Island, Nunavut
Canada

In the hyperborean landscape of Peter Pitseolak's (1902–1973) photographs, hunters pull seals from the ice and children nestle in their mother's amautis, the animal skin parkas used to carry and keep them warm. Between 1939 and 1973, Peter made some 2,000 images on the southwest coast of Baffin Island in Nunavut, the vast and largely Inuit territory of Canada. The negatives were expertly developed and printed in collaboration with his wife, the artist Aggeok Pitseolak (1906–1977). Freezing and bursting with reflective snow, the climate of the Arctic challenged the photographers. Peter fashioned a lens filter from sunglasses, and he and Aggeok crafted temperature-controlled darkrooms inside iglus and tents; a flashlight covered in red cloth was used as the safelight.

Tremendous cultural shifts occurred in the Pitseolaks' lifetime. In 1911 the first Hudson's Bay Company trading post on Baffin Island was established in Kimmirut, and in 1913 another opened in Kinngait. Contact with the traders increased and elements of traditional Inuit life receded. Tuberculosis came, eventually striking Peter's first wife, Annie. Before she died, the couple had seven children; just two daughters survived. Missionaries and schools arrived in Nunavut, and the Canadian government pushed its administrative reach across the territory.

When Peter was a boy, he crossed paths with Robert J. Flaherty, an American prospector, photographer, and filmmaker. The camera Flaherty carried made a lasting impression. By all accounts, from a young age Peter was sharply aware of the transformations around him and determined to infuse the old and current ways into the collective memory of future generations of Inuit. Photography, he understood, could accomplish that.

When the Inuit were selectively portrayed by outsiders as simplistic and static, instead of represented as a complex culture with a range of actualities during a time of massive change, Peter documented his reality. "Peter was in every way the consummate historian," wrote Amy Adams, the author of "Arctic and Inuit Photography."[1] Along with the negatives he shielded from Arctic elements, Peter carefully built an archive of diaries, birth and kinship records, and audio recordings of stories and songs.

The photographs Peter and Aggeok created refute outsiders' visions and show how their relatives and community lived in the camps. They hunted, fished, cared for children, looked after sled dogs, and engaged with one another and Peter's camera.

Evidence of a culture in flux is not denied. Detail-rich portraits present Inuit in caribou and sealskin clothing alongside radios, clocks, oil drums, and white workers from the trading posts. Aggeok, Peter's muse, poses in beaded amautis and floral print cotton dresses, and plays the accordion. Her hair is braided, except in a small sequence of indoor portraits where it unfurls past her waist in splendid waves; wearing a surprisingly summery white dress, she radiates lightness. Peter was fond of self-portraits, and many were made using a homemade cable release or with Aggeok's finger pressing the shutter button. He confidently appears with various cameras (he reportedly owned six in his lifetime), reading a book, demonstrating how to set a fox trap, and in snow-swept sceneries dressed in parkas or cardigans and a captain's hat.

Peter's photographs document the last days of the camp system before the Inuit of Baffin Island were separated from their nomadic lifeways and forced into settlements. The warmth of the camp community and the enormity of its loss is unmistakable in the pictures.

With the assistance of his photographs, Peter produced colorful drawings and ivory carvings. He often incorporated text into the drawings, the only Kinngait artist known to do so at the time. Recruiting family and campers as actors, he set up intricate scenes illustrating Inuit legends and fading subsistence practices, then photographed the action frame by frame. The series were intended for the historical record and to be used as templates for his graphic art, many of which he contributed to the West Baffin Eskimo Co-operative (WBEC), established in 1959. Known today as the Kinngait Co-operative, the venture has played a pivotal role in the development and international marketing of influential Inuit artists, including quite a few of the Pitseolaks' friends and kin, several of whom are seen in Peter's archive. Aggeok's prints and graphite drawings are held in collections throughout Canada.

Jimmy Manning (b. 1951), Peter and Aggeok's grandson based in Kinngait, is a documentary photographer who portrays thriving Inuit culture. In the 1970s, he was an art buyer for the WBEC before becoming the manager of its printmaking

---

Peter Pitseolak with his 2222 camera at home, Keatuk camp, Baffin Island, Nunavut, 1947.
PHOTOGRAPH BY AGGEOK PITSEOLAK.

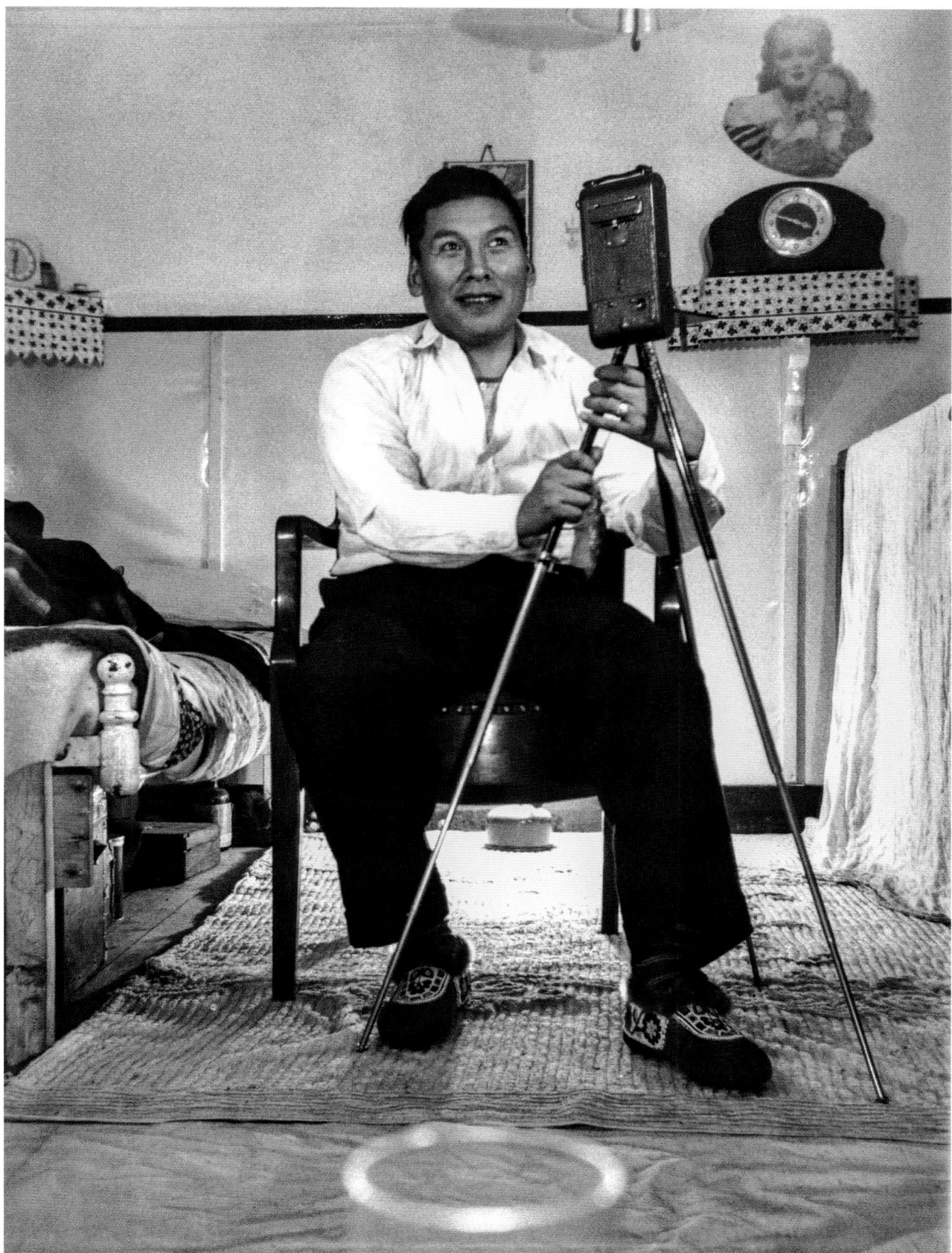

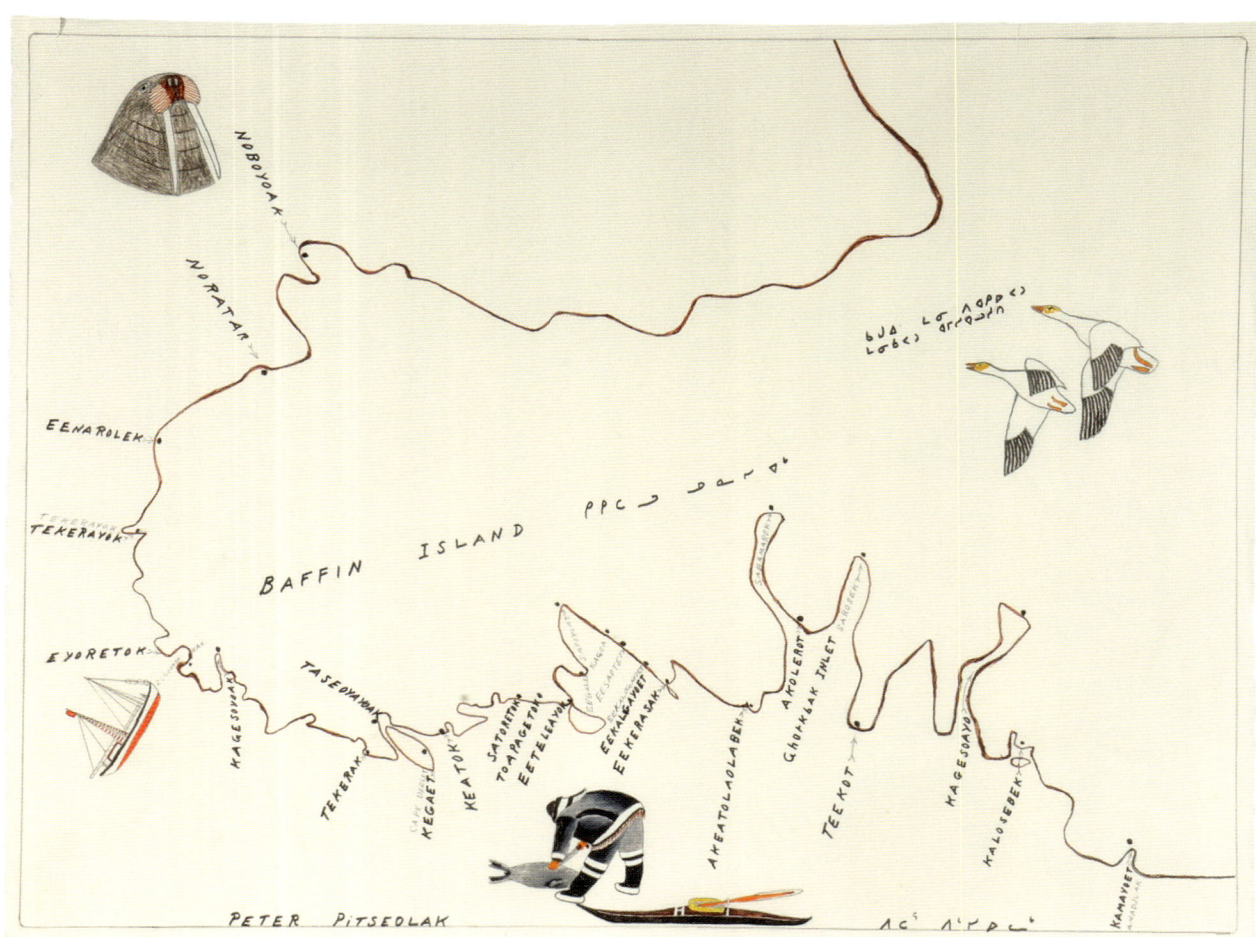

studios, where he frequently photographed the artists at work. The Pitseolaks' nephew Itee Pootoogook (1951–2014), who also lived in Kinngait and was involved with the studios, was well known for his drawings of contemporary Arctic life. Like his uncle, he used photography as the base for his drawings and as final pieces.

Dorothy Harley Eber, a writer who worked closely with Peter late in his life, said that what was "most important" to Peter was to "render true-to-life representations of the Inuit world. This was his aim both in his photography and in his graphic work."[2]

Peter's final act as an artist and historian was authoring *People from Our Side: A Life Story with Photographs and Oral Biography*. First published in 1975, four years after his death, the book contains a manuscript originally written by Peter in Inuktitut syllabics and then translated into English. Peter narrates tales of his ancestors, his itinerant youth, and the

developments that forever altered Inuit existence. There are transcriptions of interviews between him and Eber, and the volume is illustrated by his photographs.

Reflecting on all that he witnessed and experienced, Peter wrote, "I know people were happier in the old days. But I know for sure they were not happy every day…I am not tired of living or tired of people."[3]

—Sarah Stacke

Print of a map showing camps along the coast of Baffin Island, Nunavut, 1973.
DRAWING BY PETER PITSEOLAK.

Opposite: Mary Ezekiel, wife of Aggeok's son Ashevak, carrying her son Palaya in her amauti, Keatuk camp, Baffin Island, Nunavut, c. 1958.

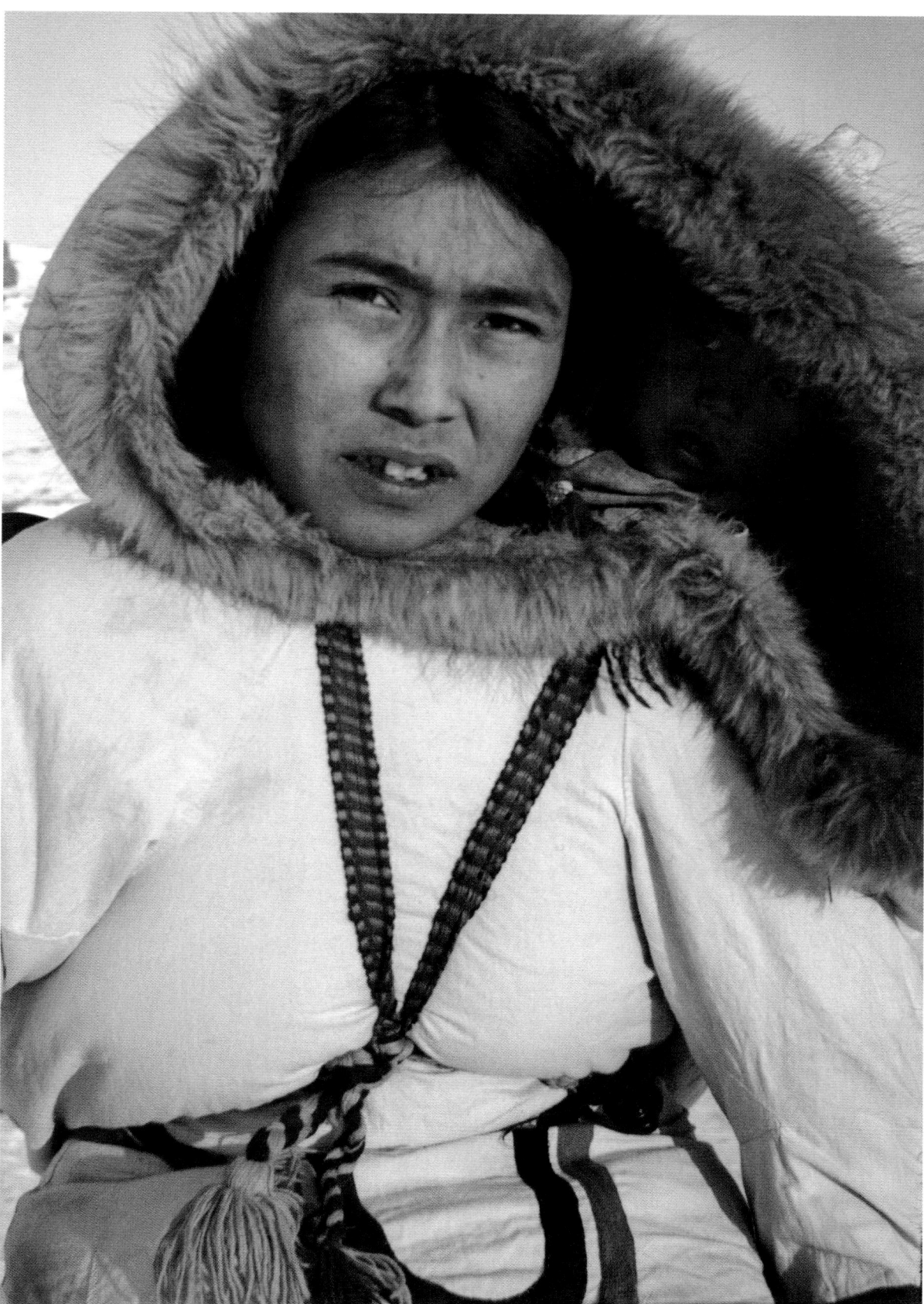

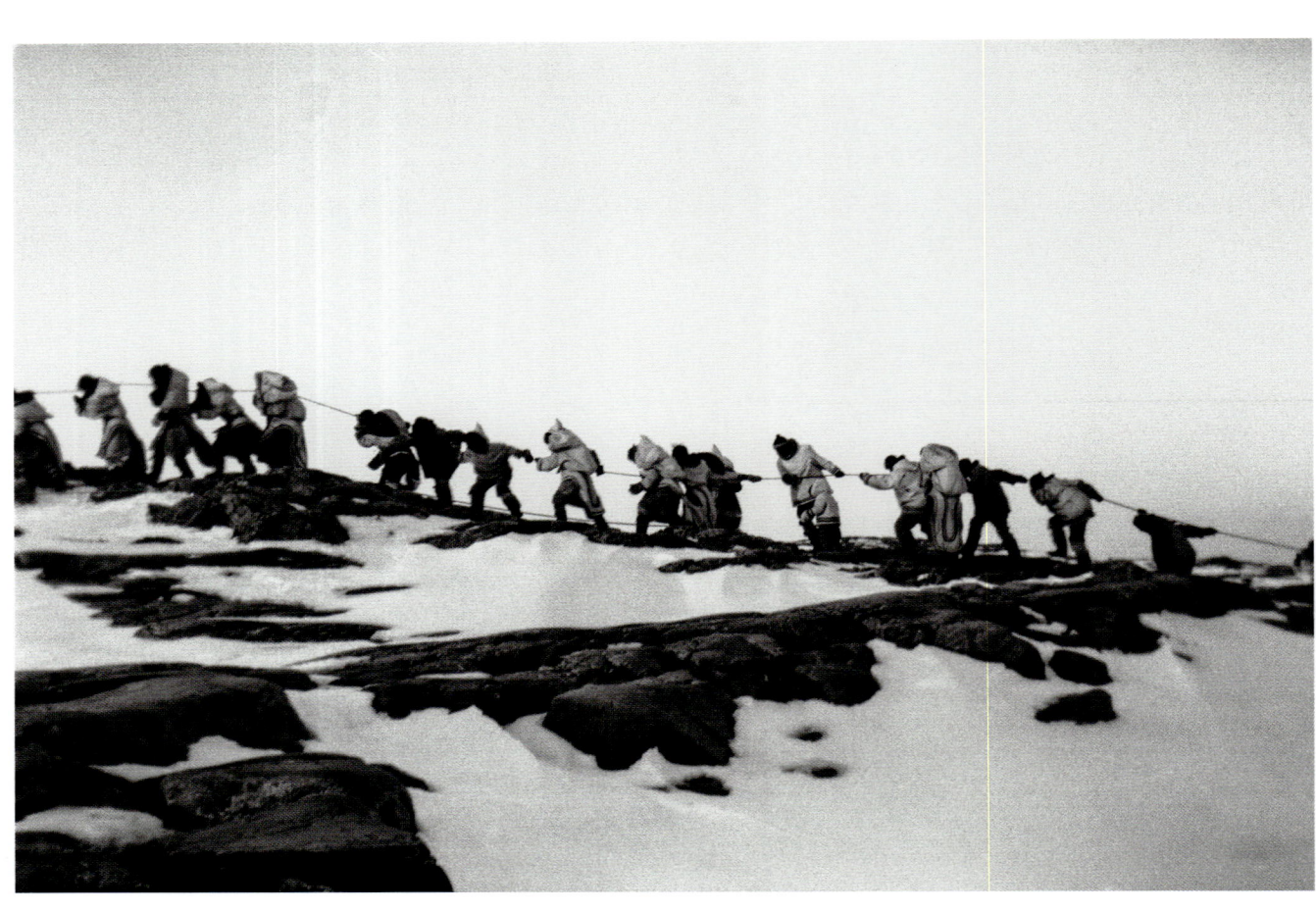

Inuit campers hauling Peter Pitseolak's Peterhead boat (used to hunt walrus) ashore at Keatuk camp, where ten families lived under Peter's leadership, Baffin Island, Nunavut, 1946.

Opposite: Hunters pulling a seal from the ice, Keatuk camp, Baffin Island, Nunavut, 1944.

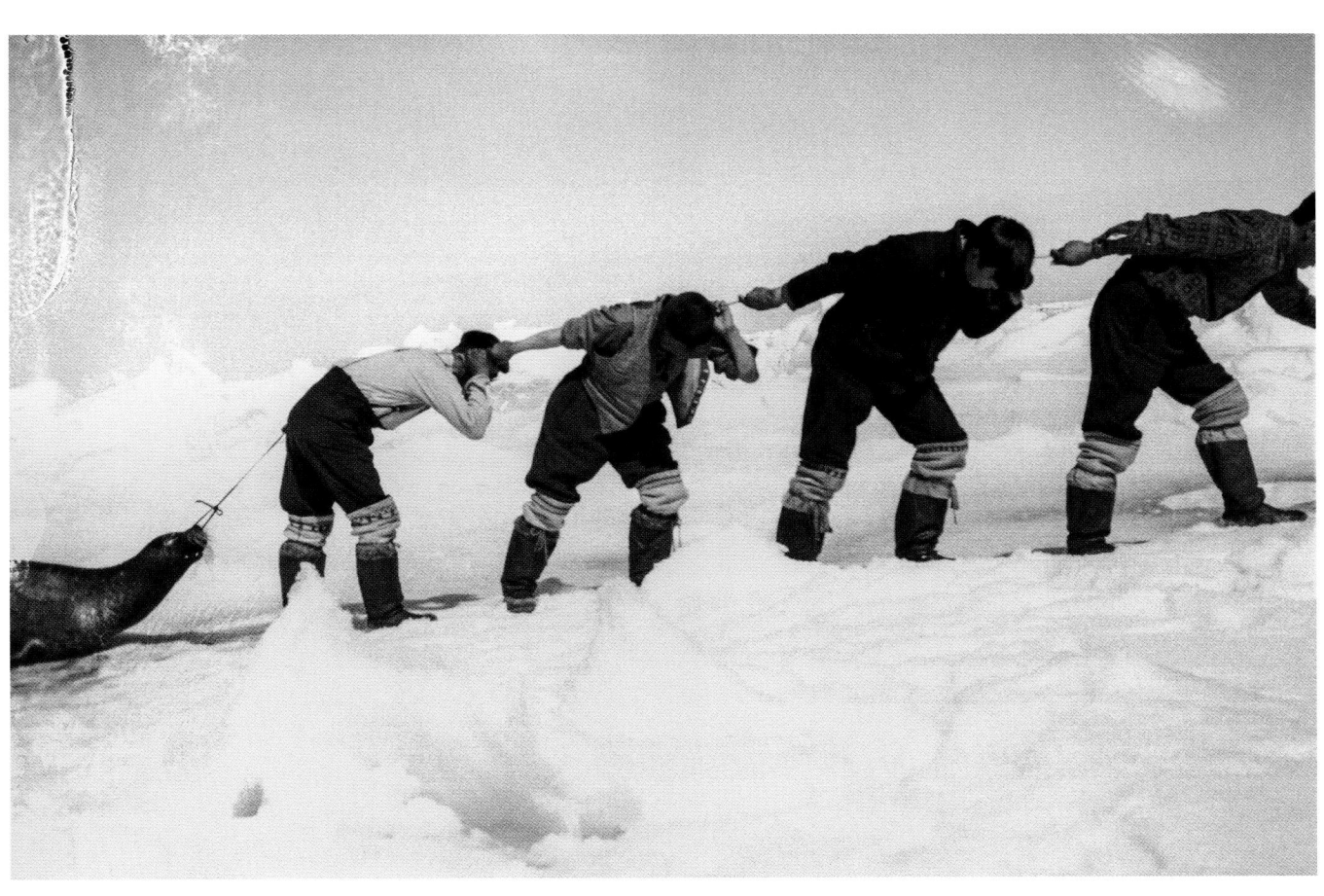

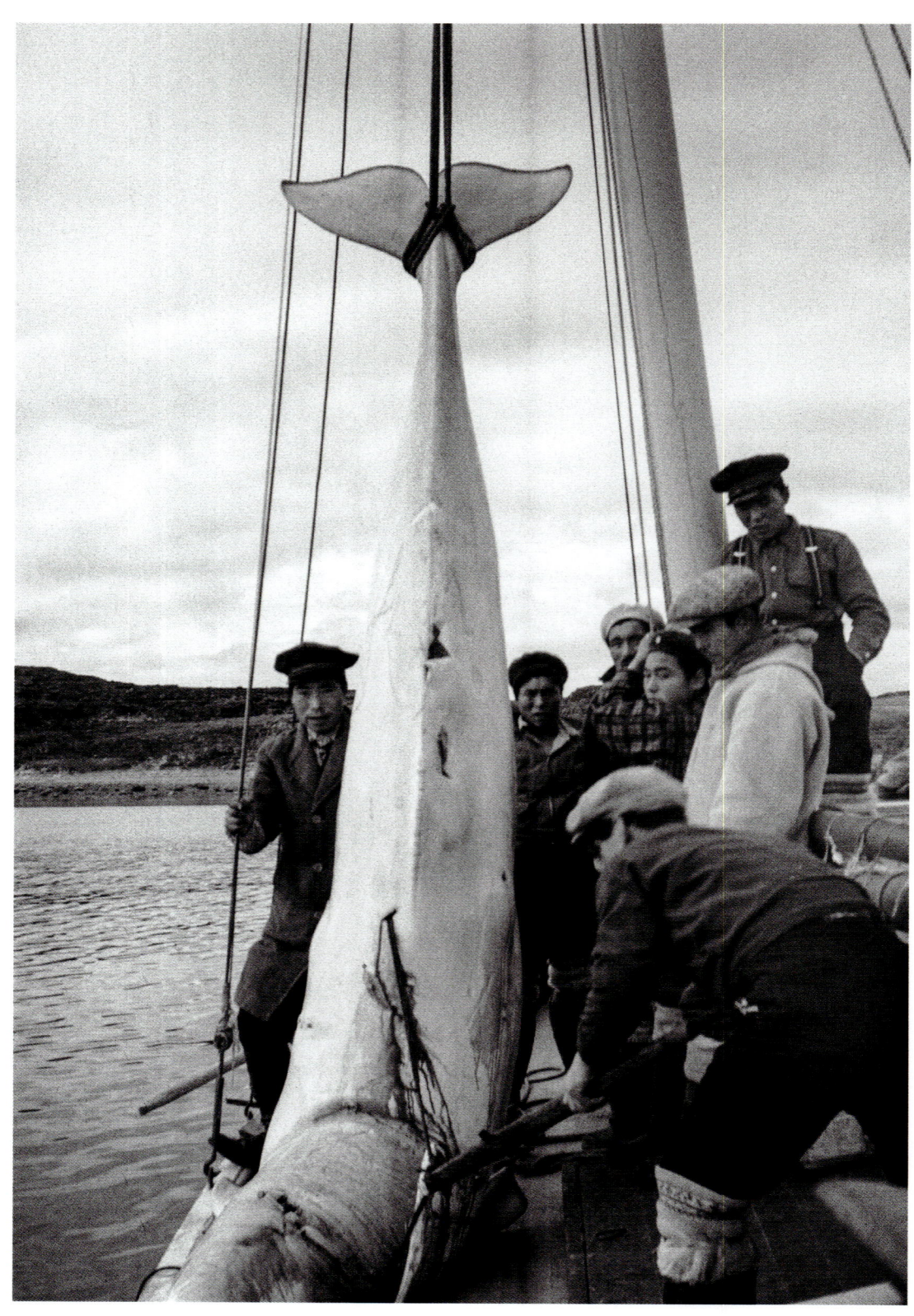

A white whale hoisted onto a boat, Baffin Island, Nunavut, c. 1940–60.

Opposite: Peter Pitseolak's daughter Kooyoo wearing an amauti,
Keatuk camp, Baffin Island, Nunavut, 1945.

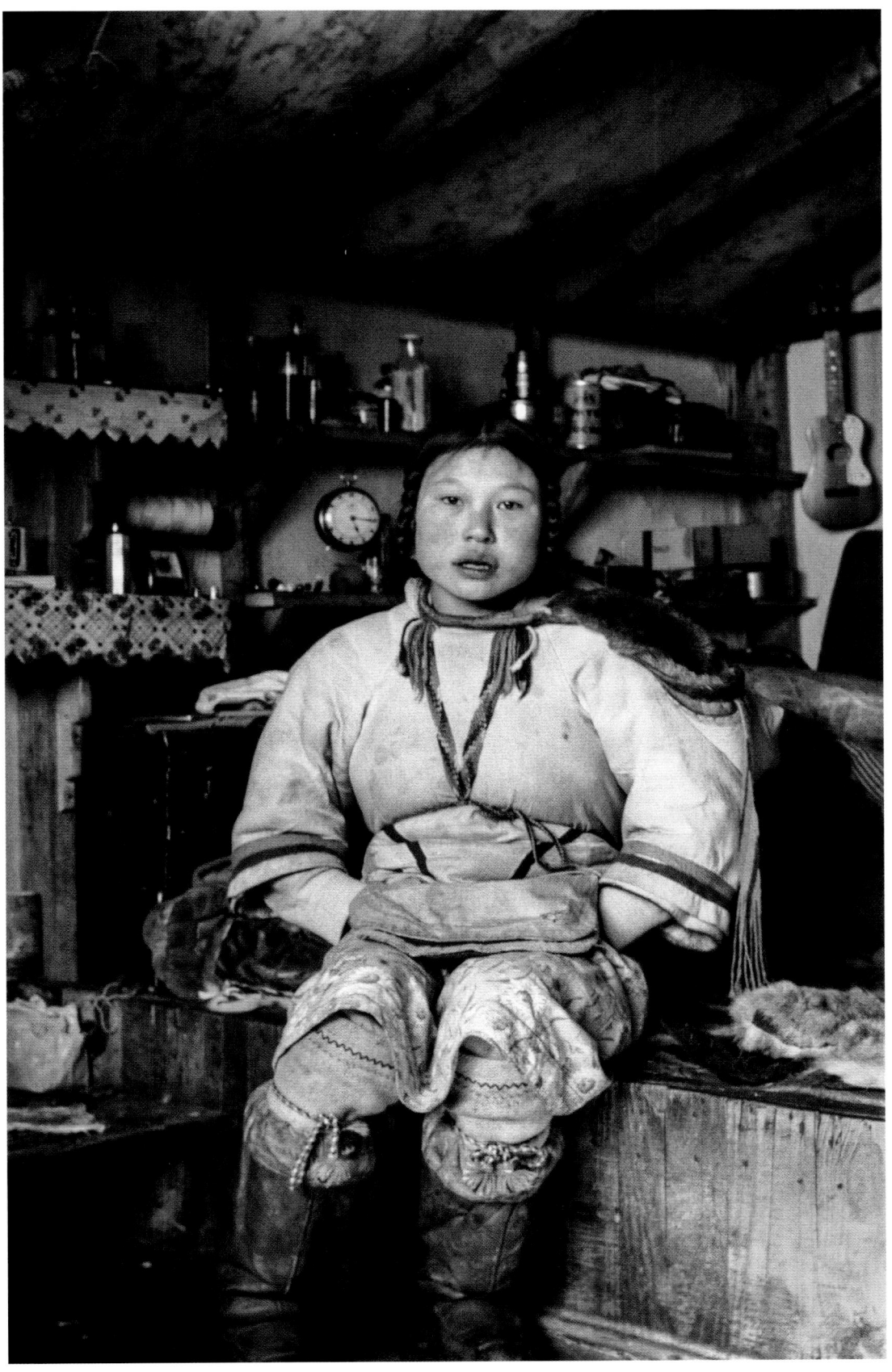

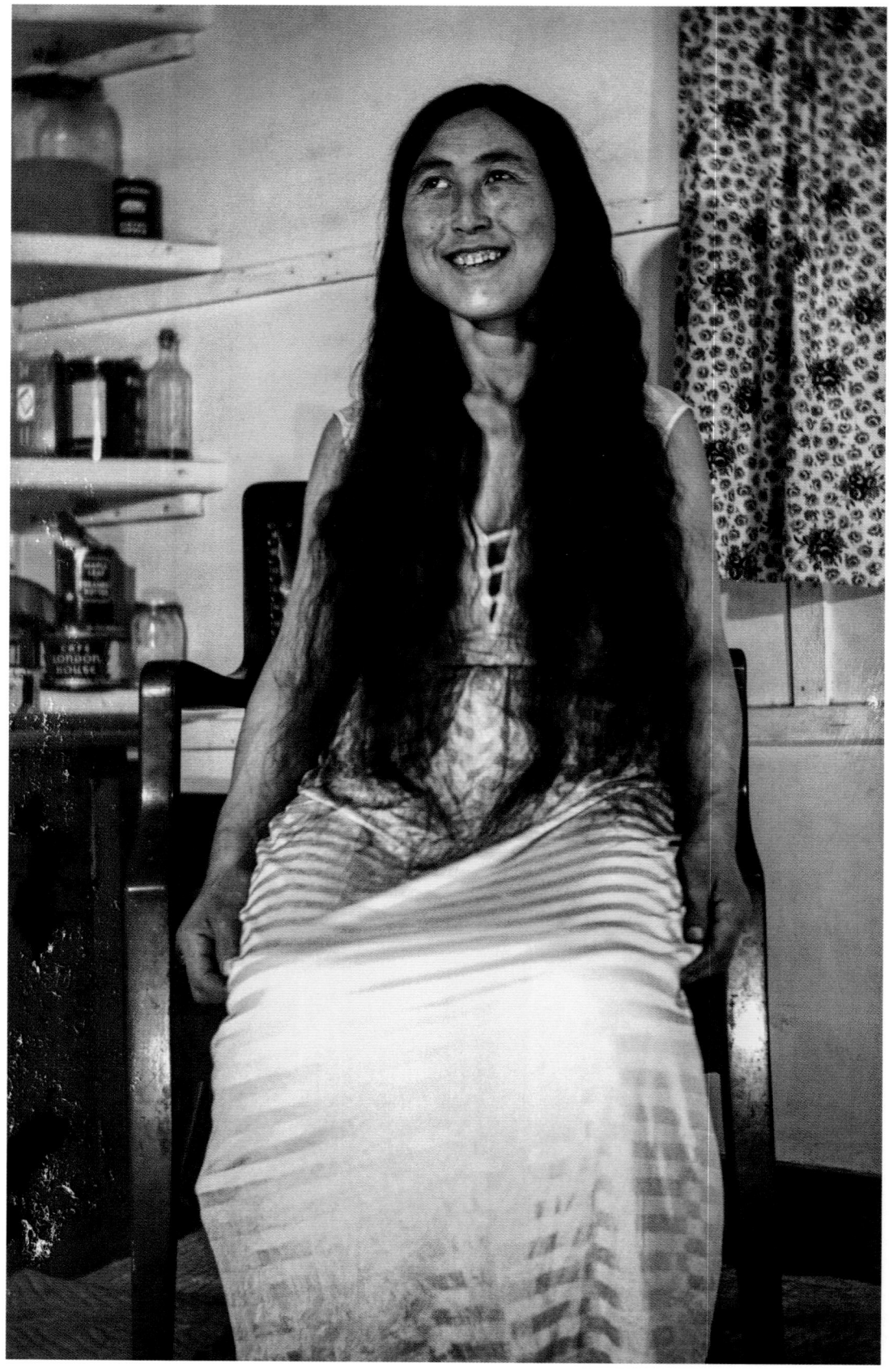

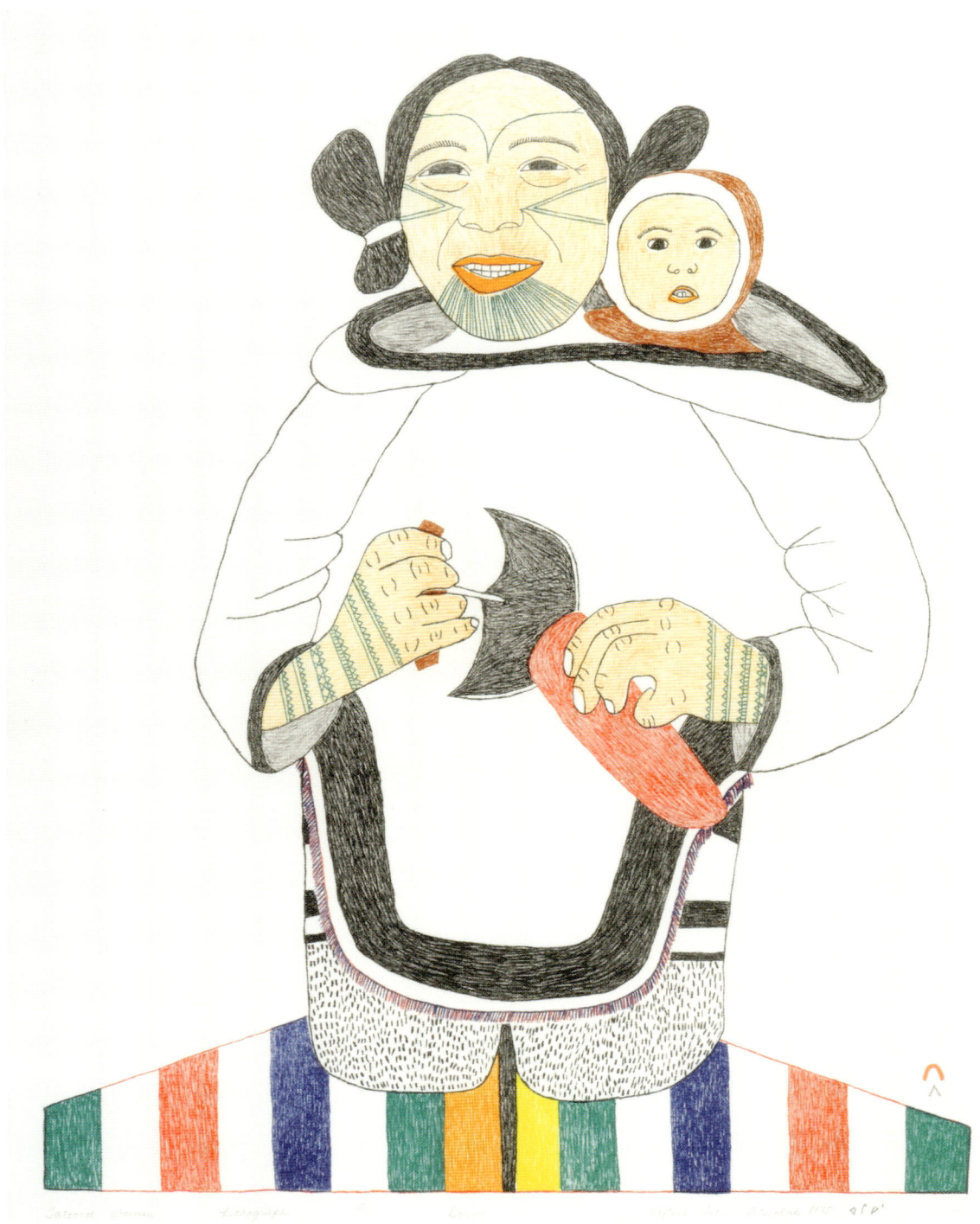

Print of a tattooed woman holding an ulu (knife) and
wearing an amauti, c. 1975–77.
DRAWING BY PETER PITSEOLAK.

Opposite: Aggeok Pitseolak in a white dress at home,
Keatuk camp, Baffin Island, Nunavut, c. 1940–60.

PHOTOGRAPHS AND DRAWINGS BY PETER AND AGGEOK PITSEOLAK. CANADIAN
MUSEUM OF HISTORY. 2000-188, 2007.46, 2000-697, 2000-154, 2000-331, 2000-355,
2000-1370, 2000-1412, 1977-067-005

FÀ:BÔ (AMERICAN HORSE) / HORACE MONROE POOLAW

Kiowa (Cáuigú)
Anadarko, Oklahoma
United States

Horace Poolaw (1906–1984) once said, "I don't want to be remembered through my pictures; I want my people to remember themselves."[1] He exhibited his photographs only a single time, at the Southern Plains Indian Museum in Anadarko in 1979, and it took the curator months to persuade him to agree to the show. "Poolaw kept his pictures close," observed one historian.[2]

In 1989, five years after Poolaw's passing, Stanford University contacted his daughter, Linda Poolaw. With 2,000 of her father's negatives—many made of spontaneously combustible nitrate film—still stored in cardboard boxes, she wondered how he would feel about her collaborating with the university to reveal his photographic legacy. When *War Bonnets, Tin Lizzies, and Patent Leather Pumps: Kiowa Culture in Transition, 1925–1955* opened in 1990, "no one was more proud than the family of Horace Poolaw," recalled Linda.[3] Leading up to the exhibition, the undergrads working with her traveled to Oklahoma and, hoping to identify the people and places in Poolaw's catalog, placed prints of his images in the hands of the Kiowa (Cáuigú). Recognizing their kin, some wept. Others reveled in resurfaced memories.

By the early 2000s, the University of Science and Arts of Oklahoma (USAO) had offered to house Poolaw's collection and named a room in its library after him. In 2008 and 2009, on a mission led by professors Tom Jones (see page 214) and Nancy Marie Mithlo, his negatives were digitized by students from the University of Wisconsin-Madison. Their efforts culminated in *For a Love of His People: The Photography of Horace Poolaw*, a 2014 exhibition cocurated by Jones and Mithlo and organized by the Smithsonian National Museum of the American Indian.

Poolaw's years behind his large-format cameras encompassed both world wars, the Great Depression, the Indian Citizen Act, the Indian Reorganization Act, and the Civil Rights Movement. His work has often been received by the public as a document of the Kiowa's compulsory entry into mid-20th-century mainstream American life, but Linda insists her father did not plan to record Kiowa culture in transition, as the Stanford exhibition title suggests.[4]

The body of work Poolaw created is firmly rooted in family and community, specifically his own in and around Anadarko, Oklahoma. It presents a portrait of the artist—his values and pride in his Tribe—and the Kiowa as agents of change, choosing what new technologies to adopt in the everyday and in their continuously unfolding traditions. He "gives us a glimpse into a Native community positioned in an ever-changing world," Jones aptly pointed out.[5]

Poolaw made a disarming portrait of his younger sister, Trecil, whom he adored, in a polka-dot-patterned top with Blackie the dog in her arms. He photographed his mother with her hair pulled into two tight braids, holding a toddler-sized Linda wearing all white. His son Robert displays his Boy Scout medals for the camera, and his son Jerry stands in front of a tipi in his U.S. Navy uniform, the "Dixie cup" hat replaced with a feather headdress. "Poolaw's camera doesn't privilege the past over the present; it celebrates each equally," said writer Rebecca Bengal.[6] His carefully composed, sometimes theatrical, and frequently joyful pictures show Elders, dancers in regalia, sports teams, women with bob haircuts and chic dresses, funerals, backyard birthday parties, and friends lingering around their nice cars.

Photography never fully supported Poolaw or his family. He worked as an Oklahoma State Trooper and, in 1943, enlisted in the U.S. Army Air Forces, teaching aerial photography at MacDill Field in Florida. After the war he raised cattle. In the 1930s, Poolaw became the official photographer of the American Indian Exposition in Anadarko, a gathering that still exists today. For a while, he made postcards with his images and sold them. Though Poolaw spent hours tucked into his home darkroom developing his negatives, he couldn't afford to make a lot of prints. The postcards, many labeled with, "American Indian Exposition, Anadarko, Oklahoma, Poolaw," were an exception. Another, more telling, title he stamped on his prints read "A Poolaw Photo, Pictures by an Indian."

Every year, the expo begins with a parade. In 1941, Poolaw photographed three Kiowa beauty queens filing through Anadarko atop a stout automobile. He made the picture from a moderate distance, letting topical details flood the frame: paraders on horseback, a grain elevator, electrical and telephone

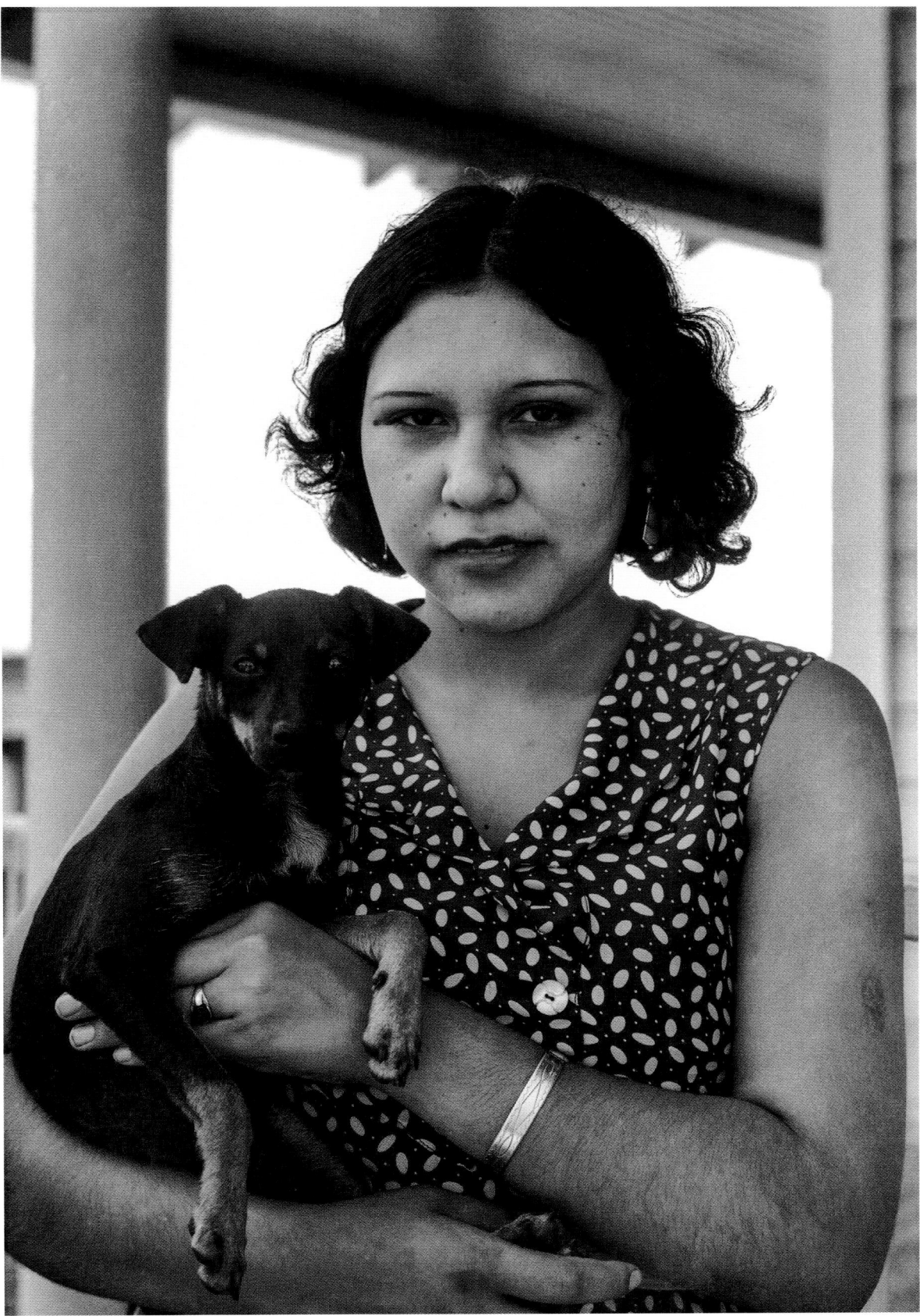

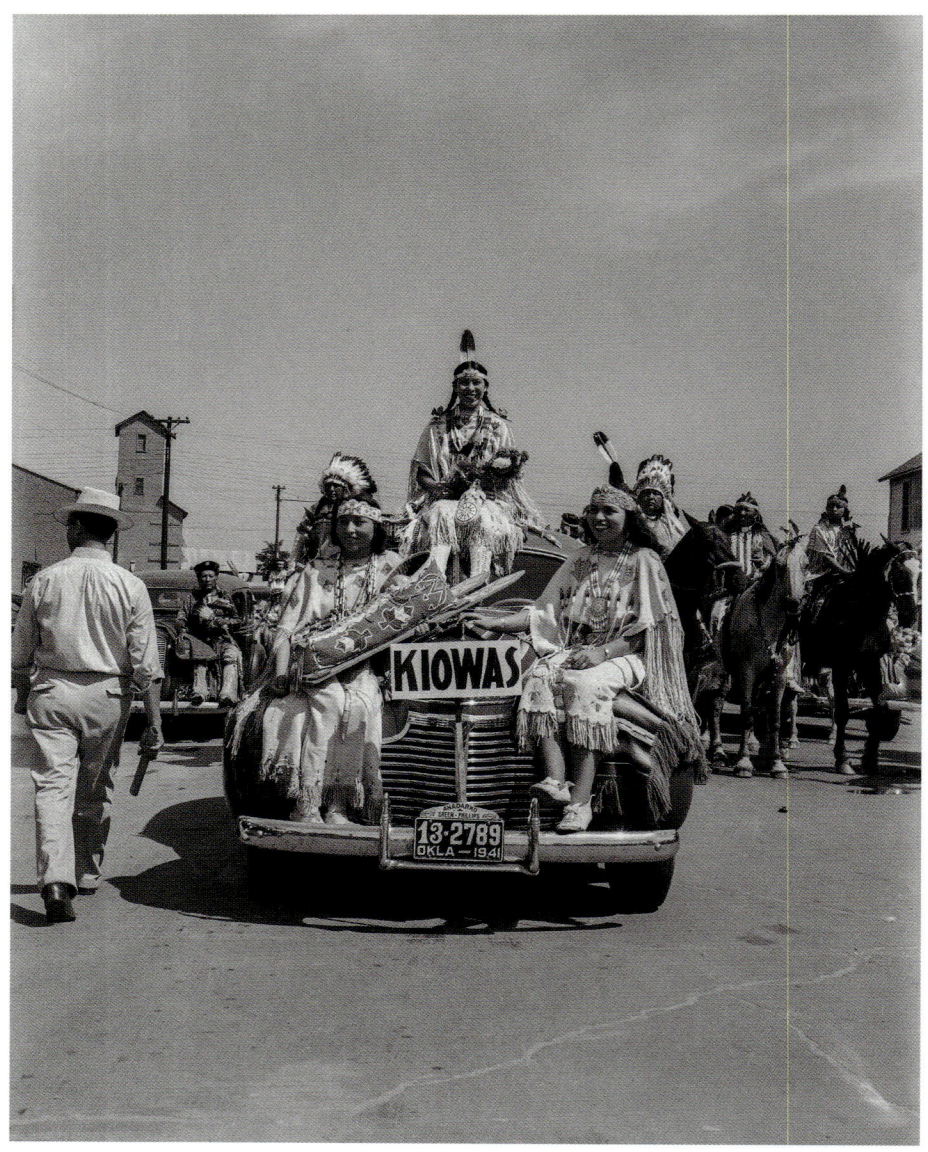

wires on the horizon, a man in street clothes, an Oklahoma inscribed license plate. "He thwarts any attempts to squint our eyes and seek nostalgia for a mythologizing past," remarked scholar David W. Penney.[7]

Poolaw started making photographs when he was a teenager and continued for five decades. His father, who went by Kiowa George, was a calendar keeper for the Tribe, chronicling the year's noteworthy events with drawings—keys that can "unlock the collective mind" of the Tribe and its families. "Horace Poolaw's photographs," said his grandson Thomas Poolaw, "serve as an extension of the Kiowa calendar."[8]

—Sarah Stacke

Juanita Daugomah Ahtone (left), Evalou Ware Russell (center), Kiowa Tribal Princess, and Augustine Campbell Barsh in the American Indian Exposition parade, Anadarko, Oklahoma, 1941.
PHOTOGRAPH BY HORACE POOLAW. COURTESY OF THE ESTATE OF HORACE POOLAW AND THE UNIVERSITY OF SCIENCE AND ARTS OF OKLAHOMA, NASH LIBRARY.

Opposite: Kiowa Tribal Princess Libby Ann Hines Hall at the American Indian Exposition, Anadarko, Oklahoma, 1948.
PHOTOGRAPH BY HORACE POOLAW. COURTESY OF THE ESTATE OF HORACE POOLAW AND TOM JONES.

Opposite: George Ashley, Wichita, at the American Indian Exposition, Anadarko, Oklahoma, c. 1945–47.
PHOTOGRAPH BY HORACE POOLAW. COURTESY OF THE ESTATE OF HORACE POOLAW AND TOM JONES.

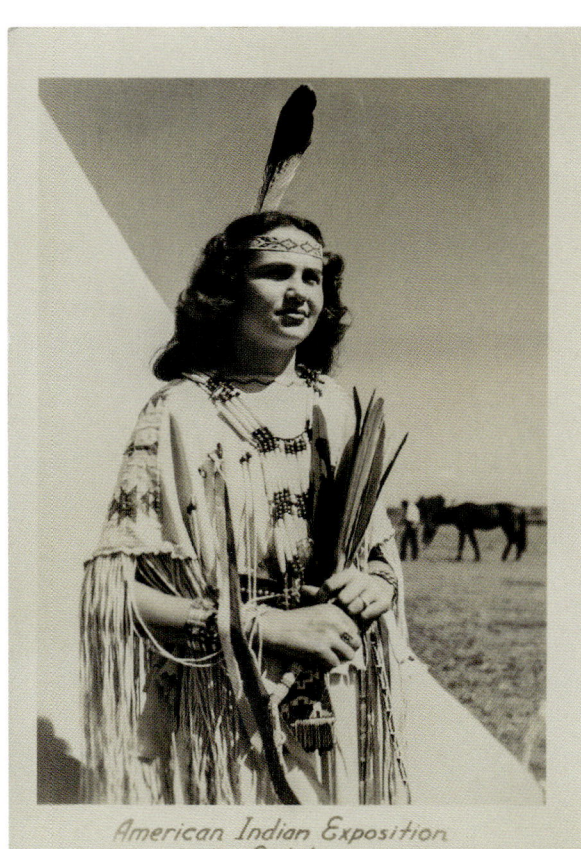

American Indian Exposition
Anadarko, Oklahoma   Poolaw

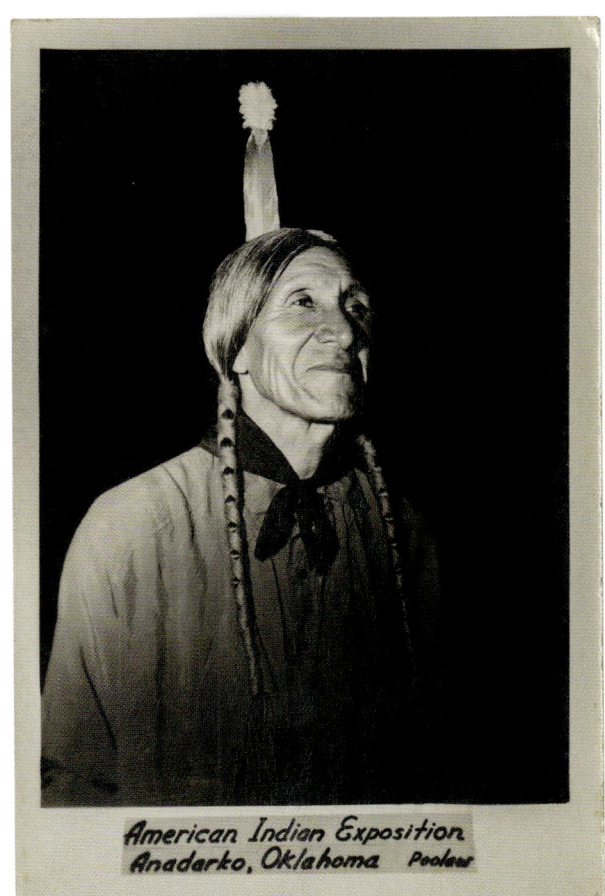

American Indian Exposition
Anadarko, Oklahoma   Poolaw

JAMES "JIM" PATRICK BRADY

Métis
Alberta and Saskatchewan
Canada

In the summer of 1967, Métis leader and photographer James "Jim" Patrick Brady (1908–1967) and Cree Band Councillor Absolom Halkett went prospecting in remote northern Saskatchewan and never returned. The circumstances of their disappearance remain unsolved. Many speculate the men were murdered for political reasons.

Brady was an intrepid outdoorsman and activist in Alberta and Saskatchewan, where he and his comrade Malcolm Norris are broadly acknowledged as two of the most influential Indigenous political figures of the 20th century. In the 1930s, Brady—whose beliefs blended Marxist, Socialist, and Métis nationalist ideologies—was a founding member of the Métis Association of Alberta and immersed himself in advocating for the Métis Settlements in the province. In the next decade he continued his community organizing role, moving from Alberta to northern Saskatchewan, and served overseas in World War II. After the war he worked with the Co-operative Commonwealth Federation (CFF), a political party founded by various farmer, labor, and socialist groups. Before his death, Brady invested himself in the Métis and Cree First Nations communities of Cumberland House and La Ronge, helping to establish the Métis Association of Saskatchewan.

The Glenbow Museum in Calgary, Alberta, stewards a collection of 13 feet of paper documents and 1,070 photographs Brady made throughout these four decades. Thanks to the work of Métis artist and scholar Sherry Farrell Racette and nîpisîhkopâwiyiniw (Willow Cree) writer Paul Seesequasis, among others, Brady's use of the camera as a tool for political advocacy and expression of Métis identity is gaining recognition.

The photographs in the James Brady fonds visualize the day-to-day lives of friends and family, and the places Brady lived in and visited. He strongly preferred vertical, full-length portraits, almost exclusively made in the natural prairie and forest landscapes of Alberta and Saskatchewan, or in front of dwellings. Relative Louis Garneau Jr. appears before a thicket of birch trees with his banjo, and a trio of Garneau women pose next to a snowman smoking a pipe. He made images of colleagues. A thoughtfully composed picture of Norris shows him on a camping trip, hanging fishing nets among the pines.

Between 1948 and 1951, in an effort to connect with the people of Cumberland House, where his work with the CFF's Department of Natural Resources was met with suspicion, Brady set out to make a portrait of every adult and many of the children living there. The photographs in this series embody "the spirit not only of the individual but also of the community ethos that Brady admired," explains Racette.[1]

Hundreds of Brady's photographs document Métis people living "on their home territories despite forces that sought to break that bond."[2] Bush airplanes, canoe expeditions, prospecting trips, trapping, fishing, and log cabins are abundant. Above all, Brady's deep affection for the land and respect for land-based economies and self-sufficiency emerge, indelibly linking the collection to the Métis self-determination he championed.

"His photographs," notes Racette, "form a remarkable chronicle of Métis life in the first half of the twentieth century."[3]

Brady was born on March 11, 1908, at Lake St. Vincent and raised in nearby St. Paul des Métis, Alberta. His dedication to social equality and political change was profoundly informed by his Irish father's social liberalism, his proud Métis mother, and his maternal grandfather Laurent Garneau—a rebel and patriot involved in the resistance movements of 1869–70 and 1885 alongside his good friend and Métis leader Louis Riel.[4]

When Brady vanished, the walls of his cabin were lined with more than 2,000 books. The documents, personal pages, written correspondence, and annotated photographs he left behind continue to embolden a better future.

—Sarah Stacke

Louis Garneau Jr. with his banjo, St. Paul, Alberta, c. 1931.

Charlotte Garneau, Mrs. Louis Garneau, and Helen Garneau pose beside a snowman, St. Paul, Alberta, c. 1938.

PHOTOGRAPHS BY JAMES BRADY. COURTESY OF GLENBOW ARCHIVES. PA-2218-33, PA-2218-195, PA-2218-569, PA-2218-94, PA-2218-462

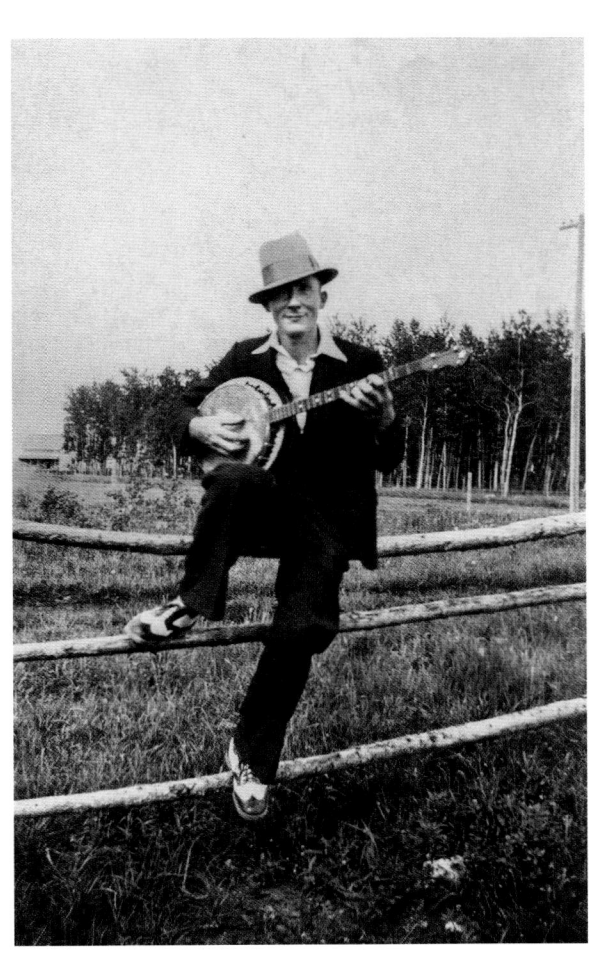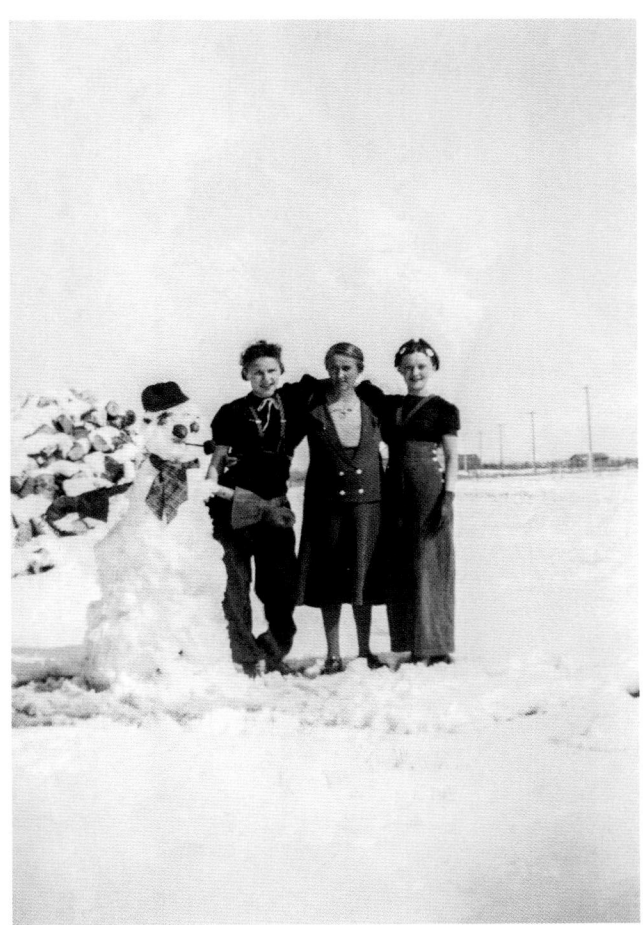

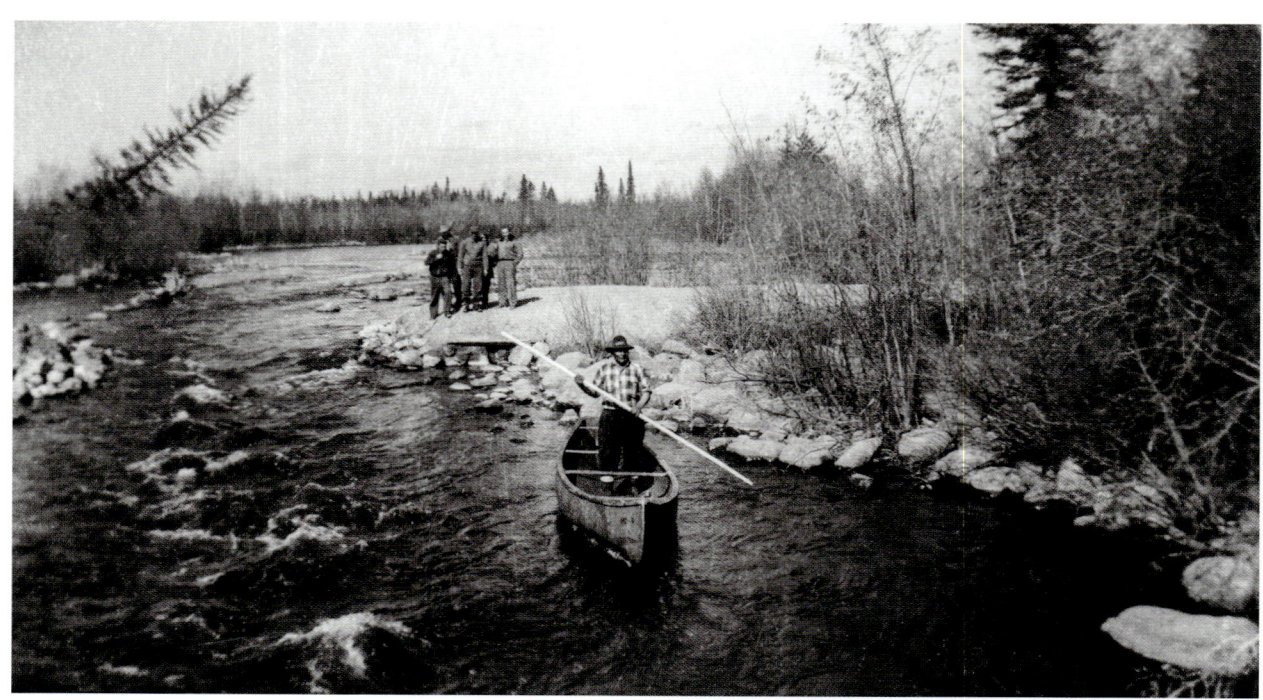

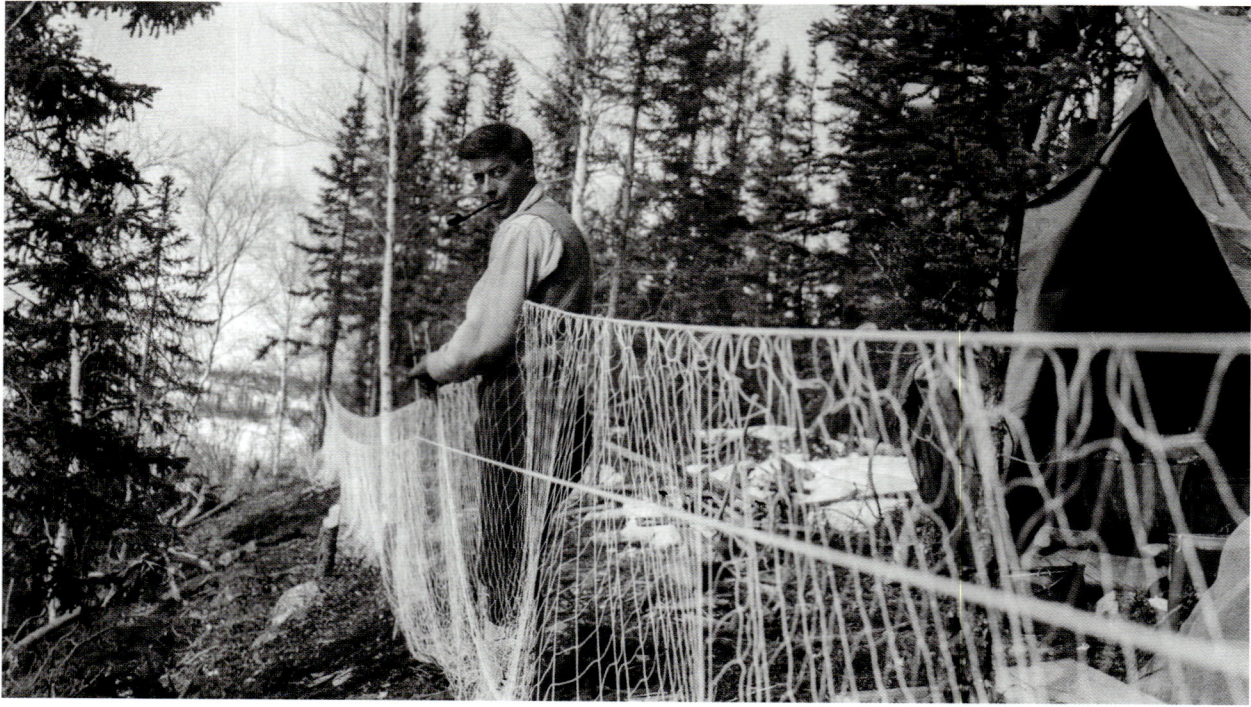

John Bird in a canoe on the Montreal River,
La Ronge, Saskatchewan, c. 1962.

Malcolm Norris hanging nets, likely Alberta or
Saskatchewan, c. 1934.

Opposite: Florence Ballantyne, Deschambault Lake,
Saskatchewan, c. 1945–55.

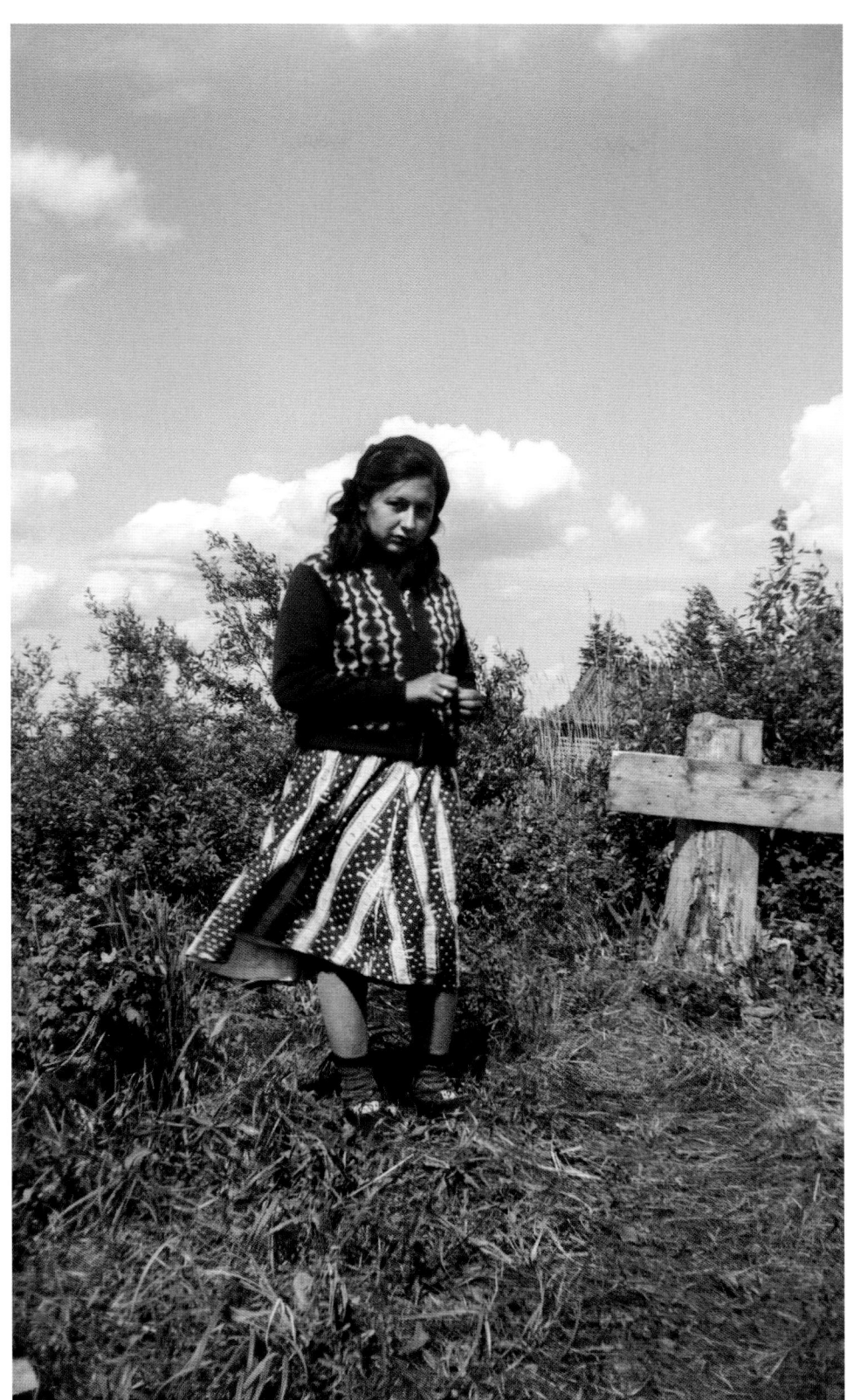

ELLA MAD PLUME YELLOW WOLF

Blackfeet
Blackfeet Nation
Montana
United States

"Ella Mad Plume Yellow Wolf's photographs are important," says her grandniece Dr. Rosalyn LaPier, an environmental historian and author. Yellow Wolf (1908–1988) photographed her daily life on the Blackfeet Nation, deliberately narrating her story for future family. At the same time, she inadvertently documented a notable era of American history through the eyes of a Blackfeet woman.[1]

Yellow Wolf was born October 4, 1908, on Little Badger Creek, on the south side of the reservation. Her parents were Elmer Mad Plume and Minnie Kaluse (or Caluse), who was Blackfeet and, the family believes, Spanish. After Kaluse and her infant son died following his birth in 1915, Yellow Wolf and her siblings lived with relatives and attended Holy Family Mission, an on-reservation Catholic boarding school. Yellow Wolf married Louis "Louie" Yellow Wolf (pronounced Low-ie) in 1939. It was her second marriage; she divorced her first husband. Louie, who was Blackfeet and African American, was the nephew of James Willard Schultz, a white American author of multiple novels and articles detailing Blackfeet life. The couple moved to Cut Bank Creek, north of Browning, where they mostly lived off the land and became full-time ranchers, an occupation they continued until their deaths, three months apart in the summer of 1988. Yellow Wolf and Louie were "constant companions," recalls LaPier.[2]

In the second week of June 1964, the largest flood in Montana's recorded history plunged the Blackfeet Nation underwater. Streams grew into broad, violent rapids. The Yellow Wolf cabin was partially swept down Cut Bank Creek, along with an unknown number of photographs. Yellow Wolf's descendants eventually donated a selection of 84 surviving photos to the Montana Historical Society (MHS). Made in the early 1940s as family keepsakes, the images confide the public with Yellow Wolf's husband, their ranching and trapping work, their rich family and community life, and their spirituality. "What makes me sad," says LaPier about losing her great-aunt's photographs in the flood, "is there were more of those, there were just a lot more of those."[3]

In the early 20th century, the U.S. government and the Catholic Church began inserting Euro-American concepts of gender roles into Blackfeet ways of life. Patriarchy was new to the Blackfeet. Historically, women were property owners, heads of households, and religious leaders. By the 1940s, Yellow Wolf "had been immersed in a society with conflicted ideas about the role of women, from her Blackfeet traditions to Catholic beliefs to American society," explains LaPier. "But some Indigenous women chose to go their own way.

"Ella was a modern twentieth-century Indigenous woman, blending traditional customs with new ways. In the early 1940s, there was nothing more modern than owning a camera and taking pictures."[4]

In a visual rebuke of the idea that women's work only belongs inside the home, Yellow Wolf appears in a self-portrait on the ranch. She's dressed in stylish and practical cowgirl wear. One hand rests on a saddle slung over a wood rail, the other touches her belt buckle. Her purposeful expression says she is exactly where she should be.

A wintertime portrait of Louie in a thick plaid shirt shows him holding over a dozen mink skins and one bobcat fur. Beaver pelts hang from his neck. Trapping was one of Louie's earliest professions, and he did nearly all of it on lands that, in 1910, became Glacier National Park. The Blackfeet retained hunting and gathering rights inside Glacier, but the park has contested this since its establishment. Photographing her husband in Glacier with the yield of his traps can be seen "as an act of resistance against the policing of Indigenous peoples utilizing their treaty rights to hunt on their historic territories," says LaPier.[5] A few of the trapping cabins Louie built in Glacier still stand today.

Labor is a prevalent theme in Yellow Wolf's pictures. With the Depression and the arrival of World War II, many Native American men sought work off the reservations as migrant farm laborers. A photograph made near Kalispell renders Blackfeet men (and one woman) in a field picking potatoes. The composition is striking. The workers form a gentle arc behind a figure crouching in the foreground, leading the eye through the frame until it ends with a tractor in the distance. In one of the later photographs at MHS, Yellow Wolf is cleaning freshly caught fish at Two Medicine Dam, a favorite spot for angling on the reservation. The dam was overcome in the 1964 flood and rebuilt two years later.

Yellow Wolf and Louie never had children of their own, but they were part of large extended families that helped and visited one another often. Kids, whether in the arms of a parent or posing with wonderment—or brows furrowed in young protest—are common in the collection. A wagonful of youthful relatives and friends, probably headed to Browning

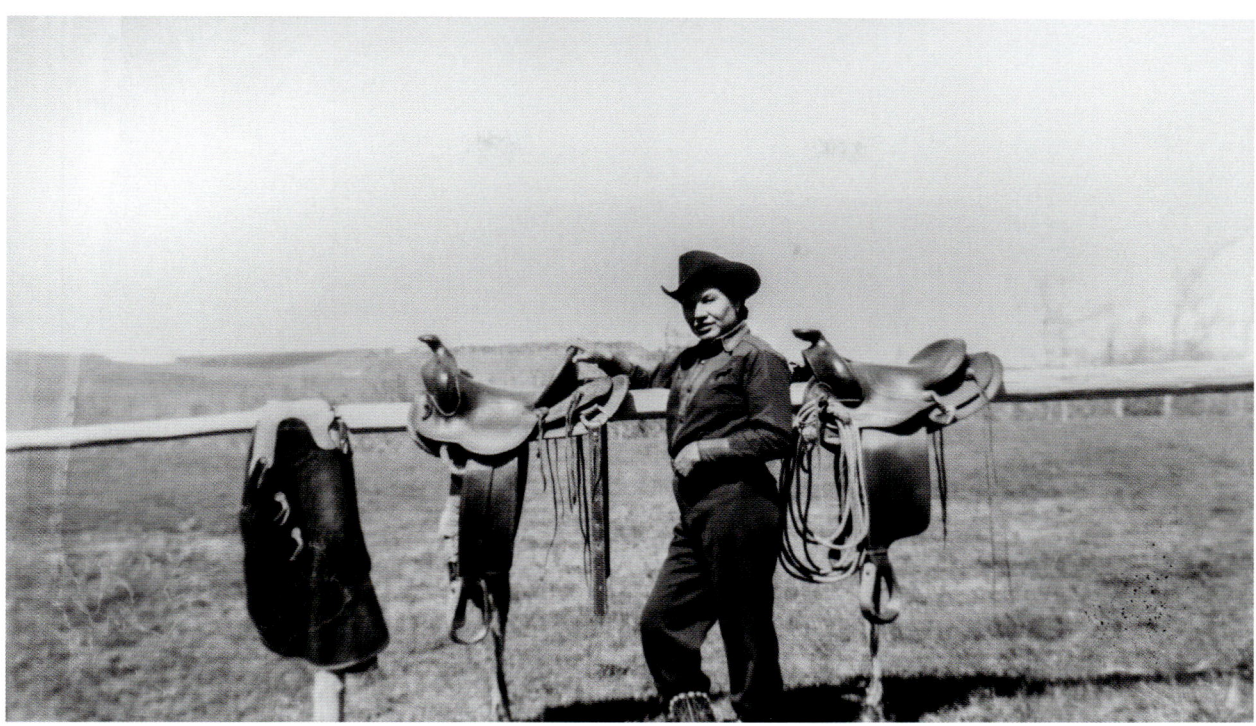

for shopping, errands, and socializing, radiates affection for their photographer.

"In terms of an act of resistance," says LaPier, "I think about those candid photographs, the photographs of people...enjoying life, versus the narrative we often hear about Indigenous communities and Indigenous life."[6]

An enchanting picture of Cups Monroe awash in evenfall light illustrates a community gathering. The passel of folk behind Monroe has likely assembled to watch a game and gamble on the outcome. At another crowded event, Yellow Wolf made a wholly candid photograph of her brother Phillip Rattler and his wife, Helen Rattler. Perhaps shy, Helen turns away from the camera, while Phillip's countenance emanates joy. "You always see these photographs of Indians never smiling," says LaPier. "That's so far from the truth."[7]

Phillip, like all of Yellow Wolf's brothers, volunteered for military service. He was part of the 43rd Tank Battalion, 12th Armored Division ("Hellcats"), in World War II and was captured by German forces, becoming a prisoner of war. After he was liberated, he spent the rest of his life on the reservation. Another photograph in the Ella Mad Plume Yellow Wolf archive at MHS portrays seven World War II soldiers from the 9th Infantry Division. The image was made by the U.S. Army in Europe, probably Germany in the spring of 1945, and very possibly pictures one of Yellow Wolf's younger brothers kneeling on the far left. As many as

25,000 Native American men fought in World War II. On the reservation, Yellow Wolf photographed military funerals for Blackfeet servicemen.

Spirituality was a major part of Yellow Wolf and Louie's life. They joined the Pentecostal Church and participated in both Christian and Blackfeet religious observances. The growing patriarchy within these activities is conveyed in a photograph Yellow Wolf made of a large church group. A cleric stands at the center, and nearly everyone around him presents as male.

Their entire lives, Yellow Wolf and Louie spoke the Blackfeet language. LaPier was 25 years old when they passed. She vividly remembers Yellow Wolf and her sisters (Victoria, LaPier's great-aunt, and Annie, LaPier's grandmother) talking, laughing, and joking—always in Blackfeet.

"On the one hand it was a hobby to take photographs," says LaPier, "but also, leaving a legacy and their own personal narrative behind was important. Photographs were a way to do that."[8]

—Sarah Stacke

Ella Mad Plume Yellow Wolf on the ranch with saddles, Blackfeet Nation, c. 1940–45.
PHOTOGRAPH BY LOUIE YELLOW WOLF. MONTANA HISTORICAL SOCIETY PHOTOGRAPH ARCHIVES. PAC 97-37.28

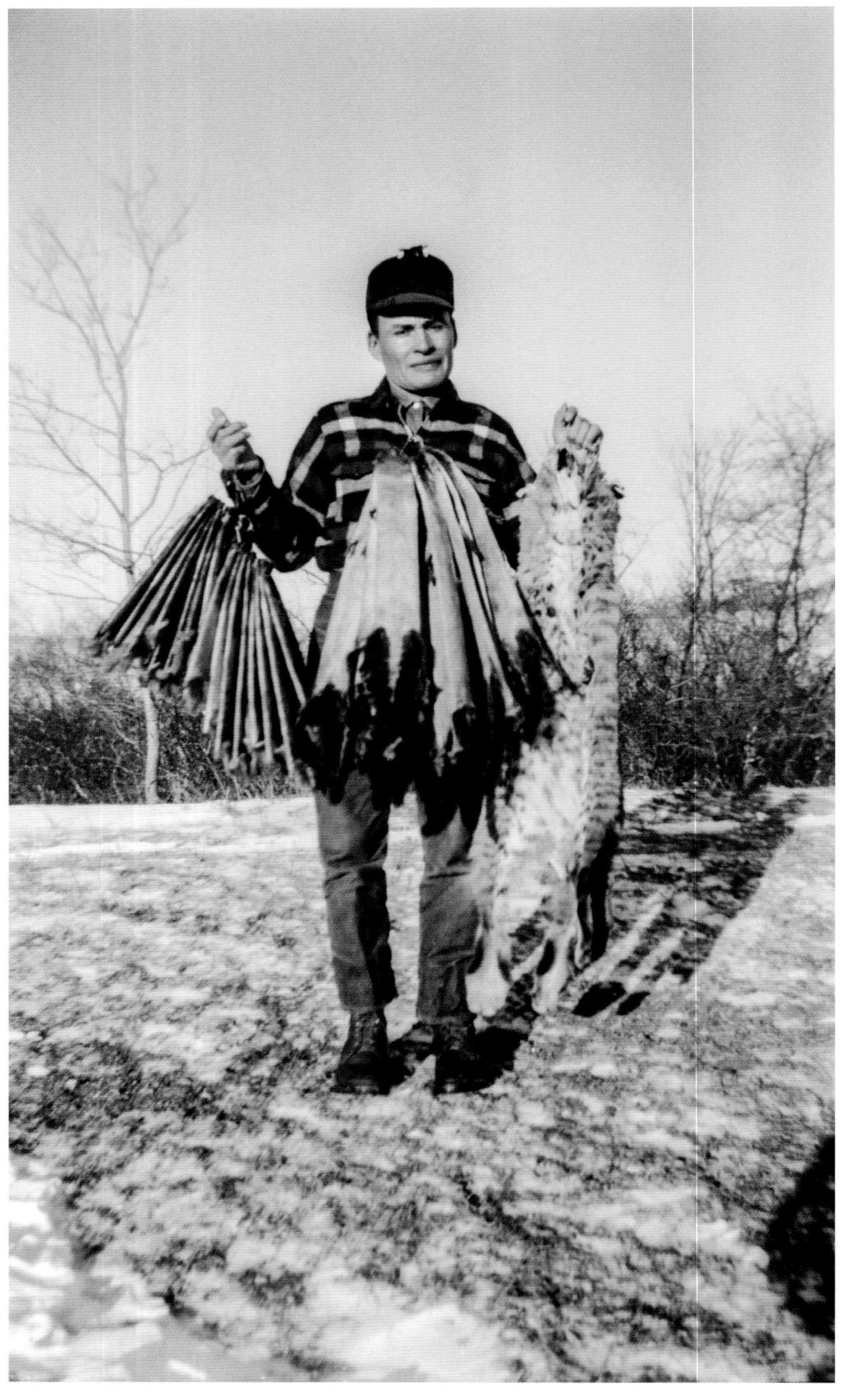

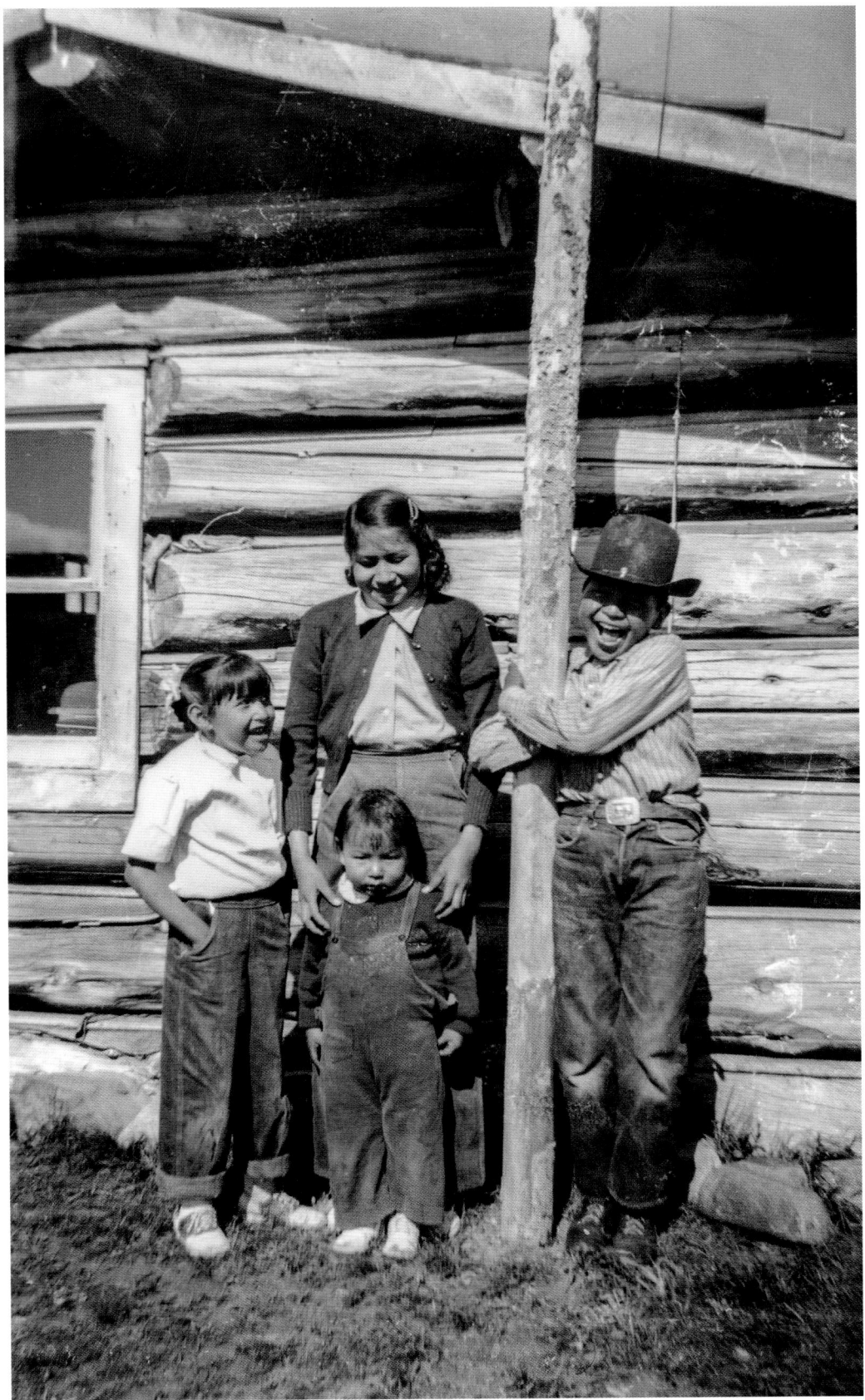

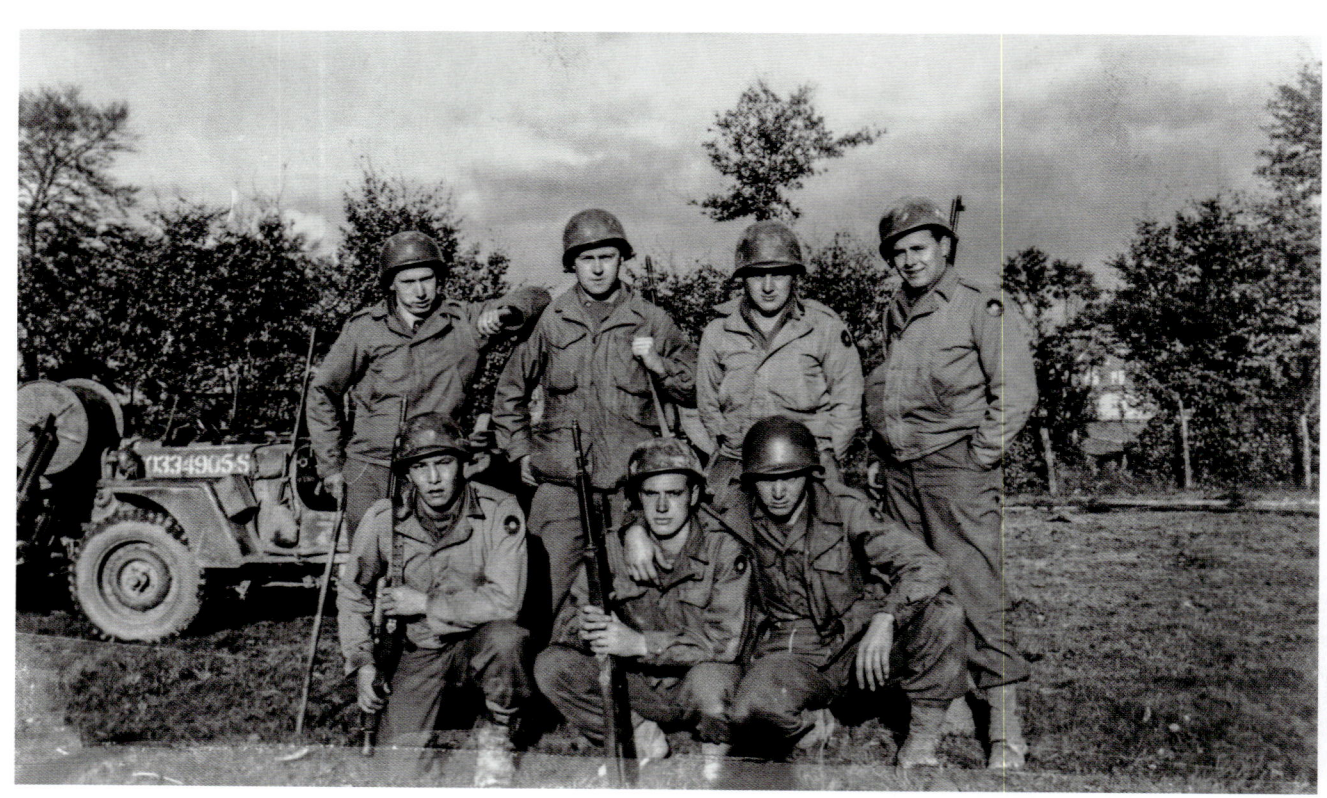

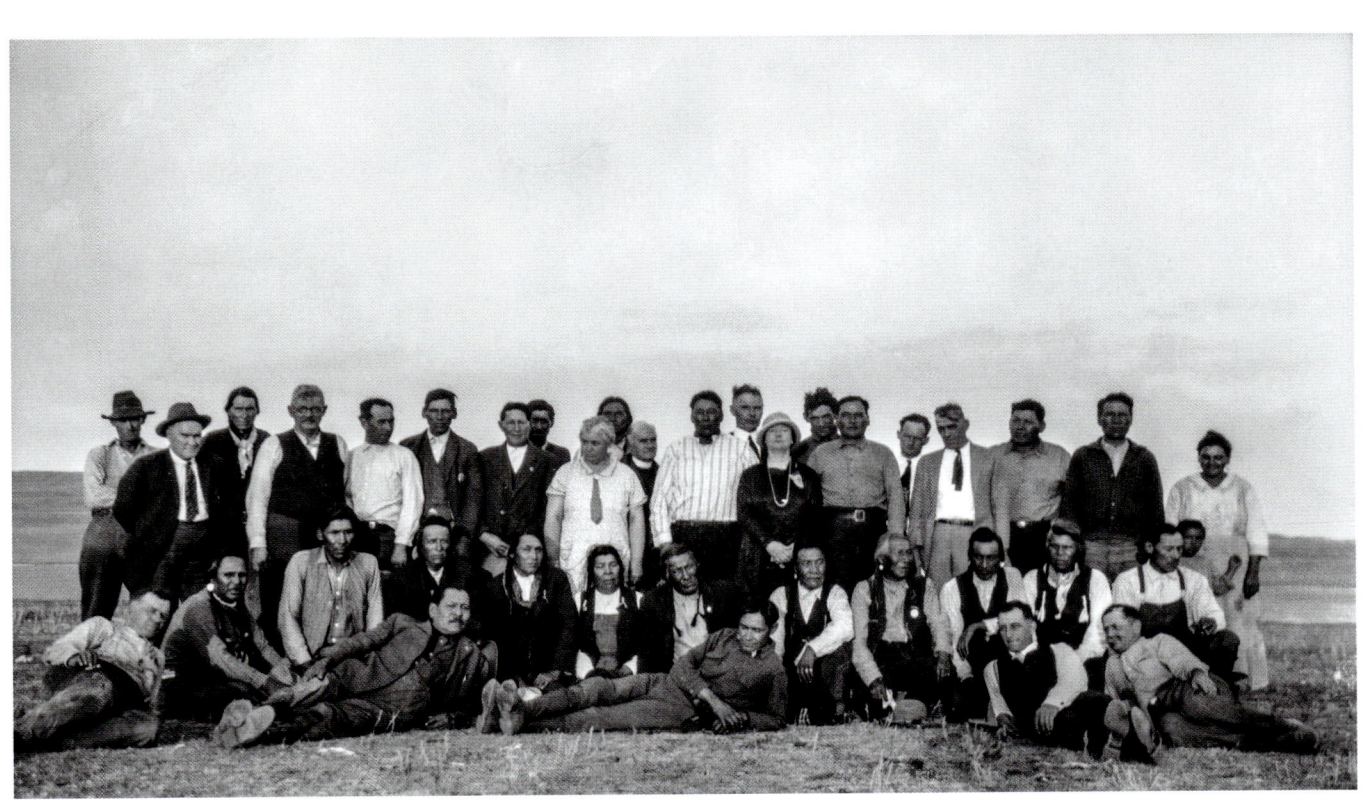

A church group, Blackfeet Nation, c. 1940–45.
PHOTOGRAPH BY ELLA MAD PLUME YELLOW WOLF. MONTANA HISTORICAL
SOCIETY PHOTOGRAPH ARCHIVES. PAC 97-37.38

Opposite: World War II U.S. Army soldiers from the
9th Infantry Division, Europe, c. 1940–45.
PHOTOGRAPH BY U.S. ARMY. MONTANA HISTORICAL SOCIETY PHOTOGRAPH
ARCHIVES. PAC 97-37.67

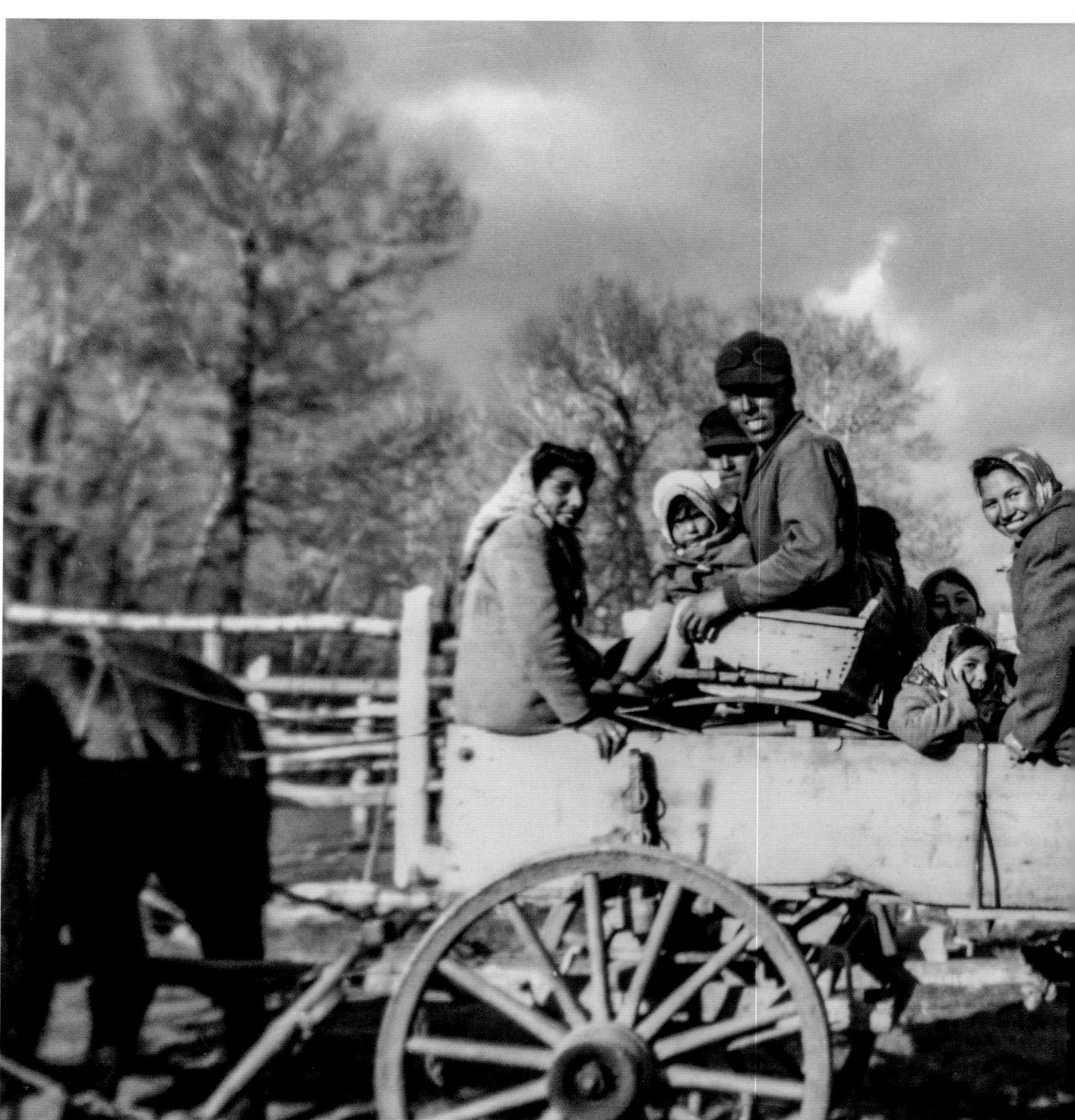

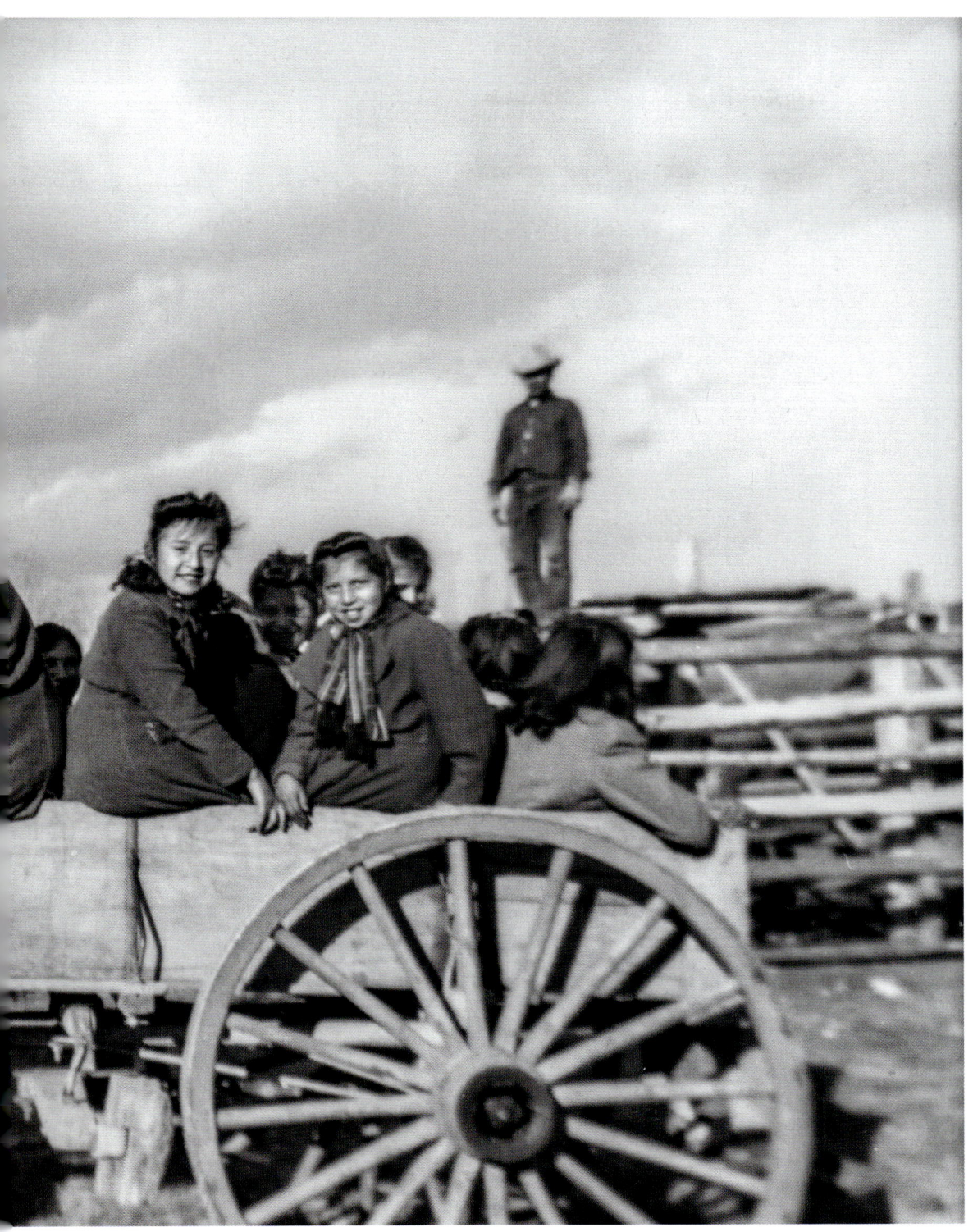

Friends and relatives from the White Grass family in
a wagon, Blackfeet Nation, c. 1940–45. It is possible Yellow
Wolf is sitting in the center in a headscarf. If that is the
case, the photograph was made by Louie.

PHOTOGRAPH BY ELLA MAD PLUME YELLOW WOLF. MONTANA HISTORICAL
SOCIETY PHOTOGRAPH ARCHIVES. PAC 97-37.43

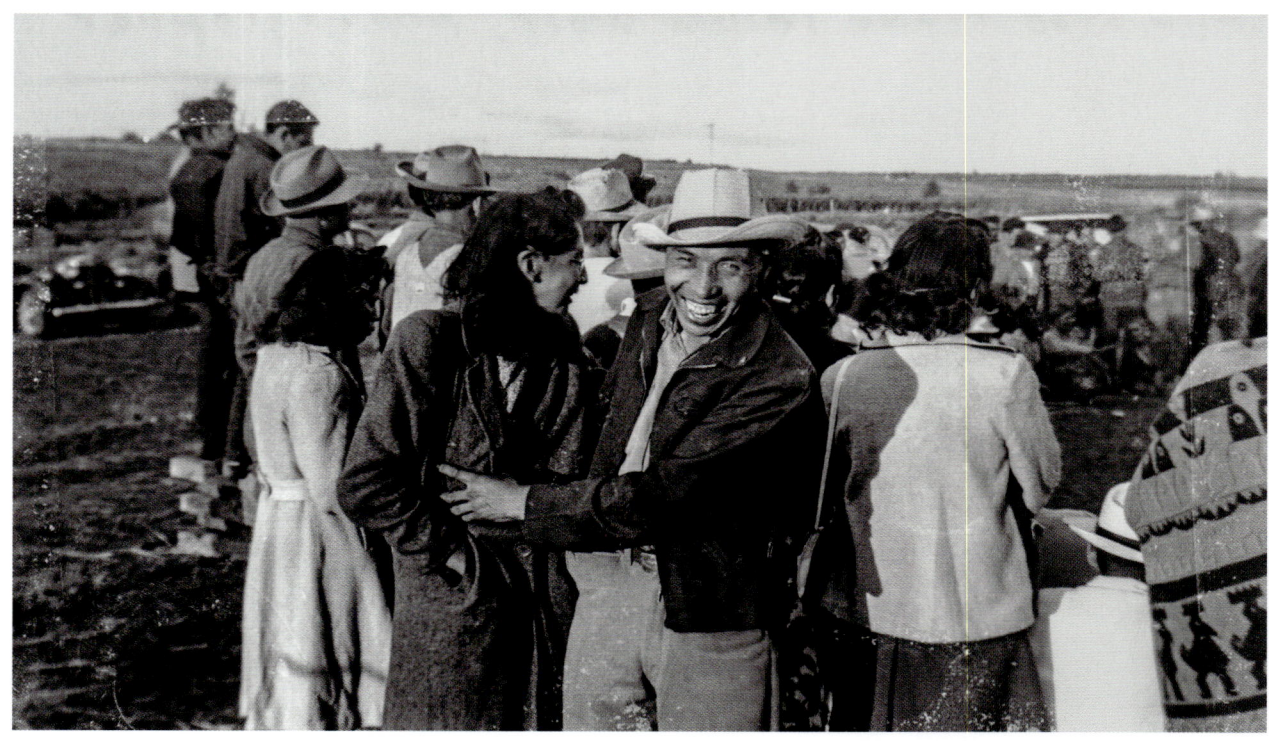

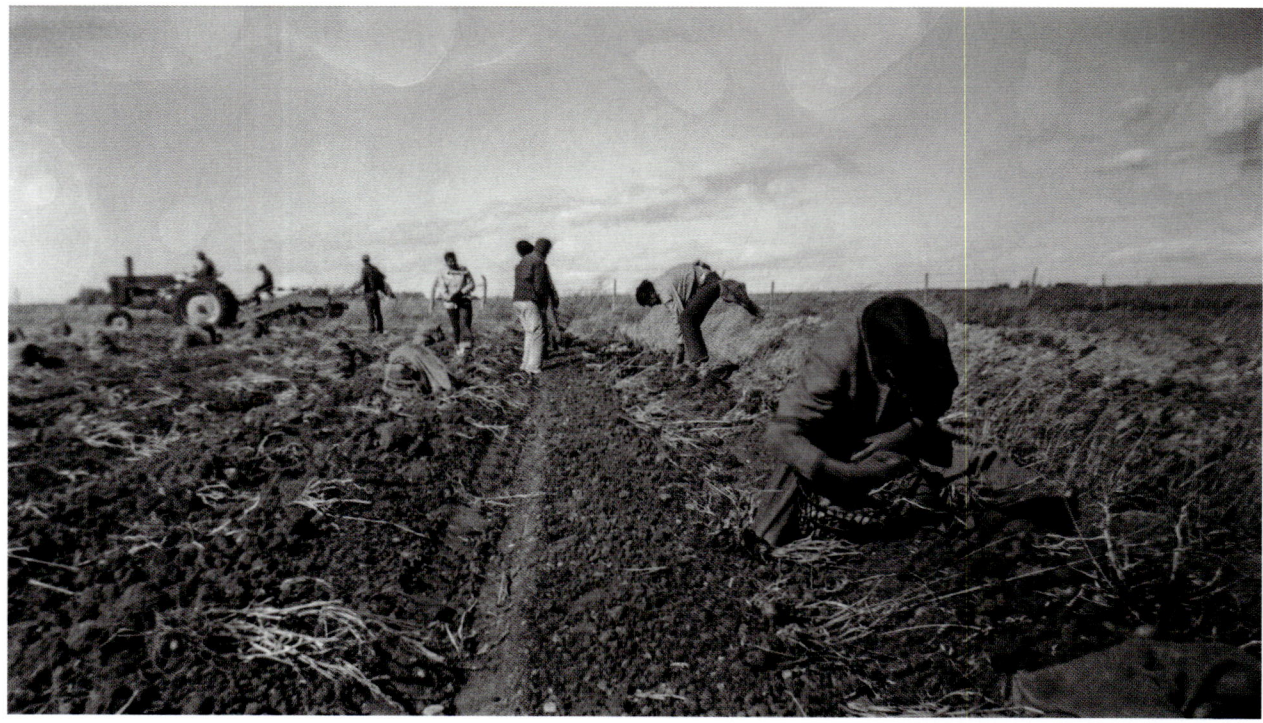

Phillip and Helen Rattler, Blackfeet Nation, c. 1940–45.
PHOTOGRAPH BY ELLA MAD PLUME YELLOW WOLF.
MONTANA HISTORICAL SOCIETY PHOTOGRAPH ARCHIVES. PAC 97-37.72

Harvesting potatoes near Kalispell, Montana, c. 1940–45.
PHOTOGRAPH BY ELLA MAD PLUME YELLOW WOLF. MONTANA HISTORICAL SOCIETY
PHOTOGRAPH ARCHIVES. PAC 97-37.81

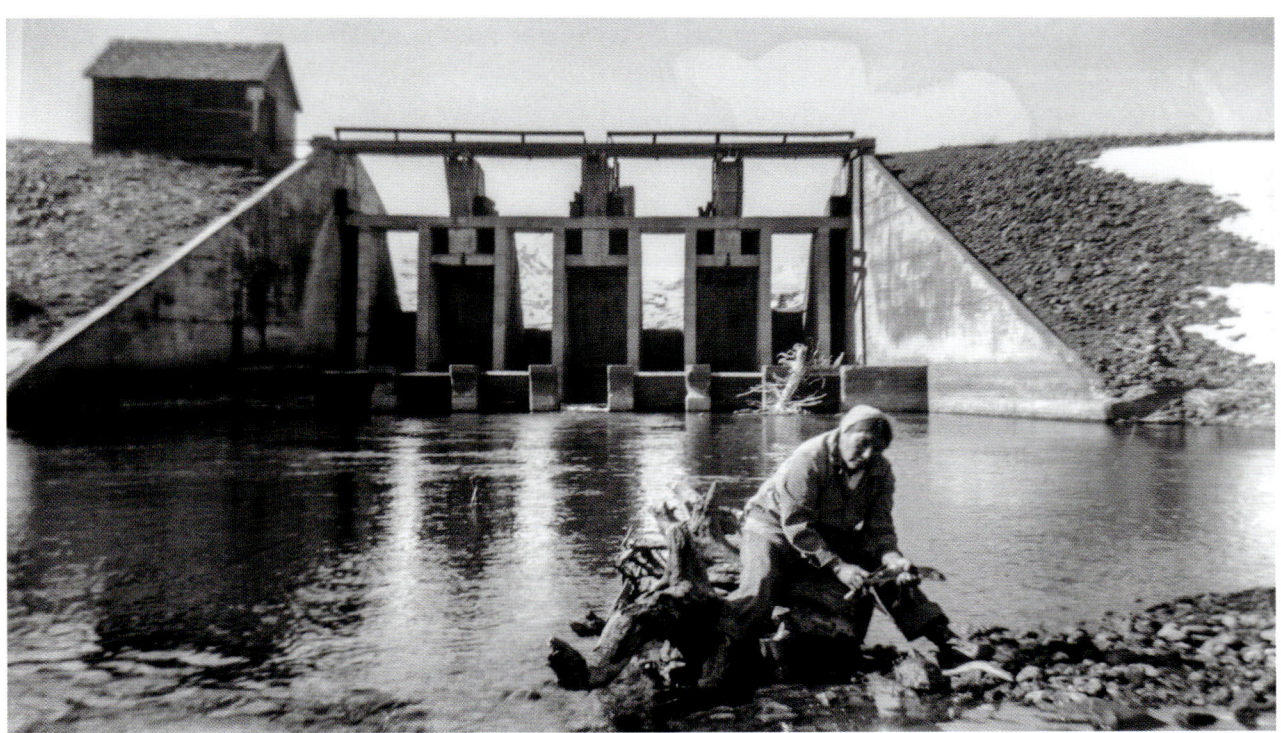

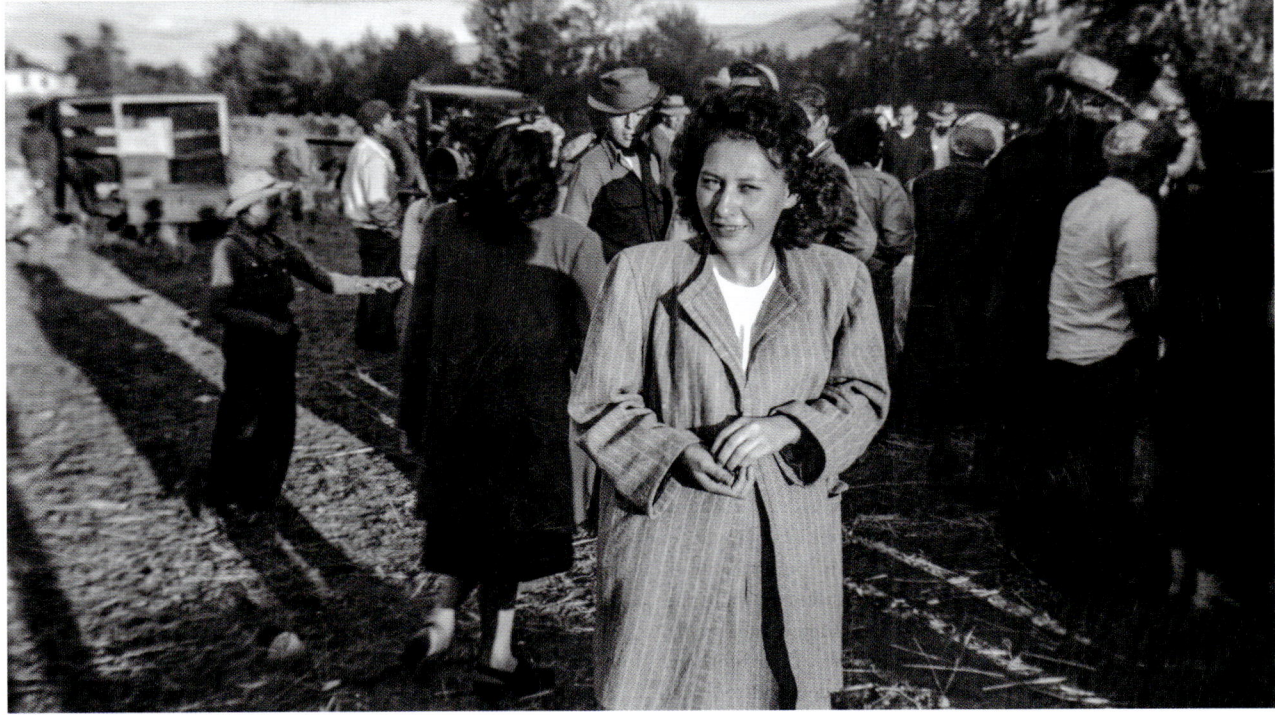

Ella Mad Plume Yellow Wolf near the dam at Lower Two Medicine Lake,
Blackfeet Nation, c. 1940–45.

PHOTOGRAPH BY LOUIE YELLOW WOLF. MONTANA HISTORICAL SOCIETY PHOTOGRAPH ARCHIVES. PAC 97-37.29

Cups Monroe, Blackfeet Nation, c. 1940–45.

PHOTOGRAPH BY ELLA MAD PLUME YELLOW WOLF. MONTANA HISTORICAL SOCIETY
PHOTOGRAPH ARCHIVES. PAC 97-37.74

MARGARET PICTOU LABILLOIS

Mi'kmaq
Ugpi'ganjig First Nation (Eel River Bar First Nation)
Chaleur Bay, New Brunswick
Canada

In the top row, fifth from the left, stands Margaret Pictou LaBillois (1923–2013). "That's her, that's my mother," exclaimed Beckie LaBillois after seeing the "School of Photography" image for the first time in 2023. "She was still a Pictou then," she added.[1]

LaBillois's contribution to the history of photography is substantial—and there are no known professional photographs attributed to her. She served in the photographic unit of the Royal Canadian Air Force (RCAF) Women's Division during World War II. Positioned at RCAF Station Rockcliffe, a picturesque base along the Ottawa River near downtown Ottawa, Ontario, LaBillois trained in aerial photography. "I could have had an office job, but I wanted to be out and about so I went into photography," she commented in 2004.[2]

LaBillois worked on photographs to map the construction of the Alaska Highway, a massive and hasty wartime project connecting Alaska to the contiguous United States through Canada's thick wilderness. She and her colleagues processed film sent from aerial photographers in Alaska, Yukon, and British Columbia, then pieced together the developed sheets on long tables. Next they drew maps based on the images, photographed the maps, and sent the new photographs back west. By her own account, LaBillois also photographed from airplanes. She remembers being told, "If you drop that camera you might as well jump after it, it will take you forever to pay for it."[3]

One of 10 siblings, LaBillois was the first member of Ugpi'ganjig (Eel River Bar)—a small coastal nation amid a vast sandbar on the south side of Chaleur Bay, New Brunswick—to graduate from high school. It was a Catholic residential school, where she was prohibited from speaking her first language, Mi'kmaq. With her diploma, she enrolled in nursing school but left to enlist in the air force. She was resolved to share the government salary with her mother, Mary Pictou (née Paul), who was the sole provider for the family. Two of her brothers, soldiers stationed in Europe, influenced her decision to enlist in another way. LaBillois believed joining the war could bring them home faster.[4] While one brother did return home, another was killed in action. After LaBillois was discharged from the air force, she and her surviving brother met in Ottawa and made the trip home to their mother, siblings, and Ugpi'ganjig

together. During her time in the service (c. 1942–44), she never met another First Nations woman.

LaBillois married Michael LaBillois, also a veteran, in 1946, and they raised 14 children. In 1970, while parenting and running a restaurant, she was elected as Chief of Ugpi'ganjig, the first woman to serve as a Chief in New Brunswick. Before assuming the position, LaBillois didn't have political ambitions.[5] It was the construction of the Eel River Dam in 1963 that led to her name on the ballot.

The dam, built immediately adjacent to Ugpi'ganjig, where the Eel River meets Chaleur Bay, halted the tidal exchange between the river's freshwater and the bay's salt water. The disruption assaulted local ecology, lifeways, and livelihoods. The number of Atlantic salmon, a cultural and dietary staple, diminished dramatically. Passage to Heron Island—a traditional site for fishing and food gathering roughly 15 miles into the bay—was nearly impossible. Because of the dam, the water was too shallow. Clam populations in the river above the dam disappeared and those below it became too polluted to dig. Without the clams, daily gatherings on the sandbars, often between several generations of families and friends, ceased. The communal digs formed the backbone of the community. "Our elders tell us that that was their main work, it was the babysitter, it was the town newspaper, it was everything," recalled local resident Jude Caplin.[6]

Families in Ugpi'ganjig fell into poverty. LaBillois and her husband, who along with their children had been digging, cooking, and selling clams every day, were forced into new occupations. Michael worked as a dock worker, while LaBillois expanded the snack shop on their land into a restaurant that offered dine-in and take-out meals.

With her education, air force experience, and reputation as someone invested in the well-being of Ugpi'ganjig, the community urged LaBillois to run against the current Chief, who reportedly never challenged the dam's construction. Initially resistant, LaBillois reflected on what had been lost with the dam, and the fate of her children and Homelands. She remembered the trips her grandfather made to Heron Island, now unreachable. When he returned, his birchbark canoe brimmed with fish, clams, eels, and berries. She thought about searching

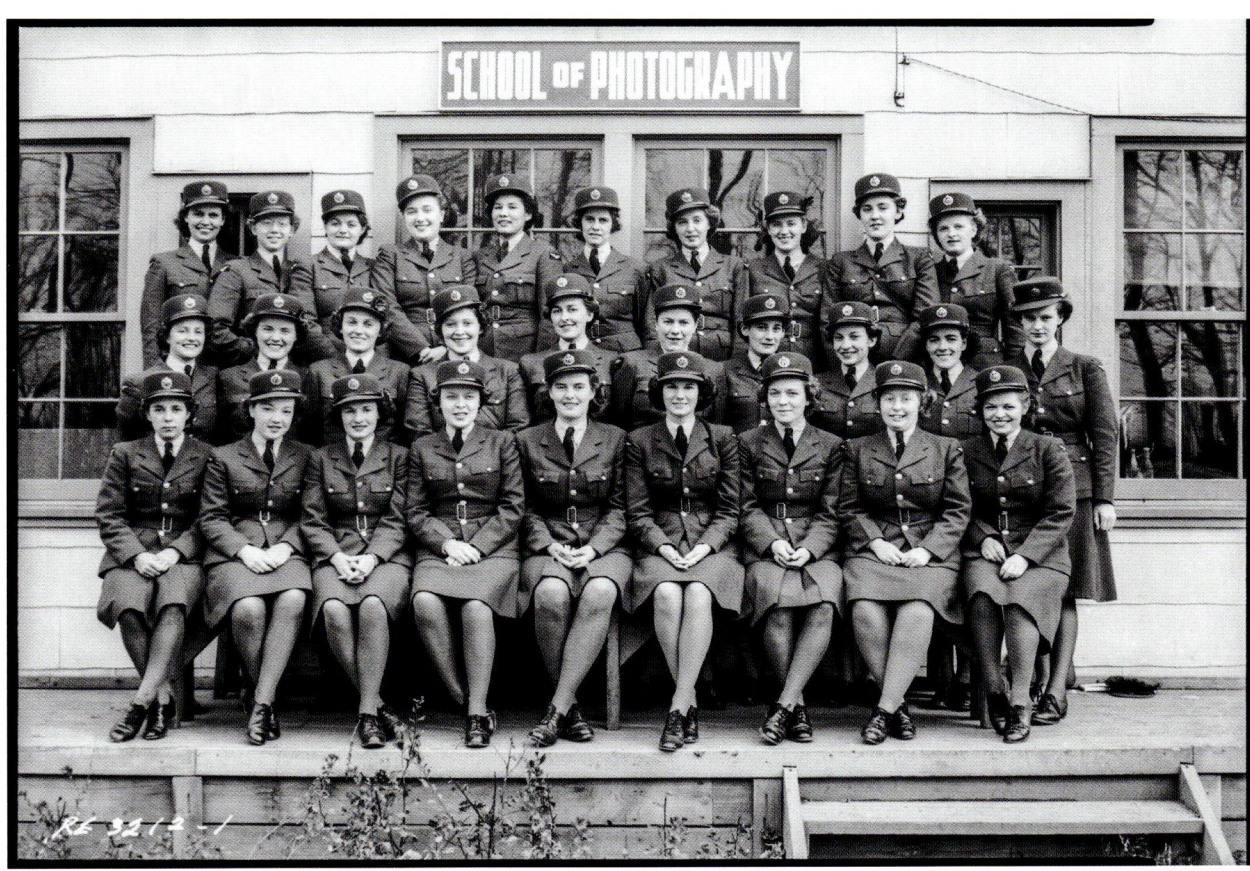

for clams as a child with her family and what it taught her. "Never sit while your sister is digging," LaBillois's mother told her. "You help her dig. You help her carry it to shore."[7]

LaBillois couldn't make the river run like it used to, but she could help Ugpi'ganjig move forward.

During her two terms as Chief, the nation reclaimed lands blanketed in ash trees and began reconnecting with their traditions. Following her tenure, LaBillois's lifework became the reviving and strengthening of Mi'kmaq language and customs. "Our language is such a vital part of our lives," she said. "It is who we are."[8] In recognition of her work as a cultural preservationist, LaBillois was the recipient of the Order of Canada in 1995 and the Order of New Brunswick in 2005. These distinguished awards were given to her by current iterations of the same federal and provincial governments that punished her for speaking Mi'kmaq in residential school.

LaBillois lived to be 89 years old.

"She was a mother to all,"[9] said Beckie and her sister Colleen Gauvin, about the sense of belonging and Mi'kmaq identity their mother nurtured in Ugpi'ganjig.

Three years before LaBillois's death, the gates of the Eel River Dam were released. A year later, the dam was removed completely. The waters of the river, flowing once again, were greeted with a traditional Mi'kmaq song.

—Sarah Stacke

"Group Photo-Class 29" picturing Margaret Pictou LaBillois, RCAF Rockliffe, Ottawa, Ontario, c. 1942.
CANADA. DEPT. OF NATIONAL DEFENCE/LIBRARY AND ARCHIVES CANADA. PA-065807

TSU-XOOG-EESH / WILLIAM LACKEY PAUL JR.

Tlingit
Southeast Alaska
United States

G rowing up with generations of legal justice leaders and having a profound sense of place in southeast Alaska informed how William Lackey Paul Jr. (1911–1974) made photographs about the world surrounding him. As the son of William Lewis Paul, the first Native attorney in Alaska, he understood the value of gathering evidence in multiple forms. His mother, Frances Lackey Paul, was a schoolteacher, community leader, dedicated documenter of southeast Alaskan culture, and an artist who "drew hundreds of pictures of Tlingit artwork in a portrait style."[1] From her, Paul drew his artistic eye, along with many lessons about the importance of serving the community. To promote Indigenous rights, he became a lawyer, just like his father and his younger brother Fred. Yet photography remained central to his identity and his expression of so many stories—of individuals, critical moments, systemic injustices, and the beauty of the Pacific Northwest and Alaska regions.

Paul integrated his legal mind with a deep wish to build awareness and empathy through photography. He accompanied his mother to document her community work with the "Spruce Root Basketry of the Tlingit" and "The Home Care of TB," projects funded by the Bureau of Indian Affairs. In the 1940s, he served six terms as secretary to the Alaska Native Brotherhood. As an attorney, he amplified justice efforts for Native populations through tangible legal advocacy. At the same time, throughout this role, he took his camera to every village he visited to make images of the people residing on the land he so loved. His son, Ben Paul (Teehiton, Raven Clan), remembered his father as living his commitment to civil rights, with vivid imprints of him "always with his camera" as he ventured into the world with a constant eye to visual documentation.

Paul built a collection of 5,000 negatives and prints—an archive that holds some of the most expansive existing records of incidents impacting Indigenous communities throughout southeast Alaska in the mid-20th century. He was committed to issues of land rights, labor, and environmental concerns surrounding fisheries, canneries, and education. In his era, Paul became one of the leading voices in the movement to protect workers, as well as the water environments affected by exploitative large-scale industrial practices in Alaska.

These five photographs reflect central tenets of Paul's life. In the first, a young "Bill Paul" holds the oar, with his brother Fred to his left, while his younger brother Robert, or "Bob," and sister Frances occupy the stern. Paul's mother or father made this image in the Ketchikan area, where Paul attended high school. Nature was right outside his doorstep throughout these formative years. Ben Paul felt certain that in his father's era, "It was a wonderful place for two teenage boys to grow up." The negative was made from medium-format 120 film (most likely with a Kodak Brownie camera), which was used for approximately 200 negatives in the family collection.

The second photograph features brother Fred in Bristol Bay in 1939. Paul made this 35mm image during a summer that symbolized his early adulthood and dedication to his studies. Both brothers fished in Bristol Bay at least three seasons in the year, to earn enough money to pay for law school at the University of Washington. In this portrait, the cigarette, hat, and head tilt work together to express personality and a distinct posture. The image conveys an ease of proximity, as Paul drew from his own family to make intimate photographs and develop his practice.

A love of water is repeated in the third photograph, which reveals a boyhood fascination with boats, alongside echoes of labor, responsibility, and industry. The layers depict the diversity

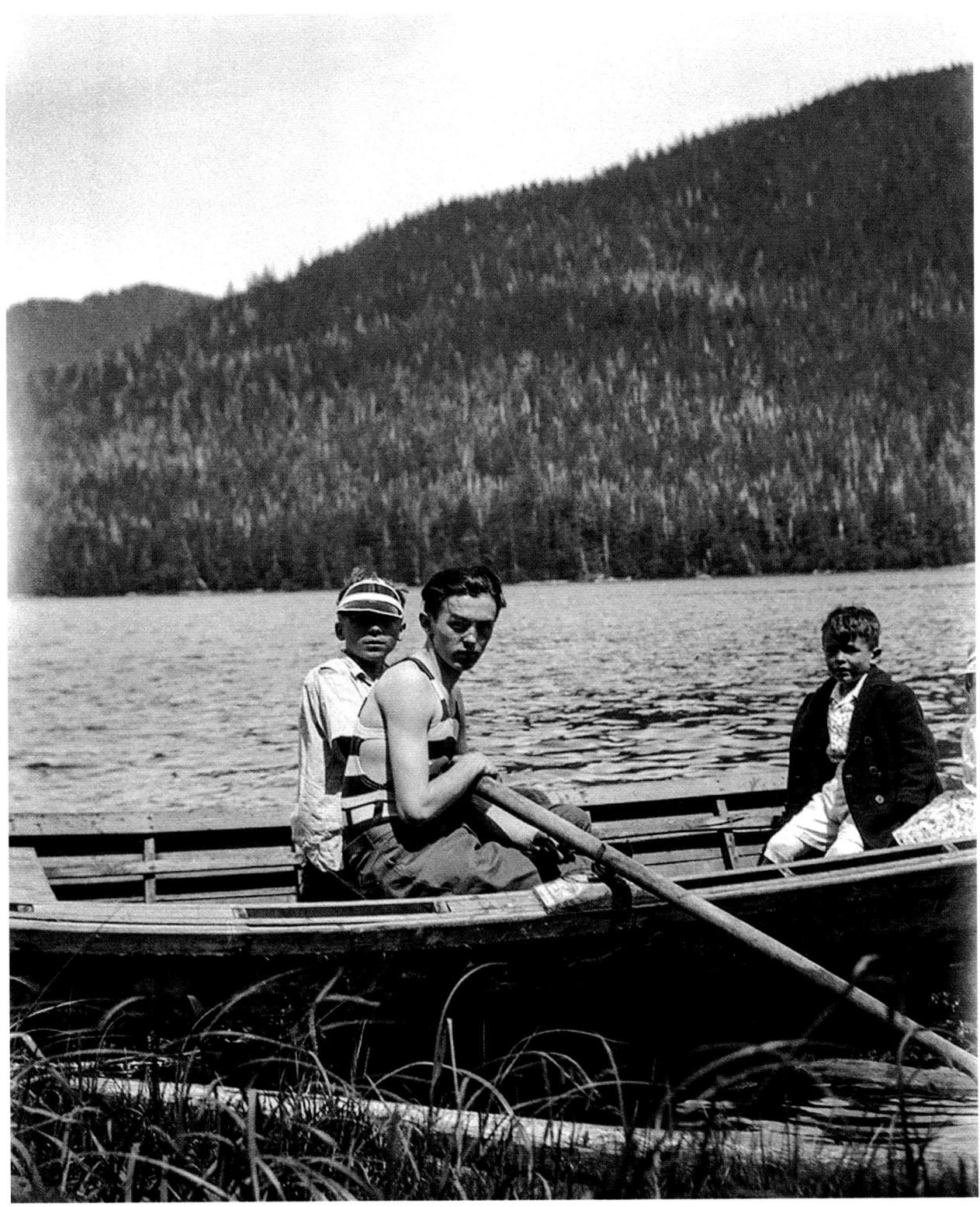

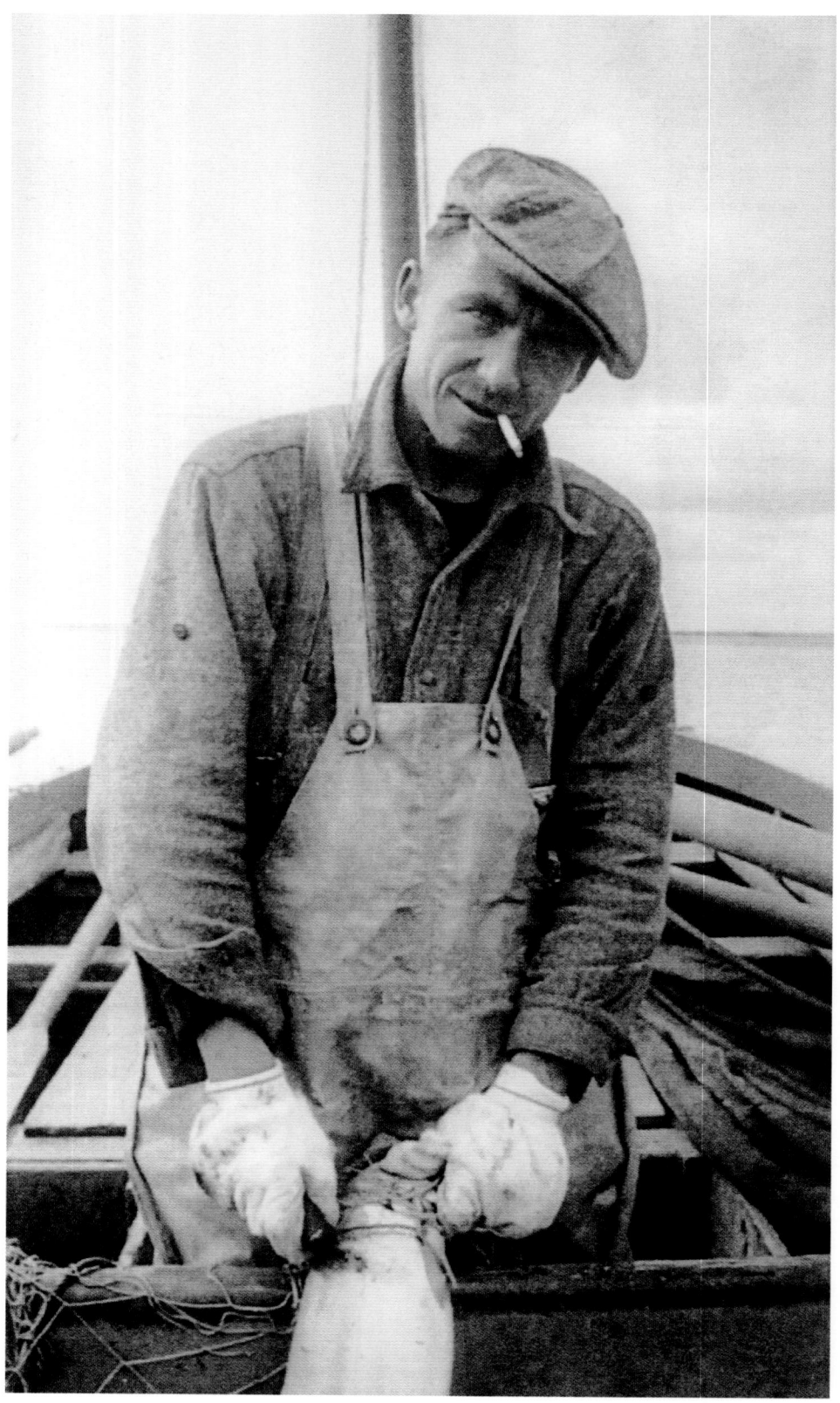

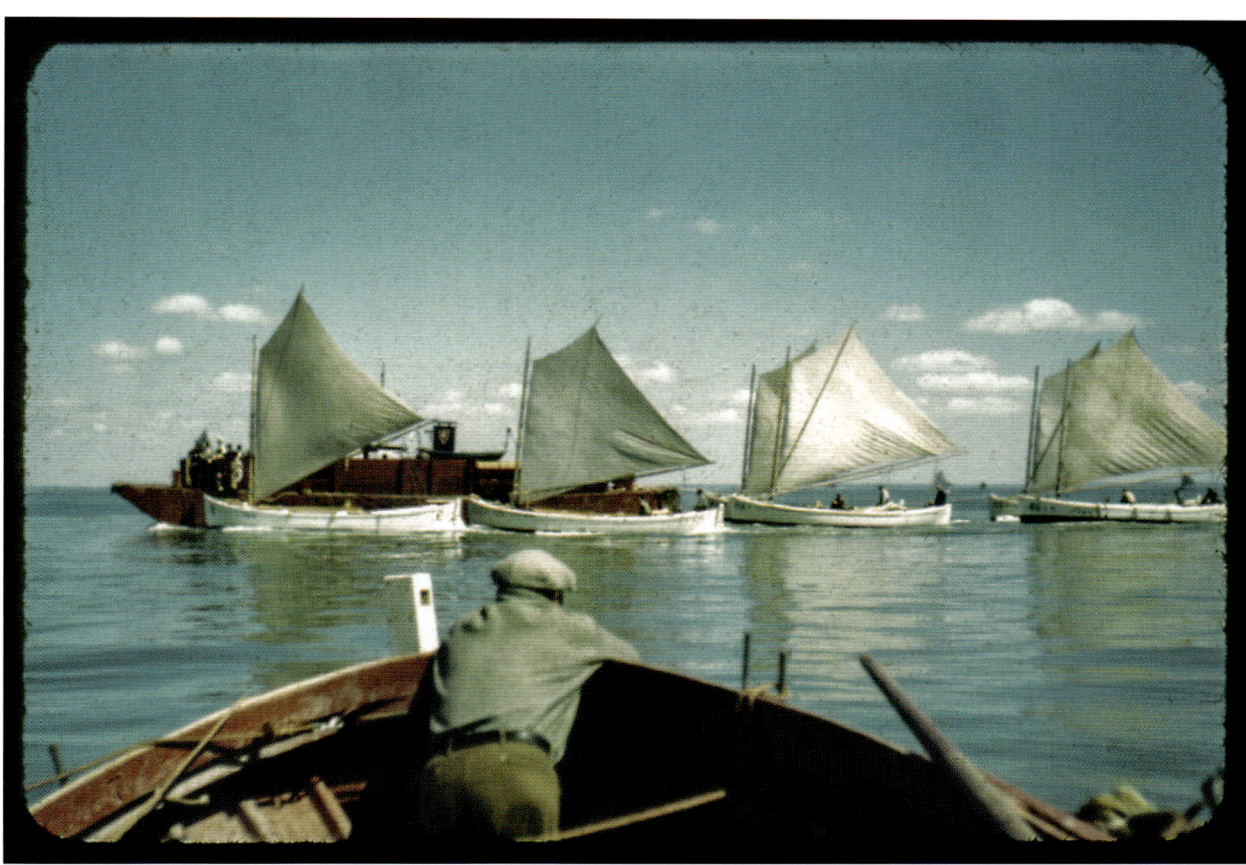

of water travel for leisure, transit, and trade. Kodachrome was just emerging when this photo was made around 1941, and Paul "explored color for the first time." The consistent palette of blue hues in striking contrast to the earth shades of warm wooden structures is arranged like a painting. Paul's own position on the boat provides a vantage point that allows a rich interplay between composition and color. He created about 100 images of Bristol Bay at this stage of his life.

The fourth and fifth photos tell a pivotal story of Paul's devotion to documenting community lives, with vivid reference to suffering and survival. Both were made in Xunaa (Hoonah), Alaska, where a 1944 fire devastated this Tlingit village. Paul traveled there from his home, at the time Juneau, to photograph the destruction in an effort to build awareness for support and recovery needs. With the acquisition of a Graflex camera, he made about 30 negatives in a 3.5" × 4.5" format. In the 1944 photograph, wreckage creates a textural sequence, with the remains of households in scattered display. The final image was made in 1946, when Paul returned to Xunaa to photograph the

rebuilding of the village. As a symbol of promise, schoolteacher E. B. Fisher stands on the roof of the new church, strategically positioned under the cross. In the background, a bright geometric pattern of newly built homes emerges on the same soil that held the immediate aftermath of the fire. Paul made notecards of this photograph for his correspondence. He wanted an image of hope and justice—conveyed in the boldness of a symbolic smiling figure atop a village—to exemplify his photography, both in style and underlying commitments. These final two photographs encapsulate Paul's unwavering dedication to visual evidence as a tool to advocate for rights and to expand the reach of artistic appreciation in his beloved community.

—Jennifer Natalie Fish

Bristol Bay, Alaska, c. 1941.

Opposite: Louis Frederick Paul, "Fred," Bristol Bay, Alaska, 1939.

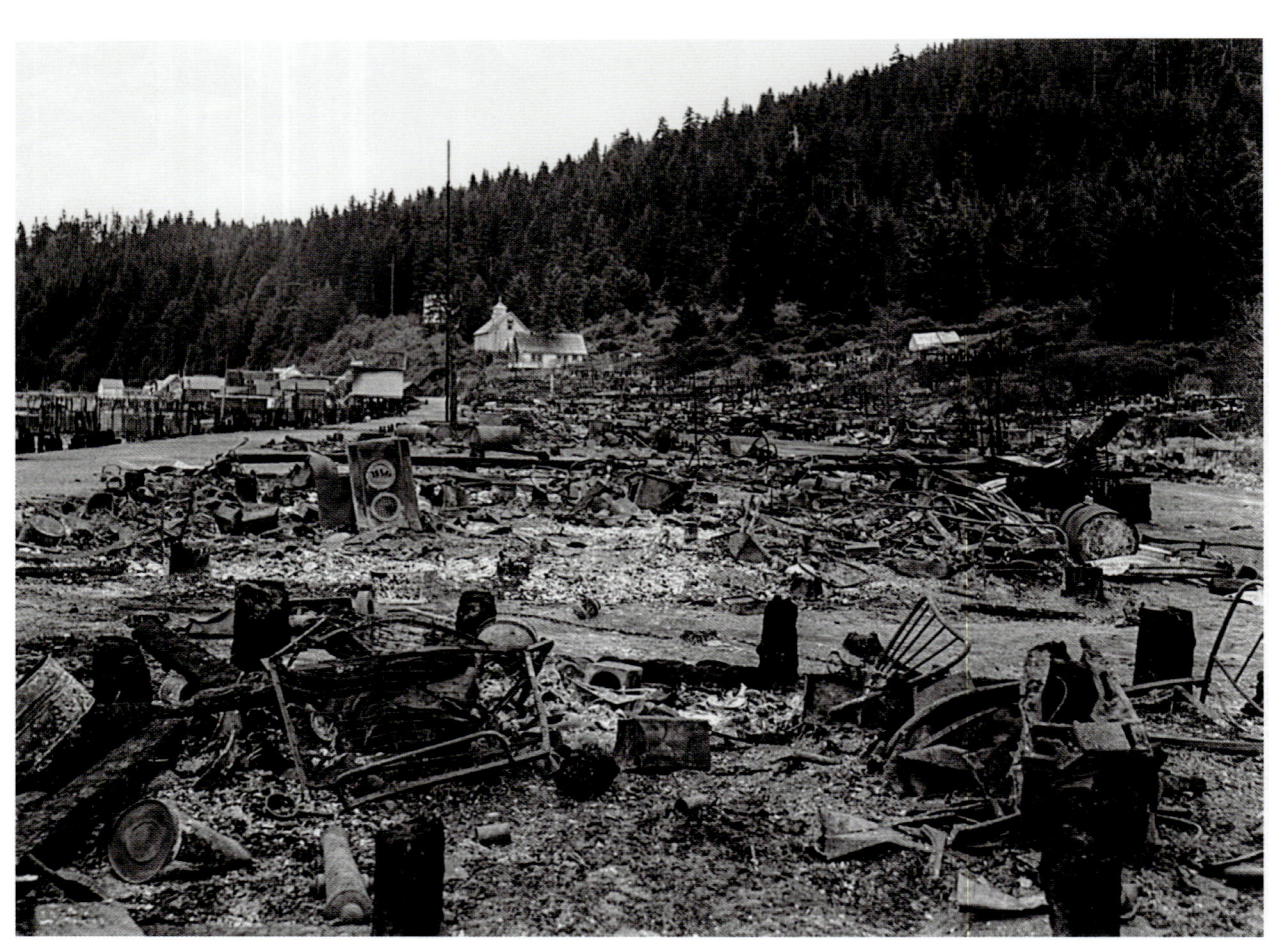

Xunaa (Hoonah), Alaska, after a fire devastated the community, 1944.

Opposite: Schoolteacher E. B. Fisher atop a newly constructed church, Xunaa (Hoonah), Alaska, 1946. The Tlingit community was rebuilt after a fire destroyed it two years earlier.

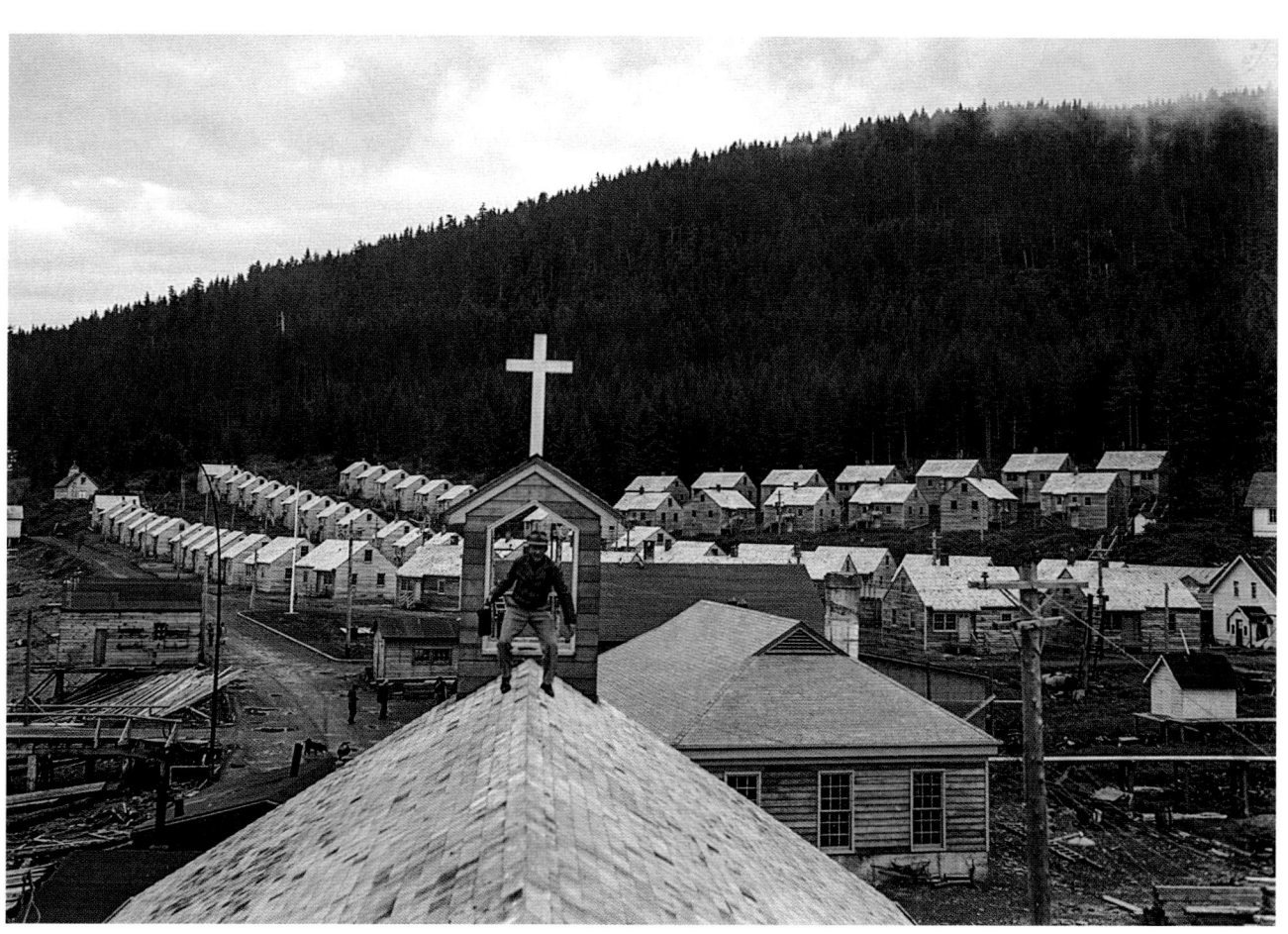

ROBERT HENRY KINGSBERY JR.

Chickasaw
Chickasaw Nation
Oklahoma
United States

Robert Kingsbery Jr. (1924–1982)—"Bob" to those who knew him—photographed the Chickasaw Annual Meeting and Festival between 1964 and 1967. The photographs, say Chickasaw artist and cultural historian Joshua Hinson, link the Chickasaw to their earliest ancestors in a precise way, through the decree to gather.

Long ago, describes Chickasaw lore, there came a time when the Chickasaw needed to move from the West. They assembled to pray for guidance from Aba' Binni'li', their Creator, and a vision was revealed to the hopayi', or prophets: brothers Chiksa' and Chahta were to lead the Chickasaw on a journey east. In the vision, Aba' Binni'li' declared to the hopayi' that the brothers would gain direction from Itti' Fabassa' Holitto'pa', a sacred pole. The pole was to be planted in the middle of camp each night. Whichever way the pole leaned the following morning, they were to resume their migration. When the pole stood straight, the people would know they had found their new Homeland.

And so, the journey began this way. Aba' Binni'li' sent Ofi' Tohbi' Ishto', a large white dog, to assist and protect them. Ofi' Tohbi' Ishto' traveled ahead, scouting for any potential threats—and healed the wounds of the injured. Eventually, the travelers encountered a mighty and ancient river. Today, this river is known as the Mississippi. They hurriedly set about constructing rafts to ferry themselves and their supplies across it. Once the crossing was over, Ofi' Tohbi' Ishto' was never seen again but would forever remain part of the story. The brothers, Chiksa' and Chahta, planted Itti' Fabassa' Holitto'pa' on the eastern bank of the river, and the people rested. In the morning, they awoke to a strange sight. Itti' Fabassa' Holitto'pa' was spinning in the ground, moving in all directions. Chahta believed the pole was straight, signaling they had reached their new home. Chiksa' believed the pole continued to lean toward the rising sun. Again, the people gathered and deliberated before reaching a decision. Those who stayed with Chahta were to be called Choctaws, and those who followed Chiksa' farther east would be known as Chickasaws.[1]

Chickasaw communities operated with large amounts of autonomy in the centuries that followed. In the 1830s, the Tribe was forcibly removed by the U.S. government from their historic Homeland in present-day northern Mississippi, northwestern Alabama, western Tennessee, and southwestern Kentucky, and pushed to present-day Oklahoma.

When Oklahoma became a state in the early 1900s, the United States severely restricted the Chickasaw Tribal government. Going forward, governors would be appointed to the Tribe by the U.S. president. After five long decades under federally appointed governors, the movement to reinstate Tribal elections gained momentum. On a fall evening in 1960, a group of more than 100 Chickasaw came together at Seeley Chapel and reconstituted the Chickasaw Tribal Council. That same night, the Tribe elected Overton James as president of the newly reformed council.[2]

Two key players in the re-formation of the Tribal council were Rev. Jesse Humes and Bob Kingsbery—photographer, politically engaged community member, and James's good friend. One of their inaugural acts was to call for a gathering every October: the Chickasaw Annual Meeting and Festival.

The Chickasaw Tribal Council, along with its supporters, worked to appoint James as governor of the Chickasaw Nation. Succeeding in 1963, James was sworn in at Seeley Chapel rather than in Washington, D.C. Shortly after the ceremony, he named Kingsbery to his advisory council, an appointment that required him to attend the Chickasaw Annual Meeting and Festival. This dovetailed with Kingsbery's enthusiasm for photography, and he produced roughly 200 photographs of the meetings and festivals on Ektachrome color film.

Kingsbery photographed from standing height (likely looking down at the viewfinder of a twin-lens reflex camera held at waist level), centered the scene in the frame, adeptly checked the exposure, and released the shutter. The collection shows Kingsbery to be present and engaged with all aspects of the event. His deceptively casual images create a rich visual documentation of the Chickasaw Annual Meeting and Festival that contains key political, cultural, and social elements.

The initial gatherings were a direct outcome of the revival of self-government and the intent to preserve it—and therefore decidedly political. "Tribal members are meeting not only as people of common blood and common culture, but also as a political body," writes Hinson in his 2008 article "Chi Ka Sha Althliha Ha Pomi Ittafaamitok: 'Our Chickasaw People Have Always Gathered Together:' Robert Kingsbery's Annual Meeting Photographs 1964–1966."[3] Kingsbery's images depict political figures such as Reverend Humes, Governor James, and Phillip Martin, who would be elected as Chief of the Mississippi Band of Choctaw Indians in 1979 and hold the title until 2007.

Other photographs more fully illuminate the cultural and social aspects of the event, like Marie Gibson stirring enormous pots of steaming pashofa, a traditional dish made with hominy and pork that Chickasaw people have served at ceremonial and cultural events for centuries. A symbol of Chickasaw identity, the dish is a bridge across time. Similarly, the multiple generations of

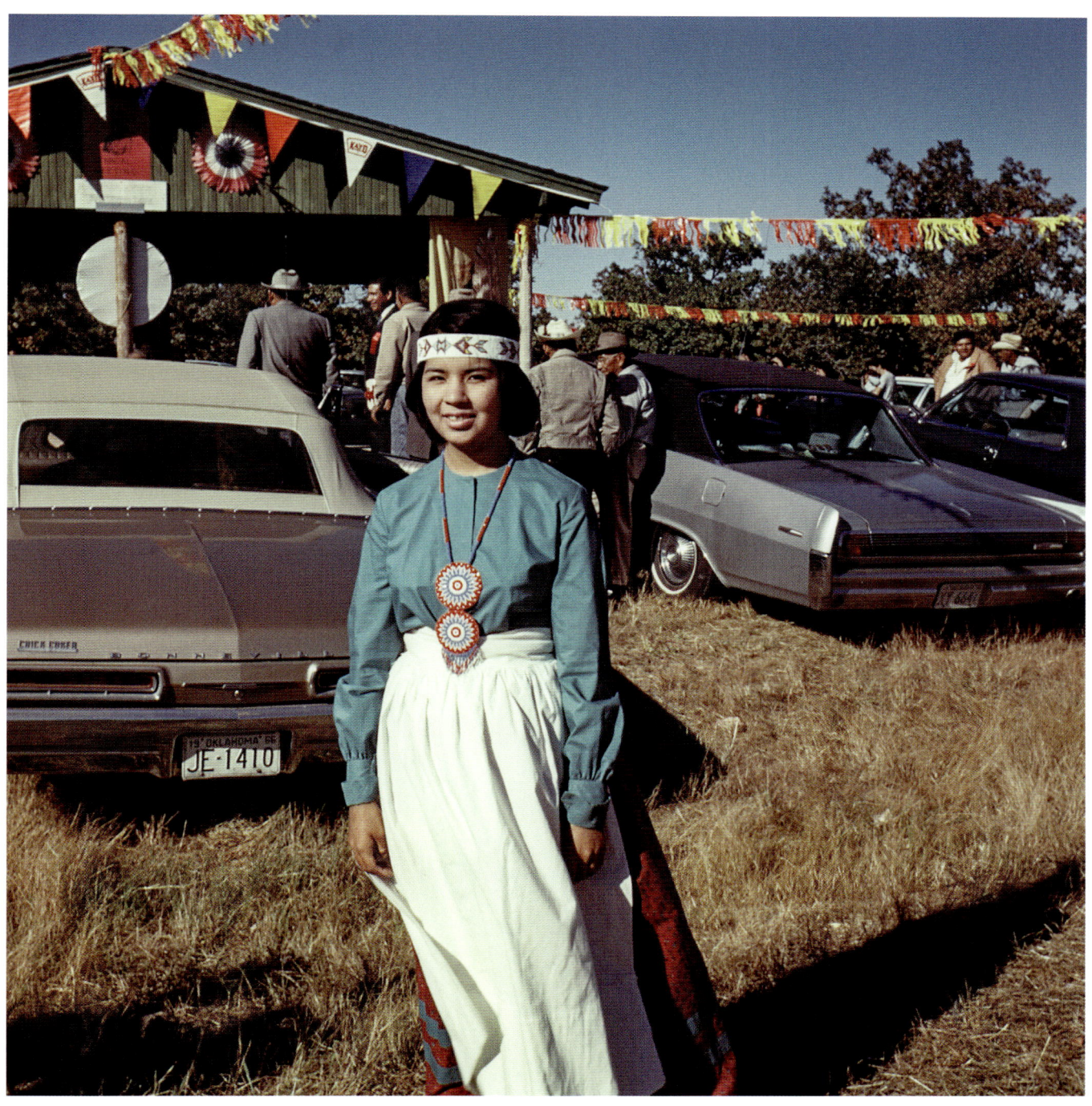

Shirley Ned wearing regalia at the 7th Chickasaw Annual Meeting, Kullihoma, Oklahoma, October 15, 1966.

PHOTOGRAPHS BY ROBERT KINGSBERY JR. COURTESY OF THE CHICKASAW NATION COLLECTION, DOCUMENTARY IMAGES OF THE CHICKASAW ANNUAL MEETINGS, 1964–67. COLLECTION NUMBER 2018.044

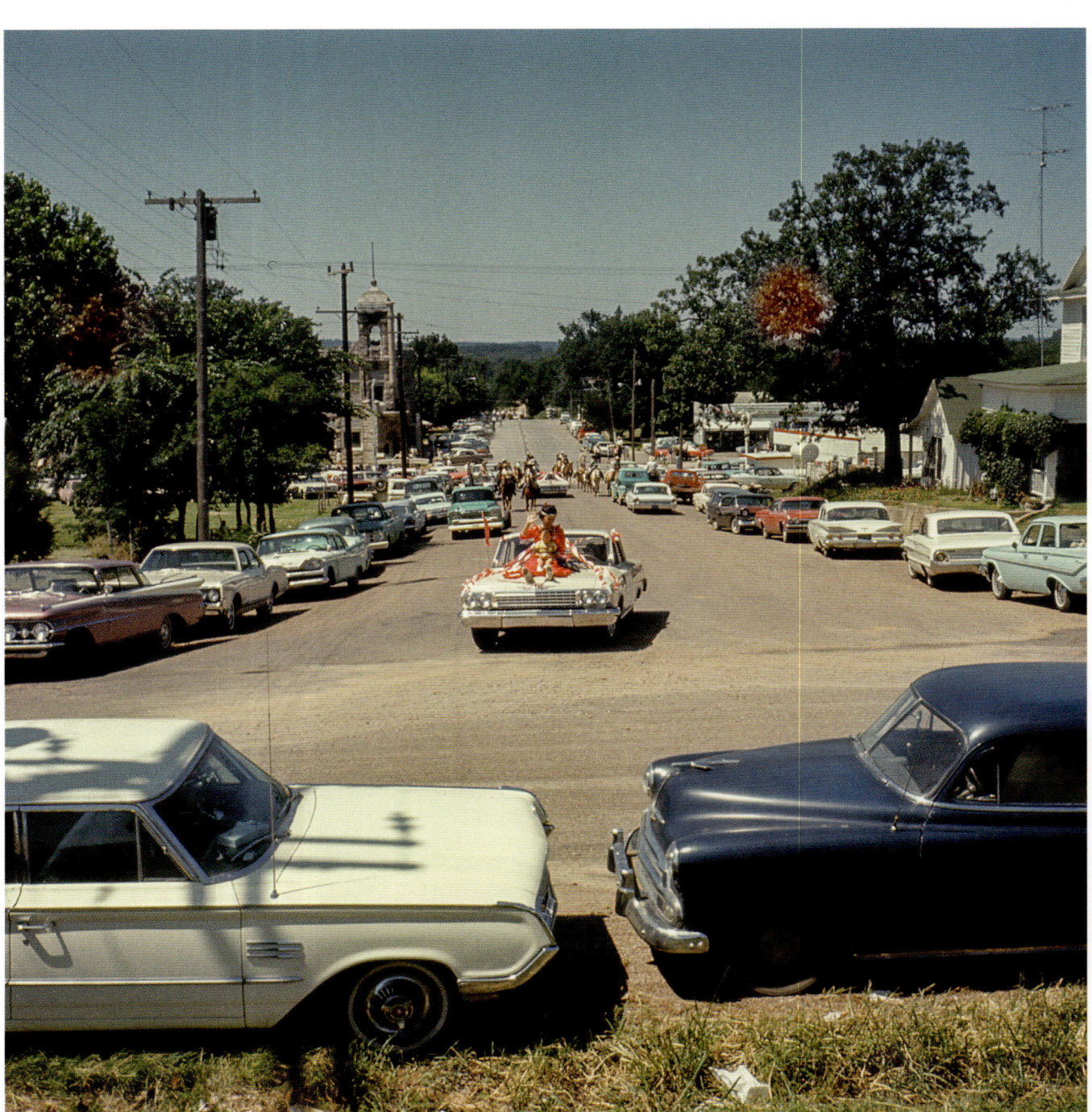

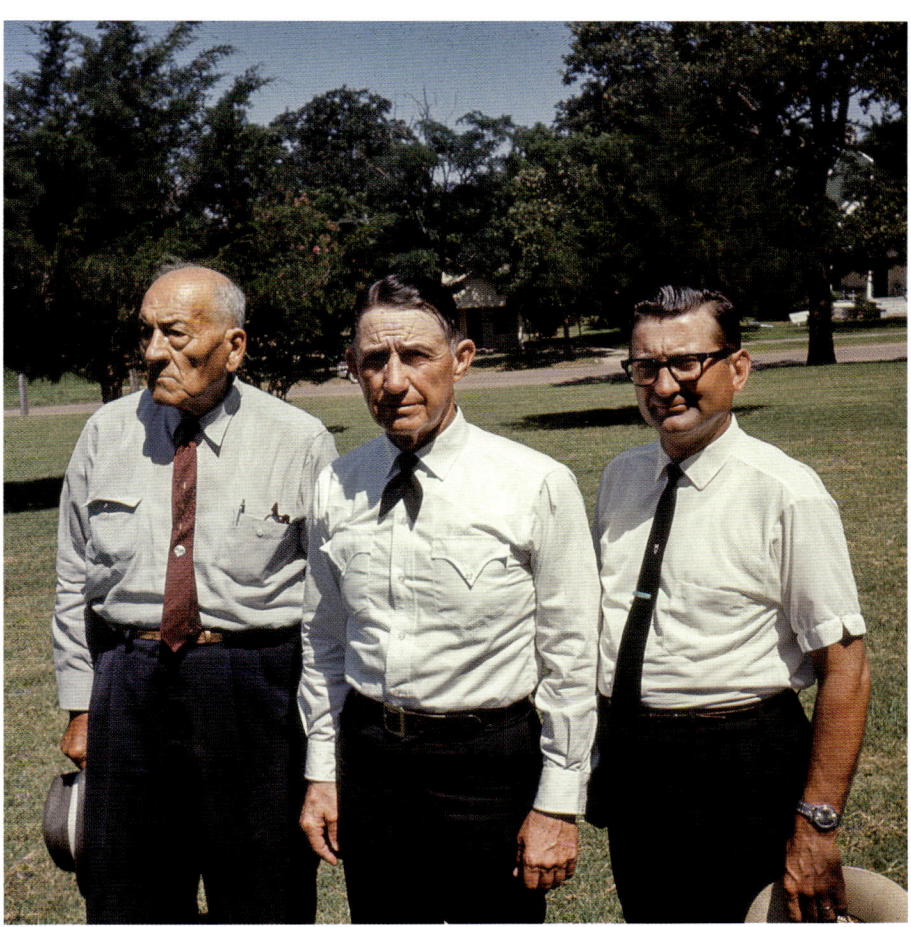

Chickasaw people in many of Kingsbery's photographs connect the past to the present—and the future. The image of Bill and Oleta Burris picnicking at the 1964 meeting with their daughters Kuhlaya and Malacha visually anchors matters of family, heritage, and belonging. The Burrises are seated in a comfortable semicircle at the back of their station wagon. The tailgate is down and plates of pashofa and glass bottles of soda are spread across it. The family pauses and looks at Kingsbery, each with a grin and a splash of sunlight on their face. In the background, kids sit in the bed of a blue Chevrolet truck, and other attendees stand on the grass in conversation.

Kingsbery's work visualizes the Chickasaw edict to gather, set forth by the ancestors and carried into today. This is the foundation of his photographs. Their heart is the fruit of centuries of Chickasaw gatherings with purpose—a respect for consensus, a commitment to fellowship, and a will to sustain Chickasaw lifeways.

—Sarah Stacke

Rev. Jesse Humes, F. L. Lewis, and Virgil Harrington at the Chickasaw Festival, Tishomingo, Oklahoma, July 3, 1965.

Opposite: View of the parade at the Chickasaw Festival, Tishomingo, Oklahoma, July 3, 1965.

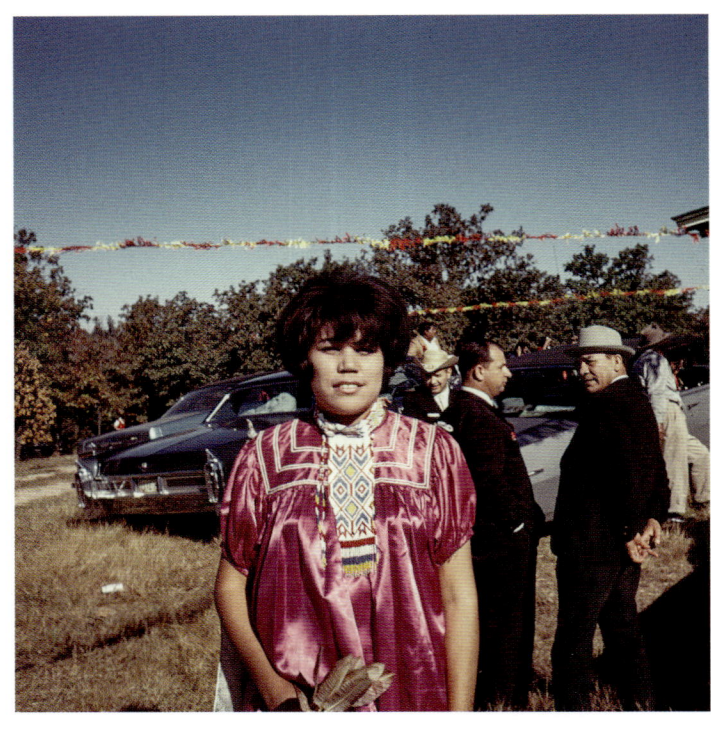

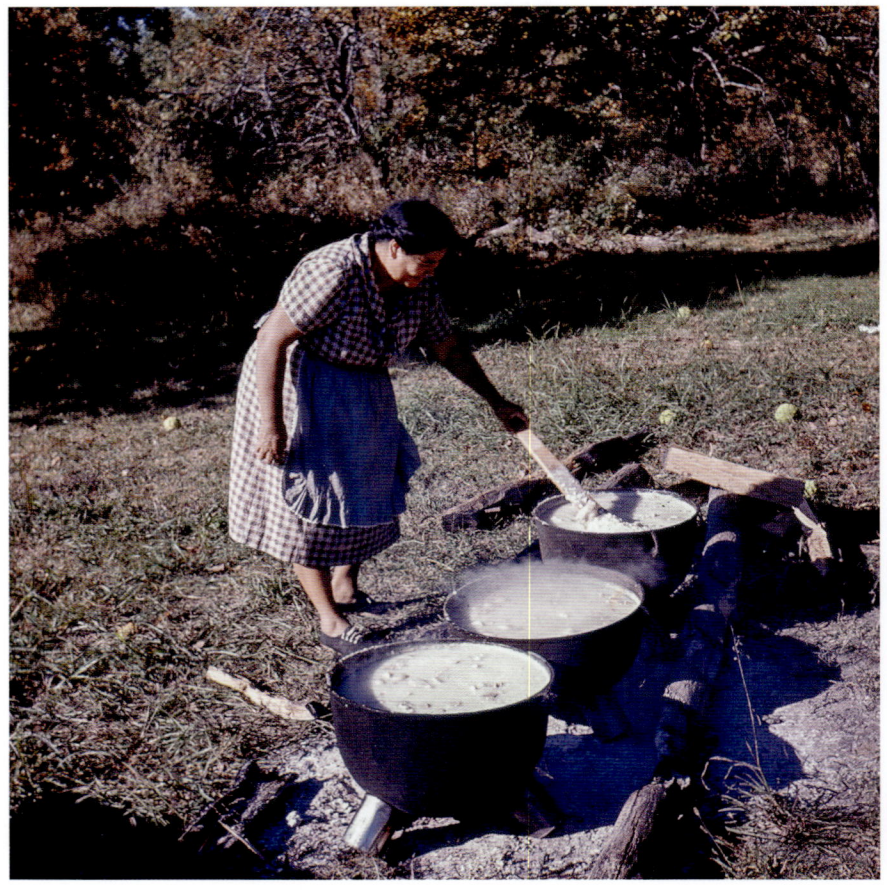

Mary Nell Poe wearing regalia at the 7th Chickasaw Annual Meeting, Kullihoma, Oklahoma, October 15, 1966.

Marie Gibson cooking pashofa for the 5th Chickasaw Annual Meeting, Seeley Chapel, Connerville, Oklahoma, October 17, 1964.

Opposite: Bill and Oleta Burris with daughters Kuhlaya and Malacha, eating pashofa and enjoying a community meal at the 5th Chickasaw Annual Meeting, Seeley Chapel, Connerville, Oklahoma, October 17, 1964.

Opposite: George Ann Robinson, an Osage citizen, at the 7th Chickasaw Annual Meeting, Kullihoma, Oklahoma, October 15, 1966.

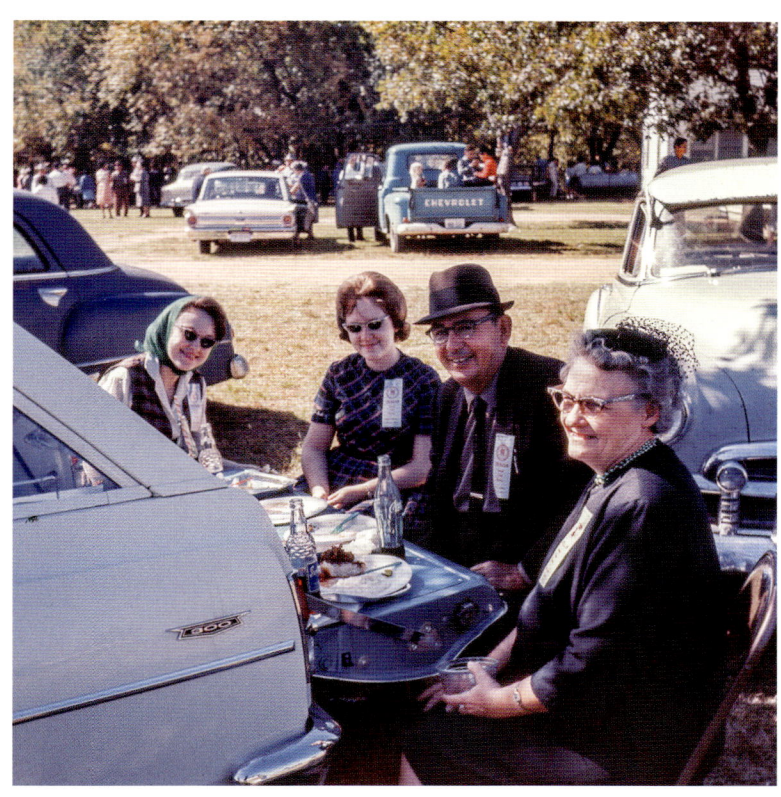

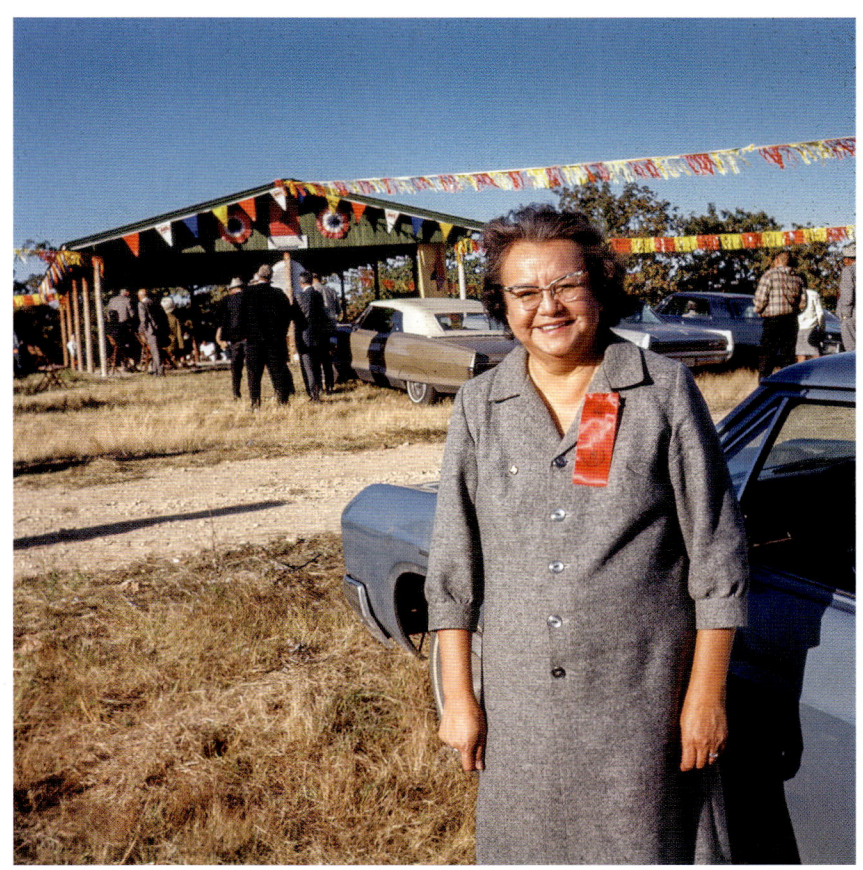

LELAND HOWARD MARMON

Laguna Pueblo
Pueblo of Laguna Nation
Laguna, New Mexico
United States

Laguna Pueblo photographer Lee Marmon (1925–2021) exposed over 100,000 frames in his lifetime. A veteran of World War II, he returned home to Laguna, New Mexico, resolved "to record the beauty of the elders and the beauty of the land lest they be forgotten," said his daughter, author Leslie Marmon Silko, in her book *Storyteller*. She described a tall Hopi basket with hundreds of photographs from the 1890s forward, made and collected by her grandfather and father. "Photographs have always had special significance with the people of my family and the people at Laguna," wrote Silko.[1]

From the late 1940s to the 1960s, Marmon focused his Speed Graphic, Rolleiflex, and Hasselblad cameras on "old timers sitting out in the sun,"[2] ceremonial and everyday activities of the Laguna and Acoma Pueblos, and the spectacular clouds and high desert plateaus of his Homeland. This body of work is Marmon's most well-known, but in his lifetime he created a wide-ranging oeuvre, including series on American Indian colleges, uranium mines and mills, prominent Native American artists, and Native American communities across the United States. In the 1950s, he documented student life at Grants High School, his alma mater. Into the 1960s, he created a healthy library of wedding photography.

From 1966 to 1982, Marmon lived in Palm Springs, California, where he was the principal photographer for the Bob Hope Desert Classic, a golf tournament that attracted celebrities, models, dignitaries, and executives. He completed assignments for *Time* magazine, the *New York Times*, the *Los Angeles Times*, and the *Saturday Evening Post*. Columbia Pictures hired Marmom as a still photographer, and he was commissioned by President Nixon and First Lady Pat Nixon to photograph a collection of New Mexican Pueblo pottery.

Compelled to return to Laguna in the early 1980s, Marmon continued making photographs and lived in the old Santa Fe railroad station on Route 66, a gift from his grandfather that was converted into a home. "His beloved Marmon family land southwest of Laguna at Dripping Springs was a frequent theme in his photographs and stories," reported *American Indian*.[3]

"I love landscape photography," said Marmon, who drove around the reservation in his old Model A truck with his dog and camera, looking for views. "I consider the genre one of the most difficult photographic endeavors. Scenic photographs I consider either good or bad. There is no in between."[4]

The Smithsonian's National Museum of the American Indian organized *Pueblo Portraits: 50 Years at Laguna Pueblo*, a solo exhibition of Marmon's work, in 1999. He published his first monograph, *The Pueblo Imagination: Landscape and Memory in the Photography of Lee Marmon*, with writings by his daughter Silko and poets Joy Harjo and Simon Ortiz in 2003. After he donated his personal papers and over 65,000 photographs to the Center for Southwest Research and Special Collections at the University of New Mexico, the university released *Laguna Pueblo: A Photographic History* in 2015. The volume highlights Marmon's skill as a storyteller by incorporating his anecdotes about how specific photographs came to be, the people and places pictured, and the Pueblo of Laguna Nation.

Arguably his most famous portrait, *White Man's Moccasins,* was made in 1954. It shows Elder Jeff Sousea, caretaker of the Laguna mission, leaning against an adobe wall. Sousea is wearing a traditional headband and beads and high-top basketball sneakers, challenging romanticized ideas about Native Americans. Likewise, in a 1961 photograph, Louise Lucas and Lupe Siow are seen kneading bread with their hair held back by headscarves. Looking closely, it's revealed the woman closer to Marmon has fashioned her scarf out of a terry cloth bath towel.

Described as free-spirited and independent, Marmon had a commitment to documenting the histories and traditions of the Laguna Pueblo through photography that has secured his place as a revered artist within Native American communities and far beyond. "I recorded…people working so hard to make a better place for their children and grandchildren to live," says Marmon. "Their faces should not fade from our memories."[5]

—Sarah Stacke

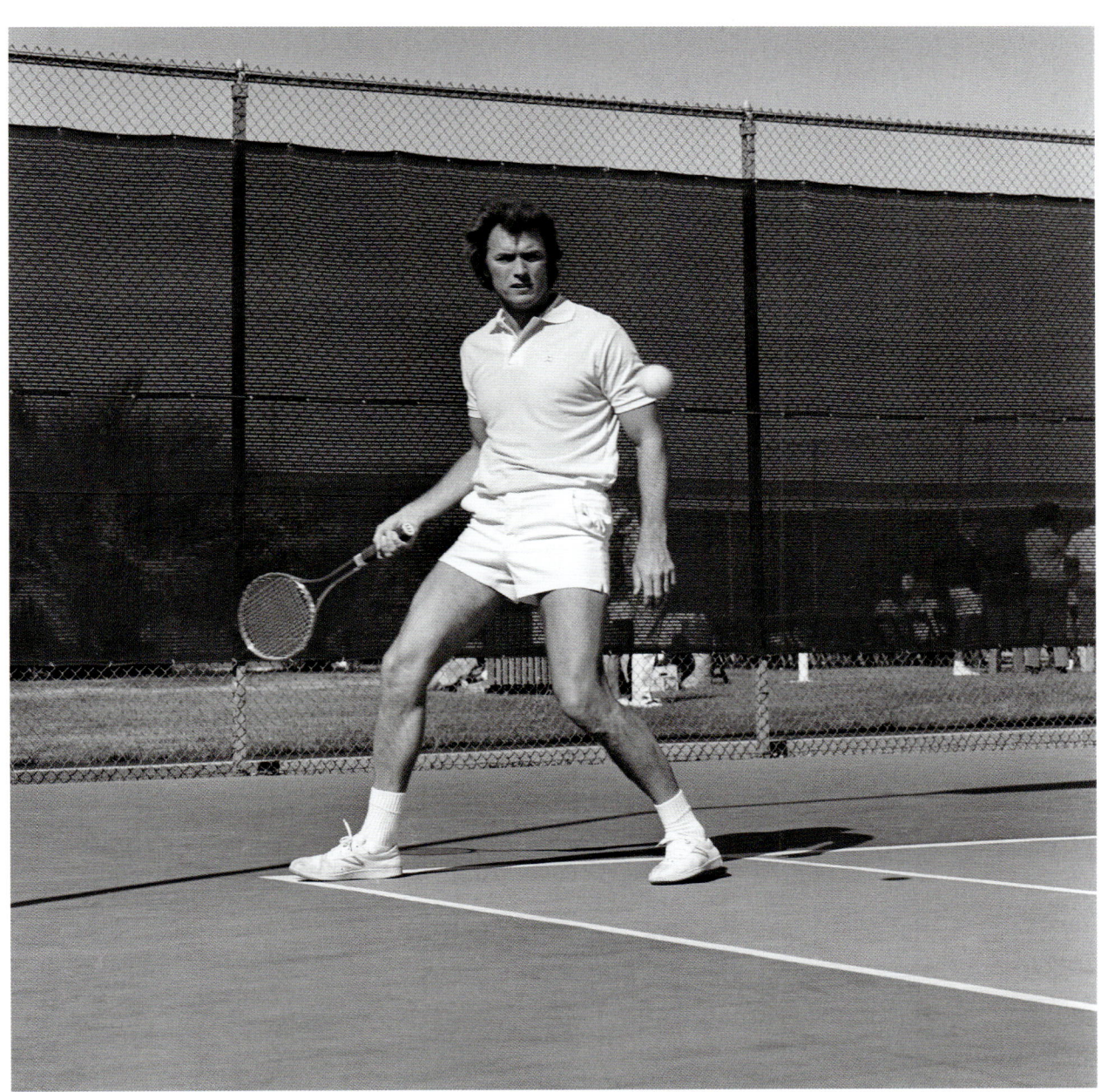

Clint Eastwood at a racquet club, Palm Springs, California,
c. 1960–70.

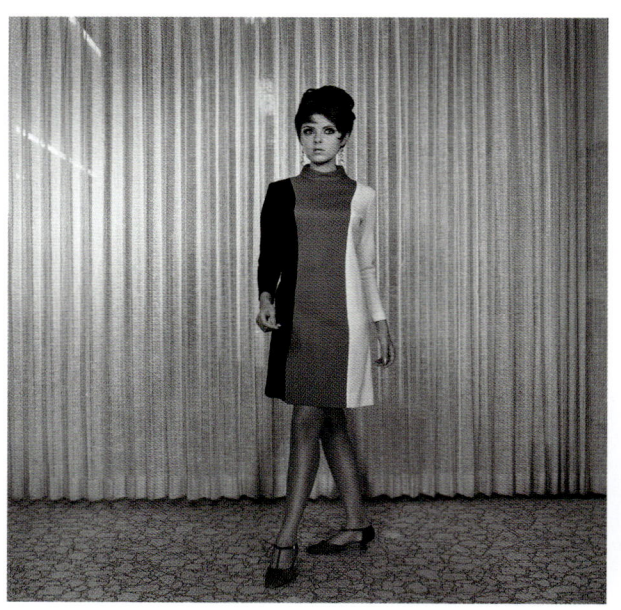 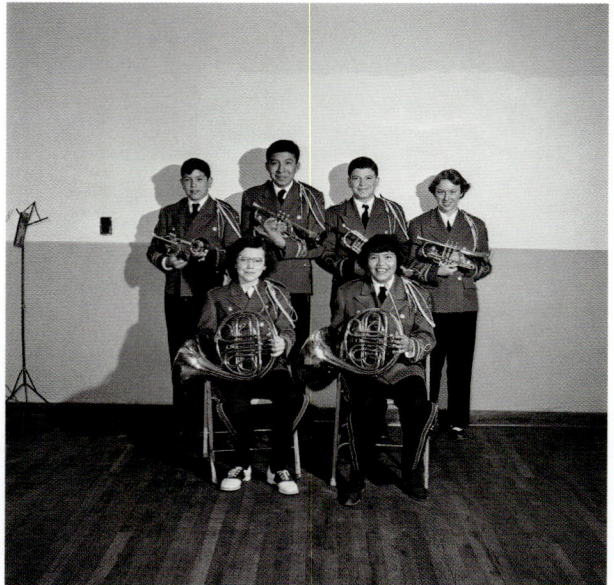

Gail Brown, Palm Springs, California, September 1967.

Grants High School, Grants, New Mexico, c. 1950.

Opposite: Grants High School, Grants, New Mexico, c. 1950.

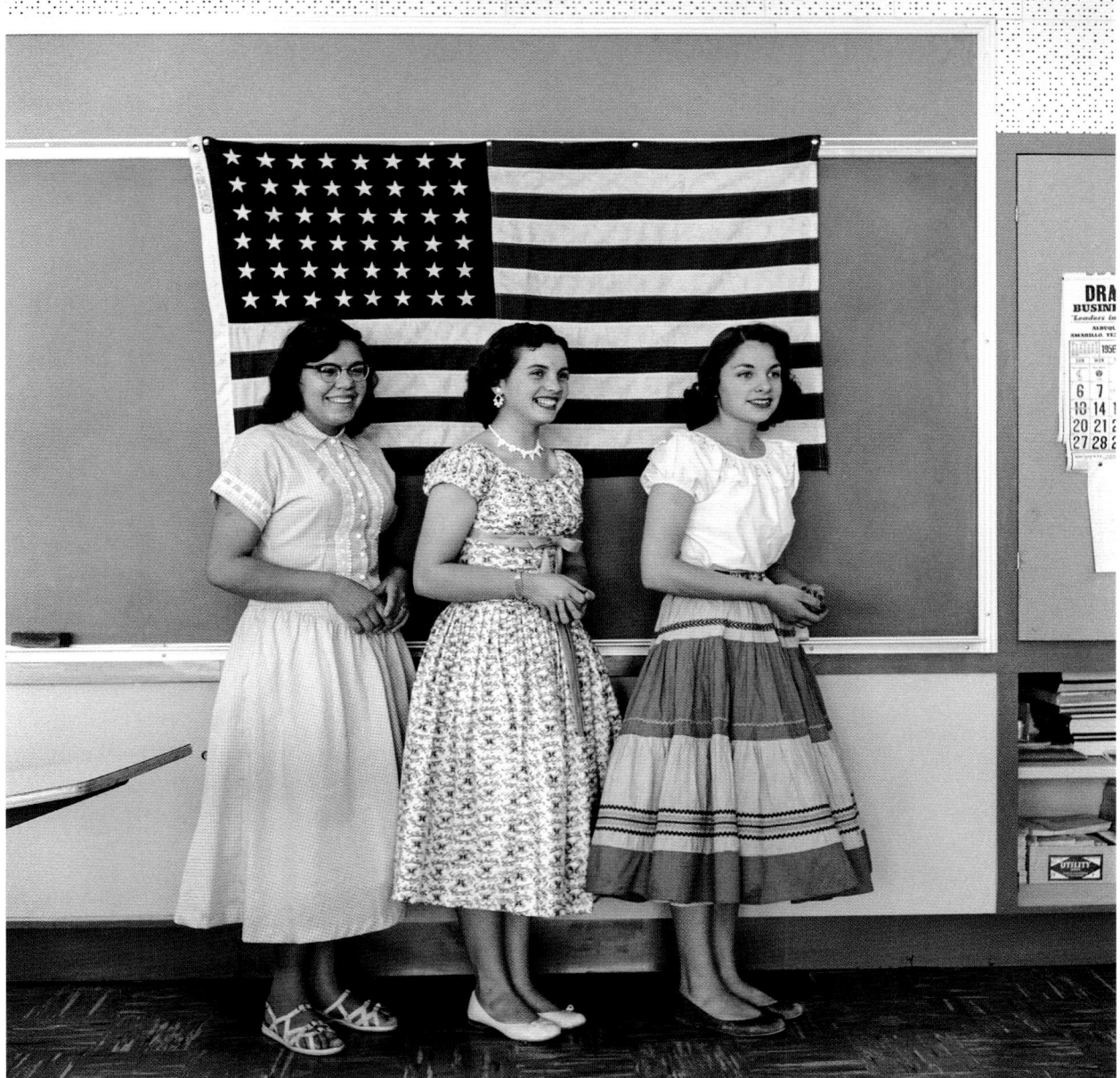

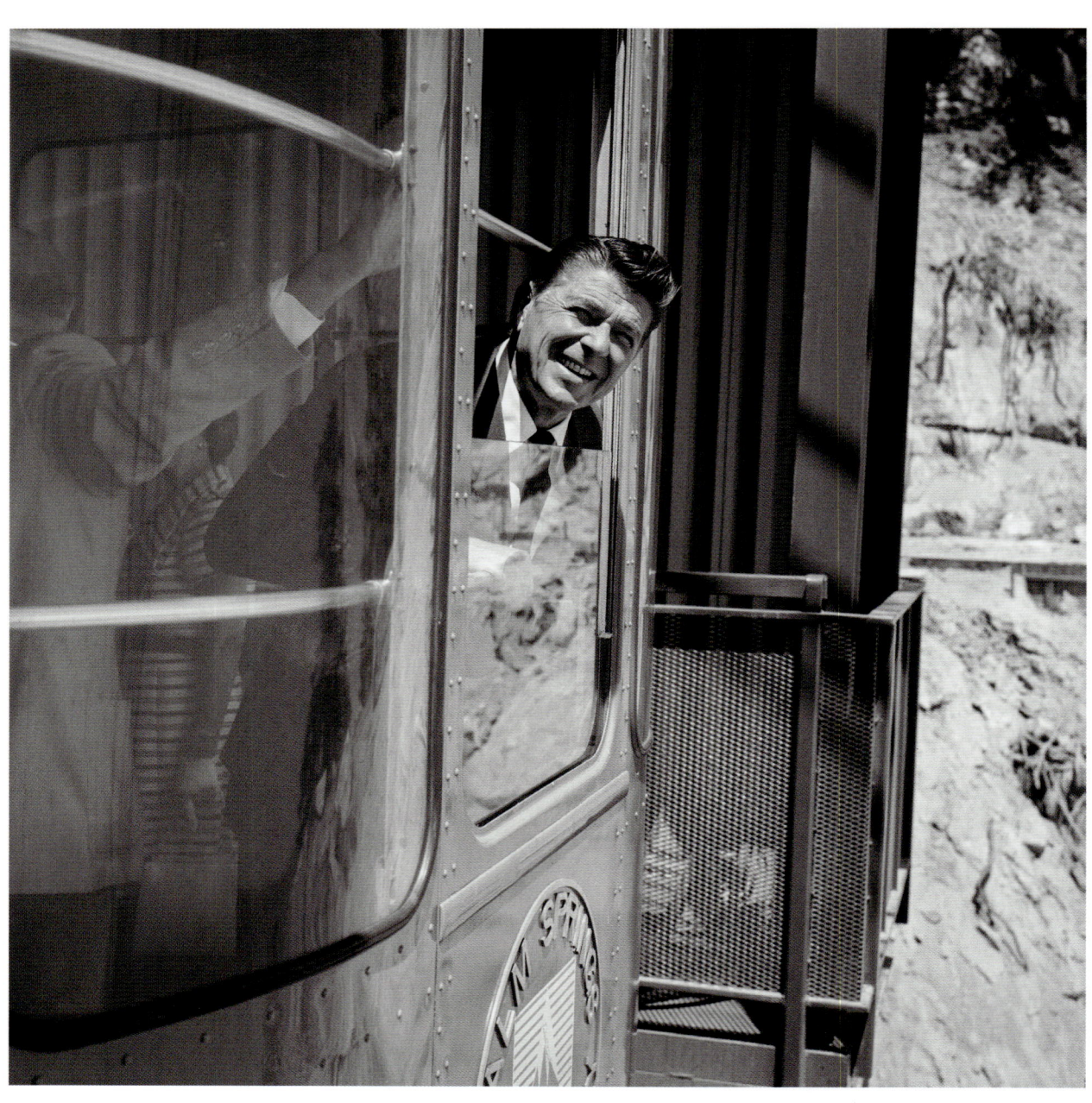

Ronald Reagan, Palm Springs, California,
September 23, 1969.

Opposite: Louise Lucas and Lupe Siow making bread,
Laguna Pueblo, New Mexico, January 1961.

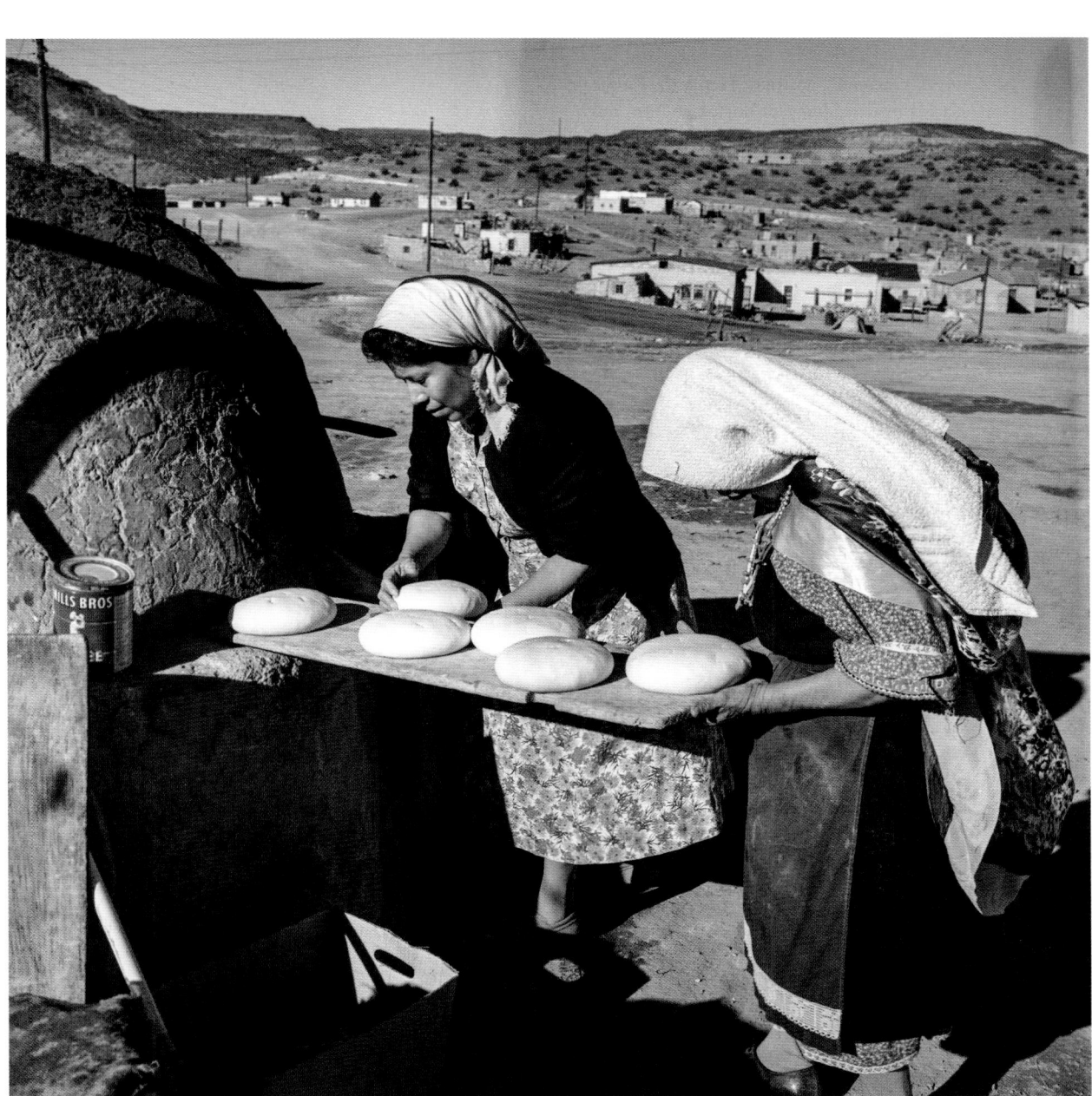

HENRY SAMUEL KAISER JR.

Athabascan
Nenana, Alaska
United States

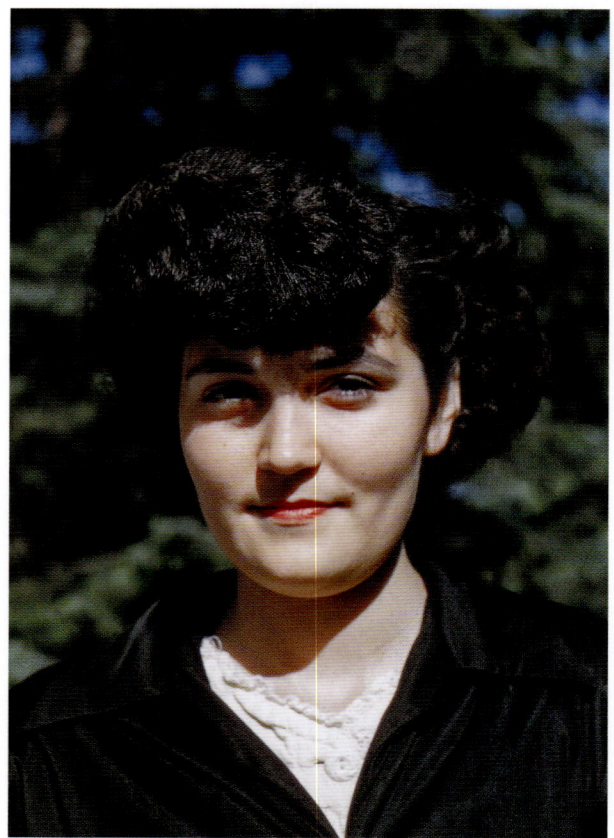

The colorful, cinematic portraits Henry S. Kaiser Jr. (1932–2011) made of buoyant doctors, nurses, teachers, and fellow patients at the Seward Sanatorium between 1950 and 1953 befit the young photographer's fervent outlook on life. Informally "the San," the 150-bed tuberculosis hospital where Kaiser rested his lungs and heart for three years was in Seward, a port city built on a pocket-size coastal plain berthed between Resurrection Bay and the foot of Mount Marathon, in southern Alaska.

When Kaiser left the San in 1953, at age 21, the doctor issued grim advice: "Stick pretty close to a rocking chair." No thank you, he said, and promptly returned north to the University of Alaska Fairbanks. Before graduating in 1960 with a degree in education, he typed an essay describing the health scares of his youth and the mindset that tendered "a world of faith in the future."[1]

Born in Fairbanks, Kaiser "was the prisoner of an undetermined heart defect," he writes, "another 'blue baby' destined to die." Kaiser, who later learned he was afflicted with a three-chambered heart, reasons he was "hanging onto life by an invisible thread."

He was raised in Nenana, a small riparian town at the confluence of the Nenana and Tanana Rivers, 55 highway miles southwest of Fairbanks, in Alaska's Interior region. For thousands of years, Nenana's townsite, situated on the traditional territory of the Tanana Athabascans, was a seasonal subsistence camp, and later a village called Toghotthele. Around 1900, European Americans began using the moniker Nenana for the settlement and the smaller river it flanked. The origins of the name are puzzling, but the term is likely derived from the Athabascan word *neenano'*, meaning "stopping-while-migrating-stream."[2] A more popular translation is "a good place to camp between rivers."[3]

The 1902 discovery of gold in Fairbanks brought fierce activity to the Interior. The following year, the head of Nenana's first non-Native family, James Duke, opened a roadhouse. A church and post office came after. In the spring of 1916, engineers of the forthcoming Alaska Railroad reached Nenana, with a stampede of workers behind them. The booming town was surveyed. Lots were auctioned and 354 sold on the first day, with 24 premium lots reserved for Duke.[4] In the fall, the laying of rails commenced, with the inaugural spike driven by none other than Duke's wife Emma.[5]

Kaiser's father, Henry Sr., who was white, arrived in 1921, the same year Nenana incorporated as a city. He and his wife, Susie Sarah Kaiser (née Smith), who was Norwegian and

Athabascan,[6] welcomed their first of four children in 1924. Their only son, Henry Jr., was ushered into the world on January 24, 1932. In February, "after a long illness," reports one Fairbanks newspaper, Mrs. Kaiser died.[7] She was buried, alongside her third daughter, at Nenana North Cemetery, in a gravesite embraced by a white picket fence. Originally established for Native folk, the bosky cemetery, where Spotted Lady's Slippers bloom profusely, rests on the slopes of Toghotthele Hill.

On New Year's Day 1949, when Kaiser was on the cusp of his 17th birthday, a fire threatened the business district of Nenana. His father, who had been elected mayor more than a decade earlier, confronted the blaze and died of a heart attack. With a smattering of c. 1920s photographs to his credit, it is perhaps Henry Sr. who passed an interest in photography to his son.

In Kaiser's college essay, he references his "parents" several times—possibly his father and a partner, conceivably the legacy of his own mother. What's clear is that Kaiser was encouraged, or inspired, to believe "time would solve all problems." His parents, for their part, relieved their son of worry about his malfunctioning heart by refusing to emphasize the bleak warnings cast by doctors. He went to school and was sent outside to play. He picked up the lifelong nickname "Bud."

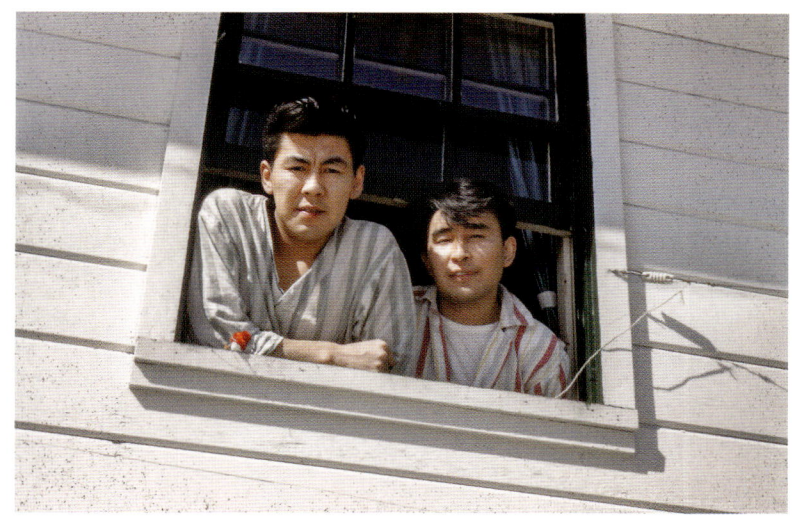

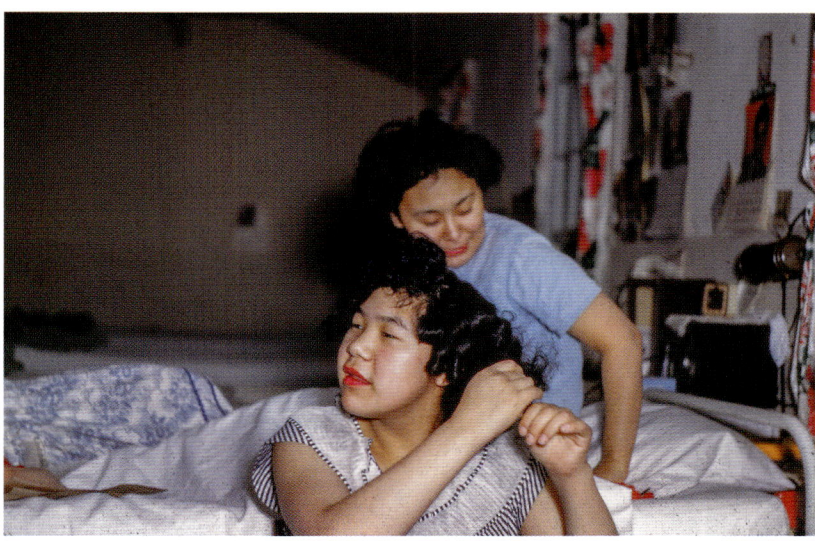

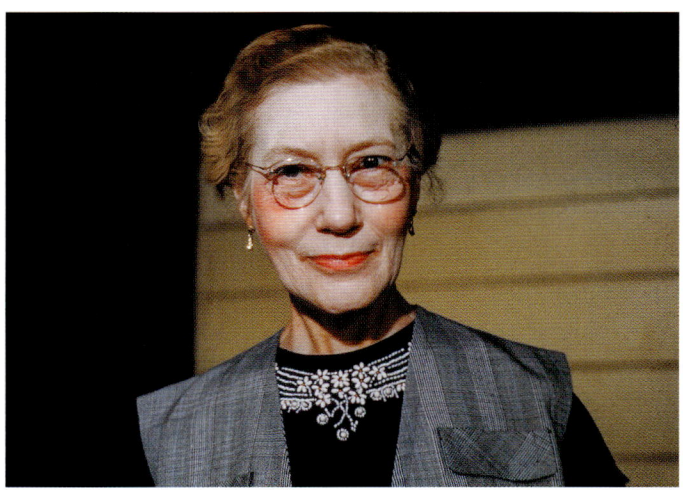

"Cher'chez Lafemme, Ward 4." Kaiser's caption, written on the slide frame, also shows an arrow pointing to the man on the right with "Tanana," and an arrow pointing to the man on the left, with "Copper Center," indicating the towns the men are from.

"Ward 6."

"Goldie Busko, Teacher."

Opposite: Gert Anayak, from King Island, Alaska. "Pretty Gertie," reads Kaiser's caption. "Where we met on the porch of Ward 3. I can still see the flowers blooming around her. July '53."

PHOTOGRAPHS BY HENRY S. KAISER JR. HENRY S. KAISER JR. PAPERS, ARCHIVES AND SPECIAL COLLECTIONS, CONSORTIUM LIBRARY, UNIVERSITY OF ALASKA ANCHORAGE.

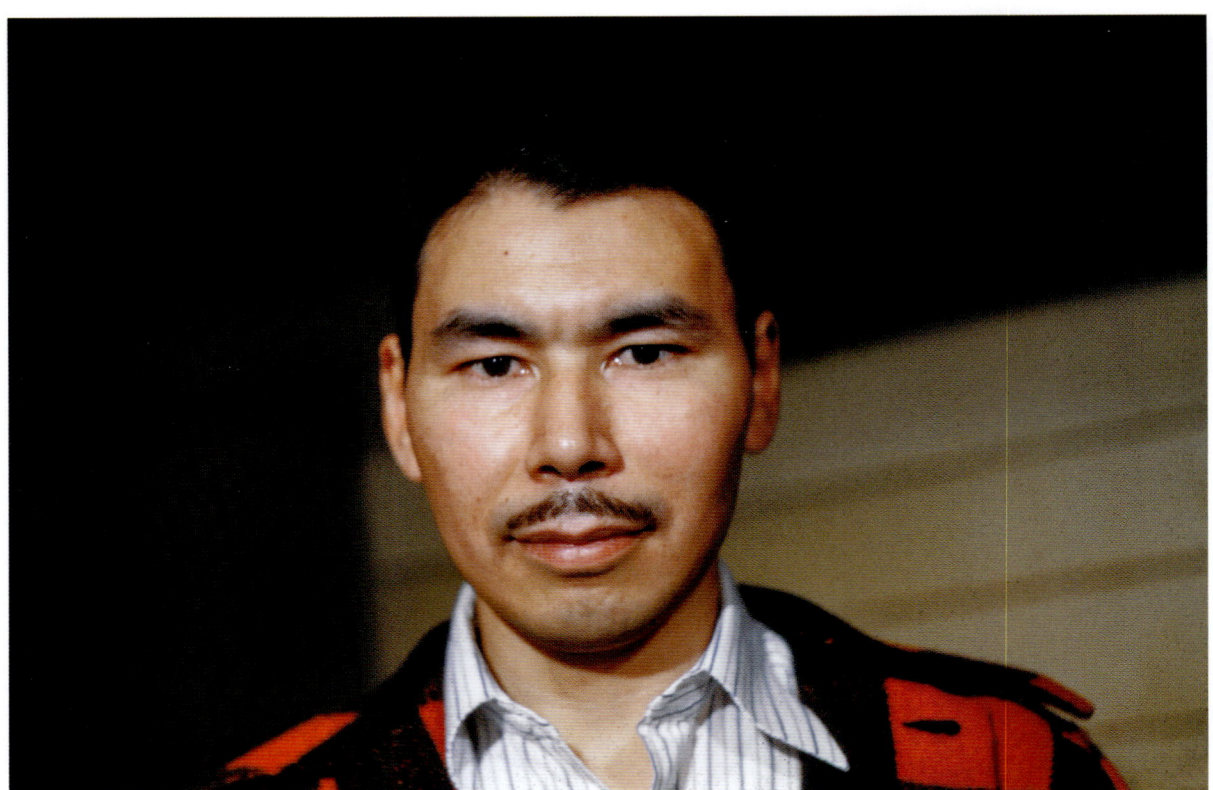

The onset of tuberculosis the same year his father died should have left him "extremely disappointed" about his fate, he says. Instead, he leaned on the words of author William Bolitho: "The most important thing in life is not to capitalize on your gains. Any fool can do that. The really important thing is to profit from your losses. That requires intelligence; and it makes the difference between a man of sense and a fool."

The answer, for Kaiser, was simple. To cure the infection, he needed a period of repose. On St. Patrick's Day 1950, Kaiser checked himself into the Seward Sanatorium, where the doctors, like in his infancy, wrote him off as a terminal case. Kaiser persisted: "Faith plus time equals victory."

At the San, Kaiser read—the Bible, biographies, historical novels, and philosophy—and with his camera, he documented

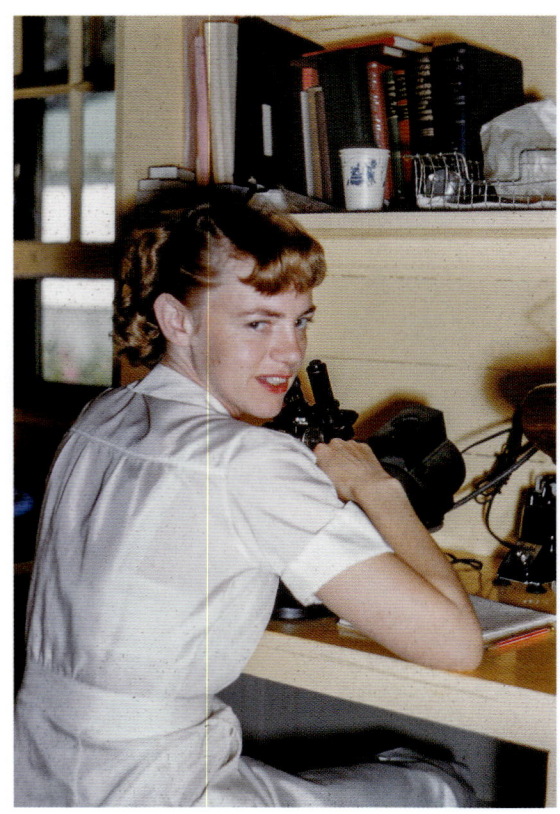

"John Topkok. Haycock, Anchorage."

"Margaret Waterhouse R.T., July 1953."

Opposite: "Copper Center: Andy Stickwan."

Opposite: "Mary Randolph, DRN."

Pages 134–135: A page from Henry S. Kaiser Jr.'s photo album with pictures from the Seward Sanatorium. A self-portrait of Kaiser, known as "Bud," is visible at the bottom of the second column. He is reading *LIFE* magazine in bed, surrounded by personal items.

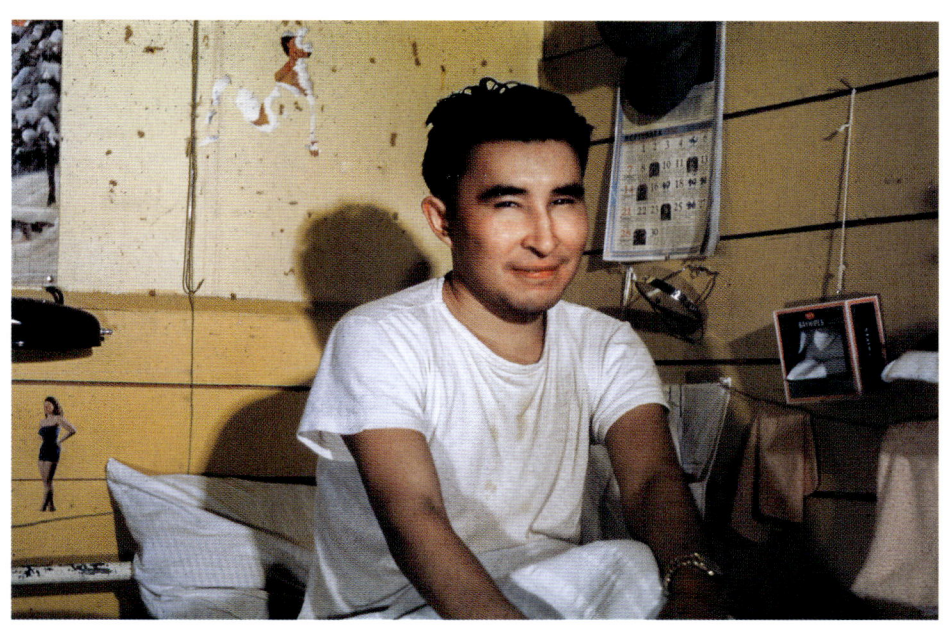

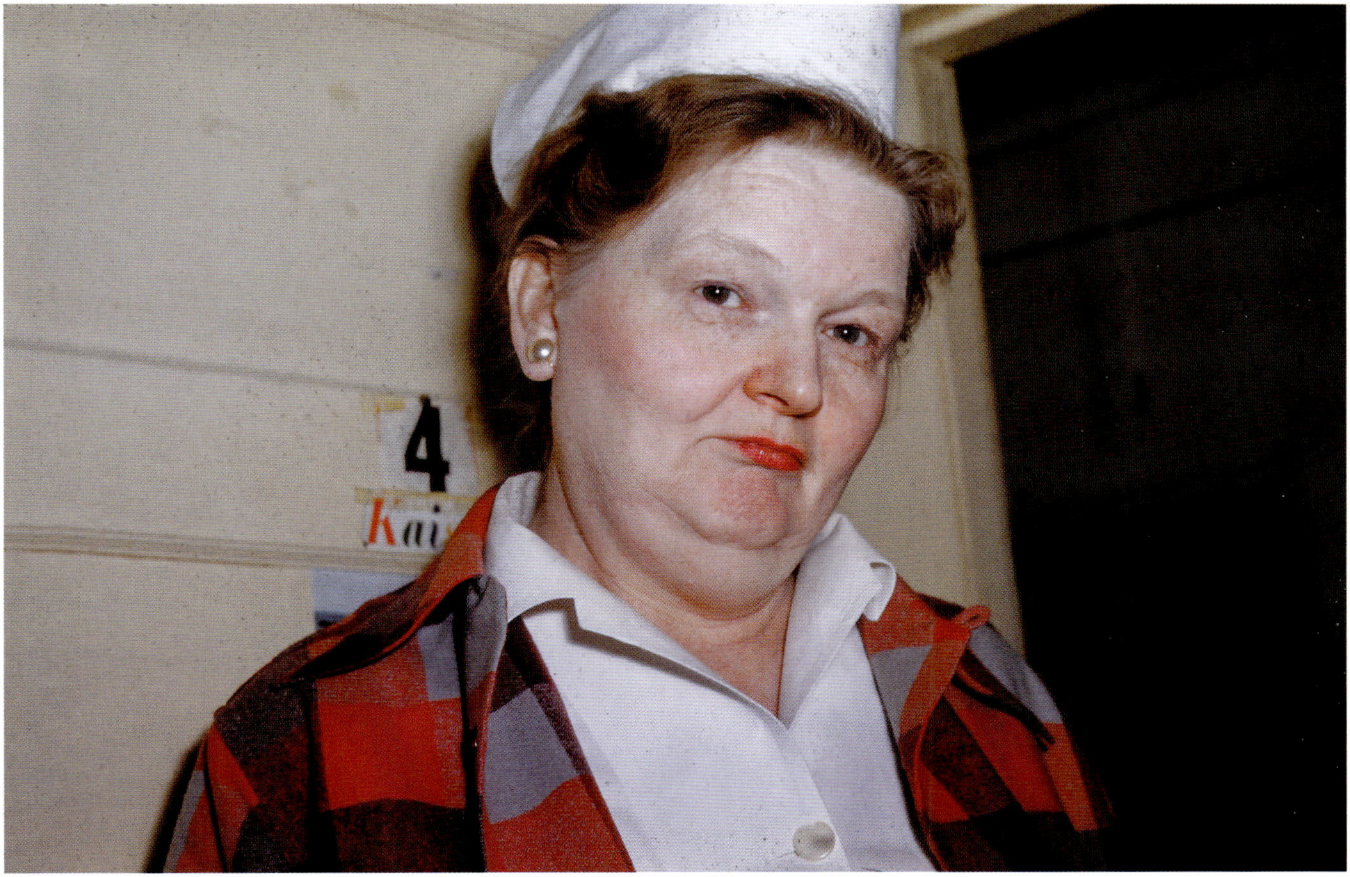

the visual tenor of his convalescence. Nearly 250 of his photographs from the San are preserved at the University of Alaska Anchorage. Almost all are flash-lit portraits. The tones are warm and saturated: yellow walls, red lipstick, purple robes, and striped pajamas. Kaiser moved in close to patients and staff, filling the frame with their faces while they grinned fondly at their photographer. He made images inside and outside the wooden wards. Pinup girls, calendars, greeting cards, dolls, and snow-capped mountains serve as background details. Julius Peterson is pictured with a single black-and-white photograph of a ship tacked to the wall above his bed.

The San, initially opened for Native Alaskans, welcomed everyone. In the margins of his 35mm Kodachrome slides, Kaiser wrote names, job titles, hometowns, and occasionally additional information like ward number. He commemorated his days in Ward 4 with a photo album of black-and-white prints, their scalloped edges hinting that the images and people pictured are pieces of a puzzle, a larger whole.

A year after he left the San, Kaiser hitchhiked to the Mayo Clinic in Rochester, Minnesota. Without an appointment, he convinced a string of cardiologists to see him. On June 11, 1954, Kaiser underwent eight hours of surgery and woke up, in his words, "re-born." His fingernails were pink instead of blue. His chest didn't rattle. Twenty days after the operation, he was released from the hospital and flew home to Alaska, where he remained until his death at age 79.

"I Hitchhiked to Heart Surgery," which is the title of Kaiser's youthful essay, marks the end of his "uncertain shaky half-life." He worked as an elementary school teacher in Nenana and Fort Richardson, where he brought "classical music, folk music, art and photography" into the classroom.[8] Landing in Anchorage, Kaiser took a job with the Bureau of Indian Affairs department of continuing education, a role that enabled him to engage with dozens of Alaska Native communities before his retirement. Through it all, he worked as a freelance journalist, photographing and writing for publications across the state, regularly producing stories that championed Native people. Throughout his life, Kaiser returned to Nenana.

In 1963, four years after Alaska became a state, Kaiser visited Rampart, the birthplace of his mother, at the Yukon River. One black-and-white photograph he made there pictures the riverfront. A small fish camp is visible on shore. The caption, encapsulating Kaiser's verve, reads, "Little boat, big boat, huge Yukon River, beautiful summer day, warm, quiet, a perfect day for photographers."[9]

—Sarah Stacke

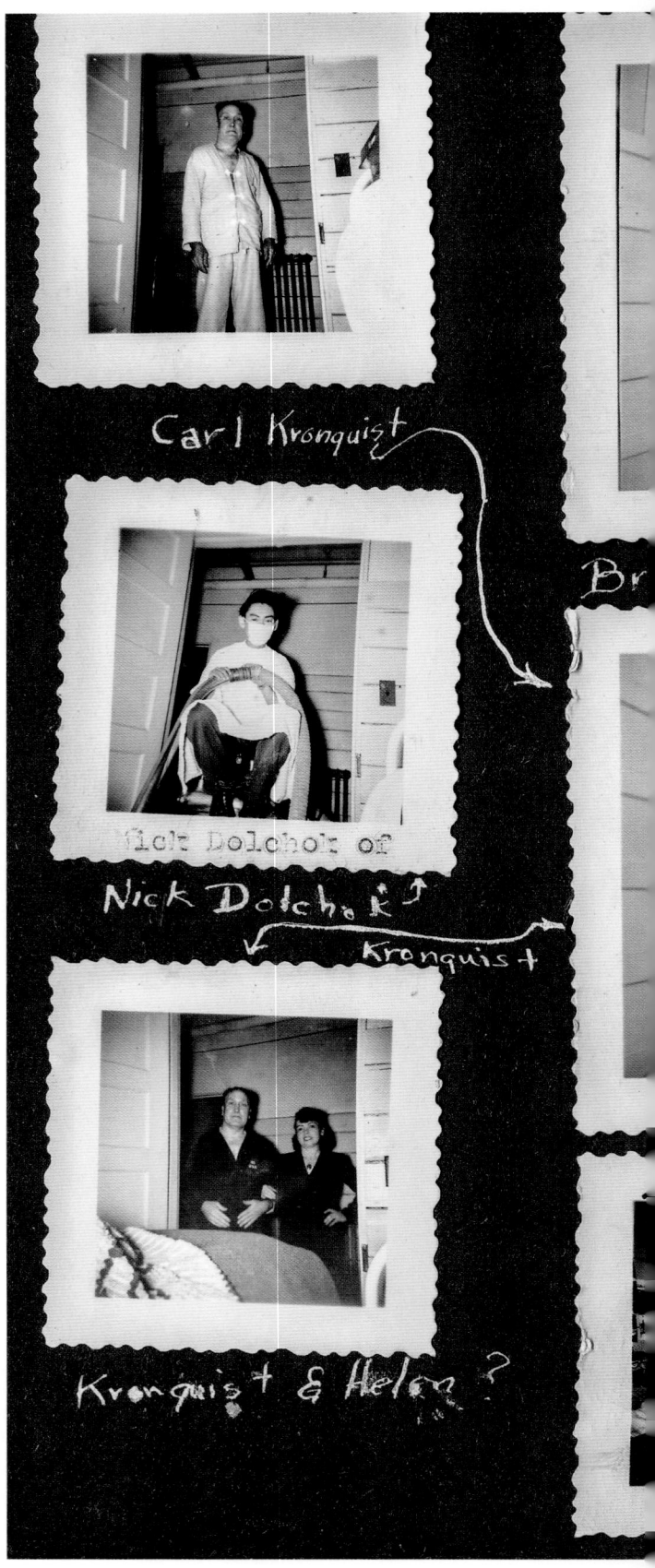

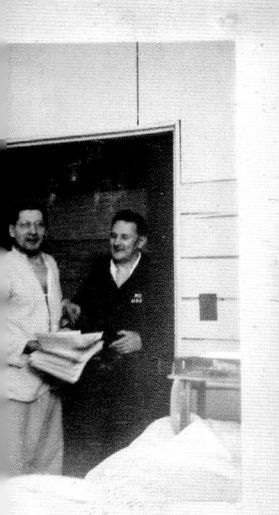

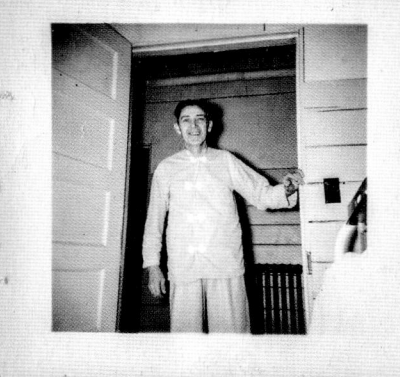

Carl Olason

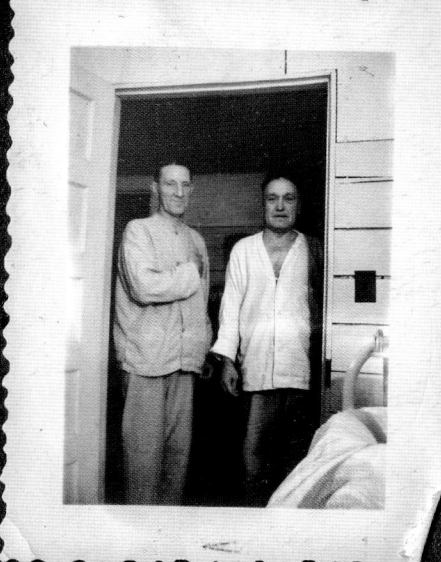

& Stream

Bennit + Kronquist

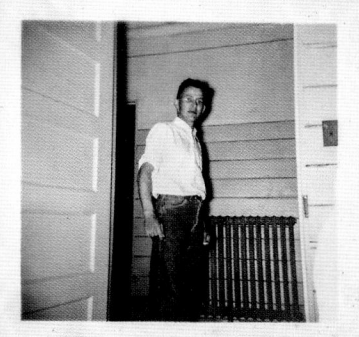

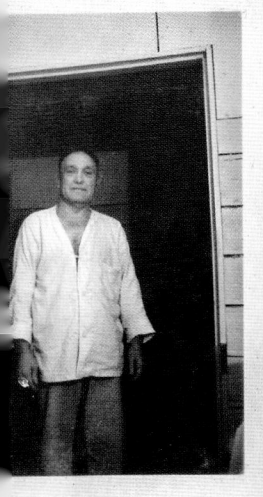

Cawthon, Joe
Orderly Wd#4

Ward

IV →

d: June '50

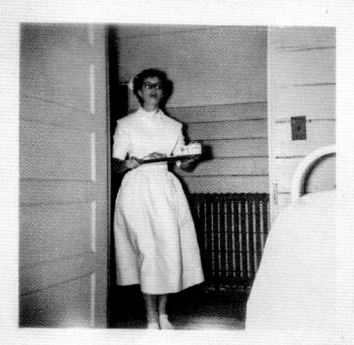

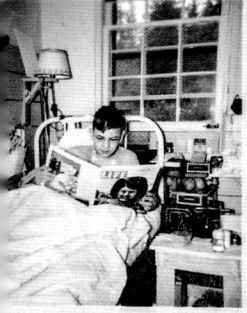

D. Brooks, R.N.
"Bud"

S BA

HERBERT RANDALL

Shinnecock, Black
Shinnecock Nation
New York State
United States

"My photography does my talking for me, I'm not much of a talker."[1]

A pervasive dance of intimacy and fierce determination distinguish Herb Randall's (b. 1936) depictions of some of the deepest struggles of racial relations in U.S. history. Amid seasons of violence and political upheaval in the 1960s Civil Rights Movement, Randall made photographs of peace and non-violence training in Mississippi. His portraits and documentary images show human resilience in the face of conflict. To tell the story of a massive social movement, he created intimate photographs that illustrated the relationships, commitments, and spirits of individuals who collectively stood for the principles of justice and racial equality. Through his images, the depth of activists' lives, choices, sacrifices, and family ties were presented as a tapestry of the diversity of people committed to political freedom struggles.

Randall drew from his identity as both Black and Native American to navigate multiple spaces. Born in Riverhead, he grew up in New York's South Bronx and later moved to the Shinnecock Nation, of which he is a citizen, on Long Island. His work is informed by intertwining struggles for Indigenous rights and racial justice.

In 1963, Randall co-founded the Kamoinge Workshop, a collective of Black photographers, in the company of some of the most established image makers of his era. The next year, he received a John Hay Whitney Fellowship—an honor that allowed him to work on a long-term project. Sanford R. "Sandy" Leigh, director of the Mississippi Freedom Summer Project in Hattiesburg, encouraged Randall to document the program's activities promoting racial equality, such as voter registration, education, and community organizing. It was his first time in the South, and Randall spent the entire summer there, at the age of 28, alongside freedom fighters and civil rights activists. This project would stretch his experience and define his photographic contributions.

From the beginning, Randall navigated this moment with a clear sense of focus and a sharp resistance to the mainstream pull to create voyeuristic images of "blood and guts" or the horrors of injustice. When he agreed to make photographs of the Freedom Summer, he recollected the strong stance he took with

Sandy: "I would say, 'Listen, I'm not doing any dogs-biting-me photographs, I don't do heroic stuff or whatever, but I will come down there and do this photograph [project], but I'm not doing the Ku Klux Klan, whatever, that's not my . . . mm-mm no.'"[2]

To create the photographs he envisioned, Randall experienced stages of immersion in the community, where he lived among those he photographed in ways that felt natural and reflective of his larger values of making images that were far more complex than mainstream representations. He strived to really "get into a place,"[3] but also described being removed from scenes in a way that kept his focus on photography. The camera became a tool for Randall's capacity to move within the Freedom Summer's programs in Hattiesburg as a respected insider-outsider.

Randall's ability to immerse himself within a community is evident in his photograph of three teenagers at the Dahmer fish fry. Here he plays with composition and his own presence in the image, as seen by the woman, Addie Ruth, who is meeting the camera's gaze. Another image portrays Rev. Jim Nance conducting voter registration, canvassing among Black households. Reverend Nance walks in unison with the community, visualized by a young man matching his stride. But by framing Nance on the railroad tracks, a short distance away from the homes, Randall also represents him as leader of the hope for change.

As he made photographs for the program, Randall continually went deeper, realizing his real purpose in photography.

"I got to a point after maybe a month or something that I needed to take some photographs that I was interested in doing…that I thought didn't necessarily document the program but I thought would certainly document that whole feeling of what is going on."[4]

That feeling took form in scenes that told a vivid story of the people and relationships in the Civil Rights Movement. His photographs revealed beautiful moments, even in times of great crisis.

"One of the main contributors to keep you going is some of those moments. They're rare, but they're important, really important."[5]

Randall's image of volunteers and locals singing at the Dahmer fish fry plays an important role in the larger story of

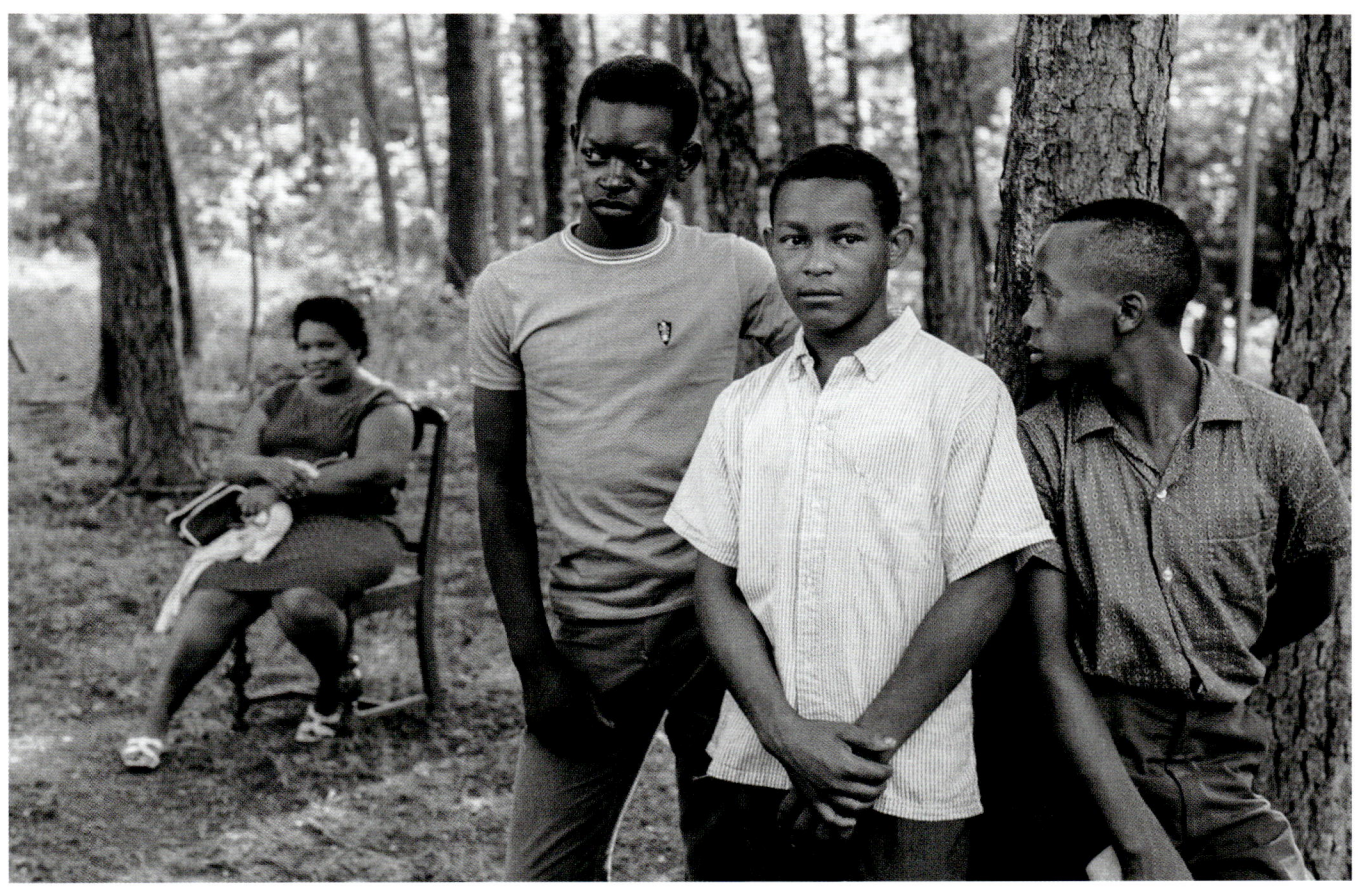

the diversity of activists committed to the civil rights revolution. This image stands in sharp contrast to the photographs of horror Randall refused to create. His lens turned to portraits of personal moments, as seen in the expression of Lorne Cress and Victoria Jackson Gray, engaged in what appears to be a critical conversation in a stark environment, softened by the presence of three ripe watermelons on the floor.

The photographs from Randall's time in Mississippi were collected into his notable book *Faces of Freedom Summer*. If these photographs talk for Herb Randall, they tell the story of a brilliant documentarian whose images emerge from the communities that held his unwavering respect. Randall's work comprises a collection of civil rights moments that visually narrate a revolution in relationships and conversations,

and the symbolic significance of gathering in a summer space that held the promise of a new landscape for humanity, far beyond Mississippi.

—Jennifer Natalie Fish

Three teenagers and Addie Ruth at a fish fry hosted by Vernon Dahmer at his home in the Kelly Settlement just outside of Hattiesburg, Mississippi, July 4, 1964. Dahmer was murdered in 1966 by the White Knights of the Ku Klux Klan for his civil rights work.

PHOTOGRAPHS BY HERBERT RANDALL. M351 HERBERT RANDALL FREEDOM SUMMER PHOTOGRAPHS, HISTORICAL MANUSCRIPTS, THE UNIVERSITY OF SOUTHERN MISSISSIPPI.

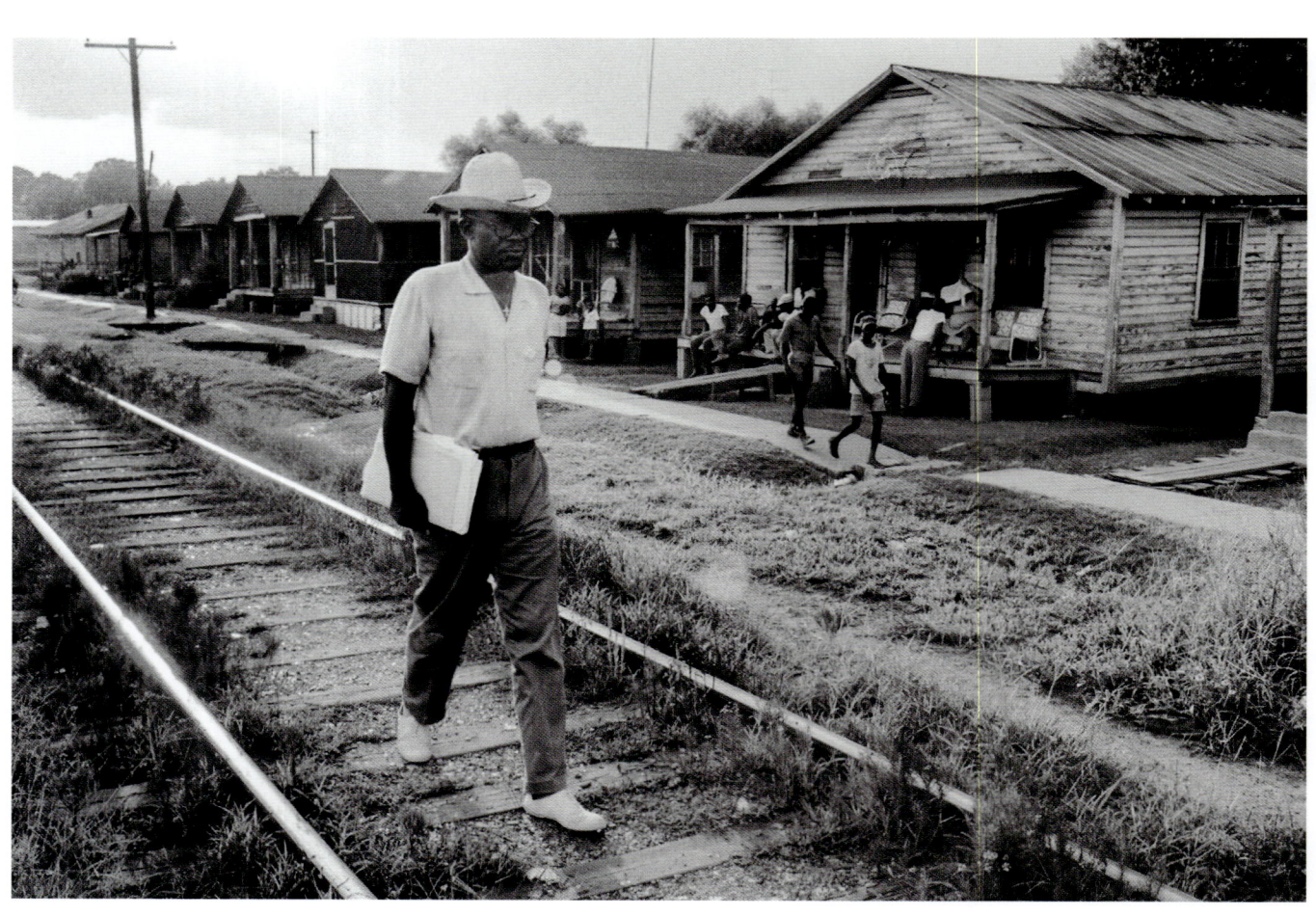

Rev. Jim Nance canvassing for voter registration, Hattiesburg, Mississippi, summer 1964.

Opposite: Volunteers and locals singing at a fish fry hosted by Vernon Dahmer, Kelly Settlement, Mississippi, July 4, 1964.

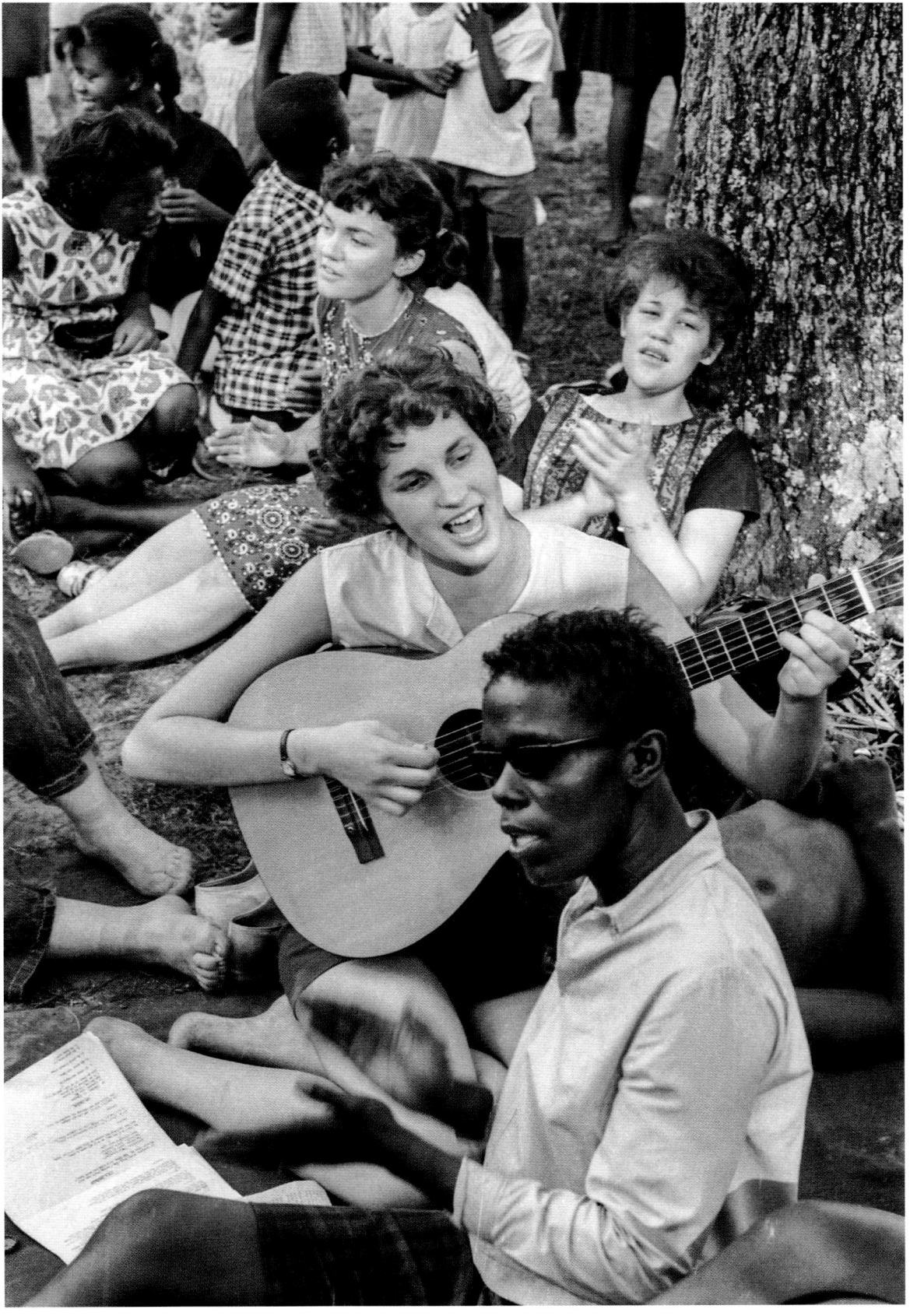

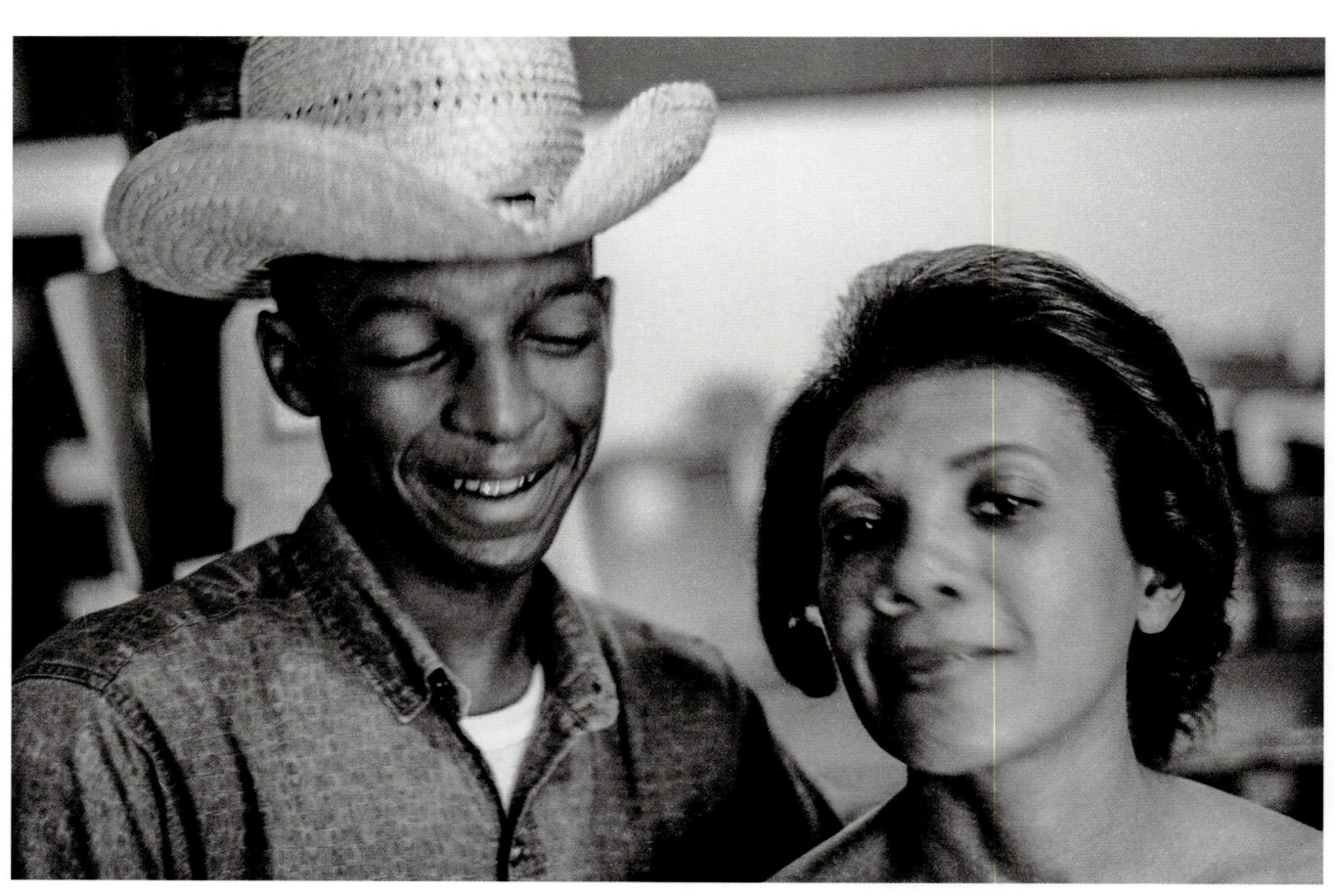

Doug Smith and Carolyn Reese, likely at the Hattiesburg
project headquarters on Mobile Street, Hattiesburg,
Mississippi, July 1964.

Opposite: Lorne Cress (left) and Victoria Jackson Gray
in Palmers Crossing, Hattiesburg, Mississippi,
July 18, 1964.

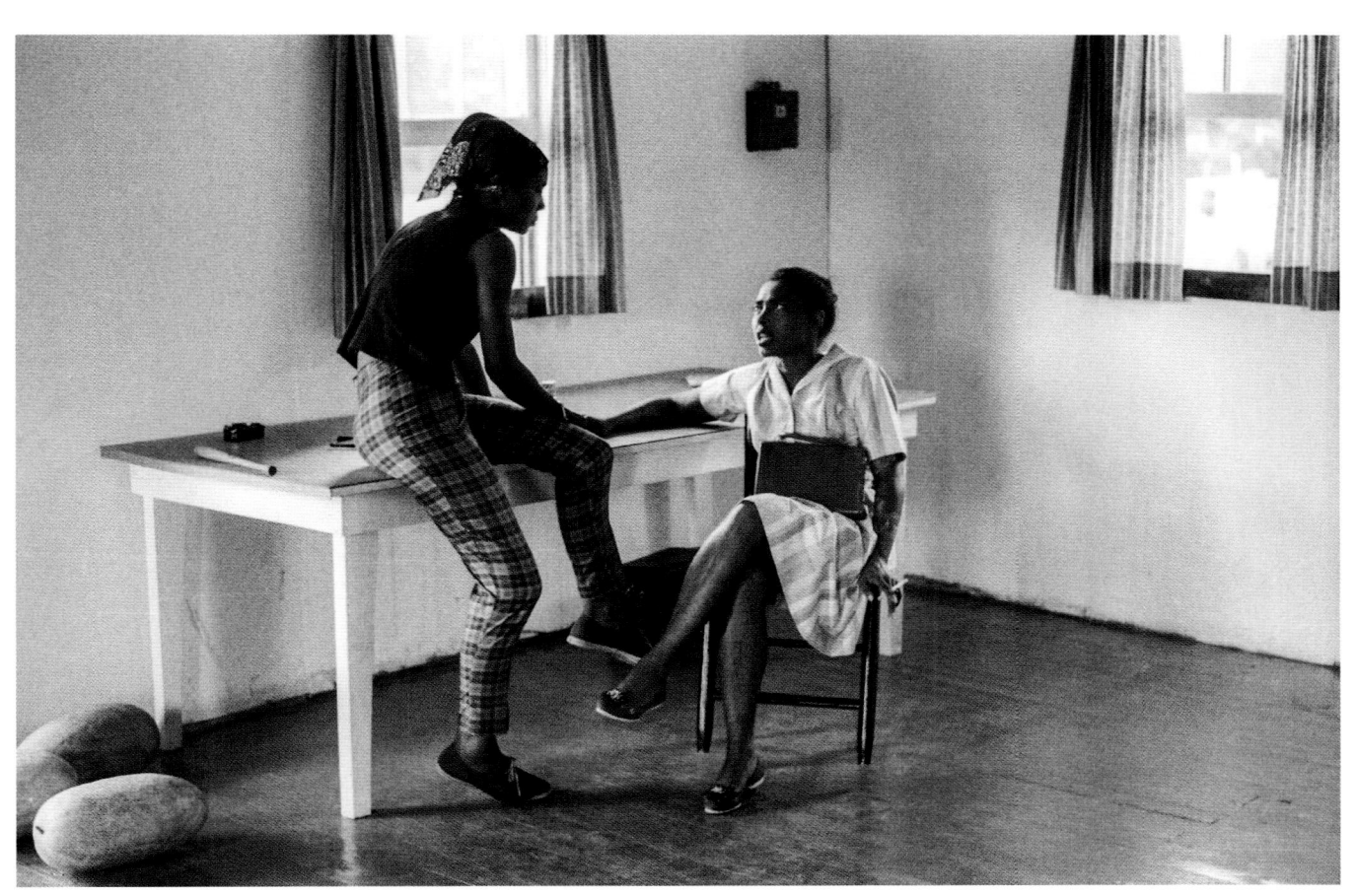

JEREMY DENNIS

Shinnecock
Shinnecock Nation
New York State
United States

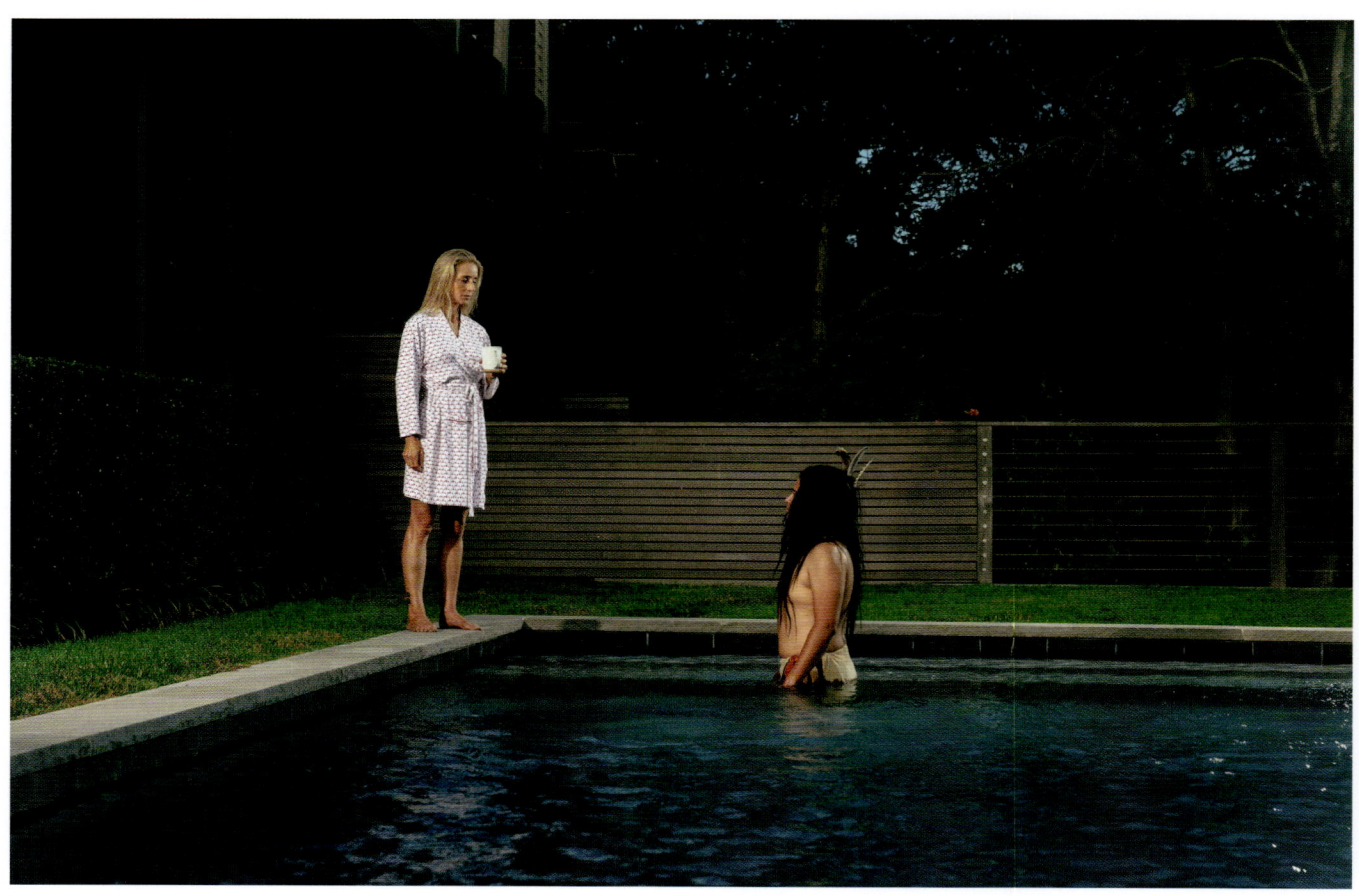

Shinnecock Nation is located on the eastern end of Long Island, New York, on a tree-covered peninsula in Shinnecock Bay, a body of water scarcely divided from the Atlantic Ocean by a slender barrier beach. The borders of the 837-acre sovereign nation follow the contours of the peninsula —they are one and the same.

The Shinnecock people have lived on Long Island upward of 10,000 years. Along with two of their immediate neighbors— the Unkechaug to the west and Montaukett to the east—they were the greatest of whalers and Wampum makers. (Wampum are beads carved from white and purple mollusk shells found in northeastern North America. A spiritual item, they are used in ceremony and when worn, associated with status.) Combined, the three distinct yet interlaced Tribes oversaw an approximately 70-mile stretch of coastal land along the southern edge of the island that reached the very eastern tip. Before European contact, roughly 11 other closely related groups were located on the island.

Throughout centuries of colonization, Shinnecock Nation— which received federal recognition in 2010 after legal debates had dragged on for more than 30 years—and Unkechaug Nation managed to retain small sections of their former territories. They are now the only recognized Tribes on Long Island. In a flagrant land grab, the Montaukett were unjustly ruled extinct in 1910 by Judge Abel Blackmar. They have been engaged in a battle to reclaim their ancestral lands ever since.

The history of land dispossession is deeply rooted in fine art photographer Jeremy Dennis's (b. 1990) practice. Except for Shinnecock Nation, where Dennis lives, the Homelands of the Shinnecock and Montaukett have turned into the fabled beachside playground for affluent, famous, and up-and-coming New Yorkers—the Hamptons.

In the filmic photograph *I Could Stand Here All Night*, Dennis emerges from a pristine Hamptons pool dressed in an "Indian" costume, while the proprietor of the estate, a svelte blonde woman in a smooth robe, looks down at him. The photograph is part of a series called Rise, in which Dennis appropriates the concept of the zombie apocalypse to reflect upon the "inherent fear that one day oppressed groups may rise and defend themselves," he explains. Rise replaces the "gory zombie figure with the American Indian, whose simple presence causes terror." [1]

"We're this inconvenient truth," Dennis tells journalist John Greiner-Ferris about his nation's proximity to the Hamptons. "You can have a nice Hampton home, you can party on the beach, but it's on stolen land, and we're right next door, 10 minutes away." Dennis likes to make the parallel that "just as zombies come back to haunt the living," Indigenous people are "still here and strong." [2]

Rise was conceived when Dennis read excerpts from a lecture by Noam Chomsky. After Chomsky was asked why the United States has a cultural preoccupation with the zombie apocalypse, he explains, "Much of it is just a recognition— at some level of the psyche—that if you've got your boot on somebody's neck, there's something wrong, and that the people you're oppressing may rise up and defend themselves." [3]

Dennis comes from a family that taught him art is important. His mother, Denise Silva-Dennis, is a painter and beadworker. His uncle is Herbert Randall, the acclaimed civil rights photographer. The "passing on of knowledge and skills" from relatives who are earnestly present in Dennis's life shaped his drive for self-exploration and, in turn, his career. "A lot of my work is just answering the question, or stating, that we are still here," says Dennis. [4]

I Could Stand Here All Night, 2021.

—Sarah Stacke

RAYMOND GREGORY DOUCETTE

Mi'kmaq
Membertou First Nation
Unama'ki (Cape Breton), Nova Scotia
Canada

Raymond Doucette (1935–2011), who went by "Ray" and "Raytel," owned and operated Raytel Photography for 35 years on Unama'ki (Cape Breton), a forested island fringed with cliffs on the Atlantic coast of Canada. When his studio opened in 1962 in downtown Sydney, the island's historical capital, it specialized in portrait, wedding, and commercial photography. By 1970, Doucette had shifted to photojournalism and regularly worked for the *Cape Breton Highlander*, *Micmac News*, and the *Atlantic Catholic*. Sadly, in 1997, most of his work was lost when his studio was devastated by a fire.

Doucette was adopted by Stephen and Mary Doucette (née Vincent), at six months old and raised in Membertou First Nation, an urban Mi'kmaq community on Unama'ki. He grew to be a devout Catholic whose "Mi'kmaq spirituality was very much a part of his persona," wrote Delores Campbell in the *Cape Breton Post* in 2012.[1] Doucette was a member of the former Church of the Sacred Heart in Sydney, the Knights of Columbus Sydney Council 1060, as well as St. Anne's parish in Membertou, the Membertou Elders, and the Membertou 55+ Club.

In 2007, Doucette received a Lifetime Achievement Award from Membertou for his contributions to the nation. Known as a soft-spoken and generous man who always carried his camera, Doucette was dedicated to photographing community and church-related events in Membertou and Sydney, including the Catholic Women's League, often for free.

Doucette's archive mirrors his affection for the people, sites, and landscapes of Unama'ki. He photographed delighted kids at a playground in Whitney Pier, a Sydney neighborhood built by immigrants from the West Indies and elsewhere, as well as Black Nova Scotians, in the shadow of a steel mill that opened in 1901 and shuttered a century later. He photographed cars cruising along the coast of Bras d'Or Lake on a summer day, with Johnstown's Sacred Heart Church, established in 1891, visible on the horizon. A 1966 photograph shows the activist and two-term Chief of Membertou First Nation Lawrence Paul, looking skeptically at three Indian Affairs representatives. Several colorful images present events on Charlotte Street, where Doucette's studio was located: a larger-than-life lobster float at the 1967 Centennial Parade; Mi'kmaq people in regalia at the 1969 Centennial Parade; sidewalks lined with shoulder-height piles of snow in 1970; the magnificently yellow Cape Breton Family Video store against a clear blue sky in 1990. And, in 1998, the year after Doucette's studio burned, he made a quiet black-and-white image of Charlotte Street at nightfall.

Doucette's "most popular"[2] image, reports the Beaton Institute, where much of his remaining archive is preserved, pictures the July 1976 Feast of Saint Anne on the tiny island of Miniku in Potlotek First Nation, less than 50 miles from Sydney. Since the 1700s, Mi'kmaq from all over the Atlantic provinces have gathered annually on the island, off the shores of Bras d'Or Lake, to celebrate Saint Anne, their patron saint. Doucette is in the middle of the action, photographing a man drumming and singing, surrounded by dancers.

In 1982, Doucette photographed the No. 12 Colliery mine in New Waterford, a town roughly 12 miles outside Sydney. The mine was the site of the worst coal mine disaster in Cape Breton history in 1917, when 65 miners were killed by an explosion. In Doucette's image we see dozens of men packed into wooden carts before descending into the mine on a narrow railway, wearing hard hats, miners' lights, and winter coats. The scene is a haunting reminder of the dangers the depths of the mine hold.

At age 76, Doucette passed away at home in Sydney, "much the way he had lived, quietly and without fanfare," wrote Campbell. He was predeceased by five siblings—three sisters in infancy and two brothers, Roy and Douglas. After learning digital photography, Doucette continued documenting his surroundings until a few days before his death. Contributing to Doucette's online memorial, his friend Sulian Herney recounts fond memories of bringing Doucette eel and moose meat. Doucette would thank Herney by emailing him pictures of the meals he cooked with the gifts.[3]

—Sarah Stacke

No. 12 Colliery, New Waterford, Nova Scotia, July 1982.
PHOTOGRAPH BY RAYTEL PHOTOGRAPHY (RAY DOUCETTE). BEATON INSTITUTE, CAPE BRETON UNIVERSITY.

Tupper Street Playground, Whitney Pier, Sydney, Nova Scotia, August 15, 1969.
PHOTOGRAPH BY RAYTEL PHOTOGRAPHY (RAY DOUCETTE). BEATON INSTITUTE, CAPE BRETON UNIVERSITY. 89-615-18810

Johnstown, Nova Scotia, July 6, 1969.
PHOTOGRAPH BY RAYTEL PHOTOGRAPHY (RAY DOUCETTE). BEATON INSTITUTE, CAPE BRETON UNIVERSITY. 89-662-18857

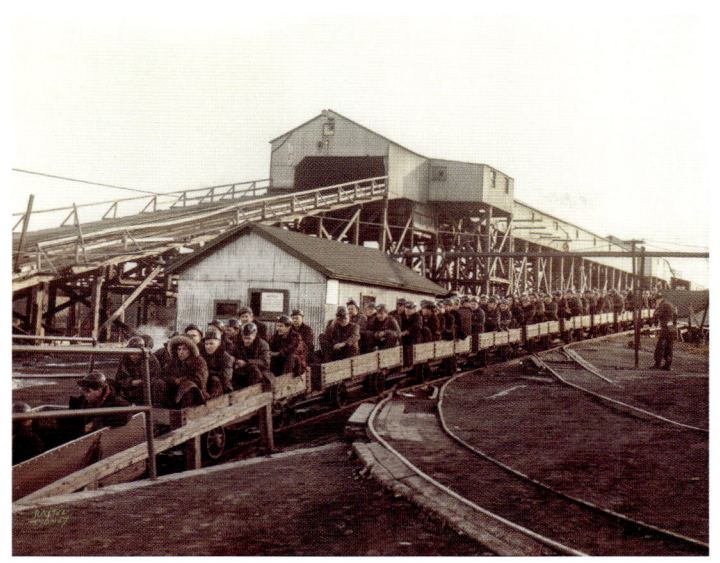

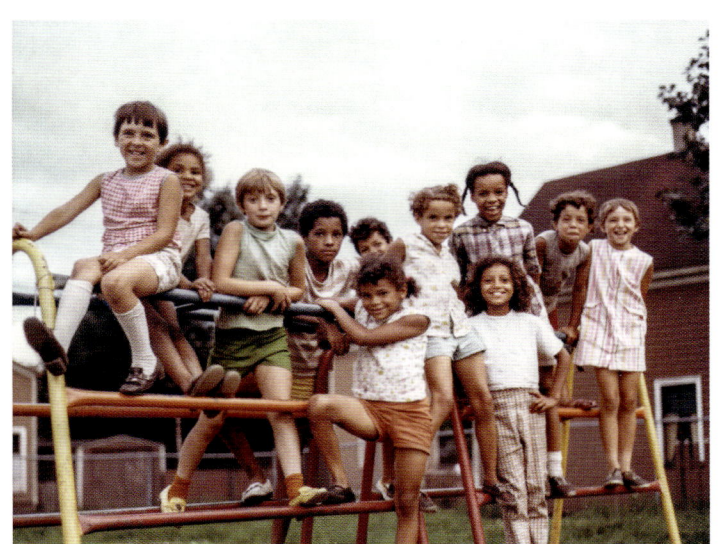

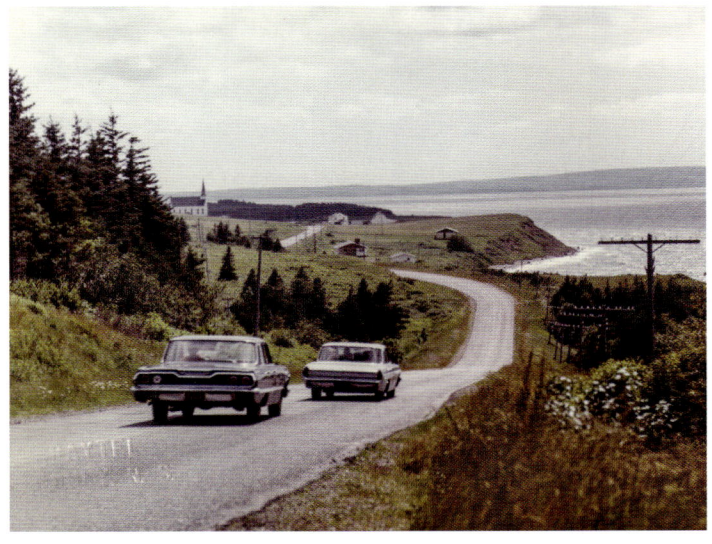

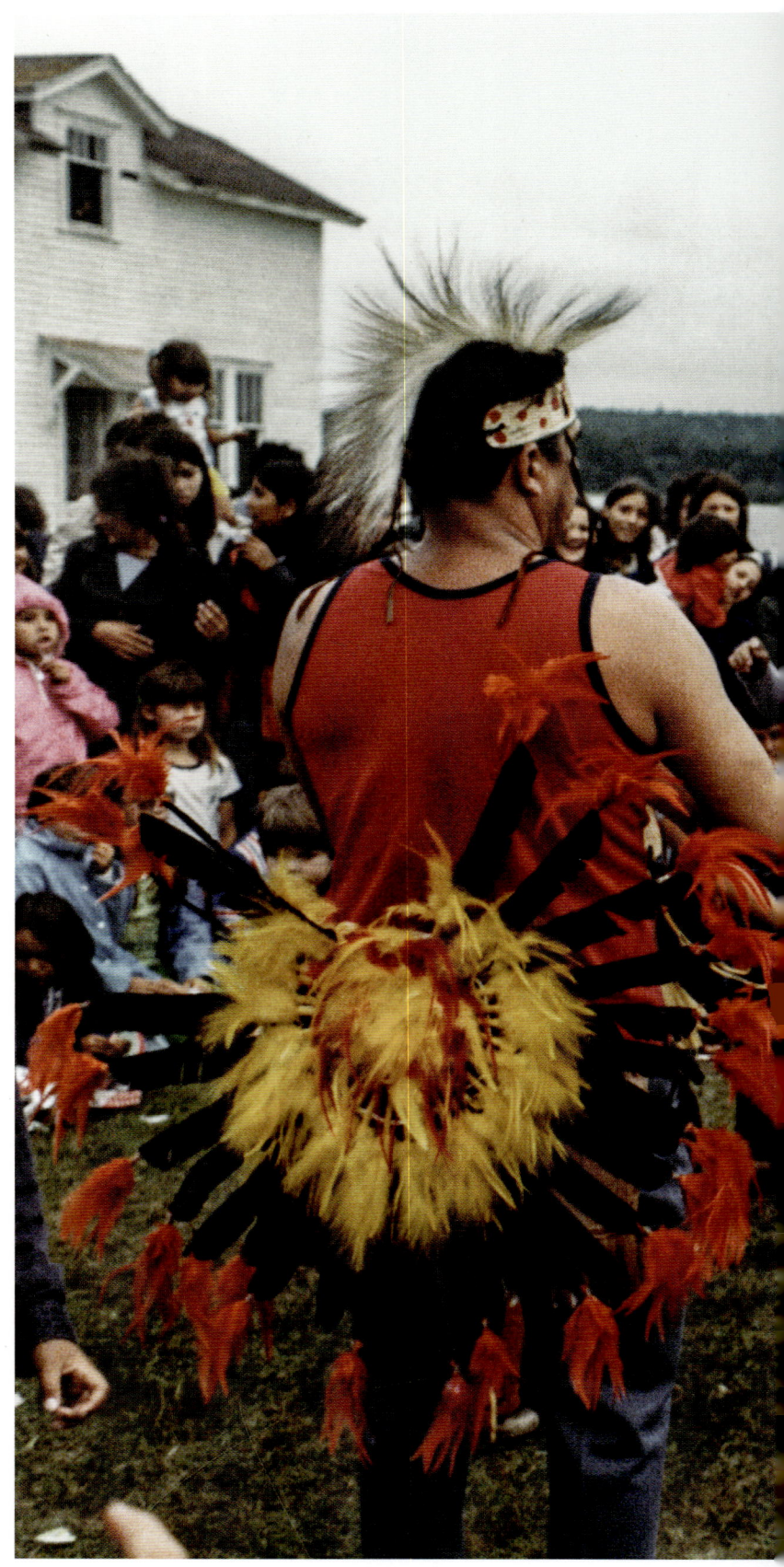

St. Anne's Mission, Potlotek First
Nation, 1976.

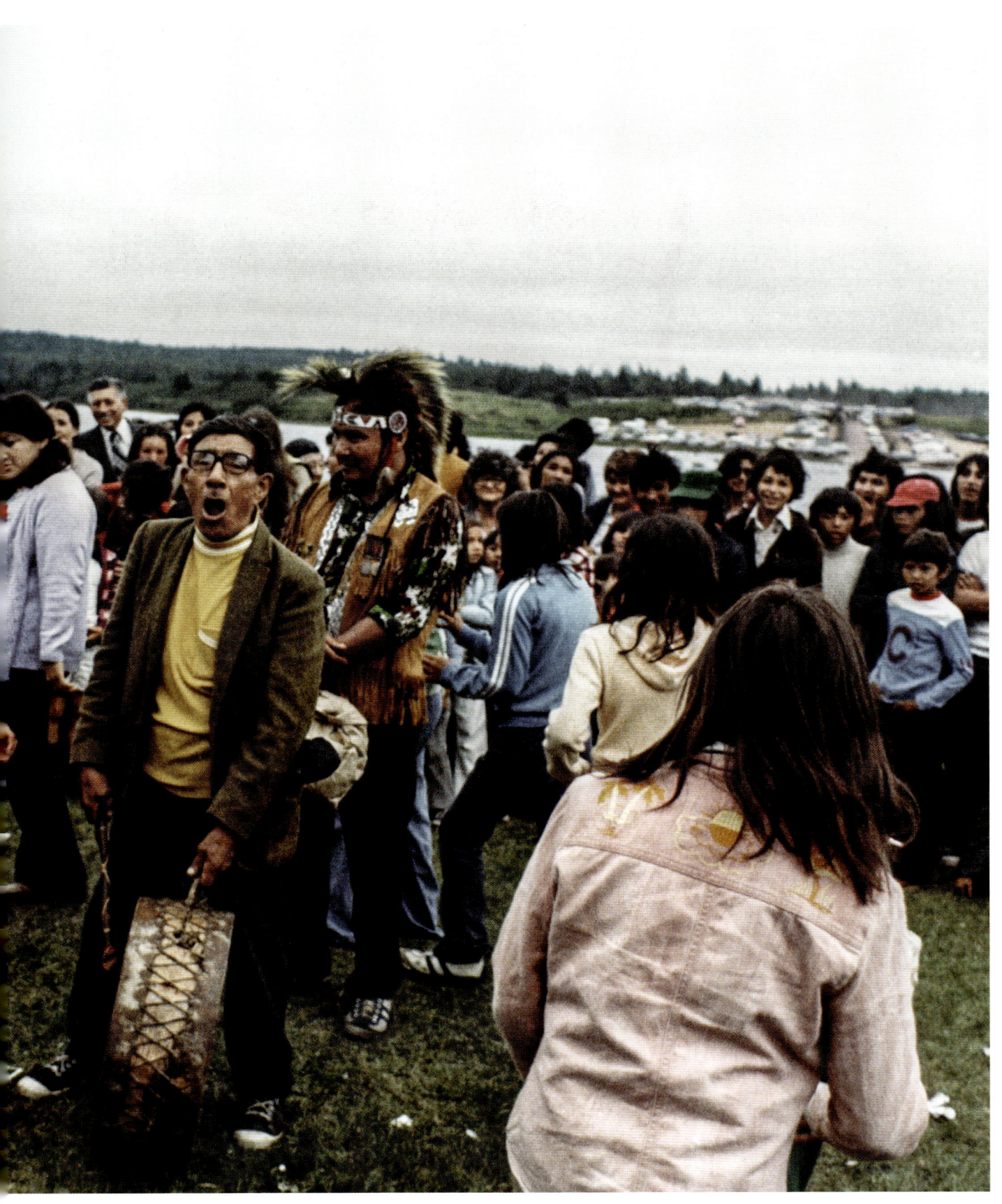

KENNETH T. MARS, JR.

Narragansett
Narragansett Tribe
South Kingstown, Rhode Island
United States

Kenneth T. Mars, Jr. (1940–2011) walked the roads of South Kingstown, Rhode Island, nearly every day, in every season, in every type of weather, for four decades. He walked to make pictures.

Between the late 1960s and the early 2000s, Mars, a tall and slender man who favored a trench coat, likely made 80,000 photos of trees and tree-lined roads. Of houses and historical buildings. Parades, parking lots, beachgoers, and baptisms. Dogs and chickens. His church. A station wagon passing by.

He used a simple point-and-click camera, presumably several different models over the years. There's no evidence he sought to upgrade his equipment; he just needed a camera that worked. After the film was developed, Mars methodically organized the prints, with the help of his dad, in dime-store albums—heaps of them in all sizes, shapes, and colors. He stored the albums in the basement of the home he shared with his parents, on wooden shelves in his bedroom, and in boxes under his bed.

What isn't known is—why? Why did Mars make the photographs?

He was a familiar presence to the people of South Kingstown. And yet, the prevailing opinion, says Erica Luke, the executive director of the local South County History Center, is that, outside of his family, "no one really knew" this man, who was at once amiable, laconic, inquisitive, and private.[1]

Born in South Kingstown on March 29, 1940, Mars was the only child of Lucille Mars (née Greenwood) and Rev. Kenneth T. Mars, Sr. The family were members of the Narragansett Tribe. When Mars was 22 years old, he began working with the custodial staff at the University of Rhode Island (URI) Memorial Student Union. Forty years later, in 2002, he retired. A handful of pages in his photo albums show colleagues, their smiles and 80s-era hairstyles arrested by the camera's flash. Mars is pictured, too. He stands next to a coworker, with his hands in the pockets of his blue work pants and alongside a man in a Rhode Island sweatshirt who playfully gives him bunny ears.

On weekends and for special gatherings, Mars served as an usher at the Peace Dale First Church of God. His father and other relatives helped build the church in the 1940s. "The Mars family were largely carpenters by trade,"[2] says Silvermoon Mars LaRose, assistant director of the Tomaquag Museum, Rhode Island's only museum entirely dedicated to telling the story of the Indigenous people of southern New England. Kenneth Mars, Sr. became the pastor of Peace Dale in the 1960s, and he and Lucille led the church for 30 years.

"There's a lot of family and community and memory attached to that church," says LaRose. And Mars, she continues, "loved family, he loved community." He and her father were first cousins and grew up together. She remembers Mars, quiet and reserved around town, becoming so animated as he recounted stories to her father from their past that the two men laughed to tears. "Ken Jr. was a riot," she recalls. "I so enjoyed being a witness to this side of his personality."[3]

When Mars wasn't at church or working at URI, he walked (he was never interested in riding a bike or driving a car) and photographed the seemingly quotidian terrain of his hometown, or diligently studied old issues of the *Narragansett Times* in the Rhode Island History room at the Peace Dale Library.

In 2011, at age 71, Mars died of undiagnosed Lyme disease. Following his death, an estimated two-thirds of the photo albums, plus the reams of notes he jotted at the library, were lost. In 2018, the remaining albums were donated to the South County History Center.

The Kenneth T. Mars, Jr. Photograph Collection totals 27,432 images. The center's staff doggedly digitized every print and album page, keeping Mars's arrangement intact. Luke is sure the constitution of the albums is purposeful. "I just can't quite put my finger on all the connections," she says. In several instances, Mars photographed a nondescript house and then went to the cemetery and photographed the headstone of the former owner. "You'd have to do the research or read local history to know there's a linkage there," Luke explains.[4]

The collection is, above all, marked by visual repetition. In album after album, thousands of nearly identical photographs appear side by side. "It's like Google Maps before Google Maps," says Luke, referring to series that show Mars's step-by-step progress along rural and city streets. The albums also illustrate the photographer's pattern of revisiting specific scenes—days, months, and years apart. "He returned to the same trees over and over," remarks Luke, "and the same buildings, the same houses."[5]

Both LaRose and Luke feel the trees are a key to understanding the photographs. "He had a particular affinity for trees," says LaRose. "Documenting their growth and seasonal cycles. That brought him joy."[6]

Whatever Mars's intentions or motivations might have been, he built a cohesive and detailed body of work that creates an intimate portrait of South Kingstown and the ways it changed, from season to season, throughout his life. Day after

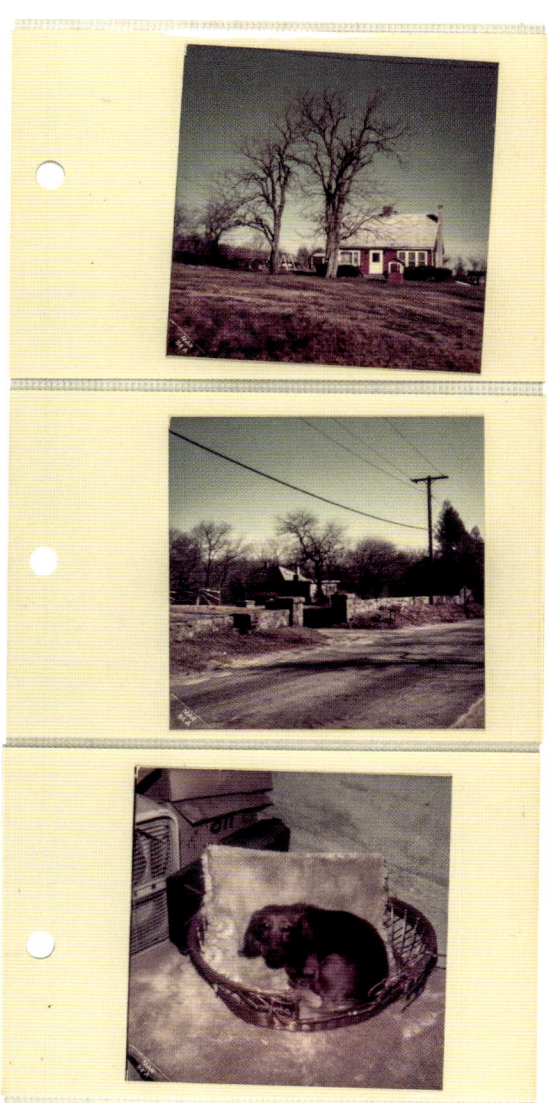

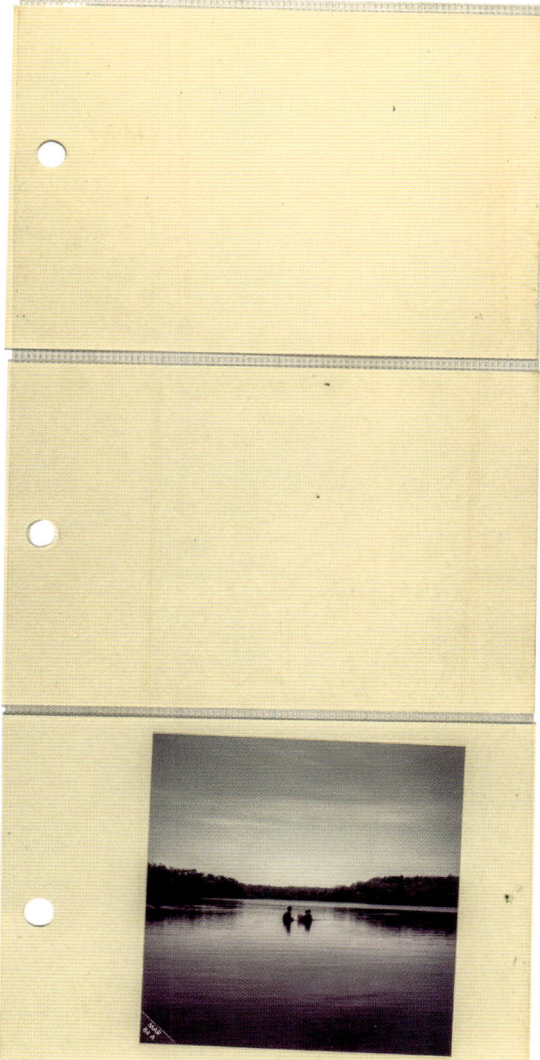

day, Mars photographed subtle glimpses of the town's people and landscape that might otherwise have stayed unseen.

A neighbor feeding a squirrel on her porch. Stone walls, telephone poles, and trees sprouting pink blossoms. A hazy blue car in the shadow of a sunny white church. Fading signs on stores, soon to be replaced. A gang of four kids racing down the street on their bikes.

"There's so many stories in his photos," marvels LaRose.[7]

Nothing was too commonplace for Mars to treasure with a photograph. He was, it seems, gratified by it all—the research, the process of making photographs, the arrangement of the albums, and what it revealed to him about his environment and his place in it. "He had a gentle spirit," says LaRose. "He leaves a legacy for other individuals to see that you can do something you love, that satisfies your heart, and that is worthwhile."

At the same time, she recognizes "how very valuable" his photographic archive is. "The fact that he was a Narragansett tribal member makes me feel just a little more proud for my community," says LaRose, "and the many unsung contributions they make to our state."[8]

—Sarah Stacke

Album 8, page 29. The third image pictures the Mars family dog.

Album 8, page 47. A baptism, presumably performed by Rev. Kenneth T. Mars, Sr.

PHOTOGRAPHS BY KENNETH T. MARS, JR. COURTESY OF THE SOUTH COUNTY HISTORY CENTER.

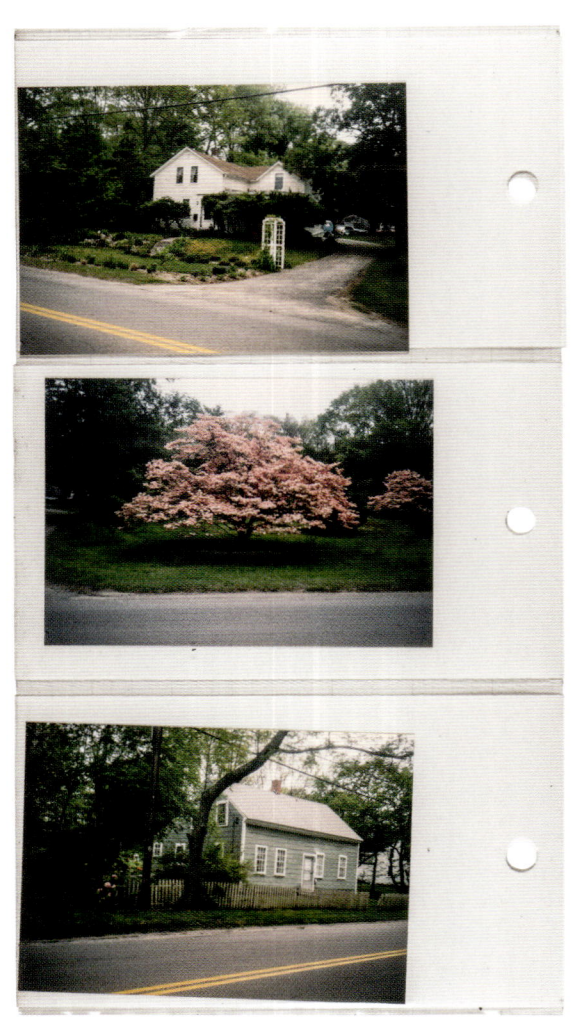

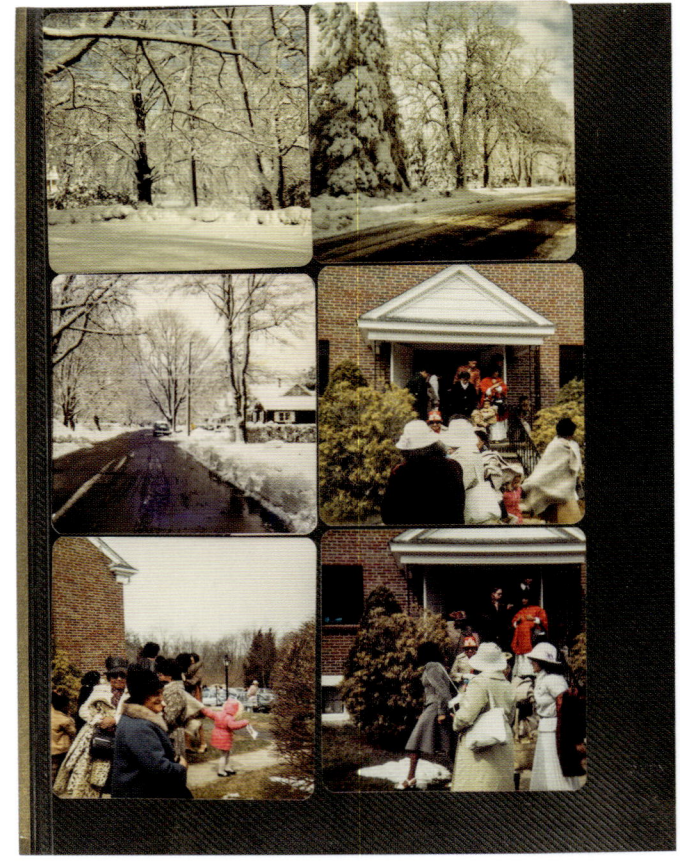

Album 27, page 104.

Album 35, page 30. Three images picture the Peace Dale
First Church of God.

150   Opposite: Album 42, page 83.

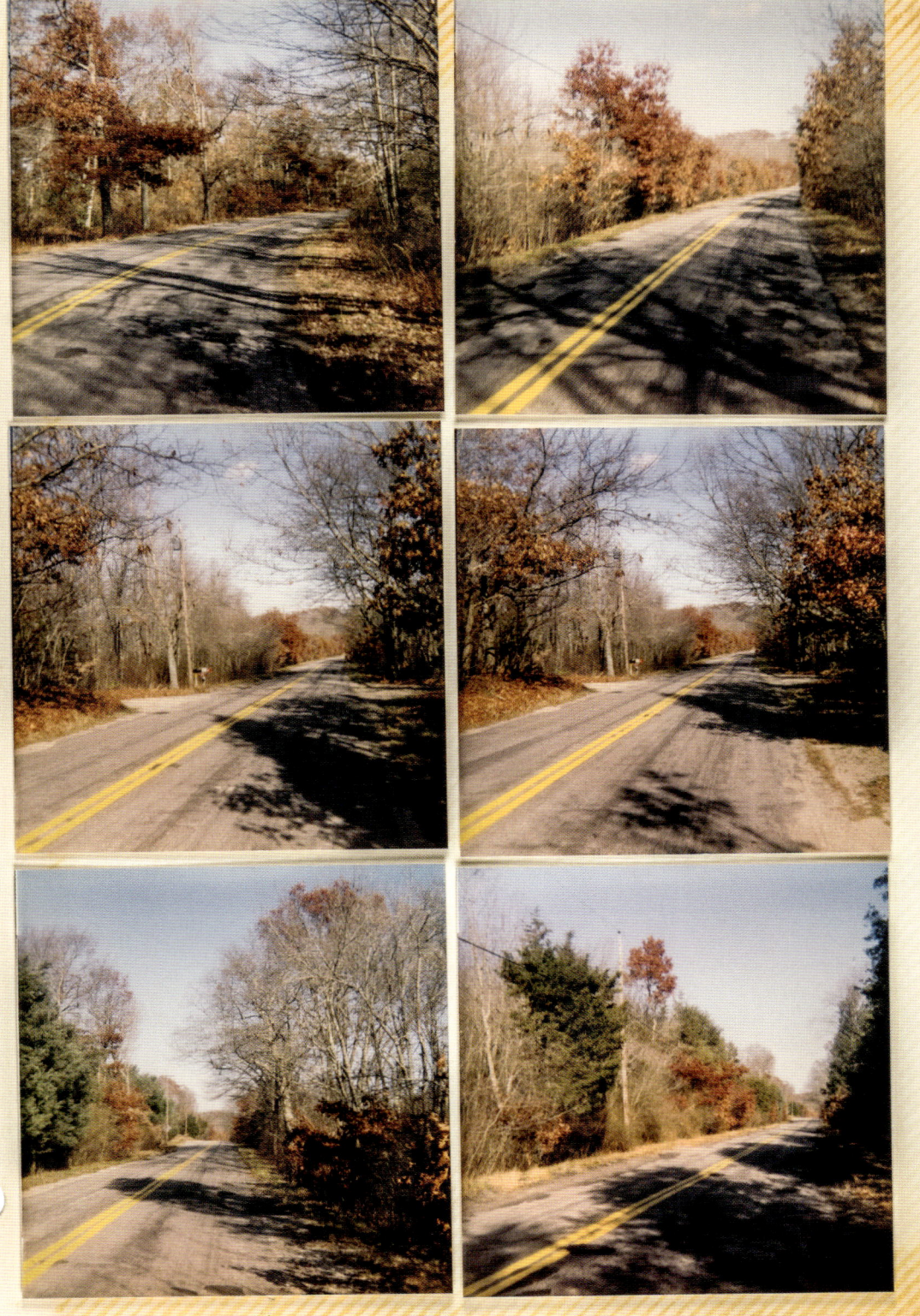

ARTHUR BEAR CHIEF

Blackfoot
Siksika Nation
Gleichen, Alberta
Canada

In the fall of 1949, at seven years old, Arthur Bear Chief (b. 1942) was taken from his family and placed in the Old Sun Residential School near Gleichen, Alberta, on the Siksika Nation. In the dorm the first night, he cried for his mother. Miss Twigg beat him until he stopped.

Sixty-seven years later, in 2016, Bear Chief published *My Decade at Old Sun, My Lifetime of Hell*, a memoir chronicling the physical, sexual, psychological, and cultural abuses he suffered at the school and their crushing aftermath. "I screwed up so bad with life. Why am I still here?…I wish someone would just kill me," he writes on the first page of the book, recalling one of many nights, alone in his basement, when he considered suicide.[1]

Between 1831 and 1996, more than 150,000 First Nations, Inuit, and Métis children were forced to enroll in Canada's residential schools. Thousands died, buried in unmarked graves, never to return home. Their families were given vague explanations, if any at all. Funded by the government and operated by the church, the schools largely shared an intent to assimilate students by eradicating their culture. Brutality was rampant within the system.

Bear Chief is a Survivor. "I am writing this book in hopes that it will help me in my journey of healing and recovery from my abuse," Bear Chief professes. "May we who survive purge ourselves of our demons and move forward together."

In 100 pages, Bear Chief relives the agony of losing his childhood, the "loving touch" of his mother, and pride in his Blackfoot identity. He's forthright about the subsequent "demons" he faced, like alcoholism, nightmares, flashbacks, and a near inability to maintain relationships with his partners and biological children.

There are moments of happiness in Bear Chief's story. He recounts a long and fulfilling career in public service throughout Canada and a midlife reconnection with his Homelands and Blackfoot language and culture. He credits his resilience to his ancestors and Elders who, he says, instilled in him a "spirit strong enough to survive."

A testament to Bear Chief's grit, the years immediately ensuing his departure from Old Sun in 1959 are marked by personal endeavors and job growth—and a period of making photographs. "I was busy exploring life," he says.

In August 1963, Bear Chief left Siksika Nation to work at a residential school in Sault Ste. Marie, Ontario, called Shingwauk Hall. It was his first off-reserve job, and the farthest he had been from home. He was just 21 years old at the time, and the boys Bear Chief looked after were hardly younger. His

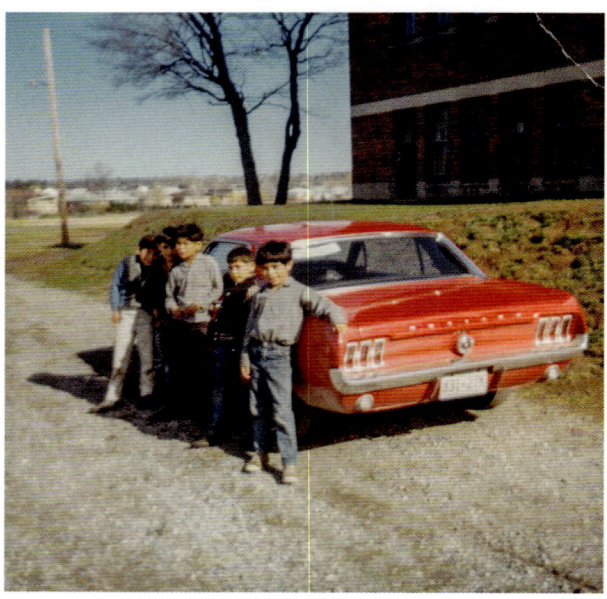

adjustment to the school was quick. "It was the same routine I had known for ten years, but now I was on the other side," he says. "One difference, though, was that I was not a monster."

Bear Chief stayed at Shingwauk Hall for a total of 28 months. He became the senior boys' supervisor. He oversaw the sports teams, taught gymnastics, and started a popular judo club that competed in local competitions. At the Sault Ste. Marie YMCA, he sharpened his own judo skills, advancing to an orange belt. And he made pictures of campus activities—keepsakes of a brief and relatively serene chapter of his life. "I truly enjoyed sports and supervising the boys," Bear Chief remarks.

The Shingwauk Residential Schools Centre (SRSC)—a cross-cultural and educational project of Algoma University that advocates for the telling of the true history of residential schools—is the steward of roughly 70 photographs Bear Chief made at Shingwauk Hall. The images are imbued with camaraderie. In photo after photo, the boys drape their arms around one another, or tilt their bodies into each other. (The school was coed, but girls rarely appear in the photos.)

One sunny image shows five boys leaning against a bright red Mustang, their heads just inches above the car. Another image shows two students in oversized coats, surrounded by glistening snow, their boots planted in shallow tire tracks. The aphyllous

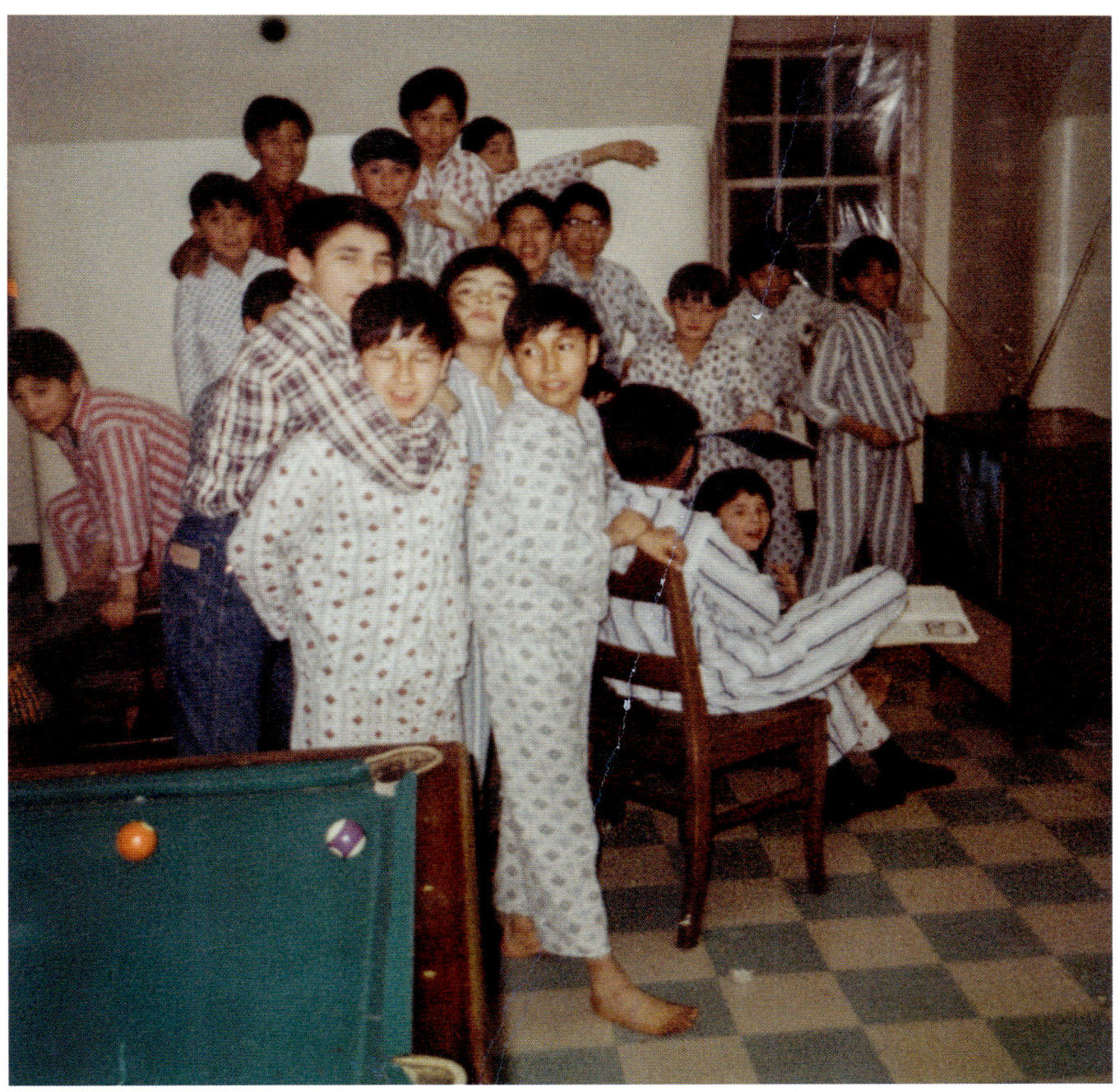

Pages 152–155: Shingwauk students, Sault Ste. Marie, Ontario,
c. 1963–70.

PHOTOGRAPHS BY ARTHUR BEAR CHIEF. COURTESY OF SHINGWAUK RESIDENTIAL SCHOOLS
CENTRE, ALGOMA UNIVERSITY.

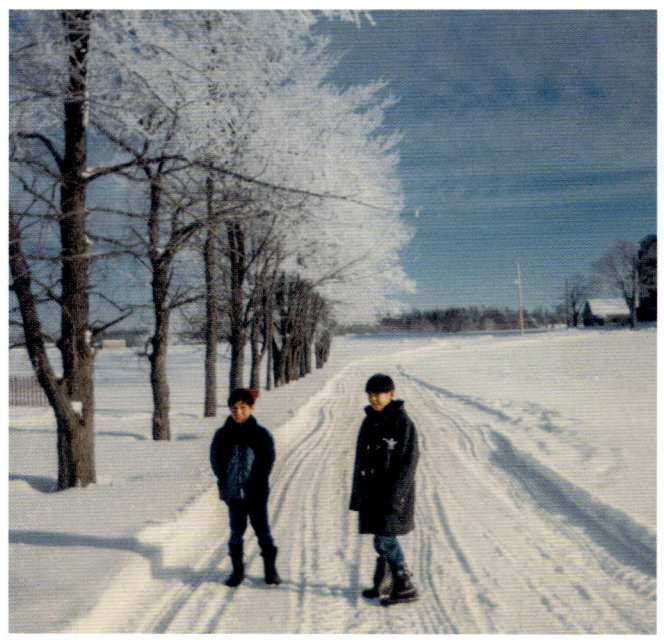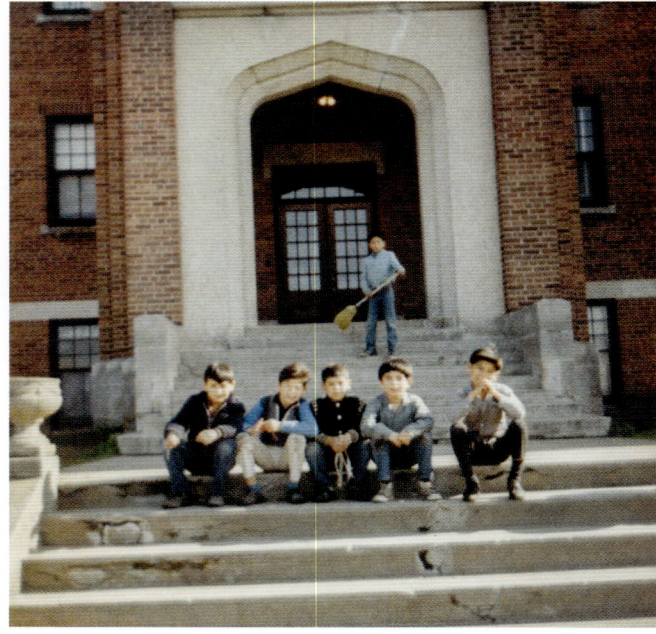

branches above them are glazed with white crystals that brush against the blue wintertime sky. Multiple photographs are made inside the dorms: a troupe of boys in their pajamas around the TV; boys piled on beds; boys practicing headstands. Bear Chief photographed Christmas celebrations and jovial rides on the backs of horses, mopeds, and snowmobiles. A host of pictures documents sports at the school, especially the judo club, with members clad in white judogis, the traditional judo uniform.

Following his stint at Shingwauk Hall, Bear Chief worked at Horden Hall, a residential school on Moose Factory Island, from 1968 to 1970. Without delay, he started a judo club for the senior boys, which expanded to include girls and youth from the island. Bear Chief continued his own training, and, in 1970, earned a brown belt, the penultimate rank in the sport.

The SRCS holds just over 20 images Bear Chief made at Horden Hall. All but one picture judo—the other is a photo of the senior boys, in dapper suits, standing outside of their dormitory. The photographs of the judo clubs at Shingwauk and Horden are "of particular note" says Krista McCracken, the researcher/curator at the SRSC, because they are some of the only images of the clubs available to the public.[2]

The remaining 10 or so photographs in the Arthur Bear Chief Collection weren't made by Bear Chief. They are classic yearbook photos, produced at Shingwauk Hall. Bear Chief held on to the palm-sized prints until 2007, when he donated his photographs from Shingwauk and Horden, which totaled just over 100, to the SRSC.

Maybe Bear Chief saw something in the promising yearbook photos that reminded him of himself. Maybe, somehow, all the photographs he made and kept were a tribute to the childhood he was denied. Perhaps they were simply mementos of a time Bear Chief looks back on with pride.

"My boys' care and safety came first, and I ensured that their stay was as comfortable and happy as it could be while they were away from their parents. After all, I was the substitute parent, and I had to be there for them."

Bear Chief used to talk to his charges about what he endured at Old Sun. "They did not believe me, but it is hard to comprehend what we actually experienced," he concedes.

"One of the most important things to understand about Residential School photography is that it only shows part of the picture," says McCracken. "Photographs," they add, "do not hold all the experiences of everyone who attended Residential Schools."[3]

—Sarah Stacke

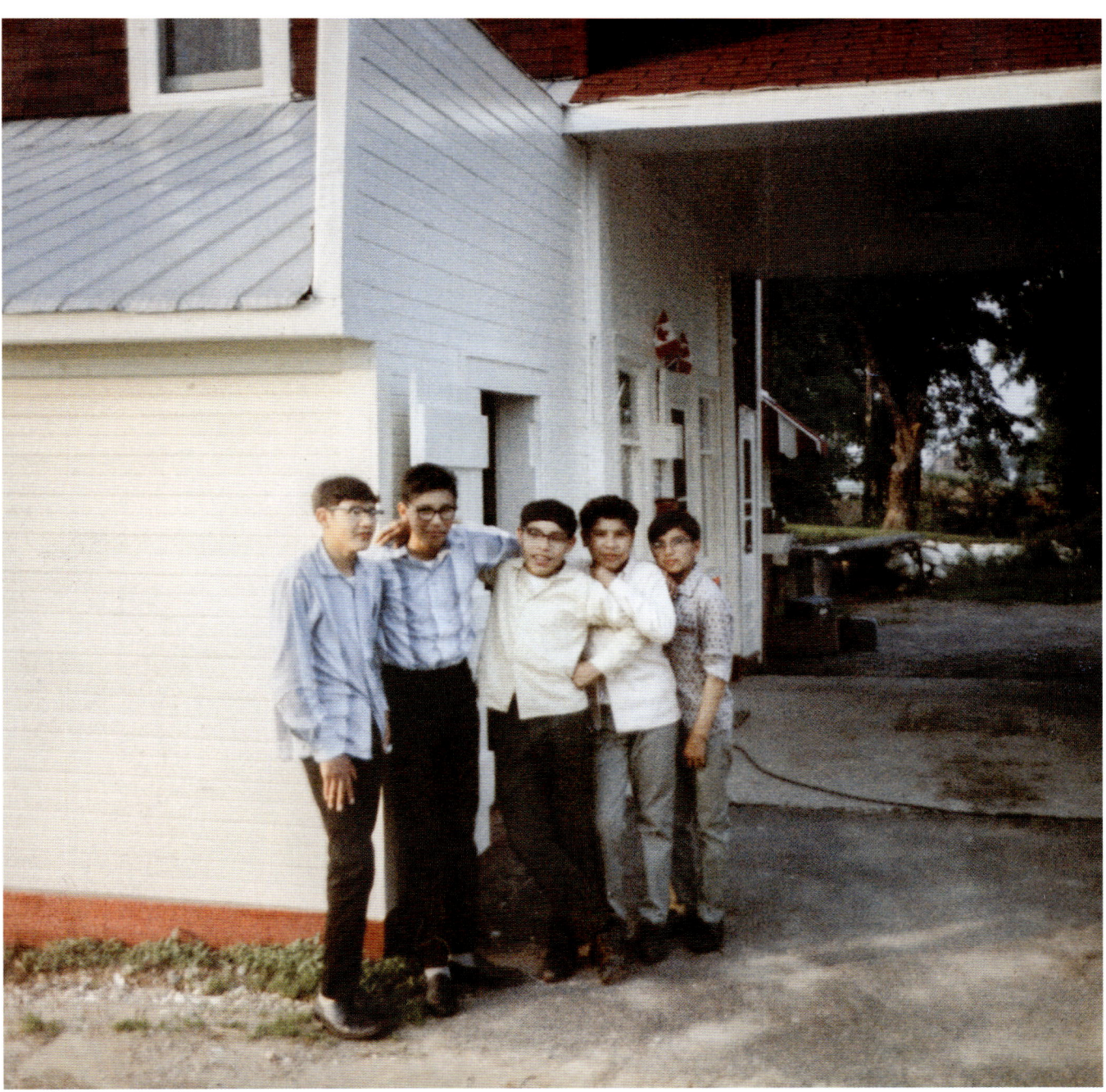

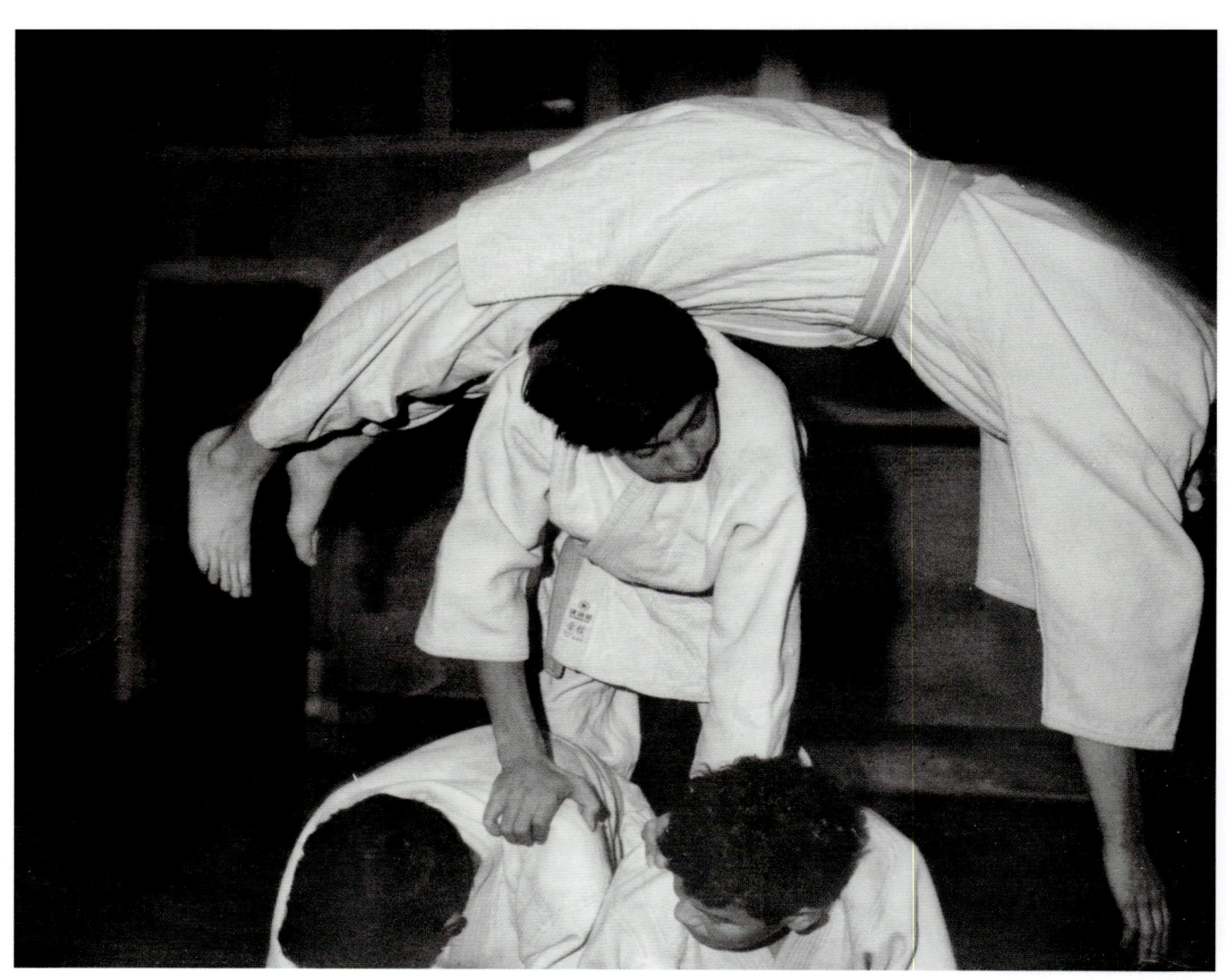

Horden judo club, Moose Factory Island, Ontario, c. 1963–70.

PHOTOGRAPH BY ARTHUR BEAR CHIEF. COURTESY OF SHINGWAUK RESIDENTIAL
SCHOOLS CENTRE, ALGOMA UNIVERSITY.

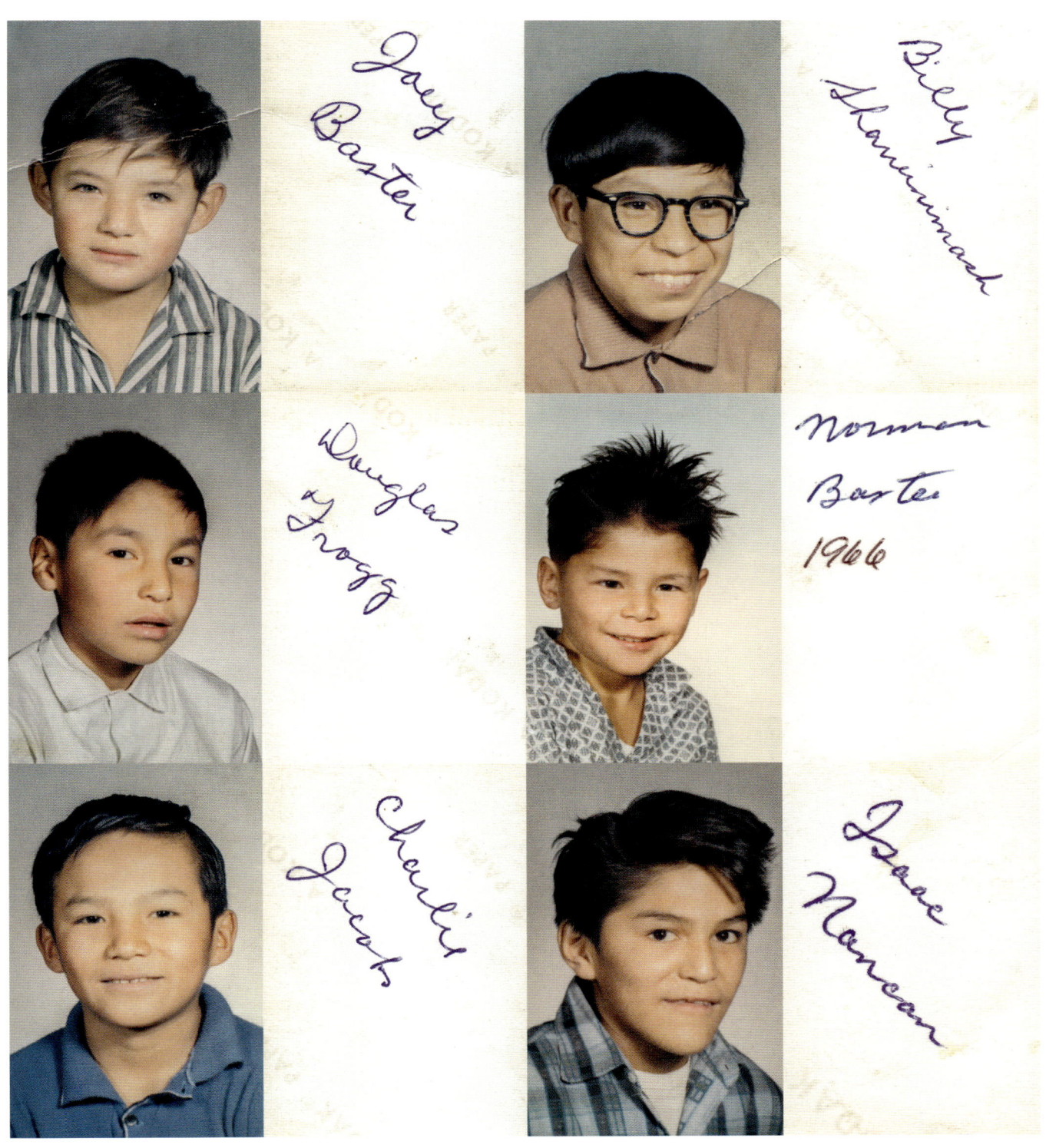

Shingwauk students Joey Baxter, Billy Shawinimash, Douglas Frogg, Norman Baxter, Charlie Jacobs, and Isaac Necan (photo is mislabeled as "Nancan"), c. 1963–70.

PHOTOGRAPHER ONCE IDENTIFIED. COURTESY OF SHINGWAUK RESIDENTIAL SCHOOLS CENTRE, ALGOMA UNIVERSITY.

DUGAN AGUILAR

Mountain Maidu, Pit River, Walker River Paiute
Susanville, California
United States

For many California Indigenous nations, a roundhouse traditionally served as the center of village life. They were usually up to 40 feet in diameter and covered with earth, bark, or shingles. For the Tuolumne Band of Me-Wuk Indians, a federally recognized Tribe in the Sierra Nevada foothills of Tuolumne County, the roundhouse endures as a gathering place for sacred events.

A photograph titled *Tuolumne Roundhouse* appears in Dugan Aguilar's (1947–2018) book, *She Sang Me a Good Luck Song: The California Indian Photographs of Dugan Aguilar*. The monochromatic image overflows with energy. Striated clouds play in the sky and the leafy trees surrounding the roundhouse take on a sentient quality. One way Aguilar felt connected to the earth was through dancers and singers, and the photographs he made provided a means to share these connections. "A spiritual soul lives not only in those who offer prayer through ceremonial song and dance, but also in those who have the gift to recognize the presence of spirit among them," observed Theresa Harlan, the editor of Aguilar's monograph. "He respects those who go into the roundhouse to pray for the world we all inhabit."[1]

Aguilar was raised on the Homelands of the Mountain Maidu, Pit River, Washoe, and Paiute peoples. He joined the Marine Corps in 1968 and served in the Vietnam War, an unsettling experience that he rarely spoke of, though he was open about the PTSD he faced. Returning home, he attended California State University, where he earned a BA in industrial technology and design. He developed his love of photography through classes at the University of Nevada and an Ansel Adams workshop taught by Adams's assistants.

Judith Lowry, Aguilar's cousin, told *American Indian* that he originally planned to photograph every Tribe in the United States, but soon realized documenting California's Native people was his life's work.[2] There are 109 Tribes in the state officially recognized by the federal government, with several non–federally recognized Tribes actively seeking recognition. Aguilar's son, Dustin, said that he hopes his father's photographs help people "see the rich cultures that have existed in California and Nevada for millennia, and how members of these groups preserve, maintain and continue tradition alongside modern, mainstream society."[3]

Aguilar was welcomed and trusted by Native communities. He photographed cultural events such as the Maidu Bear Dance, Yurok and Karuk ceremonies, and the Susanville Indian veterans' reunions, held annually in Susanville. He said the purpose of his photography was to "show Natives alive and well,"

a counterpoint to the depictions he often saw in museums and society at large.[4]

Dustin recalls his father's own embrace of life: "Despite being a very quiet person, he had an amazing sense of humor. He was an amazing hunter and athlete. He loved mountains and taught me to ski as soon as I could walk. He was just good at a lot of things, and always strived to do well. He enjoyed the arts, especially music, which he played often."[5]

Another of Aguilar's photographs shows a young Stormy Rojas participating in the Yurok Brush Dance. Barefoot and framed by lush foliage, she wears a deerskin skirt decorated with shells, and a deerskin shirt fringed at the sleeves. Multiple necklaces adorn her chest. Underneath an intricately woven cap, Rojas's hair is divided and wrapped with animal fur and hair ties. All of these details and materials represent her Yurok Tribe and their connection with the natural environment. Aguilar "illuminates the lives of indigenous California people and the relationship they keep with their homeland," said Harlan.[6]

For over three decades, Aguilar was the staff photographer for the California Indian Basketweavers' Association. Stepping into this role, he was able to document Native women upholding feminine ancestral weaving traditions. Learning that the weavers pray to the Creator for the materials they've collected and the forthcoming basket, he felt an affinity with them. This process was similar to his own approach to making photographs in the darkroom, where before entering to mix light, chemicals, and paper, he offered a prayer to the Creator for the images that would surface. "He spent a lot of time out in the darkroom," recalled Dustin.[7]

Aguilar's archive, about 25,000 negatives and prints made from the 1980s to the 2010s, is housed at the Oakland Museum of California (OMCA). Dustin, with the blessings of his family and trusted mentors, endowed the collection to the OMCA in 2022. "OMCA's focus on California's diverse cultural heritage, along with their efforts to tell undertold and untold stories, informed the choice to donate," explained Dustin. "Photography was my father's passion. I would love for people to see his work."[8]

—Tiffany Midge and Sarah Stacke

Stormy Rojas, Brush Dance, Klamath River, 1992.

Tuolumne Roundhouse, 1993.

PHOTOGRAPHS BY DUGAN AGUILAR. COLLECTION OF THE OAKLAND MUSEUM OF CALIFORNIA, GIFT OF THE FAMILY OF DUGAN AGUILAR.

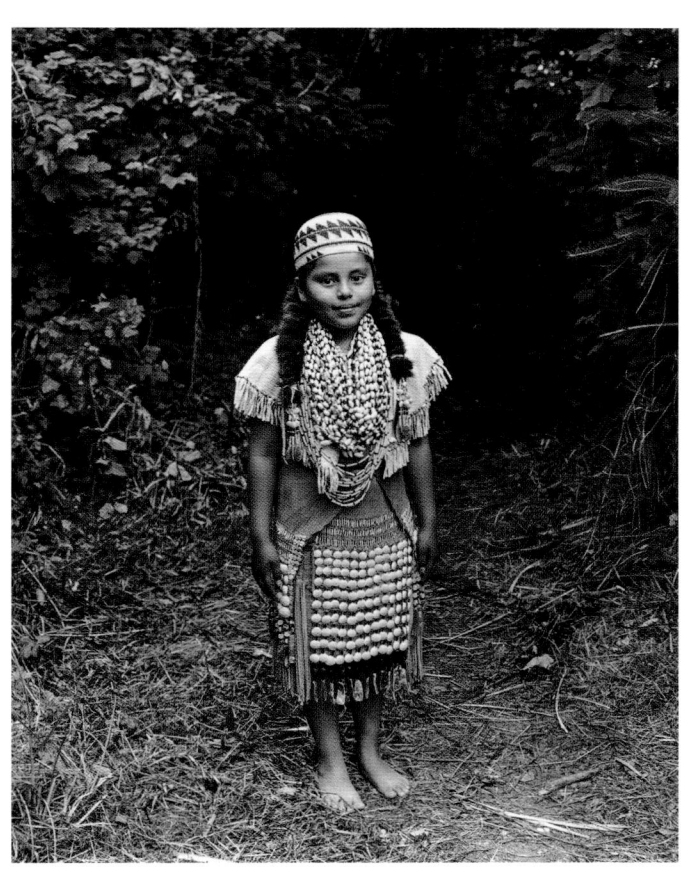
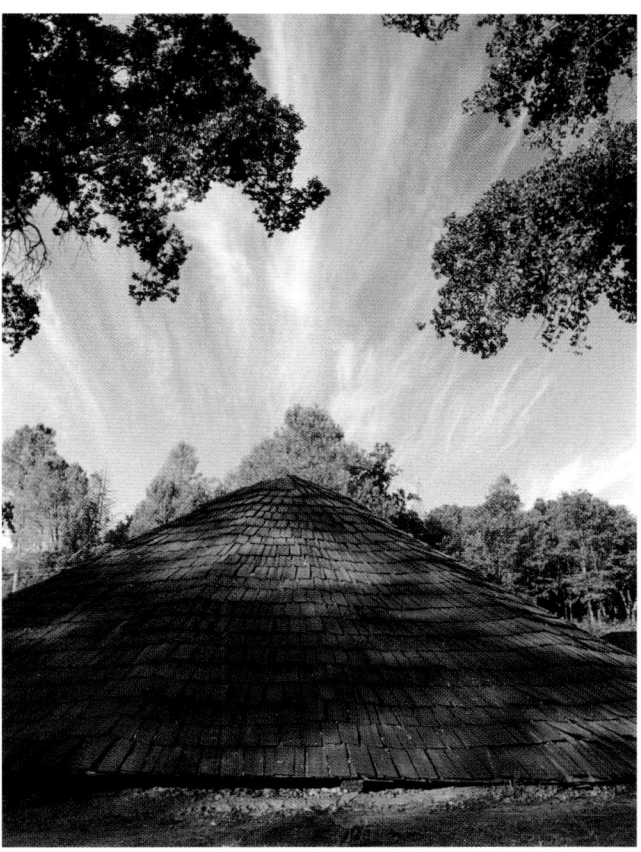

HARRY CARL SAMPSON
STEWART INDIAN SCHOOL
Over 200 Native nations from Western America
Carson City, Nevada
United States

In 1966, the Stewart Braves boys basketball team won the Nevada State Championship title 62–59 in a thrilling game against Moapa Valley High School. It was their 17th consecutive victory of the season.[1] When the team returned from Las Vegas to their campus at the Stewart Indian School, near Carson City, the homecoming was joyful. Coach James "Bud" Hurin stepped off the bus first, holding up the trophy, followed by the champions in button-down shirts and letter sweaters. Students, the marching band, the cheerleading squad, and faculty crowded around them.[2] The team's triumphant record was commemorated in the *Desert Braves* yearbook, with a two-page collage crafted with photographs of the players and newspaper clippings that declared their wins.

Open from 1890 to 1980, the Stewart Indian School saw over 30,000 students in its 90-year history. Initially intended to educate youth from Nevada's Great Basin Tribes—Washoe, Paiute, Shoshone—pupils from over 200 nations ultimately attended the school. Now the 110-acre campus is home to the Stewart Indian School Cultural Center & Museum, an establishment engaging with Stewart's complicated history.

"Stewart is one of 523 boarding schools for Native children in the U.S.," said Bobbi Rahder, the museum director. "All reflected the federal government's assimilation policy... This policy was cruel because it separated children from their families and this has caused historical trauma. There are also positive stories about students' experiences."[3]

The museum is guided by an advisory committee of Stewart alumni. "This is their school, their museum, and we are honored to work with them to make sure this important part of American history is remembered," remarked Rahder. "The mission of the museum is to honor all the experiences, and to help the families to heal from the trauma of the early years."[4]

Stewart had a long history of publications. The first school newsletter was posted in 1899 and the final one in 1980. The content reflected its evolution from an intolerant institution focused on eradicating Native American languages and cultures to a place that sought to uplift Native heritage and provide opportunities through academics, versus vocational skills, and strong extracurriculars. The mission statement of the earliest bulletin, the *Indian Advance*, read: "While it recognizes the weakness and vices of the Indian, it will attempt to mention some of his good qualities and prove that he is capable of reaching a higher state of civilization."[5] The last iteration, the *Warpath*, was authored, edited, and released biweekly by the Publications class and was filled with representative illustrations, op-eds, testimonials, campus news, an advice column, senior-class profiles, and an overall sense that the future belonged to the students.

Photography led the *Desert Braves* yearbook, produced annually from 1946 until Stewart closed; nearly every page was adorned with pictures. From its inception, the yearbook was wrought by a staff of student business managers, editors, reporters, and image makers. A hallmark of the annual was the "Snapshots" section, where compositions made from hundreds of cut-up photos filled the closing pages, presumably the hard work of the "Snapshot Editor." Over the years, dozens of photographers in training covered campus life: sports, music, clubs, classes, arts, special events, leisure, employees, and administrators. In the 1977 edition, Sonja Rogers was described as "one of the dedicated student photographers," while Dennis Quimayousie "spent long hours in the darkroom."

"Together, we worked to express our ideas and feelings in this yearbook," wrote Sonia Stone, the 1979 editor of *Desert Braves*. "Helping each other is what a part of life is all about. To find freedom in words, thoughts, and in ourselves as individuals.

ALWAYS REMEMBER . . . . .
YOU have a right to live . . . . .
to work, to play, to laugh, to cry
to be united with others, yet be proud of our individual heritages.
to just be ourselves, without suffering for it.[6]

Vital to Stewart's publications and to the history of the school, photography, and the Western United States is a student, and later a teacher, named Harry Carl Sampson (1890–1975). Kidnapped from his Northern Paiute family by Indian agents and hauled to Stewart, Sampson graduated in 1913. A star pitcher for the baseball team, he was inducted into the Stewart Hall of Fame, posthumously, in 1975. Multiskilled, Sampson learned the printing trade at Stewart and became an exceptional clarinet player. Following his studies, he was noted as the "bandmaster" in the November 29, 1913, school newspaper. By 1917, likely earlier, he was appointed the printing instructor of the *Indian Enterprise*, the then-current paper, generated in the school's print shop by "student apprentices." Sampson's title was one of three listed on the masthead, along with the superintendent and editor. He taught printing (and shoe and harness making) in the boys' trade department, too.

Some Desert Braves *image makers: Harry Stevens ('46 photographer); Mae Pete ('60 snapshot editor); Eldon Joka ('61 snapshot editor); Mary Louise Maho ('61 snapshots); Larry Phillips ('67 business manager and photographer); Ernest Sakeva ('67 sports and photographer); Harlan Jackson ('68 business manager and photographer); Paul Humphreys ('68 photographer); Florine Batala and George Ray ('75 photographers); Sonja Rogers and Dennis Quimayousie ('77 photographers); Larry Tso, Gabe Choyguha, Harry Wright, Berta Mack, Vanessa Leon ('78 photographers); Larry Tso, Julian Salcido, Evelyn Brown ('79 photographers).*

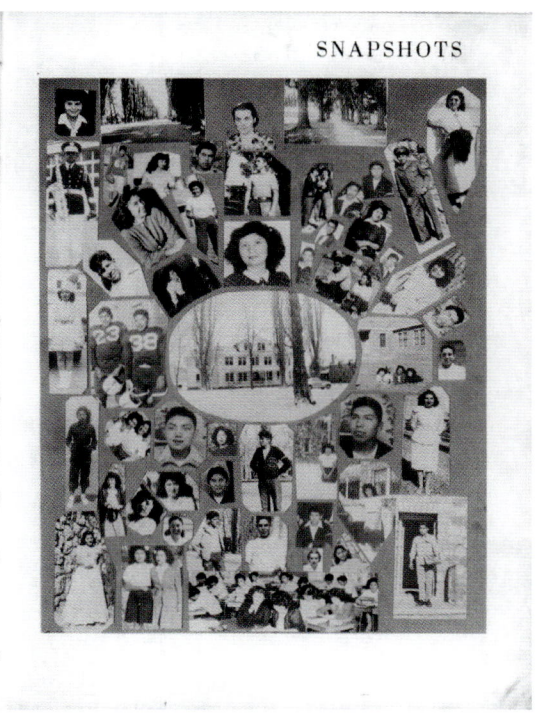

SNAPSHOTS

Sampson joined minor-league baseball teams in Nevada and California and for six decades performed as a professional clarinetist in various bands. Devoted to the well-being of his people, he was instrumental in the founding of the Reno-Sparks Indian Colony, a federally recognized nation. He was elected the nation's first chair and remained involved with Tribal council affairs. Sampson possessed remarkable wisdom about native plants and medicine central to Northern Paiute lifeways, which he cataloged and shared with generations of relatives and scholars at the University of Nevada.

"He was amazingly knowledgeable and talented," said Rahder.[7]

Sampson began photographing his surroundings in the 1910s, tucking the images away in albums. He casually pictured fandangos (festive intertribal gatherings) around the state, street scenes in Reno, circuses, subsistence activities, friends, and family. A self-taught photographer, many of his images are slightly blurry, a fitting visual metaphor for the way he was always moving from one venture to the next. The photographs continue to provide invaluable insight into his, and others', early 20th-century realities. During the 1980s, Sampson's heartfelt photographic work was published in the *Native Nevadan*, an intertribal newspaper, and was exhibited at the Nevada Historical Society. A small selection are part of the Handbook of North American Indians records at the Smithsonian's National Anthropological Archives. Several were published in Nicole Dawn Strathman's 2020 book, *Through a Native Lens: American Indian Photography.*

The Stewart Cultural Center & Museum develops exhibitions centered on school artifacts and alumni, and is a place for everyone to learn about the "contemporary art and culture of Nevada's 28 tribal nations, bands, and colonies," explained Rahder.[8] For those who attended Stewart and their relatives, it is a place to gather and collaborate. The museum looks after thousands of historical photographs awaiting awareness and annotation. These images, and all the collections at the museum, hold the stories and experiences of countless students, away from their homes, whose lives and communities were forever altered by Stewart.

—Sarah Stacke

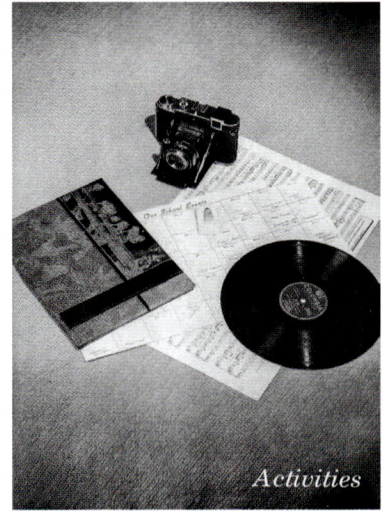

Activities

"Snapshots" page composed by the Annual Staff: Wallace Garcia, Bernyce Downey, Vivian Davis, Leong Lincoln, Lillian Tybo, Ivan George, and John Dondero. *Desert Braves*, 1949.

A still-life photograph introducing activities at Stewart. This edition's Annual Staff was Basil Jimmy, Virgil Namoki, Foster Kenton, Lauterio Valenzuela, Charlotte Antone, Verna Randall, Mary Louise Maho, Silas King, Marlene Calnimptewa, Lee Ann Emerson, and Allena Cuch. *Desert Braves*, 1962.

DESERT BRAVES YEARBOOKS AND THE *NATIVE NEVADAN* COURTESY OF THE STEWART INDIAN SCHOOL CULTURAL CENTER & MUSEUM.

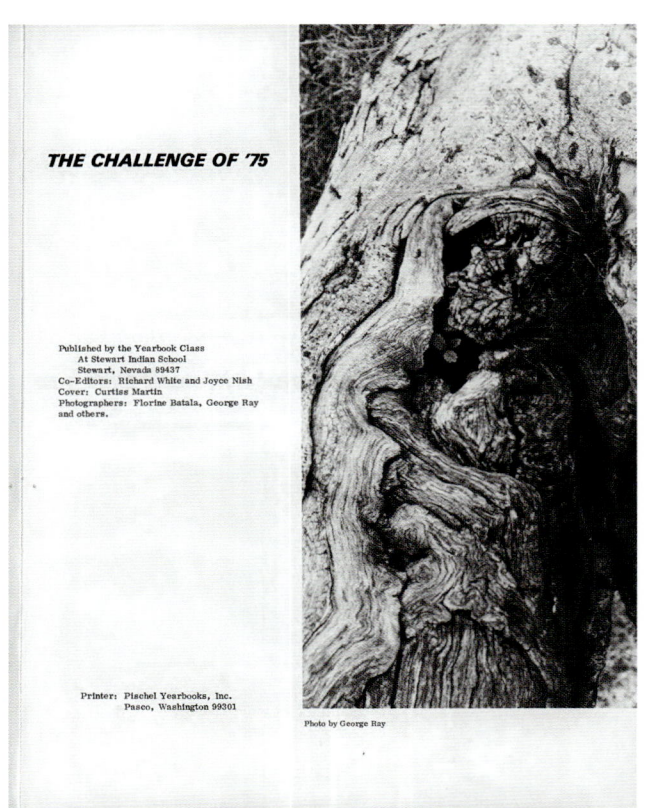

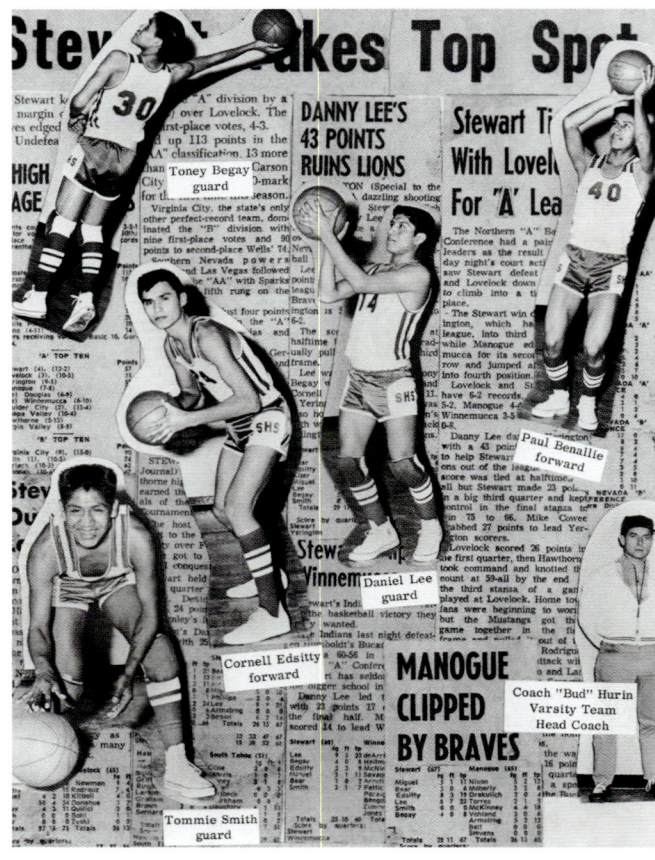

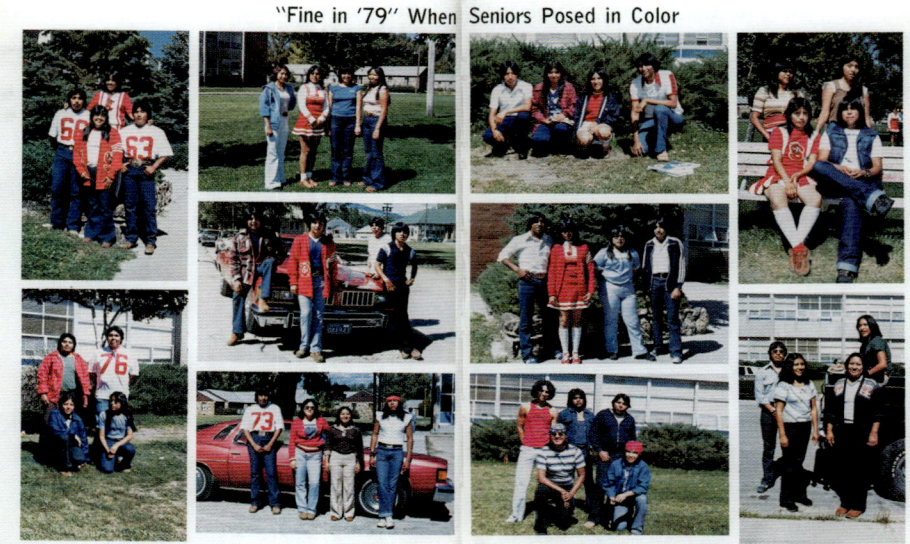

Title page with an image by *Desert Braves* photographer
George Ray. *Desert Braves*, 1975.

A collage commemorating the 1964–65 boys varsity
basketball players. The team was upset in the semifinals
of the Northern Nevada Zone Basketball Tournament, just
two wins away from playing in the state championship. The
collage was created by the Annual Staff: Kenneth Largo,
Leona Thomas, Madeline McDonald, Roybert Youvella, Wilda
Bryant, and Ruth Tommie. *Desert Braves*, 1965.

"'Fine in '79' When Seniors Posed in Color."
Published by the Yearbook Class, with editor
Sonia Stone. Photography by Larry Tso, Julian
Salcido, and Evelyn Brown, and layouts by Robert
Mahkewa. *Desert Braves*, 1979.

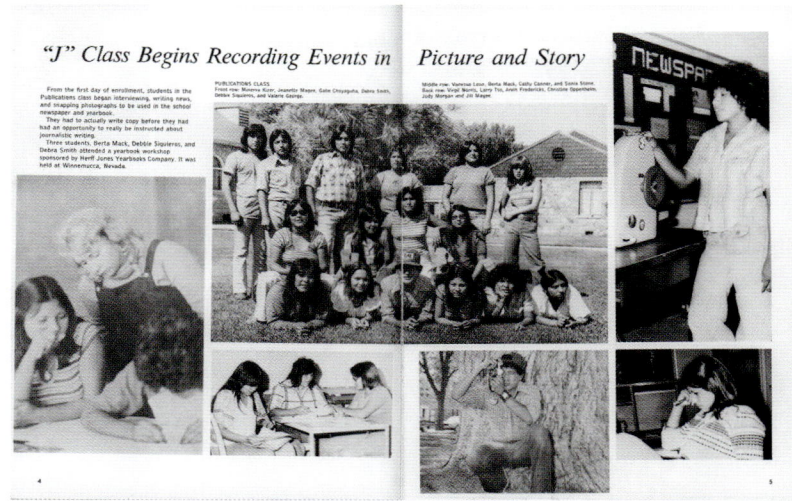

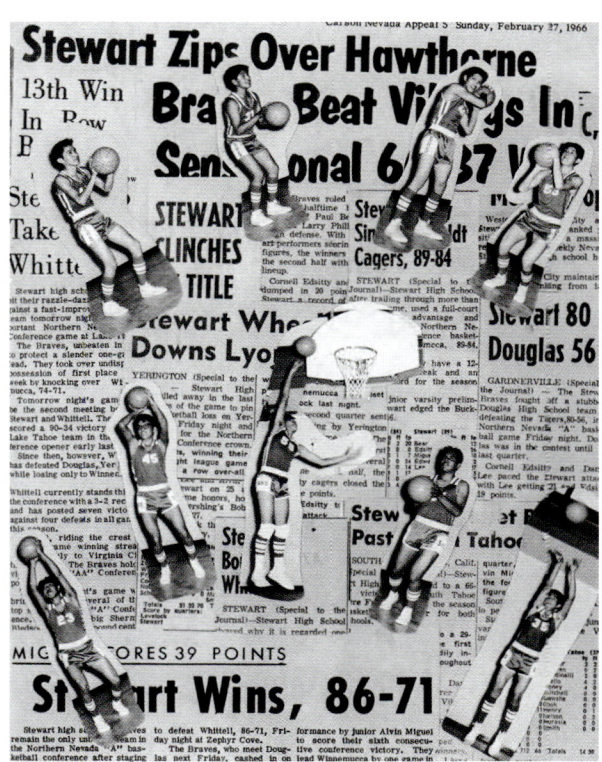

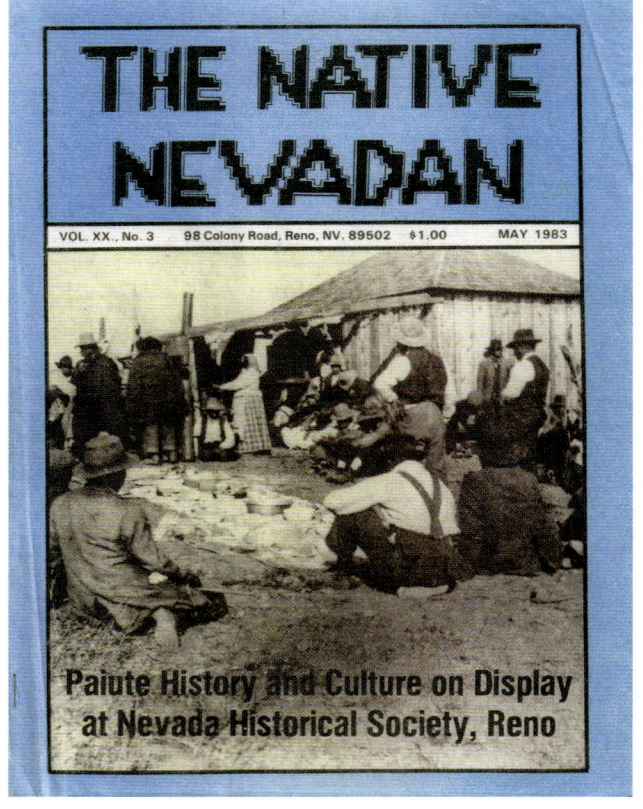

"'J' Class Begins Recording Events in Picture and Story." Published by the Yearbook Class, with editor Berta Mack. Photography by Larry Tso, Gabe Choyguha, Harry Wright, Berta Mack, and Vanessa Leon. *Desert Braves*, 1978.

A collage commemorating the 1965–66 boys varsity basketball players. The team, whose starting lineup represented five different Native nations, took home the state championship title. Senior David Lee was named most valuable player in the championship game by news media covering the event. The collage was created by the Annual Staff: Roy Youvella, Madeline McDonald, Iris Mike, Peter Begay, Carlon Ami, Faye Apkaw, and Ina Mauel. *Desert Braves*, 1966.

May 1983 cover of the *Native Nevadan* magazine featuring a photograph by Harry Sampson.

JAMES "JIM" JEROME

Gwich'in
Aklavik, Northwest Territories
Canada

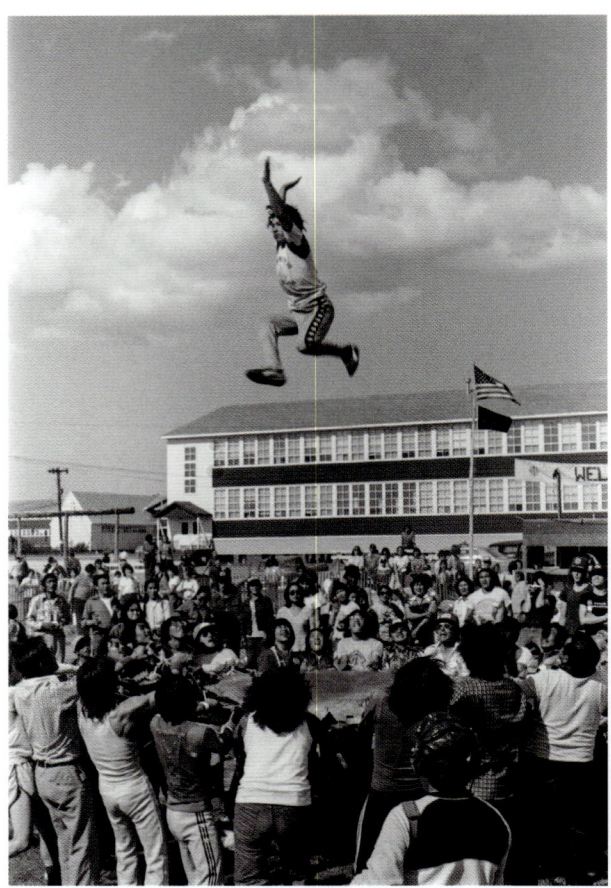

More than 3,500 black-and-white photographs made by James "Jim" Jerome (1949–1979) have been described, digitized, and made publicly available by the Northwest Territories (NWT) Archives. Many of the negatives are imperfect—scarred by the house fire that tragically took Jerome's life at 30 years old.

At the time of his death in 1979, Jerome was absorbed in funding and authoring a book about Dene Elders of the Mackenzie Valley, a sprawling and geographically rich region in Canada's Northwest Territories. Crafted from extensive interviews and photographs, the book was titled *Portraits and History of the Dene Elders*. Jerome was clear about its value.

"We want our children to retain their Dene culture and traditions through written history and photo-portraits of their Dene elders," he wrote in the project description. "We want this book to be a history book by our elders of their own history. We want future generations to have this book. They will come to understand the history of their ancestors and how their ancestors lived off the land, by the land, and with the land. We want people to have their say about their problems, their culture, and their traditions. For the first time, the Dene elders will have the opportunity to express themselves. We must do this portrait history of the Dene elders NOW, before it is lost to us forever."[1]

In the 1970s (and into the 1990s), many middle and high school students in the NWT still had to leave their families for months at a time to attend residential schools in larger communities. One letter of support for Jerome's work plainly described the cultural harm this dislocation caused. "They are taught to turn away from the Dene traditions, that most of the Dene ways are superstitious and primitive," typed Gladys Alexie of the Tree of Peace Friendship Centre. "Upon returning to their settlements for the 2 summer months, what contact they have with elders is extremely limited as most of the elders live on the land during these months, therefore making it difficult for the young people to learn that which is theirs by heritage."[2]

Two weeks before the fire, Jerome sent a letter to his partner, Elisabeth Jansen-Hadlari. The couple had a young son, Thomas. In sloping script, he told her that the project was going well, he was enjoying the interviews and portraits, and he was learning a lot. "Can you picture me as an author?" he asked. "Someday Thomas will read this book and see and know me through my portraits."[3]

Jansen-Hadlari salvaged more than 9,000 negatives from the devastation. In 1995, Thomas donated them to the NWT Archives, where they had been held in trust for him since 1982. Yet other than a handful of papers about the scope and production of *Portraits and History of the Dene Elders*, it is presumed the rest of the book's work was lost in the flames. In 2008–09, the NWT Archives partnered with the Gwich'in Social & Cultural Institute on an identification project, the result of which is the 3,500-plus photographs online with detailed information about the people, places, and activities pictured.

Born on July 31, 1949, in Aklavik, NWT, Jerome was raised near the Mackenzie River in a longtime Gwich'in camp named Nichiitsii Diniinlee (Big Rock). He spent years on the land, until he left for Grollier Hall Residential School in Inuvik. "During High School, photography was my main interest, and my spare time was often spent taking photographs and working in the darkroom," he wrote later.[4] Both of Jerome's parents died before he graduated. He traveled across Canada working as a welder, and then returned to his ancestral lands and revived his devotion to photography. In 1977, he worked for the former *Native Press* newspaper for eight months. Afterward, he pursued a freelance career.

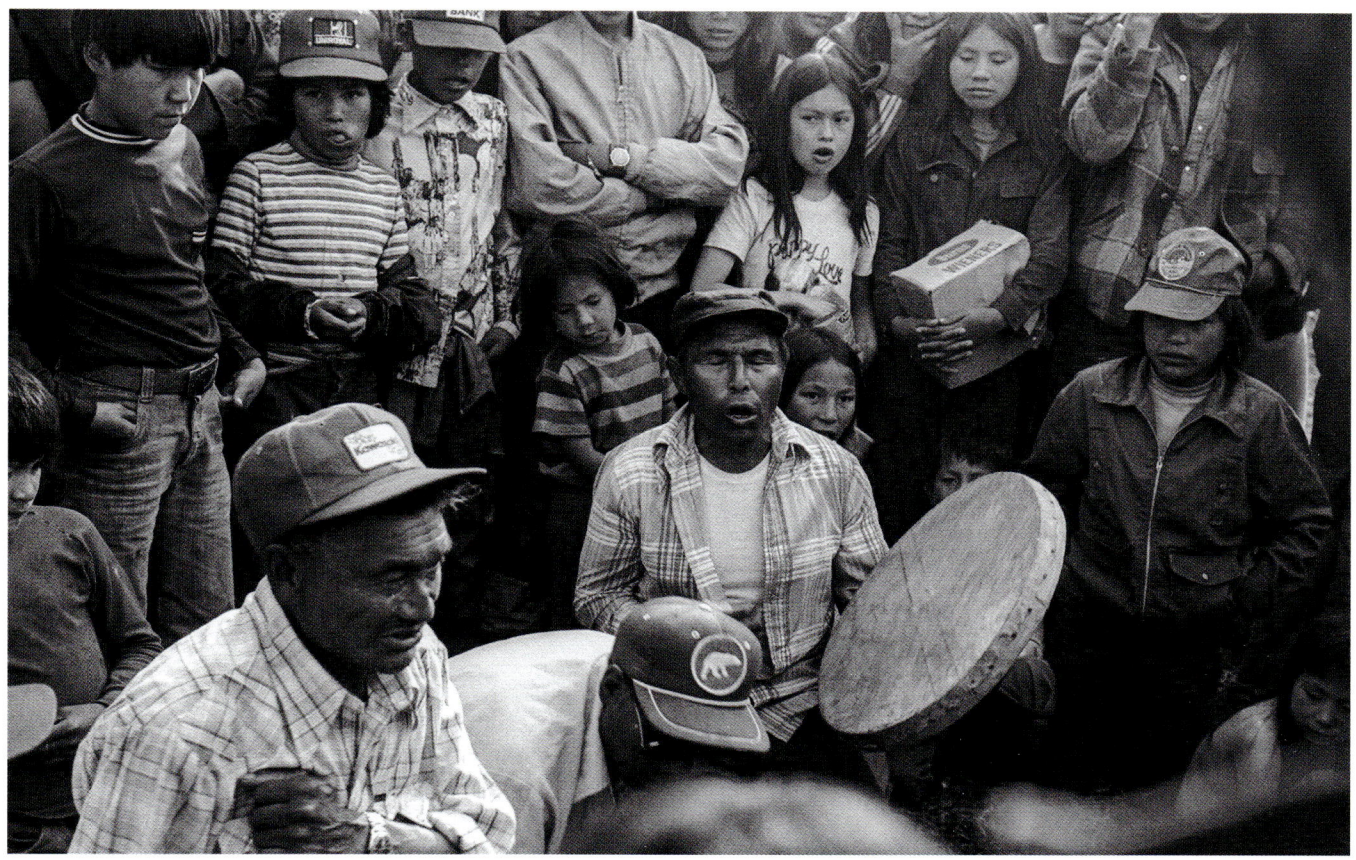

Between 1977 and 1979, Jerome made thousands of invaluable images across the NWT. In the Beaufort Delta Region, he documented traditional Gwich'in life in winter and summer camps for hunting, fishing, and trapping. Erin Suliak, the territorial archivist at the NWT Archives, said the fishing camp series are particularly meaningful. "He took photos of Elders doing the work that Gwich'in are so well-known for, especially working on and catching fish."[5] In the towns, Jerome covered everyday life and events, including the B.B. King concert in Yellowknife and the Northern Games, Arctic Winter Games, and Muskrat Jamboree in Inuvik. Portraits and self-portraits are plentiful.

"He's one of the few photographers here that really leaned into a documentary, photojournalistic style," said Pat Kane (see page 209), an Indigenous visual storyteller based in Yellowknife. "Not a lot of people up here do that kind of work."[6]

"We are forgetting our elders, our children, and ourselves! We need to know why we are here," declared Jerome.[7]

—Sarah Stacke

Men drum and play handgame at a camp for John "JC" Catholique's wedding at the Snowdrift River, Northwest Territories, 1979. Playing, seated (left to right): Louis Drybones, Joe Michel (leaning forward, polar bear hat), Billy Enzoe (drumming).
PHOTOGRAPH BY JAMES JEROME. ©NWT ARCHIVES/JAMES JEROME/N-1987-017-2725

Opposite: A young man is thrown into the air at the Northern Games during a blanket toss in front of Sir Alexander Mackenzie School, Inuvik, Northwest Territories, 1979.
PHOTOGRAPH BY JAMES JEROME. ©NWT ARCHIVES/JAMES JEROME/N-1987-017-2861

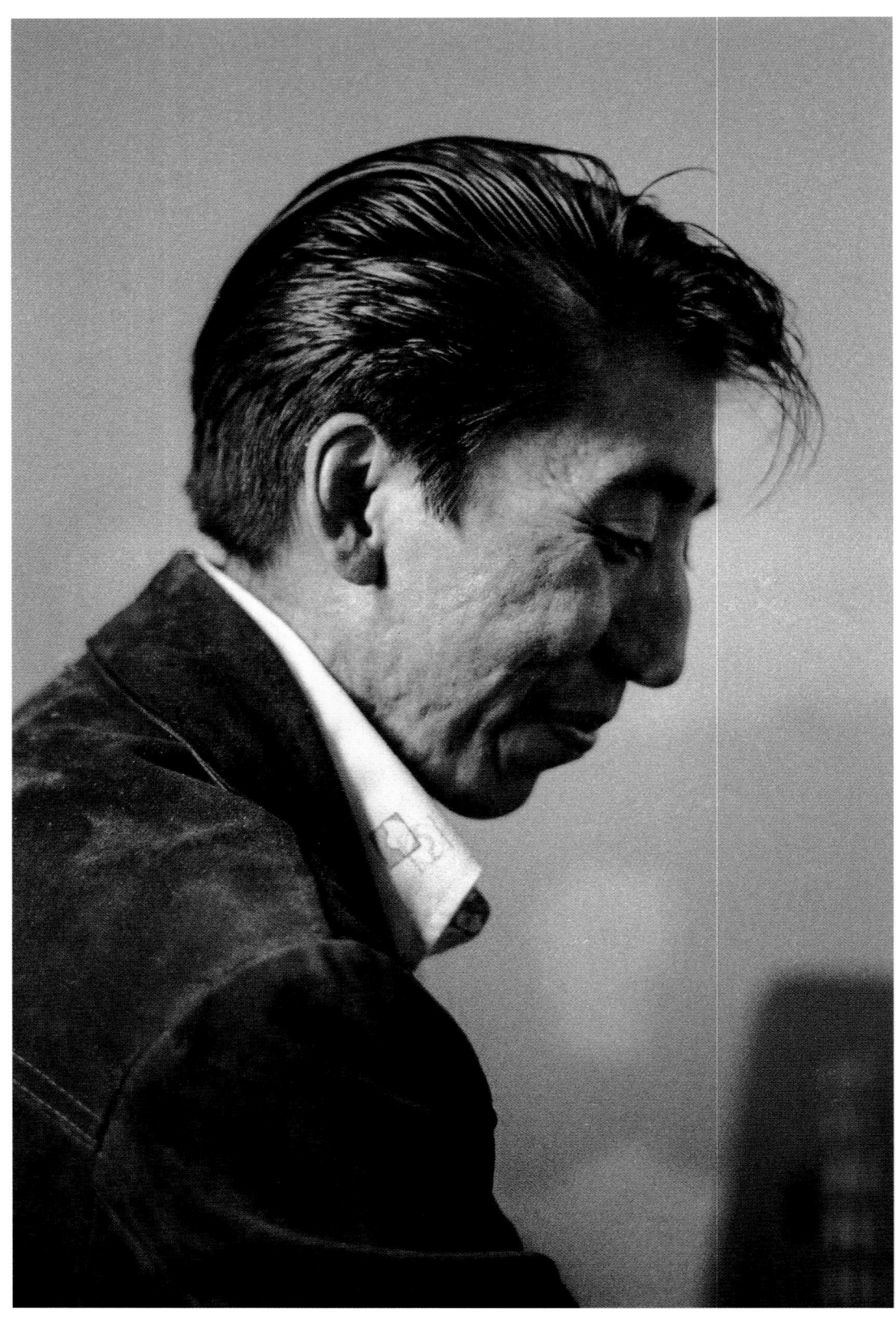

Portrait of Robert Andre, likely Northwest Territories, c. 1977–79.

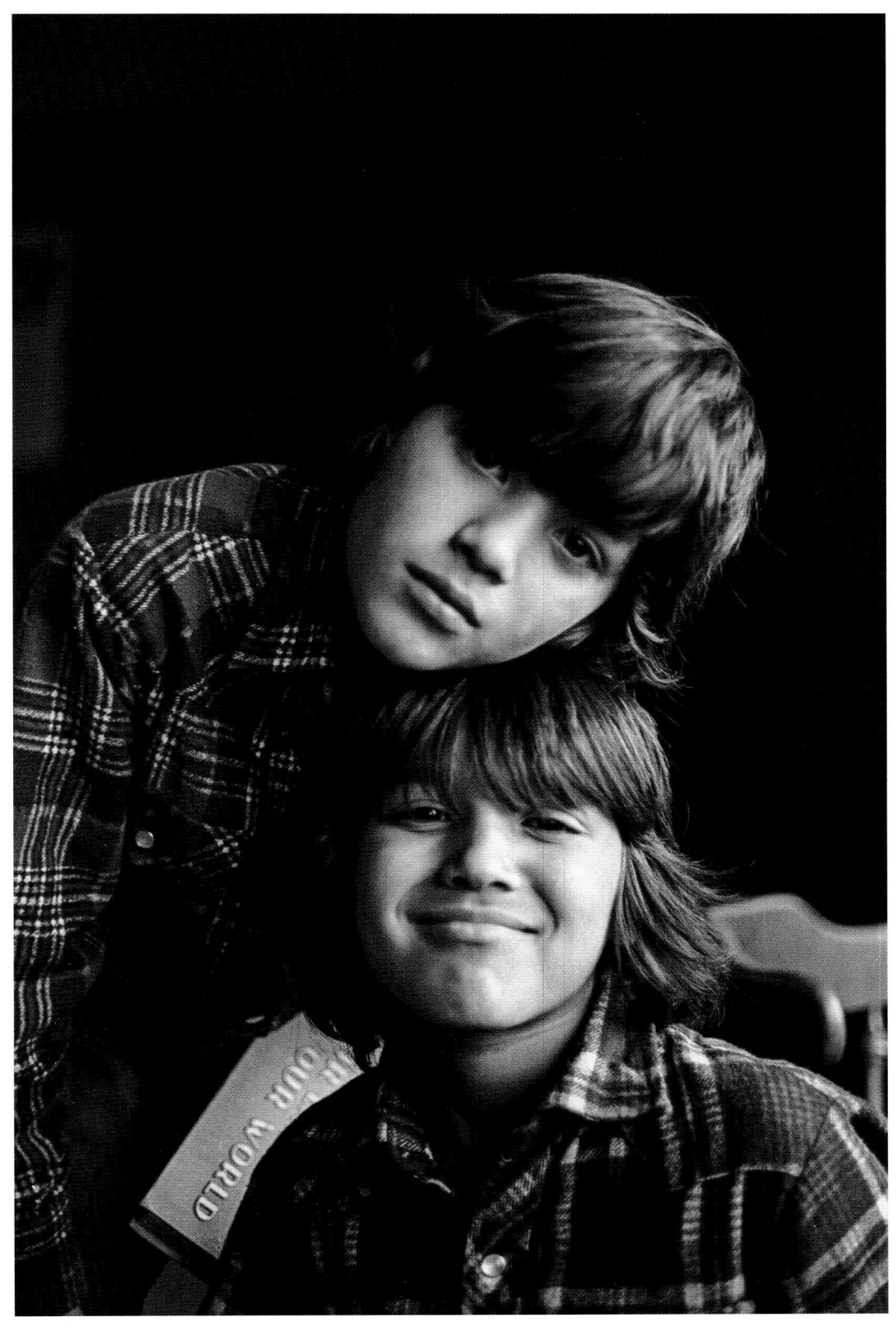

Portrait of two boys, likely Northwest Territories, c. 1977–79.

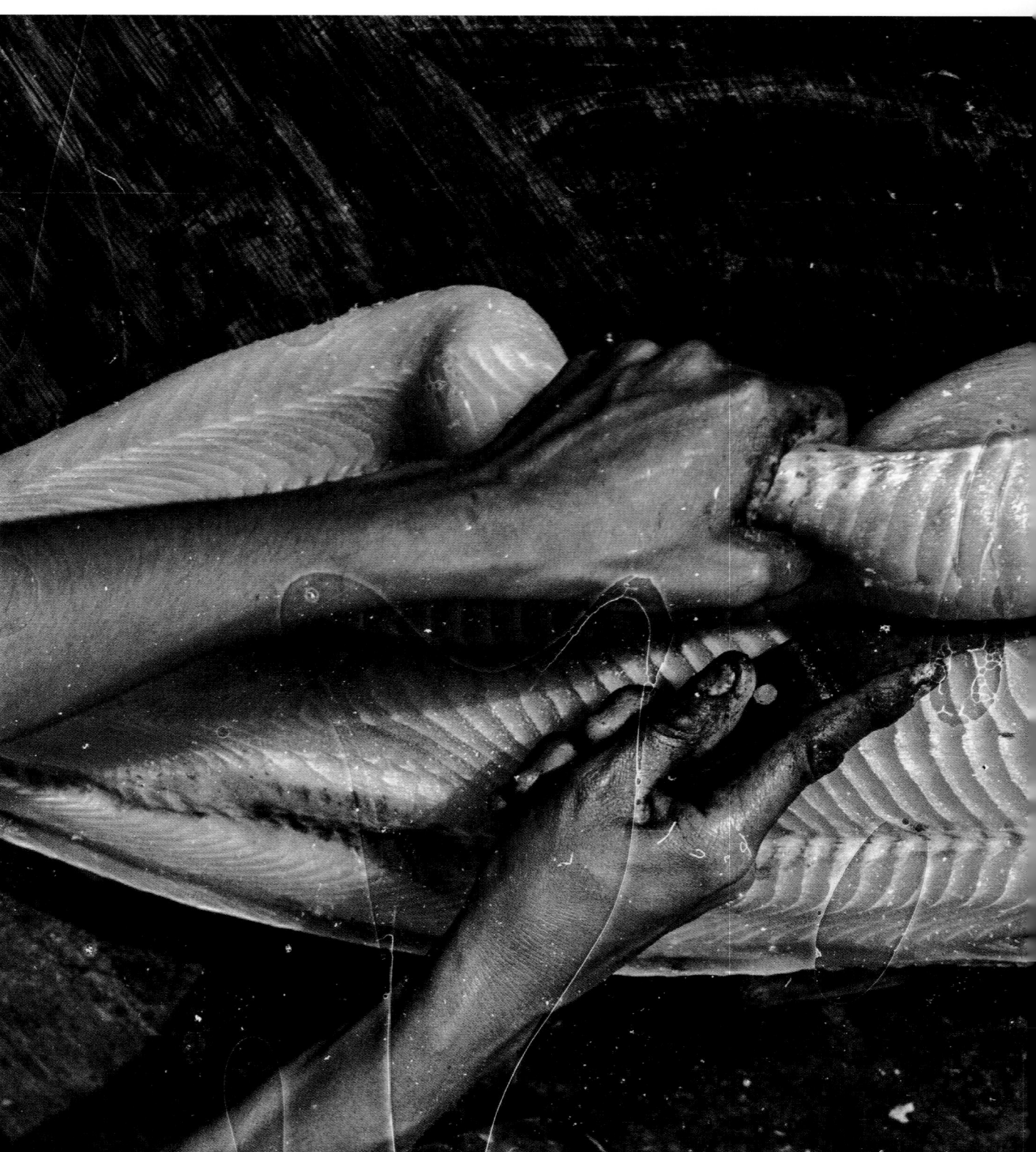

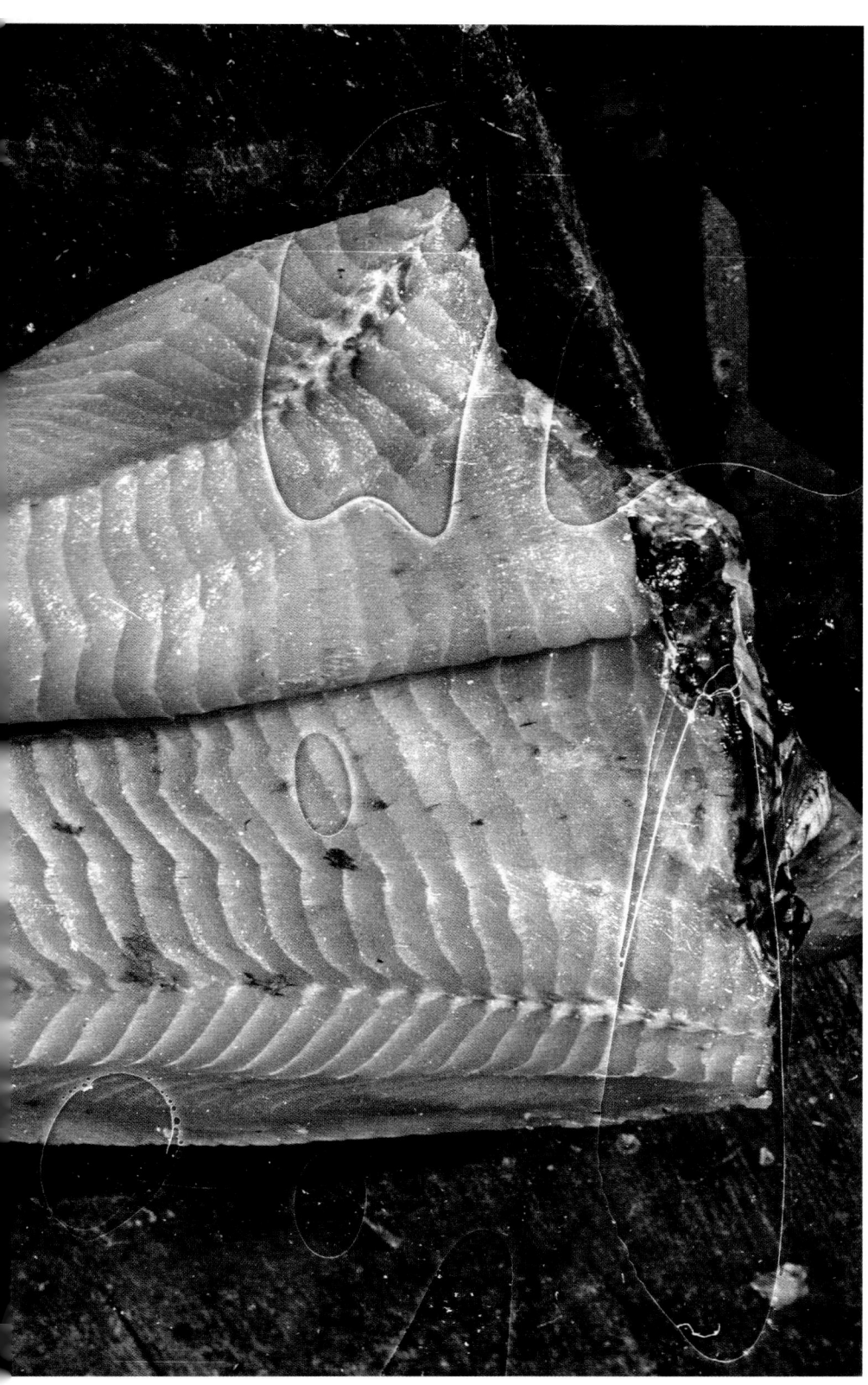

Alestine Andre cuts a large fish into fillets at her fish camp
at the Tree River, Nunavut, July 1978.

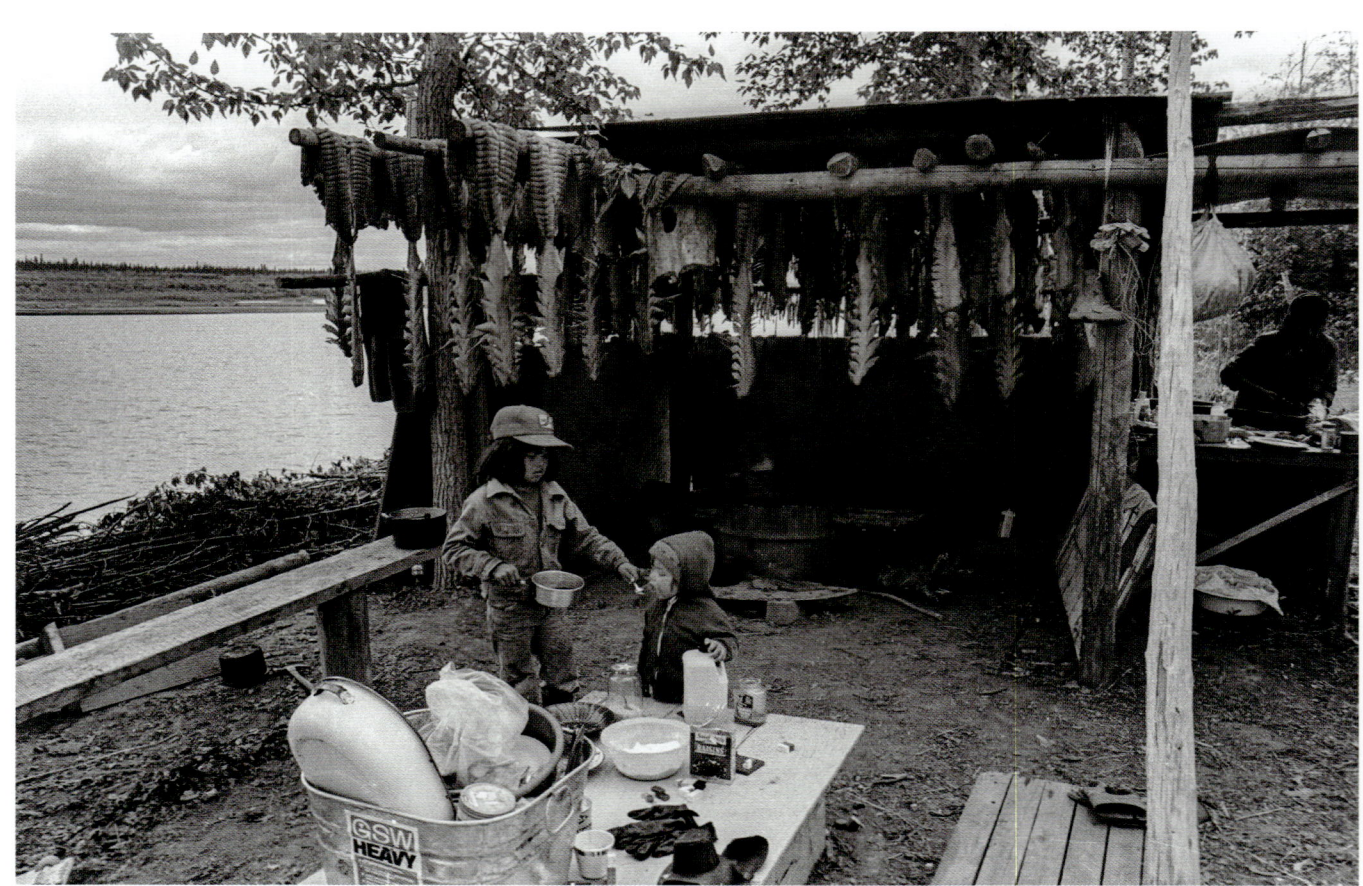

James Firth and Darcy Firth near a fish drying rack at
Laura Firth's fish camp at the Peel River, Northwest
Territories, July 1977.
PHOTOGRAPH BY JAMES JEROME. ©NWT ARCHIVES/JAMES
JEROME/N-1987-017-0274

Opposite: Three children play on the shore of Marion
Lake, Behchokǫ̀, Northwest Territories, 1977.
PHOTOGRAPH BY JAMES JEROME. ©NWT ARCHIVES/JAMES
JEROME/N-1987-017-3459

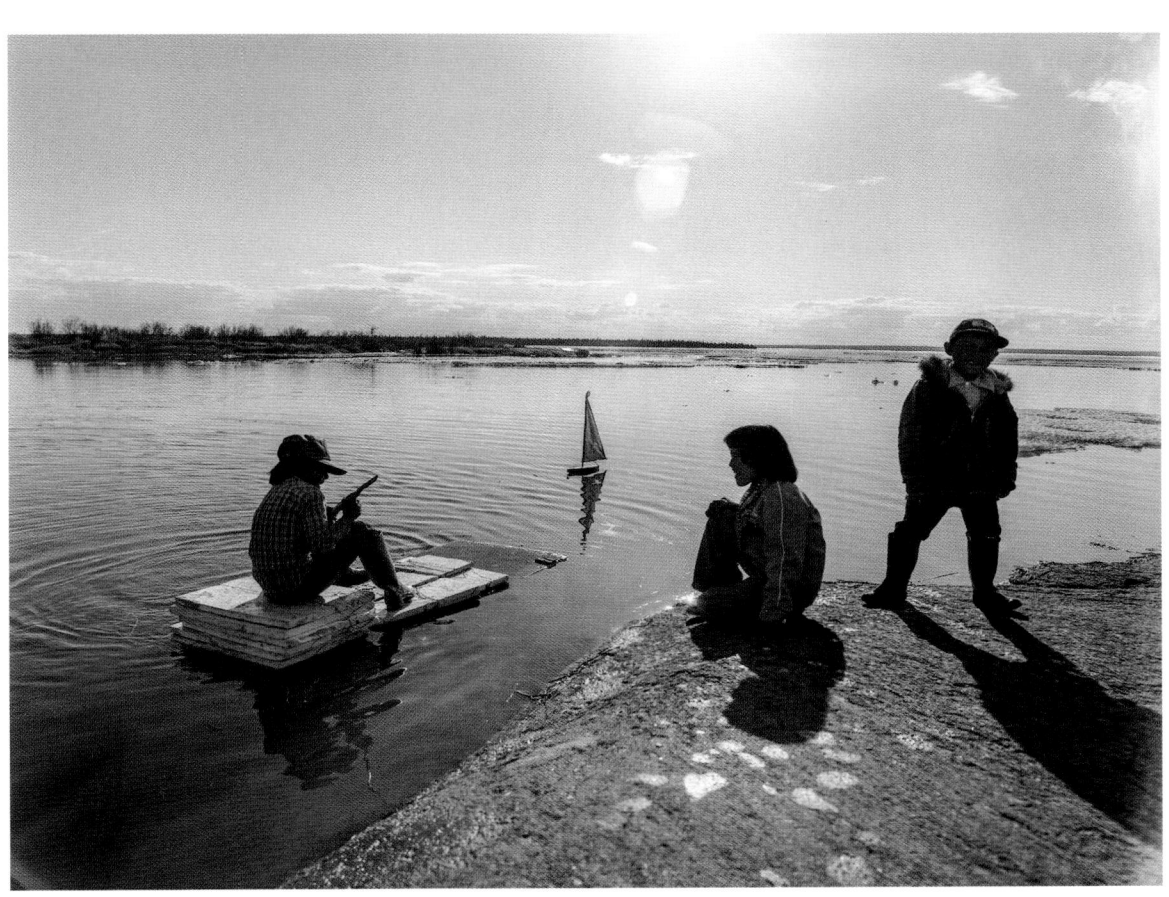

WANBLÍ TA HÓCOKA WASHTÉ (GOOD EAGLE CENTER)/
ARTHUR AMIOTTE
PORCUPINE DAY SCHOOL
Oglala Lakota
Oglala Lakota Nation
Porcupine, South Dakota
United States

Photographs and Poems by Sioux Children, a catalog featuring the work of Oglala Lakota students from the Porcupine Day School in Porcupine, South Dakota, was published in 1971 to accompany an exhibition at the Sioux Indian Museum. The image makers were guided by Arthur Amiotte (b. 1942)—now a world-renowned artist depicting Lakota life. Supplied with Instamatic cameras, the teens documented their Porcupine community. The following term, the photographs inspired the poems and prose of their schoolmates.

In an urgent multipage introduction to the catalog, Amiotte wrote about the lethal consequences of forced acculturation and the crucial relationship between art and survival. "The American Indian has tenaciously held on to his arts, not in the sense of objects alone, but rather as the fabric that binds and holds together the many dimensions of his very existence," asserted his essay.[1]

When the Porcupine Day School, operated by the Bureau of Indian Affairs, opened on the Pine Ridge Reservation, home of the Oglala Lakota Nation, in the mid-1960s, it included a robust cultural visual arts program. Amiotte was the lead instructor. The curriculum was meant to give students "a positive self-image through individual accomplishment and awareness of their own Indian cultural background," explained Amiotte, who was born on the reservation in Pine Ridge, a town about 25 miles north of Porcupine.

Amiotte taught the students about the artistic achievements of their Lakota ancestors and contemporary Native American figures. He acquainted them with the rich and diverse aesthetic pasts of Native nations across America. And he provided the instruction, tools, and culturally relevant materials for them to effectuate their own creative visions.

By Amiotte's account, the classroom, piled high with books, magazines, and supplies (dishes of beads, looms, paper, glue, jars of paint, watercolors, spun wool, an 8mm projector) always looked like a "whirlwind just hit it." The students arrived eager and energetic. "Most amazing is that amidst the tumbling into the room are such enthusiastic questions as 'What do we do today?, Where's my painting?,' or 'Gimme some lace!'," he wrote.

"Indian music is thumping from the record player…The class begins with a humming and buzzing that slowly rises to a dull roar." The Lakota language resounds between the students and the teacher's aide, Lee, "an inexhaustible source of patience."

Building off the kids' growing interest in "class activities designed to encourage experimentation and growth in self-expression and experience," photography was introduced in 1969. Alongside several photographs Amiotte made of Porcupine Day School youth working on various projects, a selection of 52 student photographs was reproduced in *Photographs and Poems by Sioux Children*. The original black-and-white prints, along with the outtakes, are preserved at the National Archives in the U.S. Department of the Interior, Indian Arts and Crafts Board records. The collection bursts with snowy country landscapes, horses, cats, Elders, friends, cozy interiors, and self-portraits.

"Artistic endeavors," wrote Amiotte in the 1971 catalog —on the brink of his celebrated career—"are marked by adventures into the unknown, flexibility in the face of change… and by resolving the disequilibrium between the self and the to-be-completed form."

The photographs and poems made at Porcupine Day School, concluded Amiotte, "reveal depths of feeling, insight, power, and an acute sensitivity for transforming a harsh world into one that is both simple and beautiful."

—Sarah Stacke

A student in Arthur Amiotte's classroom, c. 1969–71.
PHOTOGRAPH BY ARTHUR AMIOTTE.

NATIONAL ARCHIVES (RG 435-PDB). PHOTOGRAPHIC PRINTS OF THE PORCUPINE DAY SCHOOL AND ITS ART ACTIVITIES, 1969–71. DEPARTMENT OF THE INTERIOR. INDIAN ARTS AND CRAFTS BOARD. (1935–)

NATIONAL ARCHIVES (RG 435-PD). PHOTOGRAPHS AND CATALOG FOR THE EXHIBITION *PHOTOGRAPHS AND POEMS BY SIOUX CHILDREN*, 1968–70. DEPARTMENT OF THE INTERIOR. INDIAN ARTS AND CRAFTS BOARD. (1935–)

NATIONAL ARCHIVES (RG 435-PDA). PHOTOGRAPHIC PRINTS MADE BY STUDENTS AT THE PORCUPINE DAY SCHOOL, 1968–70. DEPARTMENT OF THE INTERIOR. INDIAN ARTS AND CRAFTS BOARD. (1935–)

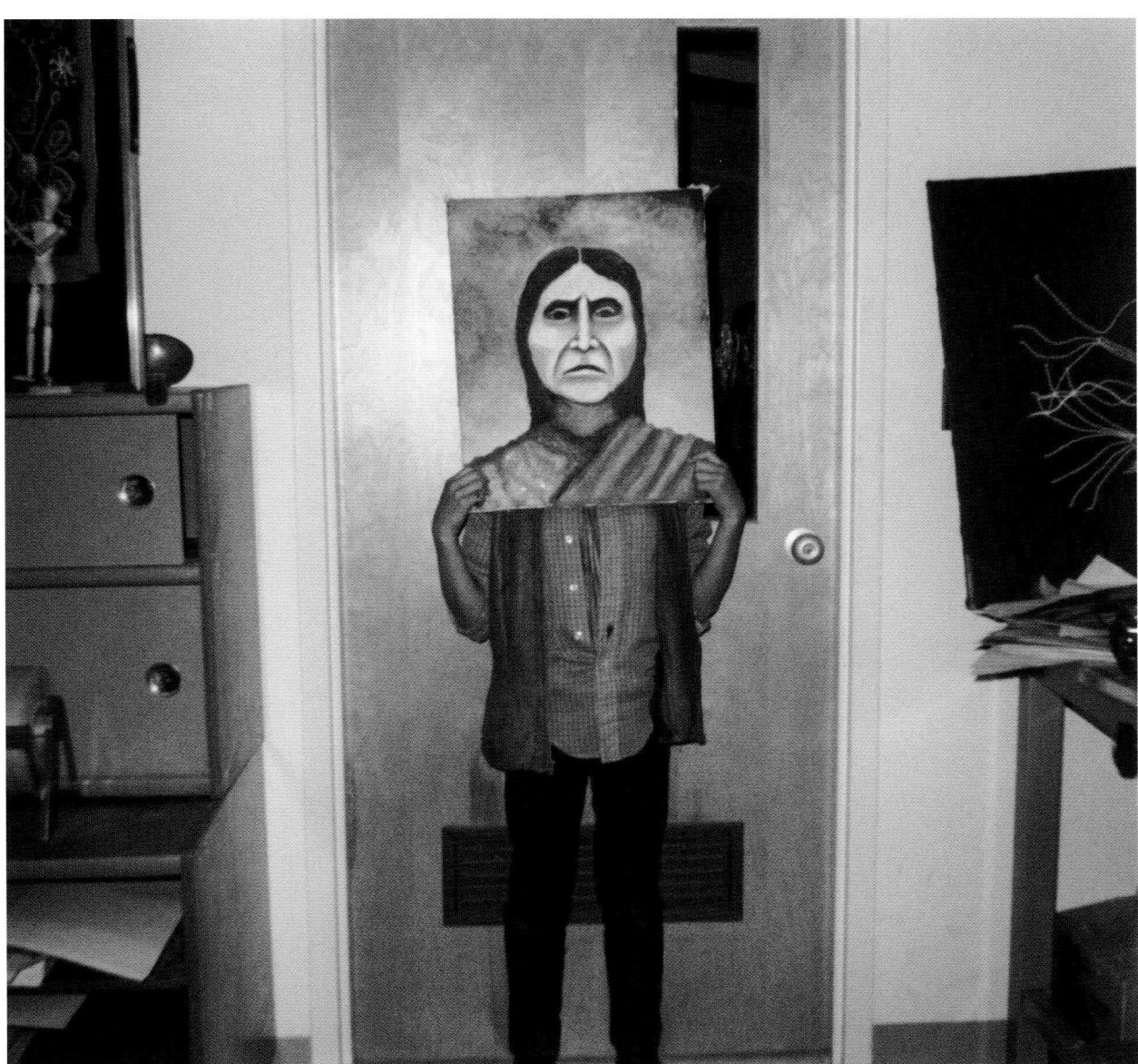

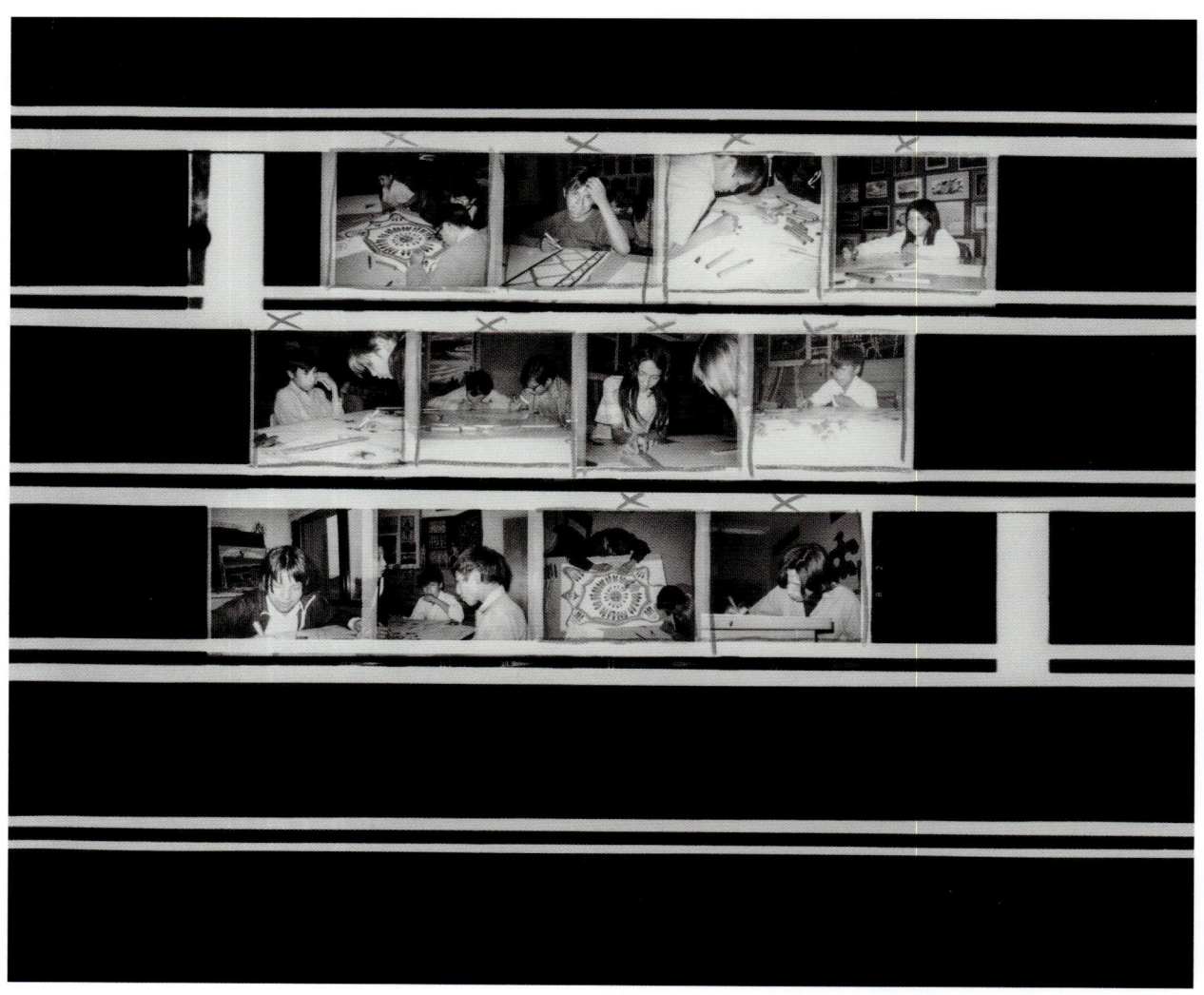

Contact sheet picturing Porcupine Day School
students, c. 1969–71.

PHOTOGRAPHS BY ARTHUR AMIOTTE.

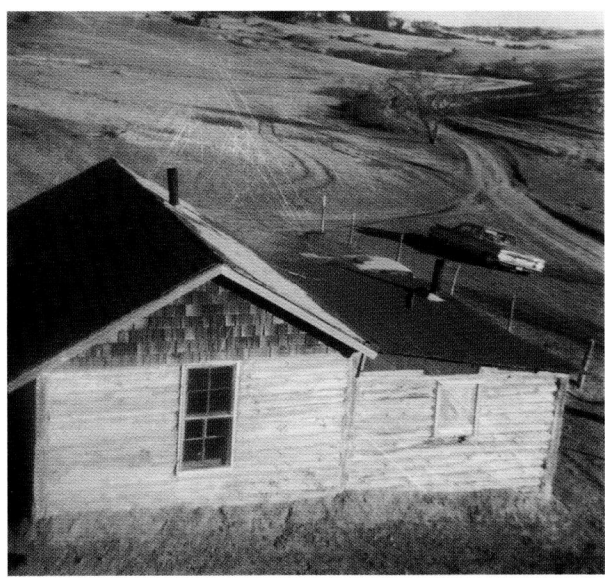

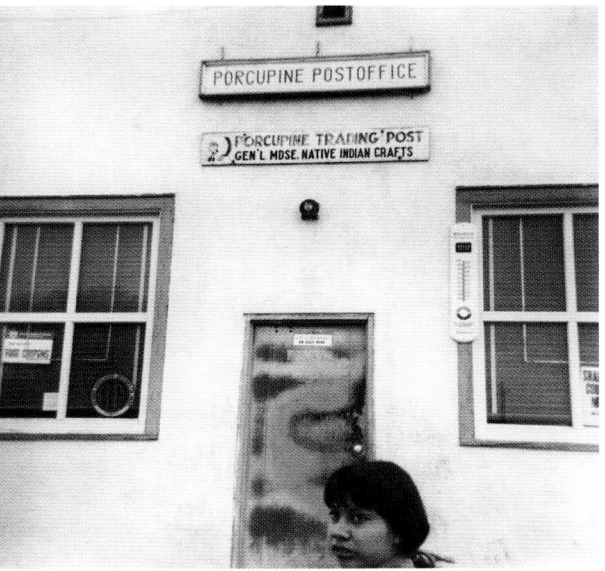

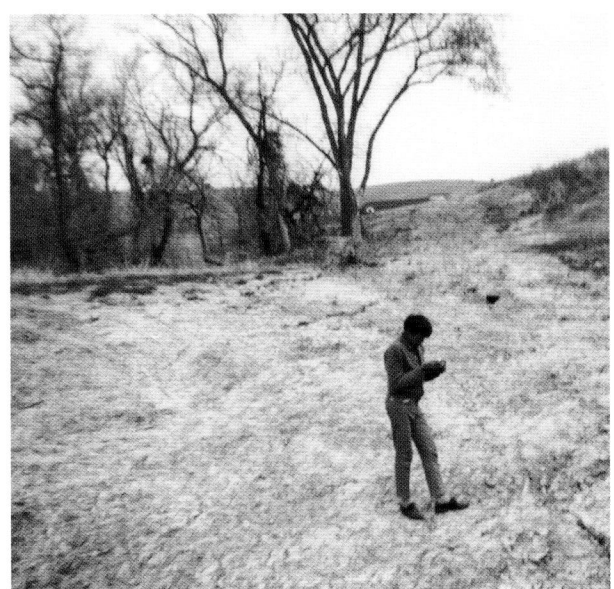

PHOTOGRAPH BY LESLIE BUSH, AGE 13, GRADE 7,
PORCUPINE DAY SCHOOL.

PHOTOGRAPH BY ETHLEEN IRON CLOUD, AGE 13, GRADE 7,
PORCUPINE DAY SCHOOL.

PHOTOGRAPH BY MANUEL IRON CLOUD, AGE 14, GRADE 8,
PORCUPINE DAY SCHOOL.

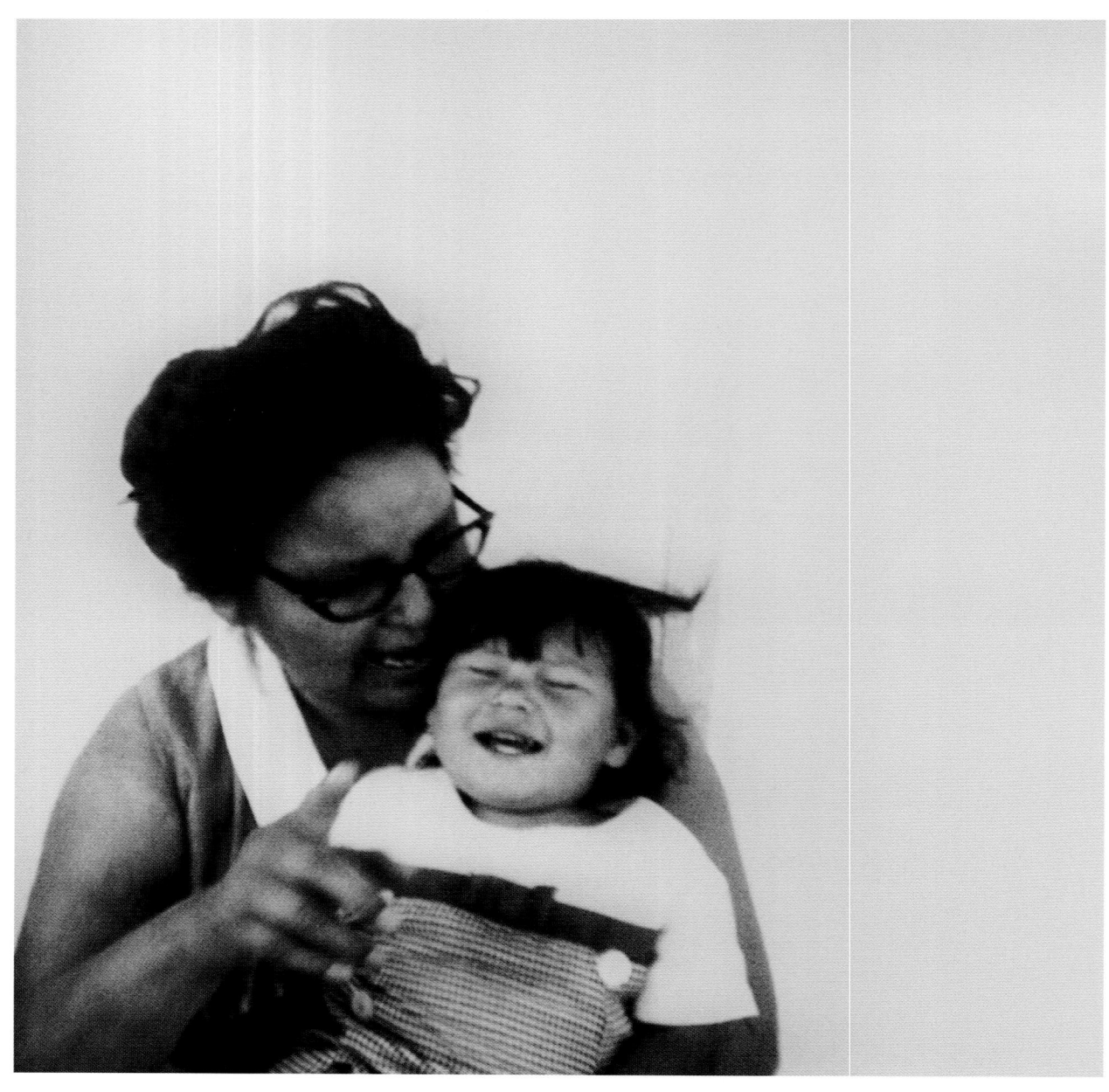

Grandma is old
Grandma is good
Grandma showed me how to use the meat grinder

Geraldine White Face, Grade 4, age 10

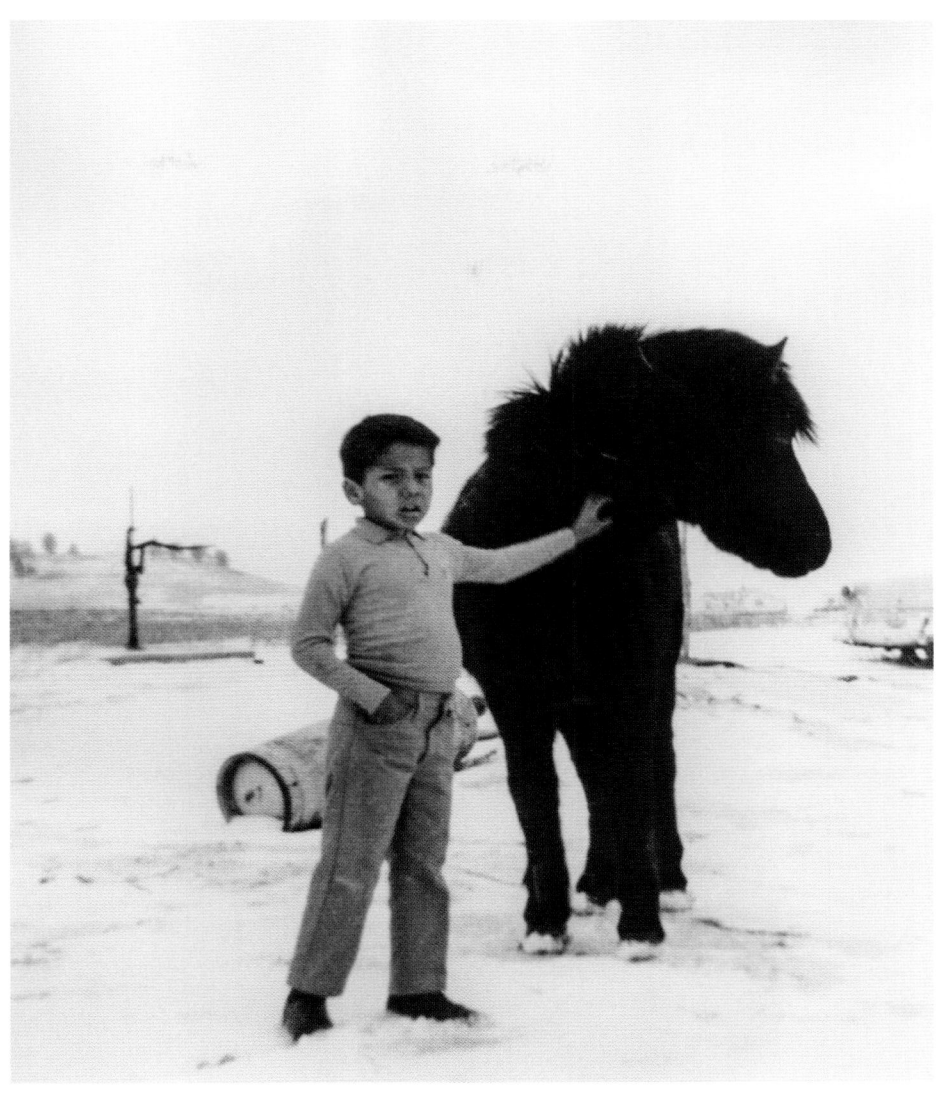

Deep in the hills there was a village where many people lived. On one big hill was a little cabin. In the little cabin lived an old man, an old woman and a little boy.

They raised a little farm. They had two cows, one horse, twenty chickens, four pigs and one dog.

One day the little boy wanted to ride the horse. The little boy said, "Come on King!" which the horse's name was. King ran up to the little boy and said, "Why did you call me?" The little boy said, "May I ride you?" The horse said, "No, you may not ride me, my back is tired." "Oh," said the little boy.

The little boy went to his dog, Ricky. The boy said, "Come, Ricky, we shall play." Ricky said, "My feet are tired of walking."

So again the little boy was going to ask the twenty chickens to play but the twenty chickens said, "We don't want to play with you." "We are too busy laying eggs so run along now," said the twenty chickens.

Again the little boy asked the two cows to play but the cows said, "We want to eat so run along." Once again he asked the four pigs to play but they said, "We are too sleepy, so run along."

So, the little boy sold all the animals.

Charlene Mesteth, Grade 4, age 9

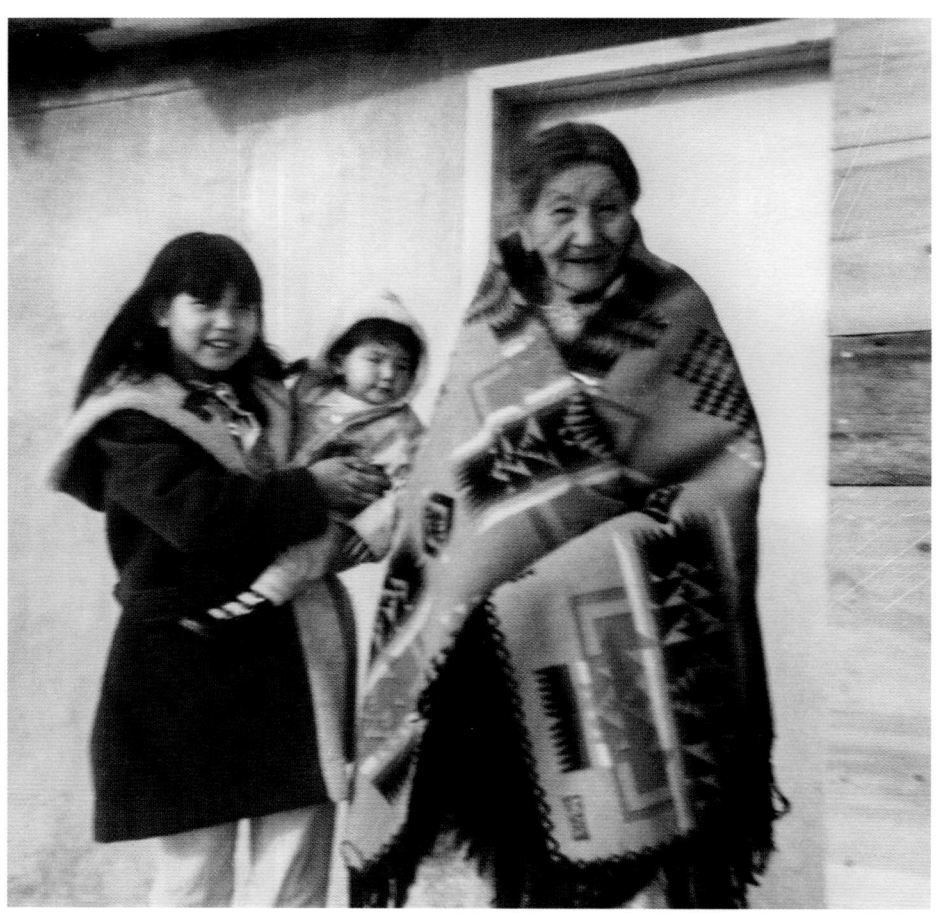

WINTER

The snow has almost come.
Every day snow will come.
Every year winter will come.
It will never stop, I say.
The hills have almost touched the sky.
Trees will be covered with sparkling snow,
for winter will be coming.
Weeds will be lying down,
for winter will be coming.
Snow will be everywhere.
Nothing can hide from the snow.
The big round rocks will be covered.
They will be whiter than anything,
for winter is coming.
The ground will be covered with snow.
The snow will cover everything.
The trees stand tall with sparkling snow.
Friends are on their way, I say.

Althea Mesteth, Grade 5, age 11

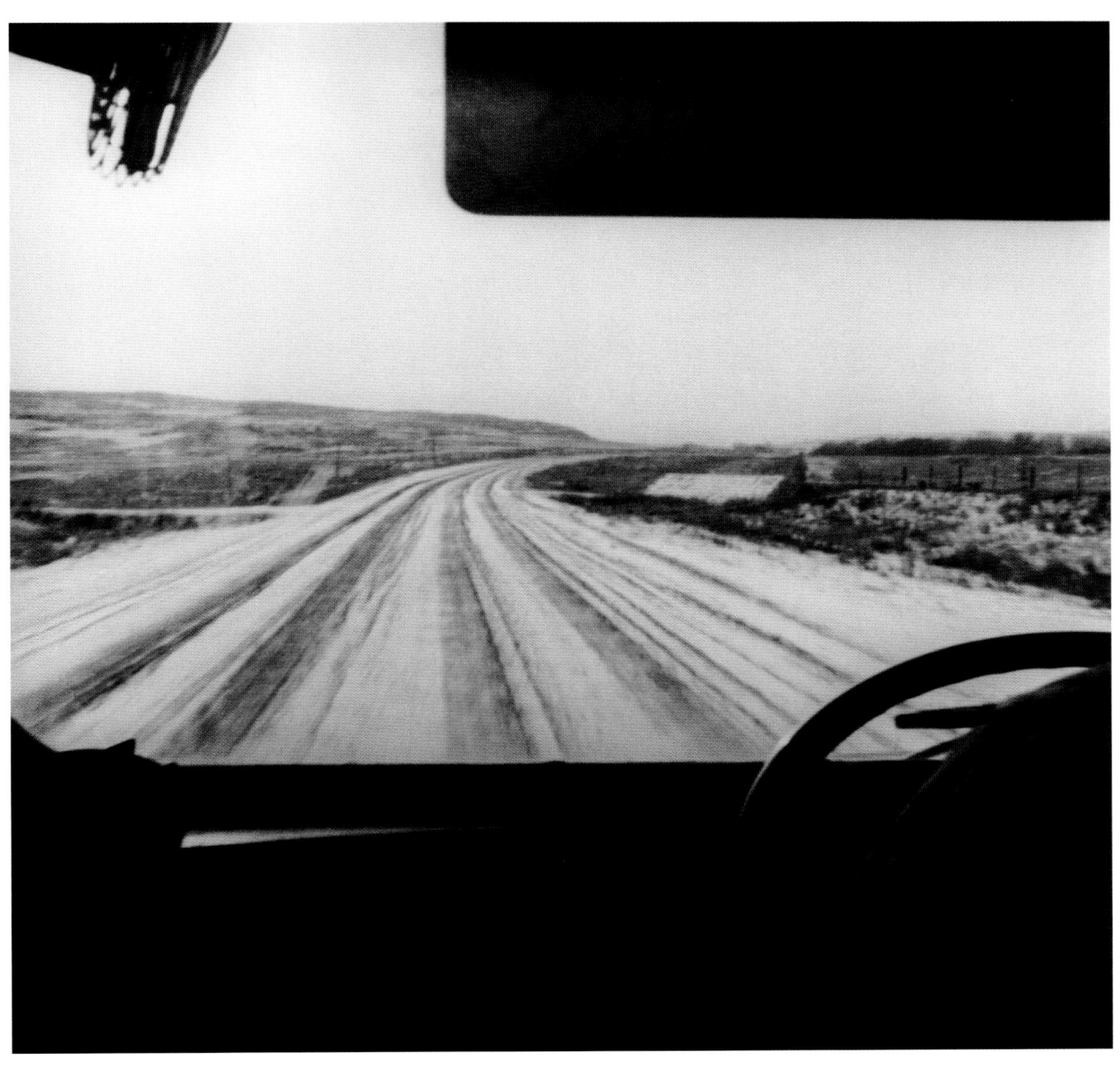

A road has no end
And never knows where or
When to stop.
The road comes and goes
Through streams, hills, and cities.
A road is where you can
Find happiness and again
You can find sadness.

      Marlene Locke, Grade 8, age 14

TAFOS
Perú

TAFOS (Talleres de Fotografía Social) was a milestone of socially engaged photography. From 1986 to 1998, a brutal period in Peruvian history, TAFOS provided photographic equipment and training to more than 270 campesinos (farmers), miners, women, men, youth, and urban folk across Perú. The rising citizen journalists, most of whom had never held a camera before, were resolved to document what they considered most important in their daily lives. With simple 35mm machines—a Yashica T3 or Nikon L35AF—they looked at political upheaval, working conditions, community activism, cultural events, family, friends, and landscapes.

The resulting photographs were disseminated locally, nationally, and internationally, and used as a catalyst for conversation and organization around conflicts within the photographers' communities. In time, the photographs played a major role in reclaiming and shaping the image of Peruvians, from Andean villages to overcrowded urban neighborhoods.

TAFOS was initiated by Thomas Müller, a German photographer, and his wife, Helga, in Ocongate, a small Quechua-speaking community near the city of Cusco, when the couple approached the Ocongate Committee of Human Rights about running a photography workshop. It was determined the committee would select 10 members to take on the role of community photographer. Müller would teach them how to use a camera. Within half a decade, the Ocongate photographers exposed 349 rolls of film covering agriculture, festivals, rituals, and activities related to community organization.

The Ayaviri workshop ran from 1988 to 1992 and coincided with the years Ayaviri, another Quechua-speaking community, began to reclaim control of its ancestral lands from the state. With 464 rolls of film, the participants photographed farmers' strikes, assemblies, and actions aimed at taking back their land. They also documented agriculture, livestock, local culture, and day-to-day life.

In the 12 years it operated, TAFOS ran nearly 30 workshops in eight different regions of Perú. Close to 200,000 images, almost exclusively black-and-white, were produced in total. Like the pilot in Ocongate, the participants belonged to local civil organizations, unions, community associations, and student or neighborhood groups, and were recruited from within their respective consortiums. The workshops, which pooled people from various organizations, typically lasted one to four years. Each program met monthly or bimonthly to share pictures and discuss plans. Occasionally, TAFOS facilitators joined in.

The intent of the workshops was autonomy. The participants decided what to photograph and they developed their own photographic styles. "The same culture [was] in front of and behind the camera—in the photographer and in the photographed —very strong and solid images were produced," Müller wrote in a description of the workshops.[1] Displays of the work were shaped by the photographers in traditional and surprising ways: at galleries, at markets, in the streets, on carts pushed through public spaces, with posters, and at community meetings.

"What TAFOS did was empower grassroots leaders to tell their stories and spread them among their own people, among the residents of their towns and cities and in the world in general," wrote Müller. "Through their work, for the first time these sectors, normally excluded from the mass media of that time, were able to participate in national debates with their own image."[2]

In the 1980s, the economy of Perú collapsed, and most of the country was living in poverty. The Shining Path, a militarized branch of the Communist Party of Perú, launched a violent, bloody attack on the Peruvian state. The government's response was ferocious. A ruthless internal conflict erupted and endured for two decades. Almost 70,000 people were killed or went missing. Statistics gathered by the Peruvian Truth and Reconciliation Commission reveal that 75 percent of the victims spoke Quechua as their first language.

The conflict spurred a massive increase in grassroots mobilization—people united to support, protect, and defend each other. It was within this environment that TAFOS was born. The camera "provided them with a way to document and decry, to explain and protest, defend and highlight the conditions in which they were living," explains Dr. Tiffany Fairey in "Building a History of Citizen Photography: The TAFOS Story." She continues, "Photography thus also became a way to explore the familiar details of their lives, to celebrate their culture, commemorate their values and traditions and reaffirm their identity."[3]

The work was risky. The country was at war and no one was more suspected of actions meant to denounce violence and rally support for change than ordinary citizens, Quechua speakers, and miners, said Müller. Using a camera to document "atrocities committed on both sides of the conflict or spreading their own culture with the pride it deserves" could easily make someone a target.[4] During critical moments when TAFOS feared the photo negatives could be confiscated or destroyed by the Shining Path or the military, they were transported by suitcase to secure locations; disks were removed from computers, and sensitive information about the photographers and their organizations was deleted.

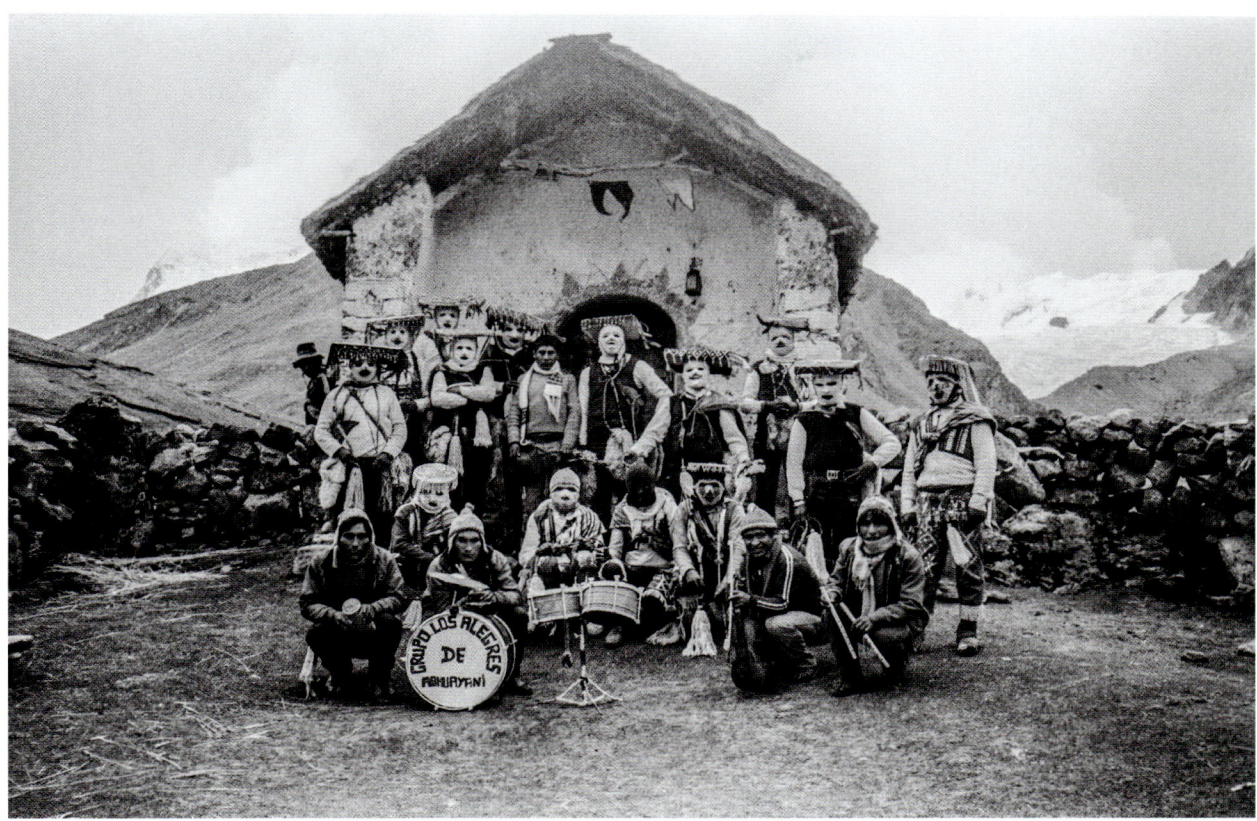

Müller believes TAFOS worked because there was a sincere demand and desire for the workshops from the people. "One of the ways to create a new social order in a fragmented country is for the people to rebuild their image, their face, their words," reads a text generated by members of TAFOS.[5] What TAFOS understood from the beginning about its participants was that "People did not need empowering, rather they needed the tools and means to further claim and realize their own empowerment," writes Fairey. TAFOS insisted that "people and politics, not just photography," were at the core of social change.[6]

Shortly after Müller closed TAFOS, he transferred all the negatives, contact sheets, prints, and documents to the Faculty of Communication Arts and Sciences of the Pontifical Catholic University of Perú (PUCP). The arrangement safeguards the collection and maintains the photographers' copyright. PUCP carefully cataloged the materials, cleaned the negatives, and opened the collection to the public. Thousands of images are available to view online, and the university actively promotes the archive through exhibitions, talks, conferences, and festivals. "The archive is central to TAFOS's ongoing legacy and significance," says Fairey.[7] Its contents secure a perspective of Perú's internal conflict, recorded by the people traditional power structures are inclined to suppress and forget.

—Sarah Stacke

Ocongate workshop, Cusco Region, Perú, c. 1987. A group likely pilgrimaging to the annual Qoyllur Rit'i festival, which occurs between May and June.
PHOTOGRAPH BY JUSTINIANO HUANCA.

PHOTOGRAPHS COURTESY OF TAFOS/PUCP PHOTOGRAPHIC ARCHIVE.

OC 129-13A, OC 11-33, OC 92-33A, OC 4-10, AY 4-29, AY 253-16A, AY 2-6, AY 176-12

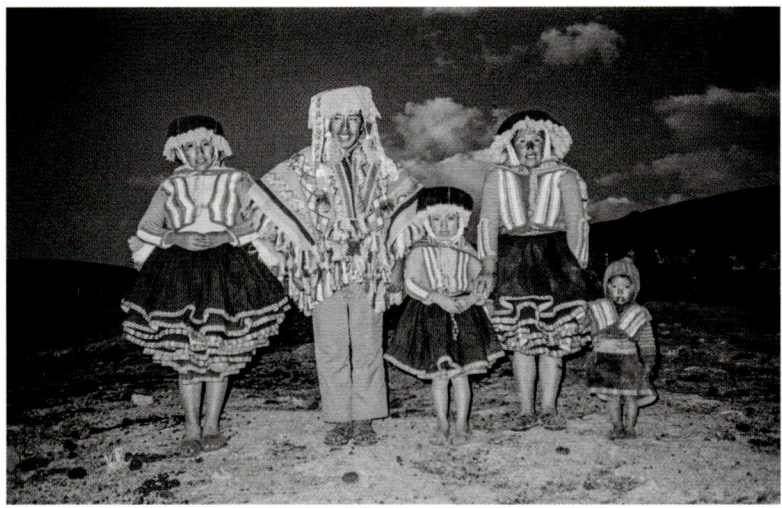

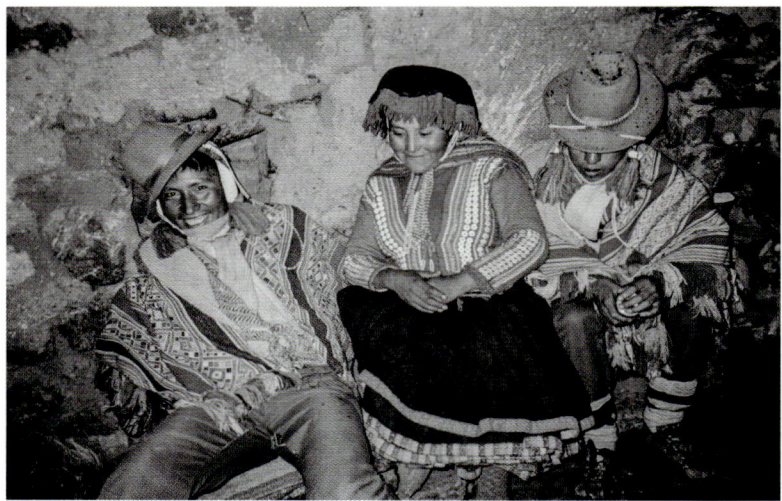

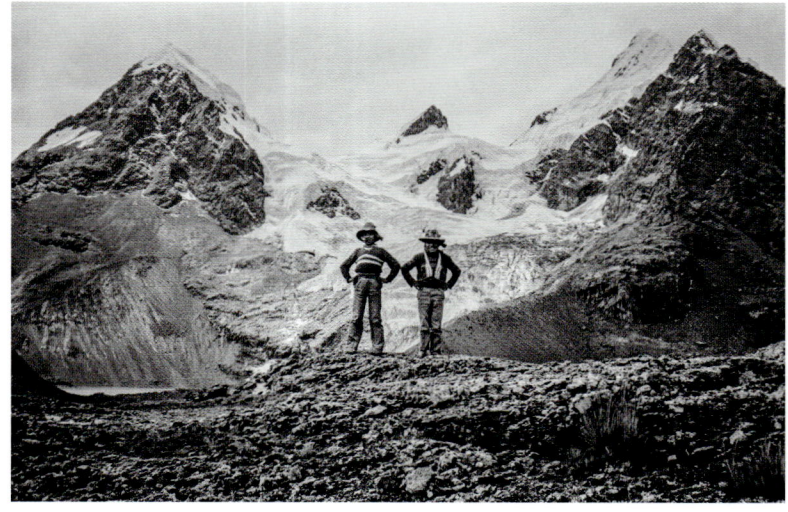

Ocongate workshop, Cusco Region, Perú, 1987.
PHOTOGRAPH BY SABINO QUISPE.

Ocongate workshop, Cusco Region, Perú, 1988.
PHOTOGRAPH BY MARIANO GONZALO.

Ocongate workshop, Cusco Region, Perú, 1987. Two children, likely in the community of Pacchanta, stand before Nevado Auzangate (Mount Ausangate).
PHOTOGRAPHER ONCE IDENTIFIED.

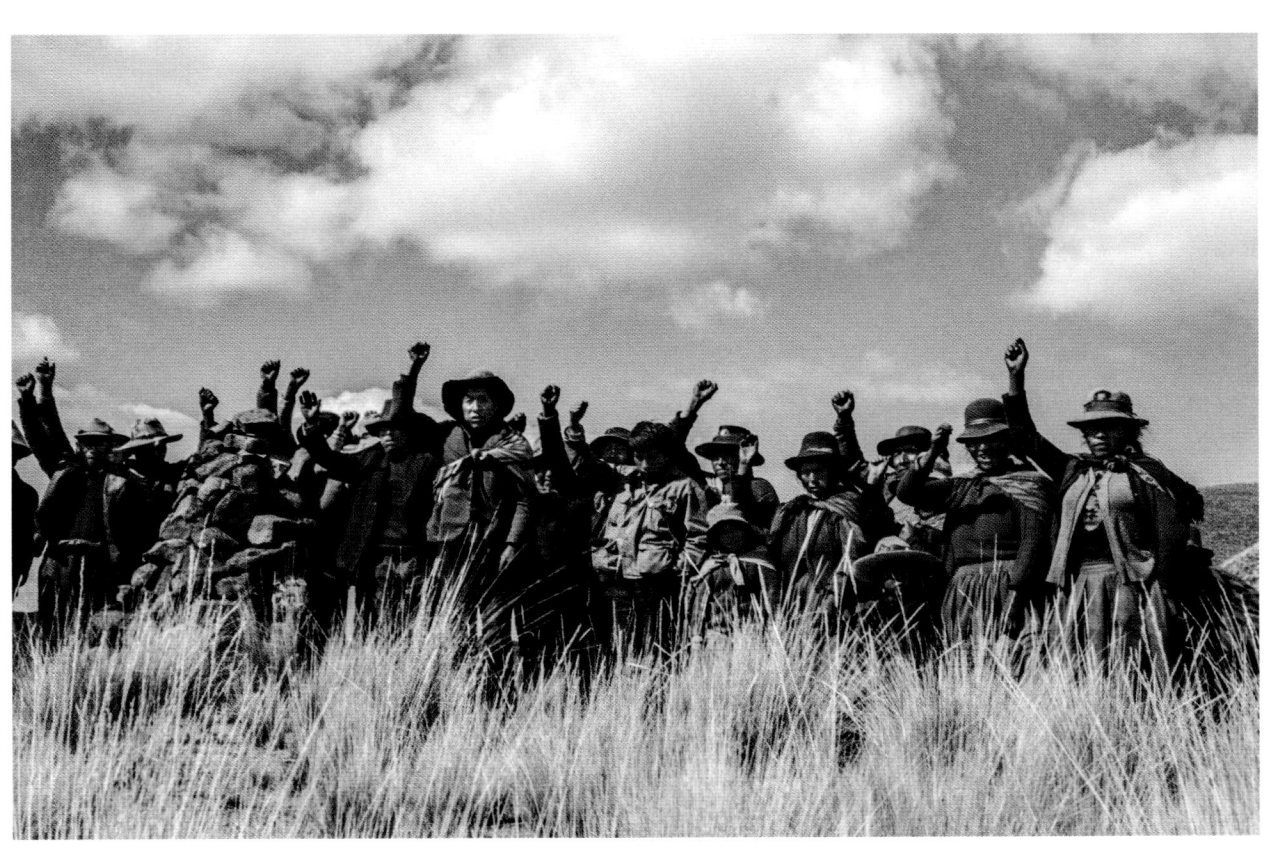

Ayaviri workshop, Puno Region, Perú, 1988.
PHOTOGRAPH BY GREGORIO ALQUI.

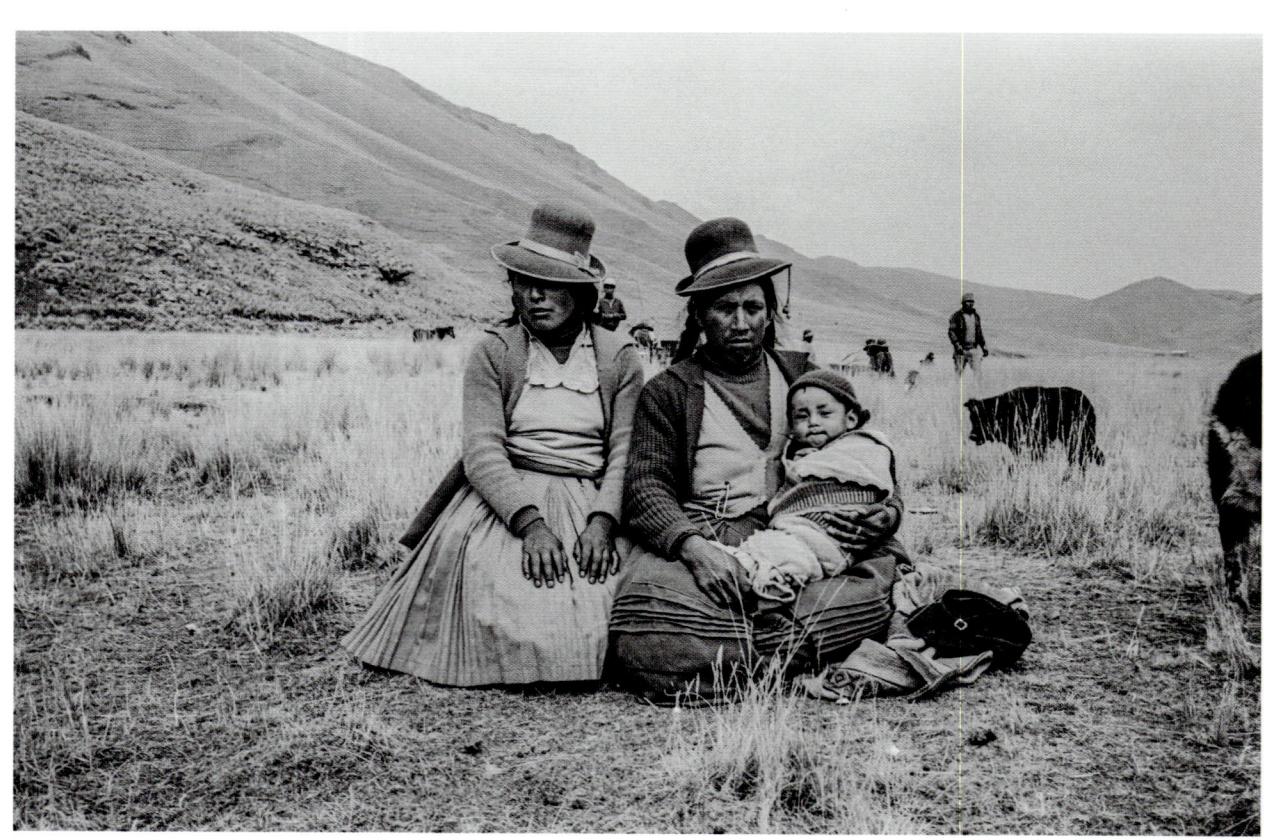

Ayaviri workshop, Puno Region, Perú, 1990.
PHOTOGRAPH BY JACINTO CHILA.

Opposite: Ayaviri workshop, Puno Region, Perú,
September 1989. Community members during the
sheep and camelid vaccination campaign, likely near
the town of Selque.
PHOTOGRAPH BY MELCHOR LIMA.

Opposite: Ayaviri workshop, Puno Region, Perú,
September 1989. Men rest on roofing material.
PHOTOGRAPH BY MAURO QUISPECONDORI.

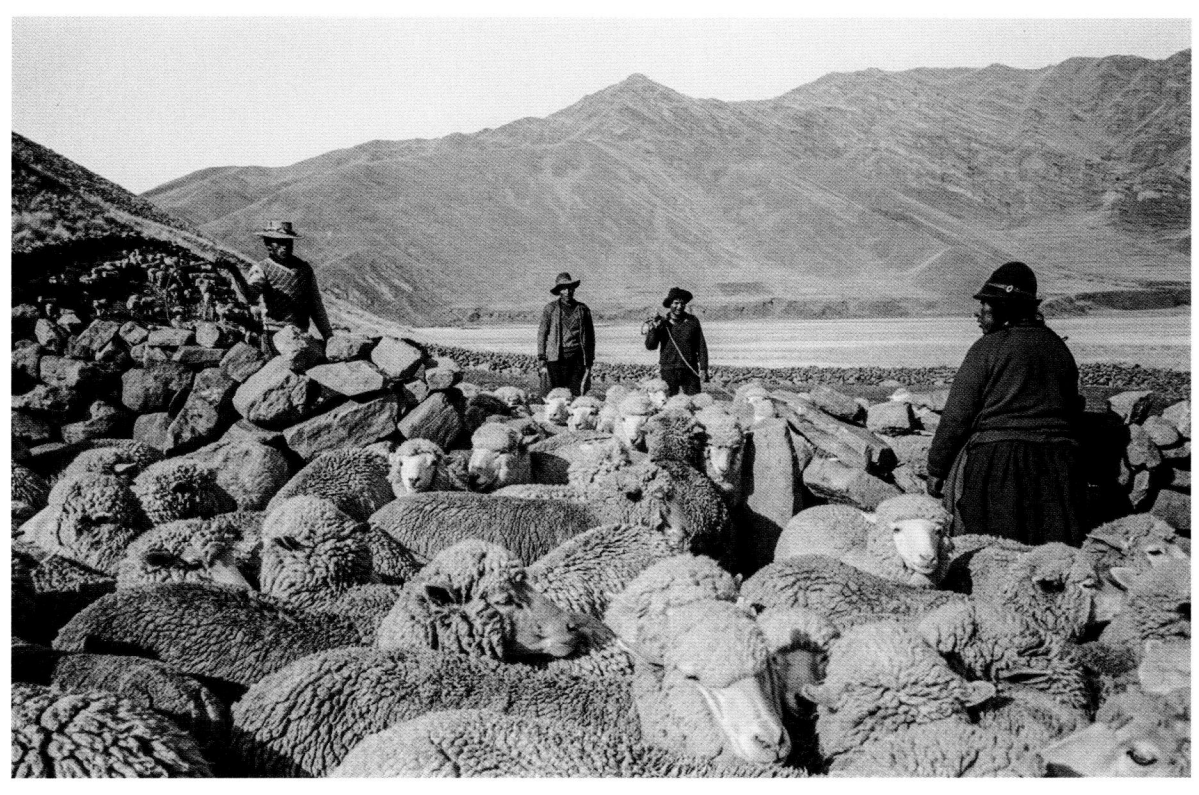

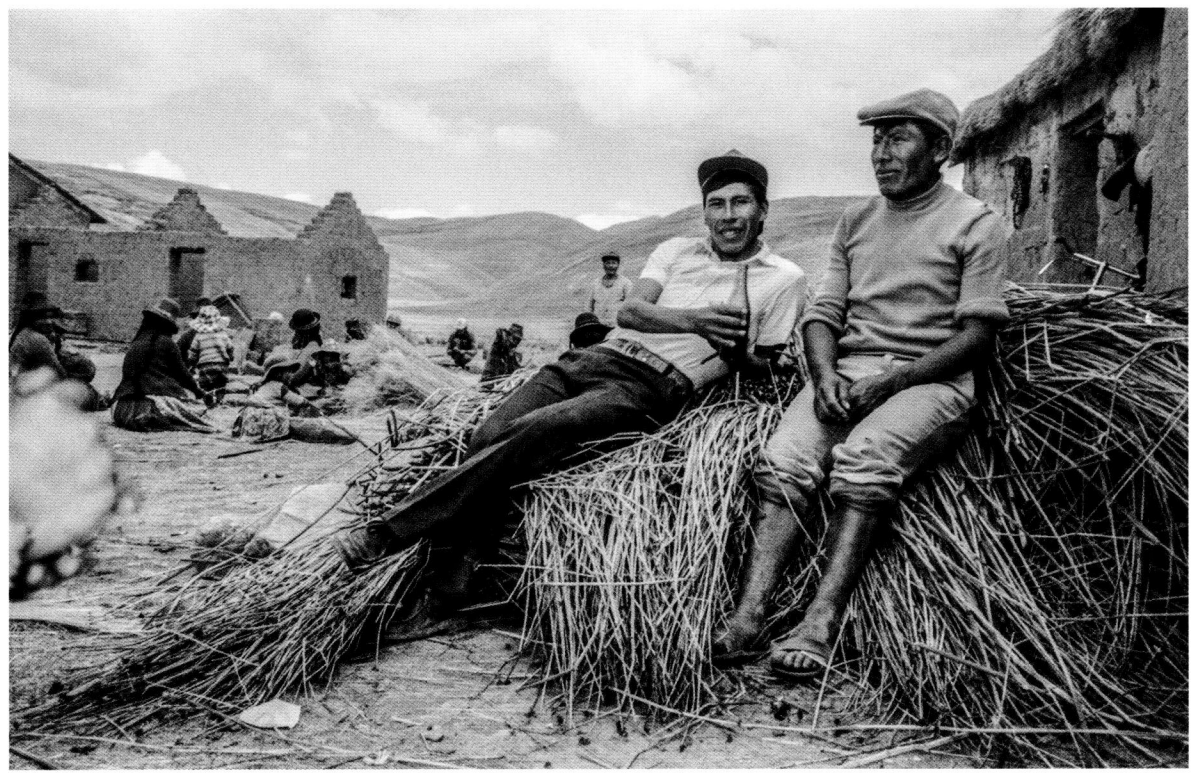

TOM FIELDS

Cherokee, Muscogee Creek
Eastern Oklahoma
United States

For photographer and visual storyteller Tom Fields (b. 1951), the intersections and tensions between cultures and belief systems offer abundant material for inspiration. His work documents the space between differing ideological viewpoints, for instance the ways the flag of the United States is considered by Native Americans. On the one hand, it represents the U.S. government's genocidal and colonial policies against Native people, but it is also a patriotic symbol of nationhood and pride that Native soldiers and Natives from military communities observe and respect. The same is true with regard to Christianity. Native people can practice Christianity and value their faith while also following the spiritual traditions of their people, even though historically, Christian-led missions and boarding schools have been the cause of major upheaval and destruction within Native populations.

"I like to photograph Native people when they cross cultural lines in today's society," says Fields. "That's where a lot of interesting visuals happen for a photographer and things need to be documented."[1]

Fields, a member of the Cherokee and Muscogee Creek Nations, isn't interested in imposing his beliefs on anyone; he considers his photographs a way to show things the way they are. Still, he recognizes his presence and describes his practice as "interpretive documentary." Fields believes the relationship between the photographer and the person photographed ultimately brings the photograph to life. "The critical balance between intrusion and respectful observance, objective reality and subjective vision, and emotional commitment create the power of the interpretive documentary image," he says.[2]

"I don't touch anything or move anything, it's whatever evolves out of that," adds Fields. "The photos should be able to speak for themselves."[3] He finds his energy and eye are best when images happen spontaneously and organically, such as the photo of Bill Frazier, the Chickasaw pastor and U.S. Marine Corps veteran mounting a flag outside Oak Grove Baptist Church in Roff, Oklahoma. At the time Fields made the photo, he was collaborating with Chickasaw writer Kelly Lunsford on a project looking at the history of eight early churches on the Chickasaw Nation.

That day was the first time Fields met Frazier. As he was photographing, with the wind whipping around, he was struck by the impression that Frazier was a Marine. And it turned out that he was right. "I have been around and photographed Marines and know how they always carry on their military ceremonies, not to glorify war but to honor the Corps and the sacrifices of their fellow soldiers," explains Fields. "Even though it's a simple, straightforward image, it carried a lot of weight of who this man was and what he was doing." Fields appreciated that Frazier was a minister and a member of the color guard, and therefore a respected member of the Chickasaw community. "It's those elements that I like to photograph," says Fields. "It's always been a favorite image."[4]

Fields, who has learned to explore what is closest to his heart, brings years of expertise and experience to his vocation. "I'm 72 years old right now. I've seen changes that have evolved since the 1960s when I started photographing a lot," he says. "I was documenting because I saw Native people interacting with life and doing it on their terms."[5]

—Tiffany Midge

Bill Frazier, a Chickasaw pastor and a U.S. Marine Corps veteran, places his American flag on the sign outside Oak Grove Baptist Church building, Roff, Oklahoma, 2010.

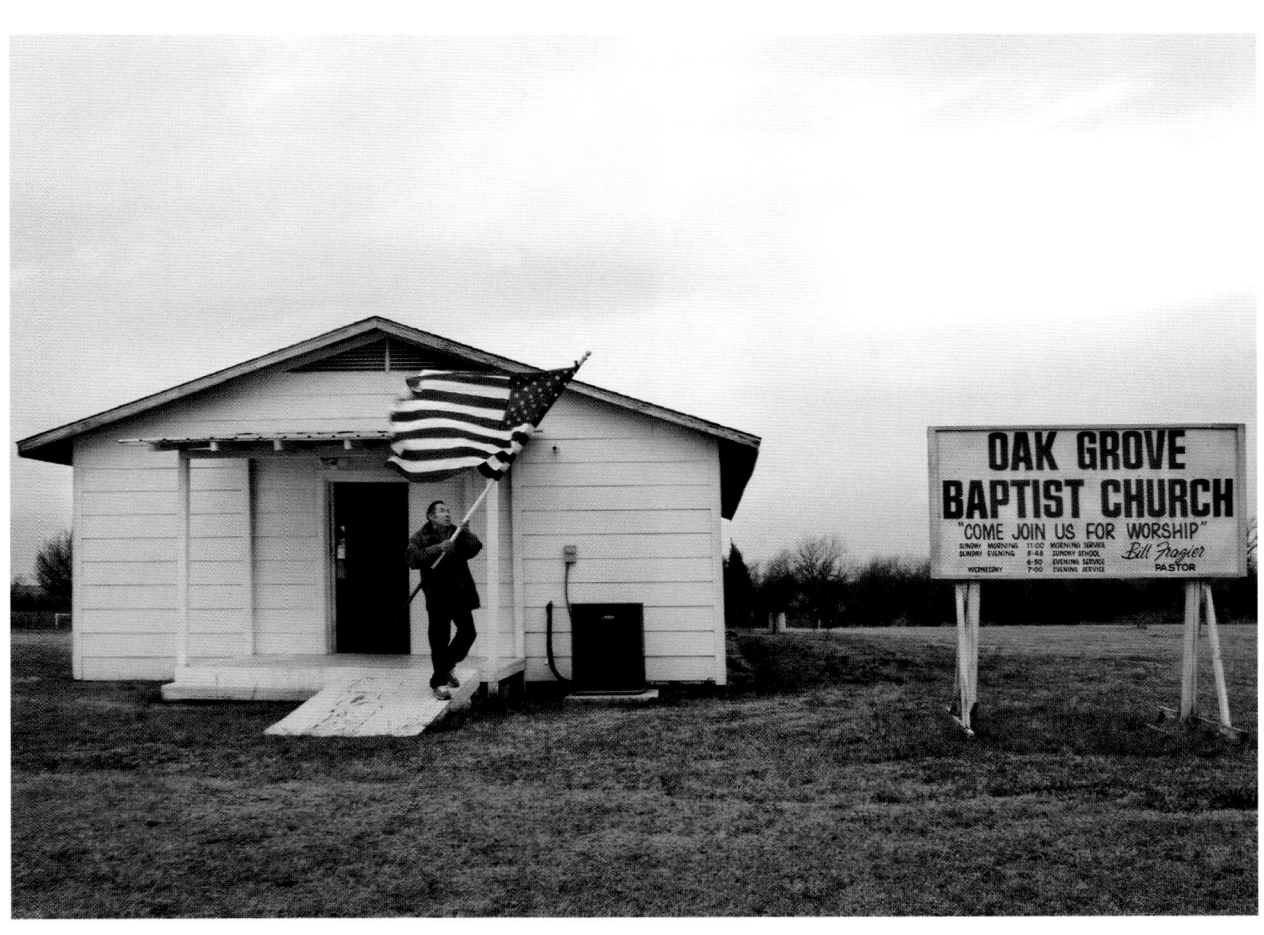

DUWAWISIOMA / VICTOR MASAYESVA JR.

Hopi
Hopi Nation
Hotevilla, Arizona
United States

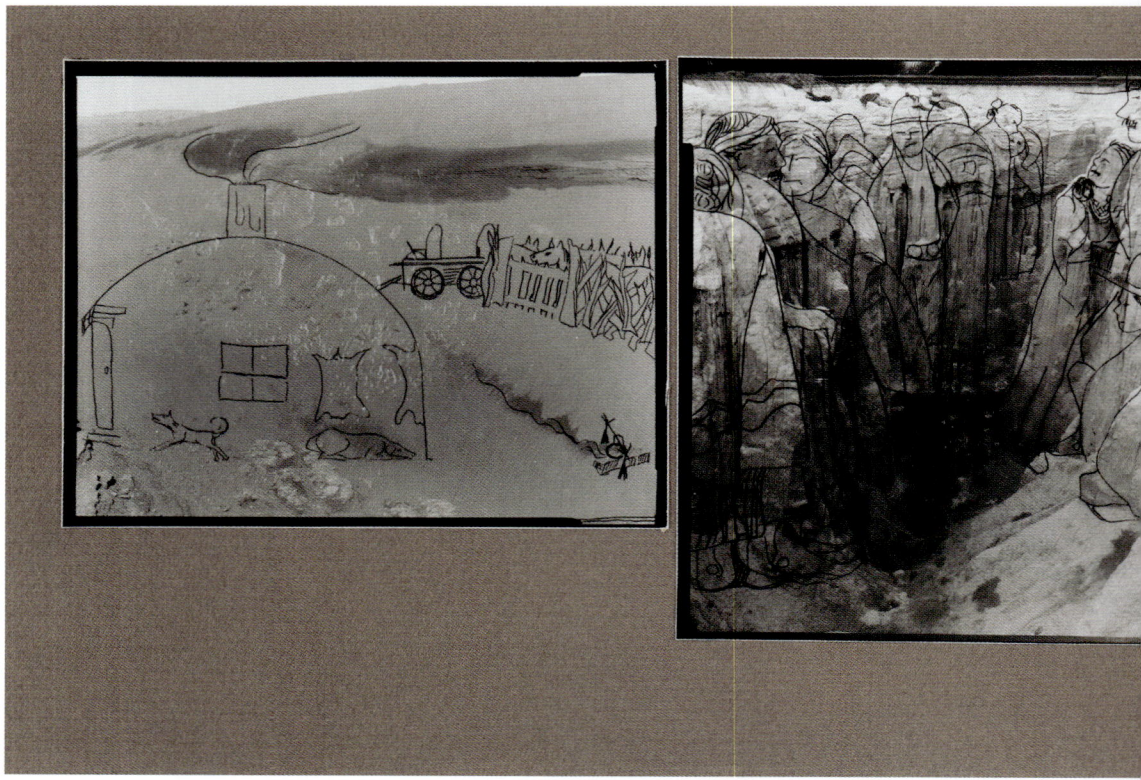

Tsinniginnie's *Hardrock Romance* is a tale "that began with a photograph," explains Duwawisioma (Victor Masayesva Jr., b. 1951).[1] The series was invoked at Coal Mine Canyon, a remote geological structure chiseled by millennia of wind and rain upon effulgent layers of orange, red, and pink sandstone. The canyon is situated where the western edge of the Hopi Nation meets Dinétah (Navajo Homeland) in what is now northeastern Arizona.

Through four photographic contact prints made from 4" × 5" negatives scratched with drawings—inspired by the abundance of petroglyphs in the region—Duwawisioma tells a story of the Hopi referencing the Nidaa' (the Navajo Enemy Way ceremony) and poking fun at their neighbors as well as the seriousness with which anthropologists study petroglyphs.

"Something as serious and important as photography must have the human accessory of buffoonery, and so it does, flourishing in Hopi stories," writes Duwawisioma in *Hopi Photographers, Hopi Images.*[2]

Raised in Hotevilla on Third Mesa, Duwawisioma went to grade school on the reservation and attended the Horace Mann School in New York City. In 1976, he graduated from Princeton University, where he studied photography with Emmet Gowin and English literature. Other than the time he was away for school, Duwawisioma has lived in Hotevilla, where for decades he has worked with youth and Elders to record Hopi culture. His substantial portfolio of photographs and films presents Hopi lifeways and heritage, while creating poetic translations of Hopi philosophy, prophesy, ritual, and history. Duwawisioma's work is central to his "lifelong quest to understand 'existence' and 'being' in terms of Hopi ancestral traditions in the modern world."[3] His forward-thinking artistic practice, honed for more than four decades, has had a significant impact on contemporary photography.

Challenging the cultural interpretations of early ethnographers and the commercialization and exploitation of his community, Duwawisioma has long envisioned the development of

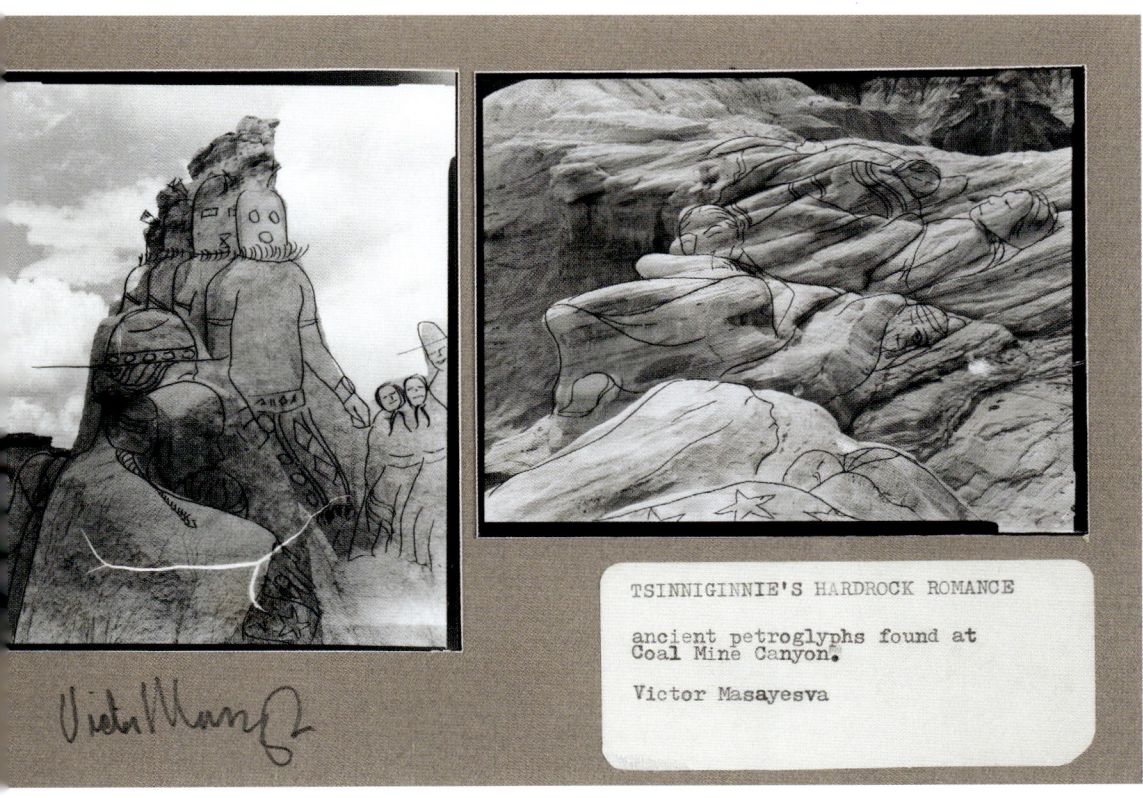

TSINNIGINNIE'S HARDROCK ROMANCE

ancient petroglyphs found at
Coal Mine Canyon.

Victor Masayesva

a new iconography originating from the storytelling and imagery of Indigenous ancestors.[4]

In the early 1980s, with extraordinary foresight of the ways many Indigenous photographers are working today, he said, "We must look to our culture for guidance, listen to our cultural conscience, and take our cue from our comprehensive tradition which has sustained our forebears over centuries. I believe we would not be far from the mark if we were to take photography as ceremony, as ritual, something that sustains, enriches, and adds to our spiritual well-being."[5]

—Sarah Stacke

Tsinniginnie's Hardrock Romance.

AMADO VILLAFAÑA CHAPARRO

Arhuaco
Sierra Nevada de Santa Marta
Colombia

To reach Naboba Lagoon, a sacred site in the Sierra Nevada de Santa Marta, Arhuaco documentarian Amado Villafaña Chaparro (b. 1956) and his companions climbed the rugged terrain toward Pico Colón. "It was raining heavily for days, making it difficult for us to continue our journey," recalls Villafaña. "The Mamos carried out spiritual work so the weather would improve, and we could continue on."[1]

The Sierra Nevada de Santa Marta in northern Colombia is the world's tallest coastal mountain range, with its highest peak, Pico Colón, reaching nearly 19,000 feet above the Caribbean Sea. Among the Arhuaco, one of four Indigenous societies living on the massif, the Mamos are spiritual and cultural authorities. They play a central role in passing on the traditional knowledge, rituals, and cosmology of the Arhuaco people, and make important decisions for the community. Ultimately, the Mamos are responsible for maintaining the harmony and balance of the universe.

Governed by the Law of Origins—a set of norms established at the beginning of time—the Arhuaco consider the Sierra Nevada de Santa Marta the "heart of the world."[2] They are spiritually obligated to defend its unique biodiversity and ecology from outside forces like mining, hydroelectric projects, deforestation, urban sprawl, and tourism. Climate change has led to the rapid loss of the Sierra Nevada's glaciers. Those that remain are considered critically endangered, in turn jeopardizing the life-sustaining rivers that rush from its peaks.[3]

Villafaña is the founder and director of the Yosokwi Collective, a media team of Arhuaco photographers, producers, and filmmakers. The collective was conceived, with the guidance of Villafaña's Mamo, to raise consciousness about the worldviews of the Arhuaco and the challenges their culture faces. "The first thing I want people to know about is the existence of the Arhuaco, who remain true to their mission, which is the protection of the Sierra Nevada, which is the protection of life itself," says Villafaña.[4]

When Villafaña and his crew trekked to Naboba Lagoon in 2014, they were creating footage for *Naboba*. Released in 2016, the applauded documentary expresses the ancestral vision of the Arhuaco in relation to the Aracataca River, which originates in Naboba and flows to the Caribbean Sea. "Water is male and female. Water has a soul. Water should be treated like a living being," reads the trailer.[5] The film, directed by Villafaña, visits sacred spaces along the river, sharing the purpose of each. "Naboba Lagoon is the mother of weaving,"[6] explains Villafaña, referring to the deeply symbolic patterns, invoked through Naboba, that Arhuaco women weave into clothing and mochilas, the traditional shoulder bags used by men to carry personal belongings.

Defending Arhuaco lands through still and moving pictures is an initiative Villafaña takes seriously. "Like any tool that doesn't come from the culture itself, the use of it implies a great responsibility so that it's used correctly," he says. "I always make the comparison with the machete. If you use a machete well, you can grow food and provide for your family. If you use it badly, you can do harm."[7]

—Sarah Stacke

Mamo Eusebio and apprentices sit by Naboba Lagoon, 2014. Making this photograph, Amado Villafaña Chaparro was thinking about his duty to transmit the Mamos' (spiritual authorities) message concerning the importance of taking care of the water.

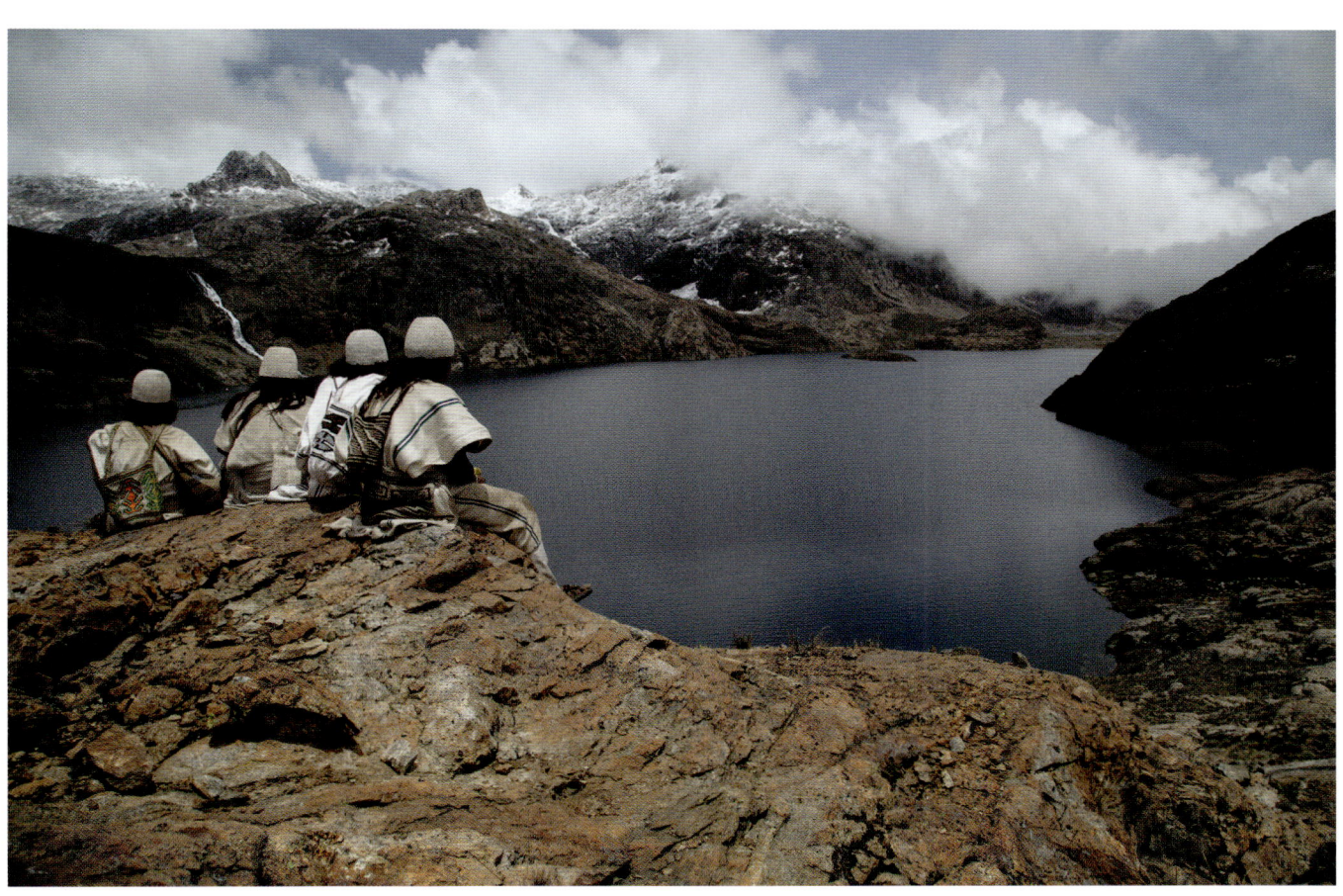

SHELLEY NIRO

Turtle Clan, Bay of Quinte Kanyen'kehà:ka (Mohawk) Nation
Six Nations of the Grand River
Ontario
Canada

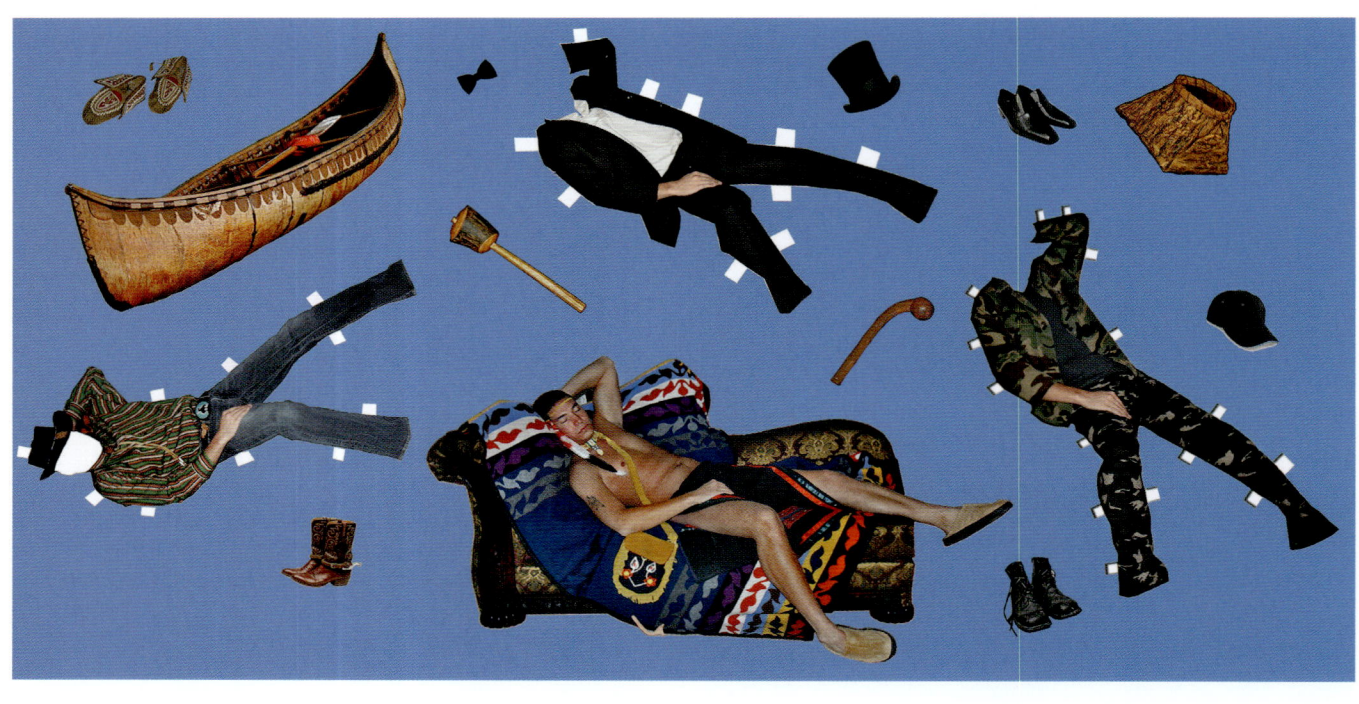

Part of a six-piece series titled Sleeping Warriors, Shelley Niro's (b. 1954) *Dressing Warrior* is a humorous mixed-media image. The artwork features an Indigenous man lying atop a colorful wool blanket with Native designs draped across a Victorian-style chaise. He's surrounded by a collection of different outfits—cowboy clothing, military uniform, formal suit—and traditional Native items, including a canoe, moccasins, and a basket. The white tabs on the outfits allude to wardrobe choices for a paper doll. The juxtaposition of these contrasting elements—Native and settler, or white—conveys the ways that Native people have adapted to a changing world. The center figure remains constant in his Indigenous selfhood while the attire he "puts on" is from white society.

Niro shares in her artist statement that before she made *Dressing Warrior*, she had been envisioning "a handsome young man sleeping in various changes of dress."[1] The original title of the work was long and clever—*Gaze of the Native North American Male as He Rests on His Postcolonial Sofa*. Jeremy Bomberry of Six Nations was the model for the Sleeping series.

With the emergence of the Idle No More movement in late 2012, Niro reconsidered her pieces of Indigenous men in repose. Idle No More is a women-led Canadian grassroots movement urging all people to honor Indigenous sovereignty and calling for the protection of the environment. She decided the pieces could still express humor and levity, but the titles had to change. "Rather than take a nonchalant poke at maleness and his slumbering, I had to address the warrior in all of us," said Niro.[2]

In *Dressing Warrior*, Niro considers the differing identities that Native people inhabit and the ways they are presented outwardly in the world. "The warrior has to embody changes in attitudes, politics and generally tries to make his own psyche bend to those devices in order to survive and live life fulfilled," she states. "It's a constant struggle."[3]

Niro is a member of the Turtle Clan, Bay of Quinte Kanyen'kehà:ka (Mohawk) Nation, Six Nations of the Grand River. Six Nations is the most populous First Nation reserve in Canada and unifies all the Haudenosaunee (Hodinǫhsǫ́:nih) nations under the Great Tree of Peace. The Haudenosaunee are known as "People of the Longhouse."

Growing up on Six Nations, Niro loved being among nature and playing in the open fields. She continuously draws upon her childhood recollections for inspiration in her art: the harsh winters, warm summers, the birdsong, and the sound of wind blowing through the leaves of the trees. Her mother, who spent her free time doing beadwork and making crafts to sell at powwows or in tourist shops, inspired and encouraged her, as did other artists in the community. Niro credits the artist Daphne Odjig, a Canadian First Nations artist of Odawa, Potawatomi, and English heritage, as one of her earliest influences.[4]

Niro's use of irony and social critique in combination with pop culture imagery establishes her as a trailblazer within the Native art world. Her work pushes back against misconceptions and stereotypes of Native people and challenges viewers to engage with serious issues. But as the *Dressing Warrior* image suggests, Niro also likes to bring viewers doses of comedy and enjoyment.

—Tiffany Midge

Dressing Warrior, 2012, from the Sleeping Warrior series.

DANA CLAXTON

Hunkpapa Lakota
Wood Mountain Lakota First Nation
Saskatchewan
Canada

Vancouver-based Hunkpapa Lakota artist Dana Claxton (b. 1959) draws inspiration from her cultural roots, the traditional spirituality of her people, and the power inherent in being an Indigenous woman. A prevalent theme in Claxton's work, which ranges from multichannel video installations, films, photography to performance, is urging viewers to "consider the ways in which Indigenous women have long been represented in museums and galleries—that is, as the anonymous makers of countless cultural belongings."[1]

Headdress–Jeneen pictures Jeneen Frei Njootli, a Vuntut Gwitchin First Nation artist. They are lavishly adorned with beaded accoutrements—hats, bags, barrettes, necklaces, bracelets—that span three generations of Vuntut Gwitchin ancestry from Old Crow, Yukon. The items, including a curtain of colorful beads worn like a veil over their face, are from Njootli's own collection.

A celebration of cultural abundance, *Jeneen* is one of five photographs in the series Headdress. Claxton says, "In these portraits, the beadworks cover and espouse the womxn's silhouettes, becoming more than just objects: the beadworks are cultural belongings, and the womxn are cultural carriers."[2] Each photograph stands alone, with its own unique and peculiar qualities, but displayed as a collection, the ensemble conveys a profound sense of wonder, joy, and delight. It is a feast for the optical senses and a wealth of colorful objects and shapes to relish and explore.

Claxton's longstanding vocation in the arts spans 30-plus years. She was born in Yorkton, Saskatchewan, and is a member of the Wood Mountain Lakota First Nation. Her work explores motifs of Indigenous beauty, the body, the spiritual, and the sociopolitical.

Claxton's aesthetics, anchored to her Hunkpapa Lakota culture, are acts of continuance that epitomize Indigenous resilience while also celebrating the ways Lakota people understand the world and themselves. In an interview with *BlackFlash*, Claxton discussed the idea of centralizing "beauty as a platform to mobilize dialogue" and contemporary Lakota voices.[3] Frequently incorporating clothing, beadwork, quillwork, and parflèche into her imagery, Claxton says, "These cultural belongings and practices are all embellished with great beauty and in some cases spiritual significance, that come with teachings of how to live a good life."[4]

—Tiffany Midge

Headdress—Jeneen, 2018.

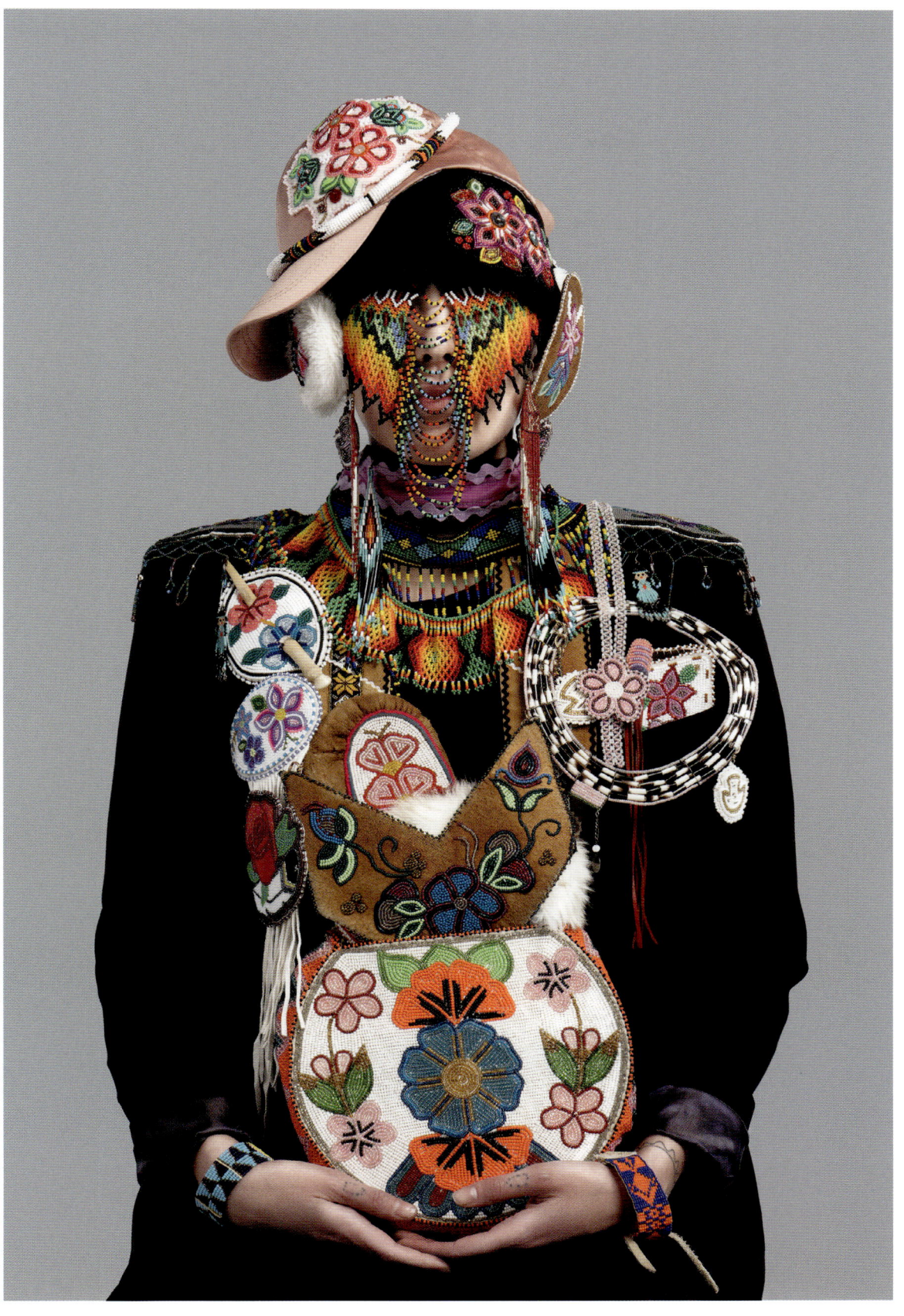

ROSALIE FAVELL

Métis
Winnipeg, Manitoba
Canada

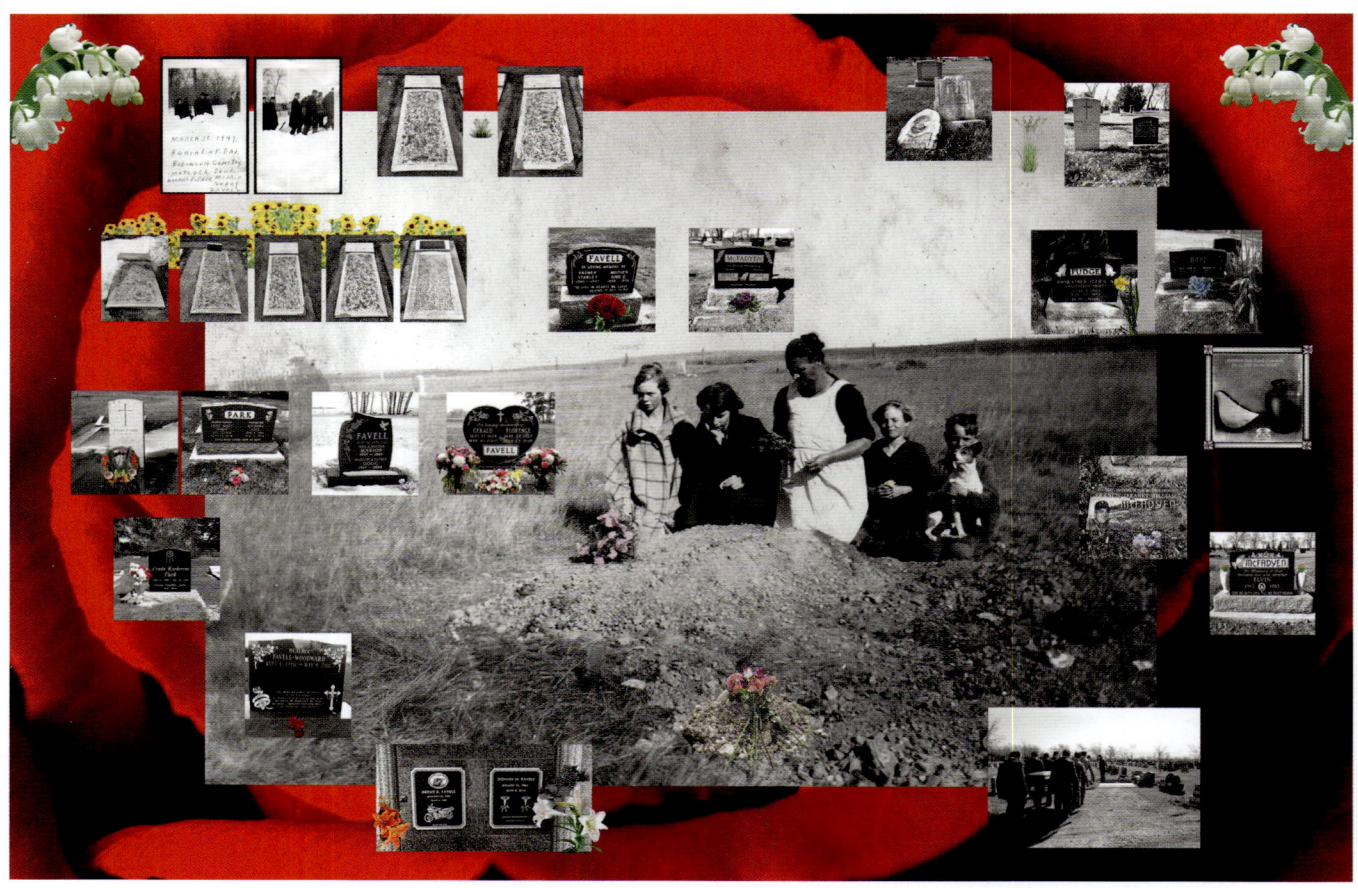

Forever in Our Hearts stands as a memorial dedicated to family members and ancestors. The photographic collage depicts burials, funerals, and a variety of inscribed headstones. The central image, the largest of the assemblage, features a woman and four children kneeling at a newly placed grave. Photo-based artist Rosalie Favell (b. 1958) found the image among her grandmother's photo albums.

The colorless sky in the main photograph speaks to the family's loss and grief. A stark contrast exists between the small black-and-white photos of headstones and the vibrant flowers —lilies of the valley, brown-eyed Susans, forget-me-nots, and more—Favell placed upon them when assembling the artwork. The entire collage is arranged against the backdrop of a single, magnified red rose.

While cemeteries aren't necessarily thought of as happy places for people to gather, Favell's recollections include pleasant times. "We've always gone to cemeteries and visited our relatives," she says. "We have picnics sometimes."[1] Favell remembers being a teenager and photographing funeral processions, like the one pictured in the bottom right of *Forever in Our Hearts*. Other photographs in the piece were made by her sister or niece. "There's a whole variety of time frames," explains Favell. "In the top left corner, there's two photos of my father's father, his burial, and the handwritten information of who was there."[2]

Favell, who is Métis, says it is an intricate identity that even some Métis people themselves don't always understand. Canada's 1982 Constitution Act recognizes three separate Indigenous groups: First Nations, Inuit, and Métis. The word *Métis* comes from the French and refers to individuals with mixed ancestry. Since the 18th century, *Métis* has described people of mixed Indigenous and European heritage, mainly in Canada. However, Métis has a broader context than simply mixed ancestry. Métis have a unique cultural identity with distinct lifeways and customs. Their ancestors are Indigenous women and European men—primarily French, English, or Scottish—who worked in the fur trade.

Forever in Our Hearts is part of Favell's lifework, a multichaptered series called Family Legacy. The work engages with a variety of photographic technologies and strategies, but the bedrock is her family's archives. Métis identity is largely defined by family, and photo albums are cherished documents. And for Favell, they are a resource in the search for her Métis roots. "My artwork reveals my journey to understand my heritage and my place within it," she says. "I am grateful to my family for the many photos that they have both taken and preserved for future generations. It is my hope that the work I have created over my lifetime will contribute to this rich family history."[3]

Of this radically personal work she says, "Through my display of images from my family's albums, I invite the viewer into my world where Indigenous peoples claim the right to exhibit their own culture and history."[4] Moreover, Favell adds, "This family archive feeds my spirit. I feel a responsibility to keep my family alive through my mining and re-presenting them."[5]

Long before colonization, Favell's Cree ancestors lived on the lands that eventually became Winnipeg and Manitoba. Her father's English forebears were fur traders, and their children became Métis, and eventually her mother's English and Scottish forebears came as settlers. "On the paternal side, the mixing of blood in my family line has been traced back to 1773 when a Cree woman named Titameg met John Favel who had arrived from England working for the Hudson's Bay," Favell explains in her essay "Holding Our Ground."[6]

Favell, who is the seventh generation from first contact, says *Forever in Our Hearts* is a "mapping out of the family" and a reminder of the prophecy that each generation affects descendants seven generations into the future. "For me, it's a very emotional, tender way of looking at the family and remembering."[7]

—Tiffany Midge

Forever in Our Hearts, 2021.

SHAN GOSHORN

Eastern Band of Cherokee Indians
Qualla Boundary
North Carolina
United States

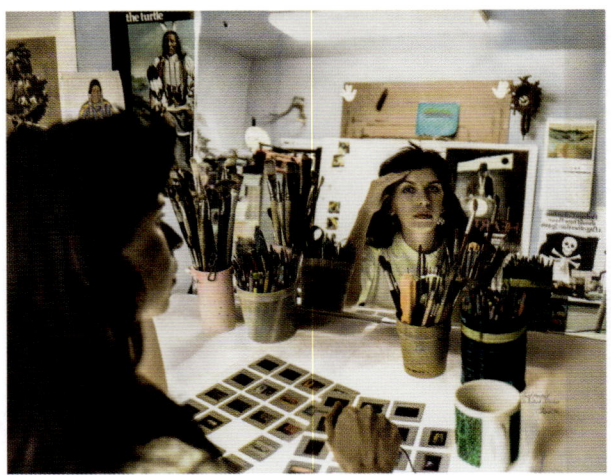

S han Goshorn (1957–2018) acknowledged she was recognized as a photographer, but that she did not think of herself as one. "I consider myself an artist who chooses the medium that best expresses a statement, usually one that addresses human rights issues, especially those that affect native people," quoted the *New York Times* in 2018.[1]

It is a variation of a sentiment that Goshorn, a citizen of the Eastern Band of Cherokee Indians (EBCI), voiced throughout her career. At the Gorman Museum of Native American Art, she clarified that she considered herself an "artist who uses a camera as a tool," much like using "paint or metal or glass." She went on to describe her relationship with photography and the craft's "unique importance" to Indian people. Since her teen years Goshorn observed and questioned anthropologists and historians gathering information about Native people without sharing the results. In the mid-1980s she joined the Native Indian/Inuit Photographers' Association (NIIPA), and for her, this community signaled a shift in representation. She said, "No longer content to just pose in front of a lens, Indians were now picking up cameras…and we were taking our own pictures of ourselves."[2]

Self Portrait in Artist Studio, made in 1996 in Tulsa, Oklahoma, exemplifies this affirmation. Goshorn's camera is placed slightly above her right shoulder. Looking at herself in a mirror, the lens sees Goshorn both in profile and straight on. Her right hand holds the shutter release. Slides and several containers filled with brushes and art utensils are strewn on the desk in front of her. Various prints of Native Americans line the walls of her studio, along with other ephemera and items: a calendar, a small cuckoo clock, a blue piece of paper scrawled with different colors of crayon and hand printed with the word *Mom*.

Coming Into Power is from a decade earlier, when Goshorn was working with paint and photo oils to hand-color black-and-white photographs, a technique she acquired as a student at the Cleveland Institute of Art. Goshorn explained she used tinting as a way to preserve the photographic element rather than painting over the image entirely. Her intention, reported the *Oklahoman*, was "to emphasize that American Indians are real people living in today's world as well as existing on a spiritual plane."[3] It was important to Goshorn that viewers understand the people she depicted, including herself, are vital and prospering in the present while also remaining rooted in the traditional.

Goshorn was raised in Baltimore, Maryland, and spent summers with her maternal grandmother on the Qualla Boundary, home of the EBCI in the Blue Ridge Mountains of western North Carolina. It was here where her interest in art began, working at the venerated Qualla Arts and Crafts cooperative. In 1981 she moved to Tulsa, Oklahoma, where she lived until her passing in 2018. She is widely known for her basket weaving, which incorporates archival photography and historical documents, such as treaties and maps. Her baskets, woven with classical Cherokee techniques, deliver political and cultural observations on Native American matters and history. Goshorn's highly impactful work continues to be exhibited in museums throughout the world.

—Tiffany Midge

Coming Into Power, 1986.

Opposite: *Self Portrait in Artist Studio*, 1996.
PHOTOGRAPHS BY SHAN GOSHORN. NATIONAL MUSEUM OF THE AMERICAN INDIAN, SMITHSONIAN INSTITUTION. 26/9971, 26/9976

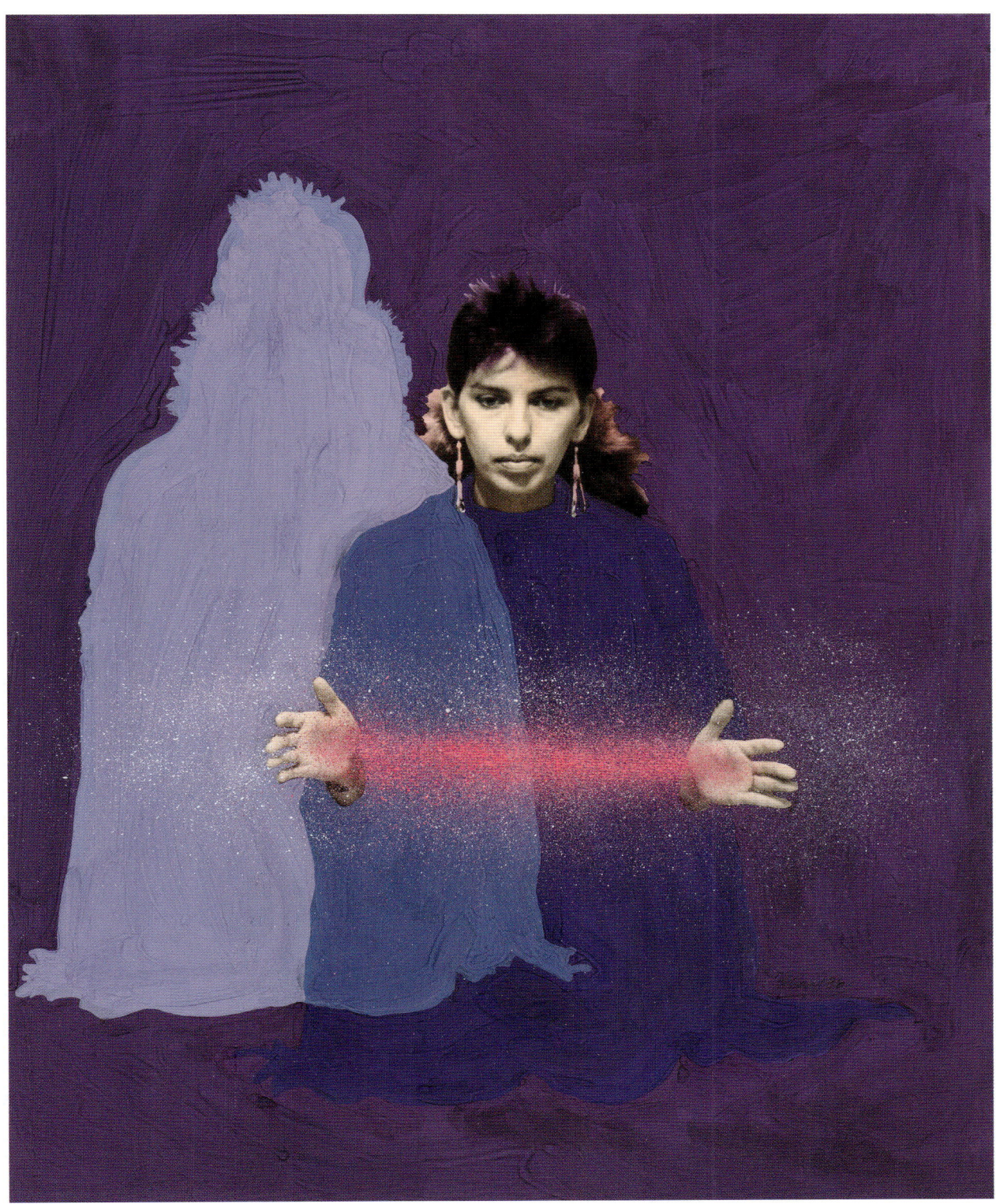

DOROTHY CHOCOLATE CARSEEN

Tłı̨chǫ Dene
Gamètì, Tłı̨chǫ Region, Northwest Territories
Canada

In March of 1985, a group of Indigenous artists came together in Hamilton, Ontario, for the Conference of Native Indian Photography. Titled "VISIONS," it was not easy for the organizers, Yvonne Maracle and Brenda Mitten, to locate potential attendees for this unprecedented event. Without an official network of Indigenous photographers, the women phoned First Nations government offices, Friendship Centres, and media outlets, and they spread information by word of mouth.

Maracle and Mitten's efforts proved successful. "Truly, VISIONS was a conference of convergence," says Métis curator Rhéanne Chartrand. "It marked the first time ever that such a diverse group of Indigenous photographers from across Canada and the United States had gathered north of the 49th parallel to present and discuss their work."[1]

Two days after the galvanizing conference ended, Dorothy Chocolate Carseen (b. 1959) and several other participants became the founding members of the Native Indian/Inuit Photographers' Association (NIIPA). When NIIPA, led by Maracle and Mitten, incorporated as a nonprofit organization in the summer of 1985, Carseen was appointed to the board of directors.

NIIPA, which operated for two decades, forged a community of Indigenous photographers and collaborators, and advocated for a "positive, realistic and contemporary image" of Indigenous peoples through the photographic arts.[2] From the NIIPA office in Hamilton, the women-run organization produced a newsletter, annual conferences, educational workshops, and exhibitions with related catalogs (*Visions, Silver Drum, No Borders,* and *Reminiscing*). In the basement of NIIPA's space, darkroom facilities were available to members, overcoming the financial barrier of accessing similar resources.

"Establishing NIIPA meant finding ways to position more Indigenous creatives behind the camera and in control of the lens," summarizes Chartrand. "Prior to the emergence of NIIPA, there was no widespread Indigenous photography movement nor an effort to support, develop, and promote Indigenous photography as art."[3]

Multiple NIIPA alumni from Canada and the United States have achieved notable artistic careers: Shelley Niro, Jolene Rickard, Martin Akwiranoron Loft, Murray McKenzie, Greg Staats, Jeff Thomas, Richard Hill, Pena Bonita, Bert Crowfoot, Larry McNeil, Jimmy Manning, Richard Ray Whitman, Rosalie Favell, Hulleah Tsinhnahjinnie, Shan Goshorn, Duwawisioma (Victor Masayesva), and others.

Carseen's graceful and naturally insightful photographs are attentive to the communal experiences of First Nations peoples in and around the Tłı̨chǫ Region of the Northwest Territories (NWT). Raised on the land near Gamètì, Carseen attended high school in Yellowknife. For more than a decade, she worked as a photographer and editor for *Native Press, Press Independent,* and *Northern Star.* Her catalog, preserved by the NWT Archives, contains many portraits, among them a charismatic frame of Eric Menicoche in a cowboy hat and denim shirt, leaning on a truck bed. Carseen photographed him from a low angle, imparting the backdrop to the clouds.

In a kinetic photograph of a wedding in Dettah, newlyweds Alice Tsetta and Louis Martin,[4] exit Kateri Tekakwitha Roman Catholic Church through a hail of rice launched into the air by guests of all ages. An illustration of St. Kateri Tekakwitha, the first Indigenous American to be recognized as a saint by the Catholic Church, hangs on the exterior of the building. Tekakwitha was born in 1656, in the Kanien'kehà:ka (Mohawk) village of Ossernenon in present-day New York State and died at age 24. She was canonized by Pope Benedict XVI in 2012.

Stored within Carseen's archive of more than 5,000 photographs is a quiet picture from a function organized by the Native Women's Association. Inside a living room, women sit in a semicircle and talk. The couches are soft, and the curtains are striped. Gentle light filters through the bare trees outside. The image was made from the point of view of someone partaking in the meeting.

An artfully seen kitchen of a tranquil home in Wekweètì calls forth memories: meals and news across a checkered tablecloth, papers for later tucked above cupboards and into cabinets, a window overlooking the rippling waters of the broad Snare River. Carseen positioned her reflection in a mirror next to the sink, a transcendent figure in the gracious, expressive room.

—Sarah Stacke

A portrait of Eric Menicoche, Fort Simpson, Northwest Territories, June 1982. Fort Simpson's traditional Dene name is Łíídlı̨ Kų́ę́.

PHOTOGRAPH BY DOROTHY CHOCOLATE CARSEEN. ©NWT ARCHIVES/NATIVE COMMUNICATIONS SOCIETY—NATIVE PRESS PHOTO/N-2018-010-10048

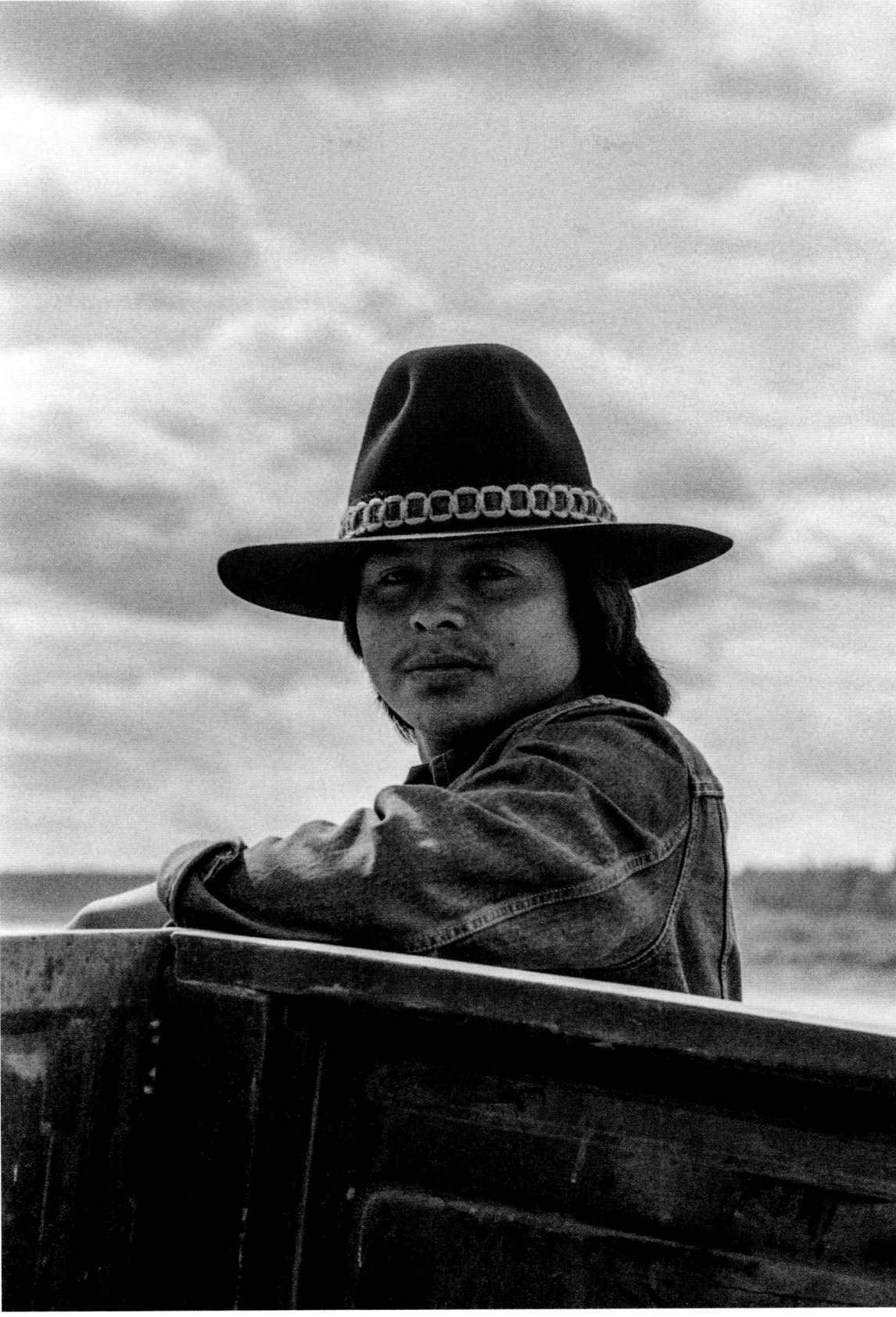

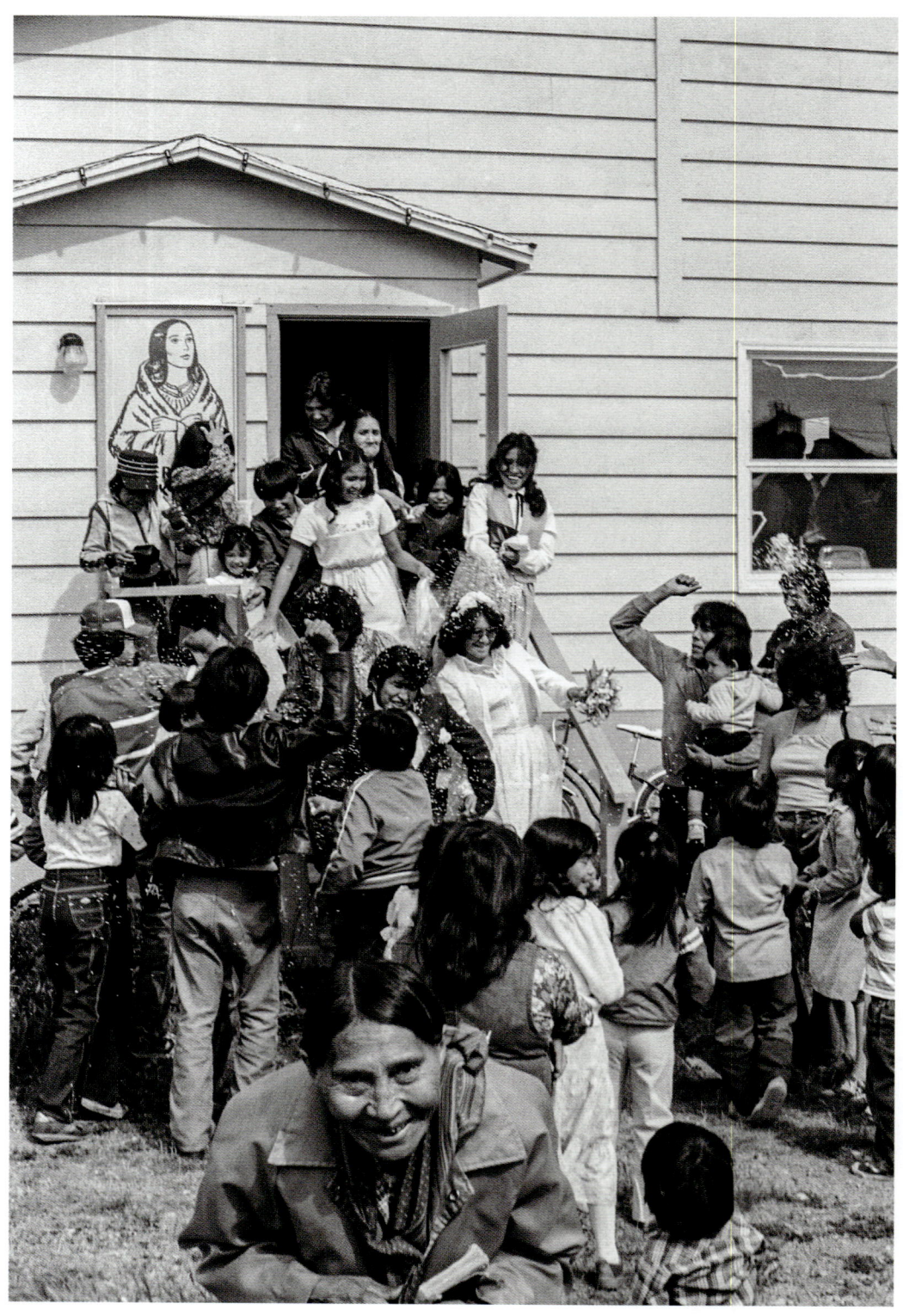

A crowd gathers outside of Kateri Tekakwitha Roman Catholic
Church as the bride and groom exit, Dettah, Northwest
Territories, July 1981. Dettah was a longtime Dene seasonal fish
camp before it became a permanent settlement in the 1930s.

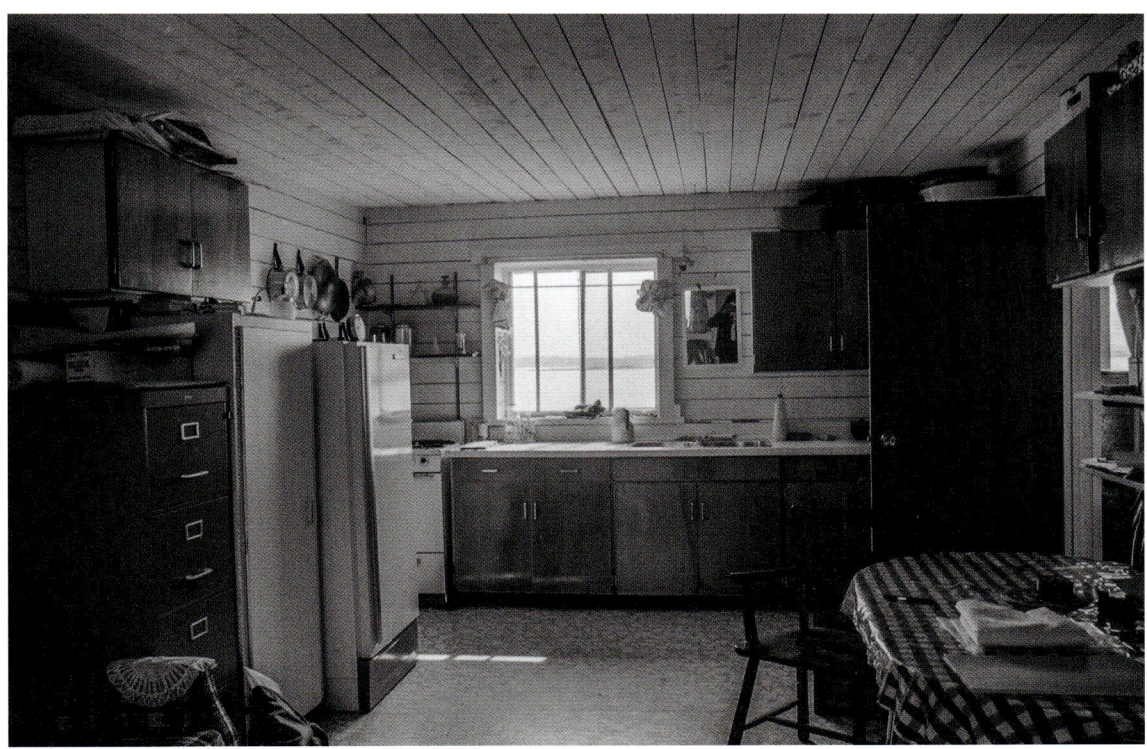

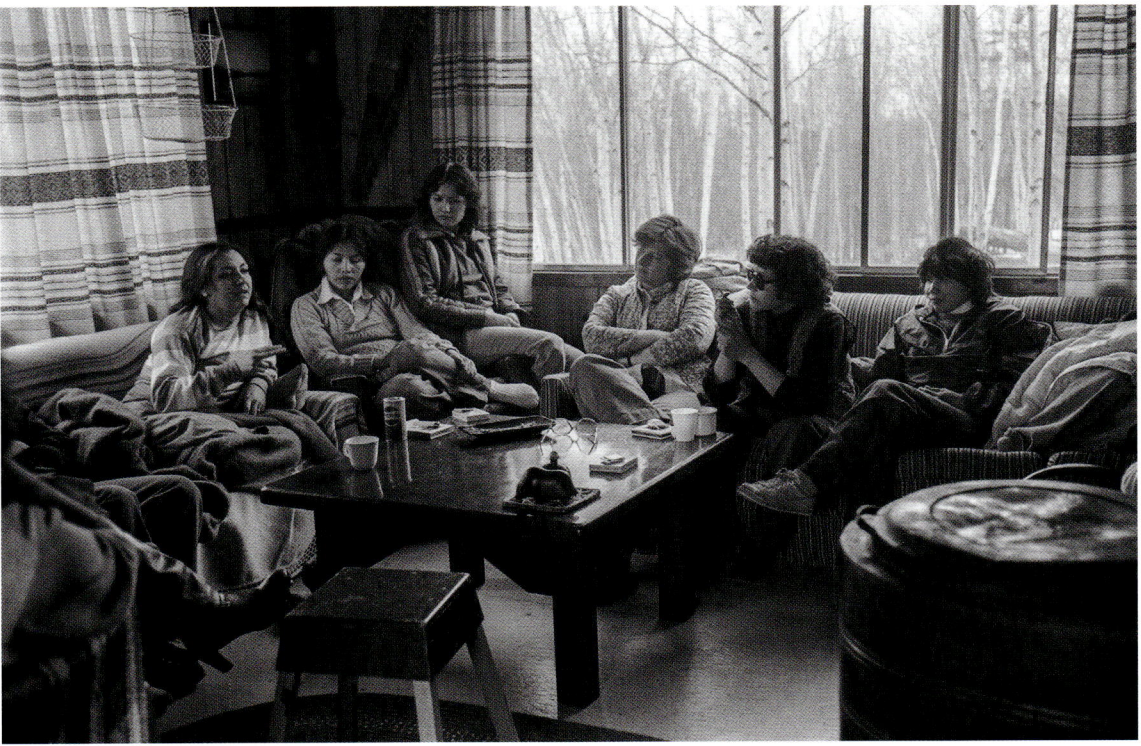

The interior of a home in Wekweètì, Northwest Territories, July 1982. Wekweètì, located at the Snare River, is the smallest and most remote of the Tłı̨chǫ Dene communities.
PHOTOGRAPH BY DOROTHY CHOCOLATE CARSEEN. ©NWT ARCHIVES/NATIVE COMMUNICATIONS SOCIETY—NATIVE PRESS PHOTO/N-2018-010-10159

Women at a Native Women's Association picnic near Prosperous Lake, Northwest Territories, May 1982.
PHOTOGRAPH BY DOROTHY CHOCOLATE CARSEEN. ©NWT ARCHIVES/NATIVE COMMUNICATIONS SOCIETY—NATIVE PRESS PHOTO/N-2018-010-09986

KIMOWAN METCHEWAIS

Cree
Cold Lake First Nations
Alberta
Canada

"Where does your art come from?" Cree interdisciplinary artist Kimowan Metchewais (1963–2011) asked his colleagues. "I want my art to be innovative, to move our voices forward, but I have to know, if I take it home to my Nation, that they can see that it carries on a long tradition."[1]

In the 1990s, Metchewais began generating a wide-ranging Polaroid collection that formed the nucleus of his practice. He organized the images by topic (Eyepieces, Mom's Wacky Mocs, Lakewater, Plants, Throat), alphabetized them in handmade boxes, and integrated them into his collages and paintings that examined connections between identity, language, history, and home. He cut the Polaroids up, taped them back together, and rephotographed them before returning everything to the collection. Metchewais relied on this personal, evolving archive for reference and source material, rather than museums, institutions, or any outside sources. The Polaroids covered the walls of his studio; he created sequences and sought links between them in a pursuit—an "investigation," Metchewais called it—to make sense of himself and the world he lived in.

"His work explores the ground, aesthetic and territorial, on which contemporary Native art and communities might stand," observed art historian Christopher T. Green.[2]

The pink bloom of a magnolia tree grows from a dark green and black background of one Polaroid. Along with eight additional studies of the flowering tree, the image is stored in Box 6, Folder 40 at the National Museum of the American Indian (NMAI) in Washington, D.C. Before Metchewais died at age 47 from a brain tumor that he lived with for sixteen years, he willed the entirety of his art, including nearly 1,000 Polaroids, to the NMAI. His brother and three of his closest friends, among them photographer Jeff Whetstone, helped the NMAI catalog his life's work.

"Metchewais drew his artistic breath from the Cree people of Cold Lake First Nations," recalled Whetstone in *Kimowan Metchewais: A Kind of Prayer*, a monograph published in 2023. "It is through this lens that the intensity of his investigation and vision offers us a narrative of the true stakes of the modernist experiment."

A Polaroid from the series Indian Handsign shows Metchewais's right hand in the center of the frame. His thumb is flush with his forefinger and his other three fingers are dispersed into a kind of plume resembling the tail feathers or wings of a bird. *FLIGHT* is penciled in all caps on the white border below the image. A smudge from a different, erased word is visible behind the letters. Metchewais was composing a language. Other gestures in Indian Handsign are labeled *LOOK, CHANGE, RECALL, GIVE*. The hand signs triangulate "a relationship between body, language, and image," noted Green.[3]

The brain tumor required Metchewais to reckon with his physical and spiritual self, and mortality, which he did through his work. After one surgery left him half paralyzed for a time, he said, "I instantly knew that I still had a vision, and that it was mysterious, and that I still felt compelled to pursue it. And I would be able to."[4]

In an untitled self-portrait made from pieces of photographs taped on ledger paper, Metchwais is dressed in jeans and a white tank top. He wears a hairpiece that falls to the floor and pools at his bare feet. Reflecting on Metchewais's work in a *New York Times* guest essay, Apsáalooke (Crow) artist Wendy Red Star writes that long hair symbolizes power in Plains culture, particularly for men. She shares a story about Long Hair, an Apsáalooke Chief "whose hair was so long, he could wrap it around the base of a tepee, or so legend goes." Radiation and surgeries had left a permanent bald spot on the back of Metchewais's head. Red Star asks, "I wonder if he was confronting his identity in these works. Are you not Native if you don't have long hair?"[5]

A compilation of two Polaroids presents the artist crouched into a boxing stance. Half of his face is obscured by the shadow of a white cowboy hat. Berry-red boxing gloves punch through the photograph like a pair of beating hearts. "My studio has been a laboratory where I have conducted an archaeology of the self. I work this way to accidentally produce live relics only to be purposefully found later," Metchewais wrote in 2009. "Live relics," he explained, are "trace elements from memory, history, and culture" that he embedded in his art. "They are alive," he continued, "because they continue to transmit influence to this day."[6]

Born in Oxbow, Saskatchewan, Metchewais began his career as an illustrator and editor at the Indigenous newspaper *Windspeaker*. He received a bachelor of fine arts from the University of Alberta Edmonton, and a master of fine arts from the University of New Mexico, Albuquerque. In 1999, Metchewais began teaching in the art department at the University of North Carolina at Chapel Hill, where he became an associate professor. He died at his mother's home in Alberta.

—Tiffany Midge and Sarah Stacke

Untitled, 1998. Photo collage on ledger paper.

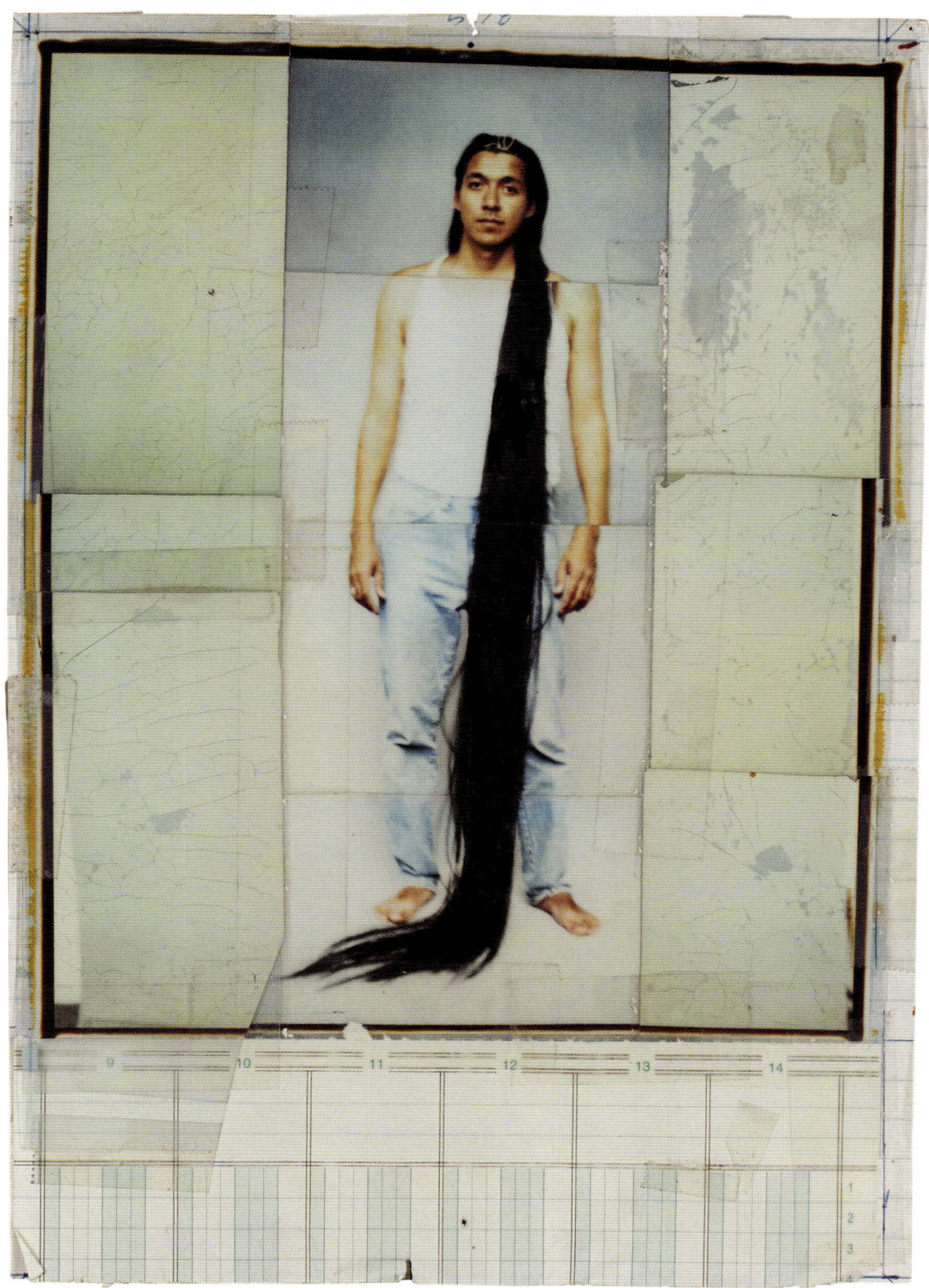

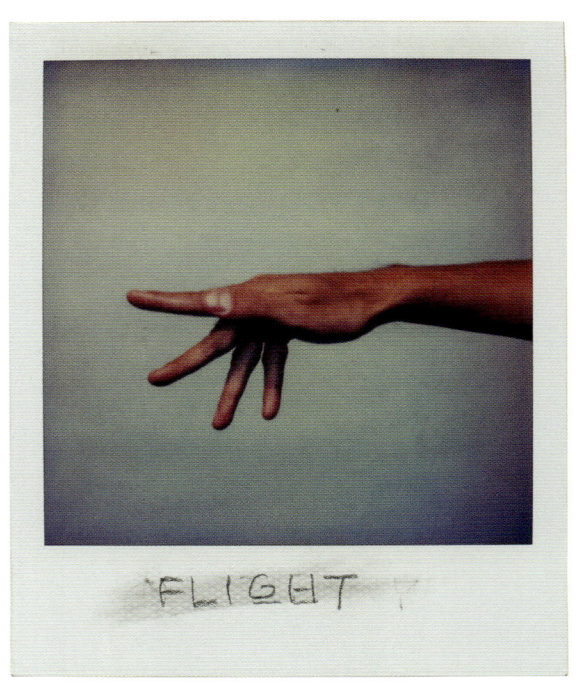

FLIGHT

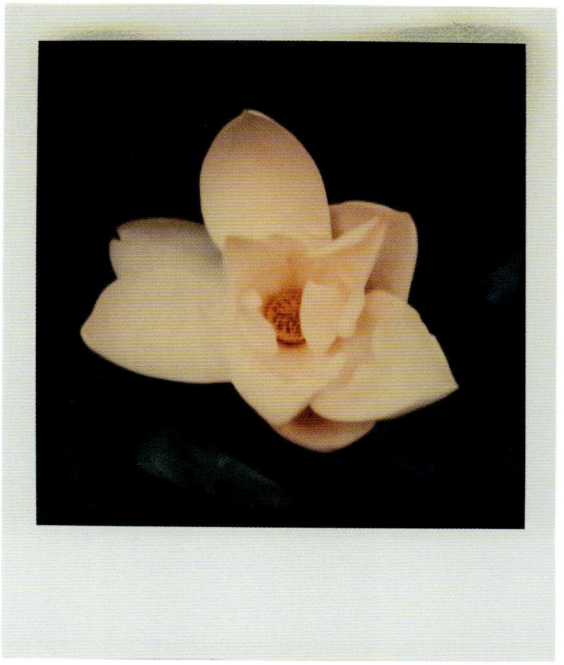

From the series Indian Handsign, Albuquerque, New Mexico, 1997.

Untitled, New Mexico, 1997.

Opposite: Untitled photograph by Enid Baxter Ryce,
Albuquerque, New Mexico, 1997.

PHOTOGRAPHS BY KIMOWAN METCHEWAIS. KIMOWAN METCHEWAIS [MCLAIN] COLLECTION,
NMAI.AC.084, NATIONAL MUSEUM OF THE AMERICAN INDIAN ARCHIVE CENTER, SMITHSONIAN
INSTITUTION. NMAI-084_001_11_001, NMAI-084_006_34_002, NMAI-084_006_40_009, NMAI-084_001_15_004

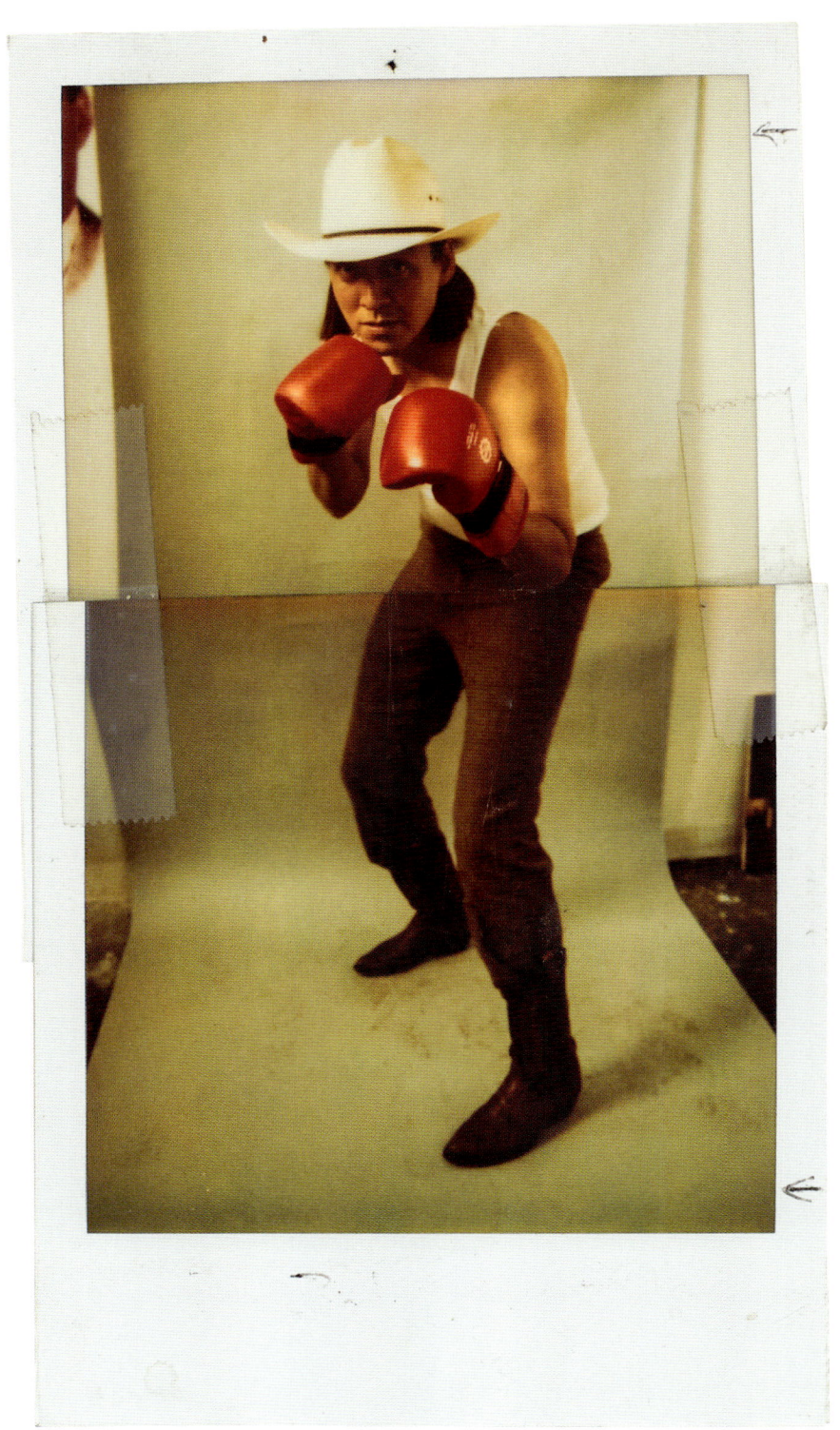

CAMILLE SEAMAN
Afro-Indigenous and European
Ølgod
Denmark

The *Lovely Monster over the Farm* is a study of atmosphere and chaos, of cloud, storm, and sky. In the foreground of Camille Seaman's (b. 1969) photograph lies the merest suggestion of a homestead and silo, while an ominous, dark, and swirling force appears above, poised to gobble them up. Seaman calls the tornado in the photograph a "lovely monster," and while it does bear remarkable similarities to monsters, something like Godzilla, calling it "lovely" suggests the adage "Beauty is in the eye of the beholder." Or maybe "Beauty is in the eye of the storm."

The imposing image was created over the course of a few hours, when Seaman was chasing a supercell storm cloud throughout rural Nebraska. From town to town, she passed by wheat fields, windmills, and barns, photographing the mesocyclone. In a 2013 TED talk, Seaman describes the encounter: "Storm chasing is a very tactile experience. There's a warm, moist wind blowing at your back, and the smell of the earth, the wheat, the grass, the charged particles. And then there are the colors in the clouds of hail forming, the greens and the turquoise blues…What really excites me about these storms is their movement, the way they swirl and spin and undulate…As I stand under them, I see not just a cloud, but understand that what I have the privilege to witness is the same forces, the same process in a small-scale version, that helped to create our galaxy, our solar system, our sun, and even this very planet."[1]

Growing up, Seaman spent summers with her grandparents on the East End of Long Island. Her grandfather was of Shinnecock and Montaukett descent, which informed much of her worldview. He taught her that all living beings are interconnected. "As a small child, he would take me into the woods and introduce me to each tree," recalled Seaman. "He said, 'This is your relative, in the same way that I am your relative. And you must respect it.'"[2] It was in this way that she came to honor and appreciate what being a good ancestor means. Her grandfather showed her that she is a part of the storms, the rain, and her environment, and it was this understanding that fostered her respect and appreciation for the natural environments she documents. She shared with PBS: "When I saw my very first iceberg in Antarctica in 2004, I remember just shaking, because I was thinking, how many snowflakes is this? How many ancestors' water is this?" Seaman realized that by photographing the sublime and frozen figures, she was making portraits of all those who came before her.[3]

Seaman's work inspires equal doses of astonishment and uneasiness. Currently based in Denmark, she has traveled to the most remote, and possibly most breathtaking, places on earth, locations largely untouched by humans but populated with polar bears, penguins, and walruses. Her haunting images of calved ice, glaciers, colossal squalls, and the ever-shifting natural environment bear witness to the effects of climate change and the impact of global warming on our planet.

"I hope that humans will realize that we are of this Earth. We only get this one. And, one day, we will realize just how special it is. I just hope it's not after we have lost so much of what makes it special," she said.[4]

—Tiffany Midge

Pages 210–211: *The Lovely Monster over the Farm*, 19:15 CST, Lodgepole, Nebraska, June 22, 2012.

PAT KANE

Algonquin Anishinaabe, Irish Canadian
Timiskaming First Nation
Yellowknife, Northwest Territories
Canada

C aribou once thrived in the hundreds of thousands in the furthermost regions of Canada's Northwest Territories (NWT). But, since the 1990s, the Barrenland herds have declined to less than ten thousand. Mining, climate change, overhunting, and a rise in predators are thought to contribute to the drop in population. This scarcity is profoundly felt in First Nations communities. For millennia, they have relied on the animal for food and cultural identification.

When Pat Kane (b. 1979) photographed a dozen caribou on the tundra near Lac de Gras, he was with 20 or so First Nations hunters, students, and Elders from Dettah—a Dene community outside Yellowknife, the capital city of the NWT. The group had traveled nearly 200 miles over wintry roads to harvest caribou, musk ox, and other animals that crossed their path.

Kane, who is based in Yellowknife, is of Algonquin Anishinaabe and Irish Canadian descent. A member of the Timiskaming First Nation, he documents the lifeways of Indigenous people in Northern Canada, with a special emphasis on the relationship between land and identity. *Dzǫ nàts'ede ha hot'e / Here Is Where We Shall Stay*, his 2023 monograph, looks at the ways the Dene of the NWT navigate a path of self-determination by addressing historical injustices committed by the Canadian government and the Catholic Church.

For more than a decade, hunting caribou in the NWT has been banned, with an exception for First Nations people who retain rights in designated zones. As Kane and the crew reached Diavik Diamond Mine, on the edge of the Arctic Circle, a large group of caribou came into view. "We got on our snowmobiles from the ice road and went inland over the tundra," recalls Kane. "The caribou scattered and ran into separate herds."[1] Kane was riding with Randy Baillargeon, a smart young hunter. It was minus 30 degrees Celsius and stormy when Baillargeon led their snowmobile over a rocky outcrop and, sure enough, a small cluster of caribou was on the other side.

"For a few minutes we just watched these animals run around and be free," says Kane. "You don't see caribou in the wild too often because they're so hard to get to, and the population is down so much. You feel a little bit in awe when you come upon a scene like that."

While Baillargeon deciphered what direction the caribou would go and how to hunt them safely, the weather shifted, and the horizon materialized through the veiled land and overcast sky. Kane raised his camera and photographed the graceful caribou traversing the Arctic tundra.

Kane, who seems as familiar with the terrain as one might be with an old friend, describes the dramatic turns of the landscape that day: "To see this beautiful stormy blue sky, mixed with clouds and white snow, is super rare. We usually get full sun, whiteout, or black darkness. It's like wow, look where we are," he remembers thinking.

—Tiffany Midge

Pages 212–213: Caribou, a source of food, clothing, and shelter for generations of First Nations people, run on the tundra near Lac de Gras, Northwest Territories, Canada, February 11, 2021.

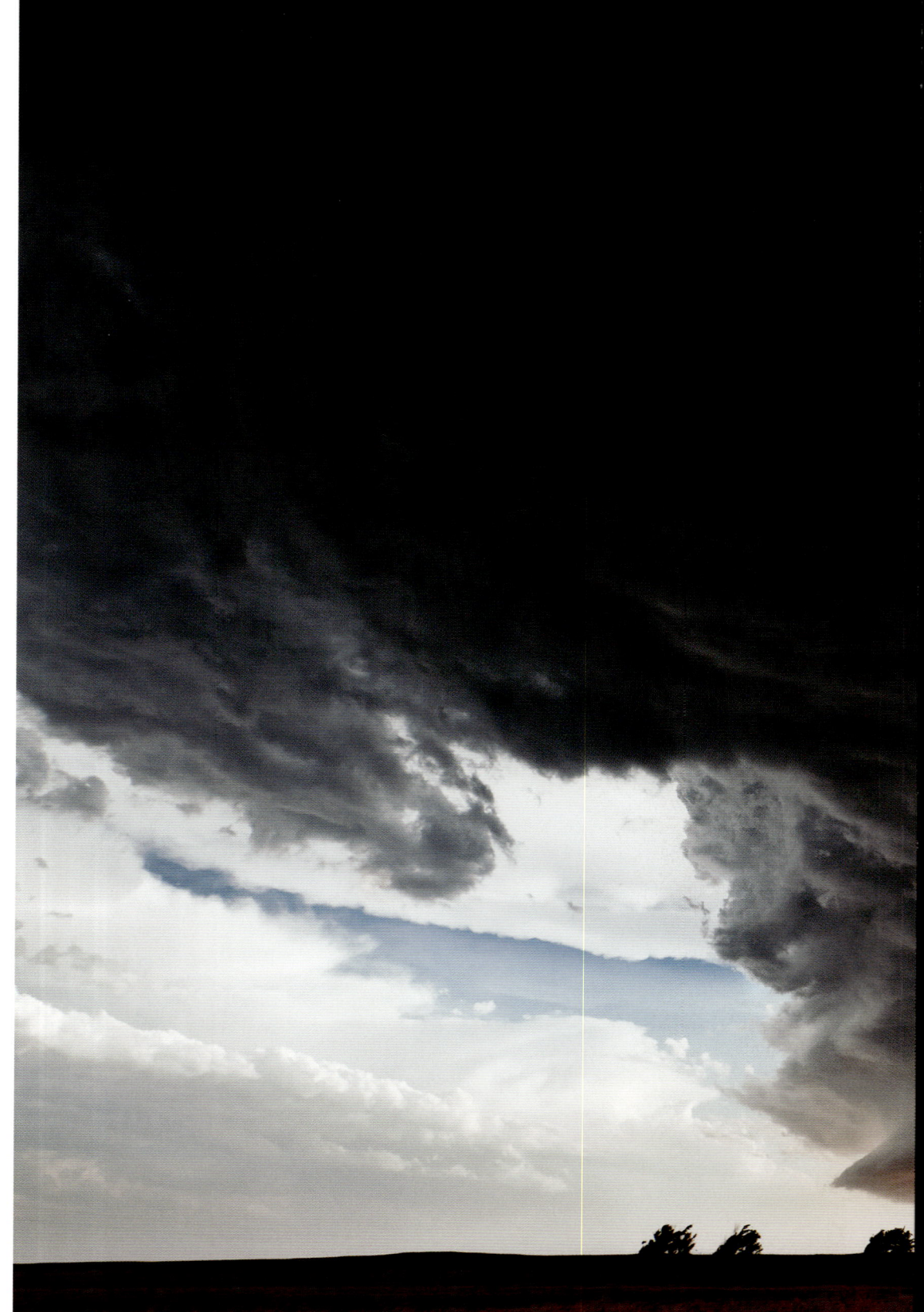

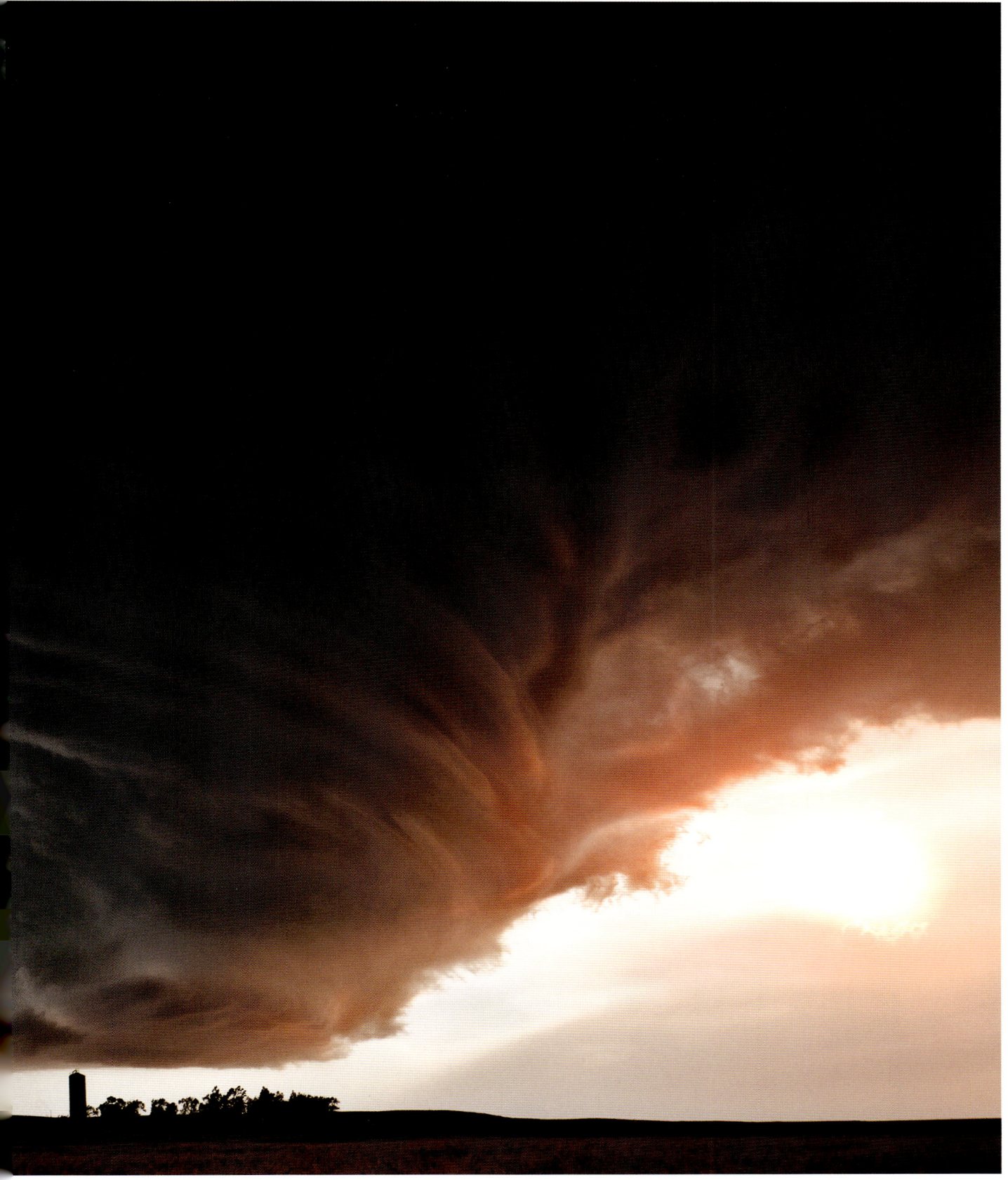

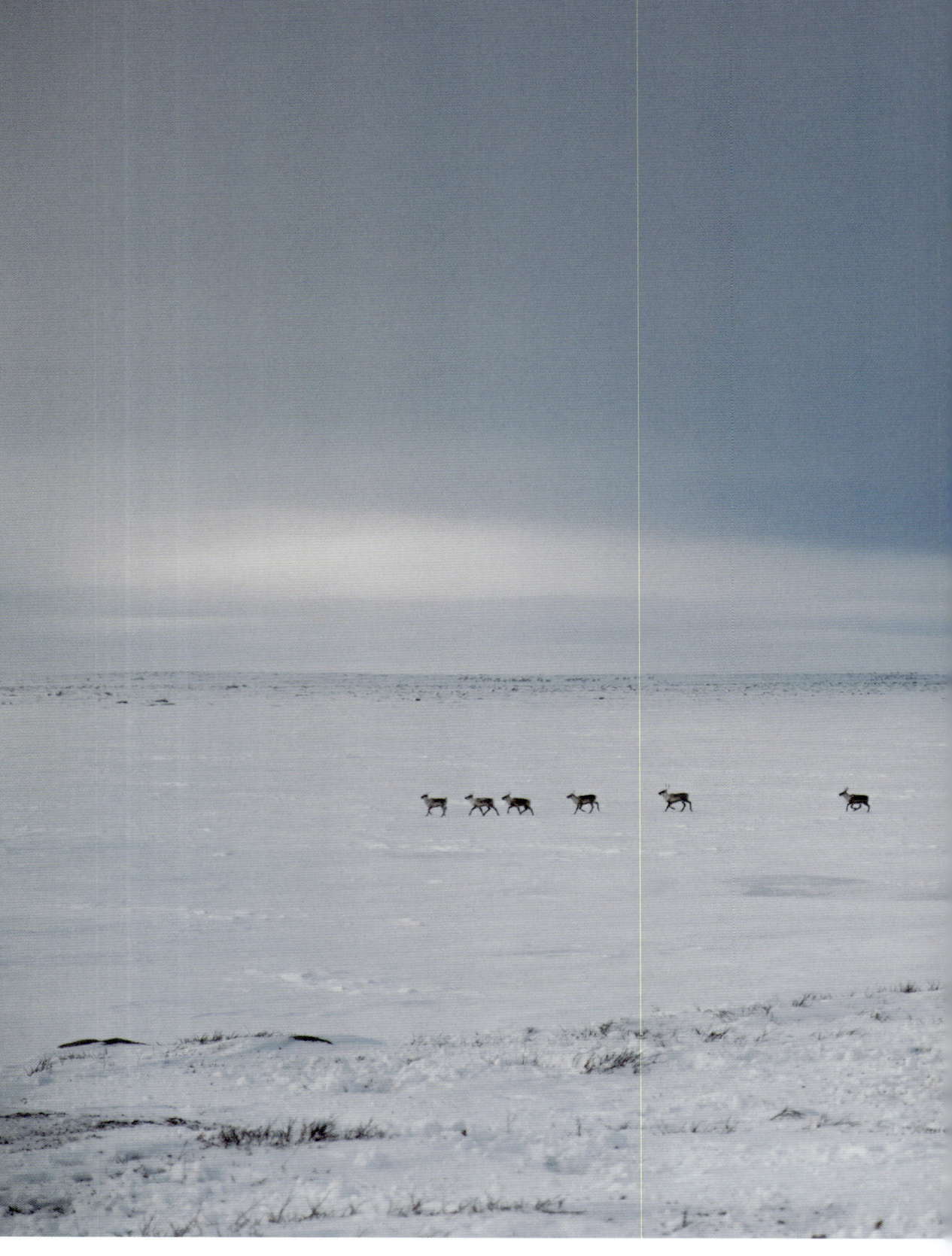

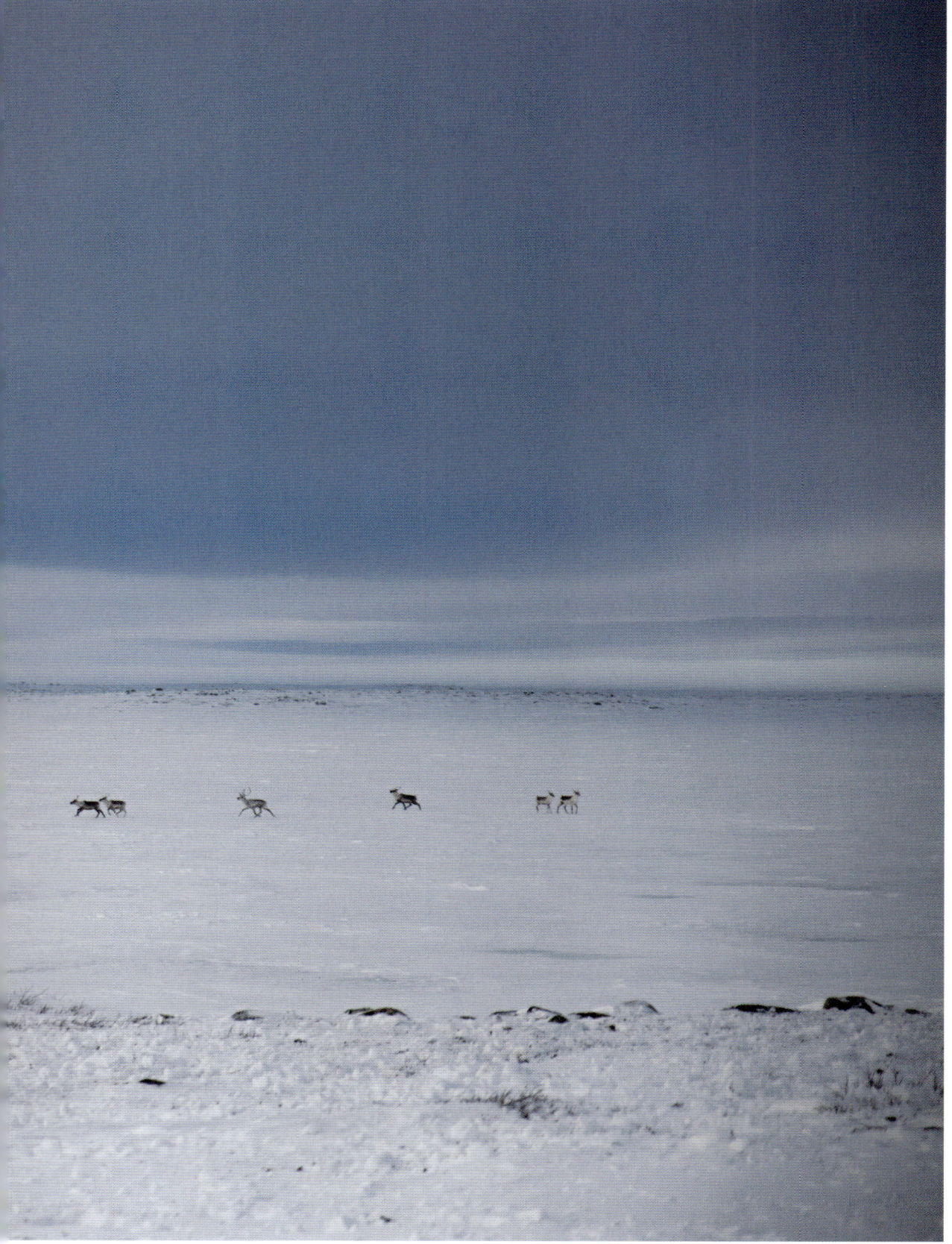

TOM JONES

Ho-Chunk
Ho-Chunk Nation
Wisconsin
United States

Tom Jones's (b. 1964) portrait of Mary Funmaker, from the series Strong Unrelenting Spirits, is an expression of Ho-Chunk identity. Her profile strikes a dramatic contrast against the black background, garnished with white beads arranged like a flowering wreath. Funmaker wears colorful beadwork and a multi-strand hairpipe necklace; a red-tipped feather extends from her silver hair. An eagle-feather fan used in ceremony and in dance anchors the photograph.

The white beadwork incorporated into the life-sized portraits that comprise Strong Unrelenting Spirits reflects traditional Ho-Chunk floral and geometric designs. Jones explained that the glimmering patterns symbolize "the spirits of our ancestors who are constantly looking over us."[1] The series was shaped by Jones's childhood experience at a ceremony in which spirits were called forth and appeared as small orbs of light floating around the room.

The beading is labor-intensive. Some portraits take Jones more than 120 hours to complete, but the effect is formidable. The first photograph Jones made for the series was of his mother, JoAnn Jones, and today Strong Unrelenting Spirits includes more than 20 images of Ho-Chunk children, women, and men. Many wear traditional Native attire, while others appear in jeans and T-shirts. It's the sitter's choice; they arrive to the session how they wish to be seen.

The ancestral Homelands of the Ho-Chunk once encompassed 10 million acres stretching between the Mississippi and Rock Rivers in what is now the Midwest. Today, the government of the Ho-Chunk Nation is headquartered in Black River Falls, Wisconsin. The nation is not situated on a reservation or one continuous land base, but owns land throughout Wisconsin, as well as Illinois. Worldwide, there are approximately 10,000 Ho-Chunk citizens.

For Jones, who is a professor of photography at the University of Wisconsin–Madison, the goal of his art is to illustrate the beauty and strength of the Ho-Chunk and help make their lives visible to the world. With works included in more than 60 exhibitions across the United States and internationally in the past decade alone, he is succeeding. In 2022, the Museum of Wisconsin Art hosted the first major retrospective of Jones's career, featuring 120 photographs from 16 portfolios spanning 25 years of a practice devoted to making art about—and ultimately for—his Ho-Chunk people.

—Tiffany Midge

Mary Funmaker, 2015, from the series Strong Unrelenting Spirits, archival digital print with glass beads.

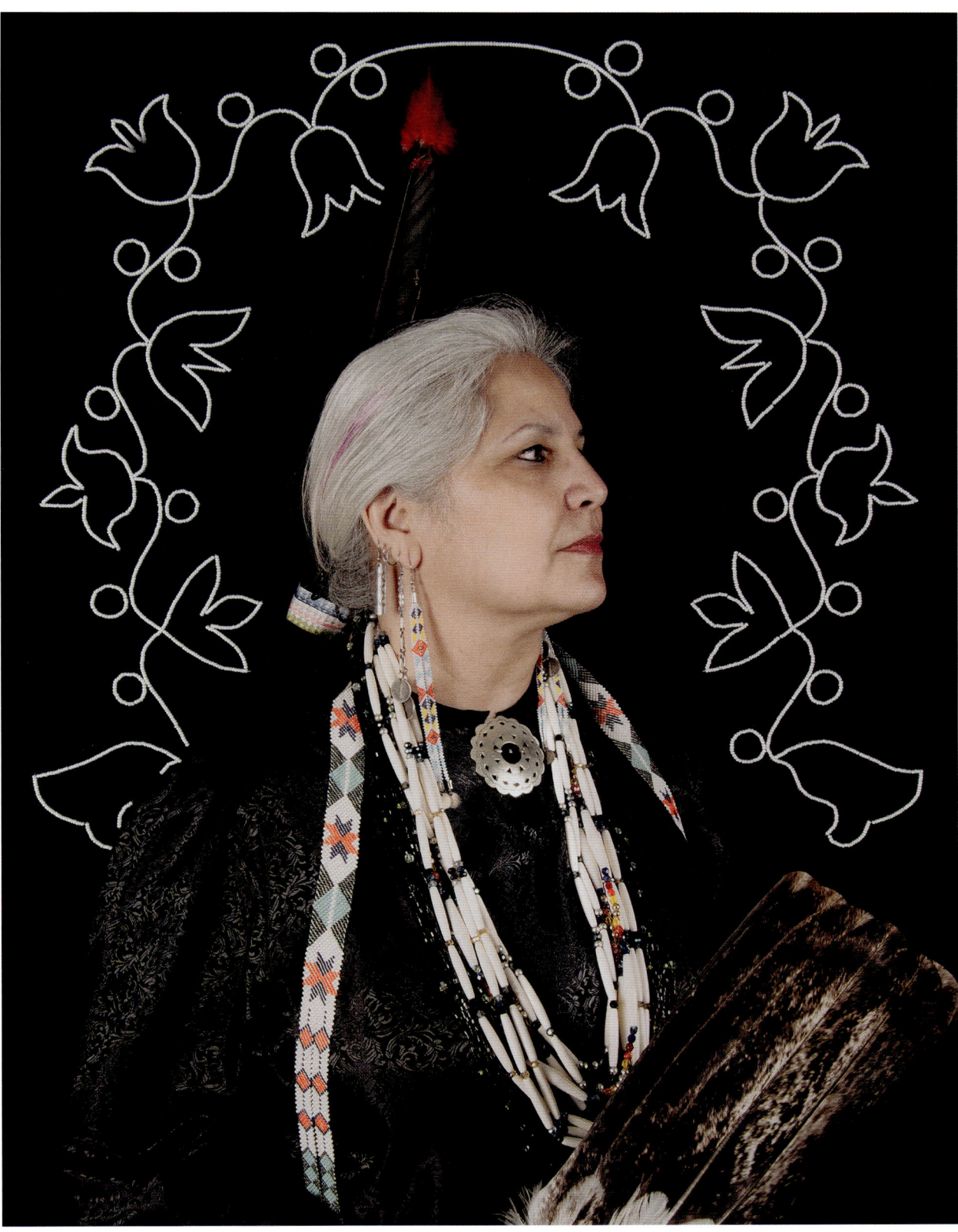

WILL WILSON

Diné
Citizen of the Navajo Nation
United States

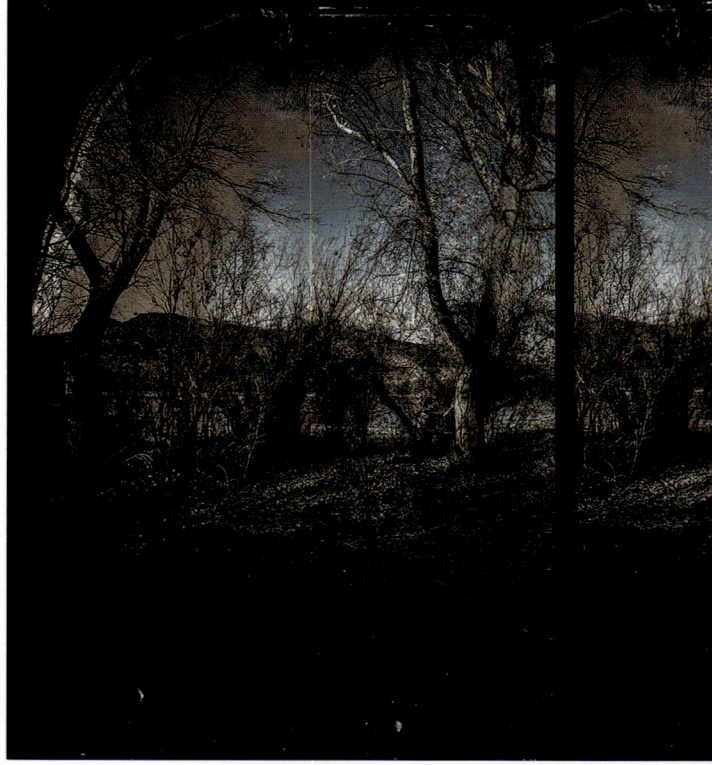

"Photography for me is about time travel," says Will Wilson (b. 1969). "Its ability to indexically register the world as it arrests time and turns space into a transient narrative object that can be altered, manipulated, and transformed continually amazes me."[1]

Wilson is a Diné photographer whose practice is focused on the continuation and transformation of Indigenous culture. By using a combination of contemporary technologies and historical photographic processes, he confronts environmental inequity and seeks to decolonize the ways in which Indigenous peoples have been represented. He spent his formative years on Naabeehó Diné Biyaad (Navajo Nation) and studied studio art and art history at Oberlin College. Later, he attended the University of New Mexico for photography, sculpture, and art history, graduating with an MFA in 2002.

His long-term portrait series Critical Indigenous Photographic Exchange (CIPX) explores self-representation using large-format (8" × 10") tintypes. Originating in the mid-19th century, Wilson says, "this beautifully alchemic photographic process dramatically contributed to our collective understanding of Native American people and, in doing so, our American identity."[2] Initially, the CIPX project was strategically framed as a response to the ongoing impact of Edward S. Curtis's photographic legacy (see page 8). Wilson explains the intent of CIPX is to "supplant Curtis's Settler gaze" with a contemporary vision of Native North America. To accomplish this, he has been inviting Indigenous artists, art professionals, and Tribal leaders to "engage in the performative ritual that is the studio portrait"[3] since 2012, collaborating with thousands of sitters to engender new forms of visual authority and autonomy.

In two artworks from Auto Immune Response, Wilson appears in the images. However, they're not intended as self-portraits. Rather, he is playing a character—the protagonist in a postapocalyptic landscape. The project "focuses on extraction and environmental degradation as one of the possible causes of the apocalypse," Wilson told Searchlight New Mexico.[4] Uranium mining and exposure have been devastating for people living in Navajo communities. The list of related illnesses is long: thyroid and respiratory diseases, renal failure, a variety of birth defects, and multiple kinds of cancer. "Almost everyone on the Navajo Nation has a relative or a friend who's gotten sick or died from uranium exposure," says Wilson,[5] whose great-uncle suffered from an unidentified

Auto Immune Response, Rio Grande: On the Consideration of Invasive Species, 2015, digitype, tintype scan, and digital capture blend.

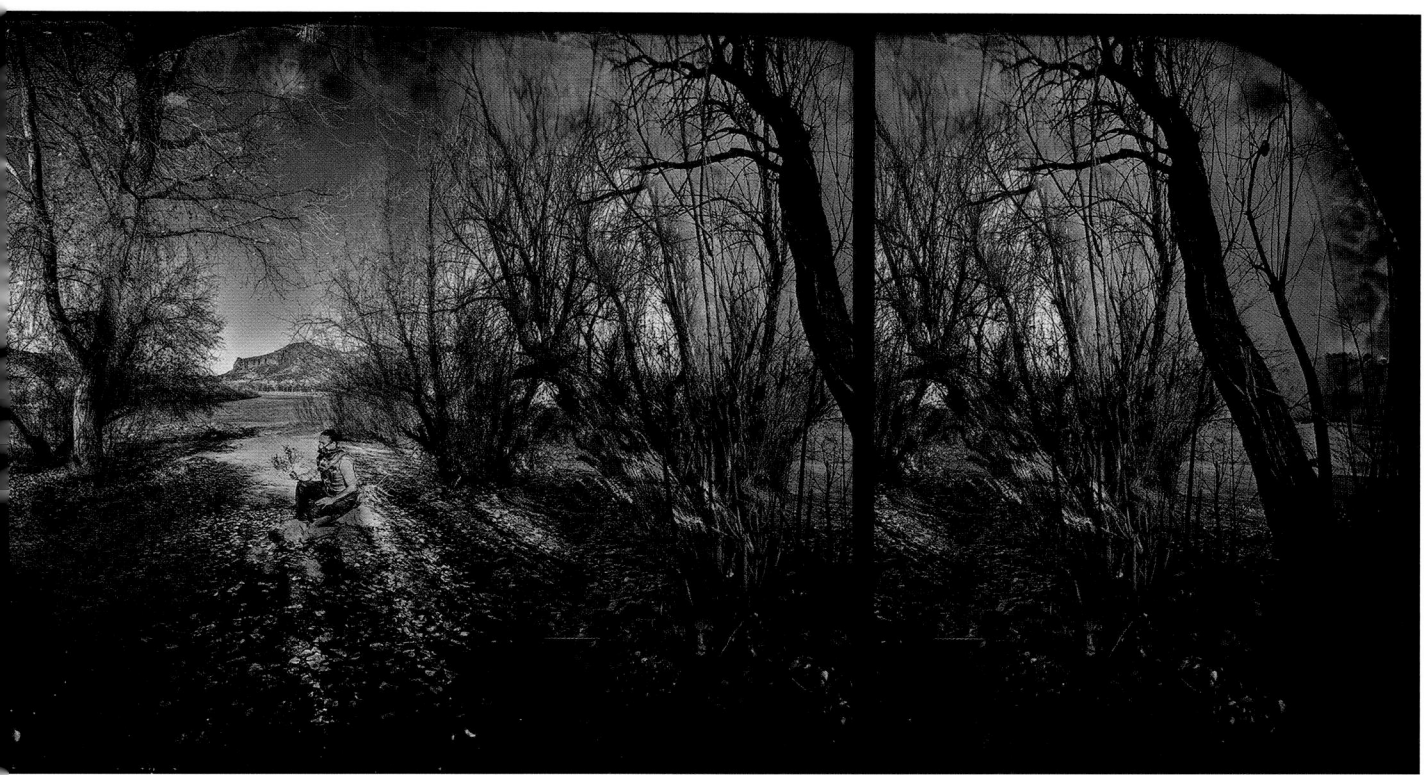

fatal cancer. Efforts by the federal government to alleviate the problems with groundwater remediation and reparations to the Navajo people who have been traumatized have been slow. Wilson knows all too well that the half-life of uranium is billions of years—the problem is not going to go away.

Amid Monument Valley's spectacular landscapes and the sacred mountains and landmarks of the Navajo Nation lies a darker story. Initially created in response to the development of the atomic bomb, there are now 500 to 1,000 abandoned uranium mines on the Navajo Nation. Photographed using drone technology, Wilson's Connecting the Dots for a Just Transition suite of images maps and documents the deserted uranium mines and radioactive waste deposits scattered across Navajo land. The Shiprock disposal cell, which holds thousands of tons of radioactive waste, sits on the site of a former uranium processing mill. The dark gray expanse seen in the foreground of Wilson's photograph is a massive containment structure for radioactive waste. Pictured on the horizon lies the mountain Tsé Bit'a'í (rock with wings), which is sacred to Diné people. Wilson hopes that Connecting the Dots will provide a historical overview of the landscape and be useful in the future.[6] "I want to give people something to look at, to understand how many of these there are," he says, "and create space for people to engage with similar ideas."[7]

—Tiffany Midge

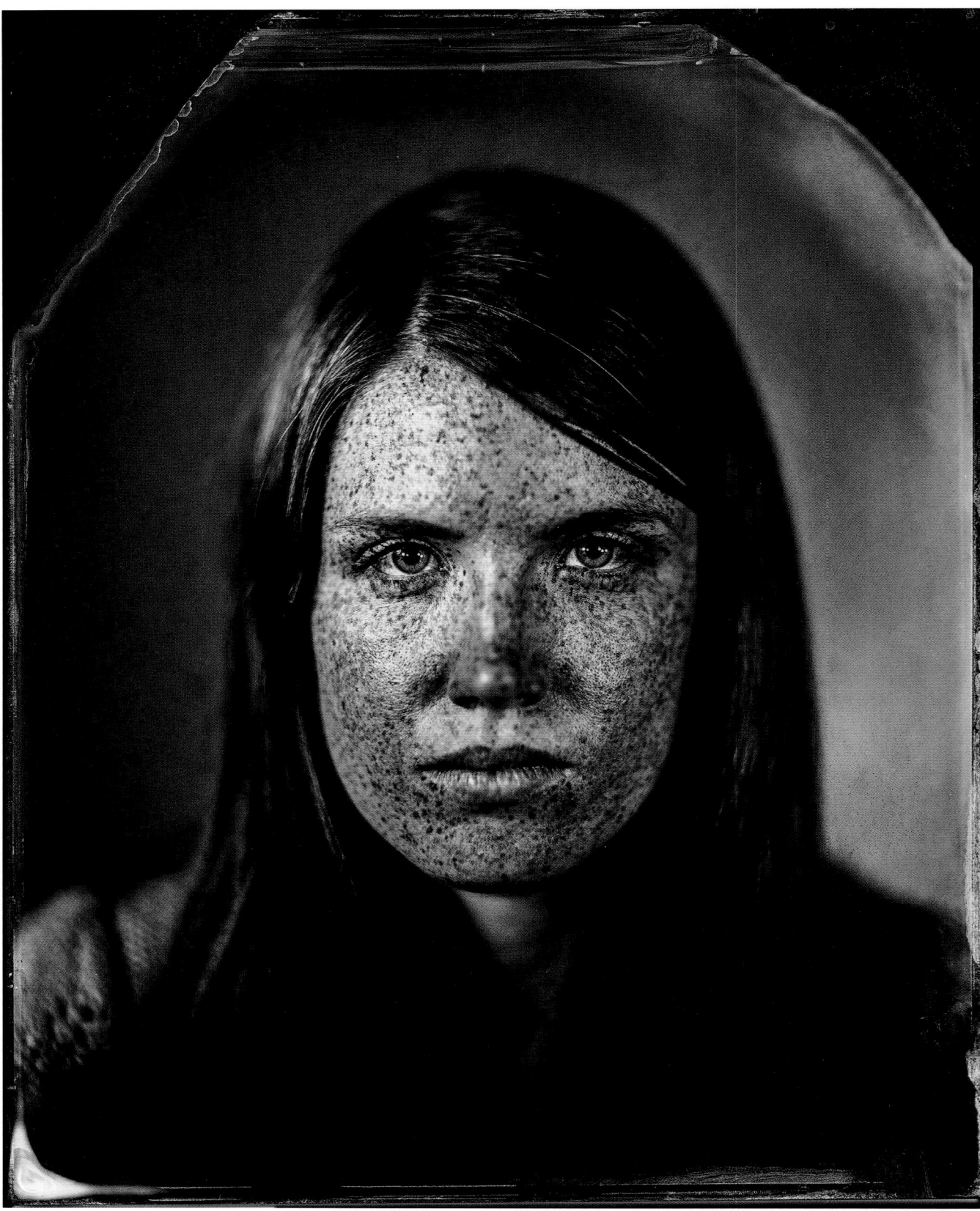

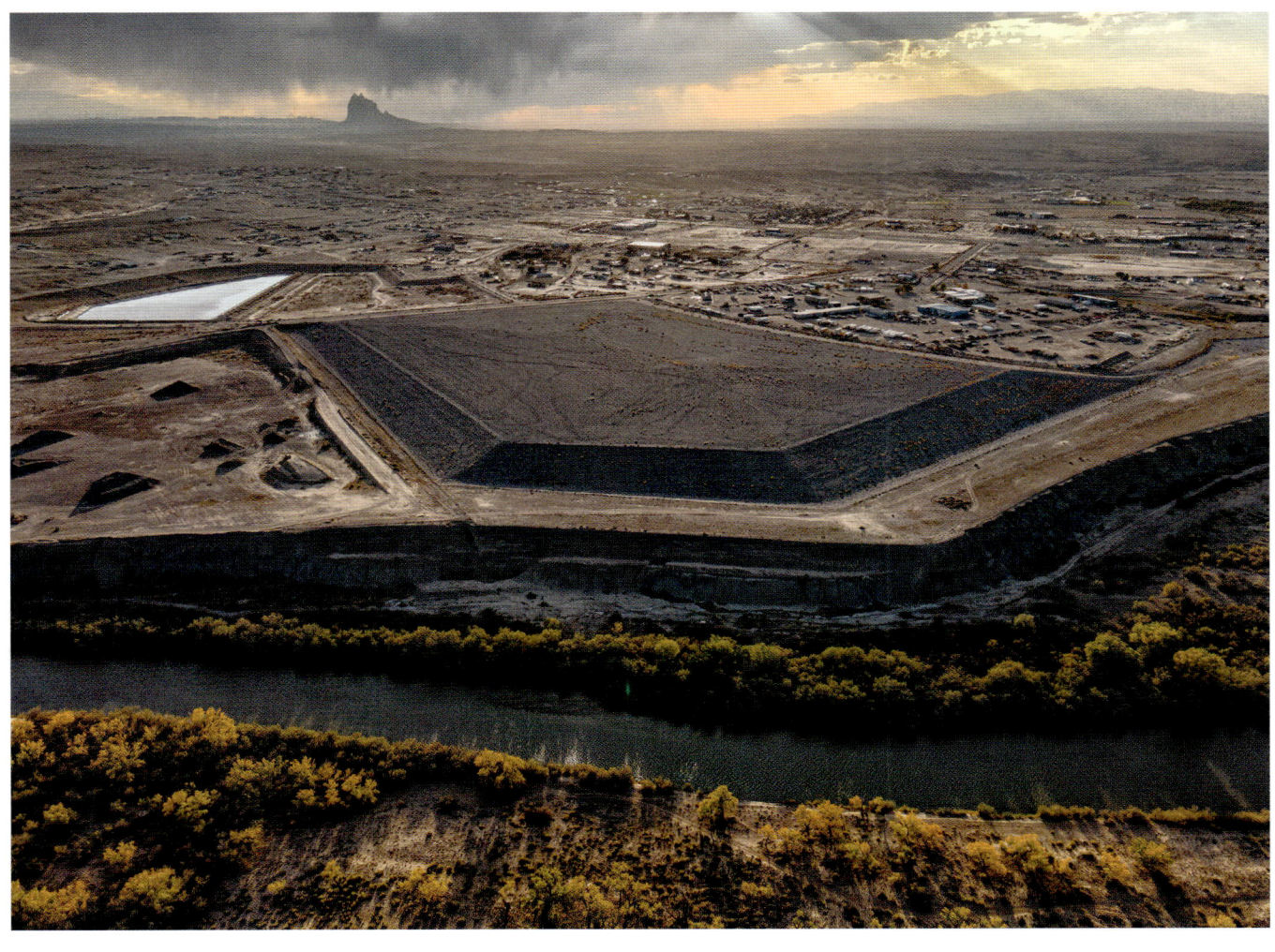

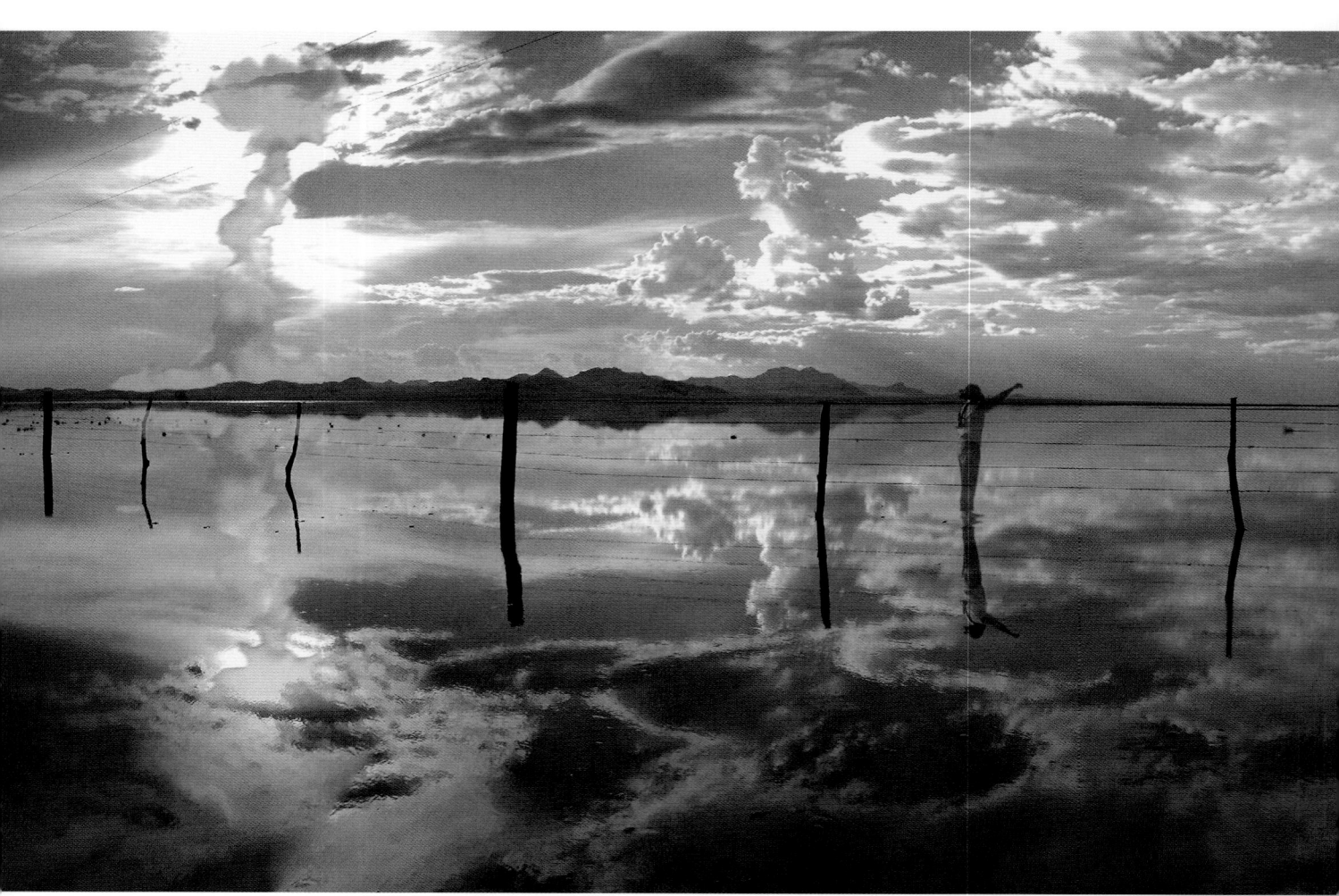

220   *Auto Immune Response No. 1*, 2004, archival pigment print.

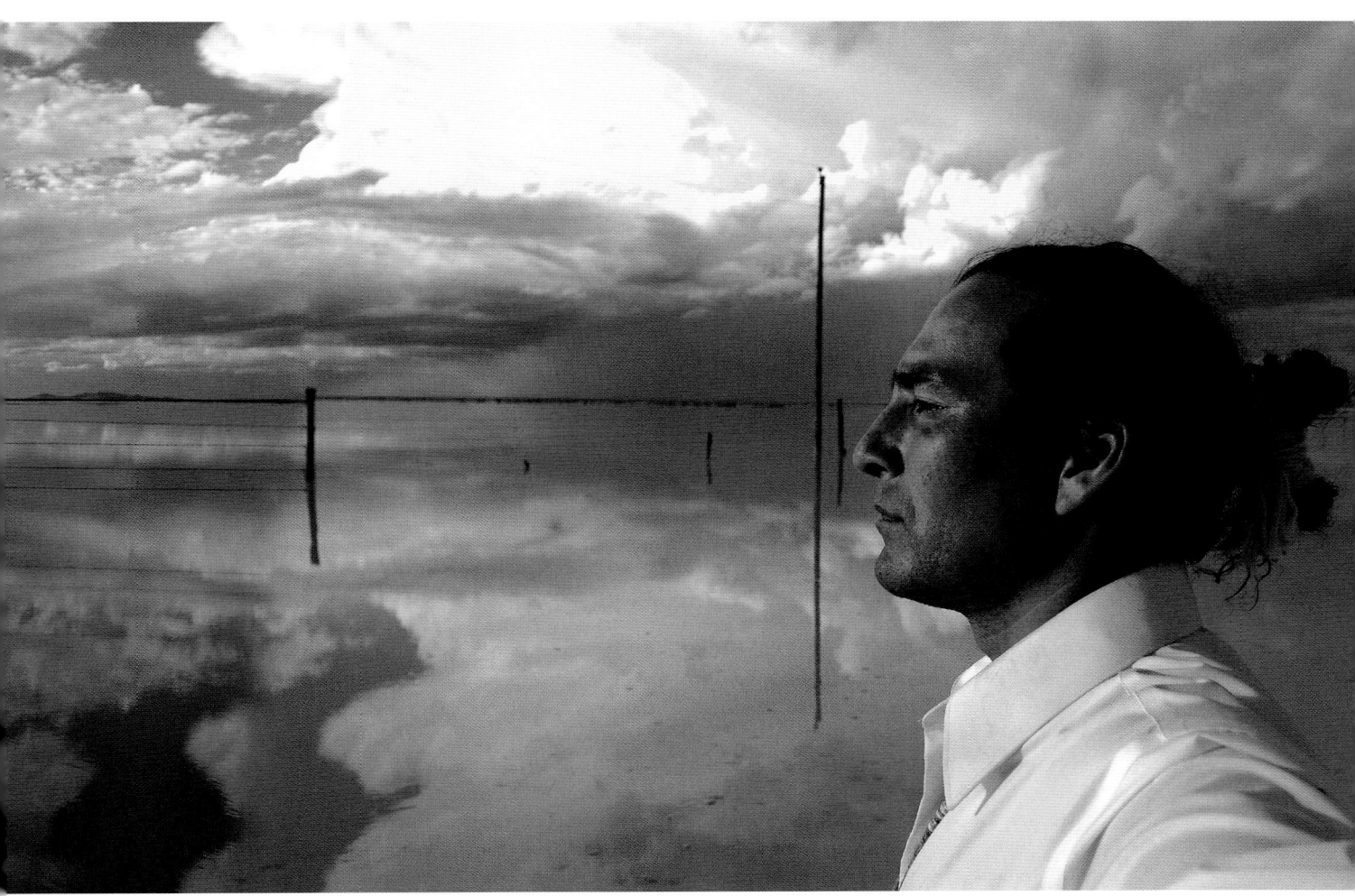

XUNKA' LÓPEZ DÍAZ

Tsotsil Maya
Joltzemen, San Juan Chamula, Chiapas
México

When Xunka' López Díaz (b. 1971) was four years old and living in Joltzemen, a Tsotsil hamlet of San Juan Chamula, Chiapas, México, her mother became ill. The natural healer saw her, but she didn't improve. Desperate for a remedy—she was pregnant with her third child—Díaz's parents traveled to the city of San Cristóbal de las Casas, where they accepted the word of God and converted to Evangelicalism. Almost instantly, in a surge of religious expulsions across the Indigenous communities of the Chiapas Highlands (and beyond), the Díaz family was banished from their home in Joltzemen. They returned to San Cristóbal, where, to survive, they made a radical shift from living off their own land to buying food and selling goods on the streets and at the market.

Twenty-five years later, in 2000, Díaz authored *Mi hermanita Cristina, una niña chamula / My little sister Cristina, a Chamula girl*, an autobiography chronicling the aftermath of her family's forced relocation. Díaz's text and captions are in three languages: Tsotsil, Spanish, and English. Alongside an essay describing the hardships she faced creating a new life in San Cristóbal, Díaz placed photographs entirely devoted to her younger sister, Cristina, who experienced a far more carefree childhood than she did. The pairing narrates the coming-of-age stories of two Indigenous evangelical women a generation apart in San Cristóbal—the same city, yet one sister fought to be recognized within its unfamiliar terrain and the other is "a new Chamulan girl…based in her own land," wrote Lourdes de León Pasquel in the foreword of the book. "In Cristina, Xunka' sees a new present where it appears the scar of the expulsion and loss of the past have been cured."[1]

Díaz photographed Cristina at home. Her face is gentle and beguiling. She's just nine years old at the time of the photos, the youngest sister of 10 siblings. Díaz is the firstborn, almost age 30. In the pictures, Cristina layers traditional skirts, sashes, and embroidered blouses with her pastel pink sweater and jelly sandals. Díaz photographs the pieces of her sister's wardrobe separately, too, a study of the garments that reflect her identity. Cristina's long hair is braided, except when she washes it in a red Coca-Cola bucket. The iconic company and the soda it produces are omnipresent in San Cristóbal. Cristina weaves bracelets, cuts vegetables, and nuzzles a black cat.

"I suffered a lot when I was growing up," wrote Díaz in *Mi hermanita Cristina*. "My little brothers and sisters did not suffer as I did."

While Díaz's mother learned to buy and sell vegetables and weave belts to vend to foreigners, and her dad worked odd jobs, Díaz cared for the children at home. She cleaned, washed clothes, and taught herself to make tortillas. "In this way, my parents could eat when they got home from work because they did not have time to make their own food," she wrote. Díaz started school when she was 10. Her classmates showed her how to make bracelets, and Díaz began selling them at hotels and restaurants. She learned to work alongside other women and to defend herself with rocks and electrical cords from ill-intentioned men. At 16, she finished her studies and for the next nine years made a living selling bracelets. Her father found steady work as a carpenter, and her mother secured a stall at the market. They bought two lots of land and built a house. Díaz accepted a job teaching Indigenous women to read and write Spanish at a cooperative called Sbeik Jchanvunetik. It was here, in 1996, that photography entered her life, when the Chiapas Photography Project (CPP) partnered with Sbeik Jchanvunetik.

CPP was founded in San Cristóbal in 1992 by Carlota Duarte, a Mexican American artist—with an MFA from the Rhode Island School of Design—and a Catholic sister with the Society of the Sacred Heart. The project's goal was to provide access to photographic equipment and training to Indigenous Maya peoples in the state of Chiapas, a population whose stories have long been told by others. "I hoped to create a space where individuals and communities would feel free to explore their own use and understanding of photography," wrote Duarte in the introduction to Díaz's book. "In *Mi hermanita Cristina*, Xunka' has shown us how photography can make a significant contribution to the way in which people write their own history."

"Since 1992, more than 500 indigenous men and women from diverse ethnic groups and religious backgrounds have learned how to use photography as a mode of personal expression" reported Duarte in 2018, about CPP.[2] The photographers have published books, exhibited work internationally, and become skilled at the business and archiving practices inherent in the careers of professional photographers.

"I did not know that I was going to work as a photographer," reflected Díaz. "I had never seen women take pictures."

—Sarah Stacke

Untitled, "Cristina washing her hair."

Li jpimil koton xchi'uk yak'il chukile / Mi sueter y la trenza / My sweater and the tie.

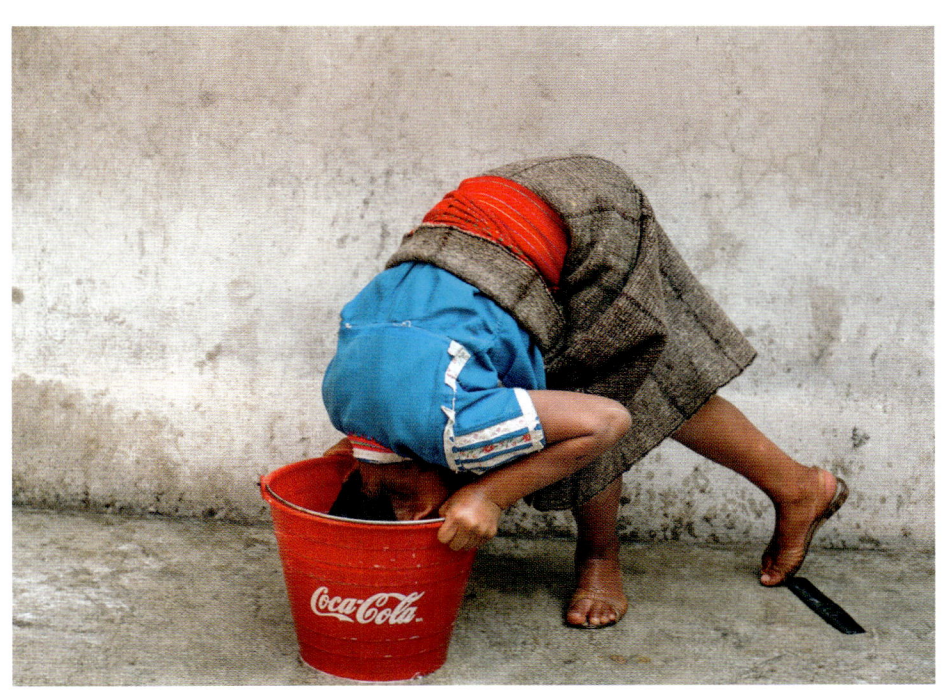

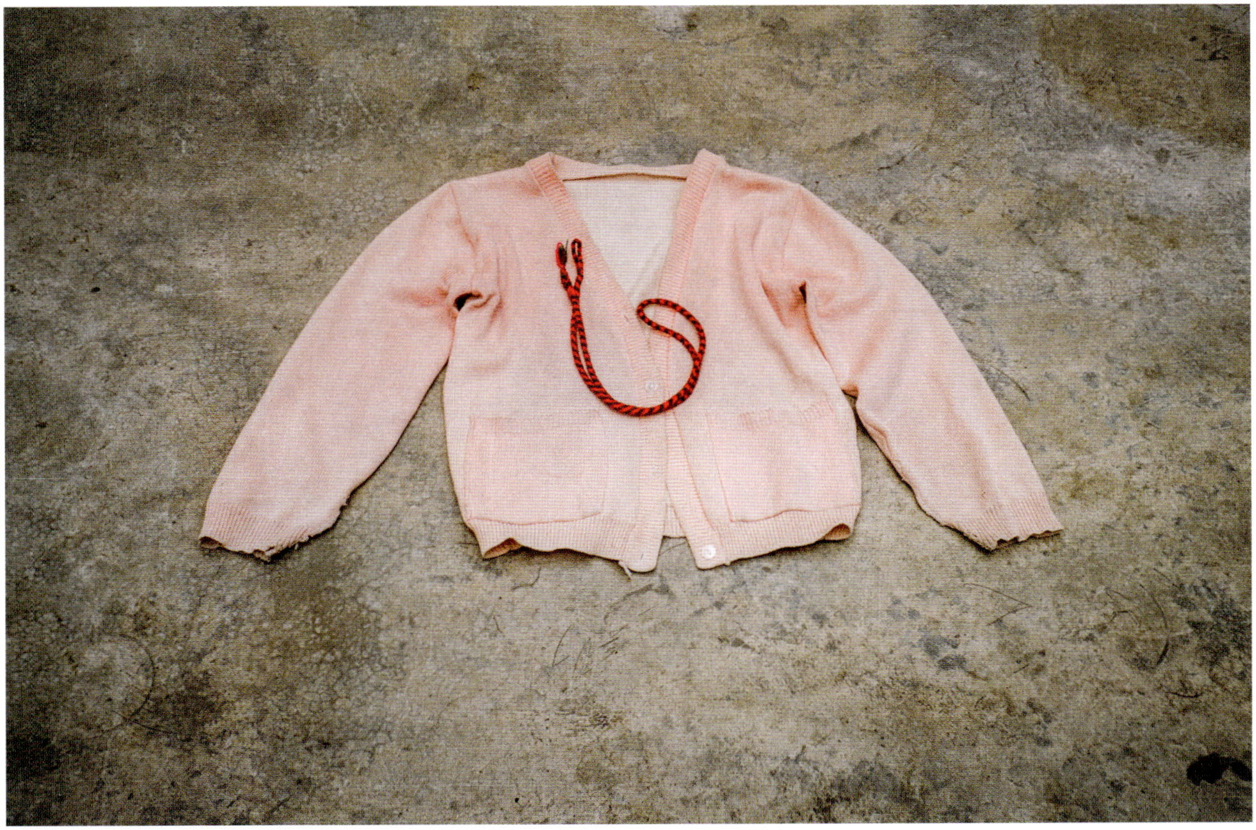

MARUCH SÁNTIZ GÓMEZ

Tsotsil Maya
Cruztón, San Juan Chamula, Chiapas
México

In her 1998 monograph, *Creencias de nuestros antepasados* (*Beliefs of Our Ancestors*), Maruch Sántiz Gómez (b. 1975) uses photography and text to visualize over 40 traditional beliefs of her Tsotsil Maya culture. A photograph of a sombrero next to a campfire is paired with the words, "It is not good to fan a fire with a hat because the owner of the hat might get a headache or feel dizzy." An image of a kettle warns, "If you eat directly from the pot, you can become a glutton."[1]

Sántiz Gómez began gathering and penning the creencias in the early 1990s, when she was a visiting artist with Sna Jtz'ibajom, a writers' collective in San Cristóbal de las Casas dedicated to preserving Mayan languages and promoting literacy. She was introduced to photography in 1993 at age 17 through the Chiapas Photography Project, and realized it could help make the customs of her forebears accessible to Tsotsil people who couldn't read. Historically, illiteracy rates among remote Indigenous communities in Chiapas have been high. The decision to invariably combine the photographs and lyrical sayings came from the realization that more of the images needed explanation than she anticipated.[2]

The creencias were recited to Sántiz Gómez by her parents, grandparents, great-grandparents, and other Tsotsil Knowledge Keepers in and around Cruztón, her birthplace in the Chiapas Highlands, a region connected to the majestic Sierra Madre de Chiapas mountains in southernmost México. "To seek out the meanings of the creencias is to work with the elders, to rescue and maintain our ancient culture and our mother tongue," wrote Sántiz Gómez in the introduction to *Creencias de nuestros antepasados*.

Her textured black-and-white photographs center household scenes—a ball of yarn, baskets of provisions, tortillas cooking, adults working, children playing, animals—on earthen backdrops, fusing the wisdom represented with the Maya lands from which it is inseparable.

Written in Tsotsil and translated into Spanish and English, the texts accompanying the photographs reveal practical admonitions born of spirituality and mortality: "It is bad to play with a ball of yarn because the garment will not turn out complete even though the thread has been counted"; "Chile seeds should not be shaked because when hugging a child he will cry a lot"; "You should not eat the first tortilla that comes off the griddle or you will become very talkative, saying bad things about other people"; "If someone dreams that they are tilling the soil it is because someone will die."

The work composing *Creencias de nuestros antepasados* has been published widely, exhibited internationally, collected by museums, and represented by the esteemed Galería OMR in México City, providing viewers worldwide a glimpse into the lore of the Maya.

Sántiz Gómez is forever committed to keeping her heritage alive for new generations of Tsotsil Maya. Today, along with her son, daughter, and a few women from Cruztón, she is handcrafting wool ponchos, shawls, sweaters, and bags using Maya techniques—and photographing every step of production. The images show sheep, shorn wool becoming thread, and the colorful flora used to make vats of natural dyes. Bundles of yarn are submerged in blue, fuchsia, and amber liquids, then hung to dry in the shade of a tree. There are looms and close-ups of intricate embroidery, and finally the finished piece.

"Photographs help, like writing, for remembering," she says.[3]

—Sarah Stacke

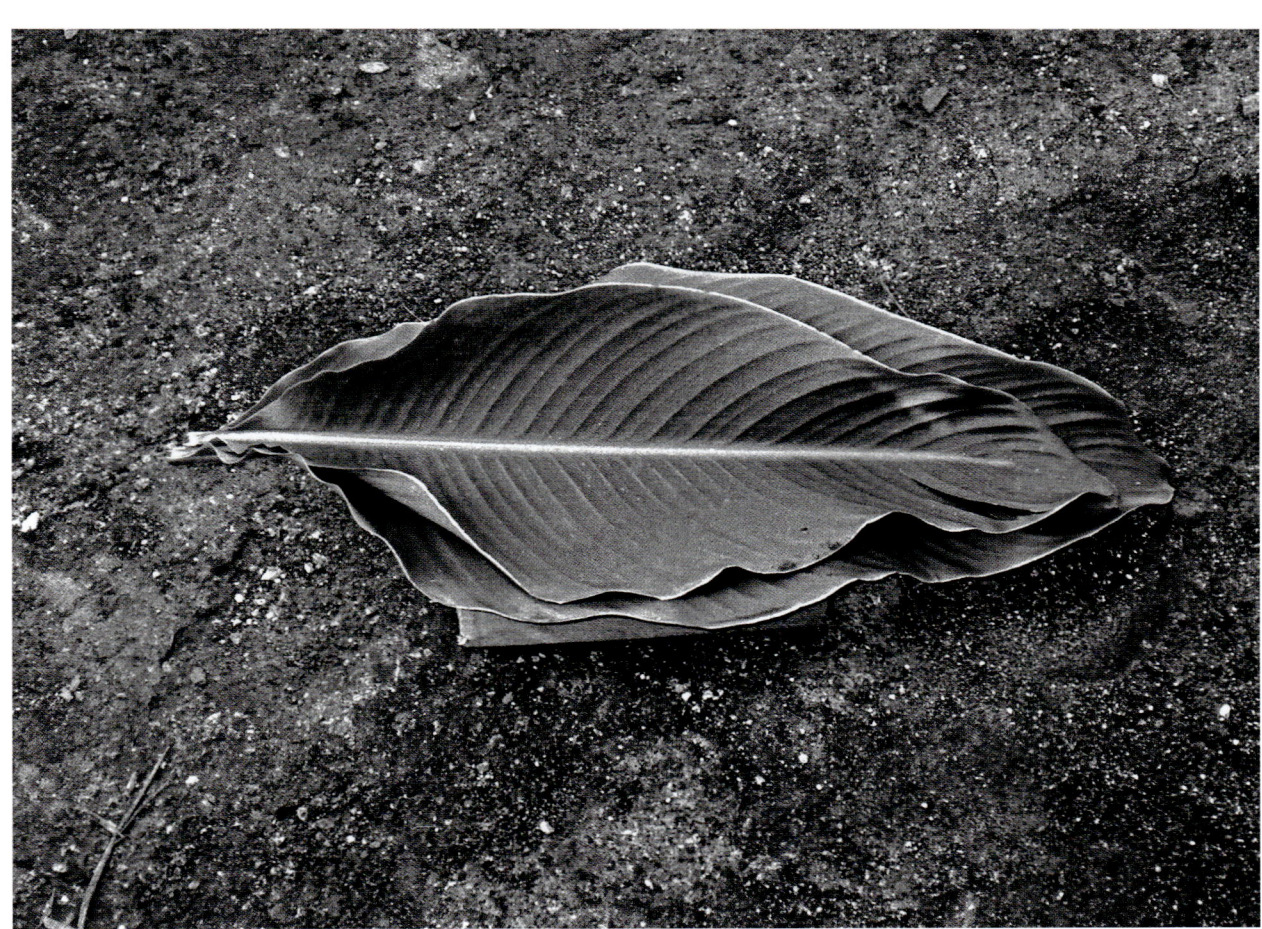

CH'UCH' | Hoja de Bejao | Bejao leaf.

No mencionar el nombre de la hoja de Bejao al envolver tamales.

> *Do not mention the name of the Bejao leaf when you make tamales.*

K'alal chbat jk'okbetik tal spix pats'e mu la xtun jbiiltastik, mi la jbiiltastike mu la xta'aj li pats'e; sepkantik la tse sepkantik la tok'on.

Al cortar la hoja de Bejao para envolver el tamal, dicen que es malo mencionar su nombre, que no se cuecen bien los tamales; salen pedazos cocidos y pedazos crudos.

> *When the Bejao leaf is cut to make tamales, it is not good to mention its name because then the tamales do not cook well; some pieces come out cooked and others raw.*

225

PIXOLAL XCHI'UK K'OK' | Fuego con el sombrero | Fire with a hat.

No soplar el fuego con el sombrero.

Don't fan the fire with a hat.

Mu la xtun jubtik o k'ok' pixolal, mi la yich' jubel o k'ok'e ti buch'u yajval pixolale ta la spas ta k'ux jol jeche' no'ox la xjimet sjol chbat.

Dicen que es malo soplar fuego con sombrero, porque al dueño del sombrero le puede doler la cabeza, o sentir mareo.

It is not good to fan a fire with a hat because the owner of the hat might get a headache or feel dizzy.

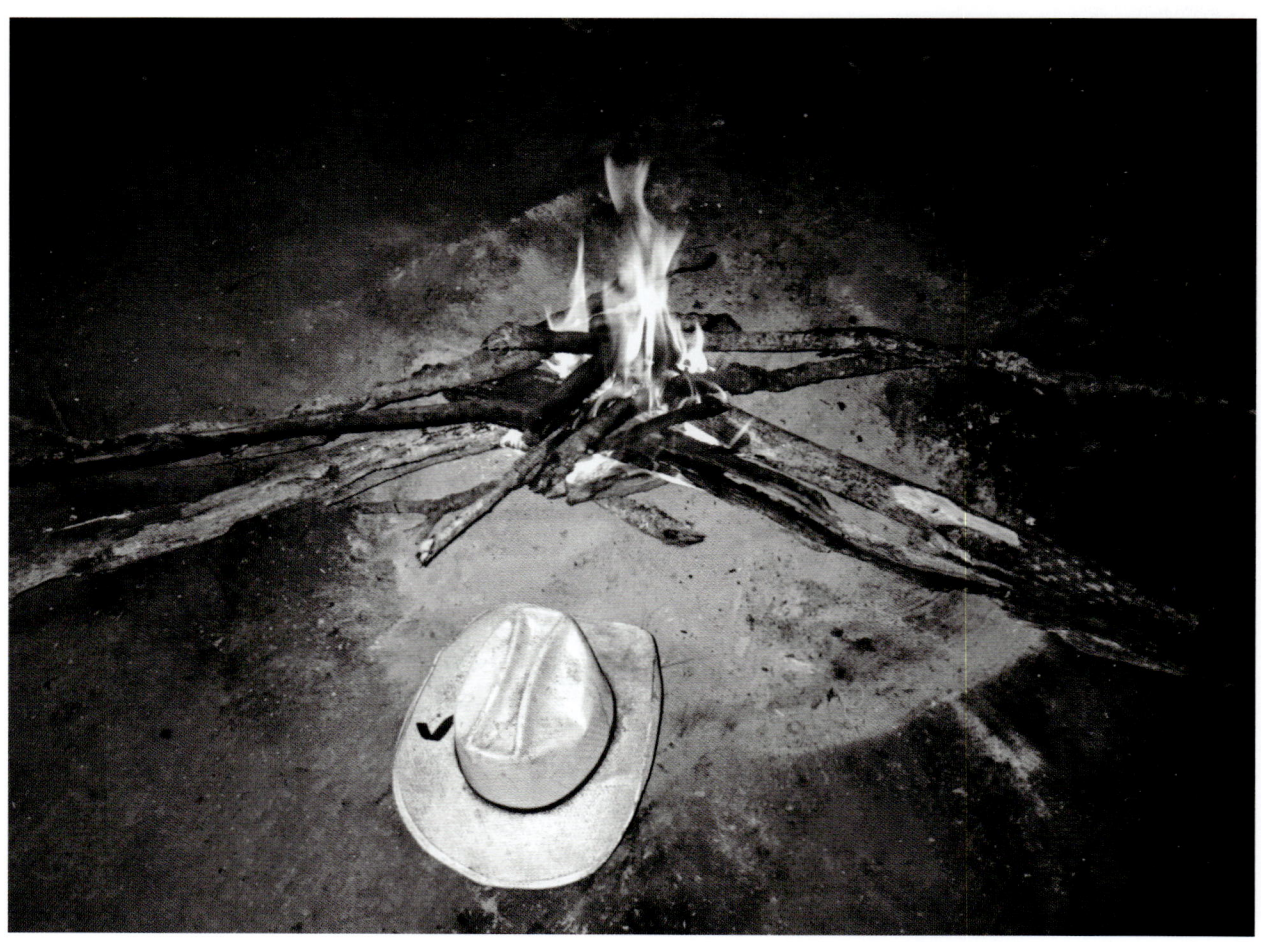

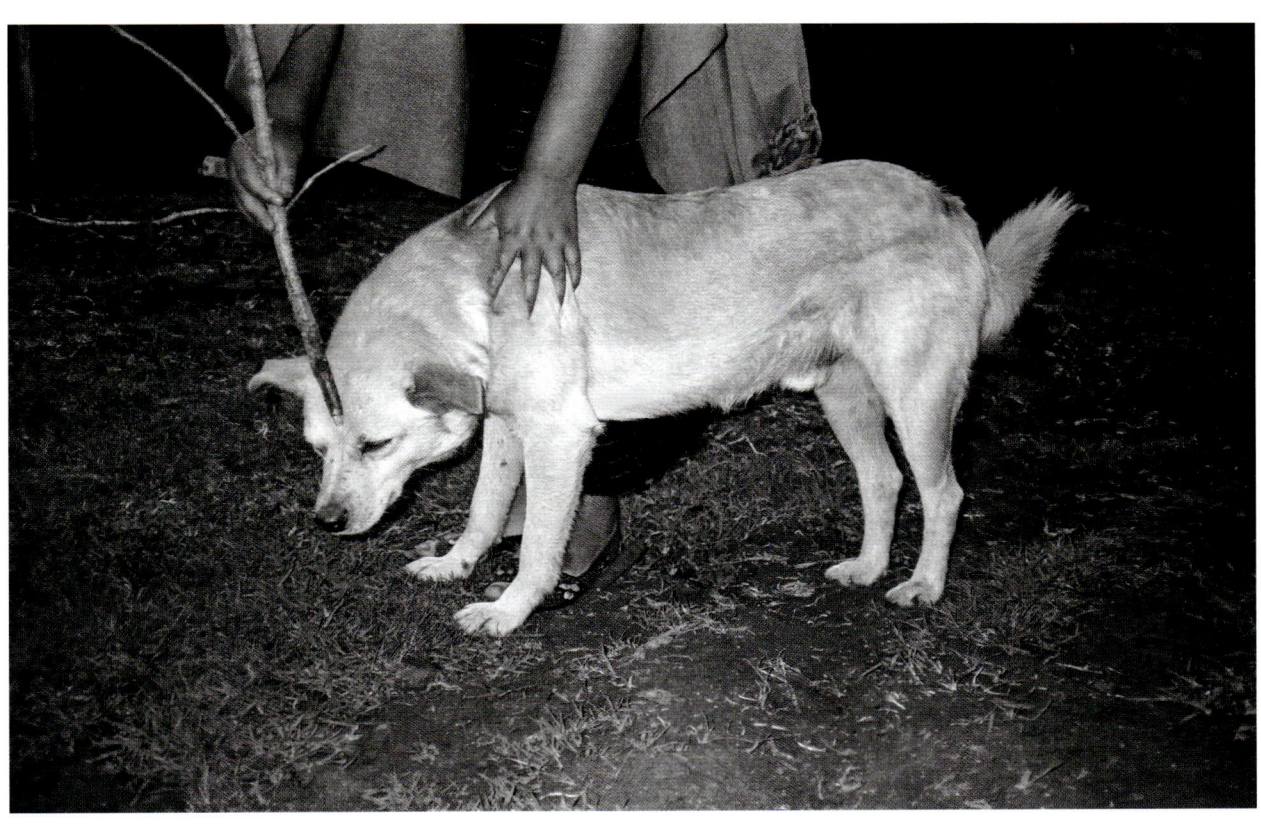

YO' MU XVOVI TS'I'E | Para que no se le pegue la rabia a un perro | To prevent a dog from catching rabies.

Yo' mu xvovi ts'i'e, chich' la kurustabel sti'ba ta xupite'.

Para que no le pegue la rabia a un perro, dicen se le hace una cruz en la frente con tizón.

To prevent rabies from infecting a dog, make a cross on its forehead with a firebrand.

CARA ROMERO

Chemehuevi
Chemehuevi Indian Tribe
Santa Fe, New Mexico
United States

Outside of the landmark Saints and Sinners, a liquor store, bar, and gathering place in Española, New Mexico, a curious scene takes place. Cara Romero (b. 1977) has staged a glowing photograph centered on the Native American trickster figure Coyote. In the theatrical composition, Coyote is turned away from the camera, surreptitiously holding a bouquet of flowers behind his back. A young woman leans on the fender of a '64 Impala lowrider; another stands alongside Coyote, her hand draped on his shoulder. The neon Saints and Sinners sign—with a pitchfork and images of an angel and devil—looms like a subtitle for the photograph, while also describing the duality and conflicting nature of Coyote. Romero sums up Coyote as "our favorite character in California Indian mythos."[1]

Author Alicia Inez Guzmán writes that Romero's image "captures that ambiguous moment when nights begin and choices are made, for better or worse, the point where the scales tip toward the mischievous. Coyote tests and teases you, signifying just that juncture."[2]

Coyote is a central character in several Native American nations throughout the West. He is most associated with getting caught up in exploits of magic, romance, gluttony, and playfulness, but with results that can bring about positive change. His foolish, and often heroic, pranks and adventures convey lessons about cultural values and ethical boundaries.

In the photograph, Romero renders a sense of the mystical merging with the material world through saturated red lighting and brilliant stars in the nighttime sky. The photograph embodies Indigenous worldviews such as metaphysical understandings of the universe and of the celestial. "I use vibrant color, experimental lighting, and photo-illustration to explore ideas of how the supernatural world overlaps with our everyday lives," says Romero.[3]

She is a member of the Chemehuevi Indian Tribe in California's Mojave Desert, and her formative years were spent both on the reservation and in Houston, Texas. Today, along with her husband and three children, she lives in Santa Fe, New Mexico.

Romero is forthright about the social and environmental issues Indigenous people face. Her photography practice challenges cultural misappropriation, environmental destruction of Native lands, and stereotypes, particularly of Indigenous women.

As in *Coyote Tales No. 1*, Romero's artistic approach combines traditional images, symbols, or old stories with contemporary perspectives. "This strategy reinforces the ways we exist as contemporary Native Americans, all the while affirming that Indigenous culture is continually evolving and imminently permanent," says Romero. "I unapologetically depict where we are now, in the present day, making sure to always respect cultural protocol and ancestral ties."[4]

—Tiffany Midge

Coyote Tales No. 1, 2017.

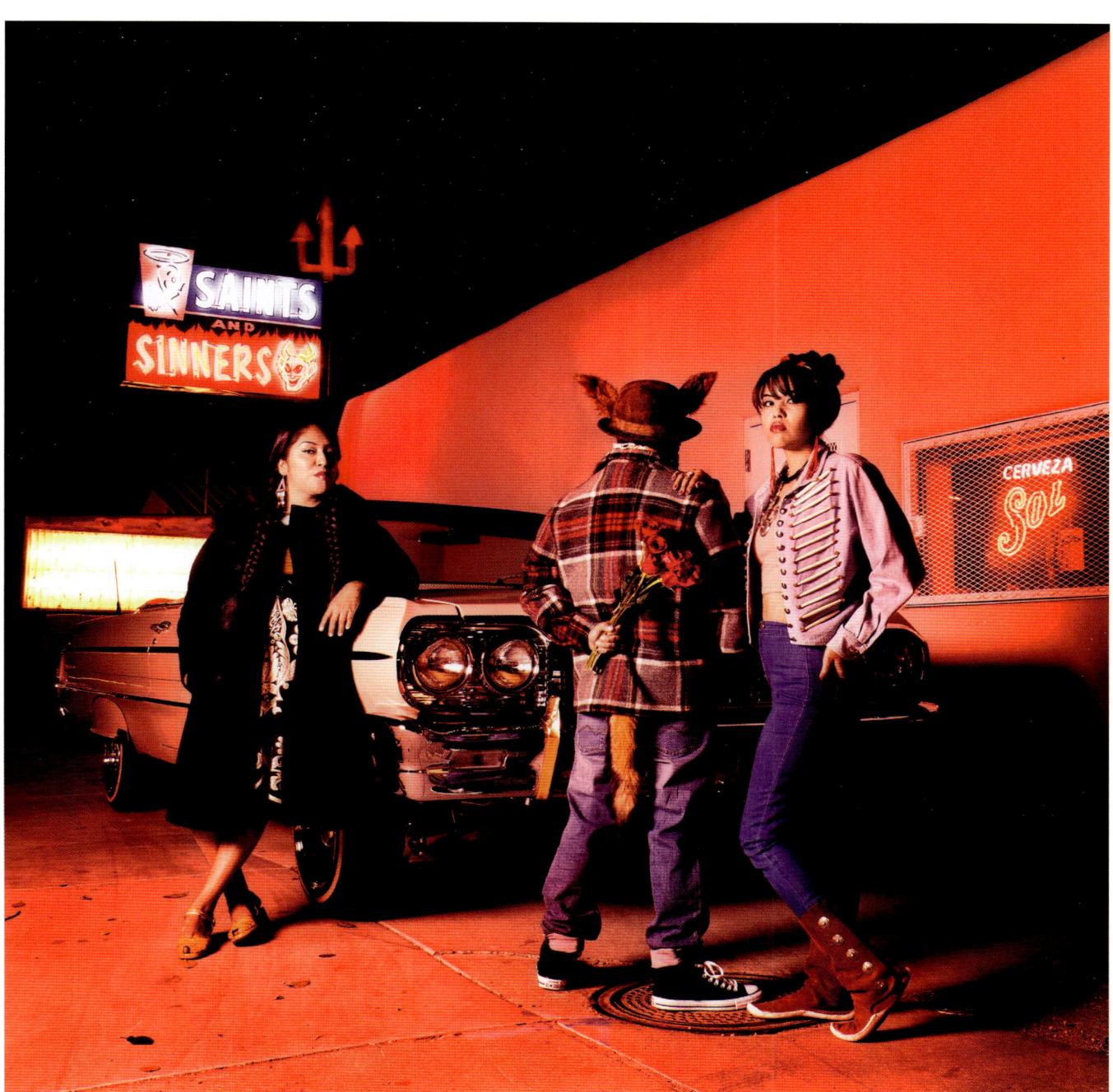

RUSSEL ALBERT DANIELS

Diné, Ho-Chunk
Salt Lake City, Utah
United States

When Russel Albert Daniels (b. 1974) photographed Genízaro descendant Maurice Archuleta in the high desert landscape surrounding the village of Abiquiú, New Mexico, he remembers thinking he was carrying out exactly what his ancestors needed him to do.

Daniels grew up with stories about a Diné forebear on his father's side, Rose Daniels, who was born in Dinétah, the Navajo Homeland, and violently taken captive by the White River Utes in the mid-1800s. Still a child, she was trafficked north to present-day Utah and Colorado and sold to Aaron Eugene Daniels, a Mormon pioneer and polygamist. She served Aaron's households for decades. Eventually, after both his wives left him, she and Aaron married and had four children. In 1889, the family relocated and enrolled with the Ute Indian Tribe of the Uintah & Ouray Reservation in northeastern Utah. Rose lived to be over 100 years old. Daniels and his siblings, who are Ho-Chunk on their maternal side, are the first of five generations to be raised off the reservation, in Salt Lake City. "We're not Ute," clarified Daniels. Rose, even after nearly a century away from Dinétah, "was Diné."[1]

"But this narrative was at odds with my public education," said Daniels, referring to the historical erasure of colonial-era Indigenous captivity and slavery in the American Southwest.[2] "What a lot of people don't know is that there was a slave trade happening here in Utah," he told journalist Scotti Hill in 2023.[3] In 1852, Utah Territory passed "An Act for the Relief of Indian Slaves and Prisoners." The statute allowed white residents to purchase Native children for "adoption" into their households for up to 20 years. The children primarily worked for Mormons as indentured domestic laborers, performing tasks necessary to maintain life on the frontier and repay the price of their purchase.

Daniels, resolved to bring this buried history and its aftermath to light, dug into the archives. After years of inquiry, "All roads pointed to the Pueblo de Abiquiú in New Mexico," he determined.[4] It was in this long-overlooked community, in 2019, that Daniels commenced La Cautiva, an ongoing documentary photography project looking at centuries of Indigenous enslavement in the Southwest. The work is rooted in the late 16th century, when the Spanish permanently settled in the region, leaving a legacy of human trafficking in their wake.

Part one of La Cautiva, titled The Genízaro Pueblo of Abiquiú, was completed in 2022 and exhibited at the Smithsonian National Museum of the American Indian. The photographs probe the collective memory and cultural renaissance shaping the Genízaro citizens of Abiquiú—people like Maurice Archuleta. The Genízaro are descendants of Native Americans enslaved by Spanish colonizers in what would become New Mexico. Beginning in the early 1600s, with funding from the Spanish Crown and reinforcement from the Catholic Church, the Spanish were compelled to "reeducate" generations of Native people. The colonizers abducted and later purchased war captives from Tribes in the region—Hopi, Comanche, Pueblo, Apache, Ute, and Diné. The captives, the majority of whom were women and children, were taken to the colonists' homes, where they were taught Spanish, converted to Catholicism, and forced into servitude. Many faced physical, sexual, and emotional abuse. The Spanish called those held in bondage Genízaro, a term derived from a Turkish word referring to ensnared youth drafted as soldiers. Indeed, some Genízaro were forcibly militarized, defending frontier outposts from raiding Tribes.

Spain's brutal campaign affected the lives of thousands of Native people, "trampling their cultural practices and spiritual beliefs," said Daniels.[5]

Genízaro commonly obtained freedom in adulthood, and by the 1700s one-third of the population of New Mexico was Genízaro—by then a "unique Native American and Hispanic ethnicity born from enslavement."[6] The Crown created a system of land grants that designated settlements for free Genízaro. A few, including Abiquiú, established in 1754 by relatives of Archuleta, persevered while Spain, México, and finally the United States claimed the surrounding land.

An artist, Archuleta participates in Abiquiú community events and takes pride in his Genízaro identity. "Since I was a child," he said, "I've learned our traditional stories, dances, and songs."[7] He crafts Genízaro regalia and shares his cultural knowledge generously. In the desert outside Abiquiú, with a dreamlike tuffaceous hoodoo in the background, Daniels made Archuleta's portrait in black and white. The hoodoo pictured was born of millions of years of wind and water against rock. Somewhere along the line, a boulder materialized at its top, a sentinel of the layers of history—and the human existences—it embodies. The Genízaro experience is "written in the land," Daniels told podcaster Ben Kilbourne, in 2020.[8]

Other images in The Genízaro Pueblo of Abiquiú show cultural performances, ancient pottery sherds, landscapes, and colonial churches. Many are formal or candid portraits featuring members of the community. They're a close-knit group; almost all descend from families who helped settle Abiquiú.

"Anthropologists and history books have ignored our painful past, but many Abiquiú families have continuously

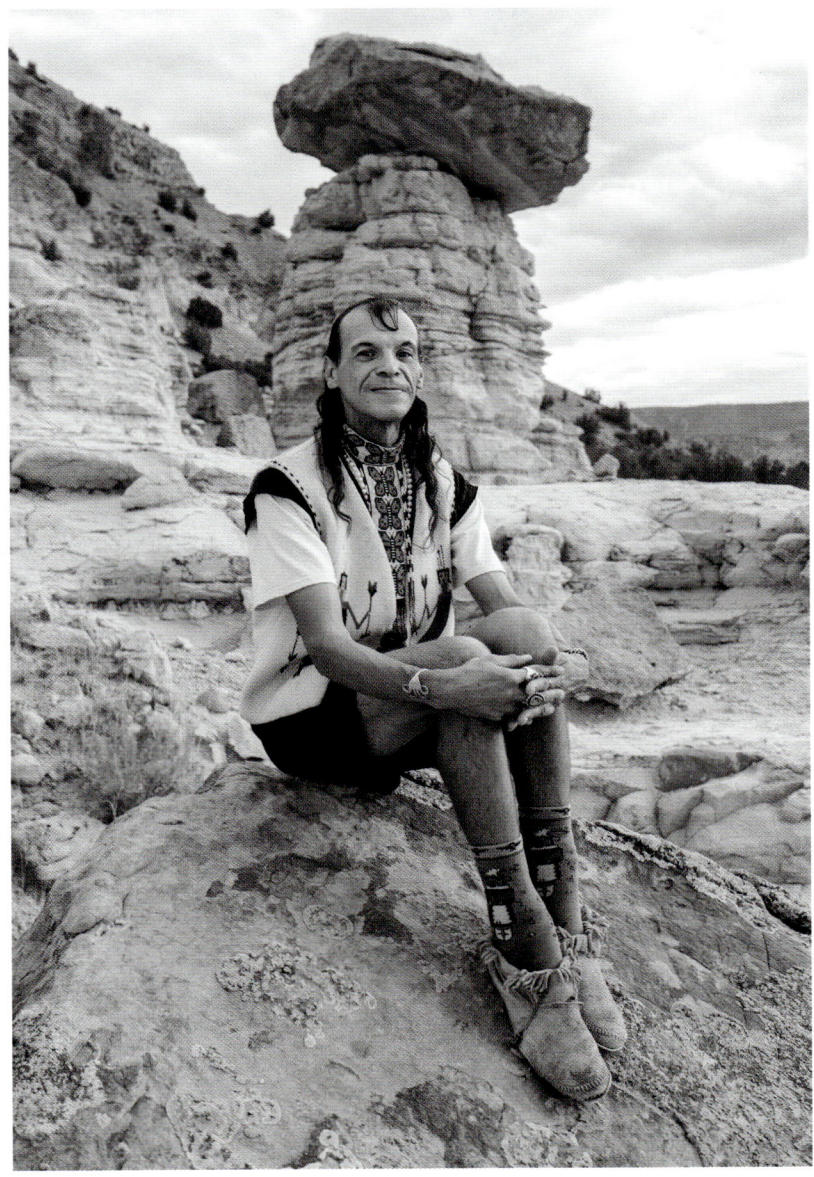

honored our Indigenous ancestry with ceremony, dancing, and feast days," reflected Isabel Trujillo, the director of the Pueblo de Abiquiú Library and Cultural Center. "Today, there is a revival and resurgence of interest in our unique Genízaro identity, culture, and history. You can't take it out of our blood."[9]

After centuries of suppression, the Genízaro are emerging from the shadows. Photography "brings visibility to what's been edited out of our common narrative," believes Daniels.[10]

His work on La Cautiva is never far from the story of his great-great-grandmother Rose—the entire series is an exercise in weaving the familial with neglected historical narratives. The saga of Rose's 19th-century enslavement led Daniels to see the omission of Spain's role in America's Indigenous slave economy, a practice that persists today in the Missing and Murdered Indigenous Relatives epidemic. "It is a continuation of trafficking Indigenous women, just like my ancestor Rose," he said.[11]

When you pay attention to the trauma and what it's done, a healing process is started, reckons Daniels.[12]

—Sarah Stacke

Artist Maurice Archuleta in 2019. Archuleta descends from an original Genízaro family in Abiquiú, New Mexico.

JOSÉ MELA

Mapuche
Santiago
Chile

José Mela (b. 1977) utilizes the camera as a conduit to re-imagine identity and interrogate a colonial photographic history that sustains stereotypical views of Mapuche people. To deconstruct these widespread stigmas, Mela collaborated with Mapuche youth to produce moving canvases where "subjects" transformed into agents of their own representation.

Along with the teenage participants in the Azentún Photography Workshop, Mela co-created images that feature the students' identities as both connected to and separate from colonial history. In the workshop, held in two locations in Santiago, Chile, the teens reflected on photographs made by Fotógrafos de la Frontera. This small group of photographers of European descent was active in the Mapuche lands of Chile's frontier region, also known as La Frontera, in the late 19th century. In Chile, Fotógrafos de le Frontera are considered the founders of ethnic photography, a practice that perpetuates problematic narratives of Indigenous peoples.[1] Mela organized Azentún, he said, "to critically and analytically revise the meaning and influence that young urban Mapuche people may attribute to these historical representations."[2]

Serie de retratos de Claudia desprendiéndose de sus ropas tradicionales mapuche (Portrait series of Claudia shedding her traditional Mapuche clothing) embodies Mela's goal to create conversations about identity through intentionally forming and transforming presentations of self. He sees identity as a process based on an individual's participation in methods of self-representation and self-affirmation.[3] In this collection of portraits, Claudia first appears in a mostly traditional depiction of Mapuche culture. Yet, as the sequence unfolds, an unraveling of the traditional dress and accessories progresses, culminating in a final image that characterizes a modern, global identity. This transformation portrays an offloading of the markers of Indigenous identity in ways that parallel the possibilities of a self-defined agency. Rather than representing the traditional as the origins of contemporary identity, Mela and Claudia have reversed this portrayal by illustrating a self-proclaimed modernity as the innermost layer. Importantly, Claudia co-created this series that celebrates the multiplicity of identities presented.

This canvas with a selection of six pictures illustrates Mela's central commitment to a "photographic practice based on the process of collective dialog."[4] Claudia's transformation within the series is a visual expression of a much larger Indigenous decolonial movement that renders each portrait a symbol of her identity and, at the same time, reflects social change.

—Jennifer Natalie Fish

Serie de retratos de Claudia desprendiéndose de sus ropas tradicionales mapuche (Portrait series of Claudia shedding her traditional Mapuche clothing), Azentún Photography Workshop, Santiago, Chile, 2015.

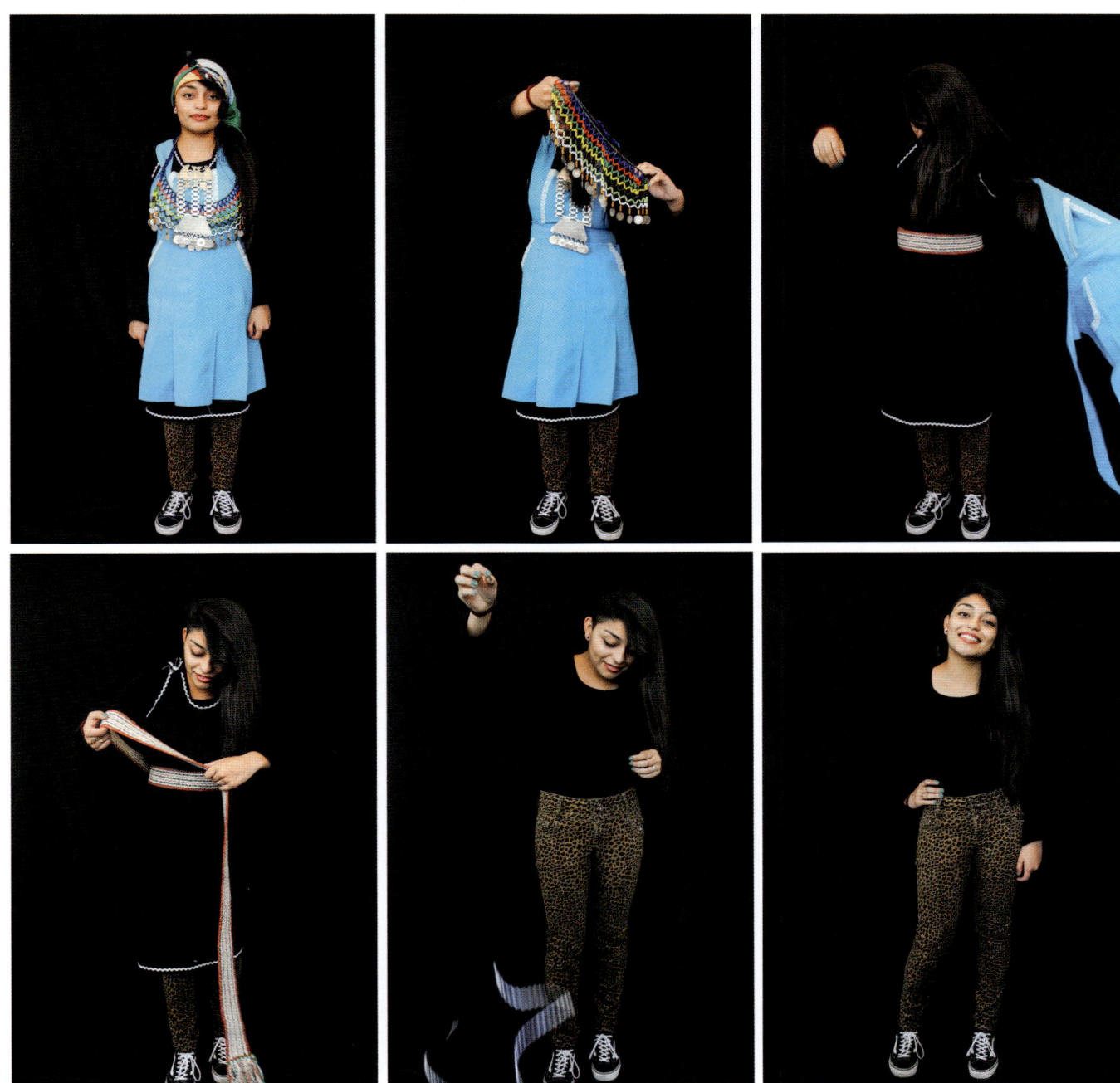

TÁHILA MOSS

Yaqui, Jewish
Yaqui Nation
Tórim, Yaqui River, Sonora
México and United States

The portrait that artist Táhila Moss (b. 1981) made of Angela Ferguson is infused with the colors of a smoldering fire. The contours of Ferguson's countenance are sharp, while a gentle, hazy light hovers over her prayerful gaze and sloped shoulders. After making the portrait, Moss produced a sizable 5' × 6' print. On its surface, atop Ferguson's head, she assembled a crown of dried Haudenosaunee (Hodinǫhsǫ́:nih) White Corn husks, seeds, ribbons, and beads.

Titled *Sovereign*, the image evokes the strength and self-determination many Indigenous women gain through their relationships with the land and traditional foods.

Ferguson is a Traditional Corn Grower and Seed Keeper from the Onondaga Nation (Onoñda'gegá' Nation), one of six nations comprising the Haudenosaunee Confederacy in present-day New York. Since 2015, Ferguson has been the director of the Onondaga Nation Farm, a self-sustaining and community-minded refuge giving rise to the nation's food sovereignty. On the farm, Ferguson and a crew of mostly women workers grow the Three Sisters of Indigenous agriculture: corn, beans, and squash. They raise buffaloes and keep bees. They forage, hunt, fish, butcher, and cook—and teach their techniques to the community.

For the Onondaga and others, traditional food is medicine. "In order for you to have balance, your food has to have balance," Ferguson says. "Your plate is a circle, and that circle is a medicine wheel for you."[1]

The heart of Onondaga Nation Farm is a secure, wood-paneled storage space, where Ferguson has gathered the seeds from well over 2,000 varieties of corn. Like an assembly of nations, the seeds, or kernels, have journeyed from across the Americas. Safely maintained in glass jars and bins, they are every shade the imagination can conjure, from slate to ochre to strawberry. Many are thousands of years old. "Some of these seeds have no more people," Ferguson told *Intercontinental Cry* in 2019. "All their people are extinct, wiped out, or absorbed into other tribes. But the food lived on."[2] Other seeds have been absent from their Tribal homes for generations. At the farm, Ferguson and the team propagate these heirloom seeds and return them to their ancestral circles—their relatives.

The seed bank makes room for the farm's preserved meats, vegetables, and fruits, "enough to feed every tribal citizen for four years," reported the *New York Times* in 2022. "This room is very powerful," Ferguson said succinctly about the independence it represents for the Onondaga Nation, as well as the seeds' ability to unify Indigenous nations and communities. "It is the epitome of food sovereignty."[3]

Moss, whose home is in her Yaqui community of Sonora, México, and in the Haudenosaunee Territory of Central New York, works across interwoven platforms to amplify the voices of the natural world and Indigenous people, particularly Indigenous women. Her photographic practice focuses on themes of Matriarchy, Indigeneity, and recuperating lifeways unraveled by colonialism. OJI:SDA' Sustainable Indigenous Futures—the women-led nonprofit organization of which she is the founder and executive director—"expands Indigenous visibility, land literacy and good health by using innovative methods of sharing ancestral knowledge."[4]

In line with the ethos of OJI:SDA', *Sovereign* is part of a larger series called My Grandmothers' Light Shines Through Me, which pays tribute to the ways women transfer wisdom across time and place. Indeed, the portrait Moss crafted of Ferguson "was created over many lands and territories."[5] It began with a long camera exposure on the Onondaga Nation Farm after the women spent an afternoon sharing reflections and beliefs. The corn husks come from a friend's garden on the Tonawanda Seneca Nation Territory (Ta:növöde' Onöndowa'ga:' Nation Territory). The piece was fully realized in the United Arab Emirates, where, in 2022, Moss was an artist resident with the Sharjah Art Foundation. While conceptualizing the tones, light, and materials that would best embody Ferguson, Moss says she was thinking about how "seeds carry the teachings of our ancestors, nourishing, and empowering us."[6] *Sovereign* was exhibited in 2023 at the Sharjah Biennial 15: *Thinking Historically in the Present*, alongside three more images of Haudenosaunee women.

OJI:SDA', the name of Moss's organization, is a Seneca word that translates to "embers of the fire." She explains: "Our personal fire is the core of our vital life energy. The embers of our fire are in connection with our ancestors before us and those to come afterwards."[7] The soft, steady yellows and oranges in *Sovereign* speak to Ferguson's calling as a Seed Keeper and unite her with Moss—two Indigenous women summoning the energy of their forebears and the land to transform the future.

—Sarah Stacke

Sovereign, 2022, from the series My Grandmothers' Light Shines Through Me. Supported by the Sharjah Art Foundation.

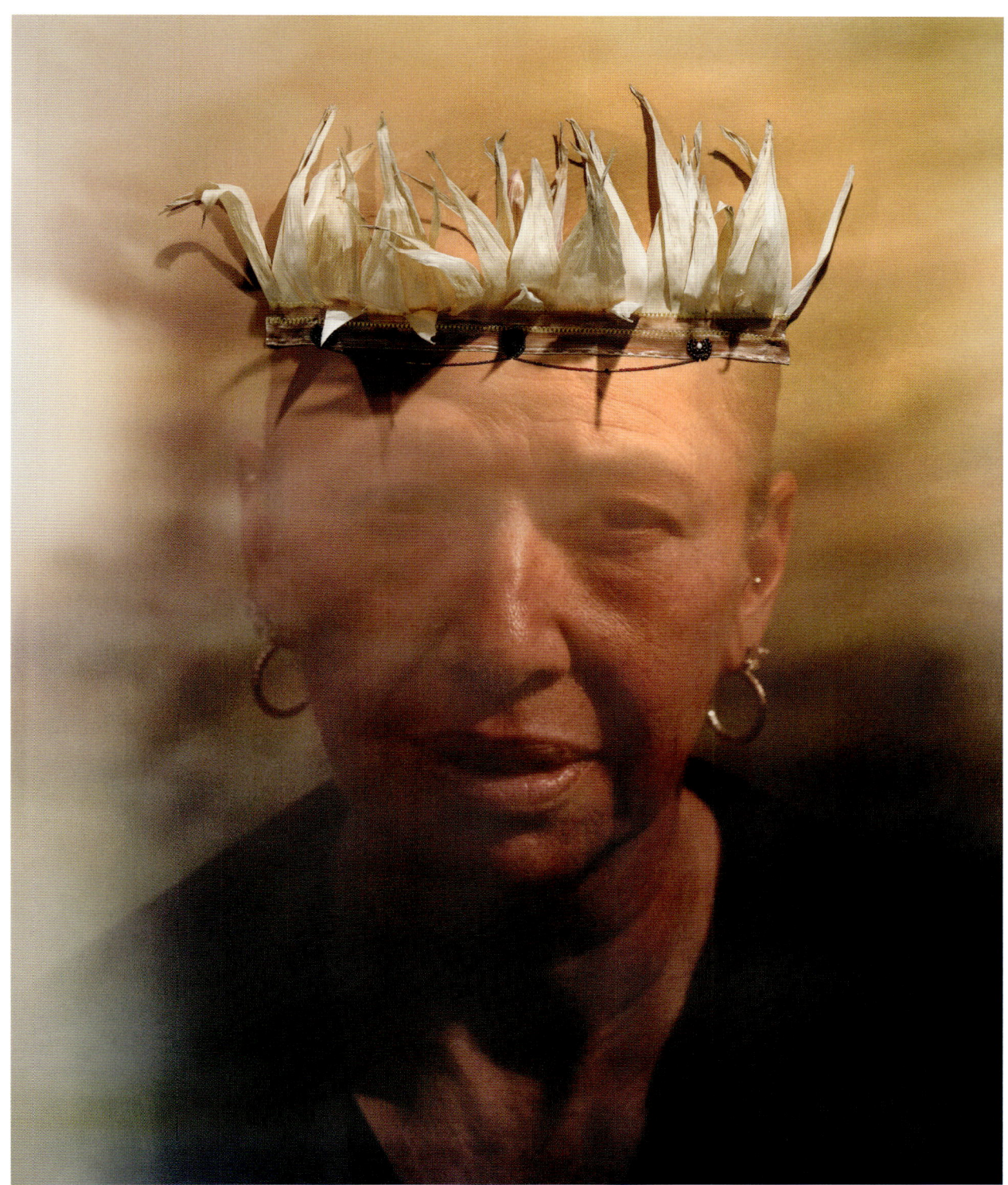

RYAN REDCORN

Osage
Pawhuska Indian Village, Osage Nation
United States

During a visit to Third Mesa, Arizona, on the Hopi Reservation, Ryan RedCorn (b. 1979) used a medium-format Hasselblad to photograph Marlee Josytewa and Amyah Lane. The young women were sitting on the steep edge of the mesa and gazing intently at Josytewa's phone, making a selfie. RedCorn is struck by the initial and misleading impression of the image. "At first glance it looks like they're ignoring the canyon for the phone, and all this splendor," says RedCorn. But, he clarifies, if you look on the phone, they're placing themselves in the "beauty and magnitude" of the landscape and recording the moment.[1]

The girls were in Third Mesa visiting their aunt and offered to guide RedCorn and the group he was with to a special, secret spot. "They were just kids being kids, wanting to show me something they thought was cool," RedCorn recalls.[2] The girls shimmied out over a rock ledge that appeared dangerous but was somewhere in the middle ground between safe and not safe. There they sat watching the sun go down.

RedCorn is Osage and was born in Tahlequah, Oklahoma. He co-founded the 1491s, the Indigenous comedy team notorious in Indian Country and beyond for their hilarious sketches. His portrait photography establishes him as a strong advocate for Native people and their depiction as vitally present in the here and now. "We're supposed to be disappearing, and it's not happening," RedCorn says in a feature for *National Geographic*.[3] RedCorn works to dismantle long-held misconceptions about Native peoples as a "vanishing race," a narrative constructed during the settling of the West that served as false justification for stealing Native people's land and other atrocities.

"Photography has a long voyeuristic and exploitative relationship with Indigenous communities," RedCorn says.[4] For his own Tribe, the Osage, that history is particularly fraught. The discovery of oil on Osage land brought great wealth to the Tribe, and with that came white men interested in marrying Osage women and inheriting their riches. Photo postcards of Osage women were produced and became a device to attract potential suitors to Osage Nation. The photographs were "sought after by white men who came to town with a specific goal of marrying an Osage woman," RedCorn says.[5] This practice had a sinister agenda that led to the extortion of money and assets from the Osage and an epidemic of related murders during a dark chapter in the Osage's history called the Reign of Terror.

Despite this tragic period, the Osage cultivated visual sovereignty through commissioning portraits, thus empowering their own narrative, RedCorn explains. "They're in charge of how they're standing, what they're wearing."[6]

RedCorn grew up with an awareness of the Osage's engagement with photography. His father, Raymond RedCorn III, collected historical photos of Osages. In the fall of 2016, he donated around 800 images, dated from 1880 to 1930, to the Osage Nation Museum.[7] RedCorn's feelings on the photographs are bittersweet—on the one hand he admires how beautiful the images are, but he also understands how many lives in the images were cut short—his great-grandfather's among them. It's a story too often reckoned with in Native communities throughout the continent: What is the price for oil, gold, uranium, land, and more? And whose lives are considered expendable in exchange for these resources?

In their own form of visual sovereignty, the young women in RedCorn's photograph, Josytewa and Lane, are asserting their presence on the land. For the casual observer, two Native girls are preoccupied with their phone, but when one looks more closely, a different story emerges. "That's why the photo is impactful," RedCorn says. "There are multiple layers of someone thinking they understand what's going on in the picture and then realizing the best possible outcome is what has actually happened."[8]

—Tiffany Midge

Marlee Josytewa (left) and Amyah Lane, Third Mesa, Arizona, on the Hopi Reservation, April 29, 2023.

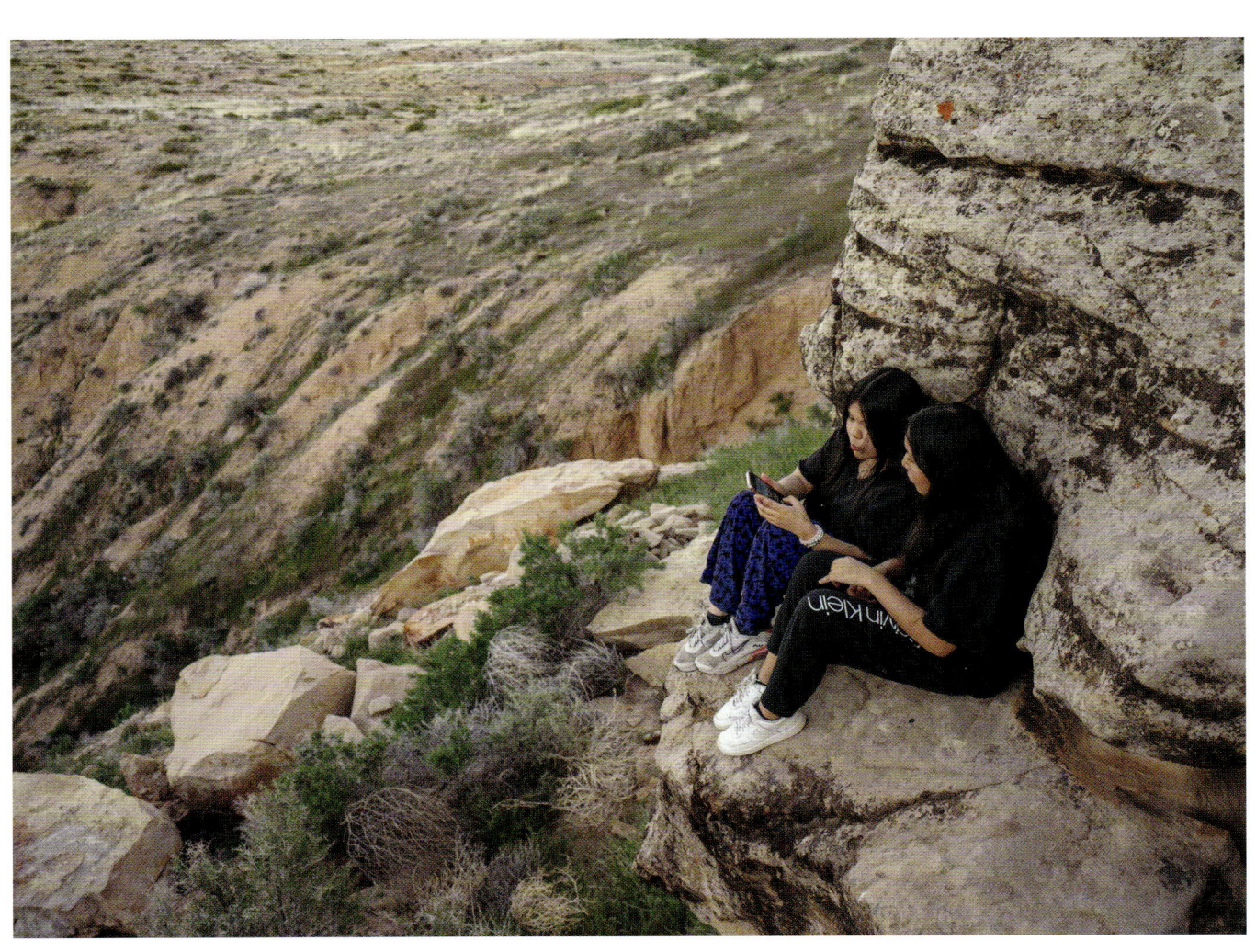

BAAHINNAACHÍSH (ONE WHO IS TALENTED) / WENDY RED STAR

Apsáalooke (Crow)
Apsáalooke Nation
Montana
United States

In the self-portrait *Spring*, Wendy Red Star (b. 1981), whose Apsáalooke (Crow) name is Baahinnaachísh, positions herself within a diorama constructed of AstroTurf, fake blooming flowers, cutouts of wild animals, and a creased backdrop showing a crisp mountain lake. Wearing a traditional red elk-tooth dress and beaded moccasins, Red Star sits stoically in the middle of the display.

Spring is a caricature of the dioramas featuring Indigenous peoples found in many natural history museums. Using wry humor, it confronts a romanticized American past of "noble savages" living in absolute harmony with nature and an American present that consigns Indigenous nations to history and invisibility. "Humor is healing to me," says Red Star about the integral role of playfulness in her artwork and Apsáalooke culture. "To have that element in my work is quite Native, or Crow, and I'm glad it comes through."[1]

As art historian Jordan Amirkhani aptly summarizes, "Red Star's early self-portraits alert viewers to the complexities alive in Native representation and bring the personal and the political into a powerful encounter."[2]

Spring is one of four photographs in Red Star's body of work Four Seasons. Accordingly, the other photographs are titled *Summer*, *Fall*, and *Winter*. She created this pivotal series when she was a graduate student in Los Angeles. Missing her home in Montana, she sought Apsáalooke matter in the city's natural history museum. She vividly recalls the path to the Native galleries: "I walked under a Brontosaurus. It was very dark." As she watched the visitors scan the Indigenous objects on display, it occurred to Red Star they'd been duped.

"The institution had set us up to think that these Indigenous communities no longer exist. To have us right next to the dinosaur bones," she observed.[3] Before leaving, she passed the museum's dioramas, many imitating Montana landscapes. Four Seasons was born.

In a 2016 iteration of Four Seasons, Red Star collaborated with her daughter, Beatrice, who was nine at the time. Beatrice designed a season (majestic mountain, pine forest, gang of animals, plastic flowers) and installed it at the Denver Art Museum. Then, she and Red Star flipped the narrative. Museumgoers were invited to insert themselves into the diorama, where Beatrice photographed *them*. "I wanted her to empower herself," explains Red Star, who centers questions of cultural heritage and the identity of Apsáalooke women in her practice.[4]

Four Seasons marks a turn toward future projects that, through extensive research, unearth Apsáalooke histories suppressed in museum and library archives. Red Star reinterprets and recuperates the material using a range of creative expression, often concurrently, including photography, collage, textiles, large-scale installation, and performance.

Red Star's practice vividly embodies her singular and urgent perspective of American society, and steadily applauds—and demands—an integral and vital place for Apsáalooke art, family, and experiences in its fabric.

—Sarah Stacke

Spring, 2006.

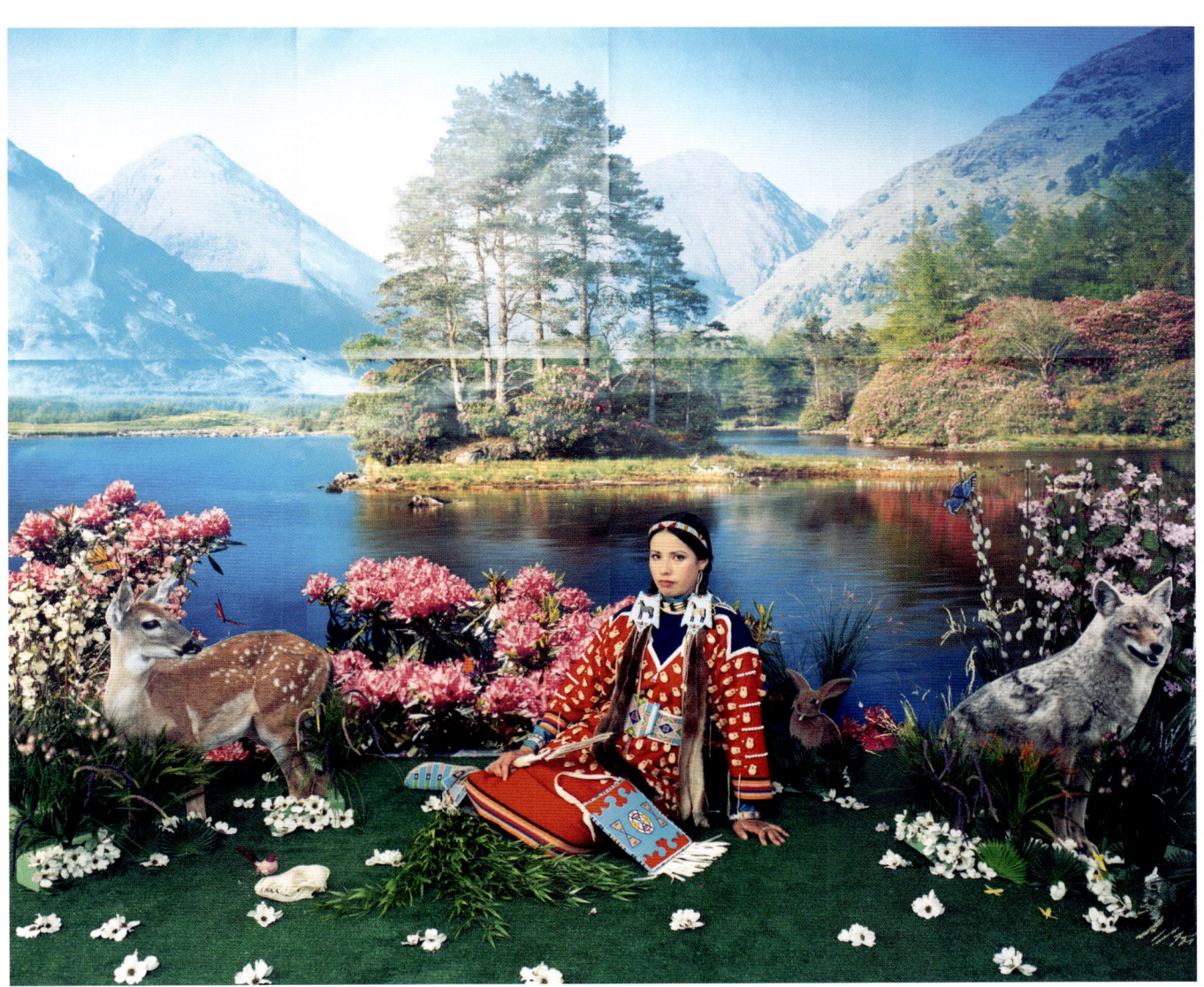

DAWN E. "DAWNEE" LEBEAU

Itazipčola Oóhenunpa (without bows and two kettle)
    of the Tetonwan Oyáte Lakota (People of the Prairie)
Wakpá Wašté Lakota Makoc'e (Cheyenne River Lakota Lands)
South Dakota
United States

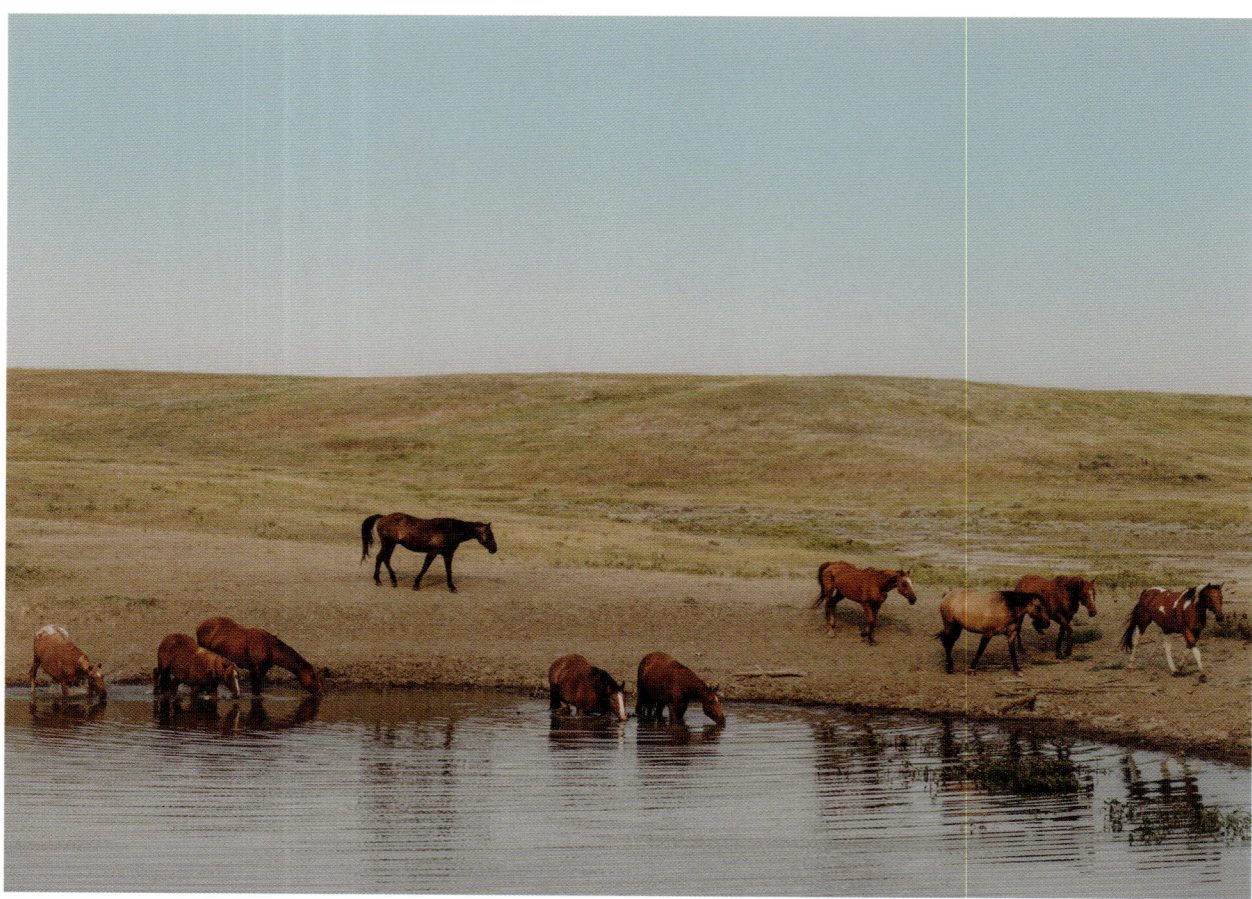

Picking up the camera and spending time outdoors documenting her Homelands provides a way to process the loss of a loved one, a way to grieve, says Dawn E. "Dawnee" LeBeau (b. 1982). These were her circumstances on the day she photographed a band of horses on the Cheyenne River Lakota Nation in South Dakota. The photo holds significance for LeBeau, a visual storyteller, because she had just experienced the passing of her father. LeBeau says that creating photos is a way to "move" with her grief. "I feel sorrow but I also feel hopeful."[1]

LeBeau felt calm and connected that day with the horses, waiting for them to drift to the right side of the water and spread out through the camera's frame. In the photograph, all the horses are positioned in the same direction. Some are drinking from the pond, while the rest tread along the shore toward some unknown, unrevealed destination, a metaphor for the emotional aftermath of her father's death.

"Horses are sacred in our Lakota culture," LeBeau says. "Šunka Wakán" translates to "four-legged" and "holy or sacred" in English, and this is meaningful, she explains, because spending time with community also includes four-legged relatives.[2]

LeBeau's late grandmother, Marcella Ryan LeBeau, Wígmuŋke Wašté Wíŋ (Pretty Rainbow Woman), was a distinguished Elder. Born in 1919, she received numerous accolades for her frontline service in the Army Nurse Corps during World War II. After returning home to the Cheyenne River Lakota Nation, she worked as a nurse for more than three decades and was an outspoken advocate for the health of Lakota communities her entire life. In 2020, Marcella was recognized by the National Congress of American Indians with a Leadership Award, and *USA Today* named her as one of the most influential women of the century. Two weeks before she began her journey to the star nation, at age 102, in 2021, she was inducted into the National Native American Hall of Fame.[3]

Like her grandmother, LeBeau is invested in the well-being of Lakota people. She was gifted her first camera in 1996—a Nikon N90s 35mm camera—when she participated in WoLakota Yukini Wicoti Tipi, a cultural immersion camp for Lakota teens. She is a lifelong resident of the Cheyenne River Lakota Nation and today uses her photography practice to create, promote, and collaborate on projects urging Lakota wellness, Lakota language, and Lakota cultural values.

In an interview for *Native Max Magazine*, LeBeau was asked how she photographs beauty. In response, she says, "Seeing Natives take pride in their traditions, learning their languages and preserving what their elders have passed on to them is beautiful."[4]

—Tiffany Midge

Šunka Wakán Otá (horses), Cheyenne River Lakota Nation, South Dakota, 2020.

BRIAN ADAMS

Iñupiaq
Anchorage, Alaska
United States

Making portraits in Alaska's Arctic region presents unique challenges. For Brian Adams (b. 1985) this meant only 40 minutes of available light the day he photographed Marie Rexford, an Iñupiaq woman living in the village of Kaktovik. "It was terrible," he recalled, laughing.[1] In the image, Rexford stands outside her house surrounded by snow and blocks of muktuk, a traditional staple of whale skin and blubber. She and her family were butchering a bowhead whale in preparation for a community Thanksgiving feast. Adams set up his tripod and made three frames while Rexford stood motionless. Because of the low light, he used the illumination of a streetlamp behind him to expose the frames on square-format film. His lens was wide open at aperture f 2.8; the shutter speed was a full eighth of a second.

Kaktovik is one of 11 whaling communities belonging to the Alaska Eskimo Whaling Commission (AEWC)—an organization that protects subsistence hunting traditions to preserve the cultural values of the Iñupiat and Siberian Yupik peoples. Whaling is illegal in most countries but remains an integral part of many Alaska Native lifeways. The harvest of the bowhead whale, states the AEWC, is "central to our culture and our identities as Alaska's First People"[2] and has been the primary food source of Alaska's Arctic coastal communities for over 2,000 years.

In a portrait made farther south in Quinhagak, a village less than a mile from the Bering Sea, three men—John Sharp, William Sharp, and Robert White—relax in a steam house. Adams was walking down the street when he saw them. He waved and the men waved back. Thinking he'd like to make a photo, but doubtful they'd agree since they were naked, Adams continued on his way. Then he had a change of heart. "If I didn't go back and at least ask, I would regret it for the rest of my life, and that image that could have been would haunt me," he recollected.[3] To his surprise, the men said yes. "They were so chill," said Adams. "I had never seen a contemporary photo of a steam house in rural Alaska and I felt like I was off to a good start with the project representing my people."[4]

Quinhagak is the first place Adams visited when he began producing his book *I Am Inuit*, published in 2017.[5] The project brought him to 20 Alaskan villages, where he documented Inuit (Iñupiat, Yup'ik, Cup'ik, and St. Lawrence Island Yupik) life through photography and short interviews.

Adams's Iñupiat family is originally from Kivalina, a community on the northwest coast. But he was raised in Girdwood, a predominantly white town south of Anchorage, where he felt disconnected from his heritage. Since becoming a photographer, he's used the medium to reconnect with his roots and extended family. Adams's inclination to celebrate his culture is evident in much of his work. In lives affected by issues of climate change, health, and cultural preservation, he welcomes moments of content and frivolity and, in doing so, confronts oversimplified portrayals of Iñupiat people.

"What I'd most like to be my life's work is portraying Alaska Native people, my people, in a way that hits as close to objective reality as possible," he told the *New York Times*. "There is hardship and there is pride. There is beauty in the land. Culture is not stagnant, and there is always change."[6]

Despite Adams's extensive travels around the state, the photographs of Rexford preparing muktuk and the men in the steam house were his first opportunity to depict these activities. "Inside Rexford's house, there's a whole crew of people butchering the bowhead whale, cutting it up into smaller pieces," he explained. "What she's doing is spreading it out to freeze; that way, when they wrap it up it doesn't congeal together. I'd never seen that process before."[7] With the steam house, he was surprised to realize he wasn't familiar with any recent representations of the custom, although it's central to the lifestyle of southwestern Alaska. "Probably because they sit in the steam houses naked," Adams joked.[8]

"Right away, when I was making them, they felt special," he said about the pair of photographs. "I couldn't wait to get the film developed and see how they came out."[9]

—Tiffany Midge

Marie Rexford preparing muktuk for a Thanksgiving Day feast, Kaktovik, Alaska, 2015.

Robert White (right), William Sharp (center), and John Sharp, Quinhagak, Alaska, 2015. "We wash our bodies, try to wash the dirt off after we work out there. Relax and get clean, I guess. It's called a steam house. We work all day and then this is where we come," the men said.

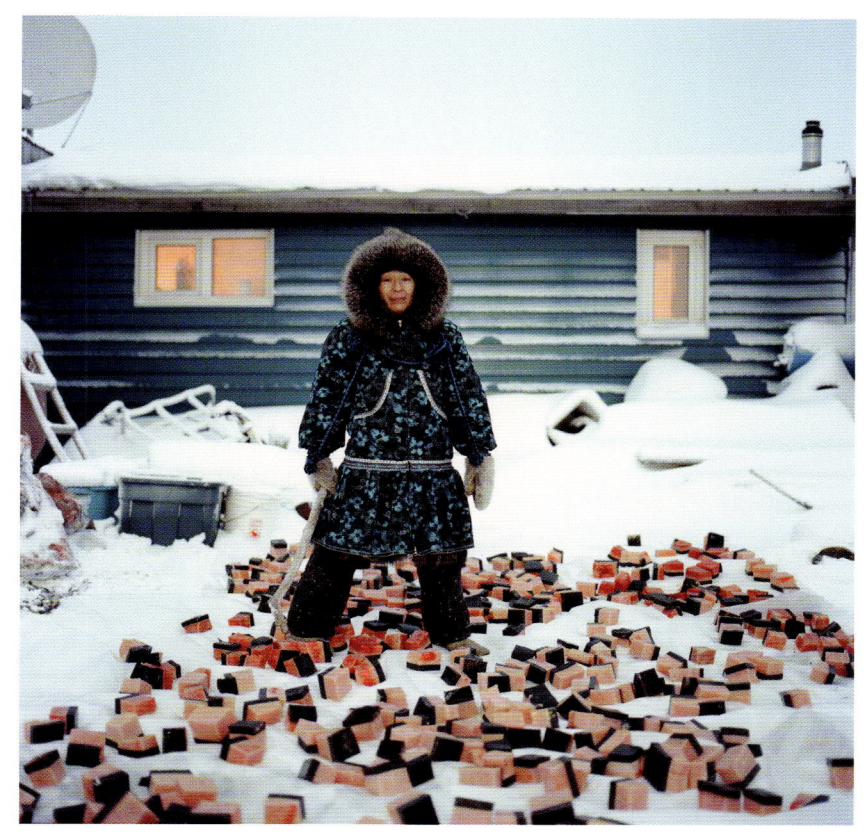

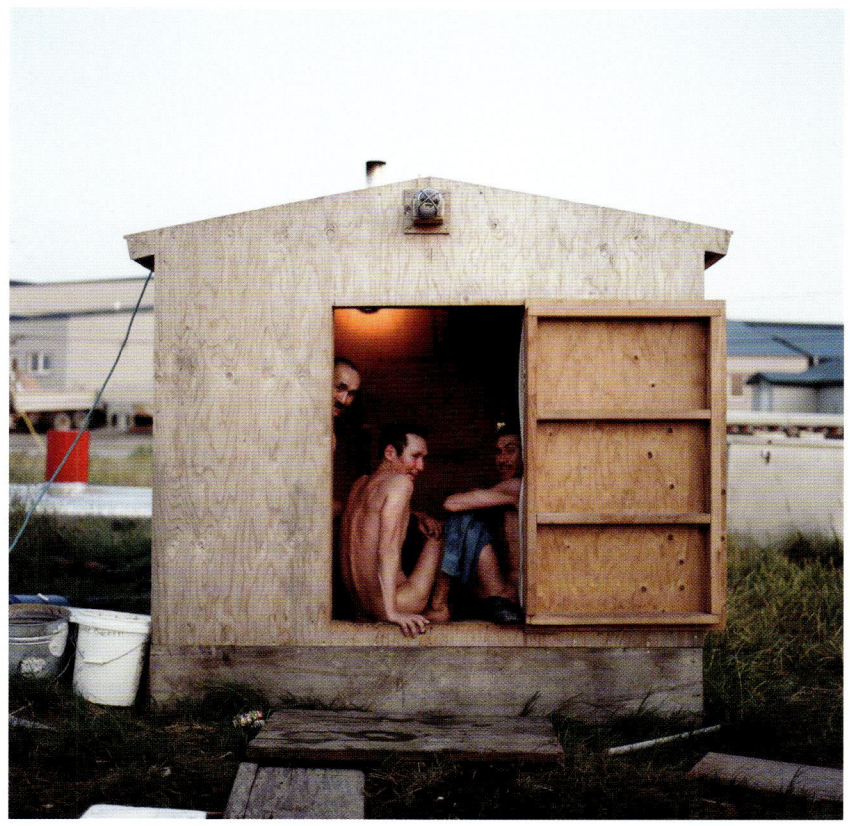

JERO GONZALES

Quechua
Cusco
Perú

"In the Peruvian Andes there are still communities that gather around a ritual, to feel bigger than any type of individuality, to thank their Apus (Deities) through dance and music for their protection and generosity," says Jero Gonzales (b. 1982).[1] With photography, Gonzales seeks to confront a world of haste, where he sees "little by little, human beings are forgetting to be 'grateful,' to thank circumstances, people and life itself."[2] Gonzales turns to documenting rituals to tell stories of Indigenous communities in celebration. With these images, he depicts humans in states of elevation, through longstanding spiritual practices carried out over centuries.

The series Pukapakuris illustrates an annual pilgrimage continued for more than 140 years by the Pukapakuri Wayri, a group of dancers from the Quechua-speaking community of Urcuspampa. Alongside tens of thousands of other pilgrims, the Pukapakuri Wayri travel to the Sinakara Valley, high in the Peruvian Andes, as part of Qoyllur Rit'i (Snow Star Festival), where they celebrate the stars, honor the local glacier, and thank the Creator for sending sacred waters. "Photography bears witness to those ephemeral moments," explains Gonzales, "from the party in general to the individual driven by the energy of the place and the ancestry; a glimpse of that liminal space where the sun meets the sky through ancestral music and dance."[3]

Gonzales considers dance one of the deepest forms of cultural expression—its enactment over thousands of years personifies reverence for Quechua legacy and survival. He describes it as a "ritual where light and movement are revealed… Ephemeral landscapes become repositories of time, and their temporal spatiality reestablishes the link with the sensory experience beyond the visible."[4] *Pukapakuri Wayri de Urcuspampa* mirrors this emphasis on light, movement, and fleeting topographies. With an intentional backlit canvas, Gonzales paints a story of individuals within a wider community. A few figures stand out, while the dancers in their entirety become a visualization of collectivity and shared cultural practice.

Gonzales places his experience of making *Pukapakuri Wayri de Urcuspampa* in direct relation to the intent of the Qoyllur Rit'i. He describes this image as "a meeting of emotions, where the photographic act helped me focus on the most essential thing in our existence, 'serenity and contemplation.'"[5] He recollects wishing to remain in this moment of ancestral connection forever. This longing allowed Gonzales to reflect on the insights generated from his visual creations. "All that remains is to be grateful to the Apus, people and circumstances that have allowed me to be here to live this moment," he says.[6]

Jero Gonzales's origins in Cusco inform the articulation and purpose of his photography. After graduating from the Centro de la Imagen in Lima, he returned to Cusco, where his work centers Quechua culture and the Andean landscape. Gonzales uses analog cameras to "realize new visual possibilities, through the exploration and combination of ancient and modern processes in the production of images."[7] He is deeply committed to his Homeland and the preservation of the Quechua language. Alongside his own work, he organizes and develops visual education workshops with children and young people from Quechua-speaking communities. Through these experiences, Gonzales uses the visual arts as a way to address identity and cultural heritage, while honoring the life stories of all participants and inspiring the next generation of photographers.

—Jennifer Natalie Fish

Pages 246–247: *Pukapakuri Wayri de Urcuspampa*, 2018, from the series Pukapakuris.

JORGE PANCHOAGA

Nasa
Popayán
Colombia

With landscapes, portraits, and close-up documentary compositions, Jorge Panchoaga's (b. 1984) photographic essay Detrás de la Montaña (Behind the Mountain) tells a story of identity, family, and migration among the Indigenous Nasa people of Colombia. Through this work, Panchoaga finds his own place in Nasa history.

When Panchoaga's grandfather was a child, he was separated from his parents. The exact circumstances are unclear, but he was raised far away by another family, and he didn't return to his Nasa village in Colombia's Cauca region until many years later.

"All the time, I wondered what I would have been if that hadn't happened to him and I was born on the reservation," said Panchoaga.[1] He began Detrás de la Montaña aspiring to piece together the past—and decipher more about the present. "I understand photography as if it were either literature or cinema. So, what I did was follow the big question I had about my grandfather's path," he explained.[2] Panchoaga faced several unknowns about his grandfather's life: why he relocated, what he faced along the way, and the extent to which he suffered before a family took him in.

A photograph of Nasa people at work in a field depicts one scene along Panchoaga's journey. Here, community members plant corn after feeding the earth with ash from burning vegetation. The image creates a visual conversation by composing the Nasa and their environment in an interconnected dialogue. The generational aspects of agricultural work represent durability and human endurance. Light is painted in the upper portion of the photograph through sublime and delicate forms made by a mix of smoke and clouds. These patterns symbolize the potential for a storm and reference a larger spiritual domain. The relationship between these ethereal shapes in upward motion contrasts with the depiction of the Nasa men and women traveling down the mountain as they work the land.

As he made photographs of the places where his grandfather lived, Panchoaga saw his family story as even more closely connected to the larger social, political, and economic conditions faced by Indigenous communities in Colombia. He began to see his grandfather's life as a "social symptom," as he surmised, "A lot of Colombians do not have fathers. That's a symptom of the civil war and drug trafficking. People are symptoms of society, and we can find reflections about what happened around them."[3] Of Panchoaga's photography, journalist David Gonzalez said, "He has created a meditation on place and identity. More important to him, he is trying to raise questions about the social, political and even criminal forces that propel migration and loss."[4]

Panchoaga shows a deep commitment to the importance of education and cultural preservation—both in photographs and archives. Trained as an anthropologist, he accompanied the Nasa community in Cauca as they established an archeological museum and published a photo book about the Calderas reservation, in a process led by archeologist Luis Gerardo Franco.

Through his own family and his social science training, Panchoaga's photographs show compelling evidence of the inseparable relationship between community and context. His photographs reveal how any understanding of culture and identity must be situated within the larger social, economic, and political terms that shape the movement of people, as well as the plight of those staking claim to lands and Indigenous histories.

—Jennifer Natalie Fish

Pages 248–249: A Nasa community planting corn, 2013, from the series Detrás de la Montaña (Behind the Mountain).

245

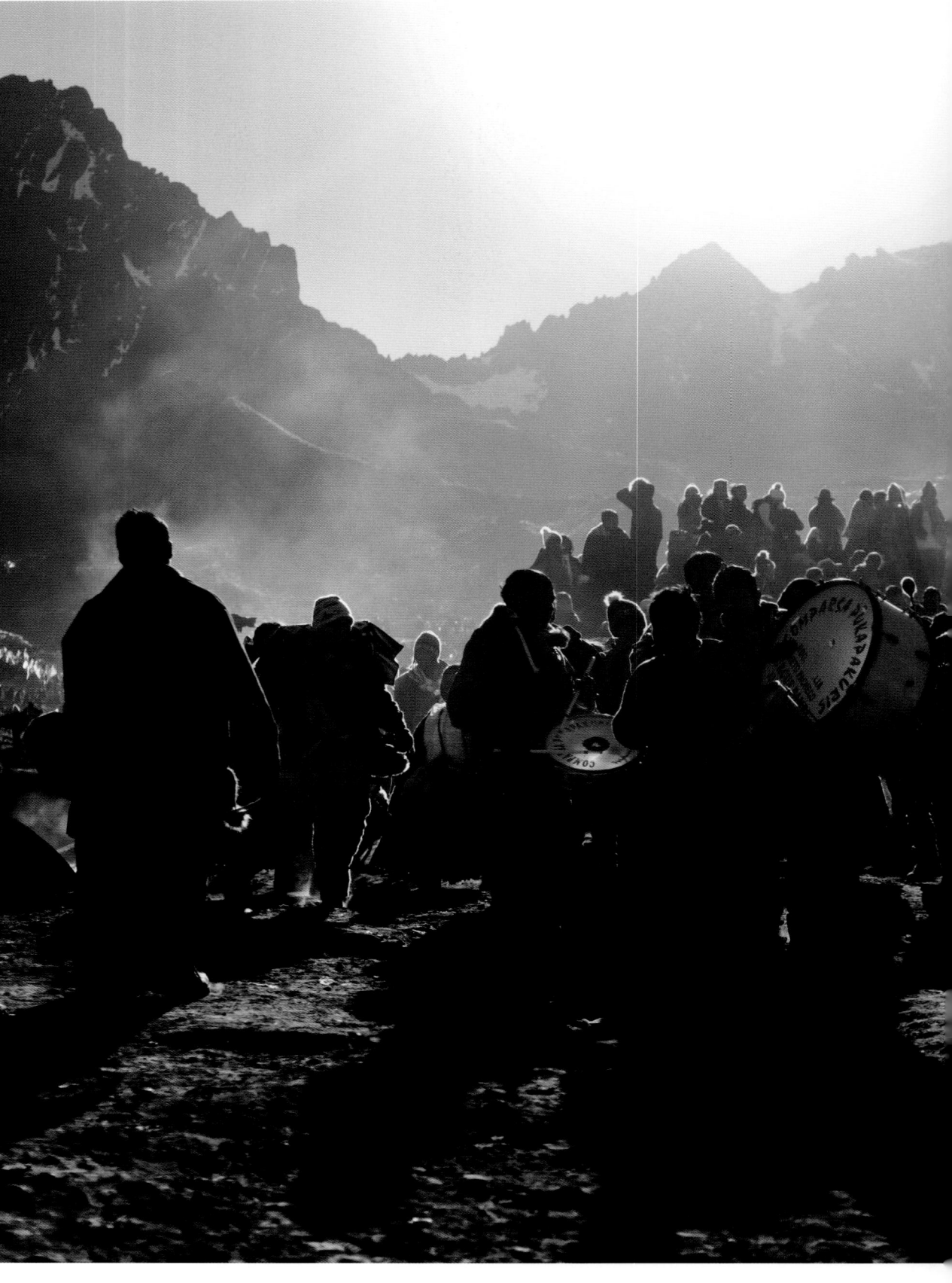

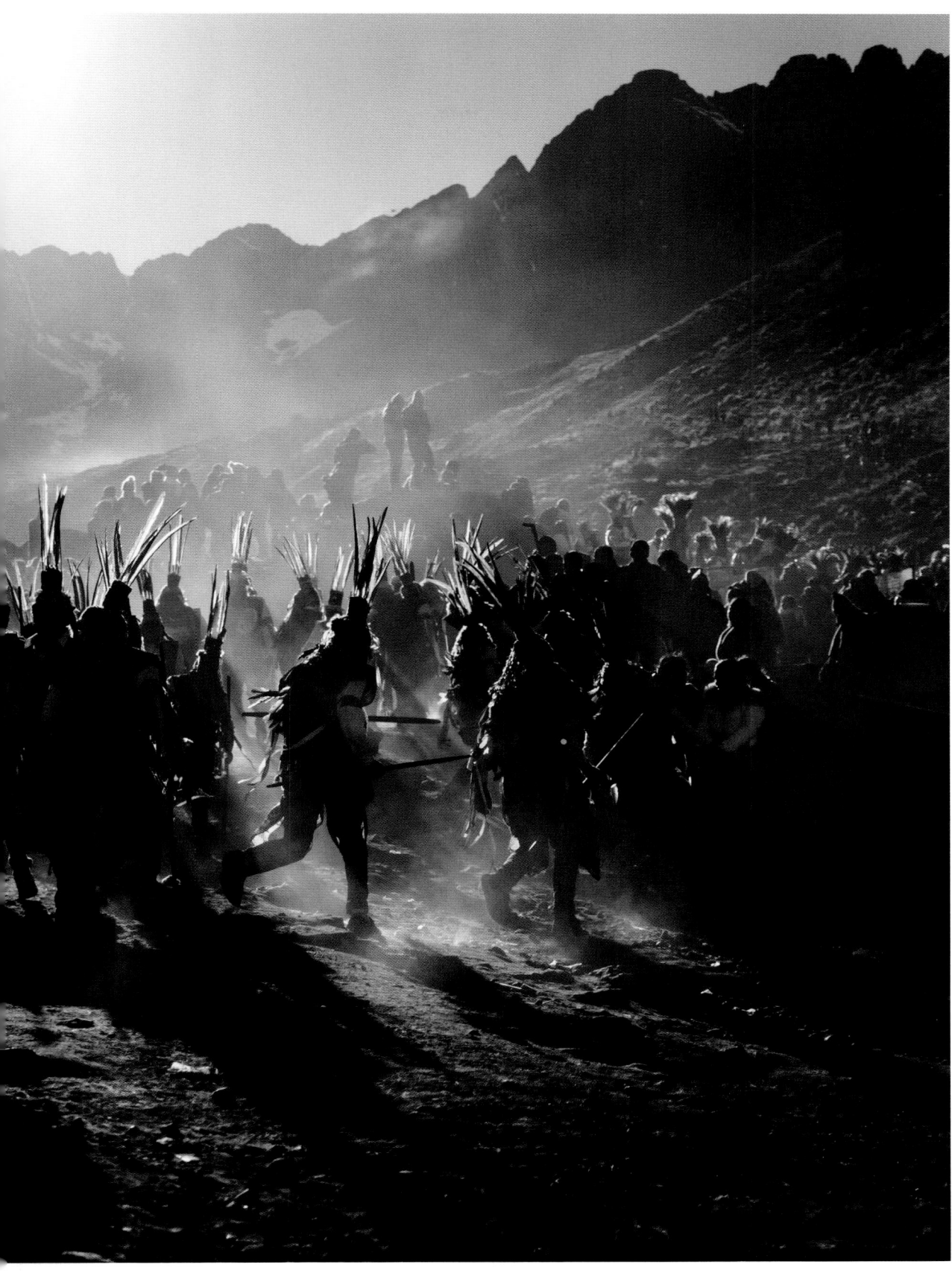

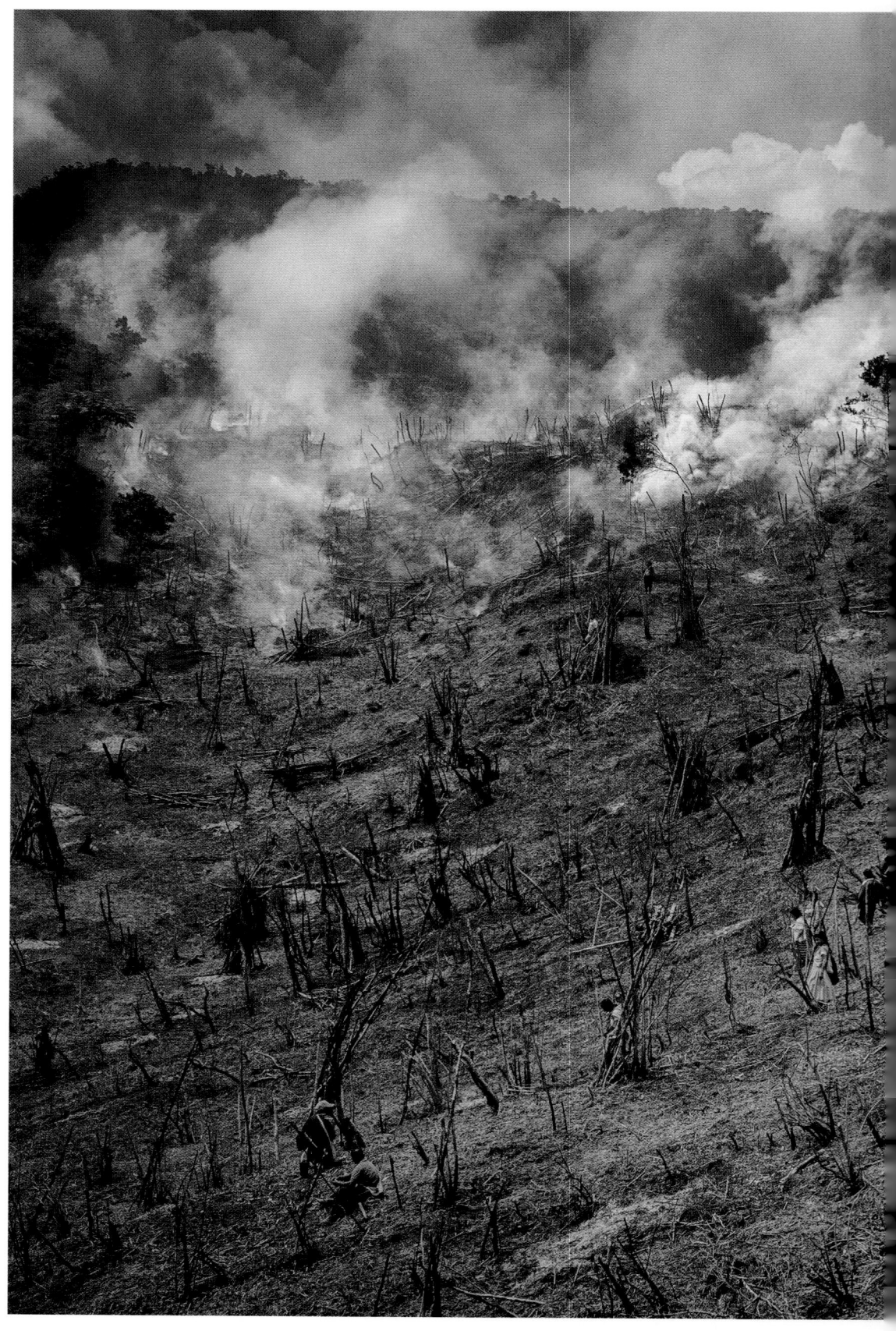

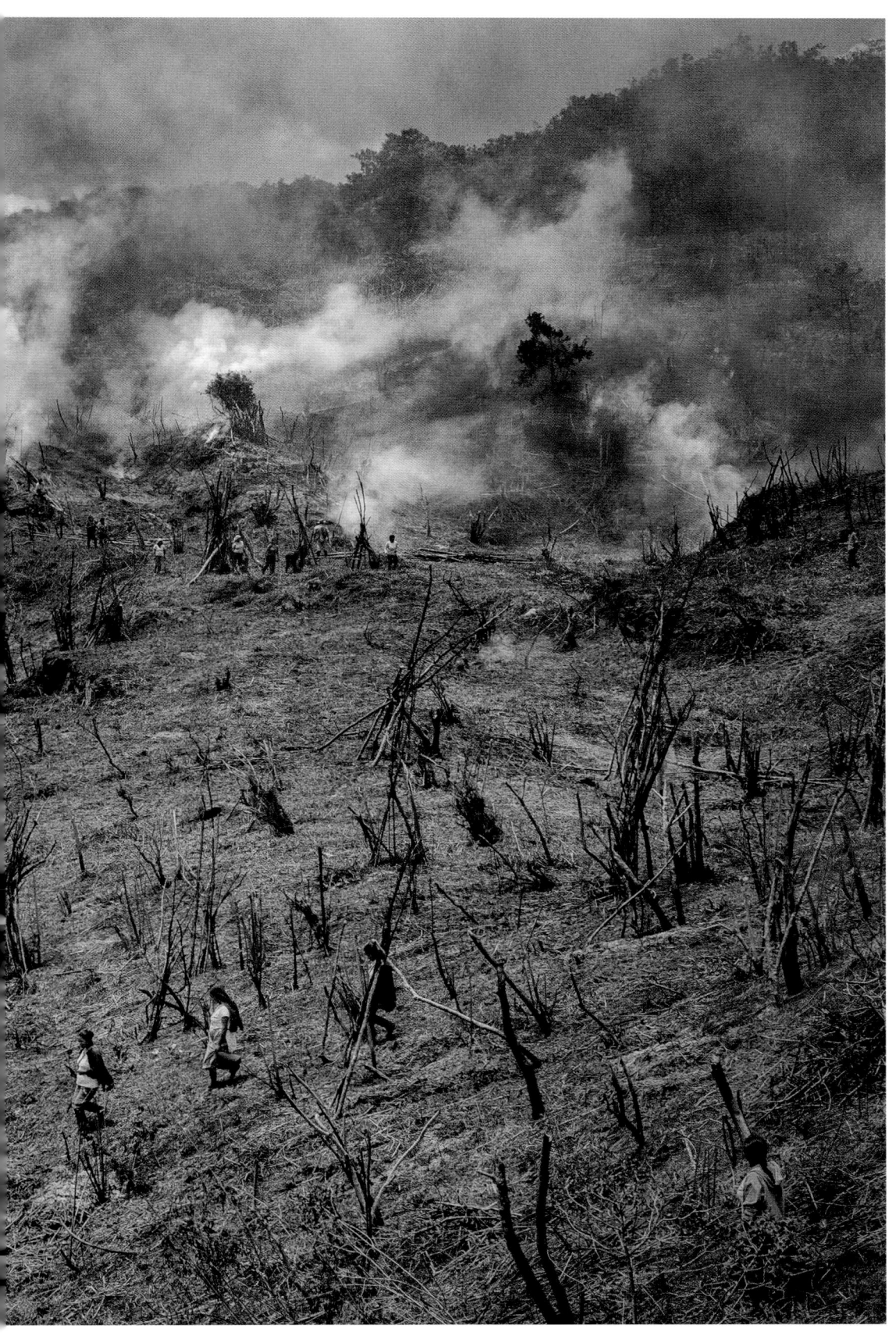

CINTHYA SANTOS BRIONES

Nahua
Tulancingo, Hidalgo
New York City, New York
México and United States

On a winter's day in Brooklyn, New York, Gisela Bravo Martinez asked her friend Cinthya Santos Briones (b. 1983), "Can you make my photograph to send to my grandchildren that don't know me, and I don't know them?" In turn, Santos Briones asked Martinez, "How do you like to be seen or represented through photography?"[1]

The exchange, in 2016, marked the start of Abuelas, a photography series by Brooklyn-based Nahua artist Santos Briones. The series looks at Mexican immigrant women who, decades ago, journeyed to the boroughs of New York City seeking opportunities for their families. Over time, they built lives and became the Elders of their communities—the abuelas. "Many have children and grandchildren living on either side of the border," says Santos Briones.[2] And yet, 20 or 30 years after the women arrived in America, they remain unseen and undocumented.

Made in the intimacy of their New York homes, each portrait in Abuelas contemplates "the women's relationship to place, and the shaping and appropriation of their environment," explains Santos Briones. The way they decorate their personal spaces, even if they just have a single room, like Martinez, speaks to the ways the abuelas carry "culture, memory, and ownership beyond borders," she adds.[3]

The portraits are made in a participatory manner. Santos Briones asks the women to choose their clothing and where in their home they wish to be photographed. They are pictured in dresses and jeans, in bedrooms, kitchens, and living rooms. The images are vibrant. "Mexican culture uses color as a social and political code," notes Santos Briones.[4] Though woven together by boldly painted walls, floral textiles, family photos, and Catholic icons, the women and their spaces emerge decidedly distinct.

The women's agency in Abuelas is essential to Santos Briones, who moved to the United States in 2012. "Even though I'm from México and I'm an immigrant, I'm not part of this community," she concedes. "I had the opportunity for citizenship and to study in the U.S., and to enter into other environments, social environments. It's really important for me to be aware of this privilege that I have."[5]

Santos Briones was raised in central México, "in a town between mountains and valleys inhabited by the Indigenous Nahua, Otomi and Tepehua communities," she writes in her artist statement. "As a migrant artist of color," she continues, "I interrogate the ways forced migration traverses and transgresses the body, consider how plants, rituals, and cultural objects intersect as they migrate alongside us, and collect and transmit restorative messages."[6]

In the 1980s, members of Santos Briones's family emigrated north in search of the elusive American Dream. The ongoing trauma of familial separation and the experiences passed down from living undocumented has, for Santos Briones, underscored the "urgency of recording and sharing our migration stories and increasing intergenerational awareness of ancestral healing knowledge."[7]

About the portrait session with Martinez, Santos Briones reflects, "It was an honor to photograph a person I admire." Well-known in Brooklyn circles for her gifts as a traditional doctor, Martinez taught her friend many techniques over the years of their acquaintance. "She is a doula, a midwife, but also a healer," acknowledges Santos Briones. "She is proud and powerful, like in the photograph."[8]

In Brooklyn, on the day of the photograph, Martinez wears golden jewelry and a black evening gown trimmed with silver sequins. She surrounds herself with splendid purple and red flowers, wall art depicting the Virgin Mary, and three giant stuffed animals (a cheetah, giraffe, and white tiger). The animals are a popular decor choice in Martinez's migrant community. "We have this notion that working-class people don't know how to live," remarks Santos Briones. "And that is a mistake. They know how to live."[9]

Two years after Martinez and Santos Briones made the portrait, Martinez moved back to México. She had health issues and was unhappy sewing clothes in a factory for less than $200 per week. "It's really difficult to be undocumented and a grandmother in your sixties or seventies," says Santos Briones. "A lot of people don't want to give you work opportunities…an Elder, a woman, undocumented, alone. You have all these categories."[10]

Similar, and similarly false, narratives of insignificance and inability frequently pulse through visual depictions of people who are a confluence of migrant, woman, and aged. Too often, they are presented as one-dimensional, or in desperate conditions. With Abuelas, Santos Briones is offering the women she photographs the chance to present themselves in a way that reflects their values and sense of identity. The way a grandmother would want her grandchildren, and all those gazing at her likeness in a frame, or flipping through the family photo album, for generations to come, to see her.

—Sarah Stacke

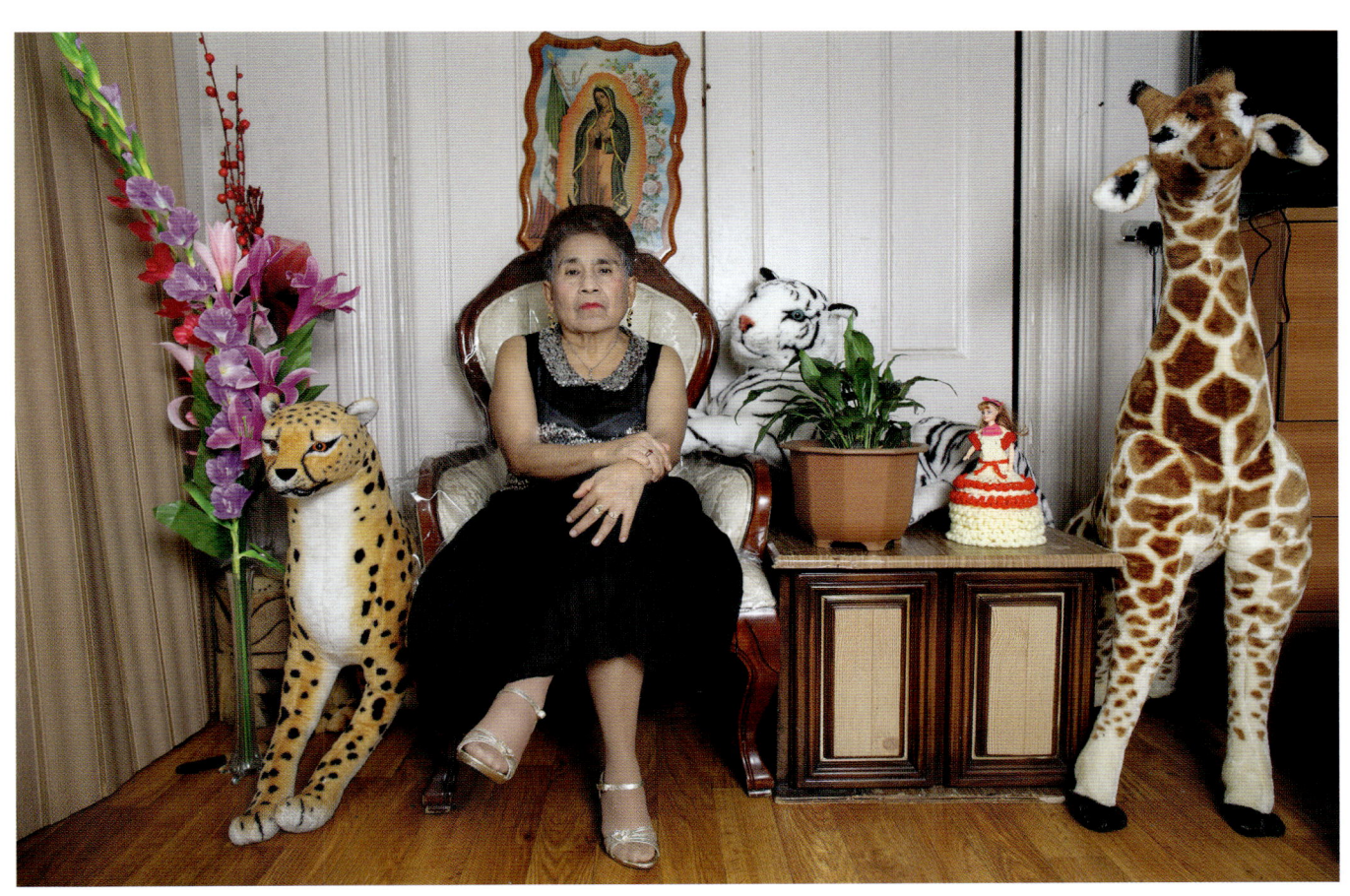

Gisela Bravo Martinez photographed in her apartment, Sunset Park, Brooklyn, New York, December 14, 2016. Born in San Bernardino, Acatlán de Osorio, State of Puebla, México, she lived in New York City for more than two decades, working in groceries and factories, though she is a professional seamstress. Martinez was known in her migrant community as a traditional healer, midwife, and physician. She was 66 years old in this photograph and a grandmother of six.

JAIDA GREY EAGLE

Oglala Lakota
Oglala Lakota Nation
Saint Paul, Minnesota
United States

In 2021, Jaida Grey Eagle (b. 1987) photographed Sean Sherman for *Vogue*. Her portrait of the renowned Oglala Lakota chef standing next to a firepit and stone wall conveys a classical, ancestral quality: The illumination from the flames creates dramatic refractions and shadows against Sherman and the masonry. Sherman, with Dana Thompson, co-founded the Indigenous restaurant Owamni in downtown Minneapolis. Derived from the Dakota word for St. Anthony Falls, Owámniyomni—meaning whirlpool or falling waters—the restaurant overlooks its namesake, the single major waterfall on the Mississippi River. The recipient of the 2022 James Beard Award for Best Restaurant, Owamni offers a menu that excludes "colonial ingredients such as beef, pork, chicken, dairy, wheat flour, and cane sugar, instead highlighting the true agricultural products of North America, such as corns, beans, squashes, wild game, birds, fish and Native plants."[1]

Both Sherman and Grey Eagle are from the Pine Ridge Reservation in South Dakota. Grey Eagle's interest in photography emerged when she was young, living there with her family. She told *Minnesota Monthly* in 2021 that she often took off with her parents' cameras and would spend hours photographing. Growing up on Pine Ridge, one of the most economically challenged communities in the United States, Grey Eagle was aware of photographers who would swoop in and document the reservation, but from a limited and questionable perspective. "When I was a teenager, there was a photographer out there who was publishing a lot of 'poverty porn' essays about my community," she recalled. These portrayals, said Grey Eagle, were flawed and incomplete and depicted Pine Ridge as dire and impoverished. Her relationship to the community was different. She witnessed connection with the land and animals, heard the Lakota language spoken, and participated in ceremonies with her family. "That's the story I'm pursuing," Grey Eagle said. "I got into wanting to do photojournalism because I'm interested in telling the truth, and not upholding white supremacy through my lens."[2]

Today, she is an acclaimed photojournalist, beadwork artist, writer, producer, and curator, residing in Saint Paul. Her work has been published in the *New York Times Magazine*, the *Washington Post*, and *Vogue*. She served as a Report for America fellow with the *Sahan Journal*, covering stories about communities of color in the Twin Cities. With a grant from Vision Maker Media, she coproduced the documentary *Sisters Rising* about Native American women working against systemic injustices. Grey Eagle aims to expand understanding of Indigenous photography. In 2023, she co-curated *In Our Hands: Native Photography, 1890 to Now*, an exhibition organized by the Minneapolis Institute of Art. "People don't know that Indigenous people have been practicing photography since the 1860s," said Grey Eagle. "I really want to uplift their work."[3]

—Tiffany Midge

Oglala Lakota chef and restaurateur Sean Sherman poses for a portrait outside the restaurant he co-founded and co-owns, Owamni, in Minneapolis, Minnesota, October 7, 2021.

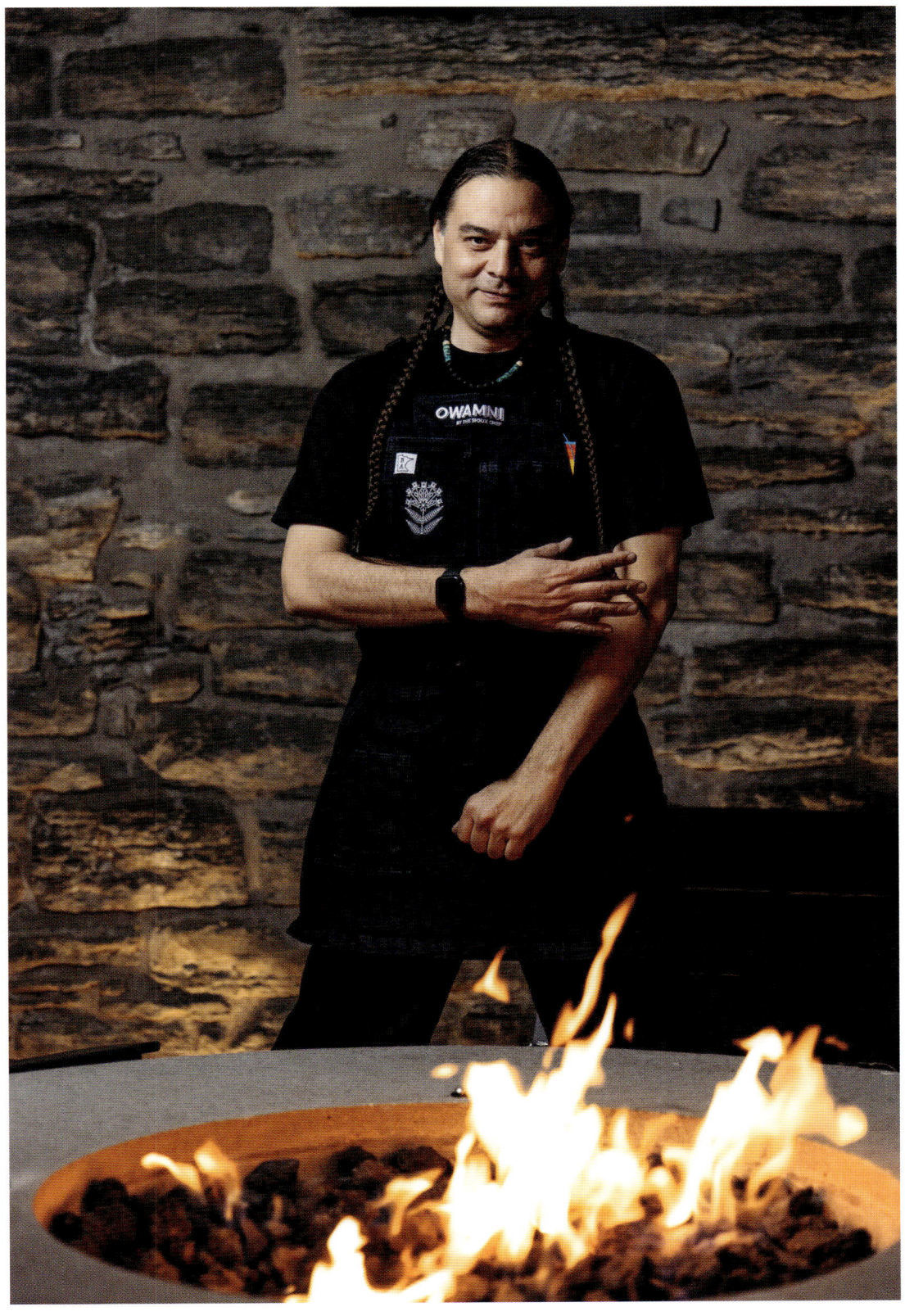

KALI SPITZER

Kaska Dena, Jewish
Unceded Lands of the xʷməθkʷəy̓əm (Musqueam), Sḵwx̱wú7mesh
    (Squamish), and səlilwətaɫ (Tsleil-Waututh) Nations
Vancouver, British Columbia
Canada

"While photographing Larissa, I was thinking about how to properly address them in all their power," says Kali Spitzer (b. 1987), an Indigenous femme queer photographer. Spitzer, who often works with people she knows, first met Larissa Grieves on the day of their portrait session. "I remember how calm and gentle Larissa's presence felt to me."[1]

The image of Grieves is part of the series An Exploration of Resilience and Resistance, which features Spitzer's community of mostly Indigenous and mixed-heritage folx. The portraits, writes artist Ginger Dunnill, are "unapologetic and make room for growth and forgiveness while creating a space where we may share the vulnerable and broken parts of our stories which are often overlooked, or not easy to digest for ourselves or society."[2] Spitzer's approach to photography is, Dunnill distills, "an exchange of trust."[3] Through this intense artistic collaboration, the personal narratives of Indigenous, Black, Brown, queer, trans, nonbinary, femme, and women's bodies are embraced, creating visual representations that are self-determined.

Centered on revitalization, healing, and celebration, Spitzer's art is most influenced by her heritage. The first line in the "Education" section of her CV reads, "1987–Present The Land & My Ancestors." From her father, a Survivor of Canada's residential schools, she is Kaska Dena from Daylu (Lower Post, British Columbia). From her mother, she is Jewish from Transylvania, Romania. "Coming from two groups of people where genocide was committed against us, and a lot of oppression, I just came out fighting," explains Spitzer, who lives on the Unceded Lands of the xʷməθkʷəy̓əm, Sḵwx̱wú7mesh, and səlilwətaɫ Nations.[4]

Grieves, whose ancestry is Nisga'a (Ganada), Gitxsan, Cree, Métis, Scottish, Swedish, and Irish, is a second-generation residential school Survivor. She identifies as two-spirit, femme, and queer. "As a queer femme imaging another queer femme," says Spitzer about working with Grieves, "there is a certain understanding in witnessing each other." The placing of Grieves's hair across her neck and shoulders is "a display of Indigenous resistance and power," she says. "It felt like the perfect way to speak to our shared histories and how we move in the world today."[5]

It's important to Spitzer that her work is viewed by people who aren't like-minded, "so they can see we're all humans," she says, "and they can have a connection with us."[6] When she exhibits An Exploration of Resilience and Resistance at galleries and museums, she likes to display the portraits as large scale as possible. The idea is to shift perspectives. Spitzer is inviting the audience to feel a little small and "appreciate and understand it is a privilege to witness us."[7] Dunnill describes the photographs' power this way: "Spitzer ignites the spirit of our current unbound human experience with all the complex histories we exist in, passed down through the trauma inflicted/received by our ancestors."[8]

Made with a large-format 8" × 10" camera and a wet-plate collodion process patented in 1856, Spitzer's images straddle eras. The specific wet-plate technique she utilizes produces tintypes. Originally known as the ferrotype, the process was popularized as the tintype, a misnomer, since no tin is used. With tintypes, portrait photography became widely available. More affordable and durable than its most notable predecessors, daguerreotypes and ambrotypes, the tintype significantly broadened society's nascent relationship to photography. Arguably in greatest use between about 1860 and 1900, the tintype was present at countless affairs, watershed events, and daily happenings. Images it generated in the second half of the 19th century and later were strategized to shape the perception and treatment of gender, race, ethnicity, and culture in North America and the world, and enact pernicious agendas.

Spitzer's biography shares that her work and the interactions behind it are "informed by the desire to rewrite the visual histories of indigenous bodies beyond a colonial lens."[9] Her choice to enlist the tintype in the 21st century enables those she photographs to root themselves in two historical records. With Spitzer, their presence and their realities are not refuted, romanticized, or othered. Instead, the ways they have existed—breathed, flourished, survived—across time are honored.

—Sarah Stacke

CEREMONY AND HEALING

These are the first words that come to mind when I think about being photographed by Kali Spitzer.

My name is Larissa Lorraine Grieves. I come from the ancestral backgrounds of Nisga'a (Ganada), Gitxsan, Métis, Scottish, Swedish, and Irish. I identify as two-spirit, femme-presenting, and queer.

I reside on the Unceded Traditional Territories of the Coast Salish, səlilwətaɬ (Tsleil-Waututh), kʷikʷəƛ̓əm (Kwikwetlem), Sḵwx̱wú7mesh (Squamish), and xʷməθkʷəy̓əm (Musqueam) Nations.

CEREMONY

Reclaiming, revitalizing, and expressing ourselves as Indigenous people is essential. So much has been taken away. When I find myself with young Indigenous people practicing their art and culture, like Kali, I hold the experience in my heart and to the most sacred levels of respect. It is ceremony, and ceremony comes in so many forms.

I DIDN'T EXPECT TO CRY

I believe our ancestors are always with us. I never truly feel alone. When I feel nervous, I ask my grandparents to be with me. That's what I did before being photographed by Kali. (If only you could hear my nervous laughter.) Kali and I had never met, and I didn't know what to expect. Meeting her, I instantly felt at ease. It was a grey and rainy day in Vancouver, but her spirit radiated comfort and she guided me into the building with security and blind trust. I knew this wasn't going to be an average experience.

BRAIDS

My hair is sacred to me. I feel that it holds all my experiences and connects me to the earth and my surroundings. When I braid my hair, I put good intentions and energy into the braids. When I braid someone else's hair, it is one of the deepest forms of affection and care. It creates a connection between good friends, family, and lovers.

Kali walked me through every part of what she was doing when she made this portrait, and she included me in the process. We made a few different photographs, but this one stuck with me. It's funny, we were trying to find a weight to hold my braid in place. We ended up with the perfect weight: a sage bundle.

DEVELOPMENT

Kali took me into the darkroom to watch the photographs transform. It was like magic. She swirled the liquids around as silver images appeared and streaks formed over the photograph. It made me feel like the spirits with us were making themselves present.

HEALING

I don't think I've ever seen myself so still. Until this portrait, I hadn't been in an environment that allowed me to trust the photographic process. I feel like I look different to myself. It is emotional to look at my face, because for the first time, I feel like I am truly witnessing my own Indigeneity. I feel my Indigeneity inside of me, but Kali has given me the opportunity to see myself in a different way. My ancestors are visible in this portrait, but most of all it makes me feel seen by myself.

—Larissa Lorraine Grieves, 2023

Larissa Lorraine Grieves, Nisga'a, Gitxsan, Métis, Swedish, Irish, and Scottish. Made in 2021 on the Unceded Lands of the xʷməθkʷəy̓əm (Musqueam), Sḵwx̱wú7mesh (Squamish), and səlilwətaɬ (Tsleil-Waututh) Nations.

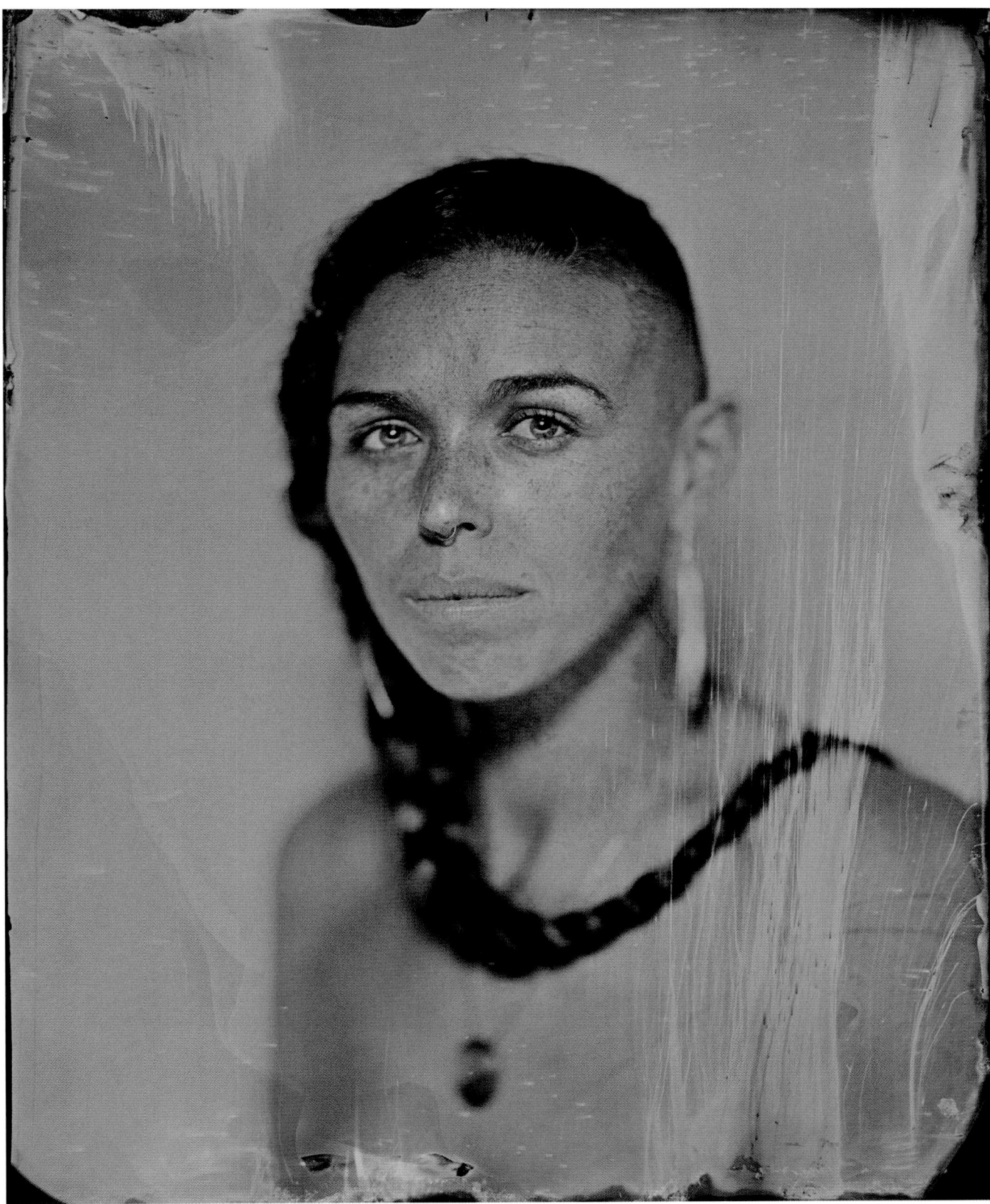

MINIK BIDSTRUP
JAKOB PETERSEN
Inuk
Upernavik
Greenland

When Minik Bidstrup (b. 1990) photographed his friend Martin Brandt Hansen at a Christmas Eve party in Nuuk, Greenland, in 2017, he was just starting to think about a career in photography. And yet, he says, the image is representative "in every way" of the work he's made as a professional: candid, flash-lit, grainy black-and-white photographs that contain subtle hints of his Greenlandic Inuit heritage and contemplate postcolonial identity.[1]

Hansen's vest is made from sealskin, a material central to Indigenous Arctic cultures. His dog, Amaroq, is a husky, though, Bidstrup points out, not a Greenland dog, an ancient husky-type sled dog that arrived with the Thule people—the ancestors of the Greenlandic Inuit—around 1,000 years ago. The Moravian star (or Herrnut star) hanging in the window is a custom inherited from German Moravian missionaries stationed in Greenland from 1733 to 1900.

"I want to use my photography to awaken people's curiosity about my culture," says Bidstrup. "Firstly, that we exist."[2]

Inuit peoples have inhabited Greenland, the largest island in the world, for approximately 4,500 years. The colonial era began in 1721 with the arrival of Hans Egede, a Danish-Norwegian Lutheran missionary. Until 1953, Greenland was a Danish colony; today it's an autonomous territory of the Kingdom of Denmark. Approximately 56,000 people live on the island, 89 percent of whom are Greenlandic Inuit.

"We are still here in the land we call home," says Bidstrup. "We may no longer be the same people the missionaries and colonizers met, but we are a people that were formed by enduring what was placed upon us."[3]

The first known photographs of Greenlandic Inuit were made in 1854 by Captain Edward Augustus Inglefield, a British naval officer and polar explorer. Thirty-five years later, in 1889, Inuk photographer John Møller opened a studio in Godthåb (now known as Nuuk). Active until 1922, Møller was considered the country's first professional photographer. He left a rich legacy of more than 3,000 glass plate negatives picturing Danish administrators and his fellow Inuit.

In a project titled, in his native Kalaallisut language, Saperasi isumaqaleritsi, or "Courageously Take a Stand," Bidstrup engages with Møller's reflections of colonial-era Greenland. Pairing Møller's images with his own, he creates diptychs that generate "photographic conversations with the past," says Bidstrup. "The theme of these conversations is centered around colonialism and its long-term effects."[4]

Bidstrup was born in Upernavik, a small town on an island of the same name, in northwest Greenland. When he was two, his family moved south to Aasiaat for four years, then to Nuuk, the country's capital city on the shores of the epic Nuuk Fjord. He remembers leafing through photo albums loaded with images his father, Jakob Petersen (b. 1957), made of their family. One image, awash in soft light, shows Bidstrup's older brother, Inuuteq, at age four or five, quietly peeling potatoes over the kitchen sink in their Upernavik home. "He's weirdly calm," observes Bidstrup. "I never saw him sitting. I think that's what drew my dad to this picture."[5]

The albums, says Bidstrup, undoubtedly influenced him. He received his first camera when he was seven, and before that played with his dad's, whether or not it had film in it. "It just kept going," he says about the way he's been drawn to photography.[6]

In the same way Bidstrup desires people to learn about his culture, he wants to know about theirs. "I had a very narrow view of what the world is," he admits. "Photography changed my life completely. It's been a reason for me to get out, to explore, to go places I've seen in other people's photographs."[7]

"There's a lot of Indigenous populations that we've stopped thinking of as Indigenous because they've been part of a national identity for so long. I'm really interested in focusing on those stories."[8]

—Sarah Stacke

Martin Brandt Hansen and Amaroq, Nuuk, Greenland, December 24, 2017.

Inuuteq Bidstrup in the kitchen of his childhood home, Upernavik, Greenland, c. 1989.

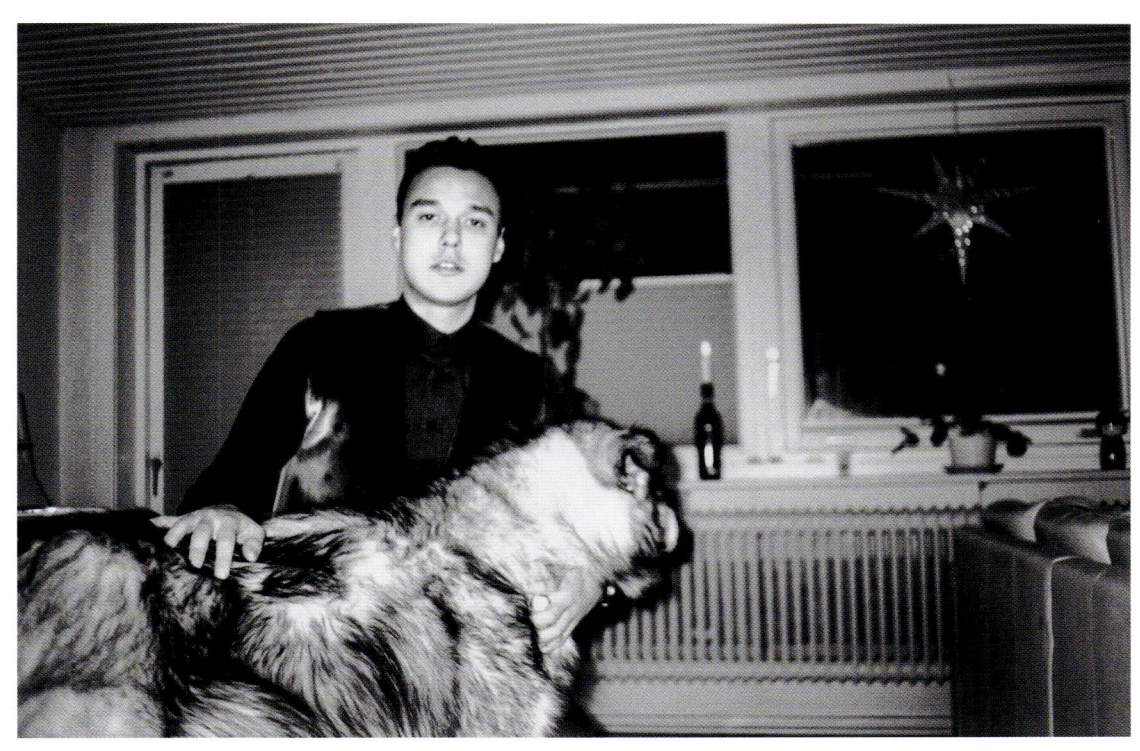

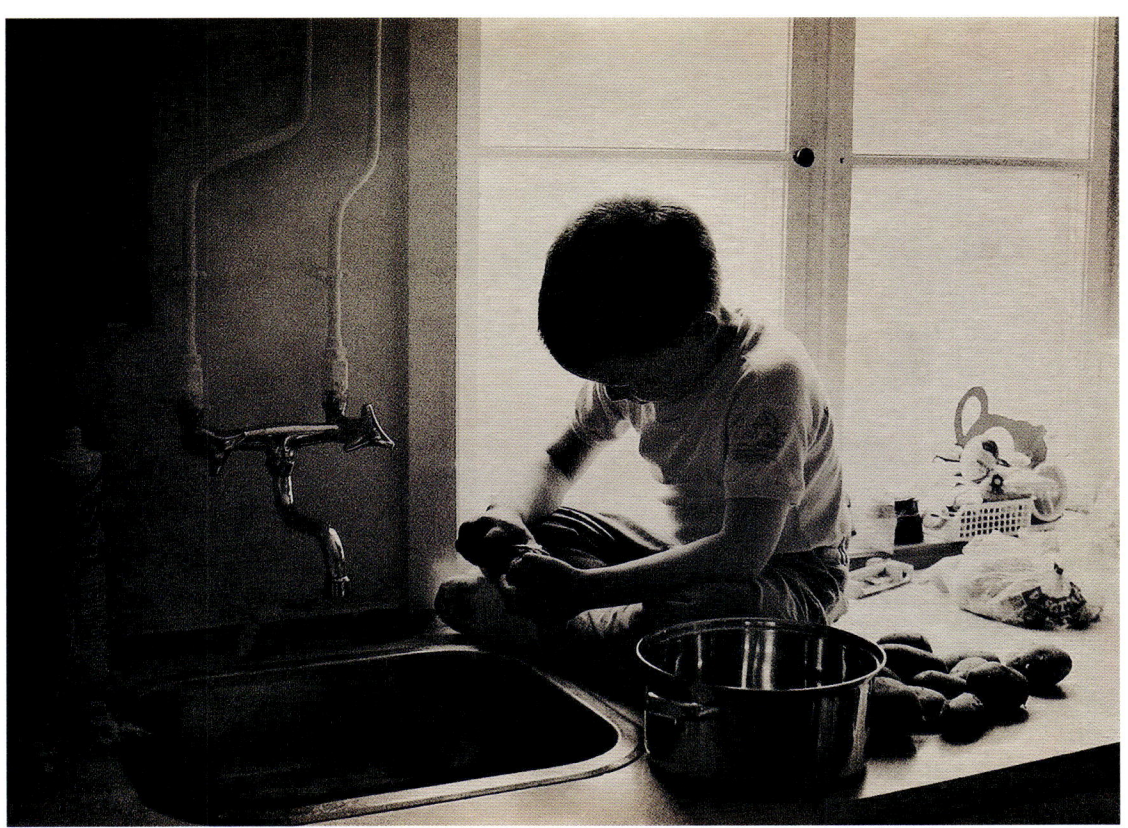

DAKOTA MACE

Diné
Naabeehó Diné Biyaad (Navajo Nation)
Albuquerque, New Mexico
United States

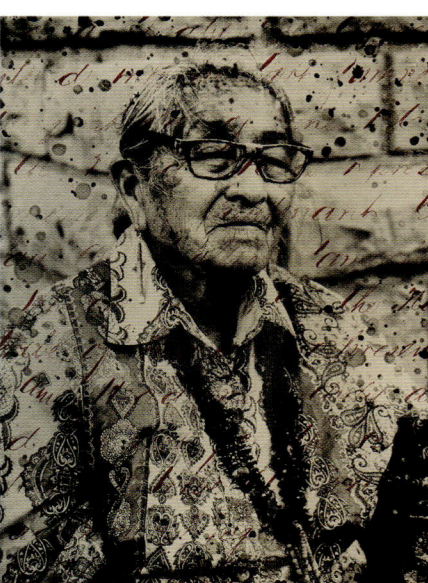 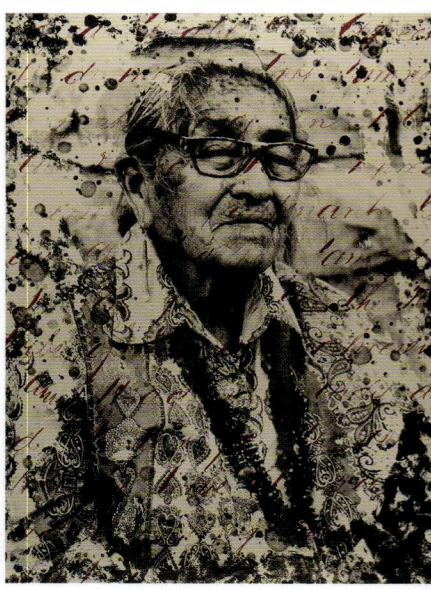

The Diné Elder featured in Dakota Mace's (b. 1991) lithograph series is Helen Nez. She is related to Mace through her maternal Clan, Redhouse, and lives in Blue Gap, Arizona, in the middle of the Naabeehó Diné Biyaad (Navajo Nation). Nez's portrait is superimposed over the first page of the Navajo Treaty of 1868, called the Naal Tsoos Saní, meaning "the Old Paper" in the Diné language. With each successive print, the image of Nez grows fainter until she almost vanishes, while the treaty text becomes more visible. The slow fade signifies "a reminder of how many of our elders' stories disappear once they are gone, especially the history that's within their words," explains Mace.[1] It also visually conveys that as U.S. policies steadily threatened the Diné way of life, Diné voices dimmed, until they were nearly eclipsed. The signing of the 1868 treaty at Bosque Redondo, also known as Fort Sumner, signaled a major shift in Diné life. "The Diné people lost their freedom and autonomy and came under the U.S. government's rule," says Mace. "Since the treaty, Diné history has been one of continuous efforts to preserve and reclaim their cultural identity and sovereignty."[2]

Nez was born in 1938 and grew up in Blue Gap, only half a mile from the Claim 28 uranium mine site, which was active in the 1950s and 1960s. When she was a young girl, the mining companies enlisted her to carry around a small device to detect uranium while she tended the sheep near her home. Diné people were regularly used by the mining companies to do this type of prospecting work. Wherever their devices found radiation, a stake was placed in the ground, determining the location of the mines. Living within such close proximity to Claim 28 has been devastating for Nez—she lost eight of her 11 children because of various kidney and lung illnesses due to the mines and uranium contamination. "Helen continues to persevere," says Mace. "She continues to be an advocate against mining…a true matriarch preserving her culture and homeland and protecting her family."[3]

Mace's Clan name, Redhouse, while powerful by way of naming and identifying her family lineage and ancestry, is also formidable by way of her art. Applied in her works frequently, the color red is a personal, familial, and dynamic choice that holds and communicates a multiplicity of meanings. "That's why you often see red in my work, because it's such a prominent color for myself family wise," clarifies Mace. "It's also a big color in terms of weaving and the medicine that we use to protect those that are traveling. There's a lot of intentional usage of that color."[4] In

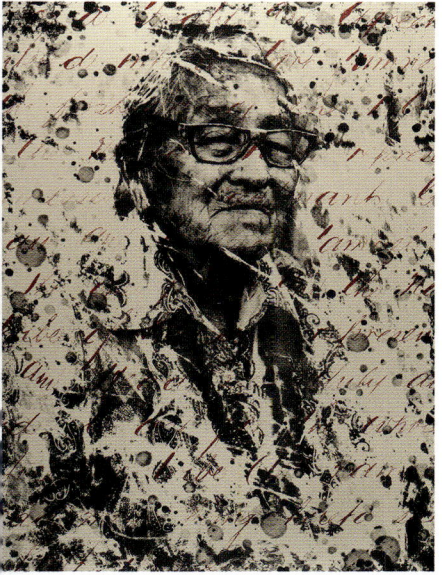
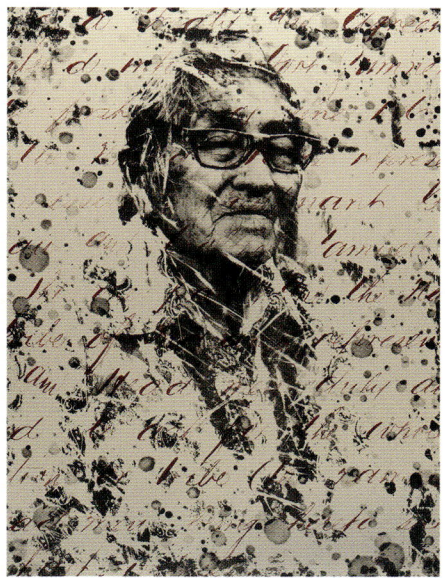
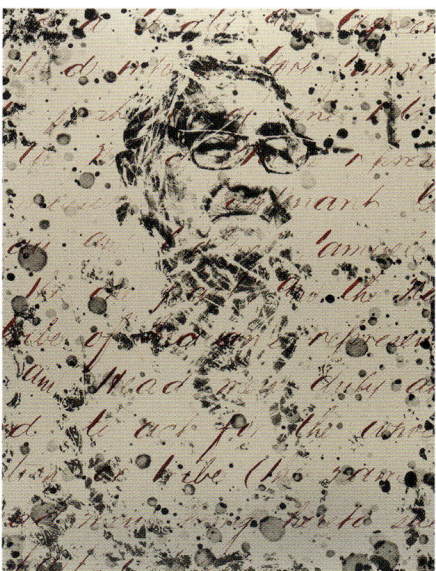

the series of Nez, the text from the Navajo treaty is scrawled in red ink.

Mace is a Diné interdisciplinary artist with a focus on translating the language of Diné history and beliefs. She received her MA and MFA degrees in photography and textile design from the University of Wisconsin–Madison, and a BFA in photography from the Institute of American Indian Arts. Her artistic practice includes alternative photography techniques, weaving, beadwork, and papermaking.

The idea for the photo lithographs featuring Nez arrived when Mace was working on a larger body of work called Dahodiyinii (Sacred Places), which retraces the stories and memories of her community and the land itself. Meeting with different Diné Elders and community members, she was deeply affected by their stories. Mace was interested in communicating the importance of the communities' relationship to the Diné Homelands and how events from the past continue to impact them today.

—Tiffany Midge

Helen Nez, 2022, from the series Naal Tsoos Saní (The Old Paper).

JOSUÉ RIVAS

Mexica, Otomi
Portland, Oregon
United States

Standing Rock, or the Dakota Access Pipeline movement #NoDAPL, began in the spring of 2016 in response to the construction of the Dakota Access Pipeline under Lake Oahe near the Standing Rock Sioux Reservation in North Dakota.

The movement drew considerable attention and sparked international dialogue about environmental protection and justice. For nearly a year, up to 10,000 people convened at a large encampment situated along the confluence of the Cannonball and Missouri Rivers on the reservation. The Water Protectors—the collective of individuals opposing the pipeline—peaceably faced off with militarized police in a series of actions aimed at impeding the pipeline's installation, bringing awareness of the potential contamination of the water supply, and serving as changemakers in the larger landscape of climate activism.

Photographer Josué Rivas (b. 1989) stayed at Standing Rock for six months, documenting the demonstrations and camp life, right up until the activists' eviction on February 22, 2017. Recalling the final day, he says, "I was experiencing the ending of something, but the beginning of something else. I started seeing a lot of grief, people burning their own tipis because they didn't want them to be taken. There was a lot of transformation happening."[1]

One photograph Rivas made at the Oceti Sakowin camp—the main camp at Standing Rock—encapsulates the intensity of those last hours. Foregrounded in the black-and-white image is a rapt man carrying an indiscernible sign; on the left is an upside-down American flag, a signal of distress. Dozens of Water Protectors bundled in hats and coats are gathered in the frame, many with raised fists. The horizon is marked with barren trees and tipis—one of which emanates plumes of black smoke skyward. The road in view is saturated with winter rain and melted snow. It is a formidable photograph that portrays a historic moment, the last day of one of the most significant environmental movements of our time.

Rivas shared that many of his choices when making images are based on intuition—that he doesn't *think* about creating photographs but instead goes by feel. With regard to the image of the Water Protectors, he acknowledges his instinct and what it could mean for generations ahead: "My intention being in front of the whole crowd was for them to remember, this is what you looked like as you were exiting and not being taken, not being defeated. This is what your pride of being here looks like. It had to be the layer of them and then the camp and then the forever. I had to see them—and not necessarily what they were leaving behind but what they planted."[2]

There were many things happening in the brief period before Rivas pressed the shutter for this iconic image. Just minutes before the 2:00 p.m. curfew imposed by law enforcement, the Water Protectors held a fire ceremony so that the camp's original fire could be kept aflame and transferred to another location on the reservation. "I remember seeing all these people cry around the fire," says Rivas. "It was this really interesting contrast of fire, the burning energy of transformation, and water—people's tears and people's emotion."[3]

Mexica and Otomi, Rivas describes himself as "an Indigenous Futurist, creative director, visual storyteller, and entrepreneur working at the intersection of art, technology, journalism, and decolonization." He explains his work "aims to challenge the mainstream narrative about Indigenous peoples, collaborate with the community, and serve as a means for transformation and collective healing."[4]

In documenting Standing Rock, Rivas, who is based in Portland, Oregon, arrived at a new understanding of his own practice, revising his purpose as a photographer. "I realized that you create spaces so that people can tell their own story," he says. "What was going through my mind was, this is for them. It belongs to them. This moment doesn't belong to me."[5]

—Tiffany Midge

People peacefully leave the Oceti Sakowin Camp, Cannon Ball, North Dakota, February 2017.

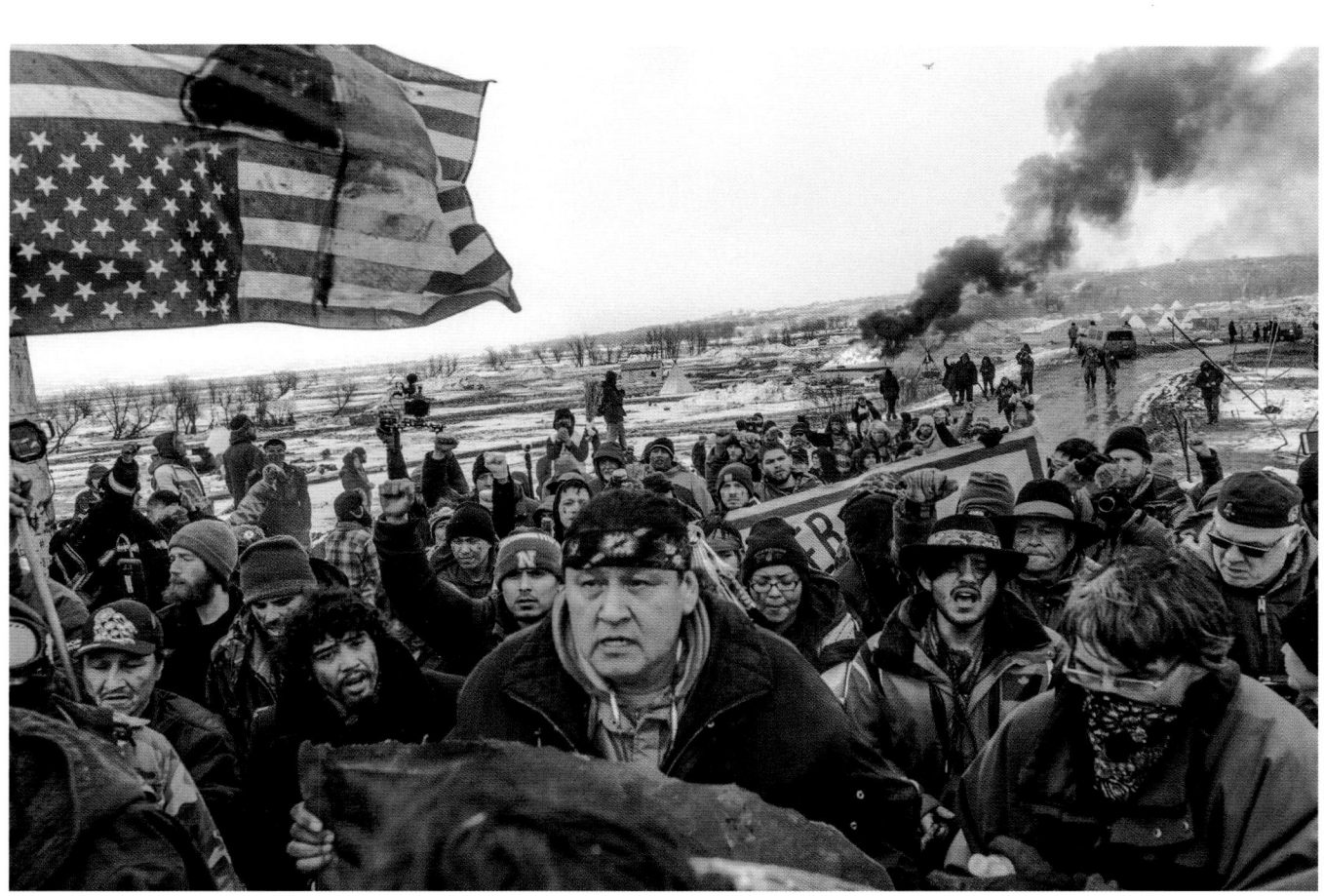

SARA ALIAGA TICONA

Aymara
La Paz
Bolivia

For decades Sara Aliaga Ticona's (b. 1989) father, an investigative photojournalist for the newspaper *El Diario*, covered social issues in Bolivia, including those affecting Indigenous communities. "I grew up seeing the world and my immediate surroundings through his photography," she says.[1]

Her father's visual and probative genes rubbed off on Ticona. Still living in the La Paz of her childhood, she uses her camera to portray Indigenous ways of life—such as those of her Aymara people—in intimate and complex ways.

In the series Water for everyone and for nobody, Ticona shares the Andean worldview of water, which cultivates a balanced and mutually beneficial relationship with the element. Unlike the popular notion that water is solely a resource, an inert liquid used for irrigation or consumption, for Ticona, and the Indigenous peoples she works with in the Andes, water is a "living being with feelings and reactions." This belief guides Ticona's empathetic relationship with water, a vital resource connecting humankind with all life on earth.

"However, in any type of interpersonal relationship, sometimes you have to argue to reach an agreement, to find harmony," says Ticona.

In the namesake image of Water for everyone and for nobody, Ticona represents an ancient Andean ritual carried out in La Paz when water manifested itself in destructive forms—hailstones or a deluge of rain. As the sky turned black and laden with clouds, guerreros (warriors) were sent to La Cumbre, a towering mountain pass where the Aymara have made offerings to Pachamama, or Mother Earth, since time immemorial. At La Cumbre, the guerreros pleaded and fought for days. They pierced the sky with ropes and rocks. They launched firecrackers into the portentous clouds, hoping to tame the angry embodiments of water.

The drama Ticona and her model survived to make the photograph is tangible within its frame. La Cumbre is the place where the climates of the Andes and the Amazon rainforest collide with tempestuous bursts of weather. "We almost died," recalls Ticona. Thick fog, fine hail, and frosty winds enveloped them. Ticona's camera was beginning to freeze, and the flash stopped working. Escaping on a motorcycle, they crashed into a ditch.

With a faceless figure silhouetted against a darkened sky, Ticona represents the legend of the guerreros and all those who still fulfill this honorable role within highland Andean communities throughout Bolivia. "Water floods the image—it's a sensation, it's fear, it's cold, and it's well-being," says Ticona. "In the end, we lived the experience of a guerrero."

—Samantha Reinders

Water for everyone and for nobody, March 24, 2022.

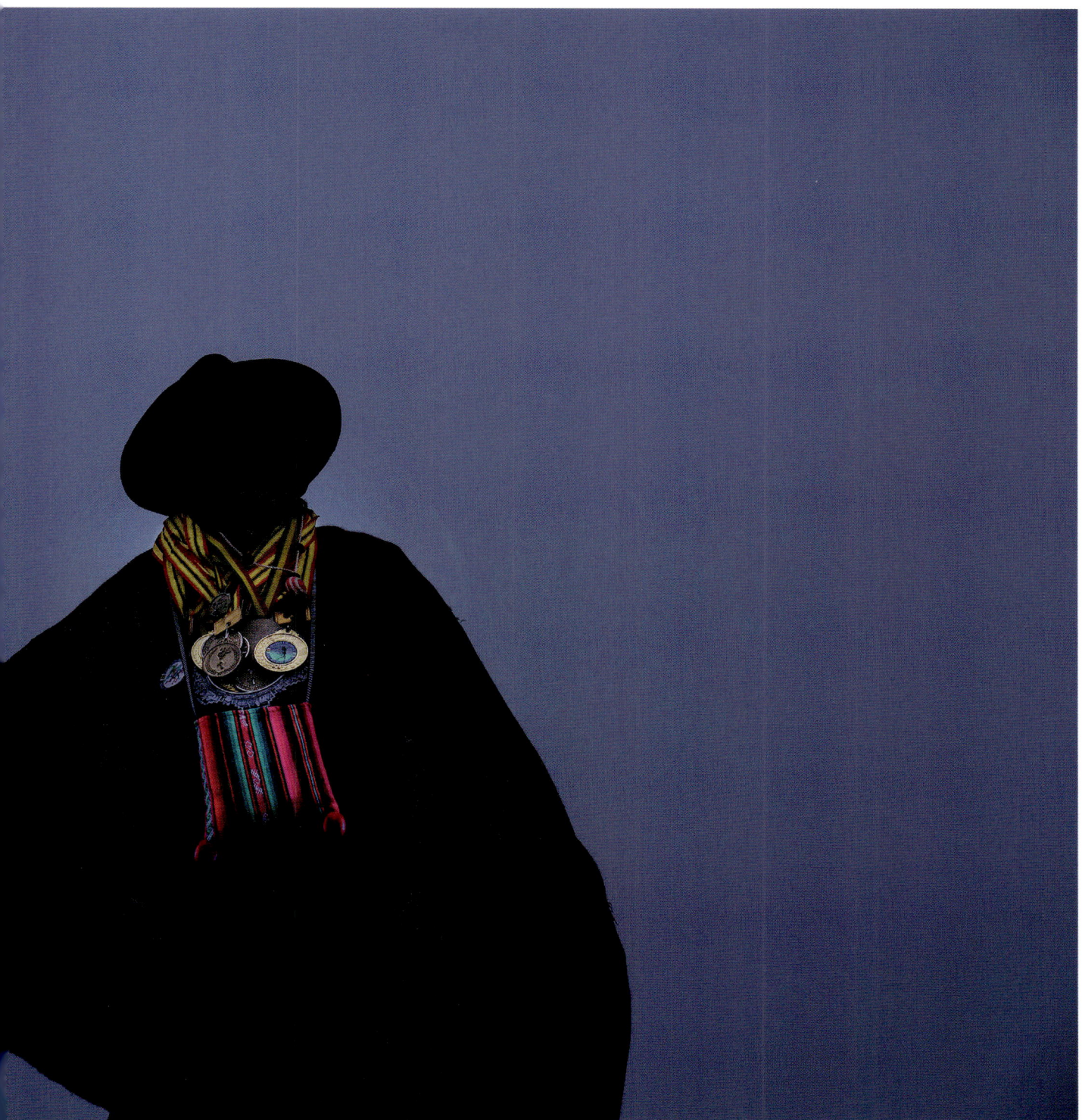

CITLALI FABIÁN

Yalalteca
Oaxaca
México

Thumbing through Citlali Fabián's (b. 1988) "My family album"—the documentary chapter of a larger body of work titled Ben'n Yalhalhj-Soy de Yalálag—the portrait of Melina Monserrat will stop you in your tracks.

Part of it is the simplicity of the composition, but it runs deeper than that. Monserrat, the young teen in the image, displays an arresting power mixed with vulnerability and a touch of shyness. She appears infinitely proud of herself and her people. Like photos in family albums the world over, this image holds much more than what it shows on the surface. It archives a memory, and a sense of place and belonging.

"For me, Melina's portrait is a beautiful summary of what it means to be Yalaltec," says Fabián. "Native cultures are often 'set' as something immutable, and I feel we have been denied the fact that we change. We are constantly influenced by, and connected to, the world. We have developed our identities beyond our 'territories.' Melina is a beautiful reflection of that to me, of our ambivalences."[1]

Fabián, who was raised in Oaxaca de Juárez, México, is of Yalaltec descent. Her work delves into the nuance of her heritage and the identity of her Yalaltec community—Zapotec people originally from Yalálag, a village in the Sierra Juárez Mountains, who now live throughout México and have strong ties to Los Angeles.

The portrait of Monserrat, who is Indigenous and Afro-Mexican, exemplifies Fabián's interest in the expansion of Yalaltec identity. Shaped by multiple backgrounds, "she signifies how rich and vibrant the culture is, and how everything is changing," says Fabián.[2]

From a young age, Fabián has been immersed in photography. The foundation of her practice was formed inside her father's photo shop, where she was surrounded by customers' vernacular images and experienced the magic that happens in a darkroom. "I remember helping develop photos, and I saw the relevance of photography in everyday life," she explains.[3]

Though Fabián's "family album" is not complete, she knows its final destination—her relatives and the Yalaltec diaspora, to help them remain united and forge new connections. She has described the series as a "universe of images," and that universe is limitless. "I'm looking at and for the essence of our identity, what connects us despite living in different latitudes," says Fabián.[4]

As more and more of Fabián's photos emerge from the chemicals of the darkroom—linking her with her father and formative youth—an important archive is built. The Yalaltec family album is getting thicker and thicker, pages heavy with contemporary memories. Indeed, after making the portrait of Monserrat, the two women learned Melina is Fabián's distant niece. "She looked like a cloud floating," remarks Fabián. "I was mesmerized by her."[5]

—Samantha Reinders

Melina Monserrat, Oaxaca de Juárez, México, June 2018.

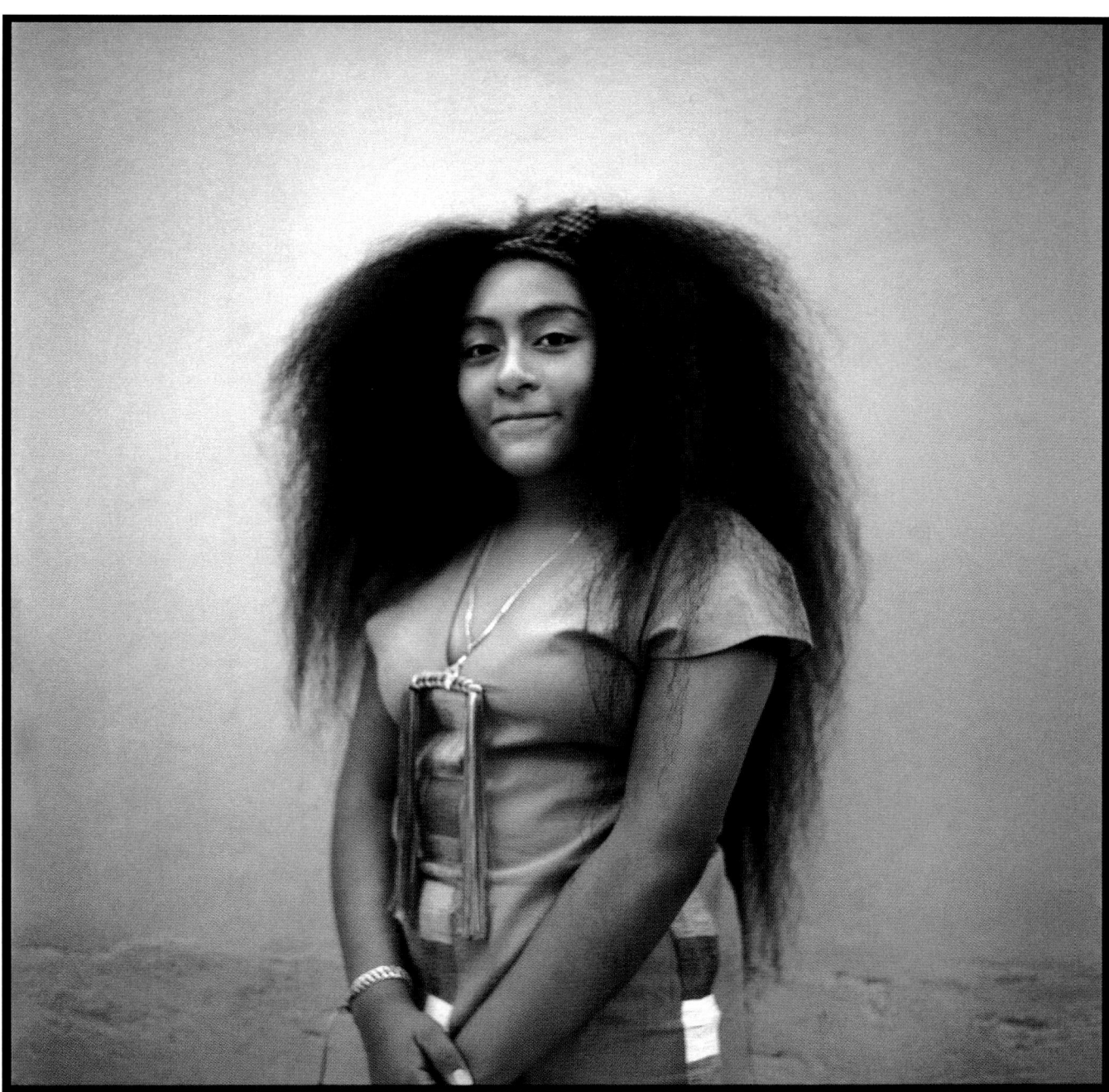

KAPULEIIKEALOONALANI FLORES

Kanaka Maoli
Moku o Keawe (Hawai'i Island)
United States

The history of photography in the Hawaiian Islands is abundant and scarcely researched, specifically that of the Native trailblazers of the medium. Unquestionably, when the islands' institutional and personal archives are duly mined, the knowledge of Native Hawaiians creating imagery in the first century of photography will broaden. From the mid-1900s forward, the record is stronger.

Kapuleiikealoonalani Flores (b. 2000), known as Kapulei, inherited the practice from her father. "When I was younger my dad was the one who always had a camera," she said. "Now I use photography to celebrate my culture…and advocate for a Hawai'i that is led by Native voices."[1]

Flores is known for her coverage of the Protect Mauna Kea Movement, a collective protecting Mauna Kea from further development and desecration, like the proposed Thirty Meter Telescope. Mauna Kea, a sacred volcano that is the highest mountain in the world from the sea floor up, is the piko (center) of Hawai'i. Since 2011, the year she turned 11, Flores and her family have organized, and participated in, many of the campaign's frontline actions. "When I say I have spent my whole life involved in the Protect Mauna Kea Movement, it's not an exaggeration," said Flores. "I can't remember a time before Mauna Kea."[2]

Flores's portfolio expands to maternity, traditional ceremonies, and Hawai'i's endemic flora and fauna. "These photos speak about our connection to our ancestors," said Flores about the scope of her work. "Showing Hawai'i through Native eyes is something I'm honored and grateful to be able to do."[3]

The first photographic process available to the public, the daguerreotype was introduced in 1839 and reached the Hawaiian Islands by May 1845. Among the maiden nobility to visit a local daguerreotypist was the reigning monarch, Kamehameha III, who was photographed with his wife and three children around 1853. Evidently, the experience left an impression on the monarch's son, Prince Lot Kapuāiwa.

He solicited a one-day apprenticeship from daguerreotypist Benajah Jay Antrim, likely in 1855.[4] It's unclear whether the prince, who ascended the throne as Kamehameha V, the last of the Hawaiian monarchs, worked behind the camera following his training.

John Kanipo'okalani Meek Jr. II is the first known professional Native Hawaiian photographer. He and his brother-in-law, Horace Crabbe, opened a studio in Honolulu in 1867. They advertised in *Ka Nupepa Kuokoa*, a Native-language daily paper—"We ask that you come down to our studio [since] we are local kids from Hawaii."[5] Two years later, in 1869, they auctioned their equipment and "hundreds of choice negatives."[6] Meek reportedly worked as a photographer until his death in 1879, at age 29 or 30. Except for one self-portrait, not a trace of the studio negatives or Meek's personal work has yet been identified.

By the 1890s, photographers were living throughout the Hawaiian Islands. Tens of thousands of their images from the 19th century to the present are awaiting study within Hawai'i's university, museum, library, and government collections. Countless more are with Native Hawaiian communities and families—like Flores's.

"Photography," said Flores, "is a way to take your power back and tell your story, your history, and your home from your perspective."[7] In one maternity photograph she made, a woman soaks in a bath of milky water. A pink bloom perches on her gravid belly, reminiscent of the many endemic flowers of Hawai'i. "Aloha 'āina: a love and connection to the land so strong you're willing to do anything to protect it, is the foundation of everything I do and who I am," she said, echoing the fierceness of those called to be guardians of lifeways—and lives.[8]

—Sarah Stacke

New Bloom, 2018.

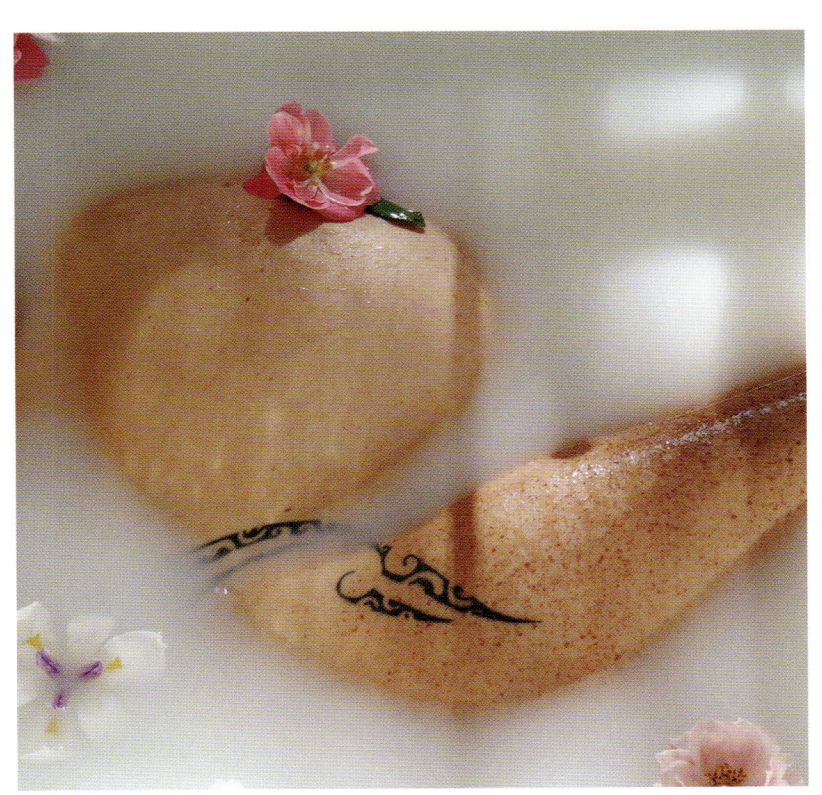

LUVIA LAZO

Zapotec
Teotitlán del Valle, Oaxaca
México

The Zapotec village of Teotitlán del Valle sits at the foothills of the Sierra Juárez Mountains in the state of Oaxaca, México. It's where photographer Luvia Lazo (b. 1990) was raised, and where she photographed Soledad Chavez on November 1, 2022—Día de los Muertos. The holiday, though cradled in death, is festive. In the image, Chavez holds a parcel of cempasúchil, or marigolds, as if inhaling their musky scent. The flowers' tangled roots descend from the clutch of her vein-laced hands—two givers of life mimicking each other. A red ribbon winds around Chavez's gray braids, and a chocolate-colored cloak hugs the curve of her back. The portrait —rich and peaceful—belies the sadness enveloping Lazo when she made it.

Less than two years before Lazo trained her camera on Chavez, her grandfather Domingo passed away. "Luvia," he said to her on the last day of his life, in their Zapotec language, "kanitlow"—I'm losing your face. In her grief, and with the realization that her grandfather's physical presence had transformed into memories, she felt the weight of the word grow.

Lazo began searching for fragments of her grandfather in the Elders of Teotitlán del Valle. She studied their hands and expressions, and the way they walked, carried baskets, or perched a hat on their head. She forged relationships, visiting the Elders in their homes and at the market. Then she photographed them.

The images have a formula. Lazo asks the person to turn away from the camera, or use whatever they happen to be holding to cover their face. This anonymity enables Lazo to invoke her grandfather and, more universally, share "the feeling of losing someone you love." But she concedes it's also an ethical decision. "When you're photographing people, you need to be really careful," she explained. "Are you the right person to show those faces?…Are those faces necessary to tell a story?"[1]

When the time arrived to name the project, it was clear: Kanitlow. This word means "everything" to me, Lazo said. It's about a "personal loss," my grandfather disappearing, but also the people in the portraits are disappearing, she added.[2]

Several of the Elders have died since Lazo photographed them, and she is keenly aware of the cultural history Kanitlow documents and examines. Playing with the arrangement of the images, she intentionally places photographs with traditional clothing next to those with more modern jeans or T-shirts. "Things vanish because everything undergoes transformations— life, but also cultures," she told writer Ana Karina Zatarain in the *New Yorker*.[3]

Marigolds are the iconic flower of Día de los Muertos. In the moment Soledad Chavez held the aureate bouquet before her, Lazo remembered a relative's words, spoken in the wake of her grandfather's death: "The destiny of all of us is that our faces are lost, and we disappear. Some of us will leave reminiscences of our being." The translation of *soledad* is "loneliness." "Here is a little bit of Soledad," said Lazo about the portrait's existence. "Soledad the name, not the loneliness of a hole in the stomach."[4]

—Sarah Stacke

Soledad Chavez, Teotitlán del Valle, México, November 1, 2022.

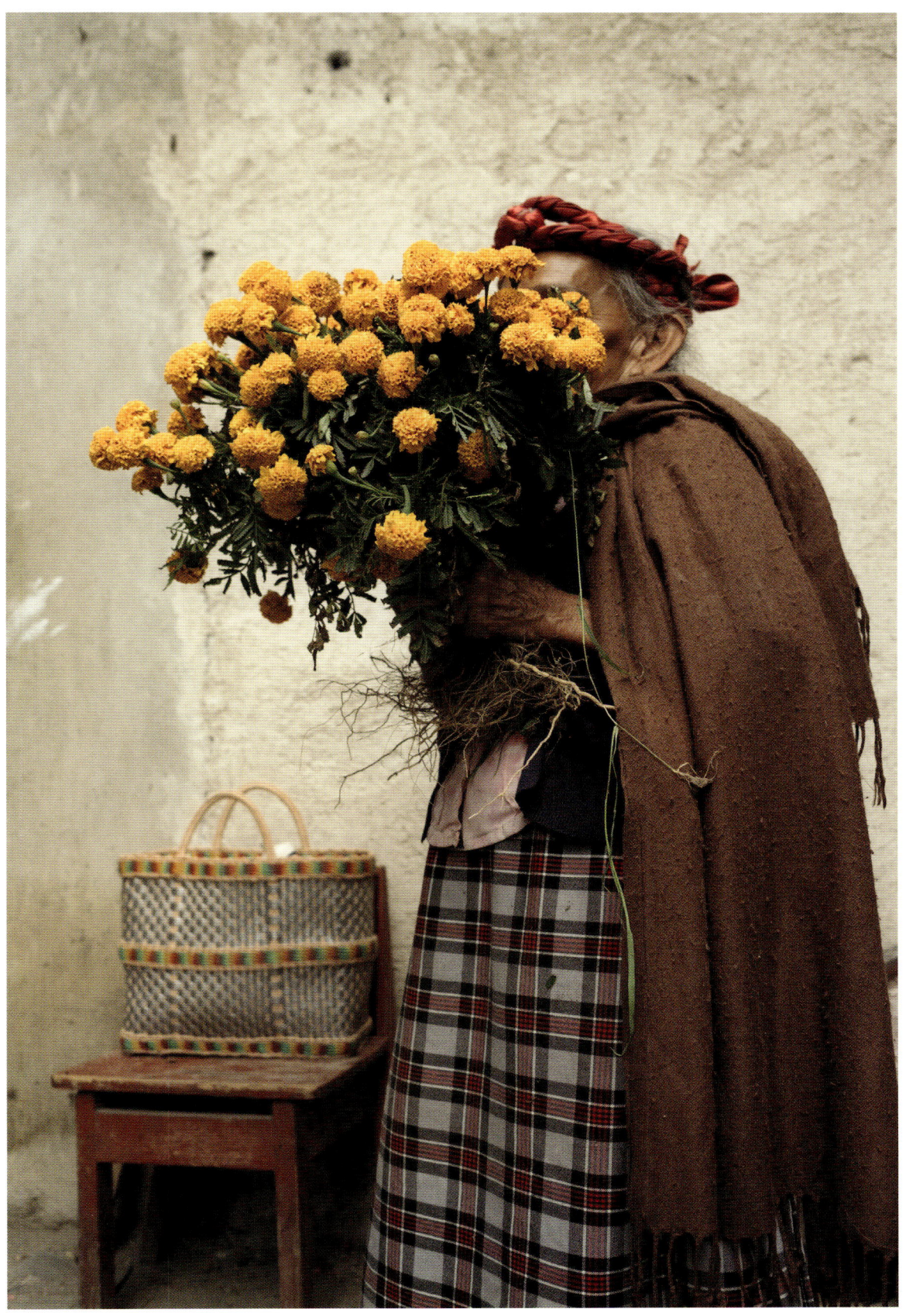

NĪA MACKNIGHT

Lakota, Anishinaabe, Scottish
Los Angeles, California
United States

Nīa MacKnight (b. 1989) combs through a steamer trunk of heirlooms that belonged to her Anishinaabe great-grandfather, John B. McGillis, whom she never met but who holds a place of eminence within her family. MacKnight, a visual storyteller and photographer, reassembles the archival items—family pictures, an eagle feather, newspaper clippings, letters, diaries—into photographic compositions that reveal a history informed by Indigenous ways of knowing, values, and lifeways.

In one of MacKnight's compositions, McGillis is wearing a handmade suit replete with large, exuberant butterflies and beaded flower blossoms; fringes detail the jacket hem, cuffs, and trouser legs. The outfit is paired with the U.S. Army cap he wore during his World War I service. MacKnight admires her great-grandfather's appearance, the way he dressed, and how he found joy in fashion. "Adorning ourselves is such a sacred art," says MacKnight. "We're holding space to celebrate our traditions. He's a style icon based on this photo."[1]

MacKnight can't pinpoint who might have made the beaded suit, whether it was a relative or McGillis's wife, but it's what he always wore for special occasions. The colorful garment reminds her of McGillis's way of life growing up in rural Minnesota, living a subsistence lifestyle. "In Anishinaabe culture, the floral motifs are central with how we express ourselves," explains MacKnight. "Integrating the emerald greens, deep maroons, and earth tones of woodlands environments is also a cultural statement."[2]

MacKnight's work aims to increase public awareness and deepen understanding of Native people and the ways they've contributed to American history. For her great-grandfather, the impact was significant. MacKnight's photographs document his military commitment; he served and fought in France during World War I. Later, he was employed with the U.S. Bureau of Indian Affairs, where he worked to provide opportunities for Native people.

McGillis left behind a vast assortment of artifacts from which his great-granddaughter was able to create timelines and narrative records, reconstructing the chapters of his life. She tells NPR, "I was confronted with the violence and trauma that my Great Grandfather experienced at the time as an Anishinaabe man forced to leave his ancestral homelands due to federal assimilation policies."[3] But among the brutal experiences of boarding school, war, and the challenges McGillis faced as a Native American within a rapidly changing world, the compositions MacKnight creates with his collection reflect a purposeful and well-lived life. "Folks like my Great Grandfather applied their Indigenous knowledge in a new way to carve out spaces for his people," says MacKnight. "His story ultimately conveys the creative tactics used by our ancestors for survival."[4]

MacKnight recalls how she and her mother would revisit the items from McGillis's trunk when the family came together for holiday dinners and gatherings. She says, "We turn to our ancestors' photographs to remind us of where we came from and why we're here today."[5] On the day she made the image of her great-grandfather in his bold suit, she and her mother, Sheridan MacKnight, felt compelled to bring it outside and see it in the light, next to the native plants growing untethered in their Los Angeles neighborhood, in what is also known as Toovangar. McGillis spent his final days nearby, before transitioning to the spirit world.

Against a backdrop of soft foliage, Sheridan holds the photograph of her grandfather in both palms, cradling a cherished Elder with reverence and care, while MacKnight invokes a modern keepsake with her camera. Like the three generations represented in the creation of the photograph, the composition bares three distinct layers. For MacKnight, chronicling one's life through photography and the making of art is an intergenerational calling, a meaningful expression of her family heritage that is both practical and celebratory.

—Tiffany Midge

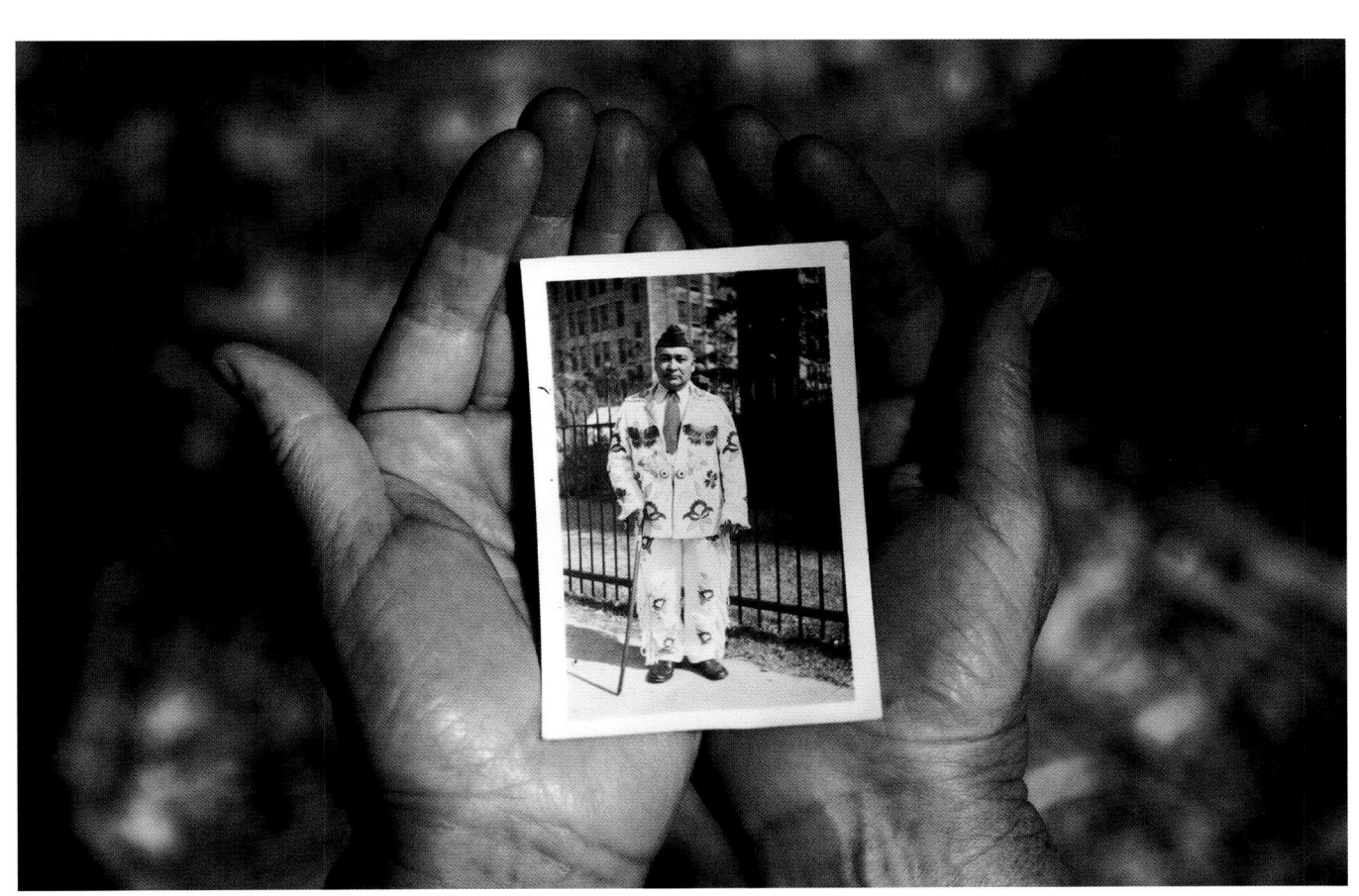

Conclusion

The extraordinary photographs of *In Light and Shadow: A Photographic History from Indigenous America* can be seen as sites of collective resistance, agency, translation, and cultural celebration. Diverse in chronology, geography, and style, all of them make the vibrant and complex experiences of Indigenous Americans visible.

There is much work left to be done. Alongside furthering the contributions of contemporary Indigenous photographers and lens-based artists, the archives are an unending source of visual narratives authored by Native people, teaching us as much about the past as what the future could be.

The photographs here whisper and roar; some are poems and others are prayers. They are contemplative, playful, and instructive. Many share rich inner lives and formative relationships with Homelands, or picture nourishing families and communities. Never static, each image and its maker directs our attention to the continuity of Indigenous knowledge and ways.

Acknowledgments

In Light and Shadow is a testament to the enduring legacy of photographs, and those who make them, across generations. Brian and I began talking about the idea that is now this book in 2019. We are humbled by the support we received to give it life.

Our utmost gratitude to the artists and descendants who generously and patiently fielded interviews, reviewed texts, and offered your time and expertise in numberless ways. The stories and perspectives you shared enriched this work beyond measure.

We are indebted to Bonnie Briant for going above and beyond and becoming a true partner in the creation of this book. Bonnie, your style and talent are tremendous.

Our deep appreciation to Magalí Druscovich, the Latin American coordinator for *In Light and Shadow*. You single-handedly extended these pages beyond North America and awed us with your abilities.

To the archivists and institutions who work tirelessly to preserve and make history available, this book (and so many more) would not be possible without you. Thank you for all that you do.

A gigantic thank you to contributing authors Tiffany Midge, Cinthya Santos Briones, Jennifer Fish, Sam Reinders, and Brenna Casey for your thoughtful and fastidious work.

Bethany Hughes, assistant professor of American Culture at the University of Michigan, thank you for coming on board as the sensitivity reader and for the insightful feedback you provided. Your careful review of the manuscript buoyed us.

In 2021, Brian and I were the recipients of the Howard Chapnick Grant, established by the W. Eugene Smith Memorial Fund. Without this support, *In Light and Shadow* would still be an idea. Our sincere thanks to Scott Thode and Elizabeth Krist.

A special note of thanks to Sheena Brings Plenty for your invaluable role in the establishment and development of the 400 Years Project; to Molly Woodward for your outstanding research; to John Edwin Mason for throwing a big curve ball into the draft of our introduction and conclusion and making them better, and to Jennifer and Brenna for your help fine-tuning these sections; to Larissa Grieves for your moving text; to Alice Gabriner for your photo editing expertise; to Mel Monsen for your wealth of McGlashan Monsen family history and your delightful messages; to Rosalyn LaPier for introducing us to Ella Mad Plume Yellow Wolf and your important anecdotes about her and Louie; to Beckie LaBillois and Colleen Gauvin for the information you provided about your incredible mother; to Ben Paul for stewarding your father's inspirational archive and sharing it with us; to Dustin Aguilar for making your father's archive available and for your tales about him; to Herbert Randall for inviting us into your home on Shinnecock Nation and the supremely enjoyable conversations; to Tom Jones for *everything* related to Horace Poolaw; to Stephen Ferry for connecting us with Amado Villafaña Chaparro and your help translating; to Carl Saytor for your unparalleled knowledge of historical cameras; to Jero Gonzales for putting us in contact with the Fototeca Andina; to Katie Humphries, Sterlin Harjo, Shari Huhndorf, and Natalia Arcos Salvo for your superb words; to Cecilia Figliuolo, archives specialist at the Still Picture Branch of the National Archives; to Erica Luke, executive director of the South County Historical Center; to Heather Hultman, senior photograph archivist at the Montana Historical Society; to Arlene Schmuland, head of Archives and Special Collections at the University of Alaska Anchorage; to Bobbi Rahder, museum director at the Stewart Indian School Cultural Center & Museum; to Carlota Duarte, founder of the Chiapas Photography Project; to Daisy Njoku, Anthropology Archives, National Museum of Natural History at Smithsonian Institution; to Krista McCracken, researcher/curator at Shingwauk Residential Schools Centre; to Black Dog & Leventhal, and to everyone else who contributed to *In Light and Shadow*.

Literary culture needs more Indigenous publishing houses, Indigenous editors, and Indigenous style guides. To those engaging with, investing in, and advocating for these realities, a heartfelt thank you.

Lastly, to Mary Stacke, for your keen and discerning eye, and to Bob Stacke, for your infectious curiosity, we are profoundly thankful. Dad, I miss you, and I wish you could have seen this book reach the shelves. To our partners and children, who experienced and nurtured the passage of this book in their own individual and steadfast ways, we are eternally grateful.

—Brian Adams and Sarah Stacke

Authors

Brian Adams (Iñupiaq) is an editorial and commercial photographer based in Anchorage, Alaska, specializing in environmental portraiture. His work has been featured in both national and international publications, and his work documenting Alaskan Native villages has been showcased in galleries across the United States and Europe. His most recent book, *I Am Inuit*, was published in December 2017. Brian is a board member of Indigevsion and a member of Diversify Photo.
www.baphotos.com
@brianadamsphotography

Sarah Stacke (Euro-American) is a photographer, author, and archival researcher based in Brooklyn, New York. Through projects created in dialogue with communities, she shares stories about relationships to the land and its histories to excavate under-considered pasts and better understand the present. Her work appears in *Harper's Magazine*, the *Nation*, NPR, the *New York Times*, the *Washington Post*, and *National Geographic*. Sarah holds an MA from Duke University, and she is a faculty member at the International Center of Photography (ICP), where she teaches courses about the use of archives in documentary work and the ways archives can shape collective memory, identity, and the future. *In Light and Shadow* is her fourth book.
www.sarahstacke.com
@sarah_stacke
@inlightandshadow_photohistory

Contributors

Designer **Bonnie Briant** has worked with institutions and publishers such as the Metropolitan Museum of Art, Bronx Documentary Center, Aperture, Damiani, Rizzoli, and David Zwirner Books. Her work has been recognized and honored numerous times by NPR and the Paris Photo–Aperture PhotoBook Awards, as well as other institutions. Some of her books have been named Book of the Year by POYi, Aperture Book Awards, and *Time* magazine.
www.bonniebriant.com
@bonniebriant

Cinthya Santos Briones is a visual artist, anthropologist, ethnohistorian, and cultural worker with Indigenous Nahua roots based in New York. Her work focuses on a multidisciplinary social practice that uses a variety of nonlinear storytelling mediums: photography, historical archives, writing, ethnography, drawings, collage, textiles, sculpture, and popular education. Cinthya holds an MFA in creative writing and photography from Ithaca-Cornell University and a certificate in Documentary Practice and Visual Journalism from the International Center of Photography (ICP).
www.cinthya-santosbriones.com
@cinthyasantosb

Brenna M. Casey, **PhD**, is an assistant professor of English at the University of Massachusetts Amherst, where she specializes in American literature and visual culture. Her previous writing has appeared in *Hyperallergic*, *Los Angeles Review of Books*, and the *New York Times*, among others.

Magalí Druscovich is a visual journalist and writer focusing on human rights, youth, and health issues, exploring trauma and resilience, specifically in Latin America. Magalí was born in 1992 in Buenos Aires and studied social communication sciences at the University of Buenos Aires and documentary photography at the International Center of Photography (ICP) in New York. Her work is published in numerous publications in Argentina and internationally. She is based in Buenos Aires.
www.magalidruscovich.com
@magalidruscovich

Jennifer Natalie Fish, **PhD**, is a professor of sociology at Old Dominion University. As a global social documentarian, she focuses on the relationship between visual and narrative stories, with an emphasis on migrant workers and Elder women's social activism. Jennifer has written five books and produced four documentary films. Her photography has been featured in the *New York Times*, *Toronto Star*, and the collections of several organizations including Human Rights Watch and the United Nations.
www.jennifernataliefish.com

Tiffany Midge is a citizen of the Standing Rock Sioux Nation and a columnist for *High Country News*. She has written reviews and profiles for *World Literature Today*, the *New Yorker*, the *Brooklyn Rail*, *First American Art Magazine*, *Indian Country Today*, and more. She is the author of *Bury My Heart at Chuck E. Cheese's* and *The Dreamcatcher in the Wry*.

Samantha Reinders is an African visual journalist, dividing her time between Cape Town and Kathmandu. She has an MA from Ohio University and is trusted by editorial, NGO, and corporate clients across the globe. She is inspired by and pursuing stories about our relation to, and impact on, the landscape we inhabit as well as notions of home, belonging, and memory. Along with her Canon, she packs empathy in her camera bag.
www.samreinders.com
@samreinders

Image Credits

Notes

INTRODUCTION

[1] *Visual sovereignty* is a term brought forth by Dr. Jolene Rickard (Skarù:ręˀ / Tuscarora), an artist, curator, and visual historian. She is an associate professor at Cornell University in the departments of History of Art and Art, and the former director of the American Indian and Indigenous Studies Program (2008–20).

[2] *Our People, Our Land, Our Images: International Indigenous Photographers* (2006), edited by Hulleah J. Tsinhnahjinnie (Taskigi, Diné), an artist and director of the Gorman Museum of Native American Art, and Veronica Passalacqua, a writer and curator at the Gorman Museum, is one of the earliest books (along with the related exhibition) to present images and artist voices from the global Indigenous community. A PDF is available at https://gormanmuseum.ucdavis .edu/shop-item/our-people-our-land-our-images-international -indigenous-photographers.

[3] *Sandwich Islands News*, February 3, 1847, 1. Quoted in Lynn Davis, *Na Pa'i Ki'i, The Photographers in the Hawaiian Islands, 1845–1900* (Honolulu: Bishop Museum Press, 1980), 13.

[4] Jolene Rickard, "Holding Ground as Nation," in *Speaking with Light: Contemporary Indigenous Photography*, eds. John Rohrbach and Will Wilson (Santa Fe: Radius, 2022), 160.

JENNIE FIELDS ROSS COBB

[1] Jon May, email exchange with Sarah Stacke, April 2023.

[2] Joan M. Jensen, "Native American Women Photographers as Storytellers," Women American Artists of the American West, https://web.archive.org/web/20050705084300/http ://www.cla.purdue.edu/WAAW/Jensen/NAW.html.

[3] Karen Shade-Lanier, "Lasting Impressions: Jennie Ross Cobb, First Female American Indian Photographer, Framed Cherokee Life in Indian Territory," *American Indian* 23, no. 3 (Fall 2022), https://www.americanindianmagazine.org/story /Photographer-Jennie-Ross-Cobb.

[4] Karen Shade-Lanier, "Lasting Impressions: Jennie Ross Cobb, First Female American Indian Photographer, Framed Cherokee Life in Indian Territory," *American Indian* 23, no. 3 (Fall 2022), https://www.americanindianmagazine.org/story /Photographer-Jennie-Ross-Cobb.

[5] "The Life and Legacy of Native Photographer Jennie Ross Cobb," *PBS News Weekend*, PBS, March 26, 2023.

[6] Nicole Dawn Strathman, *Through a Native Lens: American Indian Photography* (Norman: University of Oklahoma Press, 2020), 123.

[7] Nicole Dawn Strathman, *Through a Native Lens: American Indian Photography* (Norman: University of Oklahoma Press, 2020), 123.

[8] Nicole Dawn Strathman, *Through a Native Lens: American Indian Photography* (Norman: University of Oklahoma Press, 2020), 141.

RICHARD ALBERT THROSSEL

[1] Wendy Red Star, "People of the Earth: Wendy Red Star in Conversation with Emily Moazami," *Aperture* 240 (Fall 2020), 29, 30.

[2] Richard Throssel, "Personal," Richard Throssel Papers (2394_56_3), American Heritage Center, University of Wyoming. **Author's note:** Throssel is often identified as Métis. He was the grandson of Red River Métis who emigrated from Canada to the United States in 1841. Before moving to Montana, Throssel was raised in a community of Red River descendants in Washington State. Throssel's known ancestors were Cree, English, and Scottish, though he referred to his ancestry as Cree and French Canadian.

[3] "Famous Delineator of Life Among the Indians," *Billings Gazette* (Montana), July 2, 1911, 6, https://www.newspapers.com /image/415391510.

[4] Richard Throssel, "Personal," Richard Throssel Papers (2394_56_3), American Heritage Center, University of Wyoming.

[5] Lucy R. Lippard, "Introduction," in *Partial Recall: With Essays on Photographs of Native North Americans*, ed. Lucy R. Lippard (New York: New Press, 1992), 25.

[6] Lucy R. Lippard, "Introduction," in *Partial Recall: With Essays on Photographs of Native North Americans*, ed. Lucy R. Lippard (New York: New Press, 1992), 23.

[7] "Pictures by Richard Throssel," *Yellowstone News* (Billings, MT), February 4, 1954, 14, https://www.newspapers.com/image/954309435.

[8] Richard Throssel, Richard Throssel Papers (2394_56_3), American Heritage Center, University of Wyoming.

[9] Richard Throssel, "Personal," Richard Throssel Papers (2394_56_3), American Heritage Center, University of Wyoming.

[10] Rebecca S. Wingo, "Picturing Indian Health: Dr. Ferdinand Shoemaker's Traveling Photographs from the Crow Reservation, 1910–1918," *Montana: The Magazine of Western History* 66, no. 4 (2016), 26, http://www.jstor.org/stable/26322777.

[11] Richard Throssel, "Personal," Richard Throssel Papers (2394_56_3), American Heritage Center, University of Wyoming.

[12] Richard Throssel, "Personal," Richard Throssel Papers (2394_56_3), American Heritage Center, University of Wyoming.

BENJAMIN ALFRED HALDANE AND HENRY S. HALDANE

[1] Mique'l Icesis Askren, "From Negative to Positive: B. A. Haldane, Nineteenth Century Tsimshian Photographer," Open Collections, University of British Columbia (2006), 51, https://dx.doi.org /10.14288/1.0092671.

[2] Mique'l Icesis Dangeli, "B. A. Haldane: Inspiring Resurgence Through Images of Resistance," in *In Our Hands: Native Photography, 1890 to Now*, eds. Jill Ahlberg Yohe, Jaida Grey Eagle, and Casey Riley (Minneapolis: Minneapolis Institute of Art, 2023), 77.

[3] Mique'l Askren, "Memories of Glass and Fire," in *Visual Currencies: Reflections on Native Photography*, eds. Henrietta Lidchi and Hulleah J. Tsinhnahjinnie (Edinburgh: Museum of Scotland Publishing, 2009), 90–107.

4 Year: 1900; Census Place: Metlakatla, Southern Supervisors District, Alaska; Roll: 1830; Page: 10; Enumeration District: 0001. Alaska State Archives; Juneau, Alaska; Description: Marriage License Docket, 1917–1925; Reference Number: VS 1270. The National Archives at Washington, D.C.; Washington, D.C.; Passenger & Crew Lists of Vessels Arriving at Ketchikan, Alaska.; Record Group Title: Records of the Immigration and Naturalization Service, 1787–2004; Record Group Number: 85.

5 Mique'l Icesis Askren, "From Negative to Positive: B. A. Haldane, Nineteenth Century Tsimshian Photographer," Open Collections, University of British Columbia (2006), 7, https://dx.doi .org/10.14288/1.0092671.

6 Mique'l Icesis Dangeli, "B. A. Haldane: Inspiring Resurgence Through Images of Resistance," in *In Our Hands: Native Photography, 1890 to Now*, eds. Jill Ahlberg Yohe, Jaida Grey Eagle, and Casey Riley (Minneapolis: Minneapolis Institute of Art, 2023), 75.

7 Mique'l Icesis Askren, "From Negative to Positive: B. A. Haldane, Nineteenth Century Tsimshian Photographer," Open Collections, University of British Columbia (2006), 35, https ://dx.doi.org/10.14288/1.0092671.

8 Mique'l Icesis Askren, "From Negative to Positive: B. A. Haldane, Nineteenth Century Tsimshian Photographer," Open Collections, University of British Columbia (2006), 10, https://dx.doi.org/10.14288/1.0092671.

GEORGE HUNT

1 Judith Berman, "Hunt, George (X̱awe, 'Maxwₐlagalis, K̲'ix̲itasu, and Noł̲q'oł̲ala)," in *Dictionary of Canadian Biography* 16, University of Toronto/Université Laval, http://www.biographi.ca/en/bio /hunt_george_16E.html.

2 Margaret M. Bruchac, "My Sisters Will Not Speak: Boas, Hunt, and the Ethnographic Silencing of First Nations Women," *Curator: The Museum Journal* 57, no. 2 (April 2014), 151, https://doi.org/10.1111/cura.12058.

3 Nicole Dawn Strathman, *Through a Native Lens: American Indian Photography* (Norman: University of Oklahoma Press, 2020), 59.

4 Nicole Dawn Strathman, *Through a Native Lens: American Indian Photography* (Norman: University of Oklahoma Press, 2020), 58.

5 Margaret M. Bruchac, "My Sisters Will Not Speak: Boas, Hunt, and the Ethnographic Silencing of First Nations Women," *Curator: The Museum Journal* 57, no. 2 (April 2014), 157, https://doi.org/10.1111/cura.12058.

6 Brian Carpenter, "CNAIR Stories: The Kwakwaka'wakw Manuscripts of George Hunt," American Philosophical Society blog, May 1, 2018, www.amphilsoc.org/blog /cnair-stories-kwakwakawakw-manuscripts-george-hunt.

STOOWUKHÁA (ASTUTE ONE) / LOUIS V. SHOTRIDGE

1 Maureen Elizabeth Milburn, "The Politics of Possession: Louis Shotridge and the Tlingit Collections of the University of Pennsylvania Museum," Open Collections, University of British Columbia (1997), 324, https://dx.doi.org/10.14288/1.0088254.

2 Nora Marks Dauenhauer and Dr. Richard Dauenhauer, quoted in Maureen Elizabeth Milburn, "The Politics of Possession: Louis Shotridge and the Tlingit Collections of the University of Pennsylvania Museum," Open Collections, University of British Columbia (1997), 324, https://dx.doi.org/10.14288/1.0088254.

JOHN NAPOLEON BRINTON HEWITT

1 Kirstin Olsen, *Chronology of Women's History* (Westport, CT: Greenwood Press, 1994), 153.

2 "Dr. J. N. B. Hewitt, An Ethnologist, 77," obituary, *New York Times*, October 20, 1937, 23.

3 Elisabeth Tooker and Barbara Graymont, "J. N. B. Hewitt," *Histories of Anthropology Annual* 3 (Lincoln: University of Nebraska Press, 2007), 72, https://dx.doi.org/10.1353/haa.0.0036.

4 Joseph Bruchac, "J. N. B. Hewitt: A Voice from the Sixth Nation," *Journal of New York Folklore* 43, no. 1–2 (2017), 22.

5 Photo Lot 155, J. N. B. Hewitt Photographs of Iroquois Indians on the Six Nations Reservation, National Anthropological Archives, Smithsonian Institution, Item 4596.6 and Item I.14.

6 Gina Rappaport and Eden Orelove, "Collection Overview," *J. N. B. Hewitt Photographs of Iroquois Indians on the Six Nations Reservation, circa 1897–circa 1937* (Suitland, MD: National Anthropological Archives, 2016).

7 John R. Swanton, "John Napoleon Brinton Hewitt," *American Anthropologist* 40, no. 2 (April 1938), 289, 287, https://doi.org/10.1525/aa.1938.40.2.02a00090.

8 Elizabeth Tooker and Barbara Graymont, "J. N. B. Hewitt," *Histories of Anthropology Annual* 3 (Lincoln: University of Nebraska Press, 2007), 72, https://doi.org/10.1353 /haa.0.0036.

ROBERT GEORGE BEAULIEU

1 Alan R. Woolworth, Research Notebooks on Minnesota Photography and Photographers, 1988–95, vol. 6, The Clement Hudon Beaulieu Family, manuscripts collection, Minnesota Historical Society, www2.mnhs.org/library/ findaids/00339a.xml.

2 Alan R. Woolworth, Research Notebooks on Minnesota Photography and Photographers, 1988–95, vol. 6, The Clement Hudon Beaulieu Family, manuscripts collection, Minnesota Historical Society, www2.mnhs.org/library/findaids/00339a.xml.

3 Alan R. Woolworth, Research Notebooks on Minnesota Photography and Photographers, 1988–95, vol. 6, The Clement Hudon Beaulieu Family, manuscripts collection, Minnesota Historical Society, www2.mnhs.org/library/findaids/00339a.xml.

4 Year: 1920; Census Place: White Earth, Becker, Minnesota; Roll: T625_823; Page: 9B; Enumeration District: 20.

5 Anton Treuer, *The Assassination of Hole in the Day* (Minneapolis: Minnesota Historical Society Press, 2011), Kindle edition, epilogue.

[6] Alan R. Woolworth, Research Notebooks on Minnesota Photography and Photographers, 1988–95, vol. 6, The Clement Hudon Beaulieu Family, manuscripts collection, Minnesota Historical Society, www2.mnhs.org/library/findaids/00339a.xml.

MARTHA MCGLASHAN MONSEN

[1] Mel Monsen Jr., Martha McGlashan Monsen's grandson, estimates that 70 percent of the photographs in the collection were made by his grandmother or her camera, and the others collected.

[2] Mel Monsen Jr., interviews with Sarah Stacke, 2023–24.

[3] Zenia Stepetin (née Monsen) was born on Akutan Island in 1912.

[4] Mel Monsen, Facebook, April 20, 2023, https://www.facebook.com/mel.monsen.

[5] Mel Monsen, "Excerpts from Jasper Sayre's diary, a copy of which is in Katmai National P&P museum collection," Facebook, August 19, 2021, https://www.facebook.com/mel.monsen.

[6] McGlashan and Monsen family photographs, Archives and Special Collections, Consortium Library, University of Alaska Anchorage.

CUSCO SCHOOL OF PHOTOGRAPHY

[1] Jorge Coronado, *Portraits in the Andes: Photography and Agency 1900–1950* (Pittsburgh: University of Pittsburgh Press, 2018).

[2] Deborah Poole, "Figueroa Aznar and the Cusco Indigenistas: Photography and Modernism in Early Twentieth-Century Peru," *Representations* 38 (Spring 1992), 52.

[3] Albert Giesecke, quoted in Andrés Garay Albújar, ed., *Cusco revelado: Fotografías de Max T. Vargas, Max Uhley y Martín Chambi* (Berlin: Instituto Iberoamericano de Berlin, 2017), 133. Translation by Brenna M. Casey.

MARTÍN CHAMBI AND FAMILY

[1] Manuel Chambi, "Martín Chambi: Artesano de la luz," *Tierradentro (Arte, Ideologia, Realidad)* no. 4 (1987), 7. Quoted in Andres Garay Albújar, ed., *Cusco revelado: Fotografías de Max T. Vargas, Max Uhley, Martín Chambi* (Berlin: Instituto Iberoamericano de Berlin, 2017).

[2] Quoted in Andres Garay Albújar, ed., *Cusco revelado: Fotografías de Max T. Vargas, Max Uhley, Martín Chambi* (Berlin: Instituto Iberoamericano de Berlin, 2017), 135. Translation by Brenna M. Casey.

[3] Peruska Chambi, interview with Magalí Druscovich, May 10, 2023. Translation by Brenna M. Casey.

NETTIE ODLETY AND LUCY SAUMTY

[1] Nicole Dawn Strathman, *Through a Native Lens: American Indian Photography* (Norman: University of Oklahoma Press, 2020), 116.

[2] Nicole Dawn Strathman, *Through a Native Lens: American Indian Photography* (Norman: University of Oklahoma Press, 2020), 118.

[3] Mary J. Silva, "Nettie 'Cah-Gook' Odlety, Kaulay Family Tree," Ancestry.com, https://www.ancestry.com/family-tree/person/tree/58090911/person/170093186660/story.

[4] Wall text for a photograph of Nettie Odlety by Lucy Saumty, *In Our Hands: Native Photography, 1890 to Now*, exhibit at Minneapolis Institute of Art, October 22, 2023–January 14, 2024.

[5] "Final Rites for Pioneer Citizen: Funeral Services Are Held for Bessie Saumty Kickingbird on Friday Afternoon," *Mountain View Times* (Oklahoma), May 22, 1941, 1.

[6] Indian Census Rolls, 1885–1940 (database online), Lehi, UT, USA, Ancestry.com, 2007. Original data: "Indian Census Rolls, 1885–1940," National Archives Microfilm Publication M595, 692 rolls, NAID: 595276, Records of the Bureau of Indian Affairs, Record Group 75, National Archives, Washington, D.C.

[7] Andrew McKenzie, Daniel Harbour, and Laurel J. Watkins, "The Life of Satanta: Told at a Roundtable of the Kiowa Culture Program," *International Journal of American Linguistics* 88, no. S1 (April 2022), S93.

YISÀUM (TWICE LOOKED AT) / PARKER PAUL MCKENZIE

[1] Parker P. McKenzie and William C. Meadows, "The Parker P. McKenzie Kiowa Orthography: How Written Kiowa Came Into Being," *Plains Anthropologist* 46, no. 177 (2001), 238.

[2] Parker P. McKenzie and William C. Meadows, "The Parker P. McKenzie Kiowa Orthography: How Written Kiowa Came Into Being," *Plains Anthropologist* 46, no. 177 (2001), 238.

[3] Nicole Dawn Strathman, *Through a Native Lens: American Indian Photography* (Norman, University of Oklahoma Press, 2020), 110.

[4] Daniel Harbour and Laurel J. Watkins, "The Linguistic Genius of Parker McKenzie's Kiowa Alphabet," *International Journal of American Linguistics* 76, no. 3 (2010), 309–333. Parker P. McKenzie and William C. Meadows, "The Parker P. McKenzie Kiowa Orthography: How Written Kiowa Came Into Being," *Plains Anthropologist* 46, no. 177 (2001), 233–48.

[5] Diacritical marks were added by hand before computer keyboards supplied them.

[6] Daniel Harbour and Laurel J. Watkins, "The Linguistic Genius of Parker McKenzie's Kiowa Alphabet," *International Journal of American Linguistics* 76, no. 3 (2010), 331.

[7] Before his death, Parker McKenzie donated their full photographic collection, approximately 330 photographs, with explanatory notes on each image, to the Oklahoma Historical Society.

KAASH KLAÕ / GEORGE JOHNSTON AND FREDDIE JOHNSTON

[1] All quotes in this section are from *Picturing a People: George Johnston, Tlingit Photographer*, directed by Carol Geddes (1998; Montreal: National Film Board of Canada) www.nfb.ca/film/picturing_a_people_george_johnston/.

PETER PITSEOLAK AND AGGEOK PITSEOLAK

[1] Amy Adams, "Arctic and Inuit Photography. Part Two: Through the Looking-Glass: The Photographs of Robert J. Flaherty and Peter Pitseolak," *Inuit Art Quarterly* 15, no. 3 (Fall 2000), 18.

[2] Dorothy Harley Eber, "Peter Pitseolak and the Photographic Template," in *Imaging the Arctic* (Seattle: University of Washington Press, 1998), 57.

[3] Peter Pitseolak, Dorothy Harley Eber, and Ann Hanson, *People from Our Side: A Life Story with Photographs and Oral Biography* (Montreal: McGill–Queen's University Press, 1993), 148.

FÀ:BÒ (AMERICAN HORSE) / HORACE MONROE POOLAW

[1] Laura E. Smith, *Horace Poolaw, Photographer of American Indian Modernity* (Lincoln: University of Nebraska Press, 2016), xiv.

[2] Martha A. Sandweiss, "Family Pictures, Family Stories," in *For a Love of His People: The Photography of Horace Poolaw*, ed. Nancy Marie Mithlo (Washington, D.C.: National Museum of the American Indian, 2014), 16.

[3] Linda Poolaw, "For a Love of His People," in *For a Love of His People: The Photography of Horace Poolaw*, ed. Nancy Marie Mithlo (Washington, D.C.: National Museum of the American Indian, 2014), 40.

[4] Rebecca Bengal, "To Walk in Both Worlds," *Aperture* 240 (Fall 2020), 37.

[5] Tom Jones, "A Poolaw Photo, Pictures by an Indian," in *In Our Hands: Native Photography, 1890 to Now*, eds. Jill Ahlberg Yohe, Jaida Grey Eagle, and Casey Riley (Minneapolis: Minneapolis Institute of Art, 2023), 113.

[6] Rebecca Bengal, "To Walk in Both Worlds," *Aperture* 240 (Fall 2020), 40.

[7] David W. Penney, "Why Horace Poolaw's Indians Won't Vanish," in *For a Love of His People: The Photography of Horace Poolaw*, ed. Nancy Marie Mithlo (Washington, D.C.: National Museum of the American Indian, 2014), 61.

[8] Thomas Poolaw, "Horace Poolaw: Photographer, Mentor, Grandfather," *Great Plains Quarterly* 31, no. 2 (Spring 2011), 148.

JAMES "JIM" PATRICK BRADY

[1] Sherry Farrell Racette, "'Enclosing Some Snapshots': James Patrick Brady, Photography, and Political Activism," *History of Photography* 42, no. 3 (July 2018), 280, https://doi.org/10.1080/03087298.2018.1519938.

[2] Sherry Farrell Racette, "'Enclosing Some Snapshots': James Patrick Brady, Photography, and Political Activism," *History of Photography* 42, no. 3 (July 2018), 286, https://doi.org/10.1080/03087298.2018.1519938.

[3] Sherry Farrell Racette, "'Enclosing Some Snapshots': James Patrick Brady, Photography, and Political Activism," *History of Photography* 42, no. 3 (July 2018), 272, https://doi.org/10.1080/03087298.2018.1519938.

[4] Murray Dobbin, *The One-and-a-Half Men: The Story of Jim Brady and Malcolm Norris, Metis Patriots of the 20th Century* (Vancouver: New Star Books, 1981).

ELLA MAD PLUME YELLOW WOLF

[1] Rosalyn LaPier, "Ella Mad Plume Yellow Wolf: Photographs by a Native American Woman in the Early 1940s," *Montana* 71, no. 4 (Winter 2021), 1.

[2] Rosalyn LaPier, interview with Sarah Stacke, March 9, 2023.

[3] Rosalyn LaPier, interview with Sarah Stacke, March 9, 2023.

[4] Rosalyn LaPier, "Ella Mad Plume Yellow Wolf: Photographs by a Native American Woman in the Early 1940s," *Montana* 71, no. 4 (Winter 2021), 28.

[5] Rosalyn LaPier, "Ella Mad Plume Yellow Wolf: Photographs by a Native American Woman in the Early 1940s," *Montana* 71, no. 4 (Winter 2021), 28.

[6] Rosalyn LaPier, interview with Sarah Stacke, March 9, 2023.

[7] Rosalyn LaPier, interview with Sarah Stacke, March 9, 2023.

[8] Rosalyn LaPier, interview with Sarah Stacke, March 9, 2023.

MARGARET PICTOU LABILLOIS

[1] Beckie LaBillois and Colleen Gauvin, interviews with Sarah Stacke, 2023.

[2] Grace Poulin, *Invisible Women: WWII Aboriginal Servicewomen in Canada* (Thunder Bay, ON: D. G. Poulin, 2007), 89–90.

[3] Judy Bowman, "Margaret LaBillois," *My Handcrafted Life*, September 13, 2013, https://judybowman2.wordpress.com/2013/09/30/margaret-labillois/. **Author's note:** LaBillois was stationed in Rockcliffe throughout her service. Before the war, one of the major operations at Rockcliffe was military aerial photography used to map Canada. Though most aerial survey activities at Rockcliffe were suspended during the war, many aircraft were used in transportation and aeronautical experimentation, as well as training exercises. There were opportunities for LaBillois to periodically join an aircrew.

[4] Charlene LaBillois, "Ugpi'ganjig Elder Helps Family and Country," *Gespisiq* 3, no. 3 (Fall 2005), 12.

[5] Michelle Porter, *Rebel Women of the East Coast: Daring to Go Beyond the Limits* (Canmore, AB: Altitude Publishing, 2005).

[6] "N.B. First Nation Hopeful over Dam's Removal," CBC News, July 7, 2010, https://www.cbc.ca/news/canada/new-brunswick/n-b-first-nation-hopeful-over-dam-s-removal-1.952307.

[7] Michelle Porter, *Rebel Women of the East Coast: Daring to Go Beyond the Limits* (Canmore, AB: Altitude Publishing, 2005), 89.

[8] Judy Bowman, "Margaret LaBillois," *My Handcrafted Life*, September 13, 2013, https://judybowman2.wordpress.com/2013/09/30/margaret-labillois/.

[9] Beckie LaBillois and Colleen Gauvin, interviews with Sarah Stacke, 2023.

TSU-XOOG-EESH / WILLIAM LACKEY PAUL JR.

[1] All quotes in this section are by Ben Paul, son of William Lackey Paul, interview with Jennifer Natalie Fish, February 8, 2024.

ROBERT HENRY KINGSBERY JR.

[1] Special thanks to Chickasaw Nation for the information they provided about this history (Justin D. Lofton, Brian Cooke, Joe Thomas, Dana Lance, Keri Paniagua, Brent Oxford, Joanna John, Bruce Fish, Amanda Hudson).

[2] "Annual Meeting Traces Roots to Seeley Chapel Movement," *Chickasaw Times* (Oklahoma), August 2019, https://chickasawtimes.net/Web-Exclusives/Annual-Meeting-traces-roots-to-Seeley-Chapel-movement.aspx.

[3] Joshua Hinson, "Chi Ka Sha Althliha Ha Pomi Ittafaamitok: 'Our Chickasaw People Have Always Gathered Together': Robert Kingsbery's Annual Meeting Photographs 1964–1966," *Journal of Chickasaw History and Culture* 11, no. 2 (Spring 2008), 73.

LELAND HOWARD MARMON

[1] Leslie Marmon Silko, *Storyteller* (New York: Penguin Books, 2012), Kindle edition, There is a tall Hopi basket with a single figure.

[2] Lee Marmon, *The Pueblo Imagination: Landscape and Memory in the Photography of Lee Marmon* (Boston: Beacon, 2003).

[3] Alexandra N. Harris, "Memories of Lee Marmon: A Lifetime of Photographic Storytelling in New Mexico," *American Indian* 22, no. 2 (Summer 2021), https://www.americanindianmagazine.org/story/memories-of-lee-marmon.

[4] Lee Marmon and Tom Corbett, *Laguna Pueblo: A Photographic History* (Santa Fe: University of New Mexico Press, 2015), 153.

[5] Lee Marmon and Tom Corbett, *Laguna Pueblo: A Photographic History* (Santa Fe: University of New Mexico Press, 2015), 100.

HENRY SAMUEL KAISER JR.

[1] All quotes from Henry Kaiser Jr. in this section are from "I Hitchhiked to Heart Surgery, Henry S. Kaiser, Jr.," Henry S. Kaiser Jr. papers,

Archives and Special Collections, Consortium Library, University of Alaska Anchorage.

[2] William Bright, *Native American Placenames of the United States* (Norman: University of Oklahoma Press, 2004), 322.

[3] "A Brief History of Nenana," City of Nenana, www.cityofnenana.com /about-1.

[4] "New Government Town of Nenana," *Alaska Citizen,* August 28, 1916, 7, https://www.newspapers.com/image/893845062.

[5] Offical Publication of the Alaskan Engineering Commission, "Construction and Operation of the Alaska Railroad and the Development of the Resources Tributary," *Alaska Railroad Record* 1. no. 4 (1916), https://library.alaska.gov/hist/hist_docs /docs/asl_ANCH_3-1_Alaska_Railroad_Record_1916.pdf.

[6] On the 1910 U.S. census, Mrs. Kaiser's tribal affiliation is listed as "unknown." On the 1930 census, it is Athabascan, as it is for Henry Samuel Kaiser Jr. and his siblings on the 1940 census.

[7] "Mrs. H.S. Kaiser Passes Away at Nenana Home," *Fairbanks Daily News-Miner* (Alaska), March 23, 1932, 6, https://www.newspapers.com /image/4525157.

[8] "Henry Kaiser Obituary," *Anchorage Daily News*, August 2–3, 2011, www.legacy.com/us/obituaries/adn/name/henry-kaiser -obituary?id=18532738.

[9] Henry S. Kaiser Jr. papers, Archives and Special Collections, Consortium Library, University of Alaska Anchorage.

HERBERT RANDALL

[1] "Herbert Randall: 'The Photographer,'" *American Experience*, season 26, episode 5, PBS, June 24, 2014.

[2] Herbert Randall, interview with Sarah Stacke on Shinnecock Nation, April 27, 2023.

[3] Herbert Randall, interview with Sarah Stacke on Shinnecock Nation, April 27, 2023.

[4] Herbert Randall, interview with Sarah Stacke on Shinnecock Nation, April 27, 2023.

[5] Herbert Randall, interview with Sarah Stacke on Shinnecock Nation, April 27, 2023.

JEREMY DENNIS

[1] Jeremy Dennis, "Rise," https://www.jeremynative.com/portfolio/rise/.

[2] John Greiner-Ferris, "Horror Movie Imagery Meets Indigenous Identity," *Provincetown Independent*, February 2, 2022, https://provincetownindependent.org/arts-minds/2022/02/02 /horror-movie-imagery-meets-indigenous-identity/.

[3] Scott Kaufman, "Noam Chomsky: Zombies Are the New Indians and Slaves in White America's Collective Nightmare," RawStory, February 14, 2014, https://www.rawstory.com/2014/02 /noam-chomsky-zombies-are-the-new-indians-and-slaves-in-white -americas-collective-nightmare/.

[4] Jeremy Dennis, "Jeremy Dennis; Katie Hovencamp; November 05, 2019," *Artscene with Erika Funke*, SoundCloud, WVIA Public Media audio, https://soundcloud.com/wvia-public-media /jeremy-dennis-katie-hovencamp-november-05-2019.

RAYMOND GREGORY DOUCETTE

[1] Delores Campbell, "Raytel's Photos Helped Document Cape Breton's History," *Cape Breton Post* (Nova Scotia), February 11, 2012.

[2] Beaton Institute, email exchange with Sarah Stacke, April 2023.

[3] "Ray (Raytel) Doucette," obituary and death notice, InMemoriam.ca, 2011, www.inmemoriam.ca/view-announcement-268620-ray-raytel -doucette.html.

KENNETH T. MARS, JR.

[1] Erica Luke, interview with Sarah Stacke at South County History Center, November 17, 2022.

[2] Silvermoon Mars LaRose, email interview with Sarah Stacke, October 2023.

[3] Silvermoon Mars LaRose, email interview with Sarah Stacke, October 2023.

[4] Erica Luke, interview with Sarah Stacke at South County History Center, November 17, 2022.

[5] Erica Luke, interview with Sarah Stacke at South County History Center, November 17, 2022.

[6] Silvermoon Mars LaRose, email interview with Sarah Stacke, October 2023.

[7] Silvermoon Mars LaRose, email interview with Sarah Stacke, October 2023.

[8] Silvermoon Mars LaRose, email interview with Sarah Stacke, October 2023.

ARTHUR BEAR CHIEF

[1] All quotes from Arthur Bear Chief in this section are from Arthur Bear Chief, *My Decade at Old Sun, My Lifetime in Hell* (Athabasca, AB: AU Press, 2016).

[2] Krista McCracken, email interview with Sarah Stacke, October 2023.

[3] Krista McCracken, email interview with Sarah Stacke, October 2023.

DUGAN AGUILAR

[1] Theresa Harlan, "Dugan Aguilar: A Photographic Journey from the Heart," in *She Sang Me a Good Luck Song: The California Indian Photographs of Dugan Aguilar*, ed. Theresa Harlan (Berkeley: Heyday, 2015), 13, 22.

[2] Alexandra Harris and Chag Lowry, "He Gave Us Good Medicine: Native California Through the Eyes of Photographer Dugan Aguilar," *American Indian* 23, no. 3 (Fall 2022), www .americanindianmagazine.org/story/Photographer-Dugan-Aguilar.

[3] Dustin Aguilar, email interview with Sarah Stacke, March 2024.

[4] Theresa Harlan, "Dugan Aguilar: A Photographic Journey from the Heart," in *She Sang Me a Good Luck Song: The California Indian Photographs of Dugan Aguilar*, ed. Theresa Harlan (Berkeley: Heyday, 2015), 13.

[5] Dustin Aguilar, email interview with Sarah Stacke, March 2024.

[6] Theresa Harlan, "Dugan Aguilar: A Photographic Journey from the Heart," in *She Sang Me a Good Luck Song: The California Indian Photographs of Dugan Aguilar*, ed. Theresa Harlan (Berkeley: Heyday, 2015), 13.

[7] Dustin Aguilar, email interview with Sarah Stacke, March 2024.

[8] Dustin Aguilar, email interview with Sarah Stacke, March 2024.

HARRY CARL SAMPSON
STEWART INDIAN SCHOOL
[1] Len Holdren, "Stewart Wins 'A' Tournament: Braves 62–59 Winners Over Moapa Hoopsters," *Nevada State Journal* (Reno), March 13, 1996, 21, https://www.newspapers.com /image/1011047304.

[2] Stewart Indian School, "1966 State 'A' Basketball Championship Season," YouTube, May 28, 2020, https://www.youtube.com /watch?v=q4JA9dDeYEU&t=115s.

[3] Bobbi Rahder, email interview with Sarah Stacke, January 2023.

[4] Bobbi Rahder, email interview with Sarah Stacke, January 2023.

[5] *The Indian Advance* 1, no. 1 (1899), stewartindianschool.com /museum-2/the_indian_advance/.

[6] Sonia Stone, 1979 *Desert Braves* yearbook, Stewart Indian School, Carson City, Nevada.

[7] Bobbi Rahder, email interview with Sarah Stacke, January 2023.

[8] Bobbi Rahder, email interview with Sarah Stacke, January 2023.

JAMES "JIM" JEROME
[1] James Jerome, *Portraits and History of the Dene Elders*, ©NWT Archives /James Jerome/N-1987-017-1-5.

[2] Gladys Alexie, "Re: *Portraits and History of the Dene Elders*," ©NWT Archives/James Jerome/N-1987-017-1-3.

[3] James, Jerome, *Portraits and History of the Dene Elders*, ©NWT Archives /James Jerome/N-1987-017-1-4.

[4] James Jerome, *Portraits and History of the Dene Elders*, ©NWT Archives /James Jerome/N-1987-017-1-5.

[5] True North FM, "In Pictures: 1970s NWT Through the Eyes of James Jerome," My True North Now, January 7, 2016, www.mytruenorthnow.com/10744/news/hay-river-news /in-pictures-1970s-nwt-through-the-eyes-of-james-jerome/.

[6] Pat Kane, interview with Sarah Stacke, April 27, 2023.

[7] James Jerome, *Portraits and History of the Dene Elders*, ©NWT Archives /James Jerome/N-1987-017-1-5.

WANBLÍ TA HÓCOKA WASHTÉ (GOOD EAGLE CENTER) /
ARTHUR AMIOTTE
PORCUPINE DAY SCHOOL
[1] All quotes in this section from Arthur Amiotte are from Myles Libhart and Arthur Amiotte, *Photographs and Poems by Sioux Children from the Porcupine Day School, Pine Ridge Indian Reservation, South Dakota* (Rapid City, SD: Tipi Shop, 1971).

TAFOS
[1] Thomas Müller, "1986 TAFOS," thomasmullerperu.com/en/projects /personal_projects/tafos/.

[2] Thomas Müller, "1986 TAFOS," thomasmullerperu.com/en/projects /personal_projects/tafos/.

[3] Tiffany Fairey, "Building a History of Citizen Photography: The TAFOS Story," *Photography and Culture* 13, no. 1 (2020), 61, 63.

[4] Thomas Müller, "1986 TAFOS," thomasmullerperu.com/en/projects /personal_projects/tafos/.

[5] Tiffany Fairey, "Building a History of Citizen Photography: The TAFOS Story," *Photography and Culture* 13, no. 1 (2020), 64.

[6] Tiffany Fairey, "Building a History of Citizen Photography: The TAFOS Story," *Photography and Culture* 13, no. 1 (2020), 57.

[7] Tiffany Fairey, "Building a History of Citizen Photography: The TAFOS Story," *Photography and Culture* 13, no. 1 (2020), 76.

TOM FIELDS
[1] Tom Fields, interview with Sarah Stacke, April 19, 2023.

[2] Donna Garcia, "Indigenous Photographers Week: Tom Fields," Lenscratch, November 21, 2022, lenscratch.com/2022/11 /tom-fields/.

[3] Tom Fields, interview with Sarah Stacke, April 19, 2023.

[4] Tom Fields, interview with Sarah Stacke, April 19, 2023.

[5] Tom Fields, interview with Sarah Stacke, April 19, 2023.

DUWAWISIOMA / VICTOR MASAYESVA JR.
[1] Victor Masayesva Jr., *Husk of Time: The Photographs of Victor Masayesva* (Tucson: University of Arizona Press, 2006), 38.

[2] Victor Masayesva and Erin Younger, *Hopi Photographers, Hopi Images* (Tucson: University of Arizona Press, 1983), 11.

[3] "*Duwawisioma (Victor Masayesva Jr.)*: Màatakuyma," An exhibition at the Andrew Smith Gallery in Tucson, November 30, 2023– March 23, 2024, https://www.andrewsmithgallery.com/exhibitions /victormasayesva/Matakyuma/index.html.

[4] "Victor Masayesva, Jr," Electronic Arts Intermix, 1997, www.eai.org /artists/victor-masayesva-jr/biography.

[5] Victor Masayesva and Erin Younger, *Hopi Photographers, Hopi Images* (Tucson: University of Arizona Press, 1983), 11.

AMADO VILLAFAÑA CHAPARRO
[1] Amado Villafaña Chaparro, interview with Sarah Stacke, January 9, 2024. Translation by Stephen Ferry.

[2] Nadya Hernández, "Yosokwi Productions Uses Visual Media to Share the Realities of Indigenous Community in Colombia," International Journalists' Network, November 5, 2015, ijnet.org/en/story /yosokwi-productions-uses-visual-media-share-realities-indigenous -community-colombia.

[3] Gena Steffens, "Indigenous Protectors of These Sacred Peaks Have Kept Others Out—till Now," *National Geographic*, May 3, 2021, www.nationalgeographic.com/history/article /indigenous-protectors-sacred-peaks-secret-until-now ?loggedin=true&rnd=1707344560036.

[4] Amado Villafaña Chaparro, interview with Sarah Stacke, January 9, 2024. Translation by Stephen Ferry.

[5] *Naboba* (2016), MUBI. https://mubi.com/en/us/films/naboba.

6 Amado Villafaña Chaparro, interview with Sarah Stacke, January 9, 2024. Translation by Stephen Ferry.

7 Amado Villafaña Chaparro, interview with Sarah Stacke, January 9, 2024. Translation by Stephen Ferry.

SHELLEY NIRO

1 Shelley Niro, "Sleeping Warrior" artist statement shared with Sarah Stacke, April 2023.

2 Shelley Niro, "Sleeping Warrior" artist statement shared with Sarah Stacke, April 2023.

3 Shelley Niro, email interview with Sarah Stacke, April 2023.

4 Becky Rynor, "An Interview with Shelley Niro," *National Gallery of Canada* magazine, August 15, 2017, www.gallery.ca/magazine /artists/interviews/an-interview-with-shelley-niro.

DANA CLAXTON

1 Robin Laurence, "Dana Claxton," Border Crossings, May 2019, bordercrossingsmag.com/article/dana-claxton.

2 Dana Claxton, "Headdress 2018–2023," www.danaclaxton.com /artwork/headdress.

3 Toby Katrine Lawrence, "Locating Sioux Aesthetics Through the Sioux Project—Tatanka Oyate: Conversations with Dana Claxton," *BlackFlash*, May 9, 2018, blackflash.ca/2018/05/09/locating-sioux -aesthetics-through-the-sioux-project-tatanka-oyate-conversations -with-dana-claxton-by-toby-katrine-lawrence/.

4 Toby Katrine Lawrence, "Locating Sioux Aesthetics Through the Sioux Project—Tatanka Oyate: Conversations with Dana Claxton," *BlackFlash*, May 9, 2018, blackflash.ca/2018/05/09/locating-sioux -aesthetics-through-the-sioux-project-tatanka-oyate-conversations -with-dana-claxton-by-toby-katrine-lawrence/.

ROSALIE FAVELL

1 Rosalie Favell, interview with Sarah Stacke, April 25, 2023.

2 Rosalie Favell, interview with Sarah Stacke, April 25, 2023.

3 Rosalie Favell, "Holding Our Ground," *Rosalie Favell's Family Legacy*, (Winnipeg, MB: Winnipeg Art Gallery, 2021), 10.

4 Rosalie Favell, "Holding Our Ground," *Rosalie Favell's Family Legacy*, (Winnipeg, MB: Winnipeg Art Gallery, 2021), 10.

5 Rosalie Favell, "An Enduring Passion," in *In Our Hands: Native Photography, 1890 to Now*, eds. Jill Ahlberg Yohe, Jaida Grey Eagle, and Casey Riley (Minneapolis: Minneapolis Institute of Art, 2023), 133.

6 Rosalie Favell, "Holding Our Ground," *Rosalie Favell's Family Legacy*, (Winnipeg, MB: Winnipeg Art Gallery, 2021), 9.

7 Rosalie Favell, interview with Sarah Stacke, April 25, 2023.

SHAN GOSHORN

1 Alex Lemonides, "Shan Goshorn, Whose Cherokee Art Was Political, Dies at 61," *New York Times*, December 20, 2018, www.nytimes .com/2018/12/20/obituaries/shan-goshorn-dead.html.

2 All quotes in this paragraph: Gorman Museum of Native American Art, "Shan Goshorn, Pawnee Woman in Field, from Earth Renewal Series," Gorman Museum of Native American Art, August 17, 2021,

gormanmuseum.ucdavis.edu/collection-piece /shan-goshorn-pawnee-woman-field-earth-renewal-series.

3 John Brandenburg, "Artist Combines Painting, Photos," *Oklahoman*, July 22, 1988, www.oklahoman.com/story/news/1988/07/22 /artist-combines-painting-photos/62645181007/#tbl-em -lnr84g3430xvoywx9p7.

DOROTHY CHOCOLATE CARSEEN

1 Rhéanne Chartrand, "Native Indian/Inuit Photographers' Association," Building Cultural Legacies Hamilton, https://buildingculturallegacies .ca/artist/native-indian-inuit-photographers-association-niipa/.

2 "Mandate," Native Indian/Inuit Photographers' Association, https://web.archive.org/web/20030810222150/https://creative -spirit.com/mandate.htm.

3 Rhéanne Chartrand, "Native Indian/Inuit Photographers' Association," Building Cultural Legacies Hamilton, https://buildingculturallegacies .ca/artist/native-indian-inuit-photographers-association-niipa/.

4 Dorothy Chocolate Carseen, interview with Tiffany Midge, September 18, 2023.

KIMOWAN METCHEWAIS

1 Jeff Whetstone, "Stories on the Ground," in *Kimowan Metchewais: A Kind of Prayer* (New York: Aperture, 2023), 11.

2 Christopher T. Green, "Kimowan Metchewais: A Kind of Prayer," in *Kimowan Metchewais: A Kind of Prayer* (New York: Aperture, 2023), 259.

3 Christopher T. Green, "Kimowan Metchewais: A Kind of Prayer," in *Kimowan Metchewais: A Kind of Prayer* (New York: Aperture, 2023), 262.

4 Christina Wegs, "Grow All over Again: A Film about Kimowan Metchewais," https://vimeo.com/462339112.

5 Wendy Red Star, "Seeing Myself in the Work of an Artist I Never Met," *New York Times*, February 3, 2023, https://www.nytimes.com/2023/02/03 /opinion/kimewon-metchewais-native-american-art.html.

6 Kimowan Metchewais, "In Search of Live Relics in Cold Lake," in *Kimowan Metchewais: A Kind of Prayer* (New York: Aperture, 2023), 237, 238.

CAMILLE SEAMAN

1 Camille Seaman, "Photos from a Storm Chaser," TED talk, February 2013, ted.com/talks/camille_seaman_photos_from_a_storm_chaser ?language=en.

2 Camille Seaman, "Brief but Spectacular: Camille Seaman Photographer," *PBS NewsHour*, video transcript, pbs.org/newshour/brief/419438 /camille-seaman.

3 Camille Seaman, "Brief but Spectacular: Camille Seaman Photographer," *PBS NewsHour*, video transcript, pbs.org/newshour/brief/419438 /camille-seaman.

4 Camille Seaman, "Brief but Spectacular: Camille Seaman Photographer," *PBS NewsHour*, video transcript, pbs.org/newshour/brief/419438 /camille-seaman.

PAT KANE

1 All quotes in this section are from Pat Kane, interview with Sarah Stacke, April 27, 2023.

TOM JONES

[1] Tom Jones, "Strong Unrelenting Spirits," www.tomjonesho-chunk
.com/portfolio-collections/my-portfolio/strong-unrelenting
-spirits.

WILL WILSON

[1] "Will Wilson: Citizen of the Navajo Nation," Native Arts
& Cultures Foundation, www.nativeartsandcultures.org
/will-wilson.

[2] Will Wilson, "Will Wilson: About Me," willwilson.photoshelter.com
/about.

[3] Will Wilson, "Will Wilson: About Me," willwilson.photoshelter.com
/about.

[4] Jennifer Levin, "Extending the Frame: The Art, Vision and Activism of
Photographer Will Wilson," Searchlight New Mexico, March 2,
2023, searchlightnm.org/extending-the-frame-the-art-vision-and
-activism-of-photographer-will-wilson/.

[5] Jennifer Levin, "Extending the Frame: The Art, Vision and Activism of
Photographer Will Wilson," Searchlight New Mexico, March 2,
2023, searchlightnm.org/extending-the-frame-the-art-vision-and
-activism-of-photographer-will-wilson/.

[6] For more information on the Connecting the Dots project, please visit:
www.dineconnect.org.

[7] Jennifer Levin, "Extending the Frame: The Art, Vision and Activism of
Photographer Will Wilson," Searchlight New Mexico, March 2,
2023, searchlightnm.org/extending-the-frame-the-art-vision-and
-activism-of-photographer-will-wilson/.

XUNKA' LÓPEZ DÍAZ

[1] Lourdes de León Pasquel, "Dos hermanos, dos historias,"
in *Mi hermanita Cristina, una niña chamula / My little sister
Cristina, a Chamula girl* (México: Archivo Fotográfico Indígena;
Centro de Investigaciones y Estudios Superiores en Antropología
Social; Consejo Estatal para la Cultura y las Artes de
Chiapas, 2000), 15.

[2] Carlota Duarte, "A Place in the World: The Chiapas Photography Project
in a Context of Poverty and Wealth," *Yale ISM Review* 4.1 (Winter
2018), https://www.ismreview.yale.edu/volume-4-1
-winter-2018/a-place-in-the-world-the-chiapas-photography
-project-in-a-context-of-poverty-and-wealth.

MARUCH SÁNTIZ GÓMEZ

[1] Maruch Sántiz Gómez, *Creencias de nuestros antepasados* (México:
Centro de la Imagen; CIESAS; Casa de las Imagenes, 1998).

[2] Maruch Sántiz Gómez, "Maruch Sántiz Gómez," interview with Carlota
Duarte, *Aperture* 154 (Winter 1999): 20–29.

[3] Maruch Sántiz Gómez, "Maruch Sántiz Gómez," interview with Carlota
Duarte, *Aperture* 154 (Winter 1999), 20.

CARA ROMERO

[1] Gussie Fountleroy, "Cara Romero: Tapping the Regenerative Power
of Art," *Trend*, June 1, 2022, trendmagazineglobal.com/cara
-romero/.

[2] Alicia Inez Guzmán, "The Profound Photography of Cara Romero,"
New Mexico Magazine, December 7, 2021, www.newmexico
magazine.org/blog/post/cara-romero/.

[3] Cara Romero, "Statement," www.cararomerophotography.com/about.

[4] Cara Romero, "Statement," www.cararomerophotography.com/about.

RUSSEL ALBERT DANIELS

[1] Zion Canyon Mesa, "Photography as Medicine—Russel Albert
Daniels," *In Site*, podcast, November 9, 2020, zioncanyonmesa.org
/podcast-archive/2020/10/8/russel-albert-daniels-interview.

[2] Russel Albert Daniels, interview with Sarah Stacke, March 20, 2023.

[3] Scotti Hill, "Russel Albert Daniels Exposes Native Enslavement
and Genocide in the Southwest," *Southwest Contemporary*,
October 8, 2023, southwestcontemporary.com
/russel-albert-daniels-native-enslavement/.

[4] Russel Albert Daniels, interview with Sarah Stacke, March 20, 2023.

[5] Russel Albert Daniels, "The Genízaro Pueblo of Abiquiú," Developing
Stories, Native Photographers in the Field, National Museum of the
American Indian, https://americanindian.si.edu/developingstories
/daniels.html.

[6] Russel Albert Daniels, "La Cautiva," russeldaniels.com/cautiva.

[7] Russel Albert Daniels, "The Genízaro Pueblo of Abiquiú," Developing
Stories, Native Photographers in the Field, National Museum of the
American Indian, https://americanindian.si.edu/developingstories
/daniels.html.

[8] Zion Canyon Mesa, "Photography as Medicine—Russel Albert Daniels,"
In Site, podcast, November 9, 2020, zioncanyonmesa.org
/podcast-archive/2020/10/8/russel-albert-daniels-interview.

[9] Russel Albert Daniels, "The Genízaro Pueblo of Abiquiú," Developing
Stories, Native Photographers in the Field, National Museum of the
American Indian, https://americanindian.si.edu/developingstories
/daniels.html.

[10] Zion Canyon Mesa, "Photography as Medicine—Russel Albert
Daniels," *In Site*, podcast, November 9, 2020, zioncanyonmesa.org
/podcast-archive/2020/10/8/russel-albert-daniels-interview.

[11] Phoebe Farris, "An Interview with Photojournalist Russel Albert
Daniels," *Cultural Survival*, March 2, 2013, culturalsurvival.org
/news/interview-photojournalist-russel-albert-daniels.

[12] Zion Canyon Mesa, "Photography as Medicine—Russel Albert
Daniels," *In Site*, podcast, November 9, 2020, zioncanyonmesa.org
/podcast-archive/2020/10/8/russel-albert-daniels-interview.

JOSÉ MELA

[1] Margarita Alvarado, "La Huella Luminosa de los Fotógrafos de la
Frontera," in Abel Alexander et al., *Historia de la fotografía en Chile:
Rescate de huellas en la luz* (Santiago, Chile: Centro Nacional del
Patrimonio Fotográfico, 2000), https://www.memoriachilena.gob.cl
/archivos2/pdfs/mc0042370.pdf.

[2] José Mela, "The *Azentún* Photography Workshop: A Proposal for Self-
Representing the Urban Mapuche Teenagers in Santiago de Chile,"
Visual Anthropology 33, no. 5 (2020), 412–425, www.tandfonline
.com/doi/abs/10.1080/08949468.2020.1824974.

[3] José Mela, "The *Azentún* Photography Workshop: A Proposal for Self-
Representing the Urban Mapuche Teenagers in Santiago de Chile,"
Visual Anthropology 33, no. 5 (2020), 412–425, www.tandfonline
.com/doi/abs/10.1080/08949468.2020.1824974.

[4] José Mela, "The *Azentún* Photography Workshop: A Proposal for Self-
Representing the Urban Mapuche Teenagers in Santiago de Chile,"

Visual Anthropology 33, no. 5 (2020), 412–425, www.tandfonline
.com/doi/abs/10.1080/08949468.2020.1824974.

TÁHILA MOSS

[1] Táhila Moss, interview with Angela Ferguson, 2020.

[2] Garet Bleir, "Indigenous Corn Keepers Are Helping Communities Recover
and Reunite with Their Traditional Foods," *Intercontinental Cry*, January
17, 2019, intercontinentalcry.org/indigenous-corn-keepers-are-helping
-communities-recover-and-reunite-with-their-traditional-foods/.

[3] Kevin Noble Maillard, "On Remote Farms and in City Gardens, a Native
American Movement Grows," *New York Times*, August 26, 2022, www
.nytimes.com/2022/08/26/dining/native-american-agriculture.html.

[4] "Mission," OJI:SDA', ojisda.org/vision-and-mission.

[5] Táhila Moss, interview with Sarah Stacke, January 23, 2024.

[6] Táhila Moss, interview with Sarah Stacke, March 30, 2023.

[7] "What Does Our Name Mean?" OJI:SDA', ojisda.org/vision-and
-mission.

RYAN REDCORN

[1] Ryan RedCorn, interview with Sarah Stacke, May 10, 2023.

[2] Ryan RedCorn, interview with Sarah Stacke, May 10, 2023.

[3] Rachel Brown, "For This Native Community, Photography Has
Harmed—and Healed," *National Geographic*, March 19, 2020,
https://www.nationalgeographic.com/culture/article
/photography-tells-osage-nation-story-past-and-present.

[4] Rachel Brown, "For This Native Community, Photography Has
Harmed—and Healed," *National Geographic*, March 19, 2020,
https://www.nationalgeographic.com/culture/article
/photography-tells-osage-nation-story-past-and-present.

[5] Rachel Brown, "For This Native Community, Photography Has
Harmed—and Healed," *National Geographic*, March 19, 2020,
https://www.nationalgeographic.com/culture/article
/photography-tells-osage-nation-story-past-and-present.

[6] Rachel Brown, "For This Native Community, Photography Has
Harmed—and Healed," *National Geographic*, March 19, 2020,
https://www.nationalgeographic.com/culture/article
/photography-tells-osage-nation-story-past-and-present.

[7] Ryan RedCorn, note to Sarah Stacke, February 2024.

[8] Ryan RedCorn, interview with Sarah Stacke, May 10, 2023.

BAAHINNAACHÍSH (ONE WHO IS TALENTED) / WENDY RED STAR

[1] Abaki Beck, "Decolonizing Photography: A Conversation with Wendy
Red Star," *Aperture*, December 14, 2016, aperture.org/editorial
/wendy-red-star/.

[2] Jordan Amirkhani, "Setting the Stage," in *Wendy Red Star: Delegation*
(New York: Aperture, 2022), 139.

[3] San Francisco Museum of Art, "Artist Talk | Wendy Red Star on 'Four
Seasons' and Reclaiming Indigenous Narratives," interviewer Shana
Lopes, YouTube video, 53:30, youtube.com/watch?v=19L4P1INPro.

[4] San Francisco Museum of Art, "Artist Talk | Wendy Red Star on
'Four Seasons' and Reclaiming Indigenous Narratives," interviewer

Shana Lopes, YouTube video, 53:30, youtube.com
/watch?v=19L4P1INPro.

DAWN E. "DAWNEE" LEBEAU

[1] Dawnee LeBeau, interview with Sarah Stacke, May 11, 2023.

[2] Dawnee LeBeau, interview with Sarah Stacke, May 11, 2023.

[3] "Marcella LeBeau of Eagle Butte, South Dakota," obituary, Kesling
Funeral Home, www.keslingfuneralhome.net/obituary
/marcella-lebeau.

[4] Dawnee LeBeau, "Native Women in Photography:
Dawnee LeBeau," *Native Max Magazine*,
nativemaxmagazine.com/native-women-in-photography
-dawnee-lebeau.

BRIAN ADAMS

[1] Brian Adams, interview with Sarah Stacke, May 10, 2023.

[2] Alaska Eskimo Whaling Commission, "Our Story," https://www.aewc
-alaska.org/our-story.

[3] Brian Adams, interview with Sarah Stacke, May 10, 2023.

[4] CatchLight Staff, "Behind the Lens with Brian Adams," CatchLight,
January 15, 2021, www.catchlight.io/news/2021/1/15
/behind-the-lens-with-brian-adams.

[5] Brian Adams, photog., and Julie Decker, ed., *I Am Inuit* (Salenstein,
Switzerland: Benteli, 2017).

[6] Rena Silverman, "An Insider's View of Alaskan Inuit," *Lens*,
New York Times, March 8, 2017, archive.nytimes
.com/lens/lens.blogs.nytimes.com/2017/03/08
/among-alaskas-inuits-dispelling-televisions-reality/.

[7] Brian Adams, interview with Sarah Stacke, May 10, 2023.

[8] Brian Adams, interview with Sarah Stacke, May 10, 2023.

[9] Brian Adams, interview with Sarah Stacke, May 10, 2023.

JERO GONZALES

[1] Jero Gonzales, "Pukapakuris" artist statement shared with Sarah Stacke,
April 2023.

[2] Jero Gonzales, "Pukapakuris" artist statement shared with Sarah Stacke,
April 2023.

[3] Jero Gonzales, "Pukapakuris" artist statement shared with Sarah Stacke,
April 2023.

[4] Jero Gonzales, email interview with Sarah Stacke, November 2023.

[5] Jero Gonzales, email interview with Sarah Stacke, November 2023.

[6] Jero Gonzales, email interview with Sarah Stacke, November 2023.

[7] "Pukapakuris by Jero Gonzales," Xapiri Ground, https://www
.xapiriground.org/bulletin/pukapakuris.

JORGE PANCHOAGA

[1] Jorge Panchoaga, interview with Magalí Druscovich, May 12, 2023.
Translation by Magalí Druscovich.

[2] Jorge Panchoaga, interview with Magalí Druscovich, May 12, 2023.
Translation by Magalí Druscovich.

3 David Gonzalez, "Lost, at Home in Colombia," *New York Times*, June 17, 2015, archive.nytimes.com/lens.blogs.nytimes .com/2015/06/17/lost-at-home-in-colombia.

4 David Gonzalez. "Lost, at Home in Colombia," *New York Times*, June 17, 2015, archive.nytimes.com/lens.blogs.nytimes .com/2015/06/17/lost-at-home-in-colombia.

CINTHYA SANTOS BRIONES
1 Cinthya Santos Briones, interview with Sarah Stacke, May 12, 2023.

2 Cinthya Santos Briones, "Abuelas," www.cinthya-santosbriones.com /abuelas.

3 Cinthya Santos Briones, "Abuelas," Immigrant Artist Biennial Virtual Exhibitions, https://virtual2020 .theimmigrantartistbiennial.com/home-land/cinthya -santos-briones.

4 Cinthya Santos Briones, note to Sarah Stacke, November 2023.

5 Cinthya Santos Briones, interview with Sarah Stacke, May 12, 2023.

6 Cinthya Santos Briones, "Artist Statement," http://www.cinthya -santosbriones.com/about.

7 Cinthya Santos Briones, "Artist Statement," http://www.cinthya -santosbriones.com/about.

8 Cinthya Santos Briones, interview with Sarah Stacke, May 12, 2023.

9 Cinthya Santos Briones, interview with Sarah Stacke, May 12, 2023.

10 Cinthya Santos Briones, interview with Sarah Stacke, May 12, 2023.

JAIDA GREY EAGLE
1 Owamni, "Our Philosophy," owamni.com/our-menu/.

2 Reed Fischer, "Champions of Change in Minnesota: Jaida Grey Eagle," *Minnesota Monthly*, January 11, 2024, minnesotamonthly .com/lifestyle/champions-of-change-in-minnesota-jaida-grey-eagle/.

3 Reed Fischer, "Champions of Change in Minnesota: Jaida Grey Eagle," *Minnesota Monthly*, January 11, 2024, minnesotamonthly .com/lifestyle/champions-of-change-in-minnesota -jaida-grey-eagle/.

KALI SPITZER
1 Kali Spitzer, interview with Sarah Stacke, April 10, 2023.

2 Ginger Dunnill, quoted in Kali Spitzer, "About," www.kalispitzer.com /about.

3 Ginger Dunnill, "To Breathe In Our Brilliance and Shine Out Resilience," in *An Exploration of Resilience and Resistance* (Vancouver: Grunt Gallery, 2019). Exhibition catalog.

4 Kali Spitzer, "Healing BIPOC People Through Photography: Kali Spitzer," *Colorado Voices*, PBS video, March 24, 2013, pbs.org/video/healing-bipoc-people-through -photography-kali-spitzer-mx7un5/.

5 Kali Spitzer, interview with Sarah Stacke, Arpil 10, 2023.

6 Kali Spitzer, "Healing BIPOC People Through Photography: Kali Spitzer," *Colorado Voices*, PBS video, March 24, 2013, pbs.org/video/healing-bipoc-people-through -photography-kali-spitzer-mx7un5/.

7 Kali Spitzer, "Healing BIPOC People Through Photography: Kali Spitzer," *Colorado Voices*, PBS video, March 24, 2013, pbs.org/video /healing-bipoc-people-through-photography-kali-spitzer-mx7un5/.

8 Ginger Dunnill, "Process & Intention: Interview with Kali Spitzer," *Broken Boxes*, podcast, July 28, 2021, brokenboxespodcast.com /podcast/2021/7/28/process-amp-intention-interview-with-kali-spitzer.

9 Kali Spitzer, "About," www.kalispitzer.com/about.

MINIK BIDSTRUP AND JAKOB PETERSEN
1 Minik Bidstrup, interview with Sarah Stacke, January 9, 2024.

2 Minik Bidstrup, interview with Sarah Stacke, January 9, 2024.

3 Michele Abercrombie, "This Photographer Pairs New and Old Images to Converse with Greenland's Colonial Past," *The Picture Show*, NPR, July 27, 2021, https://www.npr.org /sections/pictureshow/2021/07/27/1005142017/this-photographer -pairs-new-and-old-images-to-converse-with-greenlands -colonial-.

4 Minik Bidstrup, "The Daily Edit–400 Years Project: Sarah Stacke," aPhotoEditor, July 20, 21, https://www.aphotoeditor. com/2021/07/20/the-daily-edit-400-years-project-sarah-stacke/.

5 Minik Bidstrup, interview with Sarah Stacke, January 9, 2024.

6 Minik Bidstrup, interview with Sarah Stacke, January 9, 2024.

7 Minik Bidstrup, interview with Sarah Stacke, January 9, 2024.

8 Minik Bidstrup, interview with Sarah Stacke, January 9, 2024.

DAKOTA MACE
1 "A Conversation with Dakota Mace," interview with Jody Clowes, *Wisconsin People & Ideas* (Spring 2023), www.wisconsinacademy.org /magazine/winter-spring-2023/watrous-gallery /conversation-dakota-mace.

2 Dakota Mace, "Naal Tsoos Saní," www.dakotamace.com/naal-tsoos-san.

3 Dakota Mace, "Naal Tsoos Saní," www.dakotamace.com/naal-tsoos-san.

4 Dakota Mace, interview with Sarah Stacke, April 17, 2023.

JOSUÉ RIVAS
1 Josué Rivas, interview with Sarah Stacke, May 9, 2023.

2 Josué Rivas, interview with Sarah Stacke, May 9, 2023.

3 Josué Rivas, interview with Sarah Stacke, May 9, 2023.

4 Josué Rivas, "Josué," www.josuerivasfoto.com/josue.

5 Josué Rivas, interview with Sarah Stacke, May 9, 2023.

SARA ALIAGA TICONA
1 All quotes in this section are from Sara Aliaga Ticona, interview with Magalí Druscovich, February 6, 2024. Translation by Magalí Druscovich.

CITLALI FABIÁN
1 Citlali Fabián, interview with Samantha Reinders, December 18, 2023.

2 Citlali Fabián, interview with Sarah Stacke, June 7, 2023.

3 Kerry Manders, "Women Talk: Citlali Fabián," Women Photograph, February 14, 2019, www.womenphotograph.com/news/2019/2/14 /women-talk-citlali-fabian.

[4] Kerry Manders, "Women Talk: Citlali Fabián," Women Photograph,
February 14, 2019, www.womenphotograph.com/news/2019/2/14
/women-talk-citlali-fabian.

[5] Citlali Fabián, interview with Sarah Stacke, June 7, 2023.

KAPULEIIKEALOONALANI FLORES

[1] Kapulei Flores, "What I'm Fighting to Protect," *Assembly*, a Malala Fund
publication, October 20, 2021, assembly.malala.org/stories
/what-im-fighting-to-protect.

[2] Kapulei Flores, "What I'm Fighting to Protect," *Assembly*, a Malala Fund
publication, October 20, 2021, assembly.malala.org/stories
/what-im-fighting-to-protect.

[3] Kapulei Flores, "What I'm Fighting to Protect," *Assembly*, a Malala Fund
publication, October 20, 2021, assembly.malala.org/stories
/what-im-fighting-to-protect.

[4] Peter E. Palmquist and Thomas R. Kailbourn, *Pioneer Photographers of the
Far West: A Biographical Dictionary, 1840–1865* (Redwood City, CA:
Stanford University Press, 2000).

[5] Lynn Ann Davis, *Na Pa'i Ki'i: The Photographers in the Hawaiian Islands,
1845–1900* (Honolulu: Bishop Museum Press, 1980), 11.

[6] Lynn Ann Davis, *Na Pa'i Ki'i: The Photographers in the Hawaiian Islands,
1845–1900* (Honolulu: Bishop Museum Press, 1980), 11.

[7] Kapulei Flores, *Kapulei Flores on Keeping Her Culture and Tradition Alive
in Hawai'i*, Missing Perspectives, November 30, 2021,
www.missingperspectives.com/posts/kapuleiflores/.

[8] Kapulei Flores (@Brightlings_), Instagram, July 8, 2022,
instagram.com/p/CfxSnQ5rFz0/.

LUVIA LAZO

[1] Luvia Lazo, "Photoville Education Field Trips: Luvia Lazo,"
Photoville Festival, Brooklyn Bridge Park, New York,
June 8, 2022, photoville.nyc/event
/photoville-education-field-trips-luvia-lazo.

[2] Luvia Lazo, "Photoville Education Field Trips: Luvia Lazo,"
Photoville Festival, Brooklyn Bridge Park, New York,
June 8, 2022, photoville.nyc/event
/photoville-education-field-trips-luvia-lazo.

[3] Ana Karina Zatarain, "The Power of Portraits with Hidden Faces," *Photo
Booth*, *New Yorker*, March 30, 2022.

[4] Luvia Lazo, interview with Sarah Stacke, November 9, 2023.

NĪA MACKNIGHT

[1] Nīa MacKnight, interview with Sarah Stacke, April 15, 2023.

[2] Nīa MacKnight, interview with Sarah Stacke, April 15, 2023.

[3] Nīa MacKnight and Elizabeth Gillis, "He Fought for Self-
Determination in a Time of Assimilation. He Left These Objects,"
The Picture Show, NPR, December 25, 2021, www.npr.org/sections
/pictureshow/2021/12/25/1060806892/indigenous-photographer
-reflects-on-identity-with-project-on-great-grandfather.

[4] Nīa MacKnight and Elizabeth Gillis, "He Fought for Self-
Determination in a Time of Assimilation. He Left These Objects,"
The Picture Show, NPR, December 25, 2021, www.npr.org/sections
/pictureshow/2021/12/25/1060806892/indigenous-photographer
-reflects-on-identity-with-project-on-great-grandfather.

[5] Nīa MacKnight, interview with Sarah Stacke, April 15, 2023.

Selected Bibliography

INTRODUCTION

"Fototeca Andina. Yuyayninchis: fotografías inéditas de César Meza y Horacio Ochoa." Independencia: Bienal de Arte de Cusco. https://bienaldecusco.art/fototeca-andina-yuyayninchis-fotografias -ineditas-de-cesar-meza-y-horacio-ochoa/.

Gattuso, John, ed. *A Circle of Nations: Voices and Visions of American Indians.* Hillsboro, OR: Beyond Words, 1993.

Silver Drum: Five Native Photographers. Hamilton, ON: Native Indian/ Inuit Photographers' Association, 1986.

Norbert, Eileen, ed. *Menadelook: An Inupiat Teacher's Photographs of Alaska Village Life, 1907–1932.* Seattle: University of Washington Press, 2016.

Rohrbach, John, and Will Wilson, eds. *Speaking with Light: Contemporary Indigenous Photography.* Santa Fe: Radius, 2023.

Strathman, Nicole. *Through a Native Lens: American Indian Photography.* Norman: University of Oklahoma Press, 2020.

Tsinhnahjinnie, Hulleah J., and Veronica Passalacqua. *Our People, Our Land, Our Images: International Indigenous Photographers.* Berkeley: Heyday, 2007.

Ahlberg Yohe, Jill, Jaida Grey Eagle, and Casey Riley, eds. *In Our Hands: Native Photography, 1890 to Now.* Minneapolis: Minneapolis Institute of Art, 2023.

JENNIE FIELDS ROSS COBB

Chavez, Will. "Images from the First-Known Native American Female Photographer." *High Country News,* March 25, 2022. https://www .hcn.org/issues/54-4/indigenous-affairs-photos-images-from-the-first -known-native-american-female-photographer/.

RICHARD ALBERT THROSSEL

Albright, Peggy. *Crow Indian Photographer: The Work of Richard Throssel.* Albuquerque: University of New Mexico Press, 1997.

Bengal, Rebecca. "To Walk in Both Worlds," *Aperture* 240 (Fall 2020): 32–41.

Lippard, Lucy R., ed. *Partial Recall: With Essays on Photographs of Native North Americans.* New York: New Press, 1992.

BENJAMIN ALFRED HALDANE AND HENRY S. HALDANE

Askren, Mique'l Icesis. "From Negative to Positive: B. A. Haldane, Nineteenth Century Tsimshian Photographer." Open Collections, University of British Columbia. http://hdl.handle .net/2429/17858.

Dangeli, Mique'l Icesis. "Bringing to Light a Counternarrative of Our History: B. A. Haldane, Nineteenth-Century Century Tsimshian Photographer," in *Sharing Our Knowledge: The Tlingit and Their Coastal Neighbors,* edited by Sergei Kan. Lincoln: University of Nebraska Press, 2015.

"Mique'l Dangeli—Re-Developing the Work of B. A. Haldane, 19th Century Tsimshian Photography." YouTube, February 14, 2018. https://www.youtube.com/watch?v=Ufww9sy6SGs.

GEORGE HUNT

Boas, Franz. *The Social Organization and Secret Societies of the Kwakiutl Indians.* In *Report of the United States National Museum for the Year Ending June 30, 1895,* 309–738.

Hunt, Sarah / Tłaliłila'ogwa. "Looking for Lucy Homiskanis, Confronting Emily Carr: Restoring Nature, Gender, and Belonging on the Northwest Coast." *BC Studies: The British Columbian Quarterly* 217 (Spring 2023): 7–33. https://doi.org/10.14288/bcs.no217.197905.

STOOWUKHÁA (ASTUTE ONE) / LOUIS V. SHOTRIDGE

Williams, Lucy, and David McKnight. "Through the Eyes of Louis Shotridge: Sharing Alaska's Native Tlingit History: A Digital Archive Project at Penn." International Federation of Library Associations (IFLA), August 6, 2008. iportal.usask.ca/record/14462.

JOHN NAPOLEAON BRINTON HEWITT

Curtin, Jeremiah, and J. N. B. Hewitt. *Introduction to Seneca Fiction Legends and Myths.* Washington, D.C.: Government Printing Office, 1919. https://www.loc.gov/item/19026413/.

Hewitt, J. N. B. *A Constitutional League of Peace in the Stone Age of America: The League of the Iroquois and Its Constitution.* Washington, D.C.: Government Printing Office, 1920. Wellcome Collection. https://wellcomecollection.org/works/vhnua6x6.

Hewitt, J. N. B. *Iroquoian Cosmology First Part.* Washington, D.C.: Government Printing Office, 1904. https://www.loc.gov /item/19013699/.

ROBERT GEORGE BEAULIEU

Klein, Alex. "The VOICE of PROGRESS: A Conflicted Message of Resistance in the White Earth Reservation's First Newspaper." *Minnesota History* 65, no. 5 (2017): 188–200. http://www.jstor.org/stable/26368694.

Treuer, Anton. *The Assassination of Hole in the Day.* Minneapolis: Minnesota Historical Society Press, 2011. Kindle edition.

MARTHA MCGLASHAN MONSEN

Goforth, Pennelope J. *Sailing the Mail in Alaska: The Maritime Years of Alaska Photographer John E. Thwaites, 1905–1918.* Anchorage: Cybrrcat Productions!, 2003.

CUSCO SCHOOL OF PHOTOGRAPHY

Coronado, Jorge. *Portraits in the Andes: Photography and Agency 1900–1950.* Pittsburgh: University of Pittsburgh Press, 2018.

Garay Albújar, Andrés, ed. *Cusco revelado: Fotografías de Max T. Vargas, Max Uhley y Martín Chambi.* Berlin: Instituto Iberoamericano de Berlín, 2017.

Poole, Deborah. "Figueroa Aznar and the Cusco Indigenistas: Photography and Modernism in Early Twentieth-Century Peru." *Representations* 38 (Spring 1992): 39–75.

MARTÍN CHAMBI AND FAMILY

Chambi, Manuel. "Martín Chambi: Artesano de la luz." *Tierradentro (Arte, ideologia, realidad)* no. 4 (1987): 5–12.

Chambi, Martín. *Martín Chambi: Photographs, 1920–1950.* Foreword by Mario Vargas Llosa, introductions by Edward Ranney and Publio López Mondéjar. Washington, D.C.: Smithsonian Institution, 1993.

Cohen-Aponte, Ananda. "Forging a Popular Art History: *Indigenismo* and the Art of Colonial Peru." *Res: Anthropology and Aesthetics* 67–68 (2016/2017): 273–89.

"Hablemos de la vida y obra de Julia Chambi." *Lima en Escena*, October 25, 2021. https://limaenescena.pe /hablemos-de-la-vida-y-obra-de-julia-chambi/.

NETTIE ODLETY AND LUCY SAUMTY
McKenzie, Andrew, Daniel Harbour, and Laurel J. Watkins, eds. *Plains Life in Kiowa: Voices From a Tribe in Transition.* Special issue, *International Journal of American Linguistics* 88, no. S1 (April 2022).

YIŚÀUM (TWICE LOOKED AT) / PARKER PAUL MCKENZIE
McKenzie, Parker P., and William C. Meadows. "The Parker P. McKenzie Kiowa Orthography: How Written Kiowa Came Into Being." *Plains Anthropologist* 46, no 1 (2001): 233–248.

SOTERO CONSTANTINO JIMÉNEZ
Constantino Jiménez, Sotero, and Carlos Monsiváis. *Foto Estudio Jiménez.* México, D.F.: Ediciones Era, 1983.

PETER PITSEOLAK AND AGGEOK PITSEOLAK
Adams, Amy. "Arctic and Inuit Photography. Part Two: Through the Looking-Glass: The Photographs of Robert J. Flaherty and Peter Pitseolak." *Inuit Art Quarterly* 15, no. 3 (Fall 2000): 4–19.

Bellman, David, ed. *Peter Pitseolak (1902–1973) Inuit Historian of Seekooseelak.* Montreal: McCord Museum, 1980.

Harley Eber, Dorothy. "Peter Pitseolak and the Photographic Template." *Imaging the Arctic.* Seattle: University of Washington Press, 1998.

Pitseolak, Peter, Dorothy Harley Eber, and Ann Hanson. *People from Our Side: A Life Story with Photographs and Oral Biography.* Montreal: McGill–Queen's University Press, 1993.

JAMES "JIM" PATRICK BRADY
Nest, Michael Wallace, Deanna Reder, and Eric Bell. *Cold Case North: The Search for James Brady and Absolom Halkett.* Regina, SK: University of Regina Press, 2020.

Seesequasis, Paul. "Enclosing Some Snapshots: The Photography of Métis Activist James Brady: A Virtual Exhibition." Glenbow, March 10, 2020. www.glenbow.org/blog/enclosing-some-snapshots -the-photography-of-metis-activist-james-brady/.

LELAND HOWARD MARMON
Marmon, Lee. *The Pueblo Imagination: Landscape and Memory in the Photography of Lee Marmon.* Boston: Beacon, 2003.

Marmon, Lee, and Tom Corbett. *Laguna Pueblo: A Photographic History.* Santa Fe: University of New Mexico Press, 2015.

HERBERT RANDALL
Randall, Herbert, and Bobs M. Tusa. *Faces of Freedom Summer.* Tuscaloosa: University of Alabama Press, 2001.

KENNETH MARS, JR.
Gravelle, Kendra. "SCHC Unveils Photographs by Kenneth Mars, Jr." *Narragansett Times*, February 16, 2018.

Kulman, Alina. "The Lens of Kenneth T. Mars: The Life and Images of a Narragansett Photographer." *College Hill Independent* 42 (February 2021): 15–17.

South County History Center. "Kenneth T. Mars, Jr. Photograph Collection." Kingston, RI. https://southcountyhistorycenter.org /mars-photograph-collection.

ARTHUR BEAR CHIEF
Bear Chief, Arthur. *My Decade at Old Sun, My Lifetime in Hell.* Athabasca, AB: AU Press, 2016.

DUGAN AGUILAR
Aguilar, Dugan, and Theresa Harlan. *She Sang Me a Good Luck Song: The California Indian Photographs of Dugan Aguilar.* Berkeley: Heyday, 2015.

Hogeland, L. Frank, and Kim Hogeland. *First Families: A Photographic History of California Indians.* Berkeley: Heyday, 2007.

JAMES JEROME
Seesequasis, Paul. *Blanket Toss under Midnight Sun: Portraits of Everyday Life in Eight Indigenous Communities.* Toronto: Knopf Canada, 2019.

DUWAWISIOMA / VICTOR MASAYESVA JR.
Masayesva, Victor, Jr. *Husk of Time: The Photographs of Victor Masayesva.* Tucson: University of Arizona Press, 2006.

Masayesva, Victor, and Erin Younger. *Hopi Photographers, Hopi Images.* Tucson: University of Arizona Press, 1983.

SHELLEY NIRO
Bennett, Melissa, Greg A. Hill, and David W. Penney. *Shelley Niro: 500 Year Itch.* Ottawa, ON: Musée des beaux-arts du Canada, 2023.

DANA CLAXTON
Arnold, Grant, Kathleen S. Bartels, and Dana Claxton. *Dana Claxton: Fringing the Cube.* Vancouver, BC: Figure 1; Vancouver Art Gallery, 2019.

Claxton, Dana, Brian J. Porter, Edward Burtynsky, Leila Timmins, and Gaëlle Morel. *Dana Claxton.* Göttingen, Germany: Steidl, 2021.

ROSALIE FAVELL
Favell, Rosalie, Donna McAlear, Christiane Becker, and Barry Ace. *I Searched Many Worlds.* Winnipeg, MB: Winnipeg Art Gallery, 2003.

DOROTHY CHOCOLATE CARSEEN
#nofilterneeded: Shining Light on the Native Indian/Inuit Photographers' Association, 1985–1992, curated by Rhéanne Chartrand, McMaster Museum of Art, January 2–March 24, 2018. https://museum .mcmaster.ca/niipa/.

No Borders: Works by Four North American Native Photographers. Hamilton, ON: Native Indian/Inuit Photographers' Association, 1991.

Reminiscing. Hamilton, ON: Native Indian/Inuit Photographers' Association, 2000.

Silver Drum: Five Native Photographers. Hamilton, ON: Native Indian/ Inuit Photographers' Association, 1986.

Visions: From Contemporary Native Photographers. Hamilton, ON: Native Indian/Inuit Photographers' Association, 1986.

Szikora, Erin. "Visual Sovereignty and the Making of NIIPA: Tracing an Archival History of the Native Indian/Inuit Photographers' Association (1985–2005/2006)." Submitted to CCAD University in partial fulfillment of the requirements for the degree of Master of Arts in Contemporary Art, Design and New Media Art Histories, Toronto, Ontario, Canada, 2020. https://openresearch.ocadu.ca /id/eprint/2959/7/Szikora_Erin_2020_MA_CADN_MRP%20 %28006%29.pdf

KIMOWAN METCHEWAIS

Metchewais, Kimowan, Christopher T. Green, Emily Moazami, and Jeff Whetstone. *Kimowan Metchewais: A Kind of Prayer*. New York: Aperture, 2023.

Wegs, Christina. "Grow All over Again: A Film about Kimowan Metchewais." https://vimeo.com/462339112.

PAT KANE

Kane, Pat. *Dzǫ nàts'ede ha hot'e / Here Is Where We Shall Stay*. Translated to Wıìlıìdeh Yatıì by Margaret Mackenzie. Boreal Collective Press, 2023.

TOM JONES

Jones, Tom, and Graeme Reid. *Tom Jones: Here We Stand*. West Bend, WI: Museum of Wisconsin Art, 2022.

Jones, Tom, Michael Schmudlach, Matthew Daniel Mason, and Amy Lonetree. *People of the Big Voice: Photographs of Ho-Chunk Families by Charles Van Schaick, 1879–1942*. Madison: Wisconsin Historical Society Press, 2011.

WILL WILSON

Mithlo, Nancy, Will Wilson, and Patsy Phillips. *Manifestations: New Native Art Criticism*. Santa Fe: Museum of Contemporary Native Arts, 2011.

Rohrbach, John, and Will Wilson, eds. *Speaking with Light: Contemporary Indigenous Photography*. Santa Fe: Radius, 2023.

XUNKA' LÓPEZ DÍAZ

López Díaz, Xunka', Lourdes de León Pasquel, and Carlota Duarte. *Mi hermanita Cristina, una niña chamula / My little sister Cristina, a Chamula girl*. México: Archivo Fotográfico Indígena; Centro de Investigaciones y Estudios Superiores en Antropología Social; Consejo Estatal para la Cultura y las Artes de Chiapas, 2000.

MARUCH SÁNTIZ GÓMEZ

Sántiz Gómez, Maruch. *Creencias de nuestros antepasados*. México: Centro de la Imagen; CIESAS; Casa de las Imagenes, 1998.

BAAHINNAACHÍSH (ONE WHO IS TALENTED) / WENDY RED STAR

Red Star, Wendy, Jordan Amirkhani, Julia Bryan-Wilson, Josh T. Franco, Annika K. Johnson, Layli Long Soldier, and Tiffany Midge. *Wendy Red Star: Delegation*. New York and Dallas: Aperture; Documentary Arts, 2022.

BRIAN ADAMS

Adams, Brian, and Julie Decker. *I Am Inuit*. Salenstein, Switzerland: Benteli, 2017.

JAIDA GREY EAGLE

Ahlberg Yohe, Jill, Jaida Grey Eagle, and Casey Riley, eds. *In Our Hands: Native Photography, 1890 to Now*. Minneapolis: Minneapolis Institute of Art, 2023.

JOSUÉ RIVAS

Rivas, Josué. *Standing Strong*. Brooklyn, NY: FotoEvidence Press, 2018.

KAPULEIIKEALOONALANI FLORES

Davis, Lynn Ann. *Na Pa'i Ki'i: The Photographers in the Hawaiian Islands, 1845–1900*. Honolulu: Bishop Museum Press, 1980.

Flores, Kapulei. "What I'm Fighting to Protect." *Assembly*, a Malala Fund publication, October 20, 2021. https://assembly.malala.org/stories/what-im-fighting-to-protect.

Index

Abiquiú, New Mexico, 230–231
Achuksuk, Helena, 38
Adams, Ansel, 158
Adams, Brian, 242–243
Aguilar, Dugan, 158–159
Amirkhani, Jordan, 238
Aklavik, Northwest Territories, 164
Alaska Eskimo Whaling Commission, 242
Alaska Highway, 72, 80, 110
Alaska Native Brotherhood, 24, 112
Alaska Railroad, 130
Alberta, 96, 98, 204
Albright, Peggy, 12
Albuquerque, New Mexico, 206, 260
Aleutian Islands, Alaska, 38
Algonquin Anishinaabe, 209
American Indian Exposition, 92, 94–95
American Museum of Natural History, 22
American Museum of Natural History Library, 22–23
American Philosophical Society (APS), 22
Amiotte, Arthur (Wanblí Ta Hócoka Washté; Good Eagle Center), 172–174
Anadarko, Oklahoma, 66, 92, 94–95
Anchorage, Alaska, 132, 134, 242
Anishinaabe, 36, 272
Anislaga (Mary Ebbets), 22
Annette Island Indian Reserve, 16
Antrim, Benajah Jay, 268
Apache, 230
Apsáalooke Nation (Crow Nation), 8–15, 204, 238
Archivo Fotográfico Víctor A. Chambi López, 60–62
Archuleta, Maurice, 230, 231
Arhuaco, 190
Ashua Eshquon Dupaz (Richard Throssel), 12
Asociación Martín Chambi, 60–61
Athabascan, 130
Ayaviri workshop, 180, 183–185
Aymara, viii, 44, 264
Azentún Photography Workshop, 232
Baffin Island, Nunavut, 82–91
Baillargeon, Randy, 209
Bay of Quinte Kanyen'kehá:ka (Mohawk) Nation, 192–193
Bear Chief, Arthur, 152–157
Beaton Institute, Cape Breton University, 144–147
Beaulieu, Robert George, and family, 36–37
Behchokǫ̀, Northwest Territories, 170–171

Bengal, Rebecca, 92
Bidstrup, Inuuteq, 258–259
Bidstrup, Minik, 258–259
Blackfeet Nation, viii, ix, 100–109
Blackfoot, 152
Boas, Franz, 22–23, 24
Bolitho, William, 132
Bomberry, Jeremy, 193
Bonita, Pena, 200
Brady, James "Jim" Patrick, viii, 96–99
Bristol Bay, Alaska, 38, 112, 114–115
British Columbia, 28–29, 72, 74, 78, 81
Bruchac, Margaret M., 22
Buck, Joshua, 30
Bureau of American Ethnology (BAE), 30
Bureau of Indian Affairs (BIA), 112, 134, 172, 272
	Indian Service office, 8, 12
	Kiowa Agency office, 66
Burris, Bill and Oleta, 121, 122–123
Burris, Kuhlaya, 121, 122–123
Burris, Malacha, 121, 122–123
Calca, Perú, 50–51
California, 158–159, 161, 228
California Indian Basketweavers' Association, 158
Canadian Museum of History, 82–91
Cannon Ball, North Dakota, 262–263
Cape Breton University, 144–147
Carseen, Dorothy Chocolate, 200–203
Carson City, Nevada, 160
Cayuga (Gayogǫhó:nǫˀ) Nation, 30, 32, 33
Chaleur Bay, New Brunswick, 110
Chambi, Martín, and family, 60–63
Chambi, Peruska, 60, 63
Chambi, Víctor, 60–62
Chani, Miguel, 44–47
Charles, Abram (Chief), 30, 33
Chartrand, Rhéanne, 200
Chavez, Soledad, 270–271
Chemehuevi Indian Tribe, 228
Cherokee, 66, 198
Cherokee Female Seminary, 2
Cherokee Nation, ix, 2, 6, 186
Cherokee Temperance Society, 6
Cheyenne River Lakota Nation, South Dakota, 240–241
Chiapas Photography Project (CPP), 222, 224
Chickasaw, 64, 118, 121, 186–187
Chickasaw Annual Meeting and Festival, 118, 119–123
Chickasaw Nation, 118, 186

Chickasaw Nation Collection, 119
Chickasaw Tribal Council, 118
Chilkat River, 28
Chilkoot, 27
Choctaw, 118
Civil Rights Movement, 92, 136–137
Clapp Rider (1904), 36
Claxton, Dana, 194–195
Cobb, Jennie Fields Ross, ix, 2–7
Cold Lake First Nations, 204
Colombia, 190–191, 245, 248–249
Comanche, 230
Communist Party of Perú, 180
Conference of Native Indian Photography, 200
Connerville, Oklahoma, 122–123
Constantino Jiménez, Sotero, 68–71
Constitution Act (1982), 197
Co-operative Commonwealth Federation (CFF), 96
Corongo, Ancash, Perú, 63
Crabbe, Horace, 268
Cree, 8
Cree First Nations, 96, 197, 204
Cress, Lorne, 137, 140–141
Crowfoot, Bert, 200
Cruztón, San Juan Chamula, Chiapas, 224
Cumberland House, Saskatchewan, 96
Curtis, Edward Sherriff, 8, 22, 216
Cusco, Perú, 44, 45, 60, 62, 180, 244
Cusco Region, Perú, 181, 182
Cusco School of Photography, viii, 44–59, 60
Cut Bank Creek, Blackfeet Nation, 100, 103–104
Dahmer, Vernon, 137, 138–139
Dakota Access Pipeline, 262
Dangeli, Mique'l, 16, 18
Daniels, Russel Albert, 230–231
Dawes Act (1887), 12, 36
Dene, 164, 209
Dennis, Jeremy, 142–143
Deschambault Lake, Saskatchewan, 98–99
Dettah, Northwest Territories, 200, 202, 209
Diné, 216–217, 230, 260–261
Dinétah (Navajo Homeland), 188, 230
Doucette, Raymond Gregory, 144–147
Duarte, Carlota, 222
Dunnill, Ginger, 254
Eastern Band of Cherokee Indians (EBCI), 198
Esh Quon Dupahs (Richard Throssel), 12
Española, New Mexico, 228
Fabián, Citlali, 266–267
Fairey, Tiffany, 180–181
Favell, Rosalie, 196–197, 200
Ferguson, Angela, 234–235
Fields, Tom, 186–187
First Nations, 18, 110, 152, 193, 197, 200, 209
Fisher, E. B., 115, 116–117
Flaherty, Robert J., 82
Flores, Kapuleiikealoonalani, 268–269
Fort Rupert, Vancouver Island, British Columbia, 22
Fotógrafos de la Frontera, 232
Fototeca Andina CBC, 45–59
400 Years Project, The, viii–ix
Frazier, Bill, 186–187
Funmaker, Mary, 214–215
Galería OMR, 224
Gamètì, Tłįchǫ Region, Northwest Territories, 200

Garneau, Louis, Jr., 96–97
Geddes, Carol, 72, 80
Genízaro, 230–231
George Johnston Museum, 80
Gibson, Marie, 118, 122
Git-wen-tqul, British Columbia, 26
Gitxsan, 254, 255, 256
Glacier National Park, 100, 102, 104
Gleichen, Alberta, 152
Glenbow Archives, 96–99
Glenbow Museum, 96
Gonzales, Jero, 244, 246–247
Gorman Museum of Native American Art, 198
Goshorn, Shan, 198–199, 200
Gowin, Emmet, 188
Grants, New Mexico, 126–127
Gray, Victoria Jackson, 137, 140–141
Greenlandic Inuit, 258
Grey Eagle, Jaida, 252–253
Grieves, Larissa Lorraine, 254–257
Grollier Hall Residential School, 164
Gwich'in, 164, 165
Gwich'in Social & Cultural Institute, 164
Haines, Alaska, 24–25
Haldane, Benjamin Alfred, ix, x, 16–21
Haldane, Henry S., 16–21
Hamilton, Ontario, 200
Hansen, Martin Brandt, 258–259
Harjo, Joy, 124
Harlan, Theresa, 158
Harley Eber, Dorothy, 84
Hattiesburg, Mississippi, 136–141
Haudenosaunee (Hodinǫhsǫ́:nih), 30, 32, 34, 193, 234
Hawai'i, viii, x, 268
Haycock, Alaska, 132
Her Dreams Are True (Julia Bad Boy), 8, 14
Hewitt, John Napoleon Brinton, 30–35
Hidalgo, México, 250
Hill, Richard, 200
Hinson, Joshua, 118
Ho-Chunk Nation, 214, 230
Holy Family Mission, Montana, 100
Homiskanis, Lucy (T'łaliłi'lakw), 22
Hopi Nation, 124, 188, 230
Hopi Reservation, 188, 236–237
Horden Hall, 154, 156
Hotevilla, Arizona, 188
Hudson's Bay Company, 82, 197
Huchuy Qosqo, Perú, 46–47
Humes, Jesse, 118, 121
Hunkpapa Lakota, 194
Hunt, George, ix, 22–23
Hunter's Home, 6
Idle No More movement, 193
Illinois River, 2, 6–7
Indian Citizen Act, 92
Indian Reorganization Act, 92
Indian Territory, 6, 64
Inland Tlingit, 72
Institute of American Indian Arts, 261
Inuit, and Inuk, 82–91, 152, 197, 242–243, 258–259
Iñupiaq, 242
Inuvik, Northwest Territories, 164–165
Isthmus of Tehuantepec, Oaxaca, 68–71
Itazipčola Oóhenunpa (without bows and two kettle), 240

Jerome, James "Jim," 164–171
Johnston, Freddie, 72–81
Johnston, George (Kaash Klaō), 72–81
Johnston, Shorty and Annie, 80
Johnston Town, British Columbia, 72, 74–75, 78–81
Johnstown, Nova Scotia, 144–145
Joltzemen, San Juan Chamula, Chiapas, 222
Jones, Tom, 92, 94, 214–215
Josytewa, Marlee, 236–237
Juárez, Benito, 68
Juchitán de Zaragoza, Oaxaca, 68
June Fourteenth Reservation Day Celebration, 36, 37
Kaatxwaaxsnéi (Florence Dennis), 24
Kaiser, Henry Samuel, Jr., 130–135
Kaktovik, Alaska, 242–243
Kalispell, Montana, 100, 108
Kamoinge Workshop, 136
Kanaka Maoli, 268
Kane, Pat, 165, 209–213
Kaska Dena, 254
Kelly Settlement, Mississippi, 137, 138–139
Kamehameha V (Prince Lot Kapuāiwa), 268
Ketchikan, Alaska, 16, 112–113
Ketchikan Museums, x, 16–21
King Island, Alaska, 130–131
Kingsbery, Robert Henry, Jr., 118–123
Kinngait, Baffin Island, Nunavut, 82, 84
Kinngait Co-operative, 82
Kiowa (Cáuigú) Nation, 64, 66, 92, 94
Kiowa (Cáuijòɡà) language, 66
Kiowa Culture Program, 64
Klukwan, Alasaka, 24, 26
Kullihoma, Oklahoma, 119, 122
Kvichak, Alaska, 42–43
Kudeit.sáakw, 24
Kwakwa̱ka̱'wakw Territory, 22–23
La Paz, Bolivia, 264
La Ronge, Saskatchewan, 96, 98
LaBillois, Margaret Pictou, 110–111
Lac de Gras, Northwest Territories, 209, 212–213
Laguna, New Mexico, 124
Lakota, 194, 241, 252, 272
Lampone, Josie, 64
Lane, Amyah, 236–237
language, extractive, x
LaPier, Rosalyn, 100–101
LaRose, Silvermoon Mars, 148–149
Law of Origins, 190
Lazo, Luvia, 270–271
Lebeau, Dawn E. "Dawnee," 240–241
LeBeau, Marcella Ryan (Wigmuŋke Wašté Wíŋ; Pretty Rainbow Woman), 241
Lewis, F. L., 121
Library and Archives Canada, 111
Lippard, Lucy, 8
Lodgepole, Nebraska, 208, 210–211
Loft, Martin Akwiranoron, 200
López Díaz, Xunka', 222–223
Los Angeles, California, 238, 266, 272–273
Louis Shotridge Digital Archive, 24
Lucas, Louise, 124, 128–129
Lyons, Phoebe, 32
Mace, Dakota, 260–261
Machu Picchu, Perú, 44, 60–61
MacKnight, Nīa, x, 272–273

MacKnight, Sheridan, 272–273
Mamos, 190
Manitoba, 196–197
Manning, Jimmy, 82, 200
Manuel Álvarez Bravo Photographic Center, 68–71
Mapuche, 232–233
Maracle, Yvonne, 200
Marmon, Leland Howard, 124–129
Mars, Kenneth T., Jr., 148–151
Mars, Kenneth T., Sr., 148, 149
Martín Chambi Digital Catalog (Catálogo Digital Martín Chambi), 60
Martin Monsen Regional Library, 39
Martinez, Gisela Bravo, 250–251
Masayesva, Victor, Jr. (Duwawisioma), 188–189, 200
McCracken, Krista, 154
McGillis, John B., 272–273
McKenzie, Murray, 200
McKenzie, Parker Paul (Yiŝàum; Twice Looked At), 64, 66–67
McNeil, Larry, 200
Meek, John Kanipo'okalani, Jr. II, ix, 268
Mela, José, 232–233
Membertou First Nation, 144
Menicoche, Eric, 200–201
Metchewais, Kimowan, 204–207
Métis, viii, 96, 152, 196–197, 200, 254–256
Métis Association of Alberta, 96
Métis Association of Saskatchewan, 96
Metlakatla, Alaska, x, 16–21
Mexica, 262
Meza, César, 44, 56–59
Mi'kmaq, 110–111, 144
Minneapolis, Minnesota, 252–253
Minneapolis Institute of Art, 252
Minnesota, 36, 134, 272
Minnesota Historical Society, 36, 37
Mississippi Freedom Summer Project, 136–141
Moccasin Game, 36
Mohawk (Kanien'kehà:ka) Nation, 30, 31, 200
Moku o Keawe (Hawai'i Island), 268
Møller, John, 258
Monroe, Cups, 101, 109
Monsen, Martha McGlashan, 38–43
Monsen, Melvin, Jr., 38, 42–43
Monsen, Nicky, 38, 42–43
Monsen, Oscar, 38, 42–43
Monsen, Zenia, 38–39
Monserrat, Melina, 266–267
Montana, viii, ix, 8, 100, 238
Montana Historical Society (MHS), 100, 101–109
Montaukett, 143, 208
Moose Factory Island, Ontario, 154, 156
Mora, Fidel, 44, 48–51
Moss, Táhila, 234–235
Mountain Maidu, 158
Mountain View, Oklahoma, 64, 66, 92–93
Müller, Thomas, 180–181
Muscogee Creek, 186
Museum of Wisconsin Art, 214
Naabeehó Diné Biyaad (Navajo Nation), 216, 260
Naal Tsoos Saní, 260
Naboba Lagoon, 190–191
Nahua, 250

Naknek, Alaska, 38–43
Nance, Jim, 136, 138
Narragansett Tribe, 148, 149
Nasa, 245
Nass River valley, British Columbia, 18–19
National Archives, U.S. Department of the Interior, Indian Arts and Crafts Board, 172–179
National Congress of American Indians, 241
National Native American Hall of Fame, 241
Native Indian/Inuit Photographers' Association (NIIPA), 198, 200
Native Women's Association, 200, 203
Navajo Nation, 216, 217
Navajo Treaty (1868), 260, 261
Nedrow, New York, 32
Nelson Act (1889), 36
Nenana, Alaska, 130, 134
Nevada, 158, 160, 161
Nevada Historical Society, 161
New Mexico, 230
New Waterford, Nova Scotia, 144–145
New York City, 188, 250–251
New York State, 30, 136, 142–143, 200, 234
Nez, Helen, 260–261
Niro, Shelley, 192–193, 200
Nisga'a, 16
Nisga'a (Ganada), 254–256
Nisutlin River, Yukon, 72–73
Njootli, Jeneen Frei, 194–195
No. 12 Colliery mine, 144–145
Norris, Malcolm, 96, 98
North Carolina, 198
Northern Pacific Railway, 36
Northern Paiute, 160–161
Northwest Territories, 164, 166–167, 209
Northwest Territories (NWT) Archives, 164–171, 200–203
Nuuk, Greenland, 258–259
Oak Grove Baptist Church, 186
Oakland Museum of California (OMCA), 158–159
Oaxaca, México, 68–71, 266, 270
Oaxaca de Juárez, México, 266–267
Ochoa, Horacio, 44, 52–55
Ocongate workshop, 180–182
Odjig, Daphne, 193
Odlety, Nettie, 64–65, 66, 67
Oglala Lakota Nation, 172, 252
OJI:SDA' Sustainable Indigenous Futures, 234
Oklahoma, 2, 64, 66, 92, 94, 118, 186
Oklahoma Historical Society, 2–7, 64–65, 67
Old Sun Residential School, 152, 154
Oneida (Onyota'á:ka) Nation, 30
Onondaga, New York, 32
Onondaga (Onoñda'gegá') Nation, 30, 32, 234
Onondaga Nation Farm, 234
Onondaga Tuscarora, 32
Osage Nation, 122–123, 236
Osage Nation Museum, 236
Oritz, Simon, 124
Otomi, 250, 262
Owamni, 252
Owámniyomni, 252
Ottawa, Ontario, 110–111
Ozark and Cherokee Central Railway, 2
Paiute, 160
Palm Springs, California, 124–126, 128

Panchoaga, Jorge, 245, 248–249
Park Hill, Oklahoma, 2, 4
Paul, Ben, 112–115
Paul, Frances, 112–113
Paul, Fred, 112–113, 114–115
Paul, Lawrence, 144
Paul, Robert "Bob," 112–113
Paul, William Lackey, Jr. (Tsu-Xoog-Eesh), 112–117
Paul, William Lewis, 112
Pawhuska Indian Village, 236
Peace Dale First Church of God, 148, 150
Peel River, Northwest Territories, 170
Penn Museum, 24–29
Penney, David W., 94
Perú, viii, 44, 46–59, 180–185
Peruvian Truth and Reconciliation Commission, 180
Petersen, Jakob, 258–259
Phoenix, Arizona, 64–65, 67
Phoenix Indian School, 64–67
Pico Colón, Colombia, 190
Pifer, Florence, 8, 12
Pine Ridge Reservation, 172, 252
Pit River, 158
Pitseolak, Aggeok, 82–91
Pitseolak, Peter, 82–91
Pontifical Catholic University of Perú (PUCP), 181
Poolaw, Horace Monroe (Fà:Bô; American Horse), 92–95
Poolaw, Linda, 92
Poolaw Unap, Trecil, 92–93
Pootoogook, Itee, 84
Popayán, Colombia, 245
Porcupine, South Dakota, 172–179
Porcupine Day School, 172–179
Port Simpson, British Columbia, 18
Portland, Oregon, 262
Potlotek First Nation, 144, 146–147
Powell, John Wesley, 30
Presbyterian Mission School, Alaska, 24
Prosperous Lake, Northwest Territories, 203
Protect Mauna Kea Movement, 268
Pueblo, 230
Pueblo de Abiquiú Library and Cultural Center, 231
Pueblo of Laguna Nation, 124, 128–129
Pukapakuri Wayri, 244
Puno Region, Perú, 183–185
Qoyllur Rit'i, 181, 244
Qualla Arts and Crafts cooperative, 198
Qualla Boundary, 198
Quechua, viii, 44, 60, 180, 244
Quimayousie, Dennis, 160, 161
Quinhagak, Alaska, 242–243
Racette, Sherry Farrell, 96
Rahder, Bobbi, 160–161
Rainy Mountain Boarding School, 66
Randall, Herbert, 136–141, 143
Rattler, Phillip and Helen, 101, 108
Raytel Photography, 144–147
RCAF Station Rockcliffe, 110
Red Star, Wendy (Baahinnaachíish; One Who Is Talented), 8, 204, 238–239
RedCorn, Ryan, 236–237
Reign of Terror, 236
Religious Crimes Code (1883), 24

Reno-Sparks Indian Colony, 161
Rexford, Marie, 242–243
Rickard, Jolene, 200
Riel, Louis, 96
Rivas, Josué, 262–263
Roff, Oklahoma, 186–187
Rogers, Sonja, 160, 161
Rojas, Stormy, 158–159
Romero, Cara, 228–229
Ross, Frances, 66, 67
roundhouse, 158
Royal Canadian Air Force Women's
    Division, 110
Ruth, Addie, 136–137
Saint Paul, Minnesota, 252
Salt Lake City, Utah, 230
salvage ethnography, 22
Sampson, Harry Carl, 160–163
Santa Fe, New Mexico, 228
Santiago, Chile, 232–233
Sántiz Gómez, Maruch, 224–227
Santos Briones, Cinthya, 250–251
Saskatchewan, 96, 98, 194, 204
Sault Ste. Marie, Ontario,
    152–155
Saumty, Lucy, 64–65
Sbeik Jchanvunetik, 222
Schultz, James Willard, 100
Seaman, Camille, 208, 210–211
Seesequasis, Paul, 96
Seneca (Onöndowa'ga:')
    Nation, 30, 234
Sequoyah, 66
Seward Sanatorium, 130–135
Shade-Lanier, Karen, 2, 6
Sharjah Art Foundation, 234
Sharp, John, 242–243
Sharp, Joseph Henry, 8
Sharp, William, 242–243
Sherman, Sean, 252–253
Shingwauk Hall, 152–155, 157
Shingwauk Residential Schools Centre
    (SRSC), Algoma University,
    152–157
Shining Path, 180
Shinnecock Nation, 136, 142–143, 208
Shiprock, New Mexico, 219
Shoshone, 160
Shotridge, Louis V. (Stoowukháa; Astute One),
    24–29
Siberian Yupik, 242
Sicuani, Canchis, Cusco, Perú, 60–61
Sierra Nevada de Santa Marta, 190
Siksika Nation, 152
Silko, Leslie Marmon, 124
Sioux Indian Museum, 172
Siow, Lupe, 124, 128–129
Sir Henry Wellcome Collection, 18, 20–21
Six Nations of the Grand River, 30, 31, 33, 34,
    192–193
Skeena River, British Columbia, 18
Sḵwx̱wú7mesh (Squamish) Nation, 254,
    255, 256
səlilwətaɬ (Tsleil-Waututh) Nation,
    254, 255, 256
Smith, Erminnie Adele Platt, 30

Smithsonian National Museum of the American
    Indian (NMAI), 12, 92, 124, 198–199,
    204–207, 230
Smithsonian National Anthropological
    Archives, 31–35, 161
Sna Jtz'ibajom, 224
Snow, Whitney, ix
Snowdrift River, Northwest Territories, 165
South Kingstown, Rhode Island, 148
Southeast Alaska, 18, 27, 28–29, 112
Southern Plains Indian Museum, 92
Spitzer, Kali, 254–257
St. Paul, Alberta, 96–97
Staats, Greg, 200
Standing Rock Sioux Reservation, 262
Stewart Indian School, 160–163
Stewart Indian School Cultural Center &
    Museum, 160–163
Stone, Sonia, 160, 162
Susanville, California, 158
Sydney, Nova Scotia, 144–145
Taant'a K̲wáan (Tongass people), 27
TAFOS (Talleres de Fotografía Social), 180–185
TAFOS/PUCP Photographic Archive, 181–185
Tahlequah, Oklahoma, 2–3, 5, 6–7, 236
Tekakwitha, Kateri, 200, 202
Teotitlán del Valle, Oaxaca, 270–271
Tepehua, 250
Teslin, Yukon, 72–78, 80–81
Teslin Lake, 74–75
Tetonwan Oyáte Lakota (People of
    the Prairie), 240
Third Mesa, Arizona, 188, 236–237
Thomas, Jeff, 200
Throssel, Richard Albert, 8–15
Thule, 258
Thwaites, John E., 38
Ticona, Sara Aliaga, 264–265
Timiskaming First Nation, 209
Tishomingo, Oklahoma, 120–121
Tłı̨chǫ Dene, 200, 203
Tlingit, ix, 22, 24, 72, 80, 112, 115–117
Toledo, Francisco, 68
Tomaquag Museum, 148
Tonawanda Seneca Nation Territory
    (Ta:nöwöde' Onöndowa'ga:' Nation
    Territory), 234
Tórim, Sonora, 234
Treaty of Washington (1855), 36
Tree River, Nunavut, 168–169
Tsimshian Nation, ix, 16, 18
Tsinhnahjinnie, Hulleah, 200
Tsotsil Maya, 222, 224
Tsukwani, (Francine T'łat'łaławidzamga), 22
Tucker, Mae W., 30
Tulancingo, México, 250
Tuolumne Band of Me-Wuk Indians, 158
Tulsa, Oklahoma, 198
Tuscarora (Skarù:rę²) Nation, 30, 32
Tutelo, 30
Ugpi'ganjig First Nation (Eel River Bar First
    Nation), 110–111
Uintah & Ouray Reservation, 230
Unalaska, Alaska, 38–39
Unama'ki (Cape Breton), Nova
    Scotia, 144

Unangan, 38
University of Alaska Anchorage, Archives and
    Special Collections, Consortium Library,
    38–43, 130–135
University of New Mexico, Center for
    Southwest Research and Special
    Collections, 124–129
University of Science and Arts of Oklahoma
    (USAO), 92–93, 94
University of Southern Mississippi, Historical
    Manuscripts, 137–141
University of Wyoming, American Heritage
    Center, 8–15
Unkechaug Nation, 143
Upernavik, Greenland, 258–259
uranium mines, 124, 216–217, 236, 260
U.S. Marine Corps, 186
Ute Indian Tribe, 230
Vancouver, British Columbia, 22–23, 254, 255
Vancouver Island, British Columbia, 22–23
Vargas Llosa, Mario, 60
Vietnam War, 158
Villafaña Chaparro, Amado, 190–191
Vision Maker Media, 252
Vuntut Gwitchin First Nation, 194
Wakpá Wašté Lakota Makoc'e (Cheyenne River
    Lakota Lands), 240
Walker River Paiute, 158
Washoe, 158, 160
Water Protectors, 262
Wekweètì, Northwest Territories, 200, 203
West Baffin Eskimo Co-operative (WBEC), 82
Whetstone, Jeff, 204
White, Robert, 242–243
White Earth Agency, 36
White Earth, Minnesota, 36–37
White Earth Nation, 36–37
White Earth Reservation, 36–37
White River Utes, 230
Whitman, Richard Ray, 200
Wichita, 67, 94–95
Wilson, Will, 216–221
Winnipeg, Manitoba, 196–197
Wisconsin, 214
WoLakota Yukini Wicoti Tipi, 241
Wood Mountain Lakota First Nation, 194
World War I, 64, 272
World War II, 80, 96, 100, 101, 104–105, 110,
    124, 241
xʷməθkʷəy̓əm (Musqueam) Nation, 254,
    255, 256
Xunaa (Hoonah), Alaska, 116–117
Yalalteca, 266
Yaqui Nation, 234
Yeilgooxú, 24
Yellow Wolf, Ella Mad Plume, viii, 100–109
Yellow Wolf, Louis "Louie," 100–101, 102, 104,
    106–107
Yellowknife, Northwest Territories, 165,
    200, 209
Yosokwi Collective, 190
Yukon, 72, 74, 78, 81, 110, 194
Yukon Archives, 72–81
Yukon River, 134
Yurok Tribe, 158
Zapotec, 68–69, 266, 270